I0799179

Essential Tools for Understanding the New Testament

Other books in the BYU New Testament Commentary series

The Gospel according to Mark by Julie M. Smith

The Testimony of Luke by S. Kent Brown

The Epistle to the Ephesians by S. Kent Brown

Epistle to the Hebrews by Richard D. Draper and Michael D. Rhodes

Paul's First Epistle to the Corinthians
by Richard D. Draper and Michael D. Rhodes

Paul's Second Epistle to the Corinthians
by Richard D. Draper and Michael D. Rhodes

The Revelation of John the Apostle
by Richard D. Draper and Michael D. Rhodes

Essential Tools for Understanding the New Testament

Brigham Young University
New Testament Commentary

Edited by
S. Kent Brown
and
Joshua M. Matson

BYU Studies
Provo, Utah

We dedicate this volume to John F. Hall (1951–2023), exceptional scholar, colleague, teacher, and everlasting friend.

This Commentary Series is made possible by a generous gift from John S. and Unita W. Welch.

Published by BYU Studies. To contact any member of the board of editors or BYU Studies, write to 1063 JFSB, Brigham Young University, Provo, Utah, 84602, or visit https://byustudies.byu.edu or http://www.byunewtestamentcommentary.com.

Cover images: Interior panel of the Arch of Titus, Rome, courtesy Kent P. Jackson; Papyrus 46, BP II (Chester Beatty Library), public domain via Wikimedia Commons, and the Western Wall at night, Jerusalem, November 29, 2008, photograph by Юкатан, Creative Commons Attribution–Share Alike 3.0 Unported license.

First time in print. Substantive corrections, additions, questions, or comments may be sent to byu_studies@byu.edu.

Library of Congress Cataloging-in-Publication Data

Names: Brown, S. Kent, editor. | Matson, Joshua M., editor.
Title: Essential tools for understanding the New Testament / edited by S. Kent Brown and Joshua M. Matson.
Other titles: New Testament commentary (Brigham Young University)
Description: Provo, Utah : BYU Studies, [2024]. | Series: Brigham Young University New Testament commentary | Includes bibliographical references and index. | Summary: "This volume invites readers to explore the undergirding foundations of the New Testament, leading all into the fabric of this collection of texts. The studies herein take readers into the byways of ancient law and custom, the virtues and flaws of modern translations, and the growing trove of manuscripts"-- Provided by publisher.
Identifiers: LCCN 2023052879 | ISBN 9781958854075 (hardcover) | ISBN 9781958854082 (ebook)
Subjects: LCSH: Church of Jesus Christ of Latter-day Saints--Doctrines. | Bible. New Testament--Criticism, interpretation, etc.
Classification: LCC BS2361.3 .E87 2024 | DDC 225.6--dc23/eng/20231122
LC record available at https://lccn.loc.gov/2023052879

Printed in the United States of America
10 9 8 7 6 5 4 3 2 1

About the Brigham Young University New Testament Commentary Series

Welcome to the BYU New Testament Commentary, a project by a group of Latter-day Saint specialists offering to readers a careful, new look at the biblical records that witness the life and ministry of Jesus Christ and the first generation of his church. The commentary series seeks to make the New Testament more accessible to Latter-day Saint general readers and scholars by employing much of current biblical scholarship while reflecting important LDS insights. At the same time, this effort may also be helpful to interested readers of other faiths who want to learn how a group of Latter-day Saint scholars understands the Bible. A fundamental article of faith for Latter-day Saints (Mormons) affirms the Bible "to be the word of God" while adding, understandably, that it needs to be "translated correctly" in order for it to be accurately comprehendible to modern language speakers.

These objectives have helped shape the purposes and parameters of this commentary series. Serious LDS readers of the Bible search the scriptures, looking for depth and breadth in passages whose meanings and mandates may ultimately be plain but not shallow. Such readers and interpreters are served by treatments that unite faith and research, reason and revelation, in prayerfully confronting profound and difficult issues that arise in the texts and affect one's path of progression. The New Testament has served as an influential guide to western civilization for centuries. As such, its records have long been studied by lay people and scholars alike, resulting in a rich reservoir of information that illuminates the New Testament era culturally, historically, and linguistically. Selectively, the BYUNTC builds upon this vast body of knowledge, resting on the Greek texts of the New Testament and connecting helpful elements of linguistic, literary, historical, and cultural research and traditional scholarship together with LDS scriptures and doctrinal perspectives. The combination of all these features distinguishes the BYUNTC from other commentaries, which are readily available elsewhere and which readers may also want to consult for more encyclopedic or specialized discussions.

The tone of the BYUNTC aims to be informative rather than hortatory, and suggestive rather than definitive in its interpretation. The opinions expressed in this series are the views of its contributors and should not necessarily be attributed to The Church of Jesus Christ of Latter-day Saints; Brigham Young University, where many of those involved here are headquartered; or anyone else, though these works have benefited from input and guidance from a number of colleagues, advisers, editors, and peer reviewers.

Each volume in this series sets in two parallel columns the King James Version (KJV) and a new working translation of the New Testament. Calling this a new "rendition" clarifies that it does not seek to replace the authorized KJV adopted by the Church of Jesus Christ as its official English text. Rather, it aims to enhance readers' understanding conceptually and spiritually by rendering the Greek texts into modern English with LDS sensitivities in mind. Comparing and explaining the New Rendition in light of the KJV then serves as one important purpose for each volume's notes, comments, analyses, and summaries. This effort responds in modest ways to the desire President J. Reuben Clark Jr. expressed in his diary in 1956 that someday "qualified scholars [would provide] . . . a translation of the New Testament that will give us an accurate translation that shall be pregnant with the great principles of the Restored Gospel."

Depending on their personal skills and interests, the authors of these volumes approach their scholarly sources and LDS materials differently but always with careful exposition and engaging perspectives. In several ways, they employ various interpretive tools, including semantic considerations of Greek vocabulary; cultural, historical, critical, literary, and structural analyses; and intertextual comparisons with other biblical passages, the Book of Mormon, and other scriptural works including the Joseph Smith Translation of the Bible. Observations are also proffered about the doctrinal and spiritual reception of New Testament teachings and practices in the broad LDS religious tradition.

The format also varies moderately from volume to volume regarding introductory materials and the style of commentary. Throughout, Greek and Hebrew terms appear in transliterated form in conformity with standards adopted by the Society of Biblical Literature. In some cases, a volume reproduces the Greek New Testament text based on the Greek text published by the Society of Biblical Literature (2010) or draws upon the twenty-eighth edition of the Nestle-Aland text in *Novum Testamentum Graece* (2012).

Contents

Background

Collections

Versions

Our Mission

The authors of this volume invite its readers to plumb the depths of the New Testament and reach for the top of its celestial tower—activities that will escort both students and teachers into rooms brightly lit and adorned with heavenly scenes that illuminate Jesus Christ as the Messiah. Those scenes stretch endlessly before our gaze as if looking through a window onto a verdant landscape bathed in warm sunshine. With this radiant scene in mind, the authors of this volume ask readers to explore the nooks and crannies as well as the undergirding foundations of the New Testament as we have it, leading all of us deeper into the fabric of this most important collection of texts that, to the delight of hundreds of millions, has borne record of the mortal and resurrected Christ for centuries. The studies herein will take readers into the byways of ancient law and custom, the virtues and flaws of modern translations, the growing trove of manuscripts, the enduring influence of these documents among Latter-day Saints, and the supernal value of the Joseph Smith Translation of the Bible. In a word, we are echoing the admonition of the Savior by inviting students and teachers to "hunger and thirst after righteousness" (Matt. 5:6) and thereby to come to know "the only true God, and Jesus Christ, whom thou [God] hast sent" (John 17:3).

Preface and Acknowledgments

Joshua M. Matson and S. Kent Brown

Why another book on New Testament background, particularly a collection of essays written chiefly for a Latter-day Saint audience? Do we not already possess two such volumes, *How the New Testament Came to Be,* edited by Kent P. Jackson and Frank F. Judd Jr. (2006), and *New Testament History, Culture, and Society,* edited by Lincoln H. Blumell (2019)?[1]

The answer comes in three parts. First, this volume establishes a foundation for readers that stands at the head of the massive, years-long effort of this series. Because of the Brigham Young University New Testament Commentary's thorough approach, these introductory articles aid the reader in understanding how each volume in the series engages with the ancient world and the restored gospel of Jesus Christ. Not all topics treated in the prior publications match those dealt with in this volume. Why not? We come back to the Commentary project. Because of its character, it needs a guiding volume to begin exploration of questions and events that the Commentary series will illuminate—questions and events that do not typically require explanation apart from an extensive commentary. Second, we judge that teachers and students who begin to read the studies published in this tome will come upon new, fresh ways of reading and thinking about scripture. They will discover that historical approaches and topics that illuminate the nature and origin of the Greek texts bear wondrous fruit in unexpected ways. Third, they will find answers to questions specific to a Latter-day Saint reading of the New Testament, such as what are effective approaches to the King James Version for English readers, and how might

1. Kent P. Jackson and Frank F. Judd Jr., eds., *How the New Testament Came to Be: The Thirty-fifth Annual Sidney B. Sperry Symposium* (Provo, Utah: Religious Studies Center, Brigham Young University; Salt Lake City: Deseret Book, 2006); Lincoln H. Blumell, ed., *New Testament History, Culture, and Society: A Background to the Texts of the New Testament* (Provo, Utah: Religious Studies Center, Brigham Young University; Salt Lake City: Deseret Book, 2019).

the Joseph Smith Translation of the Bible aid us when we come to scriptures that differ from our own?

Of course, books like this one don't just fall together. Unseen but steady work lies behind each contribution as well as beneath this entire collection of intriguing, instructive, and clarifying articles. At the top of any list stand two organizations—the generous people at the John A. Widtsoe Foundation and the team at BYU Studies. The Widtsoe Foundation, as it is called, provides the generous financial support that has brought one volume after another in the Commentary series to publication. On the BYU Studies side, without the committed assistance of Editor in Chief John W. Welch and his successor, Steven C. Harper, this volume would still be a mere idea enhanced by the existence of a few disparate studies. Shouldering the huge load of bringing this volume to light as a product that reflects consistency in its pages based on long-honed skills were Marny Parkin and Katie Lewis, each of whose handprints are visible in the final product. And of course, there is the cluster of student assistants whose abilities and efforts have ensured a high-quality presentation in the accompanying pages. Surrounding all these BYU Studies people, providing ongoing and timely supervision and support, were Melanie von Bose and Derek Gurr. Our deepest heartfelt thanks go to each and all of them.

Introduction

Joshua M. Matson and S. Kent Brown

Only rarely does one have an opportunity to tie the entire New Testament into a single bow. But that is precisely what has happened in this volume of collected studies—a group of sixteen colleagues setting out the intriguing and undulating landscape whose contours surround and expand one's understanding of this most important scriptural text. However, any effort to say something meaningful about the aggregate of Gospels, letters, revelations, and early Christian events immediately bumps into the rich diversity that emerges from the New Testament. This diversity, uneven in its various shapes throughout the New Testament, means unevenness in its parts. Yet the differences among the books eventually wind their way into a reservoir of stunning unity that brings readers face-to-face with Jesus Christ and his loyal followers.

The idea for this volume of studies was born fifteen years ago, and some of the initial drafts for the studies herein found their beginnings at that time. Slowly, but surely, the collection of articles has come together and now tells an illuminating story about the New Testament and the diverse world that gave birth to it, putting it on a trajectory to become what it is today. Across the world, the New Testament is still one of the most widely read of humanity's sacred writings. Latter-day Saints are among those who read, ponder, and benefit from this tome of scripture. Early on, the originators of the BYU New Testament Commentary series identified one main purpose of this book: to drive a stake into the ground that claims the New Testament as the spiritual heritage of members of The Church of Jesus Christ of Latter-day Saints. In our judgment, the articles gathered here do just that.

The BYU New Testament Commentary series is most unique in that it aims to "combine the best of ancient linguistic and historical scholarship with LDS doctrinal perspectives."[1] The first part of this volume may be

1. Brigham Young University New Testament Commentary, "The Project," accessed July 27, 2023, https://www.byunewtestamentcommentary.com/about-us/the-project/.

the most intriguing to a student of the New Testament because of that aim. Titled "A Saintly Inheritance," our authors lay out topics such as the relationship between the Book of Mormon and the New Testament, the Joseph Smith Translation of the Bible, how the Church has institutionally encouraged study of the New Testament through its publications, and how Latter-day Saint authors have presented their views on this important book of scripture both to Latter-day Saints and to those not of the faith.

In the second section of the book, titled "Background," authors explore the ever-present and ever-pressing social and religious environment that helped shape the message that now fills the pages of the New Testament. Some of its books arose out of a Judaean context that reflects the texture of belief in a world influenced by Jewish interest; one thinks of the letters of James and Jude. Others of its works drank from the waters of the Hellenistic stream that ran through the eastern Mediterranean basin, undergirding its culture from the days of Alexander the Great three centuries earlier; one thinks of Luke's book of Acts as well as the letters of Paul. A student need go no further than the opening four verses of the Gospel of Luke to see that the author sought to imitate the approach of the influential Greek historian Thucydides. Of course, Rome held sway over everything from the roads over which believers traveled to the sea lanes that allowed movement of goods and people and the Christian message, including carrying the letters of Paul and other authors to distant places.

In this light, Christian missionaries found themselves preaching to peoples of very different backgrounds. These differences shaped how the authors wrote the synoptic Gospels. Even though these Gospels share a notable number of accounts from Jesus' life and ministry, they differ from one another in how they framed their presentations. Mark wrote to believers in Rome and its hinterland who had suffered persecution under the emperor Nero (AD 54–68); Luke wrote to a wider audience of Greek speakers, beginning with his friend Theophilus; and Matthew penned his Gospel with Jewish readers in mind, as we can witness in his rather stylized genealogy based on Jesus' Davidic heritage at the beginning of his narration (see Matt. 1:1–17). Each of the contributions in the "Background" section build a firm foundation for students to better understand each of the New Testament texts in their cultural milieu.

In the book's third portion, called "Collections," the authors treat subjects related to the earliest manuscripts of the New Testament and what happened when these texts were copied and recopied. These manuscripts, and even later texts, have been the building blocks for translations of this scripture record into scores of languages, bringing the Christian hope to their readers.

Determining the most original Greek readings of passages, particularly those that have to do with key doctrines and principles, informs the accuracy of translations. For example, in Jesus' Sermon on the Mount, some manuscripts underlie a reading that says "whosoever is angry with his brother [or sister] without a cause shall be in danger of the judgment" (Matt. 5:22). Other manuscripts, including the earliest, 𝔓[64] (c. AD 200), omit the word translated "without a cause," changing completely the sense of Jesus' words. Most scholars believe that the Greek term translated "without a cause" (εἰκῆ) was added by a scribe who evidently thought that Jesus' words were too harsh. Another example comes from the final verses of Mark's Gospel. Some manuscripts preserve a longer ending, comprising 16:9–20, and others exhibit a shorter ending, dropping off at the close of verse 8. Textual critics have weighted the evidence to support the shorter ending, but Dr. John Gee demonstrates that this cannot be the case and argues that the loss of the longer ending in Mark's manuscripts is an example of the loss of "plain and precious things" from the Bible (1 Ne. 13:28, 29, 40).

Closely linked to the manuscripts of the New Testament are questions about how this collection of books became scripture and what conferred on these texts an aura of authority for establishing doctrine and shaping Church organization and ordinances. Following the deaths of the Apostles, the Christian churches needed guidance about how they were to understand Jesus' life and ministry as well as how they were to minister to the needs of members. The process of creating a canon of accepted scriptural works was intended to place them side by side with the books of the Old Testament, then in the form of the Septuagint—the Greek translation of the Hebrew Bible that included additional books known today as the Apocrypha.

During this era, the second and third centuries, many documents produced by competing Christian sects claimed to preserve the words of Jesus and his Apostles but contradicted accepted teachings. Many of these came from Gnostics, people who believed that salvation was principally due to what people knew about heavenly teachings and not due to the events of Jesus' death and Resurrection. One major, enduring question is how scarred the Christian churches were from the confrontation with Gnosticism. For afterwards, they faced the need to establish parameters that would help Christians decide whether doctrines and guiding principles were compromised.

The final division, named "Versions," examines the fabric of the King James Version, published in 1611, more than four hundred years ago, and its role as the preferred and Church-published edition of the Bible used by English-speaking members of The Church of Jesus Christ of Latter-day

Saints for both the Old and New Testaments. Because this translation is referred to in both official publications and conferences of the Church, there is a clear need to review its wonderful virtues and its occasional, nettlesome shortcomings, especially when measured against a growing number of more recent translations.

We turn first to a positive example. In Luke 1:57, we read in the KJV, "Now Elisabeth's full time came that she should be delivered; and she brought forth a son." Next, we compare the dreary language of the New English Bible: "Now the time came for Elizabeth's child to be born, and she gave birth to a son." The wording of the modern translation is vapid and without wonder, without the lofty sense that a miracle had just occurred in the life of this noble woman.[2] In contrast, an example of a shortcoming will be illuminating. In the KJV rendering of Ephesians 5:1, we read, "Be ye therefore followers of God." But the term "followers" should be rendered "imitators," changing the full extent of Paul's words. The singular of the Greek word is μιμητής (*mimētēs*). For some reason, the KJV translators shied away from the possibility that humans can imitate their God. Most other translations translate this term properly. That said, following the direction given to members of The Church of Jesus Christ of Latter-day Saints, the King James Version occupies a prominent position in any discussion on the New Testament. Additionally, as encouraged by the Church's *General Handbook* that "other editions of the Bible may be useful for personal or academic study,"[3] Andrew C. Skinner provides important background on various other New Testament translations available today.

What is important to notice about all the studies in this book is the freshness, the opening of possibilities to understanding the New Testament in new, even wondrous ways. Readers will come to grasp the majesty of the New Testament message and the dense power of the patience and persistence required to create the documents included in this scriptural work. We invite all to step toward the Savior through the pages of the New Testament with the humility expressed in the words of John the Baptist: "One mightier than I cometh, the latchet of whose shoes I am not worthy to unloose" (Luke 3:16).

---

2. Adam Nicolson, *God's Secretaries: The Making of the King James Bible* (New York: HarperCollins, 2003), 152–53; see also pp. 234–36 on John 21:4–7.

3. The Church of Jesus Christ of Latter-day Saints, "Editions of the Bible," in *General Handbook: Serving in The Church of Jesus Christ of Latter-day Saints* (Salt Lake City: Intellectual Reserve, 2023), 38.8.40.1, accessed October 5, 2023, https://site.churchofjesuschrist.org/study/manual/general-handbook/38-church-policies-and-guidelines?lang=eng#title_number139.

Commentary as Outreach

S. Kent Brown

> And looking round about upon them *all,*
> he said . . . , Stretch forth thy hand.
> Luke 6:10; emphasis added

> What I say unto one I say unto all.
> D&C 61:18

> That they *all* may be one; as thou, Father,
> art in me, and I in thee.
> John 17:21; emphasis added

Addressing a General Audience

To speak or write is rather straightforward. Even so, to tailor one's words for another person presents challenges. When authors try to illuminate scripture, they are challenged not only with their own views and biases but also the reader's hopes and expectations. Authors attempt historical accuracy, linguistic veracity, and sound doctrine as much as they are able but must acknowledge with humility that current claims could be wrong as more about ancient history, language, and doctrine is discovered and revealed. It is these grounds that will reveal a solid, respectable result. But more is needed. For in front of the work always stands the reader, who must be granted ready access to the author's best conclusions about the grand hallways and colorful, decorated rooms of scripture. The audience is paramount.

A scriptural commentary should open the reader's mind to the broad canvases of the text and the invisible corners that readers may not be aware of, both for the sake of its readers and for its own sake, since a commentary provides a tentative position about sacred matters. Because the BYU New Testament Commentary will rest largely on the King James translation, it must also preserve the expansive beauties of this translation while exploring its shortcomings, which rose chiefly from the soil of deficient early manuscripts and an incomplete grasp of the world of Jesus and his Apostles.

The Audience

The audience is seated in two places: within the Church and without. It may seem manifestly obvious that Church members represent one part of the Commentary's public. But this part of the audience cannot be taken for granted. The editors and authors of the Commentary see their enterprise as an extension of the pivotal, earlier effort published in 1979 and 1981 to add substantial guides to the manifold texts of scripture for Church members, including cross references, translation notes, the Bible Dictionary, materials from the Joseph Smith Translation of the Bible, and helpful chapter headings. In its own way, the Commentary simply expands these study aids for readers, filling them with historical detail and linguistic richness.

As an example, it is significant that at a late point in Jesus' ministry his parables became much more stern and plain, no longer hiding truths from those not ready to receive them. Luke records that during Jesus' last days he spoke the parable of the pounds while in Jericho (see Luke 19:11–27) and, later in Jerusalem, his parable about the wicked husbandmen and his saying about the rejected stone (see Luke 20:9–18). Each of these discloses the evident effort of Jesus, who was running out of time, to underscore the gravity of his message. This notable shift in tone thus uncovers important aspects of Jesus' last days—he knew that his mortal end was near, and he tried to reach his hearers by speaking bluntly. On one occasion, as an illustration that his unvarnished message was reaching his audience, hearers responded, "God forbid" (Luke 20:16).

The layout of the Commentary, with its self-declared focus on the text and its setting, will readily and effortlessly bring Latter-day Saint readers inside the teeming world of the New Testament as no other work currently does. The illuminating comments on the New Testament books, the overviews of the situations that brought them forth, and the verse-by-verse excavations will assist each reader in grasping the most important age in the history of the earth: when Jesus was born, ministered, died, and was resurrected.

The second audience, those of other faiths and persuasions, is also addressed. Why? Two reasons spring to mind. First, religious scholars not of our faith who sincerely want to understand how Latter-day Saints read and apply New Testament principles should feel invited to pick up the Commentary and find familiar grounds for opening and discussing the New Testament as an object of faith and of study. The New Testament is a common heritage shared among all of us. Second, we hope readers from other denominations will come away from any review of the Commentary with a vivid sense that Latter-day Saints take the New Testament seriously and worship Jesus as the Christ. To be sure, the Christ whom they see in the pages of the Commentary may not be the same as the Christ of Christian history and tradition. But they shall see him in familiar dress nonetheless, a real person in a real place and a real time.

By its very nature, a commentary must deal with detail, whether historical, linguistic, doctrinal, or cultural. For example, how does *The Commentary* deal with the term translated "the inn" in Luke 2:7, where Joseph and Mary sought lodging before the birth of Jesus, and the same term translated "the guestchamber," where Jesus ate the Last Supper with his Apostles (Luke 22:11)? Any solution will involve a rather technical discussion of the Greek word *katalyma* and its range of meanings in Jesus' era as well as the Joseph Smith Translation of Luke 2:7. Naturally, a detailed discussion ties to the first occurrence of the term in Luke's Gospel and runs for a half page. However, one of the challenges that an author in the Commentary must meet is making tedious details more accessible for readers. To this end, as in the case of "the inn" and the rest of Luke's story, the author of *The Testimony of Luke* broadly presents the situation that greeted Mary and Joseph in Bethlehem as far as it can be discovered from the Gospel record and from other clues that scholarship can glean from their world. In this manner, the Commentary introduces readers to both the questions and proposed solutions that face careful students on every page of the New Testament without drowning readers in tedious detail. Thus broad discussions and technical treatments stand together in the Commentary to assist readers who come to the New Testament with a variety of interests.

Issues of Interpreting the New Testament

Our interpretation of the New Testament begins with statements of belief penned by Joseph Smith in his 1842 letter to John Wentworth, the editor of the *Chicago Democrat* newspaper. Now known as "The Articles of Faith," these statements boldly declare that Latter-day Saints "believe in the same organization that existed in the Primitive Church," and in the matter of spiritual gifts listed by Paul (see 1 Cor. 12:4–11), they "believe in the gift of tongues, prophecy, revelation, visions, healing, interpretation of tongues, and so forth" (A of F 1:6, 7). Without apology, Latter-day Saints hold that spiritual gifts, including personal inspiration, not only lie behind the New Testament documents but also operated in the lives and ministries of members in the ancient Church. Concerning ecclesiastical powers that find a place in the New Testament, Latter-day Saints "believe that a man must be called of God, by prophecy, and by the laying on of hands by those who are in authority, to . . . administer in the ordinances" (A of F 1:5). Above all stands Joseph Smith's announcement that "we believe the Bible to be the word of God as far as it is translated correctly" (A of F 1:8), adding a measure of caution to how we treat the New Testament texts that have come down to us. In light of these statements, Latter-day Saint authors already possess a frame that shapes the way they approach the task of interpreting the New Testament world.

With this distinct frame, why go forward with a commentary? Will not all Latter-day Saints understand passages of scripture in basically the same way? The answer is yes and no. Latter-day Saints do share a common frame of reference. In addition, each Church member can enjoy the inspiration of the Holy Ghost as a personal teaching medium when studying scripture. But these aspects by themselves do not lead, for instance, to a historical understanding of the New Testament world nor to a grasp of the subtleties of the Greek text that can lay bare the doctrinal and cultural riches in the New Testament.

For example, Jesus evidently accepted the sacred calendar that regulated the dates when the priests in the temple celebrated festivals; Jesus attended the festivals, but to our knowledge, he did not comment on whether they were celebrated on the correct dates. After scholars discovered the Dead Sea Scrolls, they learned that the Jewish people who produced the Scrolls followed a different sacred calendar—based on the sun rather than the moon—and therefore celebrated the same festivals on different dates. They believed that the priests of the temple were corrupt and followed an apostate calendar.[1] If the Savior had thought that the temple calendar was out of line in the dates of its celebrations, particularly because he viewed the temple as his "Father's house" (John 2:16), we would expect to see a record of his objections in the Gospels. But we do not. This calendrical concern

1. On the calendar, consult Emil Schürer, *The History of the Jewish People in the Age of Jesus Christ (175 B.C.–A.D. 135),* rev. ed., ed. Geza Vermes, Fergus Millar, and Matthew Black, 3 vols. (Edinburgh: T&T Clark, 1973–1987), 1:599–601; concerning the religious significance, see Geza Vermes, *The Dead Sea Scrolls in English,* 3rd ed. (London: Penguin Books, 1987), 46–51.

is no small matter because the temple was the center of worship in Jesus' world and drew intense interest from all quarters.

As a second example, we turn to the Greek text. When the angel Gabriel visited Mary, he declared that she was "favoured" of God and had "found favour with God" (Luke 1:28, 30). Three other passages tie linguistically to the words translated here as "favoured" and "favour." All of them apply to Jesus, first in his youth and then in his adulthood. The KJV renders them as "grace" or "favour" or "gracious." In the first instance, after Joseph and Mary had located permanently in Nazareth, we read that "the child [Jesus] grew, . . . and the *grace* of God was upon him" (Luke 2:40; emphasis added). The second occurrence appears after the famous scene of the youthful Jesus teaching at the temple: "Jesus increased . . . in *favour* with God and man" (Luke 2:52; emphasis added). The third reports the reaction of the Nazareth congregation to the opening words of Jesus' discourse in the synagogue: "All bare him witness, and wondered at the *gracious* words which proceeded out of [Jesus'] mouth" (Luke 4:22; emphasis added). These three passages affirm clearly that, in Gabriel's words to Mary, she stood on a spiritual continuum with her divine son. As Jesus enjoyed celestial approval throughout his life, so Mary enjoyed the same approval in God's eyes.[2]

In pursuing its path to communicate with all, the Commentary must make a case for LDS views of the New Testament that matches the objections of critics, current or future. For starters, the publication of the Commentary will go a long way in answering a common complaint from some Christians that Latter-day Saints have produced few serious studies on the New Testament. The Commentary will also address another concern that the LDS view of Jesus is colored by the lens of a Restoration. Although it is important that the Commentary attempts to reveal the best in Christian and academic scholarship, it is also important to note that all discussions on nascent Christianity are colored by assumptions and theological positions. For instance, some Christian scholars will argue for the necessity of baptism, while others, citing the same passages of scripture, will urge that baptism is optional and, perhaps, not needed for salvation.

At the top of the doctrinal objections sits the matter of the Godhead or, to borrow traditional Christian language, the Trinity. For most other

---

2. See Barbara E. Reid, *Choosing the Better Part? Women in the Gospel of Luke* (Collegeville, Minn.: Liturgical Press, 1996), 66–67; S. Kent Brown, *Mary and Elisabeth: Noble Daughters of God* (American Fork, Utah: Covenant Communications, 2002), 42–44.

Christians, God has always been God. Moreover, resting their case on expressions such as "the Word was with God, and the Word was God. The same was in the beginning with God" (John 1:1–2), Christian scholars view Latter-day Saints as holding to a less-divine Christ, or to a somewhat-diminished Christ, resembling the Christ of the fourth-century teacher Arius, who believed that there was "a time when Christ was not"[3] and whose views precipitated the enormous theological struggles over the Godhead that beset Christianity for 150 years. Arius's viewpoint that Christ's divinity was derived from the Father met rejection in the grand Christian councils, beginning with Nicea in AD 325. Though its focus is on the New Testament, the Commentary has to articulate the differences between Arianism and LDS doctrine.

The Commentary also brings forward reasons why Latter-day Saints accept official statements such as "God the Eternal Father . . . is the literal Parent of our Lord and Savior Jesus Christ" and "Jesus Christ is the Son of Elohim [the Father] both as spiritual and bodily offspring."[4] Such statements, as some Christians read them, lessen Christ as God. Furthermore, Joseph Smith declared that "God himself was once as we are now, and is an exalted man" and "he [God] was once a man like us."[5] In the minds of some Christians, these declarations may narrow the chasm that properly divides sinless God from sinful humans. And because traditional Christian views on the Godhead arise chiefly from the pages of the New Testament,[6] the Commentary explains how Latter-day Saints interpret key passages about the Father, the Son, and the Holy Ghost.

---

3. William H. C. Frend, *The Rise of Christianity* (Philadelphia: Fortress Press, 1984), 494.

4. The First Presidency and the Council of the Twelve Apostles of The Church of Jesus Christ of Latter-day Saints, *The Father and the Son: A Doctrinal Exposition by the First Presidency and the Twelve* (June 1916), published in the *Encyclopedia of Mormonism,* ed. Daniel H. Ludlow, 4 vols. (New York: Macmillan, 1992), 1670–77, especially 1671.

5. *Teachings of the Prophet Joseph Smith,* comp. Joseph Fielding Smith, 9th printing (Salt Lake City: The Deseret News Press, 1956), 345–46; see also "Discourse, 7 April 1844, as Published in *Times and Seasons,*" 613–14, The Joseph Smith Papers, accessed July 25, 2023, https://www.josephsmithpapers.org/paper-summary/discourse-7-april-1844-as-published-in-times-and-seasons/3.

6. See the cogent observations of Jaroslav Pelikan, *Credo: Historical and Theological Guide to Creeds and Confessions of Faith in the Christian Tradition* (New Haven: Yale University Press, 2003), 127–57.

A Saintly Inheritance

The Bible and Book of Mormon—"One in Thine Hand"

Tad R. Callister

I believe that most of us are familiar with Ezekiel's prophecy that the stick of Judah (the Bible) and the stick of Joseph (the Book of Mormon) "shall become one in thine hand" (Ezek. 37:17). In direct fulfillment of that prophecy, the Book of Mormon acts as a witness or testament of Jesus Christ alongside the Bible so that together these two books of scripture "become one in thine hand" (Ezek. 37:17).

For a moment, consider the following:[1] How many straight lines can you draw through a single point? The mathematical answer is infinite. Suppose such a single point represents the Bible. Further assume that each straight line represents a different interpretation of the Bible. The reason we have so many Christian churches today is because they each interpret the Bible differently. If they interpreted it the same, they would be the same church.

Now ask yourself: How many straight lines can you draw between two points? The answer is one. Now assume that one point represents the Bible and the other point represents the Book of Mormon. There can be only one straight line, only one doctrinal interpretation, between the two. This is one reason the Book of Mormon is so important: it is a second witness of Jesus Christ—a second reference point that results in one interpretation of Jesus Christ and his teachings.

No wonder the Lord tells us, "The elders, priests and teachers of this church shall teach the principles of my gospel, which are in the Bible and the Book of Mormon, in the which is the fulness of the gospel" (D&C 42:12). These two scriptural accounts are joint, compelling witnesses of Jesus Christ, his life, and his doctrine—especially his Atonement.

---

1. Adapted from Tad R. Callister, "The Book of Mormon—a Book from God," *Ensign* 41, no. 10 (October 2011): 75, https://www.churchofjesuschrist.org/study/general-conference/2011/10/the-book-of-mormon-a-book-from-god?lang=eng.

What then are some examples of doctrinal misconceptions that existed at the time of Joseph Smith, and how do the Bible and Book of Mormon work together to clear up those misconceptions?

First Misconception: The Fall of Adam was a tragic step backward in our spiritual progress.

When Adam and Eve were cast out of the garden, the Bible records, "And the Lord God said, Behold, the man is become as one of us, to know good and evil" (Gen. 3:22). The Fall opened the eyes of Adam and Eve so they could know good and evil and thus progress in their pursuit of godhood.

The Book of Mormon confirms that Adam and Eve were in a state of spiritual neutrality in the Garden of Eden and thus could not progress and have a fulness of joy: "And now, behold, if Adam had not transgressed he would not have fallen. . . . And they [Adam and Eve] would have had no children; wherefore they would have remained in a state of innocence, having no joy, for they knew no misery; doing no good, for they knew no sin. . . . Adam fell that men might be; and men are, that they might have joy" (2 Ne. 2:22–23, 25).

The Fall opened the door to godhood. Nonetheless, most Christians believe the Fall was a tragic mistake—a giant step backward in God's eternal plan. One such proponent told me he could not accept The Church of Jesus Christ of Latter-day Saints because it teaches that the Fall was a giant step forward in humankind's eternal progress.

I asked this man, "Do you believe that the Garden of Eden was meant to be the spot where Adam and Eve would have their posterity and that this garden was meant to be their eternal heaven?"

"Yes," came the reply, "that is correct."

We then discussed that the central issue of our disagreement was this: Which is better—the heaven before the Fall—namely the Garden of Eden—or the heaven made available after the Fall and the Atonement of Jesus Christ? In other words, which is the better heaven—the one for the unfallen man and woman or the one for the man and woman who have fallen but have been redeemed by Jesus Christ?

If the heaven for the unfallen man and woman is better, then we agreed that the Fall was a tragic step backward. If, however, the heaven created for the fallen but redeemed man and woman was better, then we agreed that the Fall must have been a giant step forward.

I then asked the man, "Would Satan be a part of your proposed heaven [meaning the Garden of Eden]?"

"Of course not," came the reply. "Satan is not in heaven."

"That's interesting," I said. "Wasn't Satan in the Garden of Eden tempting Adam and Eve?"

He turned quiet.

"And furthermore, wasn't Satan *cast out of heaven* where God resides? For the Bible declares, 'And there was war in heaven: Michael and his angels fought against the dragon [Satan]; and the dragon fought and his angels, And prevailed not; neither was their place found any more in heaven. And the great dragon was cast out, . . . which deceiveth the whole world: *he was cast out [of heaven]* into the earth'" (Rev. 12:7–9; emphasis added).

I continued, "After Satan was cast out to the earth, he went to tempt Adam and Eve in the Garden of Eden. How then could the Garden of Eden be heaven, if Satan had just been cast out of heaven?"

With some honesty the man replied, "You have a point."

And thus, by scriptural definition, the Garden of Eden cannot be heaven—a truth confirmed by both the Bible and the Book of Mormon.

Second Misconception:
Baptism is not essential for salvation.

Some churches believe that God is free to offer his salvation if for some reason a person has not been baptized by the time he or she dies. This is a compassionate but incorrect conclusion because such churches don't understand the doctrine of baptism for the dead.

The Bible clearly teaches that baptism is essential for salvation. The Savior, who is the Great Exemplar, was baptized as a model for all others to follow. In addition, Jesus explained to Nicodemus, "Except a man be born of water and of the Spirit, he cannot enter into the kingdom of God" (John 3:5). Paul further taught that evidence of our commitment to Christ is manifested in the physical ordinance of baptism: "For as many of you as have been baptized into Christ have put on Christ" (Gal. 3:27).

The Book of Mormon teaches the same doctrinal truth and gives the underlying reasoning for such a command: "And now, if the Lamb of God, he being holy, should have need to be baptized by water, to fulfil all righteousness, O then, how much more need have we, being unholy, to be baptized, yea, even by water!" (2 Ne. 31:5). One of the things I love about the Book of Mormon is that it not only teaches doctrinal truths with clarity but often gives the underlying rationale for such doctrine.

Third Misconception: Baptism may be by sprinkling, pouring, or immersion.

Numerous Christian churches teach that one may be baptized by sprinkling, pouring, or immersion even though the Bible clearly teaches that baptism must be done by immersion. When the Savior was baptized, the Bible tells us he came "straightway out of the water" (Matt. 3:16), thus indicating he must have first been immersed in the water. Immersion is consistent with the intended symbolism of the ordinance—namely the death, burial, and Resurrection of Jesus Christ as taught by Paul (see Rom. 6:3–6).

The Book of Mormon is consistent in teaching this same truth. It teaches that "Alma and Helam were buried in the water; and they arose and came forth out of the water rejoicing" (Mosiah 18:14). Lest there be any question about the correct mode of baptism, the Savior, when he came to America, gave his disciples authority to baptize and taught them the related baptismal prayer. He also gave them instructions for how baptisms should be performed: "Then shall ye immerse them in the water, and come forth again out of the water" (3 Ne. 11:26).

The Christian reformers clearly understood how baptisms were performed by Christ and his disciples. Martin Luther acknowledged the symbolism of baptism when he said, "For this reason I would have the candidates for baptism completely immersed in the water, as the word says and as the sacrament signifies. . . . Thus it was also doubtless instituted by Christ."[2] John Wesley concurred: "Mary Welch was baptized, according to the custom of the first church . . . by immersion."[3] And John Calvin added his testimonial seal: "The very word baptize . . . signified to immerse; and it is certain that immersion was the practice of the ancient Church."[4] Nonetheless, this doctrinal truth, so clear in the Bible as understood by the reformers, became corrupted over time, hence the need for the Book of Mormon as a second and clarifying witness of the truth.

---

2. Martin Luther, "The Babylonian Captivity of the Church," trans. A. T. W. Steinhaeuser, in *Works of Martin Luther with Introductions and Notes,* vol. 2 (Philadelphia: A. J. Holman, 1915), 231.

3. John Winebrenner, *The Ordinances: Baptism, Feet Washing, and the Lord's Supper* (Harrisburg, Penn.: John F. Weishampel Jr., 1860), 296.

4. Winebrenner, *Ordinances,* 296.

Fourth Misconception: Infant baptism is necessary.

While many Christian churches practice infant baptism, there is not a single case of infant baptism recorded in the Bible. To the contrary, the Savior teaches us that little children should be given a blessing. Mark records that the Savior said, "Suffer the little children to come unto me, and forbid them not: for of such is the kingdom of God. . . . And he took them up in his arms, put his hands upon them, and blessed them" (Mark 10:14, 16).

The Book of Mormon is in complete accord. In fact, it preserves Christ's words as to why infant baptism is not necessary: "The whole need no physician, but they that are sick; wherefore, little children are whole, for they are not capable of committing sin; wherefore the curse of Adam is taken from them in me" (Moro. 8:8). Mormon then tells his son Moroni, "After this manner did the Holy Ghost manifest the word of God unto me; wherefore, my beloved son, I know that it is solemn mockery before God, that ye should baptize little children" (Moro. 8:9). Instead of baptizing little children, the Book of Mormon tells us that the Savior "took their little children, one by one, and blessed them" (3 Ne. 17:21).

How then did the doctrine of infant baptism get started? About the end of the second century AD, the doctrine of original sin emerged as taught by Origen and others. This doctrine taught that a baby does not have personal sin but inherits the original sin of Adam and thus must be baptized to rid the baby of that original sin. Fortunately, the Book of Mormon cleared up this misconception by explaining that the curse of Adam was removed by the Savior.

Kurt Aland, a scholar on early Christian writings, made this candid observation: "It can be no accident . . . that all our information about the existence of infant baptism comes from the period AD 200 and 250. . . . For the time before this we do not possess a single piece of information that gives concrete testimony to the existence of infant baptism. . . . To this day [1963] nobody can prove an actual case of the baptism of an infant in the period before AD 200."[5]

The Book of Mormon just keeps getting it right.

5. Kurt Aland, *Did the Early Church Baptize Infants?*, trans. G. R. Beasley-Murray (Philadelphia: Westminster Press, 1963), 101–2.

Fifth Misconception: The gift of the Holy Ghost automatically comes after confession or baptism.

Some Christian churches teach that the gift of the Holy Ghost automatically comes after confession or baptism without the laying on of hands even though the Bible teaches to the contrary. After Philip had baptized some new converts in Samaria, the Apostles "sent unto them Peter and John: who, when they were come down, prayed for them, that they might receive the Holy Ghost: (For as yet he was fallen upon none of them: only they were baptized in the name of the Lord Jesus)" (Acts 8:14–16). Note that these disciples had been baptized but had not yet received an automatic bestowal of the Holy Ghost. The Bible tells us that Peter and John "then laid their hands on them, and they received the Holy Ghost" (Acts 8:17). This was the same procedure followed by Paul. After some new disciples were baptized, "Paul . . . laid his hands upon them, [and] the Holy Ghost came on them" (Acts 19:6).

Again, the Book of Mormon is another testament that the gift of the Holy Ghost is an ordinance bestowed by the laying on of hands: "On as many as they [Christ's disciples] laid their hands, fell the Holy Ghost" (Moro. 2:3). This is one more case where there can be only one straight line—one doctrinal interpretation between two dots (the Bible and the Book of Mormon).

Sixth Misconception: The doctrine of Christ is a mystery.

Many churches might struggle with answering the question "What is the doctrine of Christ?" even though such doctrine is taught in the Bible and elaborated upon in the Book of Mormon. Peter spoke to a group of people about the Savior and his Resurrection. These people believed Peter and had faith in Jesus Christ and his Resurrection. As a consequence, the scriptures tell us, "They were pricked in their heart, and said unto Peter and to the rest of the apostles, Men and brethren, what shall we do?" (Acts 2:37). By reading the next few verses, a reader can infer their full question to Peter: "What shall we do to be saved?" (see Acts 2:40). Peter responds, "Repent, and be baptized every one of you in the name of Jesus Christ for the remission of sins, and ye shall receive the gift of the Holy Ghost." Later the scriptures tell us that these new disciples "continued steadfastly in the apostles' doctrine" (Acts 2:38, 42). In other words, Peter taught the doctrine of Christ—namely faith, repentance, baptism, receiving the gift of the Holy Ghost, and enduring or remaining steadfast to the end.

This same doctrine is taught in 2 Nephi 31. There Nephi tells us that "this is the doctrine of Christ, and the only and true doctrine of the Father, and of the Son, and of the Holy Ghost" (2 Ne. 31:21). Again, this same doctrine was taught by the Savior in 3 Nephi 27. He then concludes by saying that this doctrine is also known as "my gospel" (3 Ne. 27:21).[6]

Seventh Misconception: Revelation ended with the Bible.

At the time of Joseph Smith, many churches taught—and continue to teach—that revelation ended with the Bible. In other words, the Bible is the complete and final word of God. The prophet Amos taught, however, that "the Lord God will do nothing, but he revealeth his secret unto his servants the prophets" (Amos 3:7). Paul the Apostle wrote that the mysteries of the kingdom were "revealed unto [God's] holy apostles and prophets by the Spirit" (Eph. 3:5). This is consistent with the fact that the Epistles of the New Testament were revelations given to Christ's Apostles in order to assist them in instructing the Saints, clarifying doctrinal issues, and resolving disputes. Does anyone honestly believe that when the events of the Bible ended (approximately AD 100), there were no more needed instructions for the Saints, no more doctrines to clarify or reveal, no more disputes to resolve?

The Book of Mormon responds to those who believe that revelation was not an ongoing necessity in Christ's Church: "I [Moroni] speak unto you who deny the revelations of God, and say that they are done away, that there are no revelations, nor prophecies . . . ; Behold I say unto you, he that denieth these things knoweth not the gospel of Christ; yea, he has not read the scriptures; if so, he does not understand them. For do we not read that God is the same yesterday, today, and forever, and in him there is no variableness neither shadow of changing?" (Morm. 9:7–9). The logic of Moroni was compelling: If God had prophets and revelation in the Old Testament and prophets and revelation in the New Testament and he is the same yesterday, today, and forever, what would you expect God to have in his Church today?

6. See also 2 Ne. 29:10; 3 Ne. 11:38–40.

Eighth Misconception: Christ's Church doesn't need to be named after him.

One might ask this poignant question: At the time of Joseph Smith, how many churches were named after Jesus Christ? The Apostle Paul recognized that there were contentions among the Saints—some declaring they were disciples of Paul, and some disciples of Apollos, and others of Cephas, and some of Christ. Paul then clarified that they were all disciples of Jesus Christ: "Is Christ divided? Was Paul crucified for you? Or were ye baptized in the name of Paul?" (1 Cor. 1:13). In other words, we were all baptized in the name of Christ and thus are all disciples of Christ. Thus the logical conclusion was that they were members of Christ's Church (Acts 11:26), not Paul's or Apollos's or Cephas's church.

The Book of Mormon reinforces and clarifies that Christ's Church should be named after him: "Therefore, whatsoever ye shall do, ye shall do it in my name; therefore ye shall call the church in my name; . . . And how be it my church save it be called in my name? For if a church be called in Moses' name then it be Moses' church; or if it be called in the name of a man then it be the church of a man; but if it be called in my name then it is my church, if it so be that they are built upon my gospel" (3 Ne. 27:7–8).

The logic was so easy to understand—if Christ is the chief cornerstone of his Church, if he is our Savior and Redeemer, if he is the author and finisher of our faith, then why would his Church be called by any name other than his?

Elder James E. Talmage addressed this very issue: "There are churches named after their place of origin—as the Church of England; other sects are designated in honor of their famous promoters—as Lutherans, Calvinists, Wesleyans; others are known from some peculiarity of creed or doctrine—as Methodists, Presbyterians, and Baptists; but down to the beginning of the nineteenth century there was no church even claiming name or title as the Church of Christ."[7]

I believed Elder Talmage's conclusion was correct, but I also knew he did not have computers in his day and age, so I asked a friend, Richard Holzapfel, then a professor at Brigham Young University, to research the issue of whether any church was named after Jesus Christ at the time of

---

7. James E. Talmage, *The Great Apostasy: Considered in the Light of Scriptural and Secular History* (Salt Lake City: Deseret News, 1909), 158.

the Restoration in 1830. He sent me an email with the following discovery: "In the USA it seems there was no organization using any form of the Lord's name as a title for their church [before Joseph Smith restored Christ's Church in 1830]."

Martin Luther was keenly aware of what Christ's Church should be called, for he told his parishioners: "I ask that men make no reference to my name; let them call themselves Christians, not Lutherans. What is Luther? After all, the teaching is not mine. Neither was I crucified for anyone. . . . How then should I—poor stinking maggot-fodder that I am—come to have men call the children of Christ by my wretched name? . . . Let us abolish all party names and call ourselves Christians, after him whose teaching we hold."[8]

It seems so logical: if it is Christ's Church, it would be named after him. Both the Bible and Book of Mormon come to this conclusion.

Ninth Misconception: People cannot become perfect.

Most, if not all, Christian churches believe it is blasphemy to teach that people can become gods even though such doctrine is repeatedly taught in the Bible and confirmed in the Book of Mormon. The Savior in the Sermon on the Mount taught, "Be ye therefore perfect, even as your Father which is in heaven is perfect" (Matt. 5:48). Note the wording—not relative perfection as compared to another person, but absolute perfection as measured by the standard of our Father in Heaven. To this point, prophets and scholars have noted that the word "perfect" in Matthew 5:48 should be rendered as "complete."[9] Paul taught this same glorious truth. He said that the purpose of the Church was "for the perfecting of the saints . . . unto a perfect man, unto the measure of the stature of the fulness of Christ" (Eph. 4:12–13). The standard of perfection in these scriptural references was not humankind, but rather the Father and the Son (see also John 17:20–23 and Rev. 3:21). Paul understood this possibility and thus

8. Martin Luther, "A Sincere Admonition to All Christians to Guard against Insurrection and Rebellion," trans. W. A. Lambert, in *Luther's Works*, vol. 45, *The Christian in Society II*, ed. Walther I. Brandt (Philadelphia: Muhlenberg Press, 1962), 70–71.

9. For an enlightening examination of the meaning of the Greek word used in the New Testament for "perfect" (*teleios*), see President Russell M. Nelson's October 1995 general conference address, "Perfection Pending," *Ensign* 35, no. 11 (November 1995): 86–87.

disclosed his goal in life: "I press toward the mark for the prize of the high calling of God in Christ Jesus. Let us therefore, as many as be perfect, be thus minded" (Philip. 3:14–15).

The Book of Mormon, in one of its concluding verses, invites us to "come unto Christ, and be perfected in him, and deny yourselves of all ungodliness." And then it tells us how this lofty goal is possible: "By his grace [the enabling power of Christ's Atonement][10] ye may be perfect in Christ" (Moro. 10:32).

This seems so consistent with the goal of Christianity—namely, to become like Christ. If the goal of Christianity is to be a disciple and follower of Christ, then at what point is it blasphemous to say we can become like him? Is it okay to be 2 percent like Christ, or 50 percent or 80 percent, without being blasphemous? Once we have crossed the line and acknowledged we can become like Christ to any degree, then logic says we can continue to become like him until we are in fact perfect, as the scriptures command us to be.

Conclusion

Truly, the Bible and Book of Mormon are one in God's hand. Not only do they confirm each other but they also complement each other. The Bible teaches about the gospel being preached to the dead, proxy baptism, and three degrees of glory. The Book of Mormon helps us understand that the Savior's Atonement was infinite (a phrase not used in the Bible), clarifies that he suffered not only for our sins but also for our afflictions and temptations, and explains that he has the power not only to cleanse us and resurrect us but also to perfect us. In addition, the Book of Mormon gives us the covenants we make at baptism and the baptismal and sacramental prayers. It gives us masterful sermons on faith by Alma, the scattering and gathering of Israel by Jacob, the Savior's Atonement by King Benjamin, and Lehi's philosophical and spiritual masterpiece on the relationship between the Fall, the Savior's Atonement, and humankind's agency. These two books of holy scripture work to confirm and complement each other in every way.

Recently I met with a good friend who left the Church. I asked him if he honestly believed that Joseph Smith wrote the Book of Mormon. He

10. Craig A. Cardon, "The Savior Wants to Forgive," *Ensign* 43, no. 5 (May 2013): 15; David A. Bednar, "In the Strength of the Lord," *Ensign* 42, no. 4 (April 2012): 42; "Bible Dictionary," s.v. "Grace," The Church of Jesus Christ of Latter-day Saints, https://www.churchofjesuschrist.org/study/scriptures/bd/grace?lang=eng.

replied in the affirmative. He said that Joseph Smith was creative—a storyteller of prodigious proportions and thus had the capacity to write the Book of Mormon.

I believe there are at least two problems with such an argument. First, it is one thing to be creative. The stories of Mickey Mouse and Donald Duck are creative, but they are not necessarily inspiring. The Book of Mormon stories are not just creative but highly inspiring—such as the story of the two thousand sons of Helaman. When I first read that story as a teenage boy, I heard a voice in my mind say, "That story is true." This was my first significant witness of the truth of the Book of Mormon.

Second, the claim that Joseph Smith was a creative storyteller does not solve the question of who wrote the Book of Mormon. The real question remains: Where did Joseph get the incredible, even staggering doctrine that fills this book, page after page, especially its inspired insights on the Savior's Atonement and doctrine that was contrary to the mainstream religious beliefs of Joseph's time? Was it brilliance or revelation that produced such doctrine? If brilliance—if Joseph was a genius—why hadn't other geniuses since the Apostasy come up with some or all of these doctrinal truths? I believe it was revelation that produced these doctrinal masterpieces.

The same spirit that helps one know the Bible is true is the same spirit that helps one know the Book of Mormon is true. They are compatible witnesses of Jesus Christ's ministry and mission. That is why Nephi said, "If ye shall believe in Christ ye will believe in these words, for they are the words of Christ" (2 Ne. 33:10). I bear my solemn testimony that the Bible and the Book of Mormon are indeed the words of Christ.

Seeing into God's "Own Bosom" (D&C 35:20)

A Brief Journey through the Joseph Smith Translation of the Bible

Richard D. Draper

From its beginning, the Church has not viewed the Bible as inerrant. Joseph Smith explained that "from sundry revelations which had been received, it was apparent that many important points, touching the Salvation of man, had been taken from the Bible, or lost before it was compiled."[1] One of these revelations came in 1828, while he was translating the Book of Mormon. Concerning the Bible, the Book of Mormon stated that this sacred work, when it was initially produced, "contained the fulness of the gospel of the Lord, of whom the twelve apostles bear record; and they bear record according to the truth which is in the Lamb of God." But certain individuals abused the text and "have taken away from the gospel of the Lamb many parts which are plain and most precious; and also many covenants of the Lord have they taken away. And all this have they done that they might pervert the right ways of the Lord, that they might blind the eyes and harden the hearts of the children of men." As a result, "an exceedingly great many do stumble, yea, insomuch that Satan hath great power over them" (1 Ne. 13:23–29).

The Prophet explained his personal position on the Bible, stating that he believed it "as it read when it came from the pen of the original writers; ignorant translators, careless transcribers, or designing and corrupt priests have committed many errors."[2] Nonetheless, the work is inspired and still

1. "History, 1838–1856, Volume A-1 [23 December 1805–30 August 1834]," 183 (January 25, 1832), Joseph Smith Papers, accessed September 3, 2021, https://www.josephsmithpapers.org/paper-summary/history-1838-1856-volume-a-1-23-december-1805-30-august-1834/189.

2. "History, 1838–1856, Volume E-1 [1 July 1843–30 April 1844]," 1755 (October 15, 1843), Joseph Smith Papers, accessed September 3, 2021, https://www.josephsmithpapers.org/paper-summary/history-1838-1856-volume-e-1-1-july-1843-30-april-1844/127.

stands as an indispensable leg of the four standard works on which Church doctrine sits. But, as Articles of Faith 1:8 makes very clear, "we believe the Bible to be the word of God as far as it is translated correctly."

Joseph Smith's understanding of the flawed nature of the Bible opened the way for, as he called it, "a new translation." He did not confine his use of the word "translation" to the usual definition of rendering a text from one language to that of another. For the Prophet, the word comprised the "copying, editing, adding to, taking from, rephrasing, and interpreting" as well as the transmitting of a text.[3] More specifically, the word pointed to his own work on the King James Version (KJV) that he designed to correct misunderstood or false ideas and teachings. But his work also included the restoration of missing background material and the addition of items that were never a part of the Bible's sacred record.

The impetus to make a plainer translation did not, however, come from Joseph Smith's understanding of the Bible's errancy but from the Lord's. No record of a revelation commissioning the Prophet to do the work is known, but it can be surmised based on other scriptures (see D&C 35:20; 45:60–61; 76:15). He began the work in June 1830 and, over the next three years, engaged at least five different clerks to assist him.[4] With their help, he continued his efforts off and on until July 1833, when he declared the work finished.

There are differences between Joseph Smith's translation and the KJV in 3,410 verses. These "range from minor details to fully reconstructed chapters."[5] Some of his changes resulted from his consultation of contemporary biblical scholarship, primarily the work of Adam Clarke (1760–1832), whose eight-volume commentary covered every book of the Bible.[6] Most changes, however, were Smith's own inspired work. Inadvertently,

---

3. Robert J. Matthews, "Joseph Smith Translation of the Bible (JST)," in *Encyclopedia of Mormonism,* ed. Daniel H. Ludlow, 4 vols. (New York: Macmillan, 1992), 2:764. In Joseph Smith's day, the word primarily meant "to bear, carry or remove from one place to another," and "transfer; to convey from one to another." To render a text from one language to another was the sixth definition listed. See Noah Webster, *An American Dictionary of the English Language* (New York: S. Converse, 1828), s.v. "translate" and "translation."

4. These were Oliver Cowdrey, John Whitmer, Emma Smith, Frederick G. Williams, and Sidney Rigdon. The latter seems to have taken about 90 percent of the dictations and associated clerical work.

5. Matthews, "Joseph Smith Translation," 2:763–64.

6. Adam Clarke, *The Holy Bible, Containing the Old and New Testaments: The Text Carefully Printed from the Most Correct Copies of the Present Authorized Translation, Including the Marginal Readings and Parallel Texts, With a Commentary and Critical Notes Designed as a Help to a Better Understanding of the Sacred Writings,* 8 vols. (New York: Daniel Hitt and Abraham Paul, 1817; Nashville: Abingdon Press, 1977).

he translated two passages twice. These were Matthew 26 and 2 Peter 3:4–6. His changes to these texts were not exactly the same. In most cases, however, where "substantive content was added to the text, similar information was added in *both* of the new translations" but not with the same words and sometimes not in the same location.[7] Even so, the same textual problems were noted and similarly addressed. These changes provide us with insight into how the translation process worked. As one scholar noted,

> Joseph Smith taught that the Holy Ghost gives us "pure intelligence," which serves in "expanding the mind [and] enlightening the understanding." Under "the Spirit of Revelation," "you feel pure Intelligence flowing unto you" that can "give you sudden strokes of ideas." Perhaps it would be reasonable to propose that as Joseph Smith worked his way through Matthew 26, dictating the text to his scribe Sidney Rigdon in spring 1831 and again to his scribe John Whitmer the next fall, impressions came to his mind in the form of pure intelligence, enlightened understanding, and sudden strokes of ideas—but not necessarily in exact words. Responding to those impressions, the Prophet himself supplied the words that corrected the problem or emphasized the point or otherwise caused the verse to express the ideas that the Lord wanted it to communicate. This suggestion may explain why the duplicate translations are verbally different.[8]

The Prophet's changes not only reinforced or clarified doctrinal points but also expanded or added new material. The manuscripts show that Joseph Smith struggled to get the wording exactly right in a number of places, perhaps because he knew the importance of the project to the Lord.[9] By the time his rendition of the Bible was completed, he apparently felt confident that he had corrected the manifold problems of the King James text. In doing so, he produced a work of great value for the Restoration in clarifying a large number of biblical passages. However, its value does not stop there. One of its byproducts was additional revelations, many of which are now recorded in the Doctrine and Covenants.[10]

---

7. Kent P. Jackson and Peter M. Jasinski, "The Process of Inspired Translation: Two Passages Translated Twice in the Joseph Smith Translation of the Bible," *BYU Studies* 42, no. 2 (2003): 59.

8. Jackson and Jasinski, "The Process of Inspired Translation," 61–62.

9. Scott H. Faulring, Kent P. Jackson, and Robert J. Matthews, eds., *Joseph Smith's New Translation of the Bible: Original Manuscripts* (Provo, Utah: Brigham Young University, Religious Studies Center, 2004), 6.

10. Note the text for D&C 9:2; 35:20; 42:56–58; 45:60–62; 73:3; 76:15–18; 77:1–15; 86:1–11; 93:53; 94:10; 104:58; 124:89; and the editorial headings for sections 35, 71, 76, 77, 86, and 91.

The manuscripts reveal five kinds of changes that the Prophet made to the text. These are as follows: (1) "restoration[s] of the original text," (2) "restoration[s] of what was once said or done but which was never in the Bible," (3) "editing to make the Bible more understandable for modern readers," (4) "editing to bring biblical wording into harmony with truth found in other revelations or elsewhere in the Bible," and (5) "changes to provide modern readers teachings that were not written by the original authors."[11]

It is of note that virtually all changes the Prophet made were not directed at restoring the original texts but were doctrinal expansions and additions. "Joseph Smith's labor on the Bible was to make it not a museum piece for antiquity but a living revelation for the Saints of the latter days. He was appointed to the work by God (see D&C 76:15), and God endorsed it in strong language: 'And the scriptures shall be given, even as they are in mine own bosom, to the salvation of mine own elect' (D&C 35:20)."[12]

Joseph Smith's statement in July 1833 that he had finished the work did not mean, however, that the revision was ready for the press. Indeed, the various preserved manuscripts show that there was yet some inconsistency between passages, particularly those that had been translated twice, and they were most likely due to scribal error and inadvertence.[13] These needed to be cleared up. In addition, "work still needed to be done to refine the verse divisions and to provide consistent spelling and punctuation. And some of the individual changes had resulted in unevenness in wording that had not yet been smoothed out. In short, although the inspired work of translating had been completed by Joseph Smith as far as was intended, the text was still in need of some editing when he died."[14] Possibly due to the press of Church business, the lack of financial means, and continued persecutions, a press-ready copy was never completed, and therefore the work remained unpublished during the Prophet's lifetime.

Fortunately, the manuscripts of Joseph Smith's Bible translation were preserved by members of his family until the Reorganized Church of Jesus Christ of Latter Day Saints (now the Community of Christ) came into possession of the documents and, in 1867, published their first edition of the

11. Faulring, Jackson, and Matthews, *Joseph Smith's New Translation,* 8–10.

12. Faulring, Jackson, and Matthews, *Joseph Smith's New Translation,* 11.

13. Thomas A. Wayment, ed., *The Complete Joseph Smith Translation of the New Testament: A Side-by-Side Comparison with the King James Version* (Salt Lake City: Deseret Book, 2005), viii.

14. Faulring, Jackson, and Matthews, *Joseph Smith's New Translation,* 7–8.

work. They entitled it "The Holy Scriptures." In 1936, they printed a teacher's edition containing study helps. To this edition, they appended the subtitle "Inspired Version," which they have kept in all subsequent editions. In 1944, they issued a corrected edition that stands to this day and has proven to be very true to the manuscripts.

Through the gracious auspices of the Community of Christ, Latter-day Saint scholars and leaders beginning in the 1960s have been able to access the original material. This access has assuaged the concerns of those who held the "Inspired Version" suspect and has thereby heightened the desire of many Latter-day Saints to have access to this material. This desire was the impetus for a number of publications that showcased Joseph Smith's changes.[15] Among Latter-day Saints, the Prophet's work is known as the "Joseph Smith Translation," often noted as the JST. As a result of its importance and the growing interest by members and because of its status as scripture, the Church has incorporated many of the JST changes in the footnotes or appendix of the 1979 Latter-day Saint edition of the King James Version of the Bible.

The Brigham Young University New Testament Commentary series provides its readers with an in-depth analysis of each of the changes Joseph Smith made to the various texts comprising the New Testament. As a result, readers will gain a greater understanding of the significance of these changes and the contribution they make to many New Testament passages and the teachings of the Church.[16]

15. For examples, see Julie M. Hite and Steven J. Hite, comps., *The New Testament with the Joseph Smith Translation* (Orem, Utah: Veritas Group, 1994); and Julie M. Hite, Steven J. Hite, and Tom Melville, comps., *The Old Testament with the Joseph Smith Translation* (Orem, Utah: Veritas Group, 2001); see also Wayment, *Complete Joseph Smith Translation.*

16. For additional studies, see Robert J. Matthews, *"A Plainer Translation": Joseph Smith's Translation of the Bible; A History and Commentary* (Provo, Utah: Brigham Young University Press, 1975); Monte S. Nyman and Robert L. Millet, eds., *The Joseph Smith Translation: The Restoration of Plain and Precious Things* (Provo, Utah: BYU Religious Studies Center, 1985); Julie M. Smith, "Five Impulses of the Joseph Smith Translation of Mark and Their Implications for LDS Hermeneutics," *Studies in the Bible and Antiquity* 7, no. 1 (2015), 1–21, http://scholarsarchive.byu.edu/cgi/viewcontent.cgi?article=1045&context=sba; Kent P. Jackson, "Joseph Smith's Translation of the New Testament," in *New Testament History, Culture, and Society: A Background to the Texts of the New Testament,* ed. Lincoln H. Blumell (Provo, Utah: BYU Religious Studies Center; Salt Lake City: Deseret Book, 2019), 707–18.

Unmuting the Helping Voices

A Short History of Guiding Latter-day Saint New Testament Study

Joshua M. Matson

Introduction

Latter-day Saints revere the New Testament.[1] From the beginnings of the Restoration, members of The Church of Jesus Christ of Latter-day Saints have seized on the New Testament as their primary source for understanding the ministry and Atonement of Jesus Christ and the organization of his Church.[2] Referring to this engagement with the New Testament, philosopher Paul Hedengren wrote,

> Latter-day Saints revere the New Testament for its accounts of the birth, ministry, atonement, and resurrection of the Savior, Jesus Christ. The teachings of Jesus in the New Testament comprise the core of LDS doctrine, and their preeminence is evidenced by their frequent appearance in other LDS standard works accepted as scripture and in LDS speaking and writing. The writings of the New Testament apostles are accepted and appreciated for their doctrine and wise and inspired counsel and for documenting

---

1. "Reverence for the Bible," Newsroom, The Church of Jesus Christ of Latter-day Saints, January 25, 2008, https://newsroom.churchofjesuschrist.org/article/reverence-for-the-bible. The article emphatically states that "Latter-day Saints cherish [the Bible's] teachings and engage in a lifelong study of its divine wisdom. . . . To increase biblical understanding, the Church provides extensive resources and tools: lesson manuals, cross-reference materials, Bible maps, a Bible dictionary, and articles in various magazines. Thus, the Bible is much more than simply a collection of antiquated writings and revelations that have only scant relevance to the modern world. On the contrary, it stands in the center of Latter-day Saints' spiritual lives."

2. Brigham Young, in *Journal of Discourses,* 26 vols. (Liverpool: F. D. Richards, 1855–86), 16:71–77 (May 25, 1873); Orson Pratt, *Divine Authority, or the Question, Was Joseph Smith Sent of God?* (Liverpool: R. James, 1848), 14–16.

> the apostolic challenge of proclaiming the gospel, adhering to the original teachings of Christ, establishing the unity of the faith, and promoting the righteousness of believers in a rapidly growing Church.[3]

With such reverence, we might ask the question, How have Latter-day Saints lifted themselves and one another in coming to grips with this volume of holy writ? While numerous works have focused on how Latter-day Saints (particularly Latter-day Saint leaders) have appealed to the Bible in sermons, periodicals, scriptural coherency, and biblical interpretation,[4] scholars have largely overlooked the way in which the faithful members of The Church of Jesus Christ of Latter-day Saints have conducted their study of the Bible, the New Testament specifically, and how their study has been enhanced by the unmuting of many Latter-day Saint voices. In our discussion, we will probe the institutional influence of The Church of Jesus Christ of Latter-day Saints on its devotees' study of the New Testament throughout the Church's history. Additionally, we will examine the role of New Testament scholarship both in the wider academic arena and within the Church (namely, works officially produced by the Church and by individual Latter-day Saint members).

Our discussion will progress chronologically through five major periods of Latter-day Saint history and identify how faithful members have been influenced in their study of the New Testament.[5] Within each historical period, we will first set out how other religious communities have approached their study of the New Testament. Additionally, in each era, we will identify prominent Church personalities and analyze publications that impacted the place of the New Testament in Latter-day Saint life. At

---

3. Paul Hedengren, "Bible: LDS Belief in the Bible," in *Encyclopedia of Mormonism,* ed. Daniel H. Ludlow, 4 vols. (New York: Macmillan, 1992), 1:108.

4. See Philip L. Barlow, *Mormons and the Bible: The Place of the Latter-day Saints in American Religion,* updated ed. (New York: Oxford University Press, 2013); Terryl L. Givens, *Feeding the Flock* (New York: Oxford University Press, 2017), 257–78; Laurie F. Maffly-Kipp, "Mormons and the Bible," in *The Oxford Handbook of Mormonism,* ed. Terryl L. Givens and Philip L. Barlow (New York: Oxford University Press, 2015), 121–33; Andrew C. Skinner, "Bible," in *Encyclopedia of Latter-day Saint History,* ed. Arnold K. Garr, Donald Q. Cannon, and Richard O. Cowan (Salt Lake City: Deseret Book, 2000), 100–102.

5. As is often the case in studying the history of one or the other of the testaments in the Bible, oftentimes the historical record combines the approaches of studies to a testament to the entirety of the Bible. For this reason, especially in the contemporaneous histories of each section, while the term *Bible* is most often used, the principles apply equally to the Old and New Testaments. I have elected to maintain the general discussion of the Bible rather than insert *New Testament* in these discussions.

the end of each segment, we will attempt to measure the impact of these publications and how they influenced New Testament study in the Church. The final analysis will focus on how burgeoning resources influenced individuals and families. We will also assess how the Brigham Young University (BYU) New Testament Commentary adds to the rich history that Latter-day Saints have enjoyed by intellectually engaging in the text of the New Testament.

The Foundations of the Restored Gospel and the New Testament (1830–1844)

Americans shifted their approaches to the study of the Bible during the two centuries that predated the founding of The Church of Jesus Christ of Latter-day Saints. Although the Bible played a quintessential role in the colonization of the United States of America, the way in which it was influential oscillated. During the majority of the seventeenth and eighteenth centuries, the Bible was predominantly interpreted through the clergy and the antique Christian creeds.[6] These sources provided religious practitioners with a recognizable, acceptable, and hierarchical source of interpretation for the texts of the Bible. Americans, however, began to question these sources because of the rise of empirical methods of analyzing the world, including the role of supernatural revelation and spiritual influence.[7]

The middle of the nineteenth century witnessed an evolution in public perceptions concerning approaches to the Bible in America. Nathan Hatch observed, "The notion of the sovereignty of the people captured the imagination of the American people—common people—and wrought a serious crisis of authority within popular culture."[8] With the rise and spread of individual sovereignty throughout the United States between

6. Barlow, *Mormons and the Bible*, 1.

7. See Michael J. Lee, *The Erosion of Biblical Certainty: Battles over Authority and Interpretation in America* (New York: Macmillan, 2013), 87–88. Lee argues that some of the primary reasons for these questions were the increasing role of rationalism in the United States and the decreased emphasis on one being able to understand the Bible in its original languages. Lee concludes, "As the eighteenth century progressed, some Christians continued to place greater confidence in the potential of unassisted reason, and they subjected the Bible to empirical examination, confident that natural reason would always affirm supernatural revelation. In the process, their interpretation of the Bible gradually grew more naturalistic."

8. Nathan O. Hatch, "*Sola Scriptura* and *Novus Ordo Seclorum*," in *The Bible in America: Essays in Cultural History*, ed. Nathan O. Hatch and Mark A. Noll (New York: Oxford University Press, 1982), 64.

1780 and 1820, the balance of power over the interpretation of the Bible shifted from preacher to congregant. Historian Philip Barlow recognized this shift within religious communities, stating, "By the onset of the egalitarian age of Jackson, privately interpreted scripture rivaled or surpassed the clergy and the traditional creeds as the preeminent religious authority of the land."[9] By proclaiming themselves as sovereign in their interpretations, students of the Bible in America continued to ponder, discuss, and debate the nature of the scriptures and their application for their own lives. These biblical discussions focused on trying to "strengthen the authority of [the Bible] in light of mounting attacks [by rising skepticism and criticism]. Nonetheless, interpreting the Bible by increasingly natural and empirical means affected the way they perceived holy writ. American Protestants began to treat the Bible *more* like any other book."[10] It is within this context of studying the Bible that The Church of Jesus Christ of Latter-day Saints was established.

Joseph Smith's personal study of the Bible, particularly the New Testament, from a young age is unquestionable.[11] Smith's continued study of the New Testament included unique perspectives. Focusing on the dissemination of Smith's biblically informed language, his Christian primitivism, his selective literalistic bent of mind, his dissatisfaction with the current state of the biblical texts, and his disbelief in the Bible as the sole and final authority in doctrine produces a vivid picture of what the restored gospel provided its converts for study of the New Testament. Outside the Church's foundational scriptures—the Book of Mormon, Smith's published revelations, and the Joseph Smith Translation of the Bible (JST)—no direct publication was produced that guided Latter-day Saint study of the New Testament.

9. Barlow, *Mormons and the Bible,* 1.

10. Lee, *Erosion of Biblical Certainty,* 88, emphasis in original.

11. Although individuals often cite Lucy Mack Smith's statement that Joseph had never read the Bible prior to his theophany in 1820 and was "less inclined to the perusal of books than any of the rest of our children" (Lucy Mack Smith, *Biographical Sketches of Joseph Smith, the Prophet, and His Progenitors for Many Generations* [Liverpool: Orson Pratt, 1853], 84), a statement with which Orson Pratt concurred (see *Journal of Discourses,* 21:168–70 [September 21, 1879]), other sources emphasize that the study of the Bible was a staple in the Smith's home. See Richard L. Bushman, *Joseph Smith and the Beginnings of Mormonism* (Urbana, Ill.: University of Illinois Press, 1984), 60. Additionally, the passing reference with which Joseph refers to his encounter with James 1:5, "I was one day reading the Epistle of James" (JS–H 1:11), suggests that the reading of the Bible was a common occurrence.

Biblically Informed Language

One of the most apparent aspects of scripture in The Church of Jesus Christ of Latter-day Saints is the vernacular employed within them. Religious scholar Nicholas Frederick observed that in all of the Latter-day Saints' scriptural texts the trait "that is immediately noticeable is the presence and prominence of the King James Bible. . . . Much like the Book of Mormon, the Doctrine and Covenants appropriated the language and tone of the Bible, sanctifying the latter-day narrative by adopting the tongue of its spiritual predecessor."[12] Smith appears to have been inspired by the Lord to employ the familiar biblical language since the earliest converts to the faith associated authority and power with the voice of the Bible.[13] Such a realization stood as an enduring statement that the voice of God came in the manner of scriptural language, as the Book of Mormon and one of Smith's revelations attested.[14] This understanding that the language in which the scriptures are given is an important component of their effectiveness sets the foundation for the exclusive adoption of the King James New Testament as the official English version for Latter-day Saints.[15]

Christian Primitivism

Likewise, early Latter-day Saint teachings offered an equal place for Christian primitivism, the idea that New Testament principles and doctrines reach back to the beginning of the world.[16] In addition to the foundational documents of the Church adapting New Testament scriptural language, the Book of Mormon provides a clear window through which early Latter-day Saints could glimpse the importance of Christian primitivism. Numerous passages within the Book of Mormon, which by the account's own dating precede the events of the New Testament by upwards of six hundred years,

---

12. Nicholas J. Frederick, *The Bible, Mormon Scripture, and the Rhetoric of Allusivity* (Madison, Wisc.: Fairleigh Dickinson University Press, 2016), xxvii.

13. See Royal Skousen, ed., *The Book of Mormon: The Earliest Texts* (New Haven, Conn.: Yale University Press, 2009), xxiv.

14. See 2 Ne. 31:3 and D&C 1:24; see also "Revelation, 1 November 1831–B [D&C 1]," 126, Joseph Smith Papers, accessed August 11, 2017, http://www.josephsmithpapers.org/paper-summary/revelation-1-november-1831-b-dc-1/2.

15. See *General Handbook: Serving in The Church of Jesus Christ of Latter-day Saints* (Salt Lake City: The Church of Jesus Christ of Latter-day Saints, 2023), 38.8.40.1, https://www.churchofjesuschrist.org/study/manual/general-handbook/38-church-policies-and-guidelines?lang=eng#title_number139.

16. Marvin Hill, "The Role of Christian Primitivism: The Origin and Development of the Mormon Kingdom, 1830–1844" (PhD diss., University of Chicago, 1968).

contain descriptions of New Testament events in striking detail.[17] Joseph Smith emphasized Christian primitivism in his teachings to exemplify how the teachings of the New Testament were not only the source of true Christianity but that those principles were taught from the foundation of the world.[18]

Selective Literalism

Like other Americans, Joseph Smith questioned the degree to which the Bible should be read literally. Americans employed reason to begin questioning the literal interpretation of scripture, often concluding that scripture needed to be amended to reflect reality.[19] While some scholars of the restored gospel have perpetuated the claim that the tradition's primary tendency in studying the Bible is literalism,[20] others have redirected the focus to selective literalism.[21] Summarizing this approach to the Bible by Joseph Smith, Barlow concludes, "Although the Prophet acknowledged metaphorical interpretation and even biblical error, for him, the major events told in the Bible corresponded with external reality."[22] Barlow provides a series of examples that help identify Smith's method in distinguishing between the literal and the metaphorical aspects of scripture, but he does not expand on how Smith and other Church leaders taught such selective literalism to the followers of the faith.[23] On one occasion, Smith provided context for his selective literalism by stating, "I believe the bible as it read when it came from the pen of the original writers."[24] Although absent from Smith's teachings, the Prophet sought to train others how to study the text of the New Testament as it was penned by the original authors, including a study of the text in its original Greek language.[25]

---

17. See 1 Ne. 10:7–11; 1 Ne. 11–15; 2 Ne. 9; Mosiah 3:5–10; and Alma 7 as obvious examples.

18. Smith's translation of the Bible rewrote the story of Adam and Eve with a high degree of recognition of Jesus Christ and New Testament themes. See Moses 5:58.

19. See Ernest Sandeen, *The Roots of Fundamentalism: British and American Millenarianism, 1800–1930* (Chicago: University of Chicago Press, 1970), 107–12.

20. See Melodie Moench, "Nineteenth-Century Mormons: The New Israel," *Dialogue* 12, no. 1 (Spring 1979): 42–56.

21. See Thomas G. Alexander, "The Reconstruction of Mormon Doctrine: From Joseph Smith to Progressive Theology," *Sunstone* 5, no. 4 (July–August 1980): 24–33.

22. Barlow, *Mormons and the Bible,* 36.

23. Barlow, *Mormons and the Bible,* 36.

24. "History, 1838–1856, Volume E-1 [1 July 1843–30 April 1844]," 1755 (October 15, 1843), Joseph Smith Papers, accessed August 11, 2017, http://www.josephsmithpapers.org/paper-summary/history-1838-1856-volume-e-1-1-july-1843-30-april-1844/127.

25. "Journal, 1835–1836," 88 (December 23, 1835), Joseph Smith Papers, accessed August 11, 2017, http://www.josephsmithpapers.org/paper-summary/journal-1835-1836/89.

Dissatisfaction with Biblical Language

The JST provides examples of how Latter-day Saints were to approach the New Testament. In their work on the JST, historians observed a variety of changes that Joseph Smith made to the biblical text, such as restoring original text, restoring text that was not included in the original Bible, editing language to allow enhanced reader understanding, editing language to align with other revelations, and adding teachings that were not in the original text.[26] These changes can be summarized under two ideas: restoring lost texts and clarifying texts for modern readers.

Restoring original text from the Bible was one of Joseph Smith's primary objectives.[27] We see this reflected in Smith's belief that "ignorant translators, careless transcribers, or designing and corrupt priests have committed many errors [in the Bible]."[28] This belief coincides with the Book of Mormon prophet Nephi's statement that there were "many plain and precious things taken away from the [Bible]" (1 Ne. 13:28). This type of change to the biblical text encourages Latter-day Saints to engage in a form of the scholarly activity called textual criticism: to study and establish a more correct edition of the text.

The JST stands as an example of the Lord's desire to make the Bible accessible to all his children. The changes made by Smith reflect a modernization of the Bible translation and a joining of the biblical text to the teachings and revelations of the restored gospel of Jesus Christ. In this way, Smith exemplified his disregard for biblical inerrancy, infallibility, and status as the final word on doctrinal matters by stating, "There are many things in the Bible which do not as they now stand, accord with the Revelations of the Holy Ghost to me."[29] Barlow provides a commentary on this quotation, observing, "Such a statement implies that, for Smith, it was not so much that his revelations needed to be tailored absolutely to biblical

---

26. "Joseph Smith's New Translation of the Bible," in *Joseph Smith's New Translation of the Bible: Original Manuscripts*, ed. Scott H. Faulring, Kent P. Jackson, and Robert J. Matthews (Provo, Utah: Religious Studies Center, Brigham Young University, 2004), 8–11.

27. "History, 1838–1856, Volume A-1 [23 December 1805–30 August 1834]," 175, Joseph Smith Papers, accessed July 7, 2023, http://www.josephsmithpapers.org/paper-summary/account-of-john-april-1829-c-dc-7/2. Here in Joseph Smith's history, he refers to the Joseph Smith Translation of the Bible as "a branch of my <calling>."

28. "History, 1838–1856, Volume E-1," 1755 (October 15, 1843).

29. "History, 1838–1856, Volume D-1 [1 August 1842–1 July 1843]," 1573 (June 11, 1843), Joseph Smith Papers, accessed August 11, 2017, http://www.josephsmithpapers.org/paper-summary/history-1838-1856-volume-d-1-1-august-1842-1-july-1843/218.

data but, rather, that an imperfect Bible ought to conform to his more current and direct revelations."[30]

Disbelief that the Bible Has Sole Doctrinal Authority

Latter-day Saints believe that the New Testament is part of an ever-expanding canon of authoritative religious texts. With the addition of the Book of Mormon and revelations given through the Prophet Joseph, the process of continuing to build on the biblical canon is a central tenet in The Church of Jesus Christ of Latter-day Saints. Smith viewed this belief to be self-evident from the Bible itself, stating, "From what we can draw from the scriptures relative to the teachings of heaven we are induced to think, that much instruction has been given to man since the beginning which we have not [in our possession]."[31] Church members appear to have shared this recognition as Smith noted in his history that "much conjecture and conversation frequently occurred among the Saints, concerning the books mentioned, and referred to, in various places in the Old and New Testaments, which were now nowhere to be found."[32] The Book of Mormon affirmed this belief (see 2 Ne. 29:13), and Smith received a revelation that he introduced as part of a record of John the Beloved.[33] Smith instructed Latter-day Saints to continue to look for and accept different texts outside of the Bible.

Joseph Smith emphasized the necessity of reading the New Testament with the gift of the Holy Ghost to distinguish the literal from the metaphorical and the authentic from error. For Smith, and practitioners of the restored gospel, the Bible, and ancient scripture were insufficient on their own. Smith emphatically proclaimed this by saying, "I have an old edition of the New Testament in Hebrew, Latin, German, and Greek languages. . . . I thank God I have got this old book, but I thank him more for the gift of the Holy Ghost. I have got the oldest book in the world, but I have got the oldest book in my heart, even the gift of the Holy Ghost."[34] It is this same gift that Smith stated separated Latter-day Saints from all other

30. Barlow, *Mormons and the Bible,* 62.

31. *Evening and the Morning Star* 2, no. 18 (March 1834): 143.

32. Joseph Smith Jr., *History of The Church of Jesus Christ of Latter-Day Saints,* ed. B. H. Roberts, 7 vols. (Salt Lake City: Deseret News, 1902), 1:132.

33. "Account of John, April 1829–C [D&C 7]," 13, Joseph Smith Papers, accessed August 11, 2017, https://www.josephsmithpapers.org/paper-summary/account-of-john-april-1829-c-dc-7/1.

34. "History, 1838–1856, Volume E-1," 1972 (April 7, 1844).

religious organizations during his audience with President Martin Van Buren.[35] Without the Holy Ghost, Latter-day Saints were doomed to make the same mistakes that the ancient Christians made in failing to come to grips with and to adequately reproduce the Bible.

Joseph Smith encouraged this type of study of the New Testament within established Schools of the Prophets. These schools, which operated from 1833 to 1884, likely shared their curriculum with similarly established groups in the nineteenth century[36] and incorporated many of the additional insights that the Prophet had introduced through his inspired translation of the Bible. Smith appears to have limited this training to the leaders of the Church, perhaps with the intent that they would pass their knowledge on to the general populace of Latter-day Saints.[37] Ultimately, Smith encouraged members of the Church to "study the bible"[38] but to do so from the unique perspective of the Restoration.

The impact of this period on the study of the New Testament in The Church of Jesus Christ of Latter-day Saints was not felt immediately. Following the Prophet's martyrdom in 1844 and the splintering of the main body of Saints, most of whom followed Brigham Young, the JST was viewed with caution. The Church issued an official statement on the JST in 1868 to advise on the recent publication of the text by the Reorganized Church of Jesus Christ of Latter Day Saints entitled *The Holy Scriptures*.[39] As professor Thomas Wayment summarizes, "The key points of the Church's official position in 1868 are an allusion to the future coming forth of the New Translation under the direction of God, a clear endorsement of the inspiration that the Prophet Joseph had received while working on the Bible, and the belief that the New Translation was not complete."[40] Although initially

35. "Letterbook 2," 88 (December 5, 1839), Joseph Smith Papers, accessed August 11, 2017, http://www.josephsmithpapers.org/paper-summary/letterbook-2/93.

36. Joseph F. Darowski, "Schools of the Prophets: An Early American Tradition," *Mormon Historical Studies* 9, no. 1 (Spring 2008): 1–14.

37. Steven R. Sorensen, "Schools of the Prophets," in Ludlow, *Encyclopedia of Mormonism*, 3:1269–70.

38. "History, 1838–1856, Volume F-1 [1 May 1844–8 August 1844]," 92 (June 12, 1844), Joseph Smith Papers, accessed August 11, 2017, http://www.josephsmithpapers.org/paper-summary/history-1838-1856-volume-f-1-1-may-1844-8-august-1844/98.

39. "Joseph Smith Translation of the Bible," Gospel Topics, The Church of Jesus Christ of Latter-day Saints, accessed December 1, 2023, https://www.churchofjesuschrist.org/study/history/topics/joseph-smith-translation-of-the-bible?lang=eng.

40. Thomas A. Wayment, ed., *The Complete Joseph Smith Translation of the New Testament: A Side-by-Side Comparison with the King James Version* (Salt Lake City: Deseret Book, 2005), xii.

resisted, the later work of Robert J. Matthews would resurrect the JST within the Latter-day Saint community, leading to its incorporation into general Church circulation and study in 1979.

The Development of Sunday School Answers to the New Testament (1845–1885)

As the nineteenth century progressed, so did approaches to the study of the Bible in the United States. Christians who had previously disavowed creeds and religious hierarchy began to develop various approaches to the study of the Bible that aimed at balancing the progress of science and philosophy with traditional approaches to interpreting the biblical text. These attempts created the popular perspective that scripture contained dualism, or multiple meanings derived from the same text. As George Marsden has observed, "Almost all [American Protestants] held that the Bible contained dual meanings. . . . Hidden in the words of the original sayings might be a secondary meaning not apparent until much later when the prophecy was fulfilled."[41] This was especially true for the study of the Old Testament, which Christians contested could only be properly understood through the lens of the New Testament. Christians in America frequently employed typological interpretations upon scripture (such as seeing Old Testament figures and events as prophecies pointing towards the figure of Christ in the New Testament).[42] Often these typological interpretations were pointed toward current events in the United States. Marsden concluded, "These views continued to have great force in nineteenth-century America, as the view that the United States was the New Israel and the central cite of the spiritual preparations for the millennial age. The progress of history was thus casting new light on the meanings of God's revelation."[43]

While many American Protestant Christians were employing these methods of rationalism and dualism to find meaning in the Bible, biblical scholars emphasized principles and methods that aimed to get back to the original meaning of the text. An understanding of the authorial intent of the biblical author became the critical foundation to their understanding of the Bible.[44]

41. George M. Marsden, "Everyone One's Own Interpreter? The Bible, Science, and Authority in Mid-Nineteenth-Century America," in Hatch and Noll, *Bible in America,* 92.

42. Hans W. Frei, *The Eclipse of Biblical Narrative: A Study of Eighteenth and Nineteenth Century Hermeneutics* (New Haven, Conn.: Yale University Press, 1974), 66.

43. Marsden, "Everyone One's Own Interpreter," 93.

44. Marsden, "Everyone One's Own Interpreter," 91–92.

Moses Stuart, a nineteenth-century biblical scholar and primary proponent of discovering authorial intent, declared that if there was an intended understanding that the author placed upon the biblical text and the hearers of the biblical text were aware of the intent, there could be no dualistic or hidden meaning outside of that which was originally revealed.[45] Stuart's writings provoked a plethora of responses but illustrated the many different approaches for attributing meaning to a biblical text.

The introduction of these new approaches to the study of the Bible in the nineteenth century required Protestant American Christians to develop new methods of presenting the biblical narrative to the rising generation. Although Bibles aimed at the young and unlearned have existed since the Middle Ages, in nineteenth-century America, local sectarian publications dominated the biblical narrative for children.[46] Unlike Great Britain, where publications of children's biblical material were centralized in London and controlled by the Church of England, local congregations and denominations produced individualized children's Bibles for their laity.

Local sectarian groups also began to form Sunday Schools. One historian noted, "The Sunday school movement in America started in the early nineteenth century. . . . The organizers of the first American Sunday schools imagined they could reach poor children in order to instill social behaviors associated with religious virtue, primarily obedience."[47] In addition to these denominational Bibles and Sunday schools, scripture catechisms (short sayings organized in a question-and-answer format intended for memorization) were a primary and popular source for Bible literacy in the nineteenth century.[48]

The tradition of local publications and catechisms instructing youth and adults from the Bible carried over into the Restoration. Kenneth Alford observed, "Converts to The Church of Jesus Christ of Latter-day Saints often brought with them a catechistic background. . . . Thus catechisms

45. Moses Stuart, "Are the Same Principles to Be Applied to the Scriptures as to Other Books?," *Biblical Repository* 2, no. 5 (January 1832): 129–37.

46. Ruth B. Bottigheimer, *The Bible for Children: From the Age of Gutenberg to the Present* (New Haven, Conn.: Yale University Press, 1996), 48.

47. Randi Lynn Tanglen, "Religious Popular Culture and the Critique of Romantic Racialism in Harriet E. Wilson's *Our Nig*," in *Nineteenth-Century American Women Write Religion: Lived Theologies and Literature*, ed. Mary McCartin Wearn (London: Routledge, 2014), 80.

48. See Ruth B. Bottigheimer, "Religious Writing for Children: Catechistical, Devotional, and Biblical Writing," in *International Companion Encyclopedia of Children's Literature*, ed. Peter Hunt (London: Routledge, 2004), 271.

were a familiar religious education device to many early Latter-day Saint converts. It was a natural extension, therefore, for Latter-day Saints to create and use catechisms to teach the doctrines of the Restoration."[49] Various publications that focused on the doctrines of the restored gospel were produced throughout the nineteenth century in a catechistic format, but only two catechisms were specifically produced for the study of the Bible.

Beginning with the November 23, 1872, issue of the *Juvenile Instructor,* a serial catechism titled "Questions and Answers on the Bible" appeared within the periodical.[50] This serial provided catechisms on general biblical facts in the first serial and then published a catechism on the text of the Old Testament weekly until the November 27, 1875, edition. At this time, the publication of the series became erratic. From its inception, the series ran alongside a catechism titled "Questions and Answers on the Book of Mormon."[51] This practice continued until the January 1, 1879, edition, when it appears that catechisms were removed from the periodical's circulation schedule prior to the publication of various catechisms in book form.[52]

In addition to the serial publication of "Questions and Answers on the Bible" in the *Juvenile Instructor,* Eliza R. Snow, second president of the Relief Society and noted author, published *Bible Questions and Answers for Children* in 1881.[53] Snow explained the purpose for the volume in her own words as being an aid in "impress[ing] the minds of the children with important facts in the Old and New Testaments."[54] In the catechism, Snow posed various questions regarding the biblical text that were no different from other biblical catechisms circulating in America at the time.[55] But unlike other Christian

49. Kenneth L. Alford, "A History of Mormon Catechisms," in *A Firm Foundation: Church Organization and Administration,* ed. David J. Whittaker and Arnold K. Garr, Brigham Young University Church History Symposium (Provo, Utah: Religious Studies Center, Brigham Young University, 2011), 225–26.

50. "Questions and Answers on the Bible," *Juvenile Instructor* 7, no. 24 (November 23, 1872): 192.

51. See "Questions and Answers on the Book of Mormon and on the Bible," *Juvenile Instructor* 12, no. 2 (January 15, 1877): 17.

52. See "Questions and Answers on the Bible and on the Book of Mormon," *Juvenile Instructor* 14, no. 1 (January 1, 1879): 5. Alford recounts the rich history of the Juvenile Instructor Office publishing many of the catechisms in book and card form; see Alford, "History of Mormon Catechisms," 236.

53. Eliza R. Snow, *Bible Questions and Answers for Children* (Salt Lake City: Juvenile Instructor Office, 1881).

54. Snow, *Bible Questions and Answers,* 120.

55. See Isaac Watts, *Dr. Watts's Plain and Easy Catechisms for Children; The Shorter Catechism of the Assembly of Divines at Westminster with Explanatory Notes; and a Preservative*

publications that merely quoted the Bible, Snow's publication interpreted the Bible through the lens of her religious tradition.[56]

Although these catechisms were aimed at children, they were "not designed to be placed in the hands of children for them to study, but to assist those who have charge of children . . . [who are] expected to read a question, and another appointee to read the answer, and all the children present repeat the answer in concert."[57] This is exemplified by the heading of the first article in the *Juvenile Instructor* series, which read, "Catechism for Sunday Schools."[58] These catechisms provided a central curriculum and were the catalyst for important developments for Church members' study of the Bible during the nineteenth century. Although early Latter-day Saints held meetings of various types that involved the discussion, expansion, and study of the Bible, it wasn't until the Saints settled in the West that Church leaders founded an official arm of the Church devoted to the study of Church doctrine and authoritative texts.[59] As is evident today, the establishment of the Sunday School and its heritage for studying the New Testament continues to influence members of the Church, though the curriculum has changed drastically.

Higher Criticism and the Establishment of Church Religious Education with Academies, Seminaries, and Institutes (1885–1960)

The populace of the United States began to change in their acceptance of the Bible and Christianity as the nineteenth century began to give way to the twentieth. The complexities between faith and reason began to strain relationships between theologians, philosophers, scientists, and different religious communities that had once been complementary to one another.

---

from the Sins and Follies of Childhood and Youth (Cambridge, Mass.: Hillard and Metcalf, 1825), 19–23.

56. This is made most apparent in the early chapters of the catechism where Snow discusses the creation. After posing the question of "Who made this world?" the required response is "The Gods." This theological ideology introduced in the revelations of the Restoration is followed by another teaching of Joseph Smith when the question is posed, "How long did it take to make the world and all things in it?" The required response is "Six days." But the question is followed by "At that time, how many years long was a day?" to be responded to with "One thousand." Each of these responses was reliant upon unique Latter-day Saint doctrines of the day. See Snow, *Bible Questions and Answers,* 3.

57. Snow, *Bible Questions and Answers,* 120.

58. "Questions and Answers on the Bible," 192.

59. B. Lloyd Poelman, "Sunday School," in Ludlow, *Encyclopedia of Mormonism,* 3:1425–27.

Commenting on the growing tension between religion and science, Edwin Gaustad and Leigh Schmidt stated, "[For] theologians, science kept invading their territory, answering questions about the origin and purpose of the world, about the nature and destiny of humanity—questions that were fundamentally religious rather than scientific. [For] scientists, theology blocked the pathways to knowledge, ruling the experiments of the laboratory as off limits, improper, and even dangerous."[60] These ideological battles, best known in the field of biology over the theory of evolution, spilled over into the fields of psychology, sociology, anthropology, history, and archaeology. Scholars carried these debates forward, but the trickle-down effect of these discussions influenced adherents and almost all religious traditions that revered the Bible.

The methods and ideology of higher biblical criticism, which flourished in Germany during the nineteenth century, contributed to the growing animosity between religious approaches to the Bible and scientific ones. These methods for studying the Bible began to cross the Atlantic and find place in the United States as the century concluded. Higher criticism consisted of using rational judgment to understand the text of the Bible and its validity in recounting historical events. Richard and Kendall Soulen explain this as "an approach to the study of scripture that is centrally concerned with searching for and applying neutral, i.e., scientific and nonsectarian, canons of judgment in its investigation of the biblical text."[61] While rational approaches and the application of scientific methods were applied to the Bible long before the waning years of the nineteenth century, most American Protestants shared the belief that the Bible still contained the infallible word of God. Although they disagreed on the meaning of the infallible text, they maintained a sense of its validity as fact until the closing decades of the century.[62]

The general acceptance of the validity of the biblical texts as historical fact began to change in public perception during the last third of the nineteenth century. Textual criticism, the analysis of ancient manuscripts to identify the most plausible and oldest reading of a biblical text, came to an apex in the late 1800s. Through seeking after the elusive "original reading" or "autograph" of each biblical text, textual critics identified various mistakes

60. Edwin S. Gaustad and Leigh E. Schmidt, *The Religious History of America: The Heart of the American Story from Colonial Times to Today,* rev. ed. (New York: HarperSanFrancisco, 2002), 302.

61. Richard N. Soulen and R. Kendall Soulen, *Handbook of Biblical Criticism,* 4th ed. (Louisville, Ky.: Westminster John Knox, 2011), 20.

62. Mark A. Noll, *Between Faith and Criticism: Evangelicals, Scholarship, and the Bible in America* (Vancouver, Can.: Regent College Publishing, 2004), 11.

within the translation of the Authorized (King James) Version.[63] With the publication of the Revised Version of the New Testament in 1881 and its companion of the Old Testament in 1885, individuals began to modify their traditional conceptualization of the Bible as being infallible.[64] Additional translations of the Bible followed over the next fifty years. Scholars and religious adherents sought to create a translation that satisfied the changing needs of students of the Bible.[65] Furthermore, citizens began to have greater access to public and higher education following the American Civil War, leading to a professionalization of the academic life and a dissemination of academic ideals.[66] The rise of critical New Testament scholarship at this time threatened traditional understandings of the nature and character of Jesus Christ and the validity of Christian claims to a historically accurate and dependable New Testament text.[67]

This changed perspective among the masses led to an equal response by faith traditions who sought to reaffirm the biblical record. Despite the Bible's textual inconsistencies and blossoming Bible translations, many believed that the same scientific inquiry used by opponents to the Bible could be used to affirm it. Shalom Goldman observed,

> By the mid-nineteenth century [the higher criticism] school of interpretation, which subjected the biblical text to the same rigorous historical analysis as it did the texts of the classical world, was seen as a challenge to the belief that Scripture was divinely inspired. Churchmen and theologians feared that the subversion of biblical authority would lead to the spread of "unbelief." Many considered exploration and discovery in Palestine to be an "antidote to the poison of unbelief."[68]

Many faith traditions relied on the work of archaeologists like Archibald H. Sayce, who tested the main points made by higher critics against the

63. Peter J. Thuesen, *In Discordance with the Scriptures: American Protestant Battles over Translating the Bible* (New York: Oxford University Press, 1999), 42.

64. Ira V. Brown, "The Higher Criticism Comes to America, 1880–1900," *Journal of the Presbyterian Historical Society* 38, no. 4 (December 1960): 197.

65. Over the course of this period (1885–1960), three prominent translations of the Bible came into existence in the United States that rivaled the traditionally accepted King James Version (Authorized Version): Revised Version (1881, 1885, 1894), American Standard Version (1901), and the Revised Standard Version (1952).

66. Noll, *Between Faith and Criticism*, 32–33.

67. Raymond F. Collins, "Historical-Critical Methodology," in *Introduction to the New Testament* (Garden City, N.Y.: Doubleday, 1983), 41–74.

68. Shalom Goldman, *God's Sacred Tongue: Hebrew and the American Imagination* (Chapel Hill: University of North Carolina Press, 2004), 133.

evidence of archaeology.[69] The spread of higher criticism and a dwindling belief in the validity of the biblical texts led many Christian congregations to establish places of learning that were patterned after academies but devoted to the study of the Bible within an established and secure setting.[70] Many believing individuals pursued advanced education at approved Bible schools for the purpose of advancing their particular faith tradition's approach to biblical texts.[71]

Within this cultural milieu, Latter-day Saints also engaged in higher education, attempting to validate their own interpretations and conclusions about the New Testament. Most relevant to the study of the New Testament is the education of Elder James E. Talmage (a superintendent of classes for the religious instruction of children among the Latter-day Saints), who began to engage in higher education through the obtaining of advanced degrees in the fields of geology and education at Lehigh and Johns Hopkins Universities. Throughout his educational experience, Talmage was exposed to thoughts about religion and science that he applied to the teachings of the restored gospel. Talmage sought to make these insights accessible to members of the Church.[72] He wrote extensively through the early years of the twentieth century and in his later ministry as a member of the Quorum of the Twelve Apostles. Like scholars from other faith traditions, Talmage utilized his academic training to improve his ability to speak with an authoritative voice in both the fields of religion and science.[73]

Talmage wrote *Jesus the Christ*[74] as a response to the criticisms of this period about the New Testament, particularly against multiplying discussions

69. Thomas W. Davis, *Shifting Sands: The Rise and Fall of Biblical Archaeology* (New York: Oxford University Press, 2004), 23–27.

70. Rick Ostrander, *Head, Heart, and Hand: John Brown University and Modern Evangelical Higher Education* (Fayetteville: University of Arkansas Press, 2003), 39–41.

71. See Sandeen, *Roots of Fundamentalism*, 244.

72. When James E. Talmage was commissioned to write *Jesus the Christ*, he was instructed by the First Presidency (John F. Smith, John R. Winder, and Anthon H. Lund) to write the work so that it could "be placed within the reach of Church members and general readers." John F. Smith, John R. Winder, and Anthon H. Lund to James E. Talmage, July 18, 1905, photo by R. Scott Lloyd, https://www.churchofjesuschrist.org/church/news/church-classic-jesus-the-christ-published-100-years-ago?lang=eng.

73. See Terryl Givens, *Wrestling the Angel: The Foundations of Mormon Thought; Cosmos, God, Humanity* (New York: Oxford University Press, 2015), 218.

74. James E. Talmage, *Jesus the Christ: A Study of the Messiah and His Mission according to Holy Scriptures both Ancient and Modern* (Salt Lake City: The Church of Jesus Christ of Latter-day Saints, 1981).

that diminished the divine character and nature of Jesus Christ.[75] Influenced by other writers who preceded him,[76] Talmage wrote a response to higher criticism as it pertained to the life and ministry of Jesus Christ. Talmage's purpose is made clear in the preface to the volume: "It is particularly congruous and appropriate that the Church of Jesus Christ of Latter-day Saints—the only Church that affirms authority based on specific revelation and commission to use the Lord's Holy Name as a distinctive designation—should set forth her doctrines concerning the Messiah and His mission."[77] While Talmage provided the messages, the Church provided a platform for its dissemination.

The influence that Talmage's work has had on approaches to studying the New Testament in The Church of Jesus Christ of Latter-day Saints cannot be overstated. Discussing the reception of Talmage's work within the Latter-day Saint community, professors Richard Neitzel Holzapfel and Thomas Wayment have stated, "The immediate acceptance and popularity of *Jesus the Christ* following its publication in September 1915 are demonstrated by the release of a second edition just three months later."[78] This popularity was influenced by an endorsement the work received from the leaders of the Church. A letter published by the First Presidency concerning the work states,

> The book is more than a "Life of Christ" in the ordinary acceptation of that title. . . . We desire that the work, "Jesus the Christ" be read and studied by the Latter-day Saints, in their families, and in the organizations that are devoted wholly or in part to theological study. We commend it especially for use in our Church schools, as also for the advanced theological classes in Sunday schools and priesthood quorums, for the instruction of our missionaries, and for general reading.[79]

For nearly a century, the book maintained a rare position as an official publication of the Church and was among only a handful of volumes authorized for use by missionaries.

75. Malcolm R. Thorp, "James E. Talmage and the Tradition of Victorian Lives of Jesus," *Sunstone* 12, no. 1 (January 1988): 8.

76. Thorp explores three of the individuals that were highly influential in Talmage's writing of *Jesus the Christ*—namely, Frederick W. Farrar, J. Cunningham Geikie, and Alfred Edersheim. See Thorp, "James E. Talmage," 9.

77. Talmage, *Jesus the Christ,* iii.

78. Richard Neitzel Holzapfel and Thomas A. Wayment, *James E. Talmage's* Jesus the Christ *Study Guide* (Salt Lake City: Deseret Book, 2014), xvi.

79. James R. Clark, ed., *Messages of the First Presidency of The Church of Jesus Christ of Latter-day Saints,* vol. 4 (Salt Lake City: Bookcraft, 1970), 340.

While Talmage sought to emphasize the divinity of Jesus Christ in contrast to secular manipulations that diminished the Savior's character and nature, the work of J. Reuben Clark focused on combating the rise of secularism that sowed distrust in the biblical text and in the King James Version. Clark was highly educated, revered in the field of law, and a prolific writer. Clark, who would later serve in the First Presidency of the Church, devoted his Church leadership capacities to ensuring that the rise of secularism did not breach Church education.[80] Two publications from President Clark played a primary role in shaping the way in which Latter-day Saints approached learning about and studying the New Testament.

Presented in 1938, "The Chartered Course of the Church in Education" is one of Clark's most enduring legacies. Still maintained as suggested reading for all Church Education System personnel, the "Chartered Course" emphasizes the way in which Church seminaries, institutes, and academies are supposed to approach the study of the gospel in general. Leaving no room for misinterpretation, Clark stated,

> You are not to teach the philosophies of the world, ancient or modern, pagan or Christian, for this is the field of the public schools. Your sole field is the gospel, and that is boundless in its own sphere. We pay taxes to support those state institutions whose function and work it is to teach the arts, the sciences, literature, history, the languages, and so on through the whole *secular curriculum.* These institutions are to do this work. But we use the tithes of the Church to carry on the Church school system, and these are impressed with a holy trust. The Church seminaries and institutes are to teach the gospel.[81]

While addressed to religious educators, the discourse found a wider audience through appearances in the Deseret News, the *Improvement Era,* and in a pamphlet separately published by the Church.[82] The document "has become the most influential address to seminary and institute teachers in

80. See D. Michael Quinn, *J. Reuben Clark: The Church Years* (Provo, Utah: Brigham Young University Press, 1983), 161–72. Here Quinn emphasizes the dichotomy that existed with Clark as he attempted to balance the life of a disciple with the life of a scholar and how such a life could be replicated within others.

81. J. Reuben Clark Jr., "The Chartered Course of the Church in Education" (Salt Lake City: The Church of Jesus Christ of Latter-day Saints, 1994), 10–11, emphasis added, accessed November 1, 2023, https://www.churchofjesuschrist.org/bc/content/shared/content/english/pdf/language-materials/32709_eng.pdf.

82. The Church of Jesus Christ of Latter-day Saints, *By Study and Also by Faith: One Hundred Years of Seminaries and Institutes of Religion* (Salt Lake City: The Church of Jesus Christ of Latter-day Saints, 2015), 101–3.

the history of Church education."[83] Adhering to its call to curb secularism, Church education emphasized the necessity to maintain a course consistent with revealed truths rather than the doctrines of men.

Clark's other enduring legacy is a series of study notes defending the King James Version of the Bible. While organizing his notes for publication, President Clark delivered a general conference address on the material he was preparing to present to the Church and the world. After recounting the history of textual criticism on the New Testament and highlighting various controversies in the academic world concerning events in the life of Jesus Christ, Clark concluded, "To the Latter-day Saint, Jesus was the Christ, the Only Begotten, the Son of God, a member of the Trinity. All our modern scriptures are to this point, and the true ancient scriptures will neither take away from, nor destroy this everlasting truth."[84]

Clark's finished work, *Why the King James Version,*[85] built upon the foundation he established in his general conference address. This nearly five-hundred-page compilation of personal notes is almost exclusively interested in the New Testament. In the preface, Clark states:

> Save for some few comments on the origin of writing and alphabets and on Old Testament criticism, these *Notes* relate exclusively to the New Testament which it is now proposed to name "The New Covenant." The problem covered by these *Notes* is,—Shall the King James Version (also known as the Authorized Version) be abandoned and a Revised Version (one of the three of them, British and American) be adopted in its stead?[86]

Clark continues to explain why he has chosen to engage primarily in the New Testament rather than the entire Bible. He declares:

> The effect of the position of the Extreme Textualists as set forth in their Revisions of the Bible, is to weaken, if not destroy the Messiahship of Jesus. Incidents recorded in the King James Version have been omitted from the Revised Version; substantial parts of whole chapters . . . ; doctrines and teachings have been changed; doubts have been cast on fundamental expressions declaring the divinity and personality of Jesus the Christ; faith-destroying questions have been raised by marginal notes and by the text itself; the personality of Jesus in its Christian concept has in

83. Church of Jesus Christ, *By Study and Also by Faith,* 101.

84. J. Reuben Clark, in *Conference Reports for The Church of Jesus Christ of Latter-day Saints, Conference Report April 1954 Afternoon Meeting* (Salt Lake City: The Church of Jesus Christ of Latter-day Saints, 1954), 47.

85. J. Reuben Clark Jr., *Why the King James Version* (Salt Lake City: Deseret Book, 1956).

86. Clark, *Why the King James Version,* 1, emphasis in original.

> effect, been challenged. . . . The Latter-day Saints cannot in any way sanction even the slightest derogation of these principles. The Prophet has put his stamp of approval upon all this as contained in the New Testament of the King James translation.[87]

Clark articulates to the reader his perceptions concerning the rise of secular approaches to the New Testament as revealed through modern Bible translations. Through meticulous research, Clark details translator errors as revealed through their annotations and execution. Clark ultimately concludes, "The King James Version is the best record to these ends that has yet been revealed through the Bible."[88] While Clark's work influenced Latter-day Saints in their attitudes and approaches toward their study of the New Testament and New Testament scholarship, it is telling that Clark emphasized, "For this book I alone am responsible. It is not a Church publication."[89]

Developments within the Church brought about an expansion in Church religious education beyond Sunday School and accelerated the influence of Talmage's and Clark's works and messages against secularism. Additionally, the study of the New Testament on a regular basis introduced publications from other individuals who occupied less prominent positions within the Church. Church Commissioner of Education Joseph F. Merrill commissioned Obert C. Tanner, a prolific writer in his own right, to produce an appropriate textbook for the study of the New Testament in 1932.[90] Tanner's publication *New Testament Studies*[91] contributed to an attempt at uniformity in the curriculum for the newly established seminaries and institutes throughout the Church, although it included sectarian approaches to the text.[92] The work, along with its subdued iteration, *The New Testament Speaks,*[93] consisted of individual lessons that instructors used to guide classroom discussions on the New Testament.

---

87. Clark, *Why the King James Version,* 6–7.

88. Clark, *Why the King James Version,* 7.

89. Quinn, *J. Reuben Clark,* 171; Clark, *Why the King James Version?,* v.

90. Obert C. Tanner, Lewis M. Rogers, and Sterling M. McMurrin, *Toward Understanding the New Testament* (Salt Lake City: Signature Books, 1990), ix; Church of Jesus Christ, *By Study and by Faith,* 60.

91. Obert C. Tanner, *New Testament Studies* (Salt Lake City: Department of Education of The Church of Jesus Christ of Latter-day Saints, 1932).

92. Church of Jesus Christ, *By Study and by Faith,* 60.

93. Obert C. Tanner, *The New Testament Speaks* (Salt Lake City: Department of Education of The Church of Jesus Christ of Latter-day Saints, 1935).

In 1954, Lowell Bennion wrote the New Testament course of study for Gospel Doctrine classes of the Church Sunday Schools. This curriculum was revised and published under the title *Teachings of the New Testament* (1962) with the intent to be used as a reference guide for the New Testament. Unlike the other Latter-day Saint study guide writers, Bennion organized his book topically, covering the major themes of the New Testament: salvation through Jesus Christ, personal and social ideals taught in the New Testament for modern readers, and characteristics of the pristine Church. These writings focus mostly on the doctrinal implications of the New Testament with little reference to historical or social circumstances.[94]

During this period, the first seminaries and institutes of religion for the Church were established and played an essential role in engaging Latter-day Saints with the texts of scripture, including the New Testament. Under the direction of Joseph F. Merrill, seminaries and institutes offered concurrent classes throughout the school year in each of the four standard works of the Church.[95] John A. Widstoe, who succeeded Merrill as Church Commissioner of Education, introduced a rotating schedule where classes offered the same course of study throughout the year and rotated through the standard works during a four-year period.[96] While seminaries and institutes reverted back to the old system of concurrently teaching the standard works of the Church, Widstoe's rotation would later become the norm in Church religious education.

Seminary classes were offered concurrently with a high school education to provide a foundation of scriptural literacy to youth. Institute classes were intended to fulfill a different role. The first institute director of the Church, J. Wyley Session, had to decide the curriculum for his students at the University of Idaho in the mid-1910s. Commissioner Merrill assisted him. Sessions recounted Merrill instructing him to "enable our young people attending the colleges to make the necessary adjustments between the things they have been taught in the Church and the things they are learning in the university, to engage them to become firmly settled in their faith as members of the church."[97] The institute program, which offered

94. Lowell L. Bennion, *Teachings of the New Testament* (Salt Lake City: Deseret Book, 1956).

95. Church of Jesus Christ, *By Study and by Faith,* 61–62.

96. Church of Jesus Christ, *By Study and by Faith,* 61–62.

97. James Wyley Sessions, Oral history, interview by Gary L. Shumway and Gordon Irving, August 12, 1972, 11, James Moyle Oral History Program, Church History Library, Salt Lake City.

New Testament courses on a rotating basis in a similar way to the seminary program, began to spread to other universities.

Like a double-edged sword, mixed outcomes resulted from increased exposure to New Testament study in the Church. While students and members were exposed to the text more directly through professionalization, instructors were expected to have an advanced knowledge in the subject matter, leading some to pursue advanced degrees.[98] When instructors returned with advanced degrees from the University of Chicago in the 1930s, "they resumed their positions in the religious education programs of the Church. As the influence of the Chicago school spread, Church leaders began to see some of the harmful effects of introducing worldly scholarship into the study of the scriptures."[99] This proliferation of modern biblical interpretation in classrooms, which intended to combat the influence of secularism, invigorated the work of J. Reuben Clark and later Elder Boyd K. Packer, both of whom sought to ensure that the introduction of such material did not damage the faith of students. The question of what it meant to learn "by study and also by faith" (D&C 88:118) would greatly influence the study of the New Testament among Latter-day Saints in the coming decades.

New Testament in the Era of Contribution (1960–2018)

Various textual criticism theories and ideological approaches can cause disputes about biblical text. The explosion of publications during this time widened the divide between various Christian interpretations that influenced students of the Bible to adhere to their respective ideologies. Since 1960, no less than twenty different major translations of the Bible have become available.[100] Additionally, various commentaries on the books of the New Testament have been published along a wide range of interpretive ideologies. Making interpretation even more challenging is the plethora of commentaries, translations, and opinions that are available through the worldwide web.

While the debate between differing interpretations of the New Testament is rooted in the scientific and historical critical debates of the past,

---

98. Church of Jesus Christ, *By Study and by Faith*, 56–58.

99. Church of Jesus Christ, *By Study and by Faith*, 58.

100. Examples of these translations include, the New International Version (1978, 1984, 2011), the New American Standard Bible (1971, 1995), the New Revised Standard Version (1989), the World English Bible (2000), the English Standard Version (2001), the Living Bible (1971), Good News Bible (1976, 1992), the Clear Word Bible (1994), the Contemporary English Version (1995), God's Word (1996, 2004, 2007, 2015), The Message (2002), and many others.

some New Testament scholars established the Jesus Seminar, a type of scholarship focused on finding the historical Jesus. Jesus Seminar scholars employed higher criticism to discover the "actual" Jesus as opposed to what they deemed the glorified or exaggerated Jesus of the Gospels. They investigated the sources of the narrative about Jesus Christ with the purpose of identifying the most historically plausible and least historically plausible accounts of his life. Many questions posed by the Jesus Seminar were rooted in the synoptic problem (the relationship between Matthew, Mark, and Luke) and earlier critical views of the New Testament.[101]

As historian John Dominic Crossan has observed, "[The search for the Historical Jesus] is precisely [a] fourfold record, even if there were no external documents whatsoever, that constitutes the literary problem. If you read those four texts vertically, as it were, from start to finish and one after another, you get a generally persuasive impression of unity, harmony, and agreement. But if you read them horizontally, focusing on this or that unit and comparing it across two, three, or four versions, it is disagreement rather than agreement that strikes one most forcibly."[102] The sweeping desire to find the historical Jesus dominated New Testament scholarship for nearly five decades. While subsiding in recent years, most scholars continue to employ methods akin to those of the Jesus Seminar to validate or disprove various elements of the New Testament. It is within this cultural context that many of the most pervasive conclusions concerning the New Testament among Latter-day Saints were perpetuated.

Like Christianity at large, there exists a divide among students of the New Testament in The Church of Jesus Christ of Latter-day Saints concerning interpretation. Unlike other Christian congregations (who might solve these issues with schisms or creedal pronouncements), the Latter-day Saints are left to themselves to decide. Terryl Givens has observed this abundant degree of allowance. He states, "The absence of a clear pronouncement from the Mormon leadership on matters of scriptural interpretation means that members have a good deal of latitude in how they interpret subjects [in the Bible]."[103] The lack of an official statement requires individual Latter-day Saints to decide for themselves how they interpret the declaration, "We believe the Bible to be the word of God so

---

101. See Walter P. Weaver, *The Historical Jesus in the Twentieth Century: 1900–1950* (Harrisburg, Penn.: Trinity Press International, 1999).

102. John Dominic Crossan, *The Historical Jesus: The Life of a Mediterranean Jewish Peasant* (San Francisco: HarperCollins, 1991), xxx.

103. Givens, *Feeding the Flock*, 264.

far as it is translated correctly" (A of F 1:8). For decades, the interpretation of this statement has been constructed to support both conservative and progressive views of scripture within the Church.

Latter-day Saints, while given this wide latitude in identifying an appropriate interpretation of the scriptures, can be widely influenced by competing and compelling sources. Philip Barlow observed, "Latter-day Saints are urged to depend primarily on the scriptures rather than on works about the scriptures," but he added that "from among the many expressions of Mormon faith articulated throughout its history, one particular expression will have unofficial—perhaps even the inadvertent—but nevertheless the implied support of The Church of Jesus Christ of Latter-day Saints."[104] In this connection, Givens maintains that the unofficial support has been predominantly given to the interpretations championed by individuals like Elder Joseph Fielding Smith and Elder Bruce R. McConkie, largely due to their positions as Apostles within the Church.[105] However, Barlow's recognition that the official position of the Church is one of individual freedom is instructive. While the work of McConkie, Smith, and Clark are more recognized and often more frequently quoted, the scholarship of other Latter-day Saints can be equally inspiring.

For the most part, the New Testament scholarship in the Church from the mid-twentieth century was written from a Latter-day Saint perspective for a Latter-day Saint audience. However, many scholars shied away from being apologetic about the distinctive characteristics of the restored gospel and wrote with a voice intending to collaborate with other faiths and general biblical scholarship. Their scholarship increased New Testament literacy among Latter-day Saints. In the survey of influential works, we will discuss four categories of scholarship with specific examples.[106]

Devotional Scholarship

The first category of writings on the New Testament in this period is possibly the broadest and most interpretive—devotional scholarship. These works, like the compilation of discourses in *Jesus Christ: Son of God, Savior,*[107]

---

104. Barlow, *Mormons and the Bible,* 213, 214.

105. Givens, *Feeding the Flock,* 264.

106. Many of these works are discussed in greater detail in "Tracking New Testament Study among Latter-day Saints" by Kelsey Draper Lambert and John S. Thompson found elsewhere in this volume.

107. Paul H. Peterson, Gary Layne Hatch, and Laura D. Card, eds., *Jesus Christ: Son of God, Savior* (Provo, Utah: Religious Studies Center, Brigham Young University 2002).

address a general Latter-day Saint audience with the intent to promote faith. The authors' concern is not so much the accuracy of research and scholarship, but rather the implication of the text. The following few examples show some of the characteristics of this type of scholarship among the Latter-day Saints.

One of the most prolific Latter-day Saint authors, orators, and scholars during this period was Bruce R. McConkie. McConkie's first major work on the New Testament, the three-volume *Doctrinal New Testament Commentary,* provided a Latter-day Saint interpretation of virtually every New Testament verse.[108] In his explanation of the collection, McConkie includes a three-step key to interpreting scripture. First, one must search and read the text diligently; second, one must listen to the counsel from modern-day prophets and inspired leaders; and third, one must live worthy to have the Holy Spirit aid in understanding.[109] This pattern is a guide for his writing and his expectation of the reader in interpreting the New Testament. Most of his commentary comes directly from other scripture (the Book of Mormon and the Doctrine and Covenants) or other valid sources for Church doctrine (primarily writings and sermons of Church leadership).

In his four-volume series *The Mortal Messiah,*[110] McConkie follows a predetermined sequence of events in Christ's life, emphasizing the true identity of Christ rather than presenting a more traditional, chronological New Testament commentary. In the preface to the first volume, McConkie calls James E. Talmage one of his "most prominent predecessors" and acknowledges *Jesus the Christ* as the foundation for his series.[111] McConkie follows the New Testament Gospels chronologically and, like his *Doctrinal New Testament Commentary,* draws most of his conclusions from other scripture.

McConkie explicitly favors Protestant scholarship and relies on the same Protestant biblical commentators that Talmage did when writing *Jesus the Christ.* His approach occasionally includes academic tools and intellectual investigation, but his overwhelming emphasis is on doctrinal interpretations and implications for personal conduct and faith. He is cautious with and critical of scholarly writing. Like Talmage, his goal is to testify and persuade the reader to believe. Thus his writing is laced with personal

108. Bruce R. McConkie, *Doctrinal New Testament Commentary,* 3 vols. (Salt Lake City: Bookcraft, 1965–73).

109. McConkie, *Doctrinal New Testament Commentary,* 1:57.

110. Bruce R. McConkie, *The Mortal Messiah: From Bethlehem to Calvary,* 4 vols. (Salt Lake City: Deseret Book, 1979–81).

111. McConkie, *Mortal Messiah,* 1:xvii–xviii.

spiritual feelings and thoughts. In *A New Witness for the Articles of Faith,*[112] McConkie explains that the Bible, "as far as it is translated correctly" (see A of F 1:8), is scripture and is true. In its current state, the Bible is binding upon the Latter-day Saints. McConkie lessens the value of studying the language, customs, traditions, and lifestyle of those in the New Testament to aid in determining the intent and meaning of the message.[113] He clearly proports that interpretations given through the power of the Holy Ghost are the only true way to understand scripture.

In addition, Mick Smith's *The Book of Revelation: Plain, Pure, and Simple*[114] provides commentary on the book of Revelation that is understandable and accessible to every type of reader. His intent is to help "clarify hard-to-understand terms and phrases in a manner that is accessible to the general membership of the Church."[115] Authors like Smith come from varied backgrounds and do not always have higher academic degrees in religious studies. They seek to publish personal spiritual insights and meaning from the New Testament. W. Jeffery Marsh's primary motive in writing *His Final Hours* was to assist the reader to make direct spiritual applications from his "insights . . . that can be drawn from the final hours of the Savior's life and atoning sacrifice." [116] As exemplified by Smith and Marsh, the sources for most writing in this category come from Church officers and General Authorities like Talmage and McConkie. However, General Authorities now tend to shy away from writing volumes of scriptural interpretation, contributing instead through articles and essays in official Church publications like the *Ensign* and *Liahona.* These works, while not academic in nature, are important to consider because they shape the overall Latter-day Saint approach to the New Testament.

---

112. Bruce R. McConkie, *A New Witness for the Articles of Faith* (Salt Lake City: Deseret Book, 1985), 389–412.

113. Bruce R. McConkie, "The Bible, a Sealed Book," in *Teaching Seminary Preservice Readings: Religion 370, 471, and 475* (Salt Lake City: The Church of Jesus Christ of Latter-day Saints, 2004), 123–32. Here McConkie states, "When a knowledge of ancient languages is used properly—as a means of gaining inspiration about particular passages—it [is of merit]. . . . Those who turn to the original tongues for their doctrinal knowledge have a tendency to rely on scholars rather than on prophets for scriptural interpretations. This is perilous; it is a sad thing to be numbered with the wise and the learned who know more than the Lord" (127).

114. Mick Smith, *The Book of Revelation: Plain, Pure, and Simple* (Salt Lake City: Bookcraft, 1998).

115. Smith, *Book of Revelation,* xi.

116. W. Jeffrey Marsh, *His Final Hours* (Salt Lake City: Deseret Book, 2000), ix.

Accessible Academic Scholarship

The second category is accessible academic scholarship written with the intent to inform readers of the context and content of the New Testament. Sidney B. Sperry contributed to the understanding of the New Testament among Latter-day Saints from this more academic perspective. A scholar and educator at BYU, Sperry taught in religious education for forty years starting in 1932. Sperry's background in biblical history and languages caused him to favor a scholarly approach to biblical commentary, and in the preface to his book *Paul's Life and Letters,* he encourages members of the Church to pursue a greater understanding of scholarly issues.[117] In *Paul's Life and Letters,* Sperry chronologically addresses the Apostle's life events and details Paul's individual journeys. He cites other scriptures and relies on common knowledge for some historical context, but also takes a careful historical approach—attempting to illuminate background, conditions, and circumstances of Paul's life not readily recognizable in the biblical text. It is difficult to distinguish when Sperry's information is derived from scripture or outside sources, a noticeable shift from other writers in the Church during this time.

Although written for a Latter-day Saint audience, Sperry's work offerd an informative and unbiased view for any student of the New Testament. He largely omitted modern-day revelation or writings specific to the restored Church. However, he kept his Latter-day Saint audience in mind in his bibliography of sources by including warnings and personal comments regarding each source. Unlike Talmage and other Latter-day Saint scholars who favored Protestant scholarship, Sperry favored Roman Catholic sources.[118]

Accessible academic writing is still tuned to the needs of a student of the scriptures, as in Jay A. Parry and Donald W. Parry's book *Understanding the Book of Revelation,*[119] a verse-by-verse commentary. The Parrys' desire was "to find meaning in John's vision for our day, to seek to understand what people in the twentieth and twenty-first centuries might need or want to know about what John saw and heard."[120] Their book is based on scholarship and carefully researched (especially when it comes to Greek word origins and historical sources), but it is not rigorous academic reading.

117. Sidney B. Sperry, *Paul's Life and Letters,* 1st ed. (Salt Lake City: Bookcraft, 1955), vii–viii.

118. Sperry, *Paul's Life and Letters.*

119. Jay A. Parry and Donald W. Parry, *Understanding the Book of Revelation* (Salt Lake City: Deseret Book, 1998).

120. Parry and Parry, *Understanding the Book of Revelation,* 7.

They are careful and analytical in their approach and cite frequently from Latter-day Saint and non–Latter-day Saint sources.

More works of this type are three similar books concentrated on the teachings and doctrines of Jesus Christ. Andrew C. Skinner and W. Jeffrey Marsh's *Scriptural Parables for the Latter Days*[121] and Richard D. Draper's *The Savior's Prophecies*[122] are both based on sound research and emphasize a direct application to the modern world of scriptural teachings. Draper writes with an intent to help his readers prepare for the Second Coming by dealing "with specific historical events the Savior predicted just a few days before His crucifixion, as He sat on the Mount of Olives."[123]

Robert J. Matthews, a late professor emeritus of ancient scripture at BYU, wrote a study of John the Baptist that falls into this accessible category of academic scholarship. He wrote *A Burning Light: The Life and Ministry of John the Baptist*[124] with the intent to "cultivate a wider knowledge and a greater appreciation for" John and to increase "awareness of John's ministry in three dispensations of the gospel, in light of latter-day revelation, which gives a fuller view and a more complete knowledge than can be obtained from the Bible alone."[125] Even with his understanding of the Bible as a limited text, Matthews references multiple Bibles and makes cross-textual comparisons to explore the life and ministry of John. Like the other authors in this category, he relies on Latter-day Saint sources but is more interested in providing contextual information to illuminate the biblical text. Matthews is also a pivotal individual for the study of the New Testament in the Latter-day Saint tradition because of his work on the Joseph Smith Translation.[126] Matthews's work brought the JST out of obscurity and was primarily responsible for the additions of the JST in the 1979 Latter-day Saint edition of the King James Version.[127]

---

121. Andrew C. Skinner and W. Jeffrey Marsh, *Scriptural Parables for the Latter Days* (Salt Lake City: Deseret Book, 2002).

122. Richard D. Draper, *The Savior's Prophecies: From the Fall of Jerusalem to the Second Coming* (American Fork, Utah: Covenant Communications, 2001).

123. Draper, *Savior's Prophecies,* 3.

124. Robert J. Matthews, *A Burning Light: The Life and Ministry of John the Baptist* (Provo, Utah: Brigham Young University Press, 1972).

125. Matthews, *John the Baptist,* vii.

126. See Robert J. Matthews, *"A Plainer Translation": Joseph Smith's Translation of the Bible; A History and Commentary* (Provo, Utah: Brigham Young University Press, 1975).

127. Ray L. Huntington and Brian M. Hauglid, "Robert J. Matthews and His Work with the Joseph Smith Translation," *Religious Educator* 5, no. 2 (2004): 23–47.

Andrew C. Skinner's three-volume series, *Gethsemane*,[128] *Golgotha*,[129] and *The Garden Tomb*,[130] analyzes the details surrounding the suffering, death, and Crucifixion of Jesus Christ. Skinner's work provides in-depth personal insights and analysis, but through historical detail, word origins, and textual explanations, readers can gain extensive knowledge of ancient languages and history.

One of the Church's largest concentrated pools of current Latter-day Saint New Testament scholarship is the BYU Religion Faculty. Approximately every four years, the Department of Religious Education hosts the Sidney B. Sperry Symposium on topics dealing directly with the New Testament. The published writings from this and other symposia constitute a large source of New Testament reference and scholarship that primarily focuses on scholarly questions surrounding the New Testament text but made accessible to a general Latter-day Saint audience.[131] New Testament Sperry Symposium topics from the years 1987–2022 have focused on themes found in the Gospels, the Epistles, the Apostle Paul, the general New Testament message, social and family life during New Testament times, and the contextualization of the Messiah.

Compiled symposium essays address a broad academic, Latter-day Saint audience. The Book of Mormon, Doctrine and Covenants, and other modern-day scriptures and revelations are commonly cited and held as authoritative and essential to understanding the New Testament. Authors consider the scriptures topically, make frequent personal comments, and include spiritual insights from their own study. Authors are careful to provide historical background and context, and references to Greek and Hebrew word origins indicate original research and accurate intent.

The audience for the previous few examples is primarily comprised of informed Latter-day Saint readers seeking a closer reading of a particular aspect of scripture. As an appeal to Latter-day Saints seeking more devotional content in these works, some authors include separate topics or questions for discussion and reflection. Occasionally, academic authors discuss other biblical scholarship issues, such as authorship, language origins, and historical background, but they mostly assume a Latter-day

128. Andrew C. Skinner, *Gethsemane* (Salt Lake City: Deseret Book, 2002).

129. Andrew C. Skinner, *Golgotha* (Salt Lake City: Deseret Book, 2004).

130. Andrew C. Skinner, *The Garden Tomb* (Salt Lake City: Deseret Book, 2005).

131. "Sperry Symposium Archive," BYU Religious Studies Center, accessed November 14, 2023, https://rsc.byu.edu/conferences/sperry/archive.

Saint perspective on these issues—approaching the scriptural text with the intent to provide doctrinal meaning rather than attempt to address historical criticism.

Critical Reading Scholarship

Another category of Latter-day Saint New Testament writing aligns with the academic rigor of scholarship through critical reading. The selected works in this field are considered highly specialized research and are usually intended to be read by those who already have a basic understanding of the history and context of the New Testament. In 1983, BYU Religious Education Professor Richard Lloyd Anderson made a significant contribution to New Testament scholarship with *Understanding Paul.*[132] This volume is a valuable work on the life of Paul—built upon Sperry's *Paul's Life and Letters.* Anderson studied the life and teachings of Paul "as a witness of the great truths of the restored gospel."[133] Moving chronologically through the Epistles of the New Testament, Anderson introduced each letter with background information and authorship before moving into an exploration of the teachings.

Anderson's scholarly approach is combined with modern-day revelation and Book of Mormon references. He also includes an explanation of scripturally supported Latter-day Saint doctrines in the appendices. His biblical sources stem largely from the Greek text and the King James Version, but he refers to other translations as well.[134] A few sources for his extensive historical research include Josephus, the Loeb Classical Library, early Christian writers, and other early Church members. This work remains important because of its research and scholarly value.

Richard Holzapfel, a former professor of church history and doctrine at BYU and author of *A Lively Hope: The Suffering, Death, Resurrection, and Exaltation of Jesus Christ,*[135] states as his objective "to introduce to a nonspecialist readership some of the insights from recent New Testament research that may benefit the believer and help him or her gain a deeper appreciation for the richness of the narratives left to us as a gift

---

132. Richard Lloyd Anderson, *Understanding Paul* (Salt Lake City: Deseret Book, 1983).

133. Anderson, *Understanding Paul,* ix.

134. Anderson, *Understanding Paul,* xiii. Anderson notes in "Key to Translations" that "every New Testament quotation in this book has been checked against the Greek text."

135. Richard Neitzel Holzapfel, *A Lively Hope: The Suffering, Death, Resurrection, and Exaltation of Jesus Christ* (Salt Lake City: Bookcraft, 1999).

from the writers of the four Gospels."[136] His book is divided into two main parts, which separate the passion and Resurrection narratives as told from the perspectives of each Gospel writer—paying particular attention to the intended audience of Matthew, Mark, Luke, and John. Holzapfel's research is thorough and comes largely from non–Latter-day Saint sources. He includes historical background information and Greek translations of some words, but his emphasis is on the events themselves as depicted by the different Gospel writers.

Four years later, Holzapfel and Thomas A. Wayment jointly edited *From the Last Supper through the Resurrection,*[137] a collection of in-depth scholarly essays about the last week of the Savior's life. In Andrew Skinner's introduction to the series, he strongly states the authors' objectives to

> aim both at informing our understanding of the historical facts about the sufferings of our Lord . . . and also at answering the charges of critics and secular scholars who would try to persuade us that Jesus was not the literal Son of God, the actual Redeemer of all humankind, or that the New Testament accounts that report the last hours and acts of Jesus cannot be trusted as literal.[138]

In addition to relating the accounts from the four Gospels' perspectives, the various authors in this series focus on specific events from the last week of the Savior's life (for example, the Last Supper, Gethsemane, the Jewish and Roman arrests, the Crucifixion, the burial, and the Resurrection). Five supplementary essays provide historical context and address some of the controversial issues surrounding Christ's death (early accounts, responsibility for his death, and conspiracies).[139]

In 2006, Holzapfel and Wayment joined with Eric D. Huntsman to write one of the most comprehensive and complete single volumes on the New Testament ever published by Latter-day Saints. *Jesus Christ and the World of the New Testament*[140] is primarily a scholarly exploration into the world of the New Testament with some highlights from restored scripture and revelation.

136. Holzapfel, *Lively Hope,* xvii.

137. Richard Neitzel Holzapfel and Thomas A. Wayment, eds., *From the Last Supper through the Resurrection,* vol. 3 of The Life and Teachings of Jesus Christ (Salt Lake City: Deseret Book, 2003).

138. Andrew C. Skinner, introduction to Holzapfel and Wayment, *From the Last Supper,* xiv.

139. Holzapfel and Wayment, *From the Last Supper,* iii–iv.

140. Richard Neitzel Holzapfel, Eric D. Huntsman, and Thomas A. Wayment, *Jesus Christ and the World of the New Testament* (Salt Lake City: Deseret Book, 2006).

Describing the purpose of the volume, the authors inform the reader that the work is

> not a verse-by-verse commentary, nor does it seek to provide the ultimate interpretation of doctrine, a role that Latter-day Saints reserve for inspired apostles and prophets. . . . This effort is in harmony with the charge to seek learning by study as well as by faith (Doctrine and Covenants 88:118) and to "become acquainted with all good books, and with languages, tongues, and people" (Doctrine and Covenants 90:15). Therefore, when we apply this charge to the study of the world of the New Testament, it seems clear that learning *about* the New Testament is second only to learning *from* the New Testament.[141]

While interpretation of doctrine is reserved for the leaders of the restored gospel, personal interpretation and application of the biblical text is still the responsibility of the reader.

A recent development in Latter-day Saint studies of the New Testament is the focus on the voice of women within the text. In 2014, Camille Fronk Olson wrote an engaging volume that highlighted the place and voice of New Testament women.[142] The primary purpose of her volume was "to know Christ better by exploring his example and teachings through the eyes of the women of the New Testament. This unique perspective writes women back into history. It provides a glimpse from a different angle into the ancient world, hopefully to inspire readers toward a deeper reverence for the gift of the Savior and a greater commitment to serve him."[143] Olson emphasized that the New Testament is not a singular voice but a multifaceted and multigendered one.

Daniel Ludlow wrote a series of commentaries on all the standard works of the Church. However, he did not write about the New Testament books past the Gospel of John; his only volume about the New Testament is *A Companion to Your Study of the New Testament: The Four Gospels.*[144] Ludlow includes only the references for the verses about which he is writing rather than printing the biblical text before each section of commentary, as in Bruce R. McConkie's *Doctrinal New Testament Commentary.* Using his

141. Holzapfel, Huntsman, and Wayment, *Jesus Christ and the World of the New Testament,* 1, emphasis in original.

142. Camille Fronk Olson, *Women in the New Testament* (Salt Lake City: Deseret Book, 2014).

143. Olson, *Women of the New Testament,* 1.

144. Daniel H. Ludlow, *A Companion to Your Study of the New Testament: The Four Gospels* (Salt Lake City: Deseret Book, 1982).

Greek language background, Ludlow largely focuses on language issues, including an alternate translation for almost every verse cited.

Professors D. Kelly Ogden and Andrew C. Skinner, teamed up to create a first-of-its-kind, succinct, "one-volume study guide aim[ed] at touching upon the historical context, geography, and doctrine of the books of Acts through Revelation as a whole" in *New Testament Apostles Testify of Christ.*[145] This verse-by-verse study is filled with word origins, historical background, photographs from the Holy Land, and other Latter-day Saint scriptural references. The four-hundred-page book reads like a reference work, with a chapter devoted to each book in the New Testament, starting with the book of Acts. They followed up this volume with an identical work that covers the Gospels.[146]

John W. Welch and John F. Hall collaborated to write *Charting the New Testament*, a reference collection of charts and lists falling into eighteen different categories. The charts, tables, graphs, maps, lists, and timelines cover a huge spectrum of topics: chronology, Jewish cultural and literary backgrounds, Roman history, demographics, teachings of Christ, doctrines, journeys of Paul, word counts, linguistic comparisons (of the Gospels), people and places, time periods, lineages, and more. This collection is a thorough and useful reference for any teacher or student of the New Testament.[147]

Church-Published Reference Works

A final genre of published works to aid Latter-day Saints in their New Testament studies are reference sources, such as study guides for Sunday School and other Church classes, lesson manuals, and Gospel and general New Testament harmonies, published by the Church itself. Although this type of writing is not necessarily considered scholarship in an academic sense, it is important to mention because an analysis of the frequency and focus of any such literature pertaining to the New Testament over time will reflect the direction and position of the entire Church body. The Church began producing these manuals in connection with the creation of the

145. D. Kelly Ogden and Andrew C. Skinner, *New Testament Apostles Testify of Christ: A Guide for Acts through Revelation* (Salt Lake City: Deseret Book, 1998) vi.

146. D. Kelly Ogden and Andrew C. Skinner, *Verse by Verse: The Four Gospels* (Salt Lake City: Deseret Book, 2006).

147. John W. Welch and John F. Hall, *Charting the New Testament* (Provo, Utah: Foundation for Ancient Research and Mormon Studies, 2002).

Correlation Department in 1972 to "plan, correlate, prepare, translate, print, and distribute instructional materials and periodicals"[148] and ensure that all official Church teachings were in harmony with the doctrine of the Restoration. Additionally, "in 1972 the adult Gospel Doctrine class in Sunday school began a systematic study of the standard works of the Church," focusing on the New Testament every four years.[149] With all adults either personally studying or receiving New Testament instruction at least every four years, the Church maintains a respectable sense of biblical literacy.

Most New Testament study guides that were produced to coincide with the four-year cycle emphasized the Gospels were chronological for student reference, and followed a verse-by-verse study guide format. All such guides were for the students, providing some factual and historical background as points of interest but emphasizing Christ's doctrine as maintained by the teachings and revelations of The Church of Jesus Christ of Latter-day Saints. Much of the commentary comes from modern-day prophets' and apostles' teachings. Like the catechisms of the late 1800s, these materials aim to train Church members in Church doctrine with particular emphasis on how the restored gospel differs from the teachings of other Christian churches, especially in New Testament interpretation. This emphasis aligned with exponential Church growth around the world, necessitating a common understanding of the biblical text.

The Church's most influential and long-lasting publication during this era of contribution is the 1979 Latter-day Saint version of the King James Bible. For the first time in the history of the Church, Latter-day Saints had an edition of the New Testament that was produced with supplementary material for Latter-day Saints. Commenting on this edition of the scriptures, which were primarily produced by a committee chaired by Elders Robert J. Matthews, Thomas S. Monson, Boyd K. Packer, and Bruce R. McConkie, the purpose was stated that "not only will this new edition be helpful to the individual student reading at home, but there's never been a better classroom edition . . . with the topical guide, references, and dictionary in the Bible."[150] This publication, with subsequent versions in Spanish

148. Frank O. May Jr., "Correlation of the Church Administration," in Ludlow, *Encyclopedia of Mormonism,* 1:323–25.

149. Church Educational System, *Church History in the Fulness of Times,* 2nd ed. (Salt Lake City: The Church of Jesus Christ of Latter-day Saints, 2000), 570.

150. Lavina Fielding Anderson, "Church Publishes First LDS Edition of the Bible," *Ensign* 9, no. 10 (October 1979): 18.

(2009) and Portuguese (2015), aimed to provide Latter-day Saints with an edition of the Bible that would uniquely meet their needs, especially as the Church moved to a home-centered study of the New Testament in 2018.

Home-Centered, Church-Supported Study of the New Testament (2019–Present)

The advent of the internet, social media, digital media, and artificial intelligence during the first part of the twenty-first century formed a world in which information and knowledge are created, transmitted, and obtained at the click of a button. Such ease of access to information and knowledge led Paul McClure to conclude "that with higher levels of Internet use, individuals are less likely to pray, read sacred texts, attend religious services, consider religion personally important, or affiliate with a religious tradition."[151] Similarly, Allen B. Downey observed that the internet can negatively impact one's views of religion in two ways: "[First], for people living in homogeneous communities, the Internet provides opportunities to find information about people of other religions (and none), and to interact with them personally. [Second], for people with religious doubt, the Internet provides access to people in similar circumstances all over the world."[152] While such information and trends are beginning to be recognized by scholars and religious leaders alike, responses are ongoing and disparate.

In 2018, the First Presidency of the Church announced that, beginning in 2019 (with the New Testament), a new resource developed by the Church titled *Come, Follow Me—for Individuals and Families* would be used for the annual study of the scriptures and intended to "take a home-centered, Church-supported approach to gospel living, learning, and teaching."[153] While the Church emphasized that parents have the responsibility to teach the gospel to their children,[154] the adoption of *Come, Follow Me* as the

151. Paul K. McClure, "The Buffered, Technological Self: Finding Associations between Internet Use and Religiosity," *Social Compass* 67, no. 3 (September 2020): 461–78.

152. Allen B. Downey, "Religious Affiliation, Education, and Internet Use," *arXiv* (March 2014): 9, https://doi.org/10.48550/arXiv.1403.5534.

153. "Church Announces *Come, Follow Me* for Home, School, and Primary," *Church News,* July 6, 2018, https://www.churchofjesuschrist.org/church/news/church-announces-come-follow-me-for-home-sunday-school-and-primary?lang=eng.

154. *General Handbook,* 2.2.3, "Gospel teaching and learning are home-centered and Church-supported"; 17.2, "Each member of the Church is responsible to learn the gospel for himself or herself. In addition, parents are responsible to teach the gospel to their

primary course of study at all levels within the Church is intended to "support home-centered gospel learning as teachers inspire learners to experience the power of God's word for themselves. They invite class members to discover gospel truths in the scriptures and share their discoveries with each other 'that all may be edified of all' (D&C 88:122)."[155]

Primarily devotional in nature, the first *Come, Follow Me* resource broke down the New Testament into weekly chronological selections of chapters to study over the course of a calendar year. Each weekly section included key devotional themes, historical background, teachings by modern prophets and apostles on New Testament topics, and ideas for personal and family study of the text. While some historical, linguistic, and cultural contexts are provided at varying points throughout the *Come, Follow Me* manual, members of the Church are encouraged to refer to seminary and institute manuals that "provide historical background and doctrinal commentary for principles and accounts found in the scriptures."[156] This official resource for The Church of Jesus Christ of Latter-day Saints is intended to provide scriptural experiences for devoted members.

While scholars within the Church have continued to publish works detailing the history, culture, and languages of the world of the New Testament, the most recognizable advancement in New Testament studies during this final time period is the rise in digital media as a resource for studying the New Testament. Accompanying the *Come, Follow Me* materials in 2019 and 2023, members have access to a plethora of podcasts, YouTube channels, and social media accounts that utilize scholars within the Church to present insights on New Testament topics and scriptures. Moreso than any other time in history, Latter-day Saints have access to numerous resources to assist in their "home-centered" New Testament study. The impact of this study has been noted by numerous Church leaders during this time of transition in the Church. Elder Neil L. Andersen articulated such an impact when he said, "With the isolation of the worldwide pandemic and the help of *Come, Follow Me,* the teachings of the Savior are becoming more prominent in our homes, helping our worship of the Savior during the week."[157]

---

children. Gospel learning and teaching should be centered in the home. Church leaders and teachers support home-centered gospel learning and teaching."

155. "Church Announces *Come, Follow Me.*"

156. *Come, Follow Me—Individuals and Families, New Testament 2019* (Salt Lake City: The Church of Jesus Christ of Latter-day Saints, 2019), xi.

157. Neil L. Andersen, "My Mind Caught Hold upon This Thought of Jesus Christ," *Liahona* 47, no. 5 (May 2023): 93.

The BYU New Testament Commentary

As has been outlined above, the Latter-day Saint study of the New Testament has never been a monolithic pursuit. Throughout time, different approaches have been influenced by world perceptions and reactions. It is within this heritage that the BYU New Testament Commentary series (BYUNTC) contributes to the overall history of New Testament study in the Church. Drawing upon different perspectives from various scholars, the BYUNTC series provides readers with multiple scholarly voices about the New Textament texts and a new rendition based on the original Greek. With new renditions and commentary, the BYUNTC fulfills the commission given by Brigham Young in 1871.

> Take the Bible just as it reads; and if it be translated incorrectly, and there is a scholar on the earth who professes to be a Christian, and he can translate it any better than King James's translators did it, he is under obligation to do so, or the curse is upon him. If I understood Greek and Hebrew as some may profess to do, and I knew the Bible was not correctly translated, I should feel myself bound by the law of justice to the inhabitants of the earth to translate that which is incorrect and give it just as it was spoken anciently. Is that proper? Yes, I would be under obligation to do it. But I think it is translated just as correctly as the scholars could get it, although it is not correct in a great many instances. But it is no matter about that. Read it and observe it and it will not hurt any person in the world. If we are not to believe the whole of the Bible, let the man, whoever he may be, among the professed Christians, who thinks he knows, draw the line between the true and the false, so that the whole sectarian world may be able to take the right and leave the wrong. But the man Christ Jesus, who has revealed himself in the latter days, says the Bible is true and the people must believe it. Let us believe it, and then obey it.[158]

The BYUNTC aims to fulfill this charge and build upon the great legacy of seeking to be instructed in the way of the Lord.

---

158. Brigham Young, in *Journal of Discourses,* 14:226–27 (August 27, 1871).

Latter-day Saint Scholarship Encounters the World of the Bible

Tom R. Roberts

From the early days of Latter-day Saint (LDS) history, many members of the Church felt that education was an important part of the LDS approach to understanding and self-improvement. One thinks immediately of the School of the Prophets established early in 1833 under the leadership of the Prophet Joseph Smith (D&C 88:127). In a different vein, the 1846 appearance of a Welsh periodical titled *Prophwyd y Jubili* (Prophet of the Jubilee)[1] asserted LDS scholarship. This journal was published for two and a half years. Other periodicals followed, such as the *Ugdorn Seion* (Zion's Trumpet),[2] which was published from 1849 to 1862.

As religious traditions develop, some within their ranks often feel a need to internally examine teachings. This was certainly true in the LDS experience. Among the first of many academics to arise was Orson Pratt, who brought a scientific approach to LDS theology.[3] As the need to systematize member education arose in LDS thinking, B. H. Roberts responded to the challenge. His work *Defense of the Saints and Faith*[4] encouraged the promotion of the Book of Mormon and the Church on a public platform to counter prevailing misrepresentations.[5]

---

1. *Prophwyd y Jubili* (1846–48), Welsh Journals, The National Library of Wales, accessed October 23, 2023, https://journals.library.wales/browse/2078276/.

2. *Udgorn Seion,* Archive Viewer, accessed December 20, 2023, https://archiveviewer.org/collections/cy/zions-trumpet.

3. Robert Paul Erich, "Theology in Science: The Case of Orson Pratt," in *Science, Religion, and Mormon Cosmology* (Urbana: University of Illinois, 1992), 127–45; Edward R. Hogan, "Orson Pratt as a Mathmatician," *Utah Historical Quarterly* 41, no. 1 (Winter 1973), https://issuu.com/utah10/docs/uhq_volume41_1973_number1/s/112392.

4. B. H. Roberts, *Defense of the Faith and the Saints,* 2 vols. (Salt Lake City: Deseret News, 1907, 1912).

5. Reid L. Neilson, "Mormonism's Blacksmith Orator: B. H. Roberts at the 1893 World's Parliament of Religions," *Mormon Historical Studies* 12 (2011): 59–60.

Though no Latter-day Saint living in the nineteenth century pursued any major biblical studies, that changed in the early twentieth. In 1915, Elder James E. Talmage wrote his classic work, *Jesus the Christ*.[6] In this large volume, he added LDS scripture to the Gospel narratives and, in doing so, gave a full LDS rendition of the Savior's life and teachings. Talmage's respect for the current scholarship of his day is apparent, as evidenced by his use of Frederic W. Farrar's work *The Life of Christ*.[7] In *Jesus the Christ*, Talmage followed Farrar's thoughts that the Gospels came from independent fragmented sources but were, nonetheless, academically respectable. In 1932, Obert C. Tanner published *New Testament Studies*, which was revised in 1935 and retitled *The New Testament Speaks*.[8] This became the backbone of his work with Lewis M. Rogers and Sterling M. McMurrin entitled *Toward Understanding the New Testament*, published in 1990.[9]

Despite these excellent publications, there was still a great need for LDS scholars to advance LDS academic studies and for apologetics to contribute to the field of biblical studies. Hugh Nibley, a graduate of the University of California at Berkeley in 1938, answered the call when he accepted a post at Brigham Young University (BYU) in 1946 after serving in military intelligence during World War II. In 1960, he was offered a full professorship at UC Berkeley but decided to remain at BYU. His contributions to LDS scholarship over the next sixty years have yet to be completely realized. Nibley's writings were extensive and diverse, including accounts of Egyptian enthronements, historical background for Old Testament texts, a ritual analysis of temple texts in the New Testament, and comparisons to Book of Mormon literature. Nibley's works were later published in large tomes by the Foundation for Ancient Research and Mormon Studies (FARMS), including but not limited to *Old Testament and Related Studies*,[10] *The World and the Prophets*,[11] *Abraham in*

---

6. James E. Talmage, *Jesus the Christ* (Salt Lake City: Deseret News, 1915).

7. Frederic W. Farrar, *The Life of Christ* (London: Cassell and Company, 1887).

8. Obert C. Tanner, *New Testament Studies* (Salt Lake City: Deseret News, 1932); Obert C. Tanner, *The New Testament Speaks* (Salt Lake City: Deseret News, 1947).

9. Obert C. Tanner, *Toward Understanding the New Testament* (Salt Lake City: Signature Books, 1990).

10. Hugh Nibley, *Old Testament and Related Studies*, ed. John W. Welch, Gary P. Gillum, and Don E. Norton (Salt Lake City: Deseret Book; Provo, Utah: Foundation for Ancient Research and Mormon Studies, 1986).

11. Hugh Nibley, *The World and the Prophets*, ed. John W. Welch, Gary P. Gillum, and Don E. Norton (Salt Lake City: Deseret Book; Provo, Utah: Foundation for Ancient Research and Mormon Studies, 1987).

Egypt,[12] and *Mormonism and Early Christianity.*[13] In 1956, J. Reuben Clark Jr. also contributed to Latter-day Saint biblical scholarship by publishing *Why the King James Version,*[14] a treatise on early textual criticism of the Bible. It focused on the value of the textus receptus, the biblical document that forms the basis of the King James Version.

During the 1950s, several Latter-day Saint scholars achieved academic notice outside LDS tradition. For example, a number of non–Latter-day Saint academics began to accept Sidney B. Sperry as an expert in the writings of Isaiah due to his skill in comparing the readings from the Hebrew text and the Greek Septuagint. One of Sperry's best-known works was *Paul's Life and Letters,*[15] a widely used publication. Hugh Nibley gained recognition with his work on baptism for the dead, which was cited in the *Catholic Biblical Quarterly,*[16] and Cleon Skousen joined the ranks of academic scholars with his popular works *Isaiah Speaks to Modern Times*[17] and the *Thousand Years* series.[18]

As the Church's scholarship began to broaden, numerous scholarly publications appeared. In 1959, *Brigham Young University Studies,* a peer-reviewed, academic journal with a Latter-day Saint perspective, began publication. In 1979, John W. Welch established FARMS (now the Neal A. Maxwell Institute for Religious Scholarship), a foundation where LDS scholars could publish and collaborate with world-renowned academics. The same thing happened after the establishment of the Religious Studies Center in 1975 under the leadership of Jeffrey R. Holland.

---

12. Hugh Nibley, *Abraham in Egypt,* vol. 14 of Collected Works of Hugh Nibley, ed. Gary P. Gillum, 2nd ed. (Salt Lake City: Deseret Book; Provo, Utah: Foundation for Ancient Research and Mormon Studies, 1981).

13. Hugh Nibley, *Mormonism and Early Christianity,* ed. Todd M. Compton and Stephen D. Ricks (Salt Lake City: Deseret Book; Provo, Utah: Foundation for Ancient Research and Mormon Studies, 1987).

14. J. Reuben Clark Jr., *Why the King James Version* (Salt Lake City: Deseret Book, 1956).

15. Sidney B. Sperry, *Paul's Life and Letters* (Salt Lake City: Bookcraft, 1955).

16. Hugh Nibley, "Baptism for the Dead—II," *Improvement Era* 52, no. 1 (1949): 24–25, cited by Bernard M. Foschini, "'Those Who Are Baptized for the Dead,' 1 Cor. 15:29 (Third Article)," *Catholic Biblical Quarterly* 13 (1951): 53, 63, 71.

17. W. Cleon Skousen, *Isaiah Speaks to Modern Times* (Salt Lake City: Ensign Publishing, 1948).

18. W. Cleon Skousen, *The First 2,000 Years: From Adam to Abraham* (Salt Lake City: Ensign Publishing, 1953); W. Cleon Skousen, *The Third Thousand Years: From Abraham to David* (Salt Lake City: Ensign Publishing, 1964); W. Cleon Skousen, *The Fourth Thousand Years: From David to Christ* (Salt Lake City: Ensign Publishing, 1966).

By 1973, Elder Bruce R. McConkie, an LDS Apostle, had published a three-volume series entitled *Doctrinal New Testament Commentary*.[19] The work provided material for institute teachers, seminary teachers, and this Commentary series. The *Studies in Scriptures*[20] volumes, edited by Kent P. Jackson and Robert L. Millet, focused on the New Testament and appeared in 1986 and 1987. The Old Testament volumes were completed in 1993. Some of the contributors to these volumes were Kent P. Jackson, Kay Edwards, S. Kent Brown, Richard Lloyd Anderson, Robert L. Millet, Richard D. Draper, Andrew C. Skinner, Monte S. Nyman, David Rolph Seely, JoAnn H. Seely, and Robert J. Matthews. Many LDS scholars presented textual position papers at BYU through symposia held in honor of such scholars as Sidney B. Sperry, Truman G. Madsen, and Richard Lloyd Anderson.

During the 1990s, Latter-day Saint scholars began to join international committees and secured publications with internationally renowned publishers. Donald W. Parry, Andrew C. Skinner, and Dana Pike became the first LDS scholars to join the International Dead Sea Scrolls Committee. Donald W. Parry and Stephen D. Ricks edited a volume entitled *Current Research and Technological Developments on the Dead Sea Scrolls,*[21] a collection of articles presented at the Dead Sea Scrolls Conference. The work was published by the best-known academic publisher of antiquities, E. J. Brill, in 1996. Donald W. Parry, Jay A. Parry, and Tina M. Peterson's coauthored work, *Understanding Isaiah,*[22] brought LDS scholarship to a critical juncture between Isaiah and the Dead Sea Scrolls. In addition, Donald W. Parry and Emmanuel Tov edited *The Dead Sea Scrolls Reader* series,[23] which featured *Exegetical Texts,* also published by E. J. Brill. However, the first LDS scholar to publish works with E. J. Brill was C. Wilfred Griggs with his volume entitled *Early Egyptian Christianity: From Its Origins to 451 C.E.,*[24] published in 1990. Latter-day Saint scholars also began

19. Bruce R. McConkie, *Doctrinal New Testament Commentary,* 3 vols. (Salt Lake City: Bookcraft, 1965–73).

20. Kent P. Jackson and Robert L. Millet, eds., *Studies in Scripture,* 8 vols. (Salt Lake City: Deseret Book, 1984–88).

21. Donald W. Parry and Stephen D. Ricks, eds., *Current Research and Technological Developments on the Dead Sea Scrolls: Conference on the Texts from the Judean Desert, Jerusalem, 30 April 1995* (Leiden, Neth.: E. J. Brill, 1996).

22. Donald W. Parry, Jay A. Parry, and Tina M. Peterson, *Understanding Isaiah* (Salt Lake City: Deseret Book, 1998).

23. Donald W. Parry and Emanuel Tov, eds., *The Dead Sea Scrolls Reader,* 6 vols. (Leiden, Neth.: Brill, 2004–2005).

24. C. Wilfred Griggs, *Early Egyptian Christianity from Its Origins to 451 C.E.* (Leiden, Neth.: E. J. Brill, 1990).

to publish widely in essential academic reference materials. Some of these include the *Anchor Bible Dictionary,*[25] with articles by S. Kent Brown,[26] Edwin Firmage,[27] John F. Hall,[28] Dana M. Pike,[29] Stephen D. Ricks,[30] Stephen E. Robinson,[31] David R. Seely,[32] and JoAnn H. Seely.[33] In *The Oxford Encyclopedia of Archaeology in the Near East* is an article on "Oxyrhynchus" by S. Kent Brown;[34] in *Encyclopedia Judaica,* there is an article by Hugh Nibley on "Jerusalem."[35]

In addition, Latter-day Saint scholars began to publish commentary about the New Testament. Richard D. Draper published his work on the book of Revelation in 1991, portions of which were later used in an audio presentation.[36] In 1998, D. Kelly Ogden and Andrew C. Skinner published their work *Verse by Verse: Acts through Revelation.*[37] Following that work, Richard Neitzel Holzapfel and Thomas A. Wayment published a three-volume set, *The*

---

25. David Noel Freedmen and others, eds., *The Anchor Bible Dictionary,* 6 vols. (New York: Doubleday, 1992), hereafter cited as *ABD.*

26. S. Kent Brown, "Egypt, History of," "Egyptian, The (Person)," "Sayings of Jesus, Oxyrhynchus," "Truth, Gospel of," in *ABD,* 2:321–74, 2:412–13, 5:999–1001, 6:668, respectively.

27. Edwin Firmage, "Zoology (Fauna)," in *ABD,* 6:1109–67.

28. John F. Hall, "Antonia, Tower of (Place)," "Appeal to Caesar," "Caesar's Household," "Procurator," "Rome (Place)," "Senate," "Senator," in *ABD,* 1:274, 1:317, 1:798, 5:473–74, 5:830–34, 5:1086–87, 5:1087, respectively.

29. Dana M. Pike, "Jaakobah," "Jaareshiah," "Jaaziel," "Jaaziah," "Jassu," "Names, Hypocoristic," "Names, Theophoric," in *ABD,* 3:591, 3:591–92, 3:592, 3:593, 3:593, 4:1017, 4:1018, respectively.

30. Stephen D. Ricks, "Abortion in Antiquity," "Sheba (Person)," "Sheba, Queen of (Person)," in *ABD,* 1:31–35, 5:1169–70, 5:1170–71, respectively.

31. Stephen E. Robinson, "Adam, The Testament of," "Baruch, Book of 4," "Joseph, Prayer of," in *ABD,* 1:68, 1:622–23, 3:976, respectively.

32. David R. Seely, "Arabah (Place)," "Shur, Wilderness of (Place)," "Sin, Wilderness of (Place)," "Zin, Wilderness of (Place)," in *ABD,* 1:322–24, 5:1230, 6:47, 6:1095–96, respectively.

33. JoAnn H. Seely, "Irnahash (Place)," "Rephidim (Place)," in *ABD,* 3:456–61, 5:677–78, respectively.

34. S. Kent Brown, "Oxyrhynchus," in *The Encyclopedia of Archaeology in the Near East,* ed. Eric M. Meyers (New York: Oxford University Press, 1997), 4:194–95.

35. Hugh Nibley, "Jerusalem: In Other Religions; In Christianity," in *Encyclopedia Judaica* (New York: Macmillan, 1971), 9:1568–75.

36. Richard D. Draper, *Opening the Seven Seals: The Visions of John the Revelator* (Salt Lake City: Deseret Book, 1991); Richard D. Draper, *The Book of Revelation: Testifying of Christ,* American Fork, Utah: Covenant Communications, 2001, audio disc.

37. Andrew C. Skinner and D. Kelly Ogden, *Verse by Verse: Acts through Revelation* (Salt Lake City: Deseret Book, 2006).

Life and Teachings of Jesus Christ,[38] followed in 2010 by a one-volume work entitled *Making Sense of the New Testament.*[39] John W. Welch released his excellent work *The Sermon on the Mount in the Light of the Temple* in 2009,[40] illuminating the heart of the Gospel of Matthew. In 2015, Brent J. Schmidt published a thorough linguistic and historical history of *charis,* "grace," titled *Relational Grace,*[41] providing strong evidence that grace is a covenantal, active, and relational gift. In 2019, Thomas A. Wayment published his rendition of the New Testament,[42] including commentary for an LDS audience.

A few years ago, evangelical scholars began to notice the LDS Church's emphasis on biblical scholarship and accused BYU professors of cross-pollinating Joseph Smith's writings with biblical literature. However, when one reads Avraham Gileadi's *The Literary Message of Isaiah,*[43] only two LDS canonical scriptures are cited. Very few LDS sources are quoted in the work *Masada and the World of the New Testament,*[44] edited by John F. Hall and John W. Welch. The ongoing BYU New Testament Commentary series, now out to seven volumes, combines both LDS and non-LDS sources.

Further essays authored by LDS scholars have been published in the growing number of *Festschriften* publications, which are edited volumes honoring a specific academic colleague. Latter-day Saints have regularly contributed to academic journals, such as the *Journal of Biblical Literature,* the Society of Biblical Literature (SBL) dissertation series, the Harvard Semitic Monographs series, *Studia Pohl, Discoveries in the Judean Desert,* the *Harvard Theological Review, Novum Testamentum,* the *Jewish Quarterly Review,* and the *International Journal for the Philosophy of Religion.* Mormon Studies is considered to be an academic discipline by the SBL.

---

38. Richard Neitzel Holzapfel and Thomas A. Wayment, *The Life and Teachings of Jesus Christ,* 3 vols. (Salt Lake City: Deseret Book, 2003–2006).

39. Richard Neitzel Holzapfel and Thomas A. Wayment, *Making Sense of the New Testament: Timely Insights and Timeless Messages* (Salt Lake City: Deseret Book, 2010).

40. John W. Welch, *The Sermon on the Mount in the Light of the Temple* (Farnham, Eng.: Ashgate, 2009).

41. Brent J. Schmidt, *Relational Grace: The Reciprocal and Binding Covenant of* Charis (Provo, Utah: BYU Studies, 2015).

42. Thomas A. Wayment, *The New Testament: A Translation for Latter-day Saints* (Provo, Utah: BYU Religious Studies Center; Salt Lake City: Deseret Book, 2019); Thomas A. Wayment, *The New Testament: A Translation for Latter-day Saints, Revised Edition* (Draper, Utah: Greg Kofford Books, 2022).

43. Avraham Gileadi, *The Literary Message of Isaiah,* 2nd ed. (San Diego: Hebraeus Press, 2012).

44. John F. Hall and John W. Welch, eds., *Masada and the World of the New Testament* (Provo, Utah: BYU Studies, 1997).

By 2011, the need to have a biblical studies journal for LDS scholars was met in part by the Neal A. Maxwell Institute's journal *Studies in the Bible and Antiquity.*[45] Articles published in this journal covered many topics, including "Constructing Metaphoric Models of Salvation" by Miranda Wilcox,[46] "On Christ and Covenants: An LDS Reading of Isaiah's Prophetic Call" by David E. Bokovoy,[47] and "A Text-Critical Comparison of the King James New Testament with Certain Modern Translations" by Lincoln H. Blumell.[48] Textual criticism studies such as these added a great deal of breadth to LDS scholarship.

In 2019, Lincoln H. Blumell edited *New Testament History, Culture, and Society.*[49] This volume certainly takes a serious look at the New Testament with a wide variety of articles that go beyond mere survey-level description and present extensive research on the Jewish and Greco-Roman background of the New Testament. Contributors to Blumell's volume dealt with the synoptic and noncanonical Gospels, the Atonement, the Crucifixion, the Resurrection, women in the New Testament, New Testament worship and ritual practices, New Testament textual criticism, a history of Christianity in the second century, and the canonization of the New Testament.

In addition, the Neal A. Maxwell Institute for Religious Scholarship at BYU published *Ancient Christians* in 2022 about the first followers of Jesus Christ after his Resurrection. Readers will learn how ancient Christans lived; how they organized their worship; and what they believed about their own nature, God's nature, the Second Coming, and eternal progression. The book also provides incredible images of ancient Christian art, architecture, and manuscipts.[50]

---

45. Brian M. Hauglid and Carl Griffin, eds., *Studies in the Bible and Antiquity* 3 (2011), https://scholarsarchive.byu.edu/sba/vol3/iss1/.

46. Miranda Wilcox, "Constructing Metaphoric Models of Salvation: Matthew 20 and the Middle English Poem *Pearl,*" *Studies in the Bible and Antiquity* 3 (2011): 1–28.

47. David E. Bokovoy, "On Christ and Covenants: An LDS Reading of Isaiah's Prophetic Call," *Studies in the Bible and Antiquity* 3 (2011): 29–49.

48. Lincoln H. Blumell, "A Text-Critical Comparison of the King James New Testament with Certain Modern Translations," *Studies in the Bible and Antiquity* 3 (2011): 67–126.

49. Lincoln H. Blumell, ed., *New Testament History, Culture, and Society: A Background to the Texts of the New Testament* (Provo, Utah: BYU Religious Studies Center; Salt Lake City: Deseret Book, 2019), https://rsc.byu.edu/book/new-testament-history-culture-society.

50. Jason R. Combs and others, eds., *Ancient Christians: An Introduction for Latter-day Saints* (Provo, Utah: Neal A. Maxwell Institute for Religious Scholarship, 2022).

This brief survey is by no means an exhaustive treatment of all the books and materials written by LDS scholars in circulation. Today, the academic community benefits from the scores of LDS scholars who hold positions in a number of first-rate colleges and universities. A new generation is rising to give modern explanations to historical LDS positions as they develop this growing religious scholarship tradition.

A very brief sampling of published works authored by contributors to this volume appears at the end of this book, offering a glimpse of the breadth of interest that these highly qualified individuals possess.

Tracking New Testament Study among Latter-day Saints

Kelsey Draper Lambert and John S. Thompson

The exponential growth in New Testament studies written by members of The Church of Jesus Christ of Latter-day Saints over the last century calls for an up-to-date survey of the literature. Such can inform both Latter-day Saint and non–Latter-day Saint readers concerning the variety and scope of New Testament scholarship within that tradition. Influential works and trends, primarily from writers in the early twentieth century to those currently writing and publishing, will be highlighted.[1]

When the foundations of the modern Church were laid in the 1800s, secular approaches to the Bible were spreading and taking hold in academic and religious institutions of higher learning. Many scholars raised questions concerning the dating and authorship of the texts as well as the reality of people and events in the New Testament through historical criticism, textual criticism, and other developing methodologies. Some previous surveys of Latter-day Saint New Testament scholarship categorized the authors based on their attitudes toward these secular mainstream conclusions.

Philip Barlow's *Mormons and the Bible* highlights a range of attitudes—from those who felt there was no value in the secular conclusions (since they often marginalized or bracketed the divine) to those who embraced the secular view fully (convinced by the evidence and argumentation). Some preferred to take a middle path, believing the work of mainstream scholarship can be useful for understanding the text as long as it is used

1. Two bibliographies of New Testament studies within the Latter-day Saint tradition were compiled by BYU Studies: "'We Rejoice in Christ': A Bibliography of LDS Writings on Jesus Christ and the New Testament," *BYU Studies* 34, no. 3 (1994–95): 1–118; and "Latter-day Saint Writings on Christ and the New Testament—2002 Supplement," *BYU Studies* 41, no. 3 (2002): 86–158.

constructively, without rejecting the possibility of divine interaction, such as miracles or revelation.[2] Anthony A. Hutchinson divided Latter-day Saint authors a little more along this spectrum between fundamentalism, which he calls "harmonizing hermeneutical," and secular criticism, which he calls "critical hermeneutical."[3] Hutchinson's use of the term "harmonizing hermeneutical" as the opposite of "critical hermeneutical" is problematic since it makes the a priori assumption that efforts that demonstrate harmony in the texts must not be fully critical. Hutchinson argued that Church members typically gravitated toward fundamentalist writers because such "provides a sense of security . . . : The truth of God appears to have been the same anciently as it is today; there is a uniformity of the gospel that is universal and shared by the Old and New Testaments as well as the LDS scriptures." Conversely, he states that "the problems of scripture [that critical scholarship raises] are either homogenized into oblivion or ignored as unimportant."[4]

While clustering Latter-day Saint scholars according to their attitudes toward the conclusions of secular scholarship may be interesting and helpful to some, this kind of categorization often accompanies a tone that is divisive. Those who prefer to examine the scriptures in their claimed provenance or who allow for the possibility of divine interaction, revelation, or uniformity may be portrayed as uncritical apologists or not rigorous (regardless of how carefully they may actually engage the text and its historical-cultural setting or linguistics), while those who embrace the conclusions of secular scholarship, even when it conflicts with the claims of the text or other faith-claims, may be characterized as "more serious" and even "more reverential" toward the text (regardless of how carefully they may

2. Philip L. Barlow, *Mormons and the Bible: The Place of the Latter-day Saints in American Religion,* 2nd ed. (New York: Oxford University Press, 2013), 112–61.

3. Anthony A. Hutchinson, "LDS Approaches to the Holy Bible," *Dialogue: A Journal of Mormon Thought* 15 (Spring 1982): 99–124. Hutchinson has a PhD in New Testament studies from the Catholic University of America. His four categories of scholarship are (1) harmonizing hermeneutic, "an interpretive theory stressing the unity and inerrancy of the scriptures" (p. 100); (2) critically modified harmonizing hermeneutic, "more *a posteriori* thought, more dialectic between faith, experience, and evidence [than in group 1]" (p. 104, emphasis original); (3) critical hermeneutic with corrective tendencies, "primarily concerned with understanding ancient texts honestly and credibly" (p. 105); and (4) critical historical and philological hermeneutic, "manifests little tendency toward the harmonization or corrective interpretation shown in varying degrees by the other three groups" (p. 106).

4. Hutchinson, "LDS Approaches to the Holy Bible," 101.

actually engage the text and its historical-cultural setting or linguistics).[5] Conversely, those who value and agree with secular scholarship's conclusions may be characterized as heretical, especially when they conflict with the claims of the text or faith claims.

While fundamentalist views can indeed be too rigid—preventing one from engaging with difficult questions or considering new perspectives—many Latter-day Saints recognize that uncritically embracing secular approaches that may disqualify divine involvement or too quickly dismiss traditional views is simply another form of rigidness that can also conceal truth in a text. Notwithstanding the problems both extremes create, discerning Latter-day Saints recognize that each side embodies important principles that are relevant to fully understanding a text. In fact, a canonical statement admonishes Latter-day Saints to find balance between these two approaches and "seek learning, even by study and also by faith" (D&C 88:118).

In spite of this admonition, it appears that engagement with many controversial issues raised by secular criticism, such as authorship and dating, has been minimal in much of Latter-day Saint history.[6] This observation should be tempered by the fact that engagement with secular critical methodologies is often married tightly to secular critical premises.[7] While the Church's eighth Article of Faith, which speaks of belief in the Bible "as far as it is translated correctly," certainly invites participation in critical scholarship, today's premises put pressure on Latter-day Saint scholars to "bracket" their faith—or adjust and nuance their views on such things as revelation, translation, and other prophetic claims—in order to participate. Such bracketing or adjustments, however, will inherently and inevitably produce vastly different conclusions from those who do not. Voicing this concern, Andrew Skinner stated:

5. For example, see Barlow, *Mormons and the Bible,* 155 n. 91, 159; and Hutchinson, "LDS Approaches to the Holy Bible," 103.

6. For some perspectives on this, see Taylor Petrey, "Introduction: Latter-day Saints and Biblical Scholarship," in *The Bible and the Latter-day Saint Tradition,* ed. Taylor G. Petrey, Cory Crawford, and Eric A. Eliason (Salt Lake City: University of Utah Press, 2023), 1–15; and Philip L. Barlow and Stephen T. Betts, "The Place of the Bible and Biblical Scholarship among Latter-day Saints in the Twentieth and Twenty-First Centuries," in Petrey, Crawford, and Eliason, *Bible and the Latter-day Saint Tradition,* 19–34.

7. For an example of the difficulties navigating such premises, see John Gee, "The Implications of Some Standard Assumptions of New Testament Scholars: Responding to a Modern Anti-Christ," *Interpreter: A Journal of Latter-day Saint Faith and Scholarship* 46 (2021): 15–32.

> When scholars attempt to peel away the so-called layers, additions, or embellishments from our New Testament text to get at the "real" Jesus, the unembellished or natural Jesus, it strikes one as being a little bit like peeling away the layers of an onion to get at the real onion. Sooner or later one is left with a pile of layers, having set out from the start to miss the real thing or the "essence," or maybe not even really wanting to see what is there. We can remove the divinity from Jesus, but that is not the real, actual Jesus.[8]

Note that Skinner indicates that such outcomes are the result of efforts by those who "set out from the start" to paint a picture of Christ that is only naturalistic or secular, void of any divine possibility. The path one chooses at the beginning will largely determine how one interprets the evidence and the conclusion at which one arrives.

Due to the narrowness of secular premises, most Latter-day Saint writers have chosen to understand how the Bible relates to and illuminates their own tradition's foundation of restored truths, not how it might fit into the worldview of secularists. Some might characterize this as "less critical," but honest appraisals will note that many Latter-day Saint scholars use historical-cultural analysis, linguistics, text variants, and other critical, even secular, methodologies to help them understand the text. Of course, Latter-day Saints could and should become more involved even in the controversial issues of New Testament scholarship. Their voices are needed, but venturing onto such a path is no easy task, since the secular academy (1) has already adopted as "fact" many past conclusions based on some limited evidence and (2) often restricts what is admissible evidence and even how one should read the evidence that is admitted.

Joseph Smith declared, "I beli[e]ve the bible, as it ought to be, as it came from the pen of the original writers."[9] So attempting to understand the authorial intent of a scriptural text and avoiding the mere assertion of one's own interpretation or theology is important to most Latter-day Saints. They believe they have two helpful and complementary avenues to recover original meaning: (1) the historical, cultural, and linguistic tools of scholarship and (2) seership. Latter-day Saint canon indicates that seers "can know of things which are past" (Mosiah 8:17) among other things—that

8. Andrew C. Skinner, "Introduction: A Time That Matters Most," in *From the Last Supper through the Resurrection: The Savior's Final Hours,* ed. Richard Neitzel Holzapfel and Thomas A. Wayment (Salt Lake City: Deseret Book, 2003), xxi.

9. "Discourse, 15 October 1843," in *Documents, Volume 13: August–December 1843,* ed. Christian K. Heimburger and others, The Joseph Smith Papers (Salt Lake City: Church Historian's Press, 2022), 187.

is, they can convey the original meaning of important truths contained in ancient texts, even when scholarship is not possible or available. Since modern Latter-day Saint leaders are accepted as seers for the Church, they have an institutional trust to collectively interpret and preserve important truths in scripture from the past—conveying things as they really were.

This does not mean that Latter-day Saints believe their leaders are individually infallible concerning every detail of history or scripture, but they do trust in their collective wisdom, course corrections, and sense on scriptural matters of importance as given by divine inspiration. For this reason, many Latter-day Saint studies of the New Testament not only engage critical historical, cultural, and linguistic methods for understanding a text but may also include insights and ideas from Church leaders, especially those given by Joseph Smith, in an attempt to balance both study and faith.

Engaging the New Testament critically while maintaining one's faith perspective should be applauded in the academy because uniquely held Latter-day Saint perspectives on the New Testament contribute to the plurality of views that the secular academy claims to prize. As Latter-day Saint Church leader Elder Jeffrey R. Holland, paraphrasing Harvard's Jon D. Levenson, declared, "Bracketing one's faith has more limitations than virtues. Above all, it precludes sharing insights unique to one's faith, thereby missing the opportunity to enrich the other."[10] Kent Jackson addressed this concept particularly in the context of New Testament scholarship.[11]

Seeing that the Latter-day Saint acceptance or nonacceptance of New Testament secular conclusions may cause divisions, we felt it would be more helpful to categorize Latter-day Saint New Testament studies according to the general purposes they aim to accomplish. While there is certainly a variety of ability and engagement with scholarly tools among Latter-day Saint authors, the majority provide unique Latter-day Saint perspectives on the New Testament informed by their greater body of scripture and their faith-informed worldview of God's plan of salvation for all humankind. The studies highlighted herein include those which focus on (1) the translation and transmission of New Testament texts; (2) the historical and cultural contexts of the New Testament texts; (3) the life and ministry of Jesus

10. Jeffrey R. Holland, "The Maxwell Legacy in the 21st Century," in *Neal A. Maxwell Institute for Religious Scholarship 2018 Annual Report,* 16.

11. Kent P. Jackson, "Asking Restoration Questions in the New Testament Scholarship," in *How the New Testament Came to Be,* ed. Kent P. Jackson and Frank F. Judd Jr., Sidney B. Sperry Symposium (Provo, Utah: Religious Studies Center, Brigham Young University; Salt Lake City: Deseret Book, 2006), 27–42.

Christ, including those that focus particularly on his sermons, parables, miracles, passion, Resurrection, and more; (4) the lives and ministries of other New Testament figures; (5) the relationship of the primitive Church and apostasy to the restored Church of Jesus Christ of Latter-day Saints; (6) temple and ritual themes in New Testament texts; (7) text-based commentaries; and (8) study guides and harmonies.

Translation and Transmission of New Testament Texts

John K. Carmack explained that while the King James Version (KJV) has traditionally been the preferred translation in Latter-day Saint studies, "any responsibly prepared version could be used and might be helpful to us. It is the doctrine and the teachings in their historical setting which are useful and authoritative to Latter-day Saints."[12] While the King James translation of the Bible was culturally prominent and familiar to the earliest Latter-day Saints, it was not considered a superior translation in comparison to other translations in circulation during the early years of the Church.[13] In fact, Joseph Smith on occasion used alternate translations in his sermons and even revised and expanded the KJV texts as part of his early prophetic ministry, believing that no current translation was without error or omission. Joseph Smith even gave a revelation that provided room for members to consider truths contained in the additional books of the Apocrypha that were not included in the KJV of his day.[14]

While this openness to alternate texts and translations appeared to persist for the nineteenth and much of the twentieth century, Barlow notes that a strong coalescence around the King James Version grew when the more secular 1952 Revised Standard Version made an appearance.[15] J. Reuben Clark, a member of the Church's First Presidency, particularly defended the importance of the King James Version in his book *Why the King James Version* (1956). He offered an in-depth historical analysis of manuscripts and early biblical texts. He charted the translation of the King James Version

12. John K. Carmack, "The New Testament and the Latter-day Saints," in *The New Testament and the Latter-day Saints* (Orem, Utah: Randall Book, 1987), 2, reprinted in *Sperry Symposium Classics: The New Testament,* ed. Frank F. Judd Jr. and Gaye Strathearn (Provo, Utah: Religious Studies Center, Brigham Young University; Salt Lake City: Deseret Book, 2006), 9.

13. Barlow, *Mormons and the Bible,* 166–67.

14. D&C 91. The earliest versions of the KJV did include the Apocrypha, separated from and not considered equal to scripture.

15. Barlow, *Mormons and the Bible,* 173–198.

of the English Bible by citing numerous biblical scholars and manuscript experts and explained the Latter-day Saint preference for this version.[16]

During the four-hundredth anniversary of the King James Version of the Bible, Kent P. Jackson published in 2011 a collection of papers reviewing the history of the KJV's coming forth and its relationship to Joseph Smith's sermons, revelations, and translation projects as well as some of its reception history within the Church generally.[17] The various authors in this volume note the KJV's cultural importance to the Church and to the English-speaking world generally, but they also acknowledge the argument of mainstream scholarship that there are better sources than those to which the KJV translators had access and a better understanding of the ancient world in general. Lincoln Blumell's article "The Text of the New Testament," Thomas Wayment's article "The Endings of Mark and Revelation," and Gaye Strathern's article "Modern English Bible Translations" particularly address some of these issues. Wayment published a 2023 article that covers much of the same ground as that noted above, with some added discussion of why moving away from the KJV would be rather difficult for English-speaking Latter-day Saints.[18]

The same year that Jackson's book appeared, Blumell published another article that compares the KJV with other modern translations and explains why some verses are substantially different.[19] A similar, though not as extensive, work appeared earlier by Stan Larson.[20] Blumell's study concludes that, based on text-critical issues, in most cases the readings in the King James Version appear to be inferior to those in the more modern translation, but the study also highlights a few instances where the King James Version might actually preserve a better reading. This simply highlights the importance of considering all the sources and evidence and being thorough in one's research.

Years earlier, Richard Anderson reviewed the New English Bible translation, comparing its paraphrasing translation style to the KJV and typical

---

16. J. Reuben Clark Jr., *Why the King James Version* (Salt Lake City: Deseret Book, 1956).

17. Kent P. Jackson, ed., *The King James Bible and the Restoration* (Provo, Utah: Religious Studies Center, Brigham Young University; Salt Lake City: Deseret Book, 2011).

18. Thomas Wayment, "The King James Version and Modern Translations of the Bible," in Petrey, Crawford, and Eliason, *Bible and the Latter-day Saint Tradition,* 35–46.

19. Lincoln H. Blumell, "A Text-Critical Comparison of the King James New Testament with Certain Modern Translations," *Studies in the Bible and Antiquity* 3 (2011): 67–126.

20. Stan Larson, "Omission in the King James New Testament," *Dialogue* 11, no. 3 (Fall 1978): 125–31.

Latter-day Saint understanding, revealing that in some instances it seems to move further away from Latter-day Saint interpretations (the result of being completed by a committee of Protestant scholars), while in other instances it seems to move closer to Latter-day Saint understanding (such as translating a phrase in 1 Cor. 15:29 as "baptism on behalf of the dead").[21]

In spite of the cultural supremacy and use of the KJV throughout much of the Church's history, alternate translations of the New Testament by Latter-day Saints exist. First and foremost is Joseph Smith's translation of the Bible (JST)—primarily a revision work of the KJV that he viewed as part of his prophetic ministry to restore and provide a more accurate translation of that scripture to the world. The Prophet's complete project was first published in 1867 by the Community of Christ (formerly the Reorganized Church of Jesus Christ of Latter Day Saints) and was formally adopted by The Church of Jesus Christ of Latter-day Saints as supplemental material in their 1979 English publication of the Bible.[22] Scott Faulring, Kent Jackson, and Robert J. Matthews published the foundation work on the original manuscripts of this project.[23]

The prominent publications regarding the JST of the New Testament have focused primarily on the history of its creation and the doctrinal insights Joseph Smith's revisions and expansions provide, including some that explore whether the JST more accurately reflects what is known from ancient New Testament texts and scholarship today.[24] Although Joseph

---

21. Richard Lloyd Anderson, "The New English Bible: Three Views: The New Testament," *Dialogue* 5, no. 4 (Winter 1970): 102–5.

22. For a historical overview of the coming forth of the Joseph Smith Translation, see Robert L. Millet, "Joseph Smith's Translation of the Bible: A Historical Overview," in *The Joseph Smith Translation: The Restoration of Plain and Precious Things,* ed. Monte S. Nyman and Robert L. Millet (Provo, Utah: Religious Studies Center, Brigham Young University, 1985), 23–49.

23. Scott H. Faulring, Kent P. Jackson, and Robert J. Matthews, eds., *Joseph Smith's New Translation of the Bible: Original Manuscripts* (Provo, Utah: Religious Studies Center, Brigham Young University, 2004). For an analysis of the original documents, see Royal Skousen, "The Earliest Textual Sources for Joseph Smith's 'New Translation' of the King James Bible," *FARMS Review* 17, no. 2 (2005): 451–70. For parallel columns of the translation with the KJV, see Kent P. Jackson, ed., *Joseph Smith's Translation of the Bible: The Joseph Smith Translation and the King James Translation in Parallel Columns* (Provo, Utah: Religious Studies Center, Brigham Young University; Salt Lake City: Deseret Book, 2022).

24. Robert J. Matthews, *"A Plainer Translation": Joseph Smith's Translation of the Bible, a History and Commentary* (Provo, Utah: Brigham Young University Press, 1975); Nyman and Millet, *Joseph Smith Translation: The Restoration*; Robert L. Millet and Robert J. Matthews, eds., *Plain and Precious Truths Restored: The Doctrinal and Historical Significance of the Joseph Smith Translation* (Salt Lake City: Bookcraft, 1995); W. Jeffrey Marsh,

Smith claimed his translation revisions came from divine inspiration, some have attempted to connect them to contemporary sources.[25] The most substantial attempt to date is Thomas Wayment and Haley Wilson-Lemmon's work that draws parallels between Joseph Smith's revisions and a popular contemporary Bible commentary.[26] Kent Jackson published a careful rebuttal effectively dismantling the certainty of Wayment and Wilson-Lemmon's claims, leaving the question open concerning the source of Joseph Smith's Bible translation ideas.[27] Jackson provides a more detailed analysis of the coming forth of the Joseph Smith Translation in his *Understanding Joseph Smith's Translation of the Bible.*[28]

In non-English-speaking countries, the Church approves and relies primarily on other translations of the Bible—the two exceptions being LDS editions of Spanish and Portuguese Bibles. The 2009 Santa Biblia is based on the 1909 Reina-Valera translation, and the 2015 Portuguese-language Bible is based on the 1914 edition of João Ferreira de Almeida's translation. Both translations have modernized grammar and vocabulary and include unique Latter-day Saint footnotes, chapter headings, and indexes.

The Joseph Smith Translation: Precious Truths Restored (American Fork, Utah: Covenant Communications, 2002); Thomas A. Wayment, "Quest for Origins: The Joseph Smith Translation and Latin Version of the New Testament," in *A Witness for the Restoration: Essays in Honor of Robert J. Matthews,* ed. Kent P. Jackson and Andrew C. Skinner (Provo, Utah: Religious Studies Center, Brigham Young University, 2007), 61–91; Thomas A. Wayment, "Intertextuality and the Purpose of Joseph Smith's New Translation of the Bible," in *Foundational Texts of Mormonism: Examining Major Early Sources,* ed. Mark Ashurst-McGee, Robin Jensen, and Sharalyn D. Howcroft (New York: Oxford University Press, 2018), 74–100; Grant Underwood, "Joseph Smith's 'New Translation' of the Bible," in Petrey, Crawford, and Eliason, *Bible and the Latter-day Saint Tradition,* 47–62.

25. See, for example, Ronald V. Huggins, "Joseph Smith's 'Inspired Translation' of Romans 7," *Dialogue* 26 (Winter 1993): 159–82; and Ronald V. Huggins, "'Without a Cause' and 'Ships of Tarshish': A Possible Contemporary Source for Two Unexplained Readings from Joseph Smith," *Dialogue: A Journal of Mormon Thought* 36, no. 1 (Spring 2003): 157–79.

26. Thomas A. Wayment and Haley Wilson-Lemmon, "A Recovered Resource: The Use of Adam Clarke's Bible Commentary in Joseph Smith's Bible Translation," in *Producing Ancient Scripture: Joseph Smith's Translation Projects in the Development of Mormon Christianity,* ed. Michael Hubbard MacKay, Mark Ashurst-McGee, and Brian M. Hauglid (Salt Lake City: University of Utah Press, 2020), 262–84. See also Thomas A. Wayment, "Joseph Smith, Adam Clarke, and the Making of a Bible Revision," *Journal of Mormon History* 46, no. 3 (July 2020): 1–22.

27. Kent P. Jackson, "Some Notes on Joseph Smith and Adam Clarke," *Interpreter: A Journal of Latter-day Saint Faith and Scholarship* 40 (October 2020): 15–60.

28. Kent P. Jackson, *Understanding Joseph Smith's Translation of the Bible* (Provo, Utah: Religious Studies Center, Brigham Young University; Salt Lake City: Deseret Book, 2022).

James Faulconer provided a verse-by-verse translation of Romans chapter 1, which he later expanded to include a few more chapters.[29] His studies include the KJV side by side with his own alternate translation based on *The Greek New Testament,* fourth edition.[30]

A large-scale effort by Latter-day Saints scholars to produce a contemporary English translation of the entire New Testament is the Brigham Young University (BYU) New Testament Commentary series, of which this volume is a part, being published through BYU Studies. This multiyear, multivolume project was initially proposed to the BYU administration in 2002 by John W. Welch and S. Kent Brown and seeks to make the language and idioms of the New Testament more accessible to their readers.

Following standard formats of academic ventures similar to this one, each volume produces a new translation of the Greek (primarily based upon the Greek text published by the Society of Biblical Literature [2010] or the twenty-eighth edition of the Nestle-Aland text in *Novum Testamentum Graece* [2012]), complete with translation notes and textual variations, as well as commentary. Partly out of respect to the Church's official support for the KJV, this project includes the KJV translation in parallel columns with the "New Rendition" each author provides.

The authors of these volumes engage text-critical issues raised in secular scholarship to varying degrees. Reviewers claim that some have not engaged enough views opposing traditional understandings or contradicting explicit and implicit claims in other Latter-day Saint scripture.[31] Julie Smith's commentary on the Gospel of Mark, on the other hand, fully embraces the popular scholarly view, based on some convincing evidence to be sure, that post-Resurrection appearances and teachings of Christ at the end of Mark (16:9–20) are not original to the text but a later addition.[32] She does not

---

29. James E. Faulconer, *Romans 1: Notes and Reflections* (Provo, Utah: Foundation for Ancient Research and Mormon Studies, 1999); James E. Faulconer, *The Life of Holiness: Notes and Reflections on Romans 1, 5–8* (Provo, Utah: Neal A. Maxwell Institute for Religious Scholarship at Brigham Young University, 2012).

30. *The Greek New Testament,* 4th rev. ed. (Stuttgart: United Bible Societies, 1993).

31. Philip L. Barlow, "The BYU New Testament Commentary: 'It Doth Not Yet Appear What It Shall Be,'" *Studies in the Bible and Antiquity* 6 (2014): 67–86; D. Jill Kirby, "Between Exegesis and Homiletics: Examining the Genres at Play in an LDS Commentary," *Studies in the Bible and Antiquity* 6 (2014): 87–115; Grant Underwood, "Some Reflections on the Revelation of John in Mormon Thought: Past, Present, and Future," *Studies in the Bible and Antiquity* 6 (2014): 116–26; Mike Pope, "A Closer Look: Luke 22:43–44 and Questions of Interpretation," *Studies in the Bible and Antiquity* 6 (2014): 127–33.

32. Julie M. Smith, *The Gospel according to Mark,* Brigham Young University New Testament Commentary (Provo, Utah: BYU Studies, 2018), 871–74.

engage the cogent arguments in the academy supporting the original ending.[33] As a result, Smith does not provide any translation nor commentary for the ending of Mark, similar to other modern translations and commentaries. Lack of full engagement with the textual issues, both for or against, should not overshadow the other value and insights these works contain.[34]

Concurrent with the rollout of the BYU New Testament Commentary series, a little-known effort to provide a translation with notes of 1 and 2 Timothy, Titus, and Philemon was published by William Blacoe.[35] Additionally, a single-volume modern English translation of the entire New Testament "for Latter-day Saints" was published by BYU professor Thomas Wayment in 2018 (revised in 2022).[36] The introductory material for each New Testament book in Wayment's volume is minimal but includes information about manuscripts, structure, and themes. The substantial notes indicate variant readings, textual allusions, brief commentary, and more.

A few Latter-day Saint scholars address the main issues related to New Testament textual criticism, mostly written for lay members of the Church.[37] Some address the friction that can occur when a text's originality is called into question and the same text appears in Latter-day Saint scripture and revelation. A few scholars in recent years, most notably Thomas Wayment and Lincoln Blumell, have engaged the academic discourse concerning

33. Nicholas P. Lunn, *The Original Ending of Mark: A New Case for the Authenticity of Mark 16:9–20* (Cambridge, United Kingdom: James Clark, 2014). See also Jeff Lindsay, "The Book of Mormon versus the Consensus of Scholars: Surprises from the Disputed Longer Ending of Mark," parts 1 and 2, *Interpreter: A Journal of Latter-day Saint Faith and Scholarship* 25 (2017): 283–365.

34. For example, see positive reviews from non–Latter-day Saint theologian Stephen H. Webb, "Review of The Testimony of Luke," BYU New Testament Commentary, February 9, 2015, http://www.byunewtestamentcommentary.com/review-of-the-testimony-of-luke/; and Daniel Peterson, "A Milestone in Latter-day Saint Biblical Scholarship," *Deseret News,* February 7, 2019, https://www.deseret.com/2019/2/7/20665180/daniel-peterson-a-milestone-in-latter-day-saint-biblical-scholarship.

35. William Victor Blacoe, *Understanding the New Testament: 1st and 2nd Timothy, Titus, and Philemon* (Springville, Utah: Cedar Fort, 2011).

36. Thomas Wayment, *The New Testament: A Translation for Latter-day Saints,* rev. ed. (Draper, Utah: Greg Kofford Books, 2022).

37. Thomas A. Wayment, "A Viewpoint on the Supposedly Lost Gospel Q," *Religious Educator* 5, no. 3 (2004): 105–15; Carl W. Griffin and Frank F. Judd Jr., "Principles of New Testament Textual Criticism," in Jackson and Judd, *How the New Testament Came to Be,* 78–92; Thomas A. Wayment, "Textual Criticism and the New Testament," in *New Testament History, Culture, and Society: A Background to the Texts of the New Testament,* ed. Lincoln H. Blumell (Provo, Utah: Religious Studies Center, Brigham Young University; Salt Lake City: Deseret Book, 2019), 659–71; Lincoln Blumell, "Textual Criticism," in Petrey, Crawford, and Eliason, *Bible and the Latter-day Saint Tradition,* 230–41.

text-critical arguments and published New Testament texts appearing in various Christian sources from antiquity.[38]

New Testament word studies by Latter-day Saints have also appeared. Richard Draper provided a study of the New Testament usage of the word *hypókrisis,* "hypocrisy."[39] Brent Schmidt has published important monograph contributions on the meaning of *charis,* "grace," and *pistis,* "faith," in the New Testament, demonstrating that they originally included notions of covenantal obligation.[40]

The New Testament's shared phraseology and ideas with other Latter-day Saint scripture is a unique area that some scholars have also explored.[41]

---

38. Thomas A. Wayment, "A New Transcription of P.Oxy. 2383 ($\mathfrak{P}^{69}$)," *Novum Testamentum* 50 (2008): 351–57; Lincoln H. Blumell, "Luke 22:43–44: An Anti-Docetic Interpolation or an Apologetic Omission?," *TC: A Journal of Biblical Textual Criticism* 19 (2014): 1–35; Lincoln H. Blumell, "P.Vindob. G 42417 (= $\mathfrak{P}^{116}$): Codex Fragment of the Epistle to the Hebrews 2:9–11 and 3:3–6 Reconsidered," *Zeitschrift für Papyrologie und Epigraphik* 171 (2009): 65–69; Lincoln H. Blumell, "P.Oxy. 5478. LUKE 2.32–4, 40–42, 24.22–8, 30–38 ($\mathfrak{P}^{141}$)," in *The Oxyrhynchus Papyri Vol. LXXXIV* (London: Egypt Exploration Fund, 2020), 3–9; Lincoln H. Blumell, "Scripture as Artefact," *Oxford Handbook of Early Christian Biblical Interpretation,* ed. Paul Blowers and Peter Martens (Oxford: Oxford University Press, 2019), 7–32; Lincoln H. Blumell and Thomas A. Wayment, "The 'Number of the Beast': Revelation 13:18 and Early Christian Isopsephies," in *Book of Seven Seals: The Peculiarity of Revelation, Its Manuscripts, Attestation, and Transmission,* ed. Thomas J. Kraus and Michael Sommer (Tübingen, Ger.: Mohr Siebeck, 2016), 119–35; Lincoln H. Blumell and Thomas A. Wayment, *Christian Oxyrhynchus: Texts, Documents, and Sources* (Waco, Texas: Baylor University Press, 2015); Lincoln H. Blumell, "An Amulet Containing Acts 9:1," *Bulletin of the American Society of Papyrologists* 54 (2017): 31–43; Lincoln H. Blumell and Thomas A. Wayment, "Coptic New Testament Fragments in the Brigham Young University Collection," *Journal of the Canadian Society for Coptic Studies* 6 (2014): 59–88; Jason Robert Combs, "Christian Anti-Sabbath Polemic and the Textual Transmission of Luke 4:16 and 23:56," *TC: A Journal of Biblical Textual Criticism* 26 (2021): 29–46.

39. Richard D. Draper, "'Scribes, Pharisees, Hypocrites': A Study in Hypókrisis," in *The Disciple as Scholar: Essays on Scripture and the Ancient World in Honor of Richard Lloyd Anderson,* ed. Stephen D. Ricks, Donald W. Parry, and Andrew H. Hedges (Provo, Utah: Foundation for Ancient Research and Mormon Studies, 2000), 385–427.

40. Brent J. Schmidt, *Relational Grace: The Reciprocal and Binding Covenant of* Charis (Provo, Utah: BYU Studies, 2015); Brent J. Schmidt, *Relational Faith: The Transformation and Restoration of* Pistis *as Knowledge, Trust, Confidence, and Covenantal Faithfulness* (Provo, Utah: BYU Studies, 2022).

41. Mark D. Thomas, "A Mosaic for Religious Counterculture: The Bible in the Book of Mormon," *Dialogue* 29, no. 4 (Winter 1996): 47–68; Nicholas J. Frederick, "What Has Moroni to Do with John?," *Religious Educator* 14, no. 3 (2013): 92–109; Nicholas J. Frederick and Joseph M. Spencer, "John 11 in the Book of Mormon," *Journal of the Bible and Its Reception* 5, no. 1 (2018): 81–105; Stan Larson, "The Historicity of the Matthean Sermon on the Mount in 3 Nephi," in *New Approaches to the Book of Mormon: Explorations*

Due to such similarities, some work from the assumption that the New Testament must have had a direct influence on the formation of those texts that Joseph Smith claimed to translate from ancient sources. However, additional reasons for the commonalities should not be dismissed, including earlier traditions or common phraseology influencing both the New Testament world and those in Joseph Smith's translations.

Historical and Cultural Context

Some works in Latter-day Saint New Testament scholarship focus primarily on the historical and cultural context of the New Testament world rather than the text itself. A volume titled *Bible Lands,* published by the Church in 1986, is a good example.[42] It features maps and photographs from the ground and air (including some from space) of major Bible locations as well as commentary for the photos.

D. Kelly Ogden's *Where Jesus Walked: The Land and Culture of New Testament Times* sought to "identify all things geographical in the teachings of Jesus and the early apostles and to elucidate not only their surface meaning but also their deeper meaning—how some object or condition in the land of Jesus is comparable to human conduct or character."[43] The photos in this volume feature landscapes, objects, flora, and fauna that specifically inform the teachings found in the New Testament.

---

in Critical Methodology, ed. Brent Lee Metcalfe (Salt Lake City: Signature Books, 1993), 115–63; Nicholas J. Frederick, "Evaluating the Interaction between the New Testament and the Book of Mormon: A Proposed Methodology," *Journal of Book of Mormon Studies* 24, no. 1 (2015): 1–30; Nicholas J. Frederick, *The Bible, Mormon Scripture, and the Rhetoric of Allusivity* (Madison, N.J.: Fairleigh Dickinson University Press, 2016); Nicholas J. Frederick, "The Book of Mormon and Its Redaction of the King James New Testament: A Further Evaluation of the Interaction between the New Testament and the Book of Mormon," *Journal of Book of Mormon Studies* 27 (2018): 44–87; Nicholas J. Frederick, "The Bible and the Book of Mormon: A Review of Literature," *Journal of Book of Mormon Studies* 28 (2019): 205–36; Nicholas J. Frederick, "Finding Meaning(s) in How the Book of Mormon Uses the New Testament," *Journal of Book of Mormon Studies* 30 (2021): 1–35; Grant Adamson, "Joseph Smith, Thomas Paine, and Matthew 27:51b–53," *Dialogue: A Journal of Mormon Thought* 54, no. 4 (Winter 2021): 1–33; Grant Adamson, "Luke 22:43–44 and the Mormon Jesus: Protestant Past, KJV-Only Present," *Journal of the Bible and Its Reception* 9, no. 1 (2022): 53–73.

42. The Church of Jesus Christ of Latter-day Saints and the Jerusalem Center for Near Eastern Studies, *Bible Lands: Photographs, Maps, and Commentary* (Jerusalem: Pictorial Archive Near Eastern History, 1986).

43. D. Kelly Ogden, *Where Jesus Walked: The Land and Culture of New Testament Times* (Salt Lake City, Utah: Deseret Book, 1991), 2.

John F. Hall and John W. Welch's *Masada and the World of the New Testament* reconstruct the setting of the New Testament with the intent "to take readers back into the first-century world of Herod, Josephus, Peter, and Jesus."[44] This dedicated volume of the BYU Studies periodical provides political, legal, literary, economic, agricultural, cultural, and other background for the New Testament's Herodian age leading up to the Jewish last stand at Masada.

Richard Neitzel Holzapfel, Eric Huntsman, and Thomas A. Wayment produced an oversized, full-color illustrated reference called *Jesus and the World of the New Testament.* The volume is filled with illustrations, maps, charts, diagrams, photos of artifacts, buildings, and locations, and more. The information is presented in a chronological fashion beginning with the intertestamental period, continuing through the ministry of Christ, and concluding with the earlier and later ministries of the Apostles.

Kent Jackson edited a volume of contributions highlighting the Near Eastern background of the Bible, including a section on the New Testament.[45] This book was created primarily for use by Brigham Young University's Jerusalem Center for Near Eastern Studies and focuses principally on those cultures and political entities of the ancient Near East that intersect with the biblical text. A more comprehensive collection of articles on New Testament background is *New Testament History, Culture, and Society,* edited by Lincoln Blumell.[46] In addition to the standard political and religious landscape, this volume provides more details with respect to manuscripts, authorship, and dating, as well as social studies regarding women, marriage, family, ritual, textiles, and more.

44. John W. Welch and John F. Hall, "Introduction," *BYU Studies* 36, no. 3 (1996–97): 9.

45. Kent P. Jackson, ed., *A Bible Reader's History of the Ancient World* (Provo, Utah: Jerusalem Center for Near Eastern Studies, Brigham Young University, 2016). See also Kent P. Jackson, "Scenes from Early Christian History," in Ricks, Parry, and Hedges, *Disciple as Scholar,* 453–69.

46. Lincoln H. Blumell, ed., *New Testament History, Culture, and Society: A Background to the Texts of the New Testament* (Provo, Utah: Religious Studies Center, Brigham Young University; Salt Lake City: Deseret Book, 2019). See also Blumell's work on travel and communication in the New Testament era based on early letters: Lincoln H. Blumell, "Travel and Communication in the New Testament," in *The New Interpreter's Dictionary of the Bible* (Nashville: Abingdon Press, 2009), 5:652–56; Lincoln H. Blumell, "The Message and the Medium: Some Observations on Epistolary Communication in Late Antiquity," *Journal of Greco-Roman Christianity and Judaism* 10 (2014): 24–67; Lincoln H. Blumell, "Beware of Bandits! Banditry and Land Travel in the Roman Empire," *Journeys: The International Journal of Travel and Travel Writing* 8, no. 1 (2008): 1–20; Lincoln H. Blumell and Korshi Dosoo, "A Coptic Magical Text for Virginity in Marriage: A Witness to the Practice of Celibate Marriage from Christian Egypt?," *Harvard Theological Review* 114, no. 1 (2021): 118–42.

Most recently, Brigham Young University's symposium volume *The Household of God* focuses specifically on the social background of the family in the New Testament.[47] Some studies in this volume looked at the social structure of families relative to New Testament teachings, including issues of marriage, divorce, polygamy, and sexual minorities, while others focus on the use of family or family relationships as symbols in the New Testament.

The Life and Ministry of Jesus Christ

While some may conclude that Latter-day Saints are not Christian—primarily due to their rejection of the conclusions that postapostolic ecumenical councils made concerning the nature of the Godhead (for example, that Christ and his Father are of the same substance) and the trinitarian doctrine that grew out of such—they do believe strongly that Jesus is the Son of God, the Messiah, and central to God's plan of salvation for the world. Consequently, a large portion of Latter-day Saint studies concerning the New Testament have focused on his life and ministry.[48] Two Christ-centered works that have greatly influenced New Testament scholarship within the Church generally are those by Elder James E. Talmage and Elder Bruce R. McConkie. They are among the most widely read and frequently cited scholars with respect to the life and teachings of Jesus Christ.

Talmage's book *Jesus the Christ* (1915) represents one of the first major scholarly efforts to understand the life, doctrines, and teachings of Jesus Christ in the New Testament.[49] Many post-Talmage New Testament scholarship finds roots in this book, his pinnacle work. The members of the First Presidency of the Church commissioned Talmage to write *Jesus the Christ* and reviewed it before its publication as well. This eight-hundred-plus-page work is divided into forty-two chapters that direct light upon the

47. Lincoln H. Blumell and others, eds., *The Household of God: Families and Belonging in the Social World of the New Testament* (Provo, Utah: Religious Studies Center, Brigham Young University; Salt Lake City: Deseret Book, 2022). John Gee published a response to one of the articles in that volume, focusing on the meanings of term *eunuch* in New Testament times: John Gee, "Misusing Eunuchs," *Public Square Magazine* (November 30, 2022), https://publicsquaremag.org/sexuality-family/the-dangers-of-redefining-chastity/.

48. Those that focus principally on the life and thematic teachings of Christ will be featured in this section. Those that focus on the text of the Gospels will be categorized under Commentaries below.

49. James E. Talmage, *Jesus the Christ: A Study of the Messiah and His Mission according to Holy Scriptures both Ancient and Modern* (Salt Lake City: Deseret News, 1915).

antemortal through the millennial Jesus Christ, dissecting the entire broad mission of Christ and working chronologically through the New Testament account. Talmage also addressed the report of Christ's appearance to certain of the ancient American peoples in the Book of Mormon.

Talmage's intent with *Jesus the Christ* was to testify of and underscore the Savior's divine ministry through a careful analysis of his life and teachings, with a heavy emphasis on the validity of the restored Church today. His analysis was largely based on the scriptures themselves; a great part of the text framed his own rendering of each event or teaching from the life of Christ. He also addressed cultural, religious, political, and social conditions at the time of Christ, and this analysis incorporated various tools: linguistic, historic, literary, archaeological, cultural, contextual, and prayerful research. Many such applications can be found in the footnotes, where he explained a Greek word's origin, defined a Jewish biblical practice, or brought forward the significance of a geographical location. He frequently synthesized various teachings, events, and principles from the Book of Mormon, the Doctrine and Covenants, and the Old and New Testaments. His nonscriptural sources were mostly Protestant and historical; he drew regularly from the works of Edersheim, Farrar, Geike, and Josephus.

In his endnotes and inside his text, Talmage made little distinction between scholarship, scripture, testimony, personal insight, and other Latter-day Saint commentary. His research was thorough but not necessarily unbiased in trying to fulfill his intent. He often cited heavily from one scholar for a particular section and wrote conclusively, leaving the reader with little doubt that he himself believed his work to be settled. While reading his works, one senses his strong personal voice. Like his other writings, his tone is thoroughly Latter-day Saint, filled with testimony and personal insights. Although not officially endorsed as Church doctrine, *Jesus the Christ* is included in the approved reading for Church missionaries and is generally accepted as authoritative.

In his four-volume series, *The Mortal Messiah,* McConkie followed a New Testament harmony of events in Christ's life, emphasizing his divine roles and identity as Son of God rather than just providing a verse-by-verse commentary. In the preface to the first volume, McConkie called Talmage one of his "most prominent predecessors"[50] and acknowledged *Jesus the Christ* as the foundation for his own series. Each volume of McConkie's series is divided into thirty or more chapters covering any topic pertaining to the life of Christ, from living circumstances in Jerusalem to Jewish worship. He

50. Bruce R. McConkie, *The Mortal Messiah: From Bethlehem to Calvary,* 4 vols. (Salt Lake City: Deseret Book, 1979–81), 1:xvii–xviii.

included in his portrayal many passages from other Latter-day Saint scripture that influenced his interpretation of New Testament passages.

He openly favored Protestant scholarship and relied on the same biblical commentators as Talmage did—Edersheim, Farrar, and Geike. His approach incorporated academic tools and intellectual investigation, but his overwhelming emphasis was on doctrinal interpretations and implications for personal conduct and faith. He was cautious with and critical of scholarly writing that, in his view, was a form of higher criticism driven by secular interests. Additionally, he used Latter-day Saint scripture to illuminate the nature of the Bible and its teachings. Like Talmage, his goal was to testify and persuade the reader to believe. Thus his writing is laced with personal, spiritual feelings and thoughts.

McConkie appreciated the value of studying the language, customs, traditions, and lifestyle of those in the New Testament to aid efforts in determining the intent and meaning of the message; however, he clearly defended the power of the Holy Ghost as the principal aid in understanding scripture. The personal, spiritual influences of the Holy Ghost ultimately override all scholarly research in McConkie's writing. His audience is primarily Latter-day Saints but includes any with open hearts and the desire or intent to believe. He showed his personal style and commitment to Latter-day Saint doctrines with phrases such as "taking our cues and quotations from Edersheim, but tempering his views with the added light and knowledge revealed" and others.[51] These types of phrases brought his works into a critical light from non–Latter-day Saint reviewers. Nonetheless, McConkie is always respected for the sheer volume of his works and his rigorous publication quota.

In 1990, Obert C. Tanner with coauthors Lewis M. Rogers and Sterling M. McMurrin revised and expanded earlier works that Tanner had created for the Church's Education Department and produced *Toward Understanding the New Testament.* The authors emphasized the accounts in the Gospels, devoting eleven chapters to the life of Christ (the Gospels) and five chapters to the Epistles. They rely heavily on contemporary scholarship and "agree with those historians who hold the now common view that the Gospels have seriously distorted the picture of Judaism at the time of Jesus."[52] They provide nuanced views of the texts, highlighting what they believe are different theologies and prejudices of each writer.

51. McConkie, *Mortal Messiah,* 1:171.

52. Obert C. Tanner, Lewis M. Rogers, and Sterling M. McMurrin, *Toward Understanding the New Testament* (Salt Lake City: Signature Books, 1990), xi.

Other works that sought to provide a holistic view of the life and ministry of Jesus Christ primarily through the New Testament include W. Cleon Skousen's *Days of the Living Christ.*[53] Skousen provides some background material in his introduction and then mostly creates a narrative of the Gospels interlaced with cultural or intertextual insights and speculations. David Ridges provides a similar approach, though his narrative is interlaced frequently with large quotations from the Gospel writers and the Joseph Smith Translation; most background material comes from the LDS Bible Dictionary. Another volume by James W. McConkie and Judith E. McConkie attempts to reconstruct a historical Jesus through the lens of his interactions with various individuals and institutions in the New Testament: "The aim is to put Jesus within the context of his own times using historical methods that place emphasis on primary sources."[54] A volume featuring the stain-glass art of Tom Holdman and Holdman Studios contains several insights on the life and teachings of Christ through New Testament passages.[55]

In addition, some Brigham Young University symposia proceedings have been published that focused wholly on the life and ministry of Christ. These include studies on such things as Jesus' premortality; his roles as teacher, prophet, priest, and king; his trial, Crucifixion, and Resurrection; reception history; and the Christology found in various books of the New Testament and in the Joseph Smith Translation.[56] Like the symposia proceedings, Thomas Wayment and Richard Holzapfel's three-volume series, entitled *The Life and Teachings of Jesus Christ,* provides a collection of scholarly essays, chiefly from Brigham Young University professors of religion, concerning the background and various aspects of Jesus Christ's ministry.[57] Andrew C. Skinner's introductory essay in the third volume mentions that a purpose

---

53. W. Cleon Skousen, *Days of the Living Christ,* 2 vols. (Salt Lake City: Ensign Publishing, 1992–93).

54. James W. McConkie and Judith E. McConkie, *Whom Say Ye That I Am?: Lessons from the Jesus of Nazareth* (Salt Lake City: Greg Kofford Books, 2018), 3.

55. Brad Wilcox and others, *Come unto Me: Illuminating the Savior's Life, Mission, Parables, and Miracles* (Salt Lake City: Deseret Book, 2019).

56. Bruce A. Van Orden and Brent L. Top, eds., *The Lord of the Gospels,* Sidney B. Sperry Symposium (Salt Lake City, Utah: Deseret Book, 1990); Paul H. Peterson, Gary Layne Hatch, and Laura D. Card, eds., *Jesus Christ: Son of God, Savior* (Provo, Utah: Religious Studies Center, Brigham Young University, 2002); Eric D. Huntsman, Lincoln H. Blumell, and Tyler J. Griffin, eds., *Thou Art the Christ: The Son of the Living God, the Person and Work of Jesus in the New Testament,* Sidney B. Sperry Symposium (Provo, Utah: Religious Studies Center, Brigham Young University; Salt Lake City: Deseret Book, 2018).

57. Richard Neitzel Holzapfel and Thomas A. Wayment, eds., *The Life and Teachings of Jesus Christ,* 3 vols. (Salt Lake City: Deseret Book, 2003–6).

of this work was to answer "the charges of critics and secular scholars who would try to persuade us that Jesus was not the literal Son of God, the actual Redeemer of all humankind, or that the New Testament accounts that report the last hours and acts of Jesus cannot be trusted as literal."[58]

Many Latter-day Saint studies focus on specific aspects of Jesus' ministry—such as his birth, his last week, his miracles, his parables, his Sermon on the Mount, or his prophecies. Several studies over the decades address the timing of Jesus' birth.[59] A traditional explanation is that it was April 6 due to a seeming commemoration passage given in connection with the modern Latter-day Saint Church being formally established on April 6, 1830 (see D&C 20:1); however, this interpretation is uncertain. Other studies focus on prophecies, culture, and witnesses of the Nativity.[60]

Studies focusing on the suffering, death, and Resurrection of Christ's final week include Richard Holzapfel's *A Lively Hope: The Suffering, Death, Resurrection, and Exaltation of Jesus Christ,* with an objective "to introduce to a nonspecialist readership some of the insights from recent New Testament research that may benefit the believer and help him or her gain a deeper appreciation for the richness of the narratives left to us as a gift from

---

58. Andrew C. Skinner, "Introduction: A Time That Matters Most," in Holzapfel and Wayment, *Life and Teachings of Jesus Christ,* 3:xiv.

59. Paul N. Hyde, "A Date for the Birth of Christ," *A Symposium on the New Testament* (Salt Lake City: The Church of Jesus Christ of Latter-day Saints, 1980), 100–106; John P. Pratt, "Yet Another Eclipse for Herod," *The Planetarian* 19 (December 1990): 8–14; John C. Lefgren, *April Sixth* (Salt Lake City: Deseret Book, 1980); S. Kent Brown, C. Wilfred Griggs, and H. Kimball Hansen, "Book Review: Lefgren, John C. *April Sixth,*" *BYU Studies* 22, no. 3 (1982): 375–83; John P. Pratt (with response from S. Kent Brown, C. Wilfred Griggs, and H. Kimball Hansen), "Afterwords," *BYU Studies* 23, no. 2 (1983): 252–55; Thomas A. Wayment, "Appendix: The Birth and Death Dates of Jesus Christ," in Holzapfel and Wayment, *Life and Teachings of Jesus Christ,* 1:383–85; Jeffrey R. Chadwick, "Dating the Birth of Christ," *BYU Studies* 49, no. 4 (2010): 4–38; Lincoln H. Blumell and Thomas A. Wayment, "When Was Jesus Born? A Response to a Recent Proposal," *BYU Studies* 51, no. 3 (2012): 53-81; John A. Tvedtnes, "When Was Christ Born?," *Interpreter: A Journal of Mormon Scripture* 10 (2014): 1–33; Jeffrey R. Chadwick, "Dating the Death of Jesus Christ," *BYU Studies* 54, no. 4 (2015): 135–91.

60. Gerald N. Lund, *The Light of the World: Insights into the Birth of Christ* (Salt Lake City: Deseret Book, 2010); W. Jeffrey Marsh, *Unto Us a Child Is Born* (Salt Lake City: Bookcraft, 1994); Joseph Fielding McConkie, *Witnesses of the Birth of Christ* (Salt Lake City: Bookcraft, 1998); Robert L. Millet, "The Birth and Childhood of the Messiah," in *Studies in Scripture: Volume Five, The Gospels,* ed. Kent P. Jackson and Robert L. Millet (Salt Lake City: Deseret Book, 1986), 140–59; Jeffrey R. Chadwick, *Stone Manger: The Untold Story of the First Christmas* (n.p.: By the author, 2011); Eric D. Huntsman, *Good Tidings of Great Joy: An Advent Celebration of the Savior's Birth* (Salt Lake City: Deseret Book, 2011).

the writers of the four Gospels."[61] His book is divided into two main parts, which separate the passion and Resurrection narratives as told from the perspective of each Gospel writer—paying particular attention to the intended audiences of Matthew, Mark, Luke, and John. Holzapfel's research draws on mainstream academic sources. He incorporates historical background information and Greek translations of some words, but his emphasis lies on the events themselves as depicted by the different writers.

Jeffrey Marsh's *His Final Hours* is more application driven, seeking to help the reader obtain "insights about life that can be drawn from the final hours of the Savior's life and atoning sacrifice."[62] Similar to Holzapfel's approach, Andrew C. Skinner's three-volume series on the Savior's last week analyzes the details surrounding the suffering, death, Crucifixion, and Resurrection of Jesus Christ, providing in-depth personal insights and analysis but also historical detail, word origins, and textual explanations.[63] Eric D. Huntsman's *God So Loved the World* organizes the details of the final week by day. The volume includes art and music that celebrate those moments as well.

Over the last decade, BYU's Religious Studies Center has published the proceedings of an annual Easter conference held at the university. Each focus on various aspects of the Savior's last week, ranging from historical contexts to devotional meaning.[64]

---

61. Richard N. Holzapfel, *A Lively Hope: The Suffering, Death, Resurrection, and Exaltation of Jesus Christ* (Salt Lake City: Bookcraft, 1999), xvii.

62. W. Jeffery Marsh, *His Final Hours* (Salt Lake City, Utah: Deseret Book, 2000), ix.

63. Andrew C. Skinner, *Gethsemane* (Salt Lake City: Deseret Book, 2002); Andrew C. Skinner, *Golgotha* (Salt Lake City: Deseret Book, 2004); Andrew C. Skinner, *The Garden Tomb* (Salt Lake City: Deseret Book, 2005); combined into a single volume and published as *The Savior's Final Week* (Salt Lake City: Deseret Book, 2014).

64. Thomas A. Wayment and Keith J. Wilson, eds., *Celebrating Easter* (Provo, Utah: Religious Studies Center, Brigham Young University, 2007); Richard Neitzel Holzapfel, Frank F. Judd Jr., and Thomas A. Wayment, eds., *"Behold the Lamb of God": An Easter Celebration* (Provo, Utah: Religious Studies Center, Brigham Young University, 2008); Richard Neitzel Holzapfel and Kent P. Jackson, eds., *To Save the Lost: An Easter Celebration* (Provo, Utah: Religious Studies Center, Brigham Young University, 2009); Richard Neitzel Holzapfel and Kent P. Jackson, eds., *My Redeemer Lives!* (Provo, Utah: Religious Studies Center, Brigham Young University, 2011); Camille Fronk Olson and Thomas A. Wayment, eds., *With Healing in His Wings* (Provo, Utah: Religious Studies Center, Brigham Young University, 2013); Alonzo L. Gaskill and Stanley A. Johnson, eds., *Our Savior's Love: Hope and Healing in Christ* (Provo, Utah: Religious Studies Center, Brigham Young University, 2015); Nicholas J. Frederick and Keith J. Wilson, eds., *His Majesty and Mission* (Provo, Utah: Religious Studies Center, Brigham Young University, 2017); Charles Swift, ed., *The Tragedy and the Triumph* (Provo, Utah: Religious Studies Center, Brigham Young University 2019); Jan J. Martin and Alonzo L. Gaskill, eds., *The*

Most publications concerning Jesus' parables focus on understanding the meaning of the text through historical or cultural analysis; some also suggest allegorical and moral interpretations to make the parables more relevant to the reader.[65] John Welch's approach to the parables has set him apart from most of the others by focusing on their anagogical meaning relative to the Latter-day Saints' unique understanding of God's plan of salvation.[66] Similar to Welch's approach, a volume of collected papers published in 2007 explores the relationship of the parables specifically to the Atonement of Jesus Christ.[67] A few unique articles include Steven Harper's work on the relationship of the parable of the rich man and Lazarus to the law of consecration in one of Joseph Smith's revelations and Thomas Wayment's analysis concerning the names of the parables.[68]

Power of Christ's Deliverance (Provo, Utah: Religious Studies Center, Brigham Young University, 2022).

65. Robert J. Matthews, *The Parables of Jesus* (Provo, Utah: Brigham Young University Press, 1969); Todd M. Compton, "Heaven and Hell: The Parable of the Loving Father and the Judgmental Son," *Dialogue* 29 (Winter 1996): 31–44; Robert L. Millet and James C. Christensen (artwork), *Parables: And Other Teaching Stories* (Salt Lake City: Shadow Mountain, 1999); Andrew C. Skinner and W. Jeffrey Marsh, *Scriptural Parables for the Latter Days* (Salt Lake City: Deseret Book, 2002); Jay E. Jensen, "The Parable of the Two Sons: A Revelation about God," in *Sperry Symposium Classics: The New Testament,* ed. Frank F. Judd Jr. and Gaye Strathearn (Provo, Utah: Religious Studies Center, Brigham Young University; Salt Lake City: Deseret Book, 2006), 25–35; Jared M. Halverson, "Of Soils and Souls: The Parable of the Sower," *Religious Educator* 9, no. 3 (2008): 30–47; Jay A. Parry and Donald W. Parry, *Understanding the Parables of Jesus Christ* (Salt Lake City: Deseret Book, 2010); Gerald N. Lund, *The Parables of Jesus: Mirrors to the Soul, Windows to Eternity* (Salt Lake City: Deseret Book, 2022).

66. John W. Welch, "The Good Samaritan: A Type and Shadow of the Plan of Salvation," *BYU Studies* 38, no. 2 (1998): 50–115; John W. Welch, "Symbolism in the Parable of the Willing and Unwilling Two Sons in Matthew 21," in *Let Us Reason Together: Essays in Honor of the Life's Work of Robert L. Millet,* ed. J. Spencer Fluhman and Brent L. Top (Provo, Utah: Religious Studies Center, Brigham Young University; Salt Lake City: Deseret Book, 2016), 97–116; John W. Welch, "The Symbolism of Two Sons in the Parable of the Prodigal Son," in *Seek Ye Words of Wisdom: Studies on the Book of Mormon, Bible, and Temple in Honor of Stephen D. Ricks,* ed. Donald W. Parry, Gaye Strathearn, and Shon D. Hopkin (Orem, Utah: Interpreter Foundation, 2020), 265–90; John W. Welch, Jeannie S. Welch, Jorge Cocco Santángelo (artwork), and Hermon de Toit (artwork commentary), *The Parables of Jesus: Revealing the Plan of Salvation* (American Fork, Utah: Covenant Communications, 2019).

67. C. Robert Line and others, *Parables of Redemption: The Restored Doctrine of the Atonement as Taught in the Parables of Jesus Christ* (Springville, Utah: Horizon Publishers, 2007).

68. Steven C. Harper, "The Rich Man, Lazarus, and Doctrine & Covenants 104:18," *BYU Studies* 47, no. 4 (2008): 51–54; Thomas A. Wayment, "Names of the Parables," *Religious Educator* 4, no. 1 (2003): 97–106.

Similar to the parables, scholarly studies concerning Jesus' miracles focus on the historical or cultural background and understanding the text.[69] Most Latter-day Saints are open to the historical possibility of miracles (see Moro. 7:27–29, 37), so they do not view them only as metaphor. However, the possibility that literal miracles can still be symbolic is also explored in the literature in order to draw additional meaning and personal application.[70]

Jesus' Sermon on the Mount has received much attention over the last several decades. Leland Monson's monograph characterizes it mainly as an announcement of a higher law and seeks to provide a better "understanding of the relationship of the law and the prophets to the Sermon on the Mount."[71] In opposition to secular biblical scholars who view the sermon as a late editorial that stitched together random sayings of Jesus, John Welch demonstrates that the entire text can be seen as a unified whole relating to the temple.[72] Robert A. Cloward dismisses both Monson's and Welch's theses in favor of viewing the sermon as a missionary preparation.[73] However, temples and missionaries teach, arguably, the same concepts: God's path of salvation through a series of covenants and rites that bind the believer to both lesser and higher laws and ways of life. Consequently, the ideas presented by these three scholars are not mutually exclusive. An entire BYU symposium focused on the sermon, and the published proceedings provide insight into the sociocultural context in which it was given, the sources for many of Jesus' teachings, and the various phrases within the sermon.[74]

Richard D. Draper's *The Savior's Prophecies* focuses on "specific historical events the Savior predicted just a few days before His Crucifixion, as

---

69. John W. Welch, "Evidence for a New Testament Miracle," *BYU Studies* 37, no. 4 (1997–98), 173–75; Blair G. Van Dyke, "Miracles of Jesus in the Gospel of John," *Religious Educator* 9, no. 3 (2008): 14–29.

70. Eric D. Huntsman, *The Miracles of Jesus* (Salt Lake City: Deseret Book, 2014); Alonzo L. Gaskill, *Miracles of the New Testament: A Guide to the Symbolic Messages* (Springville, Utah: Cedar Fort, 2014).

71. Leland H. Monson, *Look to the Mount: A Study of the Sermon on the Mount* (Salt Lake City: Deseret Book, 1968), v.

72. John W. Welch, *The Sermon at the Temple and the Sermon on the Mount: A Latter-Day Saint Approach,* (Salt Lake City: Deseret Book, 1990).

73. Robert A. Cloward, "The Savior's Missionary Training Sermon in 3 Nephi," in *The Book of Mormon: 3 Nephi 9–30, This Is My Gospel,* ed. Monte S. Nyman and Charles D. Tate Jr. (Provo, Utah: Religious Studies Center, Brigham Young University, 1993), 119–36.

74. Gaye Strathearn, Thomas A. Wayment, and Daniel L. Belnap, eds., *The Sermon on the Mount in Latter-day Scripture,* Sidney B. Sperry Symposium (Provo, Utah: Religious Studies Center, Brigham Young University; Salt Lake City: Deseret Book, 2010).

He sat on the Mount of Olives," as recorded in Matthew 24.[75] The intent is to help readers learn that many of these events are already fulfilled and to prepare for the Second Coming.

The Lives and Ministries of Other New Testament Figures

Apart from the life and teachings of Jesus Christ, Latter-day Saint scholars have focused some of their studies on other prominent men and women in the New Testament. Those which focus on the texts such individuals may have created are categorized under "Text Commentaries" below.

Robert J. Matthews, a former dean of Religious Education at BYU, wrote a study on John the Baptist. Matthews intended that *A Burning Light: The Life and Ministry of John the Baptist* (1972) would "cultivate a wider knowledge and a greater appreciation for" the Baptist and increase awareness of his "ministry in three dispensations of the gospel, in light of latter-day revelation, which gives a fuller view and a more complete knowledge than can be obtained from the Bible alone."[76] Matthews referenced multiple Bibles and made cross-textual comparisons to explore the life and ministry of John. He relied heavily on Latter-day Saint sources, adopting dates and chronological references from J. Reuben Clark's Gospel harmony. Like Clark, he was not especially concerned with accuracy of dates that may have proved challenging. On the historical context of John the Baptist's death, see Cecilia Peek's article "The Death of John the Baptist."[77]

Volumes that focus primarily on the lives and teachings of various Apostles include Franklin L. West's *The Apostles and the Primitive Church* (1964).[78] West provides a narrative approach to the New Testament lives and ministry of the Apostles. Scattered throughout his narrative are frequent quotes of New Testament passages that highlight certain doctrines and practices in the early Church. *Go Ye into All the World* is a collection

75. Richard D. Draper, *The Savior's Prophecies: From the Fall of Jerusalem to the Second Coming* (American Fork, Utah: Covenant Communications, 2001), 3. See also Keith W. Perkins, "The JST on the Second Coming of Christ," in Nyman and Millet, *Joseph Smith Translation: The Restoration*, 237–49.

76. Robert J. Matthews, *A Burning Light: The Life and Ministry of John the Baptist* (Provo, Utah: BYU Press, 1972), vii. See also RoseAnn Benson and Robert J. Matthews, "John the Baptist: The Miracle and the Mission," *Religious Educator* 10, no. 2 (2009): 47–62.

77. Cecilia M. Peek, "The Death of John the Baptist," in Holzapfel and Wayment, *Life and Teachings of Jesus Christ*, 2:208.

78. Franklin L. West, *The Apostles and the Primitive Church* (Salt Lake City: Deseret Book, 1964).

of articles from BYU's Sperry Symposium that primarily explores the witnesses, teachings, and background of the New Testament Apostles after the Resurrection of Jesus.[79] A few of the articles focus on the church community in that age as well. John F. Hall's *New Testament Witnesses of Christ: Peter, John, James, and Paul* presents to his readers a well-researched historical and cultural background to the titular Apostles' ministries. His writing, in part, responds to "modern sectarian misunderstanding of apostolic authority and function, as well as to counter hypercritical scholarly technique that calls into question the authority of Peter, John, James, and Paul, and variously challenges their authorship of certain works of scripture by tradition long attributed to them."[80]

A volume of collected conference papers that focus on the life and ministry of the Apostle John and then a volume on Peter were published in 1998 and 2014, respectively.[81] Each volume explores the historical and cultural background and biographical notes of each Apostle as well as the thematic teachings contained in their writings. Frank Judd and Terrence Szink also produced a paper focusing on a lost writing of John the Beloved in a modern Latter-day Saint revelation.[82]

An influential scholar of the Church who made major contributions regarding the life of the Apostle Paul was Sidney B. Sperry (1895–1977).[83] Drawing upon biblical scholarship, Sperry's *Paul's Life and Letters* chronologically addresses Paul's life events and writings. He takes a careful historical approach in attempting to illuminate background, conditions, and circumstances of the Apostle's life. His focus was not linguistic, although he

---

79. Ray L. Huntington and others, eds., *Go Ye into All the World: Messages of the New Testament Apostles,* Sidney B. Sperry Symposium (Provo, Utah: Religious Studies Center, Brigham Young University; Salt Lake City, Utah: Deseret Book, 2002).

80. John F. Hall, *New Testament Witnesses of Christ: Peter, John, James, and Paul* (American Fork, Utah: Covenant Communications, 2002), [vi].

81. *The Testimony of John the Beloved,* Sidney B. Sperry Symposium (Salt Lake City: Deseret Book, 1998); Frank F. Judd Jr., Eric D. Huntsman, and Shon D. Hopkin, eds., *The Ministry of Peter, the Chief Apostle,* Sidney B. Sperry Symposium (Provo, Utah: Religious Studies Center, Brigham Young University; Salt Lake City: Deseret Book, 2014).

82. Frank F. Judd Jr. and Terry L. Szink, "John the Beloved in Latter-day Scripture (D&C 7)," in *The Doctrine and Covenants: Revelations in Context,* ed. Andrew H. Hedges, J. Spencer Fluhman, and Alonzo L. Gaskill, Sidney B. Sperry Symposium (Provo, Utah: Religious Studies Center, Brigham Young University; Salt Lake City: Deseret Book, 2008), 90–107.

83. Ellis T. Rasmussen, "Sidney B. Sperry," in *Encyclopedia of Latter-day Saint History,* ed. Arnold K. Garr, Donald Q. Cannon, and Richard O. Cowan (Salt Lake City: Deseret Book, 2000), 1174–75.

occasionally referred to the meaning of Greek words. He incorporated little modern-day revelation or writings specific to the restored Church, but Sperry kept his Latter-day Saint audience in mind in his bibliography of sources by including warnings and personal comments regarding each source.[84]

More than fifty years later, Thomas Wayment published another biography of Paul.[85] His approach is very similar to Sperry's volume, organizing the details of Paul's life and letters chronologically to provide historical and cultural background as he moves through time. Of course, Wayment has the advantage of fifty additional years of research to inform his writing. An earlier volume by Edwin Firmage explored the life and teachings of Paul in order to draw out principles of missionary work.[86] William Blacoe also produced a biography of Paul that is heavier on historical background and movement.[87]

A BYU Sperry Symposium dedicated to the life of Paul focuses on Paul's character and thematic teachings rather than on a chronological tracking of his travels and teachings.[88] The authors provide historical background and context along with references to Greek and Hebrew word origins, indicating an intent to convey the text accurately.

Several works focusing on women in the New Testament have been published in recent decades. One of the earliest is Jeni Holzapfel and Richard Holzapfel's *Sisters at the Well.*[89] Their volume begins with the cultural and historical background of women in the Greco-Roman world, including everyday life—birth, transition from childhood to womanhood, marriage, and family—and the view of women in the four Gospels. The woman in Jesus' genealogy, the women in Jesus' teachings, and the women with whom Jesus interacts are also highlighted.

Camille Olson's *Women of the New Testament* goes beyond the Holzapfels' work by including the women throughout the entire New Testament,

---

84. Sidney B. Sperry, *Paul's Life and Letters* (Salt Lake City: Bookcraft, 1955).

85. Thomas A. Wayment, *From Persecutor to Apostle: A Biography of Paul* (Salt Lake City: Deseret Book, 2006).

86. Edwin Brown Firmage, *Paul and the Expansion of the Church Today* (Salt Lake City: Deseret Book, 1979).

87. William Victor Blacoe, *From Saul to Paul: The Road to Apostleship* (Springville, Utah: Cedar Fort, 2014).

88. Paul Y. Hoskisson, ed., *The Apostle Paul: His Life and His Testimony,* Sidney B. Sperry Symposium (Salt Lake City: Deseret Book, 1994).

89. Jeni Broberg Holzapfel and Richard Neitzel Holzapfel, *Sisters at the Well: Women and the Life and Teachings of Jesus* (Salt Lake City: Bookcraft, 1993).

not just those that interacted with Jesus Christ.[90] Her study generally organizes the women according to their ethnic backgrounds—that is, Jewish, Samaritan, and Greco-Roman—but provides additional highlights for those in the Roman and Jewish aristocracy as well as those in Christ's lineage. Like the Holzapfels', Olson's work includes historical and cultural background of women in the New Testament world but also adds interesting historical facts about some of the women's lives beyond the New Testament when extrabiblical sources allow. Olson also penned earlier works that focused on Mary and Martha of Bethany, Mary the mother of Jesus, and those women who interacted with the Savior with respect to his power over death.[91]

Other studies of note include Susan Easton-Black and Alan Parish's work deriving principles of Christian discipleship from the example of various women in the New Testament, some in comparison to women in modern Church history.[92] Sherrie Mills Johnson and Camille Fronk Olson investigate the equality of women and men in the teachings of Paul in 1 Corinthians, rather than seeing women as subordinates to men.[93] S. Kent Brown's focused study of Mary and Elizabeth provides detail into the lives of these women through the culture and history of home, marriage, Bethlehem, and a careful reading of the New Testament texts. Catherine Taylor explores the archetypal role various women of the New Testament held in the Christian community.[94]

---

90. Camille Fronk Olson, Elspeth Young (artist), Al R. Young (artist), and Ashton Young (artist), *Women of the New Testament* (Salt Lake City: Deseret Book, 2014).

91. Camille Fronk Olson, *Mary, Martha, and Me* (Salt Lake City: Deseret Book, 2005); Camille Fronk Olson, *Mary, The Mother of Jesus* (Salt Lake City: Deseret Book, 2012); Camille Fronk Olson, "They Ministered unto Him of Their Substance: Women and the Savior," in Holzapfel and Jackson, *To Save the Lost,* 61–80.

92. Susan Easton-Black and Alan K. Parrish, "New Testament Women: The Exemplars," in *New Testament and the Latter-day Saints,* 43–59.

93. Sherrie Mills Johnson, "Paul's Teachings in 1 Corinthians on Women," in *Shedding Light on the New Testament: Acts–Revelation,* ed. Ray L. Huntington, Frank F. Judd Jr., and David M. Whitchurch (Provo, Utah: Religious Studies Center, Brigham Young University, 2009), 129–52; Camille Fronk Olson, "Submit Yourselves . . . as unto the Lord," in Huntington and others, *Go Ye into All the World,* 98–113.

94. S. Kent Brown, *Mary and Elisabeth: Noble Daughters of God* (American Fork, Utah: Covenant Communications, 2002); Catherine Gines Taylor, "Women and the World of the New Testament," in Blumell, *New Testament History, Culture, and Society,* 514–31.

The Primitive Church and Apostasy

One of the more unique contributions Latter-day Saints have made to New Testament studies generally is their scholarship attempting to demonstrate that the early Christian Church established by Jesus and his Apostles did not last very long but was corrupted and lost, necessitating a restoration of authority, rituals, covenants, laws, and doctrines that Latter-day Saints claim began with Joseph Smith. Ironically, this is an area in which the ideas of Latter-day Saints and many secular scholars converge as studies concerning changes to scripture, doctrines, and practices of the early Church have increased in the academic world.

Gordon Irving's 1973 article "Mormons and the Bible in the 1830s" (based on his 1972 University of Utah honors thesis) aggregates many of the earliest Latter-day Saint writings relative to the New Testament and recognizes that a prominent approach in these early writings was to outline the organization, practices, and basic doctrines that characterized the Church Jesus Christ organized; demonstrate that Jesus and his Apostles predicted an apostasy or falling away from these ideals; and show that these ideals have been restored in the Church that Joseph Smith organized.[95] Such an approach was central to early missionary efforts: "The journals of many converts show that they were seeking a common sense church which followed the New Testament pattern."[96]

Approaches linking the structure and teachings of the New Testament Church to the modern Church have remained a constant in Latter-day Saint scholarship since these early years. B. H. Roberts's *Outlines of Ecclesiastical History* (1902) is an extensive systematic work that reviews New Testament details concerning Jesus and his Apostles' establishment of the Church doctrines and practices in their day, the later Apostasy or falling away from those doctrines and organization, and the Restoration of the same doctrines and practices through Joseph Smith in modern times. James Talmage's *The Great Apostasy* (1909) similarly provides a brief outline on the establishment of the New Testament Church but then focuses on various causes of apostasy (both external and internal) that corrupted its original teachings, practices, and organization.

95. Gordon Irving, "The Mormons and the Bible in the 1830s," *BYU Studies* 13, no. 4 (Summer 1973): 473–88.

96. Irving, "Mormons and the Bible in the 1830s," 477–78.

Most of the historical evidence for apostasy in these earlier Latter-day Saint publications drew upon prevailing Protestant, or anti-Catholic, scholarship, which focused primarily on late-Christian and medieval sources that demonstrate Catholic corruption of doctrine and practices. Since that time, earlier manuscripts have come forth, giving a better view and understanding of the earliest periods of Christianity. Hugh Nibley demonstrates in these earliest sources that Jesus and the early Christians did not anticipate that the Church they founded would survive very long. Nibley further addresses the paucity of evidence for those who claim it did.[97]

Kent Jackson's 1996 monograph, primarily written for nonspecialists, provides broad outlines of strife and doctrinal drift the Apostles were attempting to correct as found mostly in New Testament passages. He also sketches a few major figures and church councils in the post-apostolic era before moving on to the bulk of the book, which focuses on the events of Joseph Smith's day.

Barry Bickmore's *Restoring the Ancient Church* identifies several key doctrines and practices of the modern Church and demonstrates their presence in the New Testament and earliest Christian sources while highlighting any historical conflicts that existed over specific issues.[98] Similar approaches are taken in Scott Peterson's and Tad Callister's works.[99] Jared Ludlow explored similarities of historical events, rather than beliefs and practices, that the early and modern Church experienced in their initial growth periods.[100]

---

97. Hugh W. Nibley, "The Passing of the Primitive Church: Forty Variations on an Unpopular Theme," *Church History* 30 (June 1961): 131–54; Hugh W. Nibley, "The Way of the Church," *Improvement Era* 58 (Jan.–Dec. 1955): 20–22, 44–45, 86–87, 104, 106–7, 110, 152–54, 166, 168, 230–32, 258, 260–61, 306–8, 364–66, 384–86, 455–56, 502–4, 538, 570–71, 599–600, 602–6, 650–53, 708–9, 817, 835–38, 840–41, 902–3, 968. Both articles were reprinted in Hugh W. Nibley, *Mormonism and Early Christianity* (Salt Lake City: Deseret Book, 1987), 168–208, 209–322.

98. Barry Robert Bickmore, *Restoring the Ancient Church: Joseph Smith and Early Christianity,* exp. and rev. 2nd ed. (Redding, Calif.: FairMormon, 2013).

99. Tad R. Callister, *The Inevitable Apostasy and the Promised Restoration* (Salt Lake City: Deseret Book, 2006); extensively edited and retitled as *The Blueprint of Christ's Church* (Salt Lake City: Deseret Book, 2014); Scott R. Peterson, *Do the Mormons Have a Leg to Stand On? A Critical Look at the LDS Doctrines in Light of the Bible and the Teachings of the Early Christian Church* (Orem, Utah: Millennial Press, 2014). Peterson's earlier work *Where Have All the Prophets Gone? Revelation and Rebellion in the Old Testament and the Christian World* (Springville, Utah: Cedar Fort, 2005) provides mainly a historical narrative of dispensations, with greater detail given to the period between the New Testament church and the modern Church.

100. Jared W. Ludlow, "The Book of Acts: A Pattern for Modern Church Growth," in Huntington, Judd, and Whitchurch, *Shedding Light on the New Testament: Acts–Revelation,* 1–29.

Daniel Graham and James Siebach produced an important study demonstrating that the assumption that Greek philosophy caused early Christian apostasy is unclear from the sources. Rather, the growing influence of philosophical ideas in early Christianity may have been an effect of apostasy.[101]

Grant Underwood expresses caution when interpreting what it means for the modern Church to be the "same" as the primitive Church.[102] However, he explores how there is sameness if one does not get too focused on just the nomenclature of offices but rather some specific functions of the organization that the early and the modern Church share.

Taylor Petrey's article goes beyond Underwood's caution, noted above, by advocating for approaches that (1) abandon any notion that early Christianity was a homogenous, "pure" religion before the Apostasy and focus more on its hybridity and (2) seek to make complete comparisons (including differences) more than just highlighting parallels between the early and the modern Church.[103] Petrey interprets the lack of pure hegemony in the ancient Church and some of Joseph Smith's statements as indicating their willingness to simply embrace multiple, even conflicting, viewpoints within the body of the Church and suggests this should be a model for the Church today. He does not, however, explain why the early Apostles were constantly correcting misunderstandings and false doctrines among the Saints through their letters, nor does he explain why Joseph Smith had many doctrinal revelations ratified as standards within the Church and constantly corrected modern Saints who overstepped their bounds of authority or claimed to receive revelation for the Church if hybridity was truly embraced.

Early Christians in Disarray, edited by Noel Reynolds, is a collection of articles that, like Nibley's work, considers broader scholarship as well as newly discovered manuscripts from the first Christian centuries in order to explore causes and timing of the Apostasy with greater accuracy.[104] James Faulconer's article in this volume looks specifically at the meaning of the term "apostasy" in the New Testament, concluding that it drew upon its

---

101. Daniel W. Graham and James L. Siebach, "Philosophy and Early Christianity," *Review of Books on the Book of Mormon 1989–2011* 11, no. 2 (1999): 210–20, https://scholarsarchive.byu.edu/msr/vol11/iss2/6.

102. Grant Underwood, "The 'Same' Organization That Existed in the Primitive Church," in Huntington and others, *Go Ye into All the World,* 167–86.

103. Taylor G. Petrey, "Purity and Parallels: Constructing the Apostasy Narrative of Early Christianity," in Wilcox and Young, *Standing Apart,* 174–95.

104. Noel B. Reynolds, ed., *Early Christians in Disarray: Contemporary LDS Perspectives on the Christian Apostasy* (Provo, Utah: Brigham Young University Press, 2005).

usage in the Greek Old Testament and meant "not only a rebellion against God, but specifically rebellion that rejects priesthood service, a service that was, in early Christianity, best revealed in temple priesthood and ordinances [that is, in covenants]."[105]

Daniel Belnap outlines a pattern from the teachings of Jesus concerning actions that led to apostasy in order to reveal similar patterns among early Christians reflected in the letters of Paul, Peter, and John as well as among those in the Book of Mormon who fell away.[106]

Kent Jackson published two articles analyzing several New Testament passages that predicted an Apostasy would occur within the early Church and then outlined evidence for such during and after the apostolic age.[107] A separate study by Gaye Strathearn focuses specifically on the doctrinal drift occurring in the early Christian Church concerning the nature of the body with its ramifications on the understanding of resurrection.[108]

Miranda Wilcox and John D. Young's collection of essays positions itself as an "academic perspective" on the Apostasy, in contrast to Latter-day Saint "leaders and apologists" who have dominated the cultural conversation.[109] Laying aside concerns of scholarly hubris from such labeling and disregard for the many leaders and apologists who happen to be academically trained as well, the volume does provide some helpful adjustments to apostasy narratives often heard among Church members.

In the wake of the Wilcox volume, Nicholas Frederick and Joseph Spencer suggest, based on their reading of the Book of Mormon, an additional way to interpret apostasy as Christian neglect and misunderstanding of

---

105. James E. Faulconer, "The Concept of the Apostasy in the New Testament," in Reynolds, *Early Christians in Disarray,* 143.

106. Daniel Belnap, "The Process of Apostasy in the New Testament and the Book of Mormon," in Huntington, Judd, and Whitchurch, *Shedding Light on the New Testament: Acts–Revelation,* 247–70.

107. Kent P. Jackson, "New Testament Prophecies of Apostasy," in *Sperry Symposium Classics: The New Testament,* 394–406; Kent P. Jackson, "The End of the Early Church," in *The Life and Teachings of the New Testament Apostles: From the Day of Pentacost through the Apocalypse,* ed. Richard Neitzel Holzapfel and Thomas A. Wayment (Salt Lake City: Deseret Book, 2010), 250–75.

108. Gaye Strathearn, "Sōma Sēma: The Influence of 'The Body Is a Tomb,' in Early Christian Debates and the New Testament," in Holzpafel and Wayment, *Life and Teachings of the New Testament Apostles,* 276–98.

109. Miranda Wilcox and John D. Young, eds., *Standing Apart: Mormon Historical Consciousness and the Concept of Apostasy* (New York: Oxford University Press, 2014), 8.

their relationship to covenantal Israel.[110] Gregor McHardy also published a book directly challenging some standard apostasy narratives heard among Church members.[111]

Temple and Ritual Studies

Long-standing Latter-day Saint practices of temple worship and ritual covenant-making have propelled some scholars to examine these areas of study relative to the New Testament. Such tend to focus on early Christian connections to a secret tradition or temple worship, specific rites in early Christianity, or temple themes and structure in New Testament texts. Hugh Nibley is arguably the most influential scholar for this type of approach. His works on temples generally and on early Christian relations to the temple, prayer circles, baptism for the dead, and ritual vestments in numerous sources specifically have laid a foundation upon which many scholars have built.[112]

The general importance of the temple to the earliest Christians based on New Testament texts is addressed by S. Kent Brown.[113] William Hamblin explored the possible existence of a sequence of early Christian initiation rites established by Jesus himself, as reflected in the writings of Clement of Alexandria.[114] Additional evidence for Christian baptism for the dead and

110. Nicholas J. Frederick and Joseph M. Spencer, "Remnant or Replacement? Outlining a Possible Apostasy Narrative," *BYU Studies* 60, no. 1 (2021): 105–27.

111. Gregor McHardy, *8 Myths of the Great Apostasy* (Salt Lake City: Signature Books, 2022).

112. Hugh W. Nibley, "The Early Christian Prayer Circle," *BYU Studies* 19, no. 1 (1978): 41–78; Hugh W. Nibley, "Baptism for the Dead in Ancient Times," *Improvement Era* 51 (1948): 786–88, 836; 52 (1949): 24–26, 60, 90–91, 109–10, 112, 146–48, 180–83, 212–14; Hugh W. Nibley, "The Idea of the Temple in History," *Millennial Star* 120 (1958): 228–37, 247–49, reprinted and expanded in "What Is a Temple?" and "Looking Backward," in *The Temple in Antiquity,* ed. Truman G. Madsen (Provo, Utah: Religious Studies Center, Brigham Young University, 1984), 19–51; Hugh W. Nibley, "Christian Envy of the Temple," *Jewish Quarterly Review* 50 (1959–60): 97–123, 229–40. All reprinted in *Mormonism and Early Christianity* (Salt Lake City: Deseret Book, 1987), 45–99, 100–167, 355–90, 391–434, respectively. Hugh Nibley, "Sacred Vestments," in *Temple and Cosmos,* vol. 12 of The Collected Works of Hugh Nibley (Salt Lake City: Deseret Book; Provo, Utah: Foundation for Ancient Research and Mormon Studies, 1992), 91–138.

113. S. Kent Brown, "The Temple in Luke and Acts," in *Revelation, Reason, and Faith: Essays in Honor of Truman G. Madsen,* ed. Donald W. Parry, Daniel C. Peterson, and Stephen D. Ricks (Provo, Utah: Foundation for Ancient Research and Mormon Studies, 2002), 615–33.

114. William J. Hamblin, "Aspects of an Early Christian Initiation Ritual," in *By Study and Also by Faith,* ed. John M. Lundquist and Stephen D. Ricks (Provo, Utah:

ritual prayer was outlined by John Tvedtnes, Daniel Sharp, and Kevin Barney.[115] Sharp and Barney also review scholarly literature that questions the practice of baptism for the dead among early Christians and demonstrate from a linguistic perspective how such arguments fall short. Other ritual practices in New Testament texts, such as ritual handclasps and embraces, prokynesis, anointing, standing in temples, baptism, and the Lord's Supper, are also explored.[116]

Paying particular attention to subtleties of language, noting Greek word origins and alternate translations, John Welch's monograph on the Sermon on the Mount specifically explores the temple themes and possible rites it reflects.[117] This largely grew out of an earlier study wherein a similar sermon appears explicitly in a temple context within the Book of Mormon.[118] Welch also compared the account in the Book of Mormon to early Greek copies of the New Testament, showing how it parallels and, in some cases, is more accurate than the current King James Version in Matthew.

Foundation for Ancient Research and Mormon Studies; Salt Lake City: Deseret Book, 1990), 1:202–21.

115. John A. Tvedtnes, "Baptism for the Dead in Early Christianity" and "Temple Prayer in Ancient Times," in *The Temple in Time and Eternity,* ed. Donald W. Parry and Stephen D. Ricks (Provo, Utah: Foundation for Ancient Research and Mormon Studies, 1999), 55–78, 79–98; Daniel B. Sharp, "Vicarious Baptism for the Dead: 1 Corinthians 15:29," *Studies in the Bible and Antiquity* 6 (2014): 36–66.

116. Todd M. Compton, "The Handclasp and Embrace as Tokens of Recognition," in Lundquist and Ricks, *By Study and Also by Faith,* 1:611–42; Matthew L. Bowen, "'They Came and Held Him by the Feet and Worshipped Him': Prokynesis before Jesus in Its Biblical and Ancient Near Eastern Context," *Studies in the Bible and Antiquity* 5 (2013): 63–89; Julie M. Smith, "'She Hath Wrought a Good Work': The Anointing of Jesus in Mark's Gospel," *Studies in the Bible and Antiquity* 5 (2013): 31–46; Jeffrey M. Bradshaw, "'Standing in the Holy Place': Ancient and Modern Reverberations of an Enigmatic New Testament Prophecy," in *Ancient Temple Worship,* ed. Matthew B. Brown and others (Provo, Utah: Interpreter Foundation, 2014), 71–142; Stephen D. Ricks, "The Doctrine of Baptism: Immersions at Qumran and the Baptisms of John, the Earliest Christians, and Book of Mormon Peoples," in *By Our Rites of Worship: Latter-day Saint Views on Ritual in Scripture, History, and Practice,* ed. Daniel L. Belnap (Provo, Utah: Religious Studies Center, Brigham Young University; Salt Lake City: Deseret Book, 2013), 153–72; Jeffrey M. Bradshaw and Matthew L. Bowen, "'By the Blood Ye Are Sanctified': The Symbolic, Salvific, Interrelated, Additive, Retrospective, and Anticipatory Nature of the Ordinances of Spiritual Rebirth in John 3 and Moses 6," *Interpreter: A Journal of Mormon Scripture* 24 (2017): 123–316; Bruce Chilton, "Jesus' Dispute in the Temple and the Origin of the Eucharist," *Dialogue* 29 (Winter 1996): 17–28.

117. John W. Welch, *The Sermon on the Mount in the Light of the Temple* (Farnham, Eng.: Ashgate, 2009).

118. John W. Welch, *Illuminating the Sermon at the Temple and Sermon on the Mount* (Provo, Utah: Foundation for Ancient Research and Mormon Studies, 1999).

Temple themes in the Gospel of Mark, the letter to the Hebrews, the Epistles of Peter, and the book of Revelation are highlighted in studies by Jasmin Rappleye, Catherine Thomas, Daniel McKinlay, Richard Draper, and Donald Parry, respectively.[119] The possible relationship of the Gospel of John's entire structure to the progression of the temple is explored by John Thompson.[120]

Text Commentaries

One of the larger categories of Latter-day Saint New Testament publications are commentaries that focus on explaining the meaning of the texts themselves. The great majority of these are written with lay members of the Church in mind. Many weave historical, cultural, and linguistic information into the commentaries in an attempt to recapture the original meaning of the text. Most also provide unique insights into the text that additional Latter-day Saint scripture and modern prophetic voices, especially Joseph Smith's, might add. Text commentaries usually come in two main varieties: verse-by-verse commentaries and article-length analyses of texts.

Verse-by-Verse Commentaries. One of the most influential verse-by-verse New Testament commentaries for many decades was Bruce R. McConkie's first personal major work on the New Testament entitled *Doctrinal New Testament Commentary.*[121] In the explanation of the first volume of the set covering the four Gospels (the other two volumes cover Acts to Philippians and Colossians to Revelation, respectively), McConkie spelled out a three-step key for interpreting scripture, specifically the New Testament. First, one must search and read the text diligently; second, one must

---

119. Jasmin Gimenez Rappleye, "The Messianic Sacred, Not Secret: The Son as a Hidden Name in the Gospel of Mark," in *The Temple: Past, Present, and Future,* ed. Stephen D. Ricks and Jeffrey M. Bradshaw, vol. 6 of Temple on Mount Zion series (Orem, Utah: Interpreter Foundation and Eborn Books, 2021), 171–96; M. Catherine Thomas, "Hebrews: To Ascend the Holy Mount," in *Temples of the Ancient World,* ed. Donald W. Parry (Salt Lake City: Deseret Book, 1994), 479–91; Daniel B. McKinlay, "Temple Imagery in the Epistles of Peter," in Parry, *Temples of the Ancient World,* 492–514; Richard D. Draper and Donald W. Parry, "Seven Promises to Those Who Overcome: Aspects of Genesis 2–3 in the Seven Letters," in Parry and Ricks, *Temple in Time and Eternity,* 121–41.

120. John S. Thompson, "How John's Gospel Portrays Jesus as the Way of the Temple," in *The Temple: Ancient and Restored,* ed. Stephen D. Ricks and Donald W. Parry, vol. 3 of Temple on Mount Zion series (Orem, Utah: Interpreter Foundation and Eborn Books, 2016), 307–33.

121. Bruce R. McConkie, *Doctrinal New Testament Commentary,* 3 vols. (Salt Lake City: Bookcraft, 1965–73).

listen to the counsel from modern-day prophets and inspired leaders; and third, one must live worthy to have the Holy Spirit aid in understanding. This pattern offered a guide for his writing and for his expectations of the reader.[122] In each volume of commentary, McConkie followed the New Testament chronologically, offering doctrinal explanations after every few verses. Most of his commentary comes directly from other scripture, including the Book of Mormon and Doctrine and Covenants, or other valid sources for Church doctrine. For example, he defines the "light" that came into the world mentioned in John 1:9 as the light of Christ given to every individual by referring to scriptures in the Doctrine and Covenants and the Book of Mormon.[123]

Religious scholar Daniel Ludlow wrote a series of verse-by-verse commentaries for Latter-day Saints on all the standard works of the Church. His commentary on the New Testament only included a volume on the four Gospels.[124] Appealing to his Greek language background, Ludlow largely focused on language issues, including an alternate translation of words in most verses cited.

Heavily influenced by McConkie's commentary and Edersheim's work on historical and cultural context, Keith Howick's thematic commentaries provide insight into the mission, parables, sermons, and miracles of Jesus.[125]

Kelly Ogden and Andrew C. Skinner published a verse-by-verse commentary of Acts through Revelation called *New Testament Apostles Testify of Christ.*[126] It was later retitled as part of a two-volume series on the complete New Testament.[127] These volumes are filled with word origins, historical background, photographs from the Holy Land, and other Latter-day Saint scriptural references. The four-hundred-page book reads like a

---

122. McConkie, *Doctrinal New Testament Commentary,* 1:57.

123. McConkie, *Doctrinal New Testament Commentary,* 1:73.

124. Daniel H. Ludlow, *A Companion to Your Study of the New Testament: The Four Gospels* (Salt Lake City: Deseret Book, 1982).

125. E. Keith Howick, *The Miracles of Jesus the Messiah* (Salt Lake City: Bookcraft, 1985); E. Keith Howick, *The Parables of Jesus the Messiah* (Salt Lake City: Bookcraft, 1986); E. Keith Howick, *The Mission of Jesus the Messiah* (Silverton, Idaho: WindRiver Publishing, 2003); E. Keith Howick, *The Sermons of Jesus the Messiah* (Silverton, Idaho: WindRiver Publishing, 2003).

126. D. Kelly Ogden and Andrew C. Skinner, *New Testament Apostles Testify of Christ* (Salt Lake City: Deseret Book, 1998).

127. D. Kelly Ogden and Andrew C. Skinner, *Verse by Verse: The Four Gospels* (Salt Lake City: Deseret Book, 2006); D. Kelly Ogden and Andrew C. Skinner, *Verse by Verse: Acts through Revelation* (Salt Lake City: Deseret Book, 2006).

reference work, with a chapter devoted to each book in the New Testament, starting with the book of Acts.

Given Latter-day millenarian roots, several verse-by-verse commentaries of the apocalyptic Revelation of John appear. BYU ancient scripture professor Richard D. Draper carefully analyzed the Latter-day Saint perspective of John's Apocalypse in his *Opening the Seven Seals: The Visions of John the Revelator.* He saw the need "for a clear analysis, using insights from modern scripture and prophetic utterance, of [the book of Revelation]."[128] Draper first set out the historical context and then explained the setting for the receipt of the Revelation, also including comments from modern-day scripture and prophets about the importance of reading and understanding the book. He then analyzed all twenty-two chapters from Revelation, discussing meanings and interpretations. He incorporated Greek translations of multiple words to aid in understanding their meaning. He frequently cited Bruce R. McConkie's *Doctrinal New Testament Commentary* but also added references to many other biblical scholarship writers. Mick Smith's *The Book of Revelation: Plain, Pure, and Simple* presented commentary on the book of Revelation that is understandable and accessible to every type of reader. His intent was to help "clarify hard-to-understand terms and phrases in a manner that is accessible to the general membership of the Church."[129] The same year, Jay A. Parry and Donald W. Parry published *Understanding the Book of Revelation,* another verse-by-verse commentary. Like Smith, the Parrys focus their commentary on helping lay members better understand the book of Revelation. The Parrys' desire was "to find meaning in John's vision for our day, to seek to understand what people in the twentieth and twenty-first centuries might need or want to know about what John saw and heard."[130] Their book was based on scholarship and careful research (Greek word origins and historical sources) but is not academic reading. They were careful and analytical in their undertaking and cited frequently both Latter-day Saint and non–Latter-day Saint sources. David Ridges published an edition of his commentary series entitled *The Book of Revelation Made Easier.*[131]

---

128. Richard D. Draper, *Opening the Seven Seals: The Visions of John the Revelator* (Salt Lake City: Deseret Book, 1991), ix.

129. Mick Smith, *The Book of Revelation Plain, Pure, and Simple* (Salt Lake City: Bookcraft, 1998), xi.

130. Jay A. Parry and Donald W. Parry, *Understanding the Book of Revelation* (Salt Lake City: Deseret Book, 1998), 7.

131. David J. Ridges, *The Book of Revelation Made Easier,* 2nd ed. (Springville, Utah: Cedar Fort, 2010).

Faulconer provided a verse-by-verse commentary to accompany his translation of Romans chapter 1 and expanded it to include a few more chapters later.[132] His hope in writing was to help any Latter-day Saint "understand Paul's message . . . [and] to show that Paul preaches the same gospel taught by all the prophets." His approach makes a careful reading of the text, highlighting nuances others may have missed, but his intention was mainly to "stimulate thinking and conversation about Romans, not to bring that thinking and conversation to an end by offering oracular or definitive pronouncements about what Paul's letter means."[133]

David Ridges's popular series includes a two-volume set entitled *The New Testament Made Easier,* first published in 2002 and updated to a three-volume set in 2022.[134] That same year, William Blacoe produced a verse-by-verse commentary on the pastoral letters, highlighting textual variants and scholarly insight into the text, and Ed Pinegar, Doug Bassett, and Ted Earl published a verse-by-verse source book of quotes and insights from other LDS leaders and scholars on the four Gospels.[135]

Richard Holzapfel and Thomas Wayment group verses and provide commentary similar to McConkie's format. They explain what they think the original author intended to convey by bringing historical and cultural details to bear on the text while providing some of their own insights on meaning and textual connections.[136] Robert Millet's verse commentary for Paul's writings focuses primarily on the doctrines and principles found therein and provides personal anecdotes and thoughts from other religious leaders and thinkers.[137]

The large-scale BYU New Testament Commentary series is the current ongoing effort to provide a comprehensive commentary on almost every verse in the New Testament. Beyond providing the new translations discussed above, each volume in the series attempts to recover how the original authors likely intended their texts to be read by explaining the meaning

---

132. Faulconer, *Romans 1;* Faulconer, *Life of Holiness.*

133. Faulconer, *Romans 1,* vii, ix.

134. David J. Ridges, *The New Testament Made Easier,* parts 1–2 (Springville, Utah: Cedar Fort, 2002–3); David J. Ridges, *The New Testament Made Easier,* 3rd ed., (Springville, Utah: Cedar Fort, 2022).

135. Blacoe, *Understanding the New Testament*; Ed. J. Pinegar, K. Douglas Bassett, and Ted L. Earl, *Latter-day Commentary on the New Testament: The Four Gospels* (American Fork, Utah: Covenant Communications, 2002).

136. Richard N. Holzapfel and Thomas A. Wayment, *Making Sense of the New Testament: Timely Insights and Timeless Messages* (Salt Lake City: Deseret Book, 2010).

137. Robert L. Millet, *Becoming New: A Doctrinal Commentary on the Writings of Paul* (Salt Lake City: Deseret Book, 2022).

of phrases using historical, cultural, text-variant, and linguistic details. This is usually followed by an analysis of the verses in their larger context, providing the scholars' insights into the literary composition and intertextual or thematic influences the authors may have attempted to convey.[138]

Textual Analyses. Beyond verse-by-verse commentaries, other text-focused studies often include deep analysis of a phrase, verse, block of verses, chapter, or book. Most of these appear as journal articles or book articles (many are in the publications already mentioned above). A prominent exception is the 1983 monograph by BYU religion professor Richard Lloyd Anderson, who made a significant contribution to Latter-day Saint New Testament scholarship with his *Understanding Paul.*[139] Anderson received his juris doctorate from Harvard in 1954, where he simultaneously studied Greek history, receiving a PhD in ancient history from the University of California at Berkeley. *Understanding Paul* provides details concerning the life of Paul; however, it focuses much of its attention on understanding the texts of Paul's letters. Moving chronologically through the Epistles of the New Testament, Anderson introduces each letter with background information and issues of authorship before moving into an exploration of the teachings and doctrinal issues in each. His approach is scholarly, combined with modern-day revelation and Book of Mormon references. He also tucks an explanation of scripturally supported Latter-day Saint doctrines into the appendices. His biblical sources stem largely from the Greek text and the King James Version of the English Bible, but he refers to other translations as well.[140] This work has remained important because of its thoroughgoing research and scholarly value in its field.

In 1984, editors Kent P. Jackson and Robert L. Millet, both ancient scripture professors at BYU, published a book series of articles focused on text analysis entitled *Studies in Scripture.* Two of the volumes in the

---

138. Currently published volumes include S. Kent Brown, *The Testimony of Luke* (Provo, Utah: BYU Studies, 2015); Richard D. Draper and Michael D. Rhodes, *The Revelation of John the Apostle* (Provo, Utah: BYU Studies, 2016); Richard D. Draper and Michael D. Rhodes, *Paul's First Epistle to the Corinthians* (Provo, Utah: BYU Studies, 2017); Julie M. Smith, *The Gospel according to Mark* (Provo, Utah: BYU Studies, 2018); Richard D. Draper and Michael D. Rhodes, *Epistle to the Hebrews* (Provo, Utah: BYU Studies, 2020); S. Kent Brown, *The Epistle to the Ephesians* (Provo, Utah: BYU Studies, 2023); and Richard D. Draper and Michael D. Rhodes, *Paul's Second Epistle to the Corinthians* (Provo, Utah: BYU Studies, 2023).

139. Richard Lloyd Anderson, *Understanding Paul* (Salt Lake City: Deseret Book, 1983).

140. Anderson, *Understanding Paul,* xiii. Anderson notes in "Key to Translations" that "every New Testament quotation in this book has been checked against the Greek text."

series focused on the Gospels and on Acts through Revelation.[141] Like most collected-papers publications, the articles vary in tone and scholarship from chapter to chapter. The variations depend mostly upon an author's background and intent, some incorporating historical, cultural, and linguistic analysis more than others. In the opening article of the *Gospels* volume, Jackson outlines the approach that the series writers have taken, which is an accurate reflection of the effort of most Latter-day Saint commentaries. He wrote that when studying the Gospels, one must study them in light of modern revealed truth, rely upon the Holy Ghost, learn the expressions of ancient writers (language syntax), and understand the Gospels historically within their own context.[142]

In addition to the *Studies in Scripture* volumes, the annual Sidney B. Sperry Symposium held at Brigham Young University has typically focused on the New Testament every four years. Publications of these proceedings contain many articles that provide analysis or commentary of New Testament texts.[143] The Sperry Symposium publications and *Studies in Scripture* volumes were some of the first books containing a collection of articles by various scholars and teachers of the New Testament. More collections have continued to be edited and published at a seemingly exponential pace over the last few decades, primarily by BYU religion professors and through Church-related presses (for example, Deseret Book and the BYU Religious Studies Center).[144]

More recent individual publications focusing on textual commentary include volumes by Taylor Halverson and Elder Jeffrey R. Holland.[145] Halverson provides brief analyses of select passages by highlighting historical and cultural details and making connections to patterns that will enrich the

141. Jackson and Millet, *Studies in Scripture: Volume Five, The Gospels*; Robert L. Millet, *Studies in Scripture: Volume Six, Acts to Revelation* (Salt Lake City: Deseret Book, 1987).

142. Kent P. Jackson, "Jesus and the Gospels," in Jackson and Millet, *Studies in Scripture: Volume Five*, 8–9.

143. *New Testament and the Latter-day Saints*; Van Orden and Top, *Lord of the Gospels*; Paul Y. Hoskisson, ed., *The Apostle Paul: His Life and His Testimony* (Salt Lake City: Deseret Book, 1994); Frank F. Judd Jr. and Gaye Strathearn, eds., *Sperry Symposium Classics: The New Testament.*

144. In addition to the many volumes already surveyed above, other notable volumes include Huntington, Judd, and Whitchurch, *Shedding Light on the New Testament: Acts–Revelation*; and Holzpafel and Wayment, *Life and Teachings of the New Testament Apostles.*

145. Taylor Halverson, *Scriptural Insights and Commentary: The New Testament* (American Fork, Utah: Covenant Communications, 2018); Jeffrey R. Holland, *Our Day Star Rising: Exploring the New Testament* (Salt Lake City: Deseret Book, 2022).

reader's understanding of the New Testament. Holland provides lay members with personal reflection essays and commentary in reaction to various episodes of selected New Testament chapters.

Guides and Harmonies

Another category of Latter-day Saint approaches to the New Testament is guides and harmonies. Publications in this category may provide compilations of previous scholarship or statements from Church leaders, questions for readers and teachers to consider, charts, synchronization of the four Gospels, and other helps. There may be little to no analysis presented directly to the reader; however, the selection of material and the questions asked do require some analysis on the back end and certainly form a kind of commentary.

In 1954, Lowell Bennion wrote the course of study for the Gospel Doctrine classes of the Church's Sunday Schools, *Teachings of the New Testament* (1956), later issuing a revised version of the same book that was intended to be used as a reference guide. Unlike the other study guide writers, Bennion organized his book topically, covering major themes of the New Testament: salvation through Jesus Christ, personal and social ideals, and characteristics of the primitive Church. He focused mostly on the modern implications of the teachings with little reference to historical or social circumstances.[146]

John W. Welch and John F. Hall created *Charting the New Testament* (2002), a reference collection of charts and lists falling into eighteen different categories. The charts, tables, graphs, maps, lists, and time lines cover a huge spectrum of topics: chronology, Jewish cultural and literary backgrounds, Roman history, demographics, teachings of Christ, doctrines, journeys of Paul, word counts, linguistic comparisons (of the Gospels), people and places, time periods, lineages, and more. This collection is a thorough and useful reference for any teacher or student of the New Testament.[147]

Harmonies help create a single narrative by either placing similar texts in parallel columns or by weaving together all the elements into a single text.[148]

146. Lowell L. Bennion, *Teachings of the New Testament* (Salt Lake City: Deseret Book, 1956).

147. John W. Welch and John F. Hall, *Charting the New Testament* (Provo, Utah: Foundation for Ancient Research and Mormon Studies, 2002).

148. For a review of Latter-day Saint harmonies, see S. Kent Brown, "The Four Gospels as Testimonies," in *Sperry Symposium Classics: The New Testament,* 77–91.

Since the pieces do not all fit together seamlessly, much analysis and weighing of evidence (and thus commentary via editing) must occur. Sperry's *Our Lord of the Gospels* (1954) was a large-scale harmony project. The years he spent developing and publishing a chronological harmonization demonstrate his focus on the life of Jesus Christ and the value he saw in creating a clear mental framework for the historical reality and flow of the Savior's life. Sperry's book is divided into four sections: aids for using the harmony; a 130-page chronological chart of the Gospels; the 400-page harmony itself (including Christ's appearance as spelled out in the Book of Mormon); and explanatory charts, tables, and maps. His non–Latter-day Saint sources were all Protestants, mostly Baptists. President J. Reuben Clark's explicit primary goals in *Our Lord of the Gospels* were to make it clear that Jesus Christ's life and ministry actually occurred as recorded in the Gospels and to increase the knowledge of the life and words of Jesus Christ.[149] According to President Clark, the precise order, time, and place of events is not too material. What matters most are Jesus' words and deeds.

In 1976, Thomas Mumford published a popular work that simply placed the entire text of the four Gospels in parallel columns.[150] A similar effort was published by Stephen and Julie Hite that included JST changes to the New Testament text.[151] David Yarn's harmony departed from typical parallel columns and blended all the Gospels together into one story of Jesus.[152] Similarly, John Welch provided a unique approach by harmonizing the letters of the Apostles; he arranged the Epistles thematically as one letter, shifting the reader's attention "away from the usual focus on historical context and the individual authorship of each of [the] letters."[153] Other than a preface to his work, he included no additional commentary. In-text notations indicated the Joseph Smith Translation and Greek and English word

---

149. J. Reuben Clark, *Our Lord of the Gospels: A Harmony of the Gospels* (Salt Lake City: Deseret Book, 1954), vii–viii.

150. Thomas M. Mumford, *Horizontal Harmony of the Four Gospels in Parallel Columns (King James Version)* (Salt Lake City: Publishers Press, 1976).

151. Steven J. Hite and Julie Melville Hite, *The Joseph Smith Translation of the Four Gospels: A Harmony* (Orem, Utah: S&J Publishing, 1992); see also Patrick A. Bishop, ed., *The Gospels in Harmony: The Illustrated, Combined Accounts of the Life of Christ* (American Fork, Utah: Covenant Communications, 2010).

152. David H. Yarn, *The Four Gospels as One,* rev. ed. (Salt Lake City: Deseret Book, 1982); compare with Eldin Ricks, *Story of the Life of Christ: A Harmony of the Four Gospels* (Salt Lake City: Deseret Book, 1977).

153. John W. Welch, *An Epistle from the New Testament Apostles: The Letters of Peter, Paul, John, James, and Jude, Arranged by Themes, with Readings from the Greek and the Joseph Smith Translation* (Salt Lake City: Bookcraft, 1999), xi.

origins. Todd G. Anderson compiled a two-volume New Testament harmony using modern-day scriptures. His appendices included select charts and commentary.[154]

Julie Smith's and James Falconer's study guides provide readers with questions to ponder throughout various chapters and verses.[155] The kinds of questions asked may help readers analyze the text more, notice little details, or apply the principles read. Richard Anderson's *Guide to Acts and the Apostles' Letters* is a workbook-style manual with questions to answer along with background material for each book of the New Testament beyond the Gospels.[156] Thomas Valletta provides the complete text of the New Testament along with some marginalia containing insights, historical and cultural background, or quotes from other sources.[157] Lynn Price compiled an index with details of every person in the New Testament.[158]

Conclusion

In a religion that promotes and prizes education, New Testament scholarship in The Church of Jesus Christ of Latter-day Saints has grown more prolific over the years. The categories outlined herein are by no means all-inclusive, but they do provide a glimpse into the growing diversity of scholarship pertaining to this sacred text. As interests grow and diversify, there is greater opportunity to engage with the variety of approaches to the New Testament in the academic world. Latter-day Saint scholars are increasingly grappling with the difficult issues raised by secular scholarship, even if they do not always accept their conclusions. Their larger scriptural tradition and unique worldview can provide distinctive avenues of thinking about the text that others in the academic world may not see, such as their views on apostasy or the temple. And that is a good thing.

154. Todd G. Anderson, *The Gospels Made Whole: One Complete Story of Jesus Christ* (Provo, Utah: Best Books, 1986); Todd G. Anderson, *Acts to Revelation Made Whole: One Complete Account of the Apostles and Prophets* (Provo, Utah: Best Books, 1991).

155. James E. Faulconer, *The New Testament Made Harder* (Provo, Utah: Neal A. Maxwell Institute, 2015), Julie Smith, *Search, Ponder, and Pray: A Guide to the Gospels* (Salt Lake City: Greg Kofford Books, 2014).

156. Richard Lloyd Anderson, *Guide to Acts and the Apostles' Letters* (Provo, Utah: Foundation for Ancient Research and Mormon Studies, 1998).

157. Thomas R. Valletta, ed., *The New Testament Study Guide: Start to Finish* (Salt Lake City: Deseret Book, 2018).

158. Lynn F. Price, *Every Person in the New Testament: An Alphabetic Reference and Synopsis* (Springville, Utah: Cedar Fort, 2002).

An Overview of Premodern New Testament Translations

Andrew C. Skinner

An overview of premodern New Testament translations takes us back to the ancient period when writings of the first Apostles and their immediate followers began to be collected and circulated as the authentic record of Jesus Christ, his teachings, and his Church.

The New Testament Emerges

The first time that extant sources mention the four Gospels together as "the Scriptures, . . . each of [their authors] equally being in possession of the gospel of God," appears to be in book 3 of *Against Heresies* by Irenaeus (c. AD 130–202).[1] Therein, this early church father began to lay a scriptural foundation for refuting the popular but misguided Marcion and other teachers of his time who were in error.[2]

The process of canonization seems to have proceeded fairly rapidly. The oldest known list of New Testament books deemed authoritative that matches most closely to our current canon is the Muratorian Fragment, sometimes referred to as the Muratorian Canon and named after its discoverer, Father Ludovico Muratori (1672–1750), who worked in the Ambrosian Library in Milan, Italy. It is a seventh-century AD Latin translation of a likely Greek original manuscript (c. AD 180–200). In it we see which writings were deemed authentic or canonical by the end of the second century and their order in the collection.

1. Edward Rochie Hardy, trans., "The Text: (Book III) The Faith in Scripture and Tradition," in *Early Christian Fathers,* trans. and ed. Cyril C. Richardson (Philadelphia: Westminster Press, 1953), 370.

2. John W. Miller, *How the Bible Came to Be: Exploring the Narrative and Message* (Mahwah, N.J.: Paulist Press, 2004), 127.

When first composed, the Muratorian Fragment mentioned all the books in our current New Testament except Hebrews, James, 1 and 2 Peter, and 3 John. In its current state, the beginning of the fragment is mutilated so that it begins midway through a sentence that refers to Mark's Gospel and implies the author knew of Matthew. Interestingly, the document also includes a couple of books not in our present canon, the *Wisdom of Solomon* and the *Apocalypse of Peter,* but clearly states that the *Shepherd of Hermas* was not canonical because of its recent date of composition.[3]

The Muratorian Fragment reveals much about the process of canonization and shows us that the second century was a time of fluidity, when the church and its postapostolic leaders were in the middle of determining which books were authoritative and which were not. Many factors played a role in determining authority, including the date of composition relative to the time of the actual occurrence of events; verifiable authorship; doctrinal and historical soundness when compared with eyewitness testimony (the Apostles) or with those who knew well what the eyewitnesses believed and taught; and traditional appeal or acceptability. B. F. Westcott's summary of the Muratorian Fragment is most instructive: "The writer speaks throughout of a received and general opinion. He does not suggest a novel theory about the Apostolic books, but states what was held to be certainly known. He does not hazard an individual judgment, but appeals to the practice of 'the Catholic [universal] Church.' There was not indeed complete unanimity with regard to all the writings claiming to be apostolical."[4]

By AD 200, the canonical picture was becoming clearer. The great theologian from Carthage, Tertullian (c. 160–220), was one of the first to call the Christian books of scripture "the New Testament." This is significant because he "placed the New Testament Scripture on a level of inspiration and authority with the Old Testament."[5] Tertullian's canonical list specifically mentions every New Testament book except Philemon, 2 Peter, and 3 John. He also included in his list the now-extracanonical books *Wisdom of Solomon* and *Shepherd of Hermas.*

3. R. M. Grant, "The New Testament Canon," in *The Cambridge History of the Bible,* vol. 1, *From the Beginnings to Jerome,* ed. P. R. Ackroyd and C. F. Evans (Cambridge, Eng.: Cambridge University, 1970), 300–301.

4. Brooke Foss Westcott, *A General Survey of the History of the Canon of the New Testament,* 7th ed. (London: Macmillan, 1896), 223–24.

5. Philip Wesley Comfort, ed., *The Origin of the Bible* (Carol Stream, Ill.: Tyndale House, 2003), 66.

During the first half of the third century, the towering intellect, theologian, biblical critic, and exegete Origen (c. 185–253)

> traveled widely throughout the Christian world (e.g., Rome, Athens, Syria, Cappadocia, and Arabia) and acquainted himself with the biblical material used at each location. About 230 he formulated a list of New Testament books accepted universally (*homologoumenoi*) by Christians: the four Gospels, Acts, Paul's thirteen epistles, 1 Peter, 1 John, and Revelation. He then cited those books held in dispute by some (*antilegomenoi*): Hebrews (he accepts), 2 Peter (he accepts), 2 and 3 John (he questions), James (he accepts), and Jude (he accepts). Noncanonical books [or what we *now* consider noncanonical] included in his canon are the *Didache, Epistle of Barnabas, Shepherd of Hermas,* and possibly *1 Clement* and the *Acts of Paul.*[6]

The first church leader to include all twenty-seven books of our present New Testament in his canonical list was Athanasius (c. 296–373), bishop of Alexandria. He described them in an Easter letter addressed to his parishioners in 367.[7] During the fourth and fifth centuries, several councils and synods addressed questions surrounding New Testament books that were deemed authoritative and those that were deemed questionable.[8] "While the majority of New Testament books were accepted as canonical by the middle of the second century, uncertainty regarding mainly the General Epistles remained well into the fourth century."[9] But by the time of the Damasine Council of 382 held at Rome, we find a list promulgated with exactly the same twenty-seven books as in the Letter of Athanasius and as we now find in modern Bibles, though in a different order. The Damasine order is the four Gospels, Pauline Epistles (with Hebrews), Revelation, Acts, and the other Epistles.[10]

It is important to remember that most of the canon's critical pieces were already in place by the middle of the second century. The seminal

6. Paul D. Wegner, *The Journey from Texts to Translations: The Origin and Development of the Bible* (Grand Rapids, Mich.: Baker Academic, 1999), 143.

7. Philip Schaff and Henry Wace, eds., *A Select Library of Nicene and Post-Nicene Fathers of the Christian Church,* 2nd ser., 14 vols. (Grand Rapids, Mich.: William B. Eerdmans, 1969–73), 4:551–52.

8. Barry R. Bickmore and Adam W. Bentley, "Christian Councils," in *Early Christians in Disarray: Contemporary LDS Perspectives on the Christian Apostasy,* ed. Noel B. Reynolds (Provo, Utah: BYU Press, 2005), 345–54.

9. Wegner, *Journey from Texts to Translations,* 145.

10. Alexander Souter, *The Text and Canon of the New Testament* (London: Duckworth, 1965), 178–79.

discussions and consensus-based decisions about which writings should be accorded scriptural status first occurred at the local church level, not the council or synod level. By the end of the apostolic era, the Holy Spirit was operating among branches and congregations of the Christian community to help church members recognize the work of the authorized servants and witnesses of the Lord. F. F. Bruce reminds us:

> One thing must be emphatically stated. The New Testament books did not become authoritative for the Church because they were formally included in a canonical list; on the contrary, the Church included them in her canon because she already regarded them as divinely inspired, recognizing their innate worth and generally apostolic authority, direct or indirect. The first ecclesiastical councils to classify the canonical books were both held in North Africa—at Hippo Regius in 393 and at Carthage in 397—but what these councils did was not to impose something new upon the Christian communities but to codify what was already the general practice of those communities.[11]

Some may want to disagree that the Holy Spirit was felt during this period. But the Apostle Paul declared that no one could even say Jesus is the Lord except through the influence of the Holy Ghost (1 Cor. 12:3). It seems logical that that same influence would also be present with those involved in determining which books should be part of the sacred canon—which books were authentic representations of the doctrine of Christ and which were not. The Spirit of inspiration has rested upon good men and women in all ages. To believe that the Holy Spirit was *not* present with any of the early Christian scholars during the critical two or three hundred years when the New Testament was being formed is to believe that God completely abandoned the canon to the adversary or the forces of secularism during one of the Bible's critical formative stages. Of course mistakes were made. Of course plain and precious parts of the Bible were lost. Of course it is true that less-than-able translators and copyists introduced corruptions into the texts.[12] But

---

11. F. F. Bruce, *The New Testament Documents: Are They Reliable?* (Grand Rapids, Mich.: William B. Eerdmans, 1985), 27.

12. Joseph Smith implied as much when he said, "I believe the bible as it read when it came from the pen of the original writers." "History, 1838–1856, Volume E-1 [1 July 1843–30 April 1844]," 1755 (October 15, 1843), Joseph Smith Papers, accessed July 10, 2018, https://www.josephsmithpapers.org/paper-summary/history-1838-1856-volume-e-1-1-july-1843-30-april-1844/127; compare Andrew F. Ehat and Lyndon W. Cook, comps. and eds., *The Words of Joseph Smith: The Contemporary Accounts of the Nauvoo Discourses of the Prophet Joseph* (Orem, Utah: Grandin Book, 1991), 256.

Latter-day Saints do not believe that there has ever been a time in the earth's history when humankind has been left totally to the cunning wiles, trickeries, and deceits of the adversary.

The Testaments Combined

As early church fathers and Christian historians recognized, the Church of Jesus Christ in the meridian dispensation emerged in a complex cultural milieu. This is exemplified by the titulus fastened to the cross on which Jesus was crucified: "And a superscription also was written over him in letters of Greek, and Latin, and Hebrew, This is the King of the Jews" (Luke 23:38). Though the Church arose in the Latin-speaking Roman Empire, the Greek language predominated in many areas, while Aramaic remained the primary language for many Jews. Except for the case of Matthew's Gospel, which Eusebius says was first written in Hebrew[13] (most scholars agree that this was actually Aramaic), the New Testament writers wrote in Greek. Quotations in the New Testament taken from the Old Testament do not follow the Hebrew text but the Septuagint—the Greek translation of the Hebrew scriptures.

In fact, so powerful a hold did Greek have in the Mediterranean Basin—the cradle of Christianity—that the Christians adopted the Septuagint as their own, as F. F. Bruce describes: "For the Church did not, in spite of the breach with Judaism, repudiate the authority of the Old Testament, but, following the example of Christ and His apostles, received it as the Word of God. Indeed, so much did they make the Septuagint their own that, although it was originally a translation of the Hebrew Scriptures into Greek for Greek-speaking Jews before the time of Christ, the Jews left the Septuagint to the Christians, and a fresh Greek version of the Old Testament was made for Greek-speaking Jews."[14]

No one knows exactly when the Old and New Testaments were combined into a single volume; evidence seems to suggest that exemplars existed by the mid-third century. However, the two oldest surviving complete (or almost complete) Christian Bibles date from the mid-fourth century. They are known today as the Codex Vaticanus and the Codex Sinaiticus.

> They contain most of the text of the Septuagint (the first Greek translation of the Hebrew Bible), including the books later eliminated by the Jews and

---

13. Eusebius, *The Ecclesiastical History* 3.39.16, trans. Kirsopp Lake, 2 vols. (Cambridge, Mass.: Harvard University Press, 1992), 1:297.

14. Bruce, *New Testament Documents*, 26.

> considered the Apocrypha by the Protestants, although the *Codex Vaticanus* is missing the books of the Maccabees. In addition, both codices contain all 27 books of the New Testament. The *Codex Sinaiticus* also includes the *Epistle of Barnabas* and the *Shepherd of Hermas.* The *Codex Vaticanus* was probably put together in Egypt around AD 350 and eventually ended up in the Vatican Library in Rome. The *Codex Sinaiticus* has a more exciting history. It was written in Egypt in the late fourth century and kept at St Catherine's Monastery at the foot of Jebel Musa (Mount of Moses), the peak believed to be Mount Sinai, where Moses received the ten commandments. It remained there unknown until 1844, when a visiting German scholar, Constantin von Tischendorf spotted it in a pile of trash that was waiting to be burned for fuel. When he realized what he had discovered, von Tischendorf managed to salvage most of the manuscript. Because of their antiquity and near completeness, these two fourth-century codices are of invaluable help to biblical scholars today.[15]

Scholars estimated that in its complete form the *Codex Sinaiticus* was composed of at least 730 parchment leaves, each 13 × 15 inches in size, and that the skins of approximately 360 sheep would have been needed to supply enough parchment.[16] Today, the *Codex Sinaiticus* is preserved in the British Museum in London, alongside another important codex named *Codex Alexandrinus.* The latter dates from the middle of the fifth century and came to England in 1627[17] after Cyril Lucar, patriarch of Constantinople, offered the manuscript to the English ambassador to Turkey as a gift for the monarch, James I. Lucar had obtained the codex in Alexandria, where he had been patriarch earlier, and he brought it with him to his post in Constantinople.[18]

The *Codex Vaticanus,* like *Sinaiticus,* has some parts missing. It got its name from being housed in the Vatican so long. Although its presence was known since 1475, Vatican officials discouraged work on it, and it was carried off to Paris by Napoleon but eventually returned (after 1815). Von Tischendorf also worked on it and published an edition in 1867.[19]

---

15. Stephen M. Miller and Robert V. Huber, *The Bible: A History; The Making and Impact of the Bible* (Intercourse, Penn.: Good Books, 2004), 89.

16. Miller and Huber, *Bible: A History,* 89. See also Christopher de Hamel, *The Book: A History of the Bible* (New York: Phaidon Press, 2001), 51.

17. De Hamel, *Book: A History of the Bible,* 51, gives the date as 1624.

18. David Ewert, *A General Introduction to the Bible: From Ancient Tablets to Modern Translations* (Grand Rapids, Mich.: Zondervan, 1990), 142.

19. Ewert, *General Introduction to the Bible,* 142.

Latin Versions of the Bible

As Christianity spread to all quarters of the Roman Empire, the empire began to become Christianized. But, in its turn, Christianity began to be influenced by the various cultures and the official language of the empire—Latin. It may well be the case that the Lord raised up and established the Roman Empire (and emperors like Octavian) with a relatively stable political, social, and economic foundation so that the gospel could put down roots and spread, just as the Lord undoubtedly established the American nation and Constitution to provide a stable base for allowing the restored gospel to flourish in the dispensation of the fullness of times. Even non-Latter-day Saints recognize that the Romans united several regions "under a single language and this paved the way for the spread of the gospel throughout the Roman Empire."[20] In a sense, the *Pax Romana,* "Roman peace," was Rome's gift to Christianity.

Although the Greek language prevailed over Latin throughout most of the empire until the third century, by about AD 250, Latin emerged as the major language, displacing Greek even in the church. As a concurrent development, the preeminent position of the bishop of Rome over all of Christendom was also beginning to take shape. By the last half of the third century, Latin was the language spoken by most theologians and writers. Therefore, the need for a Latin translation of the Bible from the Greek was inescapable, even though Greek manuscripts of the Bible continued to be produced and many scholars continued to work in Greek. The earliest Latin biblical texts emerged in North Africa, which had long been a center of Christianity. Cyprian (died 258), bishop of Carthage, is credited with being the first to adopt a Latin text for his work.[21]

Evidence suggests that a number of Latin versions of the Bible arose independently. There seems to have been no single standard version of the Latin (even though scholars refer to it that way for convenience). This increased the opportunities for corruptions to be introduced into the text. Thus the Old Latin versions are "not written in the polished literary language of that time but in the didactic, vernacular idiom of the cult, often reflecting the dialect of the common people. This colloquial flavor is colored also by the Greek idiom, seen in its transliteration of Greek terms."[22]

---

20. Wegner, *Journey from Texts to Translations,* 252.

21. J. N. Birdsall, "The New Testament Text," in Ackroyd and Evans, *Cambridge History of the Bible,* 1:371.

22. A. Vööbus, "Versions," in *The International Standard Bible Encyclopedia,* ed. Geoffrey W. Bromiley and others, rev. ed., 4 vols. (Grand Rapids, Mich.: William B. Eerdmans,

Bruce Metzger believes the evidence suggests that early translations were interlinear renditions with the Latin words being written above the Greek in each line.[23] All Bibles at this time were handwritten.

As the strength and population of Christianity increased within the Roman Empire, so did its influence with the emperors. In AD 313, Constantine the Great signed an edict of toleration, instantly changing Christianity from a banned religion to a favored one. Christians were no longer persecuted as they had been under Constantine's predecessor, Diocletian (ruled 284–305). Christian writings were no longer destroyed. Instead, Constantine ordered fifty Bibles for churches that he planned to build in the new capital city of the empire, Constantinople, which was old Byzantium, a long-established Greek-speaking town. Naturally, Christian observance and liturgy continued in the Greek language.[24]

In AD 332, two years after the founding of Constantinople, the emperor commissioned the renowned Christian scholar Eusebius of Caesarea to oversee the creation of these Bibles. The emperor's letter to Eusebius states that the manuscripts were to be written "on well-prepared parchment by copyists most skilful [*sic*] in the art of accurate and beautiful writing." This letter is the earliest surviving official statement on Bible-making.[25] None of Constantine's Bibles are known to have survived. However, two "exquisitely crafted Bibles from that era" did survive: *Codex Sinaiticus* and *Codex Vaticanus,* as discussed above. Scholars generally believe that it is unlikely that these codices are among the fifty Bibles produced by Eusebius.[26] But they provide biblical text scholars with helpful information regarding the history of the Bible and the period that saw Greek and Latin Bible manuscripts vying for predominance.

Jerome and the Vulgate

Into this environment came the man the world would know as St. Jerome, one of the most famous biblical scholars in history and certainly the most capable of his day. Born about AD 345 in modern Yugoslavia to Christian parents, Eusebius Hieronymus Sophronius (Jerome) went to Rome at age twelve to study classical Latin writers under the famous grammarian

---

1979–88), 4:970.

23. Bruce M. Metzger, *The Text of the New Testament: Its Transmission, Corruption, and Restoration,* 3rd. ed. (New York: Oxford University Press, 1992), 72.

24. De Hamel, *Book: A History of the Bible,* 50.

25. De Hamel, *Book: A History of the Bible,* 50.

26. De Hamel, *Book: A History of the Bible,* 50–51; Miller and Huber, *Bible: A History,* 95.

Donatus. Jerome devoted himself diligently to the task and, after a few years, traveled throughout the empire continuing his studies. He learned Greek while in Antioch for a year in 373–74. But during this time, he fell ill (almost to the point of death) and had his now-famous dream that changed his life forever. His own recollections tell the story best:

> Meantime preparations for my funeral went on; my body grew gradually colder, and the warmth of life lingered only in my throbbing breast. Suddenly I was caught up in the spirit and dragged before the judgment seat of the Judge; and here the light was so bright, and those who stood around were so radiant, that I cast myself upon the ground and did not dare to look up. Asked who and what I was I replied: "I am a Christian." But he who presided said: "Thou liest, thou art a follower of Cicero and not of Christ. For 'where thy treasure is, there will thy heart be also.'" Instantly I became dumb, and amid the strokes of the lash—for He had ordered me to be scourged—I was tortured more severely by the fire of conscience, considering with myself that verse, "In the grave who shall give thee thanks?" . . . At last the bystanders, falling down before the knees of Him who presided, prayed that He would have pity on my youth, and that He would give me space to repent of my error. He might still, they urged, inflict torture on me, should I ever again read the works of the Gentiles. . . . Accordingly I made oath and called upon His name, saying: "Lord, if ever again I possess worldly books, or if ever again I read such, I have denied Thee." . . . I profess that my shoulders were black and blue, that I felt the bruises long after I awoke from my sleep, and that thenceforth I read the books of God with a greater zeal that I had previously given to the books of men.[27]

After his dream, Jerome became a zealous Christian and proved his diligence in bringing an improved version of the Bible to the world. For the next several years (374–79), he lived an ascetic life in the Syrian Desert studying Hebrew. In 382, he became secretary to Pope Damasus, "which proved to be his date with destiny."[28] Jerome contemplated the great biblical problem of his day: the poor quality of the Old Latin manuscripts of the Bible that often differed from one another. In a letter to Pope Damasus in 383, Jerome described the problem with the existing Latin manuscripts of just the New Testament alone. In language reminiscent of Joseph Smith, Jerome said, "For if we are to pin our faith to the Latin texts, it is for our opponents to tell us *which*; for there are almost as many forms of texts as there are copies. If, on the other hand, we are to glean the truth from a comparison of many, why not go back to the

---

27. Jerome, *Letter* 22.30, in Schaff and Wace, *Select Library of Nicene and Post-Nicene Fathers,* 6:35–36.

28. "Jerome Completes the Vulgate," *Christian History,* no. 28 (1990): 12.

original Greek and correct the mistakes introduced by inaccurate translators, and the blundering alterations of confident but ignorant critics, and further all that has been inserted or changed by copyists more asleep than awake?"[29]

Thus the pope commissioned Jerome to make a new translation of the Bible, one that would establish a standard Latin text, correcting the inaccuracies and rectifying the corruptions in the Old Latin texts. It would be called the Vulgate because it was in the "vulgar," or common, tongue of the Latin people. Another motive to create the Vulgate was to ensure that the western Roman Catholic Church would be clearly Latin in orientation. With the publication of Jerome's Vulgate, it seems the Lord gave to the people of medieval Christendom that which they were ready to possess and what best served his purposes at the time. That the Lord's hand was involved during the different phases of the Bible's history seems evident. President M. Russell Ballard said, "It is not by chance or coincidence that we have the Bible today."[30]

Jerome's rendition of the four Gospels appeared in AD 383. The entire Bible was completed in 404 or 405. All totaled, Jerome labored for twenty-three years to produce his masterpiece.[31] In the midst of his work, two things happened. First, shortly after Pope Damasus's death in 384, Jerome abandoned Rome and went to the Holy Land to live. He settled in Bethlehem, living in a cave complex traditionally associated with the Grotto of the Nativity, where he wrote, studied, translated, oversaw a monastery, and advised those who had followed him from Rome.[32] Second, Jerome was dealt a severe blow when he was passed over to succeed Pope Damasus. Still he labored on, driven by some invisible force that some are inclined to call the Holy Spirit.

Though there are issues for which Jerome may be justly criticized and though some thoughtful historians do not like his personality very much, some believe his sacrifice to be a worthy and acceptable one. It is the

29. J. Stevenson, ed., *Creeds, Councils and Controversies: Documents Illustrating the History of the Church AD 337–461* (London: SPCK, 1989), 183, emphasis in original. Joseph Smith said, "I believe the bible as it read when it came from the pen of the original writers; ignorant translators, careless transcribers, or designing and corrupt priests have committed many errors." "History, 1838–1856, Volume E-1," 1755 (October 15, 1843).

30. M. Russell Ballard, "The Miracle of the Holy Bible," *Ensign* 37, no. 5 (May 2007): 80.

31. "Jerome Completes the Vulgate," 13.

32. E. F. Sutcliffe, "Jerome," in *The Cambridge History of the Bible,* vol. 2, *The West from the Fathers to the Reformation,* ed. G. W. H. Lampe (Cambridge, Eng.: Cambridge University, 1969), 83–86.

judgment of modern writers that Jerome was a brilliant scholar and a good linguist, with a firm grasp of Latin, Greek, and, to a lesser extent, Hebrew. The longer one studies Jerome, the more one develops an appreciation for the work Jerome undertook and can imagine the trials, tribulations, and hardships that came to him, as he himself described—sitting month after month, by dim light, wrestling with poor eyesight, toiling sometimes day and night to give Christians a better rendition of the word of God. Jerome recognized the monumental, even presumptuous nature of his task, but he undertook it as a genuine labor of love. In his preface to the four Gospels, he wrote the following to Pope Damasus:

> You urge me to revise the old Latin version, and, as it were, to sit in judgment on the copies of the Scriptures which are now scattered throughout the whole world; and, inasmuch as they differ from one another, you would have me decide which of them agree with the Greek original. The labour is one of love, but at the same time both perilous and presumptuous; for in judging others I must be content to be judged by all; and how can I dare to change the language of the world in its hoary old age, and carry it back to the early days of its infancy? Is there a man, learned or unlearned, who will not, when he takes the volume into his hands, and perceives that what he reads does not suit his settled tastes, break out immediately into violent language, and call me a forger and a profane person for having the audacity to add anything to the ancient books, or to make any changes or corrections therein?[33]

The Vulgate gradually won acceptance in the Western world and, by the eighth or ninth century, replaced all Old Latin versions. The climax of its acceptance came at the Council of Trent in 1546, when the Vulgate was declared to be the official Bible of the Roman Catholic Church.[34]

Jerome chose to translate in a sense-for-sense manner rather than in a word-for-word manner. However, it must be recognized that the text of the Vulgate is not uniform in all its sections; when he first started out, ironically, he relied too heavily on Old Latin manuscripts of the New Testament—some of the very texts he was attempting to correct. And, frankly, he became a better translator over time as he gained more experience.

33. Jerome, *Prefaces, The Four Gospels,* in Schaff and Wace, *Select Library of Nicene and Post-Nicene Fathers,* 6:487–88.

34. H. F. D. Sparks, "Jerome as Biblical Scholar," in Ackroyd and Evans, *Cambridge History of the Bible,* 1:518; Philip Schaff, ed., *The Creeds of Christendom,* vol. 2, *The Greek and Latin Creeds, with Translations* (New York: Harper and Brothers, 1878), 82.

Therefore, it is difficult to determine the value of the Vulgate New Testament, especially the Gospels, for textual studies.

Yet, ultimately, the Vulgate was of tremendous value. It has exercised significant influence on the language and thought of Western Christendom. It was foundational in the preparation of other premodern translations of the Bible. The Vulgate was the direct precursor to the Wycliffe Bible, which was the first Bible translated completely into English from the Latin version. Wycliffe's Bible played a key role in both the Protestant Reformation and the efforts to arrive at the King James Version.

Gothic Version

Another translation of the Bible that appeared in Europe shortly before the Vulgate, but which was far less influential, was the Gothic Version. The ancient Goths founded an empire between the Danube River and the Black Sea and were split into groups on either side of the Dniester River—the Visigoths on the west and Ostrogoths on the east. They converted to Christianity and, by AD 325, had a Gothic bishop named Theophilus representing them at the Council of Nicea. More important, however, was Wulfilas (c. 311–383), who "was ordained to the episcopate by Bishop Eusebius of Nicomedia" and became known as the "Apostle to the Goths."[35]

Wulfilas (or probably Ulfilas, Gothic for "Little Wolf") labored to produce the Gothic translation of the Bible by first creating the Gothic alphabet. About two-thirds of the alphabet is composed of Greek letters, and the rest of it is a combination of Latin characters and old Germanic runes. Wulfilas made his translation of the Old Testament from the Septuagint. The New Testament was rendered from the Greek text established at Byzantium (Constantinople) around AD 350.[36]

The value of the Gothic Version appears to be mixed. Only a few fragments of the Old Testament have been preserved. "According to Philostorgius (c. 368–430), Wulfilas left out Samuel and Kings when he translated the Old Testament because he felt its war stories would encourage the warring Goths to continue to fight."[37] In terms of the New Testament, there are only nine extant manuscripts, which are fragmentary in nature. "The most famous Gothic manuscript, known as Argentius ([that is,] the Silver Codex), from the fifth or sixth century, contains the four Gospels arranged

35. Wegner, *Journey from Texts to Translations,* 257.
36. Wegner, *Journey from Texts to Translations,* 258.
37. Wegner, *Journey from Texts to Translations,* 258.

in Western order (Matt., John, Luke, Mark) and written in silver letters on purple vellum."[38] Wulfilas was, according to Bruce Metzger, "hospitable to Arianism,"[39] a heresy that denied Christ's eternally divine existence and nature and was condemned at the Council of Nicea in AD 325. How much Wulfilas's theological views influenced his translation of the New Testament has been debated. But, as Metzger notes, "perhaps the only certain trace of the translator's dogmatic bias is found in Phil[ippians] ii. 6, where reference is made to the pre-existent Christ in terms of being *galeiko guda* (= 'similar to God'), whereas the Greek *ἴσα θεῷ* should have been rendered *ibna guda* [= 'being in very nature God']."[40]

Old Slavonic Version

During the early Middle Ages, the Slavs of eastern Europe began to be converted to Christianity. According to tradition (some say legend), the Byzantine emperor Heraclius (c. 575–641) was among the first to evangelize the region, bringing priests from Rome, and "baptized the Croats."[41] More certain is the account of an attempt to Christianize the Moravian Empire (the area of the modern Czech Republic) formed three centuries later: "The founder of the empire, Rostislav, in order to check the growth of Frankish influence in his realm, asked, in 863, for Slavonic priests to be sent from Byzantium who should conduct the services and preach in the Slavonic language of the people."[42] Before this time, Frankish church leaders had been preaching in the Germanic tongue of the Franks and conducting the liturgy in Latin.[43]

In response to Rostislav, eastern Emperor Michael III in Constantinople (ruled 842–867) sent two brothers, Constantine (826–869, also known as Cyril) and Methodius (815–885), who became the "apostles to the Slavs."[44] They preached in the Slavonic language, began training Moravian clergy, and created the Glagolitic alphabet, which was based on biblical alphabetic elements. We note Bruce Metzger's description: "It appears that Cyril

38. Wegner, *Journey from Texts to Translation,* 258.

39. Bruce M. Metzger, *The Early Versions of the New Testament: Their Origin, Transmission, and Limitations* (Oxford: Clarendon, 1977), 377.

40. Metzger, *Early Versions of the New Testament,* 377.

41. Metzger, *Early Versions of the New Testament,* 394.

42. F. F. Bruce, *The Books and the Parchments,* rev. ed. (London: Marshall Pickering, 1991), 208.

43. Bruce, *Books and the Parchments,* 208.

44. Wegner, *Journey from Texts to Translations,* 259.

[Constantine's monastic name], taking as a model the increasingly flamboyant Greek minuscule script of the ninth century, and perhaps adopting also several Latin and Hebrew (or Samaritan) signs, used his inventive powers to devise an assortment of stylized and symmetrical characters made up of little quadrangles, triangles, and circles, with appendages."[45]

It should also be noted that there have been divergent opinions expressed about which alphabet Cyril actually created. Again, Bruce Metzger wrote,

> The difficulties that the modern philologist faces, however, arise from the fact that the extant Old Church Slavonic manuscripts present us with two distinct alphabets, the Glagolitic and the Cyrillic. Which of the alphabets Cyril invented, the relationship of the two alphabets to each other, and their antecedents, are questions to which widely divergent answers have been given. Today, however, there is widespread agreement that the alphabet invented by Cyril to take to the Moravian Slavs was that now called Glagolitic. . . .
>
> The Cyrillic alphabet is, most scholars agree, of later provenance than the Glagolitic. . . . This alphabet, which is considerably less individualistic than the Glagolitic, may have been devised by St. Kliment, a pupil of Cyril and Methodius and an active missionary in Bulgaria.[46]

With a new, user-friendly alphabet in place for the writing of Slavonic, Cyril began the work of translating the New Testament. Purposely, he started with John 1:1, "In the beginning was the word,"[47] as his preparatory work (creating a new alphabet) to bring forth the new translation had demonstrated. When Cyril died in 869, he and his brother had translated probably only the Psalms, the four Gospels, and Acts from Greek manuscripts into Slavonic. Methodius was then joined by a group of priests to help him finish the task of translating the rest of the Bible, which they accomplished by the latter part of the ninth century. Unfortunately, no Old Slavonic manuscripts from this early period have survived; the oldest manuscripts date from the tenth or eleventh century.[48]

The Old Slavonic Version is of value in helping us understand the spread of Christianity and its influence on native cultures. It also helps us flesh out the history of the transmission of the biblical texts in premodern times, a period of tremendous evangelization.

---

45. Metzger, *Early Versions of the New Testament,* 402.

46. Bruce M. Metzger, *The Bible in Translation: Ancient and English Versions* (Grand Rapids, Mich.: Baker Academic, 2001), 49.

47. Metzger, *Bible in Translation,* 49.

48. Metzger, *Early Versions of the New Testament,* 403.

Early Eastern Versions—the Diatessaron

Acts 2:9–11 lists those visitors from foreign lands in Jerusalem during the first Christian celebration of Pentecost: "Parthians, and Medes, and Elamites, and the dwellers in Mesopotamia, and in Judæa, and Cappadocia, in Pontus, and Asia, Phrygia, and Pamphylia, in Egypt, and in the parts of Libya about Cyrene, and strangers of Rome, Jews and proselytes, Cretes and Arabians, we do hear them speak in our tongues the wonderful works of God." As mentioned here, some of these attendees came from the East, beyond the borders of the Roman Empire, and surely were converted to the gospel, taking the message of salvation through Jesus Christ back to their homelands. We know that Christianity spread to Syria, Mesopotamia, and Egypt very early and that it continued to spread farther east. Eusebius mentions Pantaenus, head of the catechetical school in Alexandria, who took the gospel message as far as India:

> For indeed there were until then many evangelists of the word who had forethought to use inspired zeal on the apostolic model for the increase and building up of the divine word. One of these was Pantaenus, and it is said that he went to the Indians, and the tradition is that he found there that among some of those there who had known Christ the Gospel according to Matthew had preceded his coming; for Bartholomew, one of the apostles, had preached to them and had left them the writing of Matthew in Hebrew letters, which was preserved until the time mentioned.[49]

Bible versions and translations followed soon after Christianity reached these various regions.

One of the earliest versions of the four Gospels to circulate in the East was Tatian's Diatessaron. Tatian (110–172) came from Mesopotamia, was converted to Christianity, became a father of the Syriac church, and founded a group of ascetic Christians called Encratites. It is not known whether Tatian's masterwork was originally composed in Greek or Syriac. The name *diatessaron* is Greek, meaning "through four," and weaves all four Gospels into one continuous narrative, essentially making it the earliest known harmony of the Gospels. But the Diatessaron was circulating in Syriac sometime after AD 150 and gained its popularity in large measure owing to Ephraem (c. 306–73), a Syrian church father from Edessa who wrote a commentary on the work.[50]

49. Eusebius, *Ecclesiastical History* 5.10.2–3, 1:463.

50. C. S. C Williams, "The History of the Text and Canon of the New Testament to Jerome," in Lampe, *Cambridge History of the Bible,* 2:33–34.

Syriac Peshitta

Translations of the whole Bible into Old Syriac appeared by the end of the third or beginning of the fourth century AD. "Syriac" is the general name given to Christian Aramaic, a distinctive cursive variation of the Aramaic alphabet. At the beginning of the fifth century, a new version appeared—the Syriac Peshitta. Around AD 400, early church father Theodore of Mopsuestia noted that no one really knew who its translator(s) had been. Also in the fifth century, the Syriac church split into two factions—the Nestorians (East Syriac) and the Jacobites (West Syriac)—which resulted in two major editions of the Syriac Peshitta.[51]

The earliest Old Syriac edition of the Old Testament seems to have been translated from the Hebrew but subsequently revised in accordance with the Septuagint. Regarding the New Testament, scholars have identified five different Syriac versions. But from the fifth century onward, the Peshitta became established as the standard version. At first, the Peshitta New Testament included only twenty-two books, omitting four Epistles (2 Peter, 2 and 3 John, and Jude) and the book of Revelation. "But Philoxenus of Mabbug added these books to the version of the New Testament he commissioned in 507–508."[52]

The Syriac Peshitta is a valuable tool for Old Testament textual criticism because it represents a fairly early version from a different Jewish tradition of texts. The importance of the Peshitta New Testament has at times been exaggerated, as F. F. Bruce explained: "Because the Syriac Bible is written in a variant dialect of the language that Jesus spoke, extreme views are sometimes expressed about the forms in which his sayings appear in the Syriac Gospels, as though his actual words in the language in which they were uttered might be found there. The ordinary reader, for example, may readily infer from the writings of Mr. George Lamsa that the Peshitta Gospels preserve the very words of our Lord better than the Greek Gospels do. This, of course, is quite wrong; the Peshitta New Testament is simply a translation of the Greek."[53]

---

51. T. Nicol, "Syriac Versions," in *The International Standard Bible Encyclopedia,* ed. James Orr (Chicago: Howard-Severance, 1915), 5:2883–85.

52. Wegner, *Journey from Texts to Translations,* 246.

53. Bruce, *Books and the Parchments,* 190.

Coptic Versions

Egypt was another region into which the Gospels quickly spread by the mid- to late first century AD (see Acts 2:10), and it is where papyrus fragments of the Greek New Testament have been discovered, dating to the early second century. However, the language written by native Egyptians was undoubtedly Coptic, which is the latest phase in the long history of the evolving ancient Egyptian language. Until the Christian era, Egyptian had been written in hieroglyphs and their derivatives: the hieratic and demotic scripts. The Coptic language used by Egyptian Christians is a combination of twenty-four Greek letters plus seven signs taken from a cursive variety of demotic to express sounds not found in spoken Greek. As Bruce Metzger points out, "Coptic literature is almost exclusively religious."[54]

Though six different dialects are spoken up and down the Nile River valley, the two main dialects are Sahidic (found in Upper Egypt) and Bohairic (spoken in Lower Egypt). This accounts for two extant Coptic versions of the Bible in Egypt. Sahidic was the earlier dialect in Egypt, and this version of the Bible dates to the third century AD and is rooted in the Alexandrian text-type, though it contains some unusual textual variants not found in other versions of the New Testament. For example, "Matthew 6:13 ends with 'for yours is the power and the glory forever,' instead of the more common 'for yours is the kingdom, and the power, and the glory forever.' . . . In Acts 15, the Golden Rule is stated in the negative, namely, 'do not do unto others what you would not want them to do unto you.'"[55] The Bohairic dialect of Coptic, spoken in the Delta region of Egypt, became the most developed and in time superseded the other dialects. For a time, it was the only known version of the New Testament in Egypt that was also Alexandrian in type. Both Coptic versions of the New Testament are valuable for text-critical studies and transmission history.[56]

Nubian Version

Nubia is south of Egypt and north of Ethiopia. Christian influence probably entered Nubia from the time that the Coptic church became firmly established in Upper Egypt during the third and fourth centuries AD. Assigned missionaries arrived in Nubia during the mid-sixth century. In succeeding

54. Metzger, *Bible in Translation,* 35.
55. Wegner, *Journey from Texts to Translations,* 247.
56. Wegner, *Journey from Texts to Translations,* 247–48.

centuries, churches in Nubia multiplied and numbered in the hundreds. Exactly when the Bible was translated into Nubian is not known. However, if the pattern of evangelization observed in other countries was followed in Nubia, a vernacular version appeared perhaps as early as the second half of the sixth century. The reason for such tenuous conclusions comes from the fact that evidence for the Nubian version only came to light in the early twentieth century. In 1906, sixteen mutilated pages from a parchment codex originating in Upper Egypt were purchased in Cairo. They contained a portion of a lectionary for Christmastide that included passages from the New Testament in Nubian. Toward the end of the twentieth century, other biblical fragments in Nubian came to the attention of scholars: the Gospel of John and the book of Revelation.[57]

Armenian Version

Armenia is situated directly north of Mesopotamia. It boasts of being the first nation to officially adopt Christianity as its state religion, which occurred when King Tiridates III (c. 287–314), who had formerly persecuted Christians, was converted by Gregory the Illuminator (c. 257–331) sometime around 300.[58] King Tiridates then issued a royal edict commanding all his subjects to adopt Christianity. Up to this point, the Armenian people only had books written in Syriac or Greek.[59]

There are differing traditions as to how the first Armenian version of the Bible came into existence. One source ascribes it to "St. Mesrop (d. 439), a soldier who became a missionary, who created a new alphabet, and, with the help of one Catholicus Sahak (Isaac the Great, 390–439; [Catholicus is a title meaning Primate of the Armenian Church])," translated the Bible into Armenian from the Greek texts of both the Old and New Testaments. Another tradition comes from Moses of Chorion, St. Mesrop's nephew and disciple, who states that only Sahak translated the Syriac text of the Bible into Armenian.[60] The significant element of the story is the creation (again) of a new alphabet to serve a people who needed the Bible in their own language.

> The earliest attempt to construct an Armenian alphabet was made by a certain Bishop Daniel. Since he was a Syrian, he probably took the Aramaic alphabet as a pattern. According to the historian Koriun, the alphabet

57. Bruce Metzger, *Bible in Translation,* 50–51.
58. Wegner, *Journey from Texts to Translations,* 248; Metzger, *Bible in Translation,* 40–41.
59. Wegner, *Journey from Texts to Translations,* 249.
60. Metzger, *Text of the New Testament,* 82–83.

> was found to be unsuitable for representing the sounds of the Armenian language. . . .
>
> At length and with the help of a Greek hermit and calligrapher, Rufanos of Samosata, about A.D. 406 Mesrop succeeded in producing an Armenian alphabet of thirty-six letters, twenty letters coming directly from Greek, twelve others being formed according to a Greek model, and four being taken from Syriac.[61]

Thus the foundation of all Armenian literature came about as the result of the quest for a Bible written in their language.

The Armenian version of the Bible is a fairly early translation of the Bible when compared with all the rest, and thus some of the readings may be early—which is helpful to students of the biblical text. "The Armenian version contains several books outside the standard canon; for example, . . . the *Epistle of the Corinthians to Paul* and the *Third Epistle of Paul to the Corinthians* are included in some of the New Testament manuscripts." The final official Armenian Bible is dependent on the readings of the Septuagint and the Peshitta.[62]

Armenian New Testament manuscripts present some interesting characteristics (the General Epistles appear immediately following the book of Acts) and some richer variant readings. For example, in John 5:7, the lame man at the Pool of Bethesda remarks, "While I drag myself, another steps in before me" instead of the common reading, "while I am coming." In Mark 7:25, the usual reading states that the little girl "had" an unclean spirit, while "the Armenian version says the little girl 'was pressed' or 'was squeezed' by an unclean spirit."[63] What does all this tell us about the New Testament canon in the East during the fifth century?

Georgian Version

Georgia is north of Armenia in the Caucasus Mountains. Christianity was introduced in Georgia during the fourth-century AD reign of Constantine the Great, but when or how the Bible first came into the country is not known with any certainty. Like other versions we have discussed, an alphabet had to be developed before Georgians could have the scriptures in an understandable tongue since the Georgian language is unrelated to any of those around it. Bruce Metzger believes that at least the Gospels were

61. Metzger, *Bible in Translation,* 41.
62. Wegner, *Journey from Texts to Translations,* 249.
63. Wegner, *Journey from Texts to Translations,* 249.

translated by the mid-fifth century, while other scholars, especially Sidney Jellicoe, propose that an original Georgian version appeared by the sixth century, translated from the Armenian version and later revised by comparing it with a Greek text.[64] The oldest Georgian manuscript, the Adysh manuscript of 897, contains only the four Gospels. Paul Wegner asserts that the "Georgian version is a tertiary version from either the Syriac or Armenian versions, and thus its primary value is its corroboration of the Old Syriac versions.[65]

Ethiopic Version

It is not known when Ethiopia (Abyssinia is the older name) received Christianity. The tradition that the Ethiopian official baptized by Philip (Acts 8:26–39) took the gospel back to his homeland cannot be corroborated, according to Metzger.[66] Both literary and inscriptional evidence points to the establishment of Christianity in Ethiopia by the fourth century AD. It is believed that portions of the Bible were translated into Ge'ez or Old Ethiopic by the fifth or sixth century, probably by Monophysite monks, who accepted the belief that Christ possessed only one nature and who were escaping persecutions by Byzantine rulers. The oldest extant Ethiopic text is a copy of the Gospels dating from the tenth century. The Ethiopic New Testament is different in that it includes two apocryphal books: *1 Enoch* and *Jubilees*.[67]

Arabic Versions

Beyond a couple of references in the New Testament, little is known about early Christian contacts with Arabia. The Christian historian, Eusebius, describes the appointment of a man named Moses as bishop in the region during the fourth century AD and the miraculous peace that resulted: "All the regions of the East therefore were at that time ravaged by the Saracens: but a certain divine Providence repressed their fury in the manner I am about to describe. A person named Moses, a Saracen by birth, who led a monastic life in the desert, became exceedingly eminent for his piety,

64. Sidney Jellicoe, *The Septuagint and Modern Study* (Ann Arbor, Mich.: Eisenbrauns, 1978), 261.

65. Wegner, *Journey from Texts to Translations,* 250.

66. Metzger, *Early Versions of the New Testament,* 217; Wegner, *Journey from Texts to Translations,* 250.

67. Wegner, *Journey from Texts to Translations,* 251.

faith, and miracles. Mavia the queen of the Saracens was therefore desirous that this person should be constituted bishop over her nation, and promised on this condition to terminate the war."[68] At this time, Christians from Ethiopia also began moving into the southern part of the Arabian Peninsula.

The first mention of a version of the Bible in Arabic comes from the Midrash *Sifre* on Deuteronomy 34:3, which states that the Torah came to Israel in four languages: Hebrew, Greek, Arabic, and Aramaic. But nothing else is mentioned, and the assertion is uncorroborated. The arrival and spread of Islam in the seventh century AD forced Jews and Christians living in Arabia to adopt the Arabic language, but translation of the Bible into Arabic was outlawed by Islamic law. However, it was translated secretly and sometimes reflected the influence of Docetism. (From the Greek *dokein,* "to seem or appear," Docetism is the heretical belief that Jesus possessed only a heavenly, immaterial nature and only appeared to be incarnate, only seemed to possess a physical body, and that the material world and thus one's physical body were inherently evil.) F. F. Bruce explained, "The Scriptures do not seem to have been extant in an Arabic version before the time of Muhammad (570–632), who knew the gospel story only in an oral form, and mainly from Syriac sources. These Syriac sources were marked by Docetism, which explains the statement in the Qur'an that Jesus was only apparently crucified, but did not really die."[69]

According to the latest New Testament scholarship, the translations into Arabic were made from conglomerate versions: Greek, Old Syriac, Latin, Coptic, and the Syriac Peshitta. Professor Metzger summarized the evidence regarding the Arabic versions of the four Gospels:

> According to an analysis by Ignazio Guidi of more than seventy-five Arabic manuscripts, the Arabic versions of the Gospels existing in manuscripts fall into six basic groups: (1) those made directly from the Greek; (2) those made directly from or corrected from the Syriac Peshitta; (3) those made directly from or corrected from the Coptic (usually the Bohairic dialect); (4) those made from Latin; (5) manuscripts of two distinct eclectic recensions produced by the Alexandrian Patriarchate during the thirteenth century; and (6) miscellaneous manuscripts, some of which are characterized by being cast in the form of rhymed prose made classic by the

68. Eusebius, *Ecclesiastical History* 4.36, in Schaff and Wace, *Select Library of Nicene and Post-Nicene Fathers of the Christian Church,* 2:116.

69. Bruce, *Books and the Parchments,* 206–7.

> Koran. Furthermore, more than one Arabic version has been corrected from others derived from a different basic text.[70]

The oldest known manuscript of the Arabic Bible is the Codex Vaticanus Arabicus 13, which contains a portion of the Gospels and Pauline Epistles, dating to the eighth or ninth century AD.[71]

Sogdian Version

Sogdian is an Iranian language which became the lingua franca of an extensive area in Persia and Central Asia. In the early twentieth century, a variety of Sogdian documents came to light in northwest China, including fragmentary copies of passages from Matthew, Luke, and John as well as several verses of 1 Corinthians and Galatians. These biblical texts are believed to date from the time of the Nestorian mission to Central Asia during the seventh century AD.[72]

Summary

It would be hard to overestimate the importance of endeavors to translate the Bible into the vernacular tongues of Christians in the premodern period. First, these labors were usually preceded by proselytizing work to establish the Christian church in regions not always favorable to the gospel, thus underlining the determination and bravery of those Christian translators.

Second, sometimes great effort was expended to create vernacular alphabets where none had previously existed in order to render new translations in the language of the common people. These new alphabets were impressive achievements in and of themselves. Often translations of the Bible into the vernacular significantly affected the cultures of those native inhabitants because it featured commandments to love one's neighbors and to do good continually.

Third, when people had a Bible in their own language, they were better able to withstand those times when persecution and heresy beset them. Paul Wegner noted, "Church history confirms that in areas such as Egypt and Syria, where the Bible was translated into the languages of the common people at an early stage, the Muslim conquest in the seventh century

---

70. Metzger, *Bible in Translation,* 46–47.
71. Wegner, *Journey from Texts to Translations,* 252.
72. Metzger, *Bible in Translation,* 47.

was not able to wipe out Christianity. But in areas where there were no translations (as with the Berber peoples in North Africa) hardly a trace of Christianity is left. The early church realized the importance of translating the Bible into other languages."[73]

Fourth, though vernacular translations were made long ago, they are of great advantage to those who seek to understand the history of interpretation of scripture as well as the history of the transmission of the Bible. Again, Paul Wegner informs us that "primary translations (those translated directly from the Hebrew and Greek texts) are most important, but secondary and tertiary translations have at least a limited value. . . . The most important primary translations are the Septuagint, Syriac Peshitta, and Latin Vulgate because they have been translated directly from some form of the Hebrew or Greek texts. Secondary translations are often helpful in determining the text that they have been translated from; for example, Old Latin texts are quite helpful in determining the text of the Septuagint since they were translated from some form of it."[74]

We marvel at the work of early Christians to spread the word of God far and wide into new regions among people who spoke different languages (Greek, Latin, Syriac, Coptic, Gothic, and Slavic—to name some). We pay tribute to those who gave so much of themselves to give others of varied cultures the word in their own tongues, especially considering the difficulty of transferring meaning from one language to another (Latin has no definite article, Syriac cannot distinguish between the Greek aorist and perfect verb tenses, Coptic lacks the passive voice,[75] and so on). Despite stiff challenges, the creation of many vernacular Bible translations was accomplished well before our modern age of ease, convenience, and technological advances.

73. Wegner, *Journey from Texts to Translations,* 243.
74. Wegner, *Journey from Texts to Translations,* 243.
75. Metzger, *Text of the New Testament,* 68.

Background

Uncovering the Historical Background of the New Testament

John F. Hall, Eric D. Huntsman, and Cecilia M. Peek

Introduction

Coming to relish the background of the New Testament is somewhat like adding an essential garnish to a favorite food, producing a more memorable meal. On the other hand, we students and teachers who work at understanding scripture can find deep satisfaction in the plain meaning of one passage after another. Without knowing any New Testament background, many know the joy of discovering a new comprehension of a passage, such as the two disciples experienced when they walked with the resurrected Christ toward Emmaus as he "expounded" the meaning "in all the scriptures," leaving the two almost breathless and saying to one another, "Did not our heart burn within us?" (Luke 24:27, 32). Although the New Testament can stand on its own, we find greater comprehension when we understand the world of the New Testament authors, including the noble intentions behind their writing.

The New Testament writers lived in elements of three societal systems: Judean, Hellenistic, and Roman. Books written under Judean influence include the Gospels of Matthew, Mark, John, and the Epistles of James and Jude. Other works were composed in distant Roman provinces in totally different surroundings, including the Gospel of Luke, the book of Acts, and Paul's letters. In addition, because Rome ruled the entire Mediterranean region, clear Roman influences pepper the entire New Testament. Thus knowing context can change the flavors we encounter as we seek a more memorable experience with the New Testament.

Text and Context

John F. Hall

The necessary starting point for deriving meaning, understanding, and inspiration from the New Testament is obviously a perusal of the text itself. If the text is an accurate translation from the original Greek, the language in which the New Testament was composed, the reader can reasonably accrue rewarding information. However, comprehension can increase manyfold if the text is understood in its proper context. The literal Latin meaning of "context" is "with the text"; in other words, the sense of this term points to information that must be known in order to understand the text. Said another way, the world of the author, personal considerations about the author, and the intent of the author in writing are essential determining factors in comprehending the meaning of any given text. Such considerations increase in importance proportionately to the time between when the text is written and the time it is read. Accordingly, an essential prerequisite for modern readers to better apprehend the significance of ancient texts is additional knowledge about the New Testament's context—an ancient world very different in attitude and circumstance from the modern world in which we live.

Understanding the intersecting ancient cultures, particularly the Hellenization of Judea and the political dominance of Rome, will enable readers to find more from the New Testament. It is especially valuable to understand Roman culture, government, and law because the Greek-speaking provinces in the eastern half of its empire, as well as the province of Judea, belonged to Rome. The following treatments present information about Judean, Hellenistic Greek, and Roman culture and history that clarify the context of the New Testament.

The Jewish Context of the New Testament

Eric D. Huntsman

The effects of the Babylonian exile and the unrealized hope of a glorious national restoration under the Davidic dynasty after the return were two factors that greatly influenced the religious and political contexts of New Testament writings. After earlier interference in the kingdom of Judah, the Babylonians destroyed Jerusalem in 587 BC and deported many of its nobility, priesthood, and artisans. Those that returned to the old territory of Judah, soon after Cyrus conquered Babylon c. 538/537 BC, brought with them a renewed devotion to the Mosaic law that transformed Judaism. This change was accelerated with the efforts of Nehemiah and Ezra and produced a transitional religion different from both Ancient Israel, known in most of the Old Testament, and rabbinic Judaism, known from the Mishnah and other later sources. The temple was rebuilt c. 516 BC, but the Second Temple Period that followed (515 BC–AD 70) failed to realize a truly legitimate restoration of an anointed king, resulting in messianic expectations and an eschatology that was in many ways more appropriate for the Second rather than the First Coming of Jesus Christ.

Religious Developments

Rather than leading to a loss of national identity and religion, the Babylonian captivity led to deeper attachment to the law of Moses as the means of separating the people of Yahweh from the "nations," or Gentiles, around them. Without the temple and its attendant sacrifices and rituals, the law and the writings of the prophets became a greater focus of attention, and the national disaster of 587 BC was increasingly seen as punishment for earlier unfaithfulness to God, a point stressed by both the Deuteronomic and Chronicler's histories.

The return to Judah was accomplished in stages, with groups migrating under the leadership of Sheshbazzar, Zerubbabel, Ezra, and Nehemiah. Cyrus commissioned Sheshbazzar, a "prince of Judah" (Ezra 1:8), perhaps the same as Shenazar, who was of Davidic descent (1 Chr. 3:18), to return to Jerusalem in 538 BC with the temple vessels and lay the foundations of a new temple (Ezra 1:8–11; 5:14–17).[1] Rather than finding their ancestral

1. Tamara C. Eskenazi, "Sheshbazzar," in *The Anchor Bible Dictionary,* ed. David Noel Freedman, 6 vols. (New York: Doubleday, 1992), 6:1207–9.

homeland empty, the returning exiles, or *ʿam haggôlâ,* "people of the exile," found the countryside and villages of Judah still inhabited by the *ʿam hāʾ āretz,* "people of the land," whom the Babylonians had left in the land with each deportation. The *ʿam haggôlâ* succeeded in reimposing themselves over this majority, dominating it socially and economically, and, perhaps more importantly, insisting upon its new religious practices and devotion to the law.[2] This returning aristocracy that saw itself as the true Judeans may have constituted the socioeconomic and religious-political group known as *hoi Iudaioi,* or "the Jews" in the Gospel of John. They were a leadership and landowning class somehow apart from the peasantry and urban crowds that generally received Jesus and "heard him gladly" when he silenced their leaders (Mark 12:37), and they included some well-to-do followers of Jesus, such as Lazarus and his sisters.[3]

Another group, with whom the returning exiles had even more difficult relations, was the Samaritans of the Ephraim hill country to the north of Jerusalem and Judea. The Samaritans were largely people of the tribes of Ephraim and Manasseh who were not deported with their leadership at the time of the Assyrian destruction of Israel in 721 BC. In this respect, they were analogous to the *ʿam hāʾ āretz* of Judah, but whereas Ezra and Nehemiah were largely able to reverse the effects of intermarriage between Jews and other local peoples, the mixing of the residual Israelite population to the north with Assyrian colonists had occurred too long ago. Exile had forced the *ʿam haggôlâ* to maintain their racial and religious identity by strict separation from Gentiles, and after their return to the blackened remains of Jerusalem, they refused to interact with their Samaritan cousins. Samaritan authorities opposed the rebuilding of the Jerusalem temple, and Nehemiah drove a high priest's grandson out of his city as a "Samaritan sympathizer."[4]

---

2. Everett Ferguson, *Backgrounds of Early Christianity,* 2nd ed. (Grand Rapids, Mich.: William B. Eerdmans, 1993), 376–79; Robert P. Carroll, "Israel, History of (Post-Monarchic Period)," in *Anchor Bible Dictionary,* 3:569–70.

3. Note how "the Jews" come to comfort Mary and Martha in John 11:31–46, one of the few places in the Gospel of John where *hoi Iudaioi* is used positively and does not seem to apply solely to the Jerusalem leadership of chief priests and elders. For a survey of scholarship on *hoi Ioudaioi,* see Adele Reinhartz, *Befriending the Beloved Disciple: A Jewish Reading of the Gospel of John* (New York: Continuum, 2001), 72–78; Raymond Brown, *An Introduction to the Gospel of John,* ed. Francis J. Moloney (New York: Doubleday, 2003), 161–72.

4. Ferguson, *Backgrounds of Early Christianity,* 378–79; Robert T. Anderson, "Samaritans," in *Anchor Bible Dictionary,* 5:941. See also Ezra 4.

The efforts of Nehemiah and especially Ezra to reform the restored community reflect the new emphases on the law brought back with the exiles. The postexilic books of the Old Testament—Ezra, Nehemiah, Haggai, Zechariah, and Malachi—are largely concerned with the kinds of problems addressed by these two reformers: building and maintaining the temple, avoiding intermarriage with foreigners, paying tithes, observing the Sabbath, and strictly following the law of Moses. Second Temple Judaism learned these lessons well, and establishment of "temple and Torah" were the two primary "accomplishments of the returned exiles." One can see in Matthew how these practices came to occupy, if not preoccupy, the Jewish community at the time of Christ.[5]

Another result of the reforming activities that is particularly ascribed to Ezra was the movement toward establishing an early canon of the Hebrew Bible. The efforts of "Ezra the scribe" (Neh. 8:1) to preserve and teach from these accepted writings eventually replaced the authority of the prophet and the tradition of the teaching priest with Ezra's edited texts and the practice of interpreting them by a new class of scribes. In this manner, Ezra became one of the founding figures of rabbinic Judaism.[6] The Hebrew Bible that took shape after the exile under Ezra's influence consisted of the Pentateuch and the former Prophets, and in its later, final form, it included the *Torah* (the Law, as found in the books of the Pentateuch), *Nevi'im* (the Prophets, both early and later), and *Kethuvim* (the Writings).

Because of the lack of prophetic or other generally recognized authority in the Intertestamental Period, these developments actually led to the rise of sectarianism in Judaism. While all major Jewish groups after the exile and through the time of the New Testament accepted the temple and the Torah, they differed in their view of scripture and in their acceptance of practices begun during the captivity and developed through reformation efforts, such as those of Ezra. While the origins of some of the later Jewish parties known in the New Testament arose partially as a result of political factors (see below), differences about the boundaries of the scriptural canon and certain religious practices divided major groups like the Sadducees and Pharisees. Our understanding of the actual beliefs and practices of the Sadducees may well be distorted by the lack of Sadducean sources,

5. Ferguson, *Backgrounds of Early Christianity*, 377–78.

6. W. H. C. Frend, *The Rise of Christianity* (Philadelphia: Fortress Press, 1984), 15–16; Michael Grant, *The History of Ancient Israel* (London: Weidenfeld and Nicolson, 1984), 189–91; Ferguson, *Backgrounds of Early Christianity*, 376–79.

but it is clear that they accepted only the Torah as contained in the Pentateuch, whereas the Pharisees espoused an oral as well as a written law. This distinction led to major disagreements between the two groups over issues of ritual purity, since one of the major purposes of the oral law was to avoid breaking the rules of the written law through the addition of extraneous regulations. In addition, the Pharisees accepted the Prophets and the Writings as scriptural, whereas the Sadducees did not.[7]

During Christ's ministry, he observed the law, respected the temple, and sought to deepen his followers' understanding of the teachings of the prophets, albeit without rigid devotion to the outward form that developed in the Second Temple Period. Subsequent leaders of the Church after Jesus' Ascension continued to reflect their Jewish background. Peter assumed the law and its practices and limited the teaching of the gospel to the Jews until directed otherwise by vision (Acts 10). Even then, he seems to have maintained some connection with the worldview and practices of his upbringing (Gal. 2:11–14). Jesus' brother was known as "James the Just" because of a reputation for righteousness and his observation of the law. Due to his status as leader of the Church in Jerusalem, James represented many Jewish Christians. Although the Savior had taught in his forty-day ministry that the law had been fulfilled, as he taught the Nephites in 3 Nephi 9:17–20, at least some of the Jerusalem Saints continued to use the temple as a place of prayer, and James told Paul that many Jews believed in Jesus but were still "zealous of the law," perhaps for continuing cultural reasons (Acts 21:20). Even Paul, who taught against the necessity of continuing to be zealous in obeying the law of Moses, was influenced in much of his teaching and thinking by Jewish religious and scriptural thought.[8]

Political Developments

For all the apparent successes of Second Temple Judaism in its religious "reform," it failed in the political realm to restore a legitimate national monarchy. Zerubbabel, perhaps Sheshbazzar's nephew and a more direct heir to the throne of Judah, seems to have replaced Sheshbazzar as the agent or

7. Frend, *Rise of Christianity*, 23–26; Grant, *History of Ancient Israel*, 216–17; Gary G. Porton, "Sadducees," in *Anchor Bible Dictionary* 5:892–94; Ferguson, *Backgrounds of Early Christianity*, 480–87.

8. See W. D. Davies, *Paul and Rabbinic Judaism: Some Rabbinic Elements in Pauline Theology* (London: SPCK, 1955); Daniel Boyarin, *A Radical Jew: Paul and the Politics of Identity* (Berkeley: University of California Press, 1994), 39–56, 136–57; and John McRay, *Paul: His Life and Teaching* (Grand Rapids, Mich.: Baker Academic, 2003), 360–71, 440–47.

governor of the Persian king, and it was under his direction that the temple was at last completed. Despite both of their connections with the House of David, the monarchy was not restored. Popular expectation of such, in fact, may have resulted in their dismissal and disappearance from the historical record,[9] perhaps because of popular anticipation that Zerubbabel would assume the throne of David and become a true *māšîach*—a "messiah" or "anointed king." Nehemiah, who was not a Davidide, appears next as *tirshatha* or "governor." Although the details of administration in the Persian period are obscure, no other royal scion seems to have been appointed.

In the Hebrew Bible, those who were designated as chosen and favored by God through anointing included kings, high priests, and, at least in the case of Elisha, prophets. In a sense, each of these anointed figures could be considered a "messiah" whose role was to help save Israel.[10] Whereas a Christian and Restoration understanding of the role of *the* Messiah allows us to see that such "messiahs" simply prefigured Jesus Christ, the ultimate Prophet, Priest, and King, the vicissitudes of the history of Judah and Israel after David led to an increasingly narrow messianic view that focused solely on the political salvation and prosperity of Israel. Accordingly, Israel saw the birth of Hezekiah—one of the rare, relatively righteous kings of Judah during whose reign the Lord miraculously saved Jerusalem from the Assyrians—as the fulfillment of the messianic prophecy of Isaiah (Isa. 7:14; 36:1–37; 38).[11] They failed to realize that this salvation was a type of greater salvation that would come through another Son of David, the true Immanuel (Matt. 1:22–23). Likewise, the meteoric rise of Judah and its temporary restoration of the Davidic borders of Israel under King Josiah was seen as a fulfillment of messianic hopes, once again focusing Jewish expectations on a political fulfillment of messianic prophecies. Josiah's untimely death at Megiddo was difficult for the chroniclers and scribes to explain, forcing them to interpret Josiah's death as a vicarious act on behalf of sinful Judah,[12] although this interpretation, too, failed to see it as only a type of the far greater vicarious sacrifice of the true Messiah.

---

9. Bryan E. Beyer, "Zerubbabel," in *Anchor Bible Dictionary,* 6:1084–86.

10. Grant, *History of Ancient Israel,* 212–15; Marinus de Jonge, "Messiah," in *Anchor Bible Dictionary,* 4:777–88; S. Kent Brown and Richard Neitzel Holzapfel, *Between the Testaments: From Malachi to Matthew* (Salt Lake City: Deseret Book, 2002), 211–13.

11. Antti Laato, *A Star Is Rising: The Historical Development of the Old Testament Royal Ideology and the Rise of the Jewish Messianic Expectations* (Atlanta: Scholars Press, 1997), 118–29.

12. Latto, *Star Is Rising,* 131–50.

With the dismissal of Zerubbabel and the disappointment of national expectations regarding the House of David, messianic expectations appear to have focused on the figure of the high priest, beginning with the high priest Joshua, who is conspicuous alongside Zerubbabel in Zechariah 1–6.[13] This quasimessianic status of the high priest, in the absence of a legitimate king, allowed the high priest in the postexilic period to take on the guise of the leader of the nation as well as of the temple ceremonial life. Thus the Persian province of Yehud effectively became a small temple state like others throughout the satrapy of Syria,[14] initiating a long history of collaboration between high priests and the Persian imperial power and, subsequently, the rule of the Ptolemies, Seleucids, and Romans that followed.

The shifting political tides of international politicos endangered the precarious autonomy that the Jews maintained under the administration of their high priests. After the brief rule of Alexander the Great (336–323 BC), who conquered Syria and Judea in 332 BC and, according to legend,[15] had allowed the high priest to continue and even expand his political power, Jerusalem and its environs lay on the border between Ptolemaic Egypt and Seleucid Syria. This position caused rival groups within the priestly hierarchy to champion one Hellenistic dynasty against the other. The Ptolemies held Palestine securely from 301 to 219 BC, but after that, the Seleucid monarch Antiochus III the Great (223–187 BC) began to wrest control of southern Syria and Palestine, with Jerusalem finally coming under Seleucid control in 198 BC. A pro-Seleucid faction gained control of the high priesthood and began, apparently without any Seleucid encouragement at first, a policy of Hellenization.[16] This undercut the status of the high priest among conservatives as the leader of the Jewish community, particularly under the extreme Hellenizers Jason and Menelaus, high priests with Greek names and attitudes. Jason, the last high priest of the legitimate Zadokite family, and Menelaus, who as a Benjamite was not likely from a priestly family, repeatedly tried to outbid each other by bribing the Seleucid king for the high priesthood; they subsequently fought civil wars against each other from 170 to 167 BC.[17]

---

13. Laato, *Star Is Rising,* 193–207.

14. Frend, *Rise of Christianity,* 15; Grant, *History of Ancient Israel,* 190–91; Ferguson, *Backgrounds of Early Christianity,* 378.

15 W. W. Tarn, *Alexander the Great* (Boston: Beacon Press, 1956), 41 and note 2.

16. Peter Green, *Alexander to Actium: The Historical Evolution of the Hellenistic Age* (Berkeley: University of California Press, 1990), 499–505.

17. Green, *Alexander to Actium,* 508–14.

Hence the ground for great change was already laid when Antiochus IV Epiphanes (175–164 BC) initiated a policy of extreme Hellenization in 167 BC that led to the famous revolt of Mattathias of the Hasmonean family and his sons. The miraculous success of his son Judas Maccabaeus eventually led to a series of half steps whereby the temple was cleansed and rededicated in 164 BC, autonomy was restored, and independence was eventually achieved. A Jerusalem assembly confirmed Judas's brother Simon as hereditary high priest in 140 BC, and the military successes of his son John Hyrcanus (161–143/2 BC) extended the borders of the new state effectively to its old Davidic extent. Extensive areas such as Idumea, the home of Herod's family, were forcibly converted to Judaism, and Galilee was colonized by Jews, explaining how the family of Mary and perhaps Joseph ended up in Nazareth. To many it seemed the glories of David and Solomon were being revived, leading one of the sons of John Hyrcanus, either Aristobolus (104–103 BC) or Alexander Jannaeus (103–76 BC), to adopt the title of "king" as well as high priest.[18]

The original faithfulness of the Hasmonean family to the temple and the Torah earned them a certain legitimacy that they otherwise lacked since their family, although priestly, was not of the official Zadokite branch. Similarly, their military and diplomatic successes seemed to justify the usurpation of the title of "king," even though they were in no way descended from David. Despite these inconsistencies, the fact that the Hasmoneans had delivered the Jews from religious and political oppression helped create a false messianic expectation that would outlast their own dynasty and give revolutionary movements in Judaism for the next two centuries certain messianic connections.[19] Consequently, when Jesus began to criticize the corrupt religious establishment of his day and tend to the temporal needs of people with his feeding of the five thousand, he retreated from the *ʿam hāʾ āretz* who flocked to him because he perceived that "they would come and take him by force, to make him a king" (John 6:15). This expectation and the hope that he would deliver them from the Roman occupation may also have lain at the root of the people's enthusiastic reception of him as "son of David"

18. Emil Schürer, *The History of the Jewish People in the Age of Jesus Christ,* ed. Geza Vermes, Fergus Millar, and Matthew Black, 3 vols. (Edinburgh: T. & T. Clark, 1973–87), 1:125–228; Grant, *History of Ancient Israel,* 212, 219–21; Laato, *Star Is Rising,* 258–60; Brown and Holzapfel, *Between the Testaments,* 59–65.

19. Richard A. Horsley, "Messianic Movements in Judaism," in *Anchor Bible Dictionary,* 4:791–97; Laato, *Star Is Rising,* 256–79, 357–80.

upon his triumphal entry into Jerusalem (Matt. 21:1–11; Mark 11:1–11; Luke 19:29–40; John 12:14–19).

The legitimacy of the Hasmoneans, however, was questioned from the beginning, and their rule resulted in serious divisions that persisted into New Testament times. Simon's appointment in 143 BC as high priest and ethnarch, or civil ruler, was qualified by the statement that he held his position "pending the advent of a genuine prophet" (1 Macc. 14:40) who could authoritatively recognize him as the Lord's anointed.[20] Although many saw messianic overtones in the activities of the early Hasmoneans, they were not universally accepted as such within the Jewish community. The Qumran covenanters, usually identified with the group Josephus called the Essenes, rejected the Jerusalem priesthood as illegitimate and broke from the Hasmoneans after suffering from the actions of a "wicked priest," probably Judas Maccabeus's brother Jonathan.[21] Withdrawing from Jewish society, the Qumran community awaited both a genuine anointed king, or a messiah from the House of David, and a legitimate high priest, or priestly messiah.[22]

The Pharisees also had their origins in an anti-Hasmonean movement, disputing the right of John Hyrcanus to rule and contesting later Hasmonean claims to the title of king.[23] The Psalms of Solomon, a pseudepigraphal document of the first century BC associated with the position of the Pharisees, views the Hasmoneans as usurpers to the Davidic throne and serves as a model of Pharisaic messianic expectations.[24] Unlike the Qumran community, the Pharisees did not withdraw from political life but instead attempted to reform. When the Hasmonean queen, Salome Alexandra, came to power (76 BC), she allowed the Pharisees a substantial measure of influence at court, a circumstance that persisted into the era of Roman rule at the time of Jesus.[25]

Such harmony was not the case between Jews and Samaritans. Hasmoneans created and deepened further division when John Hyrcanus, the second-century Hasmonean leader, destroyed the Samaritan temple on

---

20. Schürer, *History of the Jewish People,* 1:193–94.

21. Frend, *Rise of Christianity,* 27; Ferguson, *Backgrounds of Early Christianity,* 488; Laato, *Star Is Rising,* 285.

22. Schürer, *History of the Jewish People,* 2:550–54.

23. Schürer, *History of the Jewish People,* 1:211–14.

24. Laato, *Star Is Rising,* 279–84.

25. Ferguson, *Backgrounds of Early Christianity,* 480–81.

Mount Gerizim in 128 BC, permanently poisoning relations between the two groups.[26] However, the Sadducees cooperated with the Hasmoneans early on and continued the proven aristocratic policy of collaborating with whatever governing power was in control throughout the New Testament period until the Jewish revolt of AD 66–70 also saw the destruction of the temple and their power base.[27]

Lastly, a more obscure group in the New Testament emerged with the advent of Herod the Great. Apparently a purely political group, the Herodians, as the New Testament calls them, consisted of royal retainers and landowners who felt that Herod's sons, and perhaps a reconstitution of Herod's kingdom, provided the best hope of maintaining both limited Jewish autonomy and their own social and economic status under the Romans. In this regard, they seem to have set aside any messianic expectation and were purely political realists.[28]

26. Frend, *Rise of Christianity,* 18; Brown and Holzapfel, *Between the Testaments*, 191–92.

27. Schürer, *History of the Jewish People*, 2:413–14.

28. E. Mary Smallwood, *The Jews under Roman Rule from Pompey to Diocletian: A Study in Political Relations* (Leiden, Neth.: E. J. Brill, 1981), 163–64.

The Hellenistic Context of the New Testament

Cecilia M. Peek

Setting the Hellenistic Table

After the conquest of Tyre by Alexander the Great in 332 BC, Palestine, previously a part of the Persian Empire, came under the sway of the Macedonian king. Following the death of Alexander in 323 BC, the region was fought over by two of the Hellenistic dynasties that succeeded him: the Ptolemies in Egypt and the Seleucids in Syria. The Ptolemies generally dominated Palestine for the first century after Alexander's death, but through the military campaigns of Antiochus III from 223 to 200 BC, the Syrian Seleucids successfully gained control of the area. This control continued until the Hasmonean revolt in the 160s BC.[29] Palestine then remained a territory subject to the political control of one or another Greco-Macedonian ruler for more than one hundred and fifty years. Throughout this period, not only the Jews resident in Judea but also the Jews of the Diaspora—those great numbers of Jews who had been spread by Persian rulers throughout Asia Minor, Syria, and Egypt—interacted with new Greek rulers. They came into close contact with the Greek language, Greek education, and the arts in urban centers like Alexandria, Antioch, and Ephesus.[30] Indeed, by the early third century BC, Jews had become an important minority in Egypt, especially prominent in Alexandria, where the Jewish scriptures were being translated into Greek for the thousands of Jews now speaking Greek as their primary language.[31] In the wake of Alexander's conquests and under the shifting reigns of the Ptolemies and Seleucids, Greek cities

29. See Diodorus Siculus 18.3, 19.59.2, 19.80–86, 21.1.4, 39.6; Quintus Curtius 10.10.2; Justin, Epitome, 13.4.10–17, 31.1.1–2; and Polybius 16.18–19. For a summary discussion and particular bibliography on Alexander's assumption of control and the shifting power structure that followed his death, see Green, *Alexander to Actium,* 499 nn. 3–4; Frank W. Walbank, *A Historical Commentary on Polybius,* 3 vols. (Oxford: Clarendon Press, 1967), 2:523–25, 546–47.

30. See Green, *Alexander to Actium,* 317–18, 325, 501; Erich S. Gruen, *Heritage and Hellenism: The Reinvention of Jewish Tradition* (Berkeley: University of California Press, 1998), xiv. Compare Gerard Mussies, "Languages (Greek)," in *Anchor Bible Dictionary,* 4:197.

31. Mussies, "Languages (Greek)," 4:197. Compare Raymond E. Brown, *An Introduction to the New Testament* (New York: Doubleday, 1997), 56.

spread across parts of Palestine well within the reach of Judea,[32] and Jews of that region likewise experienced frequent and persistent contacts through government, trade, and travel with the people and culture of the ruling Hellenistic regimes. The impact of those contacts came to pervade many aspects of life in Jewish Palestine.

Determining the precise degree and nature of the impact of Hellenistic culture on Jewish society remains notoriously difficult and too great for the scope of this discussion. Ancient evidence does, however, confirm that penetration and influence were present and significant.[33] Jewish sources themselves acknowledge the Jewish assimilation and imitation of some Greek cultural models.[34] And this influence is still demonstrably present in Palestine at the time of Jesus and in the composition of New Testament texts.[35] The world in which the books of the New Testament were composed and published was a world overseen by Roman government officials but still bearing the marks of the Hellenistic culture that had ruled that world for almost two hundred years. In view of this, one must ask how the Hellenistic background and context affected the thought and behavior of New Testament authors and actors. It is impossible to answer such questions fully in this setting, but we will look to two areas as *exempla* of the types of influences at work in the text.

---

32. Erich S. Gruen, "Hellenism and Persecution: Antiochus IV and the Jews," in *Hellenistic History and Culture,* ed. Peter Green (Berkeley: University of California Press, 1993), 240–41, figure 38.

33. Since, as Gruen, *Heritage and Hellenism,* xiv, points out, the "prevailing" and, one might add, ruling "culture of the Mediterranean world could hardly be ignored or dismissed." Two views prevail. The first view maintains that Judaism was divided between two groups: the pious Jews, who opposed Greek cultural influence, and the "Hellenizing" Jews, who welcomed and encouraged it. For this view, see Schürer, *History of the Jewish People,* 1:145–46; and Fergus Millar, "Background to the Maccabaean Revolution: Reflections on Martin Hengel's *Judaism and Hellenism," Journal of Jewish Studies* 29–30 (Spring 1978): 1–21. The contrasting view holds that Greek culture encountered no significant opposition within Judaism and that Palestinian Judaism in the Hellenistic age evolved into a notably Hellenized Judaism, not meaningfully different from that of the Diaspora. For this position, see Martin Hengel, *Judaism and Hellenism: Studies in Their Encounter in Palestine during the Early Hellenistic Period,* 2 vols. (Philadelphia: Fortress, 1974), 1:6–106. The reality is probably somewhere between these poles.

34. See, for example, 1 Maccabees 1:9–15. Compare Jonathan Goldstein, "Jewish Acceptance and Rejection of Hellenism," in *Jewish and Christian Self-Definition,* ed. E. P. Sanders, A. I. Baumgarten, and Alan Mendelson, 3 vols. (Philadelphia: Fortress Press, 1981), 2:75.

35. For a summary overview, see Mussies, "Languages (Greek)," 4:202; and Brown, *Introduction to the New Testament,* 83–93.

The Language of the Authors

Since the New Testament survives as written words, we will first consider the linguistic role Hellenistic culture may have played. The conquests of Alexander the Great and the establishment of the Hellenistic kingdoms following his death resulted in the spread of the Koine Greek dialect as the *lingua franca* of the eastern Mediterranean world. Koine represented an amalgamation of major Greek dialects, with simplified grammar and a pronounced connection to the Attic dialect.[36] This conflation of dialects made Koine potentially accessible to native speakers of Greek from a wide range of locations. Similarly, the simplified grammar made the language easier for foreigners to learn.

These are critical considerations when the administration of the territories ruled by the Hellenistic kings depended upon a consistent bureaucratic language, one that could be used and understood at multiple levels of political management. While the native languages of subject lands were being used at the most local level, Koine Greek was indisputably the language of administration at the interface between the official representatives of native populations and the official representatives of the ruling monarch throughout the Hellenistic age.[37] To issue laws and enforce them, to promote commerce and make it secure, to make pleas and voice complaints, in short, to successfully negotiate the relationship between subjects and rulers, Koine Greek was the chosen language for clear communication. An underreported example is that of Jesus standing before Pilate. In none of the Gospels or other reminiscences do we come upon a memory of an interpreter standing between them. Evidently, Jesus knew Greek, as did the educated Pilate.

This has implications for our understanding of the New Testament, both for its composition and for its dissemination. In terms of the scriptural heritage and training of New Testament writers, the Jewish scriptures in which some were fluent seem to have been the Greek translation of the

36. F. Blass, *A Greek Grammar of the New Testament and Other Early Christian Literature,* ed. A. Debrunner and Robert W. Funk, trans. Robert W. Funk (Chicago: University of Chicago, 1961), 1–6. Compare Mussies, "Languages (Greek)," 4:197–98.

37. On the continued use of local native languages, see Susan Sherwin-White, "Seleucid Babylonia: A Case Study for the Installation and Development of Greek Rule," in *Hellenism in the East: The Interaction of Greek and Non-Greek Civilizations from Syria to Central Asia after Alexander*, ed. Amélie Kuhrt and Susan Sherwin-White (London: Gerald Duckworth, 1987), 4–5, 7, 23–25. On the prominence of Greek as the language of government, see Naphtali Lewis, *Greeks in Ptolemaic Egypt: Case Studies in the Social History of the Hellenistic World* (Oxford: Clarendon Press, 1986).

Hebrew Old Testament known as the Septuagint (LXX). According to the so-called *Letter of Aristeas,* King Ptolemy II of Egypt (283–246 BC) ordered the creation of a Greek version of the Jewish scriptures because, among other things, he wanted to do a favor for the freed Jewish slaves in Egypt as well as for the Jews of the Diaspora more broadly.[38] As Mussies points out, this "makes sense only if it reflects a reality in which many if not most Jews outside Palestine could not (or could not sufficiently) read and understand the Hebrew Torah, but spoke and were well versed in Greek."[39] While one cannot confidently extrapolate from Aristeas's assertion that the Jews of the Diaspora (inside and outside of Egypt) were universally better qualified to read Greek than Hebrew in the era of Ptolemy II, it does seem to have been a developing pattern—one established by the lifetime of Jesus. Certainly, several New Testament authors were intimately familiar with the Greek text of the LXX.[40]

Paul's "basic Bible" was the LXX, and when he reminds Timothy of the scriptures Timothy has known from his youth, he seems to be referring to the LXX: "But continue thou in the things which thou hast learned and hast been assured of, knowing of whom thou hast learned them; and that from a child thou hast known the holy scriptures, which are able to make thee wise unto salvation through faith which is in Christ Jesus" (2 Tim. 3:14–15).[41]

Moreover, Luke's citations of Old Testament passages regularly and explicitly recall the language of the LXX. In Jesus' birth narrative, Luke employs formulaic descriptions drawn from passages in Genesis (37:11, "his father observed the saying") and Daniel (4:28, "there came a voice from heaven").[42] Likewise, in Luke's description of the first sermon of Jesus' public ministry, given in the synagogue at Nazareth, he includes a citation of a Jubilee text from Isaiah 61:1–2 and 58:6 that is "so close to [the language] of the LXX that it seems to depend on it and not on an independent translation either from the Hebrew or from a Targum."[43]

38. *Letter of Aristeas* 39. Compare Josephus, *Antiquities of the Jews* 12.2.1, 5. While the *Letter of Aristeas* is almost unquestionably a fictional account, and therefore not a reliable indicator of the king's actual motives for—or even involvement in—the creation of the Septuagint, it does portray the reality that a Greek translation of Hebrew scripture was made in the early Hellenistic period, no doubt because it was needed.

39. Mussies, "Languages (Greek)," 4:197.

40. Compare Melvin K. H. Peters, "Septuagint," in *Anchor Bible Dictionary,* 5:1102.

41. Peters, "Septuagint," 5:1102.

42. Brown, *Introduction to the New Testament,* 234, 268, note 87.

43. See S. H. Ringe, *Jesus, Liberation, and the Biblical Jubilee* (Philadelphia: Fortress, 1985), 38.

Even Matthew, for whom evidence exists that he knew Aramaic or Hebrew or both, demonstrates influence from the LXX, as shown by some of his quotations of Old Testament prophecies. For example, Matthew 4:14–16 includes a citation of Isaiah 9:1–2, which indicates that he drew on the LXX version of the Isaiah passage.[44]

Textual evidence for use of the LXX is also found in Hebrews, 1 Peter, and the Epistle of James.[45] For those authors who did make confident use of the available Greek translation of Hebrew scripture, we may assume that some of the subtleties of Greek grammar and rhetoric mediated their relationship to and understanding of their Jewish faith.

Not only do a number of the New Testament writers demonstrate knowledge of the Greek translation of Jewish scripture, but also the writings of the New Testament books came down to us in Koine Greek. Although most of the authors were born in Judea, it is widely assumed that a number of the texts were original Greek compositions.[46] The choice of language has important implications. In the case of original Greek composition, it indicates that the writers had sufficient facility in Greek for such an undertaking. Paul, for example, exhibits a marked familiarity with basic Hellenistic rhetorical training in his epistolary style.[47] Of the four Evangelists, Luke has the best control of Greek. In his Gospel, specifically in his infancy narrative, he consciously imitates the style of the Septuagint.[48] His writing style in Acts, meanwhile, demonstrates an awareness of the "rhetorical conventions of Greek historians and some knowledge of Greek literature and thought."[49] Although numerous other examples from New Testament texts could be put forward,[50] for the purposes of this abbreviated discussion, it is sufficient to note that the surviving texts of the New Testament provide

---

44. W. D. Davies and Dale C. Allison, *A Critical and Exegetical Commentary on the Gospel according to Saint Matthew,* International Critical Commentary, 3 vols. (Edinburgh: T. & T. Clark, 1988), 1:380–86. Compare Brown, *Introduction to the New Testament,* 36.

45. Brown, *Introduction to the New Testament,* 691 with note 23, 695, 698, 718, 741–42.

46. Brown, *Introduction to the New Testament,* 36.

47. See John L. White, "New Testament Epistolary Literature in the Framework of Ancient Epistolography," in *Aufstieg und Niedergang der Römischen Welt* (New York: Walter de Gruyter, 1984), 2.25.2:1730–56. Compare Brown, *Introduction to the New Testament,* 412–13.

48. Brown, *Introduction to the New Testament,* 268.

49. Brown, *Introduction to the New Testament,* 268. Compare Henry J. Cadbury, *The Style and Literary Method of Luke,* 2 vols. (Cambridge, Mass.: Harvard University Press, 1919).

50. One may, for example, again cite 1 Peter, Hebrews, and the Epistle of James.

evidence of the writers' (or scribes') control of Koine and, in some cases, of advanced Greek rhetorical education. The choice of the Greek language has a further implication: it suggests that the authors of the New Testament books intended and anticipated a widespread dissemination of their texts throughout the Greek-speaking world of the eastern Mediterranean.

Hellenistic Philosophies

A second area where scholars believe they see evidence of Hellenistic influence on the New Testament is in philosophy. The influences are said to range from Plato to Zeno and to influence writers as diverse as John and Paul.[51]

For example, Plato's conception of the world of forms and the insubstantial imitation of it to be found in this world and in the lives of humans likely shaped John's description of Jesus as the one "who has come from above to offer true realities."[52] This does not mean that John was adopting a Platonic viewpoint, but he may have been familiar with Platonic terminology. He conveyed the notion that Jesus comes as the representative figure of a higher reality and, in his coming, reveals that higher reality to men and women and invites them to participate in it.

Epicureanism, a philosophical tradition stemming from Epicurus (342–270 BC) and developed in the Hellenistic Age, indirectly influenced New Testament thought. Epicurus sought to free people from fear and superstition, leaving no need for religion, and he believed that death was final: there was no resurrection from the dead.[53] Epicureans were among Paul's listeners in Athens (Acts 17:18, 32), "and when they heard of the resurrection of the dead, some mocked." For this Christian truth was, according to Paul, "unto the Greeks foolishness" (1 Cor. 1:23). With Epicureans in his audience, Paul may have framed his speech in part to respond to their possible objections.

Stoic philosophy, founded by Zeno of Citium, was "deeply religious and thoroughly moral."[54] According to the Stoic, the universe was guided

---

51. For a summary discussion, see F. F. Bruce, *New Testament History* (New York: Doubleday, 1971), 41–55; C. K. Barrett, ed., *The New Testament Background: Selected Documents,* rev. ed. (London: SPCK, 1987), 58–91; Brown, *Introduction to the New Testament,* 88–93.

52. Brown, *Introduction to the New Testament,* 88.

53. Brown, *Introduction to the New Testament,* 89; Bruce, *New Testament History,* 41–43; Barrett, *New Testament Background,* 78.

54. Barrett, *New Testament Background,* 65.

by a divine reason or purpose (*logos*), which should likewise guide men's lives through the application of moral values and the conquest of the self.[55] Here again scholars see important points of contact: the Stoic terms that center on the supreme *logos,* which they say is the same as Zeus, are very like the terms John brings forward to portray Jesus as the word (*logos*) from the beginning: "Thou, O Zeus, art praised above all gods: many are thy names and thine is all power forever. The beginning of the world was from thee: and with law thou rulest over all things. . . . Nor is anything done upon the earth apart from thee."[56] Here, as elsewhere, John is not equating Jesus to any Stoic notion of divinity, but drawing on descriptive language that may resonate with a Stoic audience and establish Jesus as the supreme governing power.

Paul was addressing Stoics, along with the Epicureans, in Acts 17, and he seems to be "echoing Stoic formulas."[57] When he says, "God that made the world and all things therein, seeing that he is Lord of heaven and earth, . . . seeing he giveth to all life, and breath, and all things; and hath made of one blood all nations of men for to dwell on all the face of the earth" (Acts 17:24–26), he recalls both the language of the Stoic hymn to Zeus cited above and Zeno's conception of the world community (*oikumene*) of which all men are fellow citizens. Paul's observation that "in him we live, and move, and have our being" (Acts 17:28) is an apparent quote from Epimenides's *Cretica.* His reminder to the Athenians that their own poets have said "For we are also his offspring" (Acts 17:28) repeats a view expressed in Aratus's *Phaenomina.* Elsewhere in Paul's writings, he seems to be reforming traditional Stoic and Epicurean maxims.[58]

Even the influence of Cynic philosophers may be found in the texts of the New Testament. Cynics famously engaged in so-called "diatribes," a method of discourse involving rhetorical questions, paradoxes, and other features. Paul's letters are said to demonstrate features of the Cynic diatribe, and Jesus himself is sometimes characterized as a Cynic preacher.[59]

---

55. Barrett, *New Testament Background,* 65–66; Brown, *Introduction to the New Testament,* 90; Bruce, *New Testament History,* 44–49.

56. Barrett, *New Testament Background,* 67, where the Cleanthes *Fragment* is cited.

57. Brown, *Introduction to the New Testament,* 90.

58. Specifically, in 1 Thessalonians 4.

59. On the Cynic diatribe, see Brown, *Introduction to the New Testament,* 89. On Jesus as a Cynic preacher, see F. G. Downing, *Cynics and Christian Origins* (Edinburgh: Clark, 1992).

None of this is to suggest that Christian thought expressed in the New Testament merely developed out of existing Hellenistic philosophies. However, certain early Christian writers were familiar with and conversant in the idiom of their Hellenized milieu, and they successfully employed that idiom in their missionary labors and in their writings to communicate Christ to diverse audiences. Paul knew the possibilities suggested by the Greek-speaking world. He traveled far and wide throughout it, bringing the message of Christ to the Jews of the Diaspora and to the Gentiles among whom they lived. Indeed, one may conclude that the multicultural communities and the use of Koine that resulted from Alexander's conquests made widespread dissemination of the living and written gospel message possible.

Rome and the World of the New Testament

John F. Hall

Roman government in 31 BC came under the control of a single individual, Octavian Caesar, grandnephew of Julius Caesar. Four years later, the Roman senate rewarded him with the title Augustus Caesar for successfully leading Rome through the government transition from republic to empire. Historians suggest that perhaps the most important consequence of this revolution was the establishment of an era of peace and prosperity within the borders of the empire, known as the *pax Augusta* or *pax Romana*. One wrote, "Protected by well-trained and exercised legions along the frontiers, *pax romana*, or the Roman peace, guaranteed that prosperity prevailed within. Travel and communication were facilitated by Roman roads, which connected well-developed urban centers with infrastructures maintained by an efficient government. . . . Christianity developed and expanded under these conditions. Roman government, law, society, religion, and custom influenced the inhabitants of those large portions of Europe, Asia, and Africa over which Rome exercised dominion."[60] It was in this setting of the Roman Empire that Christianity was born, the books of the New Testament were written, and Christianity was spread under the protection of Roman law and government.

During the seven centuries that preceded the age of Augustus, Rome had successfully unified Italy, brought the western Mediterranean under its control with the defeat of the Phoenician empire of Carthage, and expanded eastward, acquiring the territories of the Hellenistic Greek successor kingdoms of Alexander.[61] It was Augustus himself who incorporated the last of these kingdoms, Ptolemaic Egypt, into Rome's empire with the defeat of Cleopatra and his former colleague Antony. Out of this long process came two government innovations constituting the historical background that, if understood, explains adequately the world of the New Testament.

The first of these is the notion that citizenship, with full or partial privileges of Roman law, could be extended to other places and to persons not born in Rome. Never before had any people granted equal privilege under

---

60. John F. Hall, *New Testament Witnesses of Christ* (American Fork, Utah: Covenant Communications, 2002), 37. Also see Ronald Syme, *The Roman Revolution* (Oxford: Clarendon Press, 1939), for the best treatment of the events resulting in the reign of Augustus Caesar.

61. An excellent general survey of Rome's rise to Mediterranean dominion is M. Cary and H. H. Scullard, *A History of Rome Down to the Reign of Constantine*, 3rd ed. (London: Macmillan Press, 1975).

the law to anyone not born in their particular polity. An immigrant might live in a city for fifty years but never be included in the rights held by the native born. The Romans changed this; they were a people who esteemed the law and valued the protection it afforded. Thus they were willing to reward others with grants of citizenship.

> Roman law originated as the rulings and practices of those who acted as officials of both state and religion. Because it derived from the gods, Roman law could extend to all nations as the *ius gentium* (law of nations), which required the guarantee of fair treatment for all men, though Roman citizens exercised higher privileges and received greater prerogatives under that law. However, because Rome had developed into a city when separate peoples merged to become Romans, an innovative concept took form that citizenship was not limited to children born to Roman citizens, but could be extended to whole cities that Rome annexed in Italy, or could be granted even to individuals who by their acts and services merited Roman privileges.[62]

By the time of Christ, most free residents of Italy, many leading citizens of cities in western provinces in Gaul and Spain, and a very small number of provincials from the eastern portion of the empire had received citizenship. Notably in this eastern region—namely, in the city of Tarsus—someone in Paul's immediate family had received citizenship and passed its rights to him. In Judea, citizenship among local residents was very rare.[63] In the cities of the provinces, Roman law pertained to Roman citizens, but local law pertained to local residents. The laws of those subject to noncitizens were recognized by Rome and allowed to be practiced among such local peoples as *ius gentium.* The Sanhedrin derived their right to apply the provisions of the law of Moses to the populace of Judea from this Roman legal doctrine of local law for local residents under the concept of *ius gentium.*[64] The Roman system of provincial administration developed out of this principle of law.

With its initial acquisition of the Carthaginian holdings in Sicily, Sardinia, and Corsica, Rome organized those regions outside of Italy into separate administrative areas known as provinces. The pattern continued as

---

62. Hall, *Witnesses,* 40. The standard study of citizenship in Roman law is A. N. Sherwin-White, *The Roman Citizenship* (Oxford: Clarendon Press, 1939).

63. For estimations of percentage of citizens among the population of various provinces, see John W. Welch and John F. Hall, *Charting the New Testament* (Provo, Utah: Foundation for Ancient Research and Mormon Studies, 2002), chart 6-4.

64. See A. N. Sherwin-White, *Roman Society and Roman Law in the New Testament* (Oxford: Clarendon, 1963); and Alan Watson, *The Spirit of Roman Law* (Athens, Ga.: University of Georgia, 1995).

Rome acquired great expanses of territory and organized many provinces. Only in the eastern reaches of the empire, where local dynasts ruled as client kings loyal to Rome, was administrative practice different.

The most important provinces were governed by former chief officials of Rome, called consuls or praetors. These officials had their authority extended for a period of several years upon the completion of their terms of office in order to govern a province. Other senators or those of equestrian rank governed the less important provinces. The governor was sometimes accompanied by a state financial officer known as the *quaestor* and by personal friends who might serve as informal advisors.

The number of troops assigned to a province might be, as in the case of Judea, as small as a cohort (six hundred men) or two, the number of soldiers that formed an honor guard for Roman officials. However, in the frontier provinces along the Rhine and Danube, many thousands of highly trained legionary soldiers were necessary to prevent barbarian incursion. In the eastern provinces, only Syria—situated directly counter to the Parthian kingdom that filled the territory held today by Iraq and Iran—possessed a significant force of legions (ideally, a legion consisted of six thousand men). Sometimes three, sometimes four legions were stationed in Syria under the command of its high-ranking proconsular governor.[65] By contrast, during its era under direct Roman administration, Judea's governor was a comparatively unimportant equestrian prefect or procurator, with only a ceremonial guard to command.[66] Moreover, while the Roman administrator of Judea was "in some fashion subject to the much-higher-ranking governor of Syria, within Judea he nevertheless exercised full civil and criminal jurisdictional powers."[67]

---

65. The organization of the Roman army and the provinces of assignment for its individual legions are outlined in Welch and Hall, *Charting,* 5-1 through 5-6. Two standard studies on the Roman military are Graham Webster, *The Roman Imperial Army of the First and Second Centuries A.D.* (London: Adam & Charles Black, 1969) and H. M. D. Parker, *The Roman Legions* (London: Oxford University Press, 1928).

66. Although Roman governors began to administer Judea in AD 6 with the title of *praefectus Iudaeae,* by the year 44, after Claudius's regularization of Roman administrative posts for the provinces, the governor of Judea held the slightly higher rank of procurator. John F. Hall, "Procurator," in *Anchor Bible Dictionary,* 5:473–74. A list of Roman administrators of Judea and their ranks and terms of office is provided in Welch and Hall, *Charting,* 4-8. For general discussions on provincial government and organization in eastern parts of the empire, see Fergus Millar, *The Roman Near East, 31 B.C.–A.D. 337* (Cambridge: Harvard University Press, 1993). Also see Welch and Hall, *Charting,* 4-5.

67. John F. Hall, "The Roman Province of Judea: A Historical Overview," in *Masada and the World of the New Testament,* ed. John F. Hall and John W. Welch (Provo, Utah: BYU Studies, 1997), 329.

However, a Roman governor seldom exercised his power in relation to provincials themselves. Rather, his sphere of interest embraced the Roman citizens who might reside in a province. The problems and concerns of locals were delegated to local officials. Just as *ius gentium* allowed the exercise of local law by the provincials and their officials, local officials similarly undertook administration on behalf of local populations. This was a cardinal principle of Roman provincial administration since the organization of the first province and was applied throughout the whole empire, east and west.

> In the first century AD, subject to the emperor's *maius imperium,* or greater authority to countermand the authority of governors, the provincial governor was supreme in his province in all spheres administrative, military, or judicial. However, since the governor was accompanied by a small personal staff, his direct involvement in the day-to-day running of provincial life was very limited. In fact, he usually interposed himself only in matters that involved Roman citizens. Otherwise, the affairs of the cities and towns of provinces and the local populace were directed by local officials to whom the business of government fell. . . . As long as protection was provided for the interests of Rome and any of her citizens who may have had dealings or involvements in the province, little attention was typically apportioned to issues of provincial towns and cities.[68]

A Roman governor's interest in the affairs of a province ensured continued loyalty to Rome, continued timely collection of taxes, and continued unrestricted exercise of rights for Roman citizens. If these interests or Roman control of the province were threatened, the action of a Roman governor was swift and decisive as he interposed himself in provincial matters. Otherwise,

> Roman policy had long adhered to the perspective that local governance was the most convenient provided the status quo be maintained, including the preservation of law and order, the collection of assessed revenues, and the support of Roman foreign policy with the supply of troops when required. Rome's major concerns for the provinces were to maintain a peace in which Roman trade and commerce could be conducted and Romans could come and go in safety. Taxes were collected to support the framework of government, including the army as guardians of internal security and providers of protection from the threats of foreign powers or barbaric enemies without the empire.[69]

68. Hall, *Witnesses,* 42.
69. Hall, "Roman Province of Judea," 321.

The consistency of Roman policies and practices of government throughout all the provinces of its empire provides a cultural context within which New Testament events can be properly understood. Whether events in Judea during the lifetime of the Savior; the activities of Apostles such as Peter and Paul associated with the initial spread of the "good news" of Christianity; or the late-dated actions and teachings of John, the lone surviving apostolic witness, all happened under the same Roman law and the same principles of Roman provincial administration. While many of these events transpired in the several provinces of Asia Minor, in Greece, or in Syria, especially important are Judea and Galilee as the settings of Christ's ministry.

A crucial caveat to correctly understand the historical context of the New Testament is to guard against imaginings of modern popular culture, as expressed in certain historical novels, films, or stage productions, that ignore history and portray Roman involvement where there was none or that offer sensationalist interpretations contrary to the record of legal evidence, historical writing, and the New Testament text itself. It is important to recognize that events before the advent of direct Roman rule, AD 6 in Judea and AD 44 in Galilee,[70] cannot have directly involved Roman administrators or troops. Similarly, in order to correctly understand the events chronicled in the Gospel of John or in Acts where Jewish leaders are held responsible for acting against the Savior and his followers, one must first understand that local officials, whether Herodian rulers or the Sanhedrin, maintained militia and paramilitary law enforcement troops, administered local law, and exercised jurisdiction over local residents who did not possess Roman citizenship.[71] In these, as in other situations, the text must be read in terms of historical context to establish accurate meaning.

The Roman applications of dual legal practices also explain why these same leaders of the Jews were able to stone Stephen under provisions of local law but were prevented by Roman soldiers from doing the same to Paul (see Acts 22:24–29). The local leaders administered the local law for provincials, and the Roman governors or courts administered Roman law for Roman citizens. Additionally, in the first century, Roman law served as a protector not only of the Roman citizen Paul but also of other Christians of Jewish origin outside of Judea. These Christian converts were often the object of persecution from strict Jews who considered them to be apostates

70. Welch and Hall, *Charting,* 4-8 and 4-9.

71. John 18–19; Acts 4; Welch and Hall, *Charting,* 10-1 through 10-12; Hall, *Witnesses,* 75–76, 116.

from Judaism, and, like Stephen, they were liable to death by stoning. Outside of Judea, where local Jewish leaders administered law for provincials, Jewish prosecutors were required to pursue their attacks on Christians in the courts of other provinces, where other local laws prevailed over Roman law.

> It is abundantly clear from Acts that in the first century the persecutors of Christians were not Romans but Jews, the former brethren of so many Christians converted from Judaism. Who does not recall the many times Paul's successful proselyting of local Jewish congregations resulted in angry synagogue leaders demanding action against Paul from town administrators? While it cannot be denied that Paul's status as a natural-born Roman citizen furnished the Apostle great protection, it is also clear that even the non-citizen was accorded certain legal rights under Rome's concept of *ius gentium.*[72]

Because of Roman law, religious tolerance existed throughout the empire in the first century. Indeed, the Romans had been especially tolerant of Jewish religion. Julius Caesar himself "promulgated laws to protect the religious freedom of Jews throughout the empire, extending to the Jews an unprecedented grant of special privileges,"[73] including recognition as a legal religion, exemption from military service, and certain tax exemptions.[74] First- and second-century Christian writings "seem not to indict Rome for killing Christians, but correspond with Roman second-century documents that reveal Rome as something of a protector of Christians."[75]

The world of Rome, clearly delineated along specific administrative guidelines that applied in all the provinces of its empire and founded on the dual principle of Roman law and *ius gentium,* provided an environment conducive to the spread of Christianity in the first century. Accordingly, all legal and governmental proceedings noted in the New Testament must be examined and interpreted in the context of Roman policies.

---

72. Hall, *Witnesses,* 47.

73. Hall, "Roman Province of Judea," 324. See also Hall, *Witnesses,* 45.

74. Louis H. Feldman, *Jew and Gentile in the Ancient World: Attitudes and Interactions from Alexander to Justinian* (Princeton: Princeton University Press, 1993), 92–94.

The Pliny-Trajan correspondence is often cited as evidence of not only second-century but also first-century policy toward the persecution/prosecution of Christians, that specific evidence is required to convict of specific criminal charges. Pliny, *Epistulae* 10.96–97. Also see Harold Mattingly, *Christianity in the Roman Empire* (New York: Norton, 1967), 36–40.

75. Hall, *Witnesses,* 47.

To the Jew and Also to the Gentile

Cultural Contexts for the New Testament

Avram R. Shannon

Eschatology and Apocalypticism

"Unsure" and "unsettled" are words that characterize the time and place of the coming of Jesus Christ. The Roman Empire, which would endure for centuries afterward and whose cultural tradition still affects the world, was a relatively recent phenomenon.[1] The uncertainty of this world affected both Judaism and earliest Christianity, each of which exhibits elements of both eschatological yearning and apocalyptic thinking. Eschatology and apocalypticism are separate but related concepts, and together they represent a substantial thread that runs through much of the New Testament writings and informs how the individual books were received.

Eschatology is the interest in and wait for the end of the world (the term derives from *eschaton,* Greek ἔσχατον, a word that means "end"). Hence, "eschatology" refers to the various ways in which a given religious group understands and anticipates the end of the world. This can take many different forms, including images of destruction of the wicked or a return to a longed-for primeval event. Generally speaking, the more disenfranchised a group feels, the more likely they are to develop eschatological forms of thinking. This can be seen in the early days of the restored Church. Long before the Civil War engulfed the United States, The Church of Jesus Christ of Latter-day Saints was very concerned with eschatology and thought that Jesus Christ's Second Coming was imminent.[2] On the other hand, as the Church in America has become relatively more prosperous and gained

1. Octavian became the first Roman emperor under the name Augustus in 27 BC, between twenty and thirty years before the birth of Jesus.

2. See *Teachings of the Presidents of the Church: Joseph Smith* (Salt Lake City: The Church of Jesus Christ of Latter-day Saints, 2007), 250–59.

acceptance within mainstream society, eschatological feelings have tended to subside, although they have never fully gone away.

"Apocalyptic" properly refers to a specific ancient genre of literature. The name derives from the most famous exemplar of this kind of literature: the Revelation of John, as found in the New Testament.[3] This genre is primarily a Jewish and Christian one, although texts that can be categorized as apocalyptic do appear in other languages and cultures.[4] While the name comes from Revelation, the genre itself appears to be much older; the book of Daniel in the Hebrew Bible is one example of a Jewish apocalypse that was sufficiently early to be included in the Old Testament canon. These texts are often associated with the notion of the current world order being overturned in favor of a divinely appointed order. Groups that are looking for or waiting for that overturn are often characterized as "apocalyptic" or holding to "apocalypticism."[5] There is, therefore, some clear overlap between apocalyptic groups and eschatological groups. Sometimes apocalyptic texts and groups see the overturning of the order as part of an eschatological event, but that is not necessary. Thus there is some overlap between eschatology and apocalypticism, but they are not the same thing.

The Christianity represented in the New Testament is certainly eschatological. Matthew 24 and 25 are explicitly about the "end of the world" (Matt. 24:3).[6] Although the word *eschaton* does not appear in these verses and does not appear in the synoptic Gospels referring to some sort of end-time, it does show up that way in the Gospel of John, where Jesus speaks of "the last day" on numerous occasions (see John 6:39–40, 44, 54; 11:24; 12:48). It is clear from the context of these sermons that the "last

---

3. The Greek word translated as "Revelation" is ἀποκάλυψις (*apokalupsis*). See the excellent overview in John J. Collins, "Apocalypse: An Overview," in *Encyclopedia of Religion,* ed. Lindsay Jones, 2nd ed., 15 vols. (Detroit: Macmillan Reference, 2005), 1:409–14.

4. An example of this would be the "Potter's Oracle," which is a third-century BC Egyptian text foretelling the return of Egypt to native rule and the ousting of the Greek Ptolemies. For a discussion on seeing Lehi and Nephi's visions in the Book of Mormon through an apocalyptic lens, see Jared M. Halverson, "Lehi's Dream and Nephi's Vision as Apocalyptic Literature," in *The Things Which My Father Saw: Approaches to Lehi's Dream and Nephi's Vision,* ed. Daniel L. Belnap, Gaye Strathearn, and Stanley L. Johnson (Provo, Utah: Religious Studies Center; Salt Lake City: Deseret Book, 2011), 53–69.

5. For difficulties with this term, see Robert L. Webb, "'Apocalyptic': Observations on a Slippery Term," *Journal of Ancient Near Eastern Studies* 49, no. 2 (1990): 115–26, esp. 115–17.

6. Greek συντελείας τοῦ αἰῶνος (*sunteleias tou aionos*). The parallel passages in Mark 13 and Luke 21 do not have this phrase, although their content still has eschatological elements. This chapter is important enough for Latter-day Saint self-understanding that Joseph Smith's New Translation of this chapter circulated separately from the rest of the New Translation and was eventually collected in the Pearl of Great Price and canonized.

day" so referenced refers to some kind of end-time event. Even with the specific lack of the word *eschaton,* ancient Christians were very concerned with the end of regular human history and the victory of Jesus Christ over everything.

Orality and Literacy

The world of ancient ritual was one where orality prevailed; indeed, the passing on of ritual regulations and laws was primarily an oral event. There has been a wealth of recent studies on the nature of orality in the ancient world, in both Jewish and non-Jewish contexts.[7] These studies highlight the great fluidity that existed between the written and oral word in the ancient world. According to many early Christian scholars, even texts that quickly became "scripture"—with all the rich associations of writing and tradition connected to scriptures, such as the Gospels—possessed a basic core of oral traditions that circulated through the early Christian movement. Letters, although written for ease of transmission, were read out loud and were thus experienced as oral texts.[8] Speaking generally, in the New Testament world and the early Roman Empire, people heard literary texts, and these oral texts were later written down, codified, and studied. Therefore, there was a strong fluidity between what was oral and what was written in the ancient world.

The texts of early Judaism and Christianity were both part of this oral tradition. Paul Achtemeier suggests that the New Testament, being a product of the broader ancient Mediterranean, came about in a world of "residual orality," even in literary creations.[9] Achtemeier goes on to argue that silent reading to oneself was very rare and something that would arouse great surprise. Although Achtemeier's notion of the rarity of ancient silent reading has been called into question, his observations about the general orality of the ancient world and the fluidity between oral and written are accepted.[10] Catherine Hezser argues that oral communication between

7. John Halverson, "Havelock on Greek Orality and Literacy," *Journal of the History of Ideas* 53, no. 1 (1992): 148–63; Carl J. Couch, "Oral Technologies: A Cornerstone of Ancient Civilizations?," *Sociological Quarterly* 30, no. 4 (1989): 587–602.

8. Catherine Hezser, "Oral and Written Communication and Transmission of Knowledge in Ancient Judaism and Christianity," *Oral Tradition* 25, no. 1 (2010): 75–92.

9. Paul J. Achtemeier, "*Omne Verbum Sonat:* The New Testament and Oral Environment of Late Antiquity," *Journal of Biblical Literature* 109, no. 1 (1990): 3–27.

10. See Frank D. Gilliard, "More Silent Reading in Antiquity: *Non Omne Verbum Sonabat,*" *Journal of Biblical Literature* 112, no. 4 (1993): 689–94. For a history of the controversy and discussion, see William A. Johnson, "Toward a Sociology of Reading in

rabbis was the primary medium for shared information in the tannaitic period because there is no record of written communication between the sages of that time period; she contrasts this with early Christianity's tradition of epistles.[11]

It is common in the modern world of compulsory public education to think in terms of literacy and written transmission rather than oral transmission. In the ancient world, where writing was a professional skill practiced by a limited guild, most information would have been transmitted orally. Although writing remained an arcane skill to most inhabitants during late antiquity, there was a possibility that something written down could be read by someone who was not privy to the technical skills of the ritual practitioner, so secrecy was very common. In addition, ritual information had the added status of being privileged or secret.[12] Even if texts were written down, these kinds of texts often used a purposefully obscure language in order to safeguard their secrets.[13] Today, the nature of preservation bias means that we experience the material we do have from the ancient world through texts even when a given text was once oral.[14]

In addition, although Jewish and Christian scripture in the ancient world was eventually written down, it was primarily experienced orally.[15] Daniel Boyarin has pointed out that even the act of reading was a performance in the ancient world since texts were read out loud in community environments.[16] In Hebrew, the etymological root of the word "to read" (*qara*ʾ) is "to recite, to call aloud."[17] Reading was often a social activity as much as it

---

Classical Antiquity," *American Journal of Philology* 121, no. 4 (2000): 593–627. Johnson argues that in order to properly understand reading and orality in the ancient world, it is important to understand the discursive world that informed that reading.

11. Hezser, "Oral and Written Communication," 81–87; Catherine Hezser, *Jewish Literacy in Roman Palestine* (Tübingen, Ger.: Mohr Siebeck, 2001), 267–75.

12. Albert Henrichs, "'Hieroi Logi' and 'Hierai Bibloi': The (Un)Written Margins of the Sacred in Ancient Greece," *Harvard Studies in Classical Philology* 101 (2003): 239–40.

13. Gregory Nagy, "The Fire Ritual of the Iguvine Tables: Facing a Central Problem in the Study of Ritual Language," *Classical World* 100, no. 2 (2007): 151–58.

14. Henrichs, "'Hieroi Logi' and 'Hierai Bibloi,'" 210–11.

15. On the interplay between the written and the oral, see Elizabeth Shanks Alexander, "The Orality of Rabbinic Writing," in *The Cambridge Companion to the Talmud and Rabbinic Literature,* ed. Charlotte Elisheva Fonrobert and Martin S. Jaffee (Cambridge: Cambridge University Press, 2007), 38–57. On pages 52–53, Alexander notes that this interplay is found across a wide variety of cultural, temporal, and linguistic divides.

16. See Daniel Boyarin, "Placing Reading: Ancient Israel and Medieval Europe," in *The Ethnography of Reading,* ed. Jonathan Boyarin (Berkeley: University of California Press, 1993), 10–37.

17. This is also the root used in Arabic for the Quran.

was an academic one. An example of how this worked out appears in the New Testament. In the Gospel of Luke, Jesus opens his mortal ministry by quoting from the biblical book of Isaiah:

> And he came to Nazareth, where he had been brought up: and, as his custom was, he went into the synagogue on the sabbath day, and stood up for to read. And there was delivered unto him the book of the prophet Esaias. And when he had opened the book, he found the place where it was written, The Spirit of the Lord is upon me, because he hath anointed me to preach the gospel to the poor; he hath sent me to heal the broken-hearted, to preach deliverance to the captives, and recovering of sight to the blind, to set at liberty them that are bruised, To preach the acceptable year of the Lord. And he closed the book, and he gave it again to the minister, and sat down. And the eyes of all them that were in the synagogue were fastened on him. (Luke 4:16–20)

The people in the synagogue in Nazareth were not reading along in their own personal copies of the scriptures. Even among the people who were literate, the cost of producing scriptures by hand meant that personal reading copies would be rare. They were not nonexistent but would have been limited to the elite class. Thus most people encountered the scriptures in the context of shared oral readings, as seen in the above example from Luke. Jesus read the scriptures to the people in the synagogue, but they experienced and processed them orally.[18]

As the early Christians began to spread the good news of Jesus' Resurrection, they also spread his teachings, which circulated orally before they were written down in the Gospels and preserved in the present-day New Testament (see Mark 6:7–12).[19] Scholars have long postulated a source containing Jesus' sayings known as "Q" (from the German *Quelle,* meaning "source") that was utilized by both Luke and Matthew.[20] The discovery of the *Gospel of Thomas* among the texts at Nag Hammadi showed that this kind of sayings collection was, in fact, valued by early Christians. The

18. Hezser, *Jewish Literacy in Roman Palestine*. Hezser posits that the textual and material cultural evidence suggests that Jews around the time of Jesus were, in fact, less literate than their surrounding Greco-Roman neighbors. This has recently been challenged by Michael Owen Wise in *Language and Literacy in Roman Judaea: A Study of the Bar Kokhba Documents* (New Haven, Conn.: Yale University Press, 2015).

19. Birger Gerhardsson, *Memory and Manuscript: Oral Tradition and Written Transmission in Rabbinic Judaism and Early Christianity,* trans. Eric J. Sharpe (Uppsala, Swed.: C. W. K. Gleerup, 1961), 193–336. More recently, see the essays in Henry Wansbrough, ed., *Jesus and the Oral Gospel Tradition* (Sheffield, Eng.: Sheffield Academic Press, 1991).

20. Dale C. Allison Jr., "Biblical Literature: New Testament," in Jones, *Encyclopedia of Religion,* 2:906–7.

original words of Jesus Christ appear to have circulated among early Christians orally and were only later collected and written down.[21] This phenomenon also helps explain the similarities and differences between the Sermon on the Mount, as recorded in Matthew 5–7, and the Sermon on the Plain, as recorded in Luke 6:17–49. The teachings in both sermons are clearly related but deployed in different contexts in the two Gospels. Jesus likely dipped into these same teachings in a number of different contexts,[22] but it is also likely that his important teachings, which the Sermon on the Mount clearly frames, circulated orally among his followers. Hence, one possible solution to differences in the Gospel accounts is oral transmission.

One other element in the discussion of literacy in the ancient world is the presence of multiple languages in the Roman province of Judea. The Holy Land was, in many ways, a corridor for different empires, and each of these empires and societies left cultural and linguistic marks on the land and the people. When Jesus is hung on the cross, Pilate orders that a plaque be put up, inscribed with Hebrew, Greek, and Latin (Luke 23:38; John 19:20). Because this inscription appears to have been intended to be read by random people passing by the Crucifixion site, it gives insight to expectations of basic literacy in ancient Judea. It also gives insight into languages that the Romans expected their Judean subjects to be able to read. The presence of three languages could indicate the expectation that people would be able to read one but not necessarily all the specified languages.

The original language of the Jews was Hebrew. This is the language of the scriptures, but Hebrew also existed as a living language in the New Testament period, as evidenced by texts like the Mishnah and the Bar Kokhba letters.[23] The Jews who returned from Babylon brought back with them the Aramaic language. This language is related to Hebrew, and there was influence on both sides. Mishnaic Hebrew was influenced by Aramaic, and Jewish Aramaic was, in turn, heavily influenced by Hebrew. All of Jesus' recorded statements in the New Testament appear to be Aramaic, suggesting that this was his primary language of communication. There are times when the New Testament authors (especially John) identify a statement as

21. Allison, "Biblical Literature," 919–20.

22. The version of this sermon delivered by the resurrected Jesus at the Nephite temple in Bountiful, as recorded in 3 Nephi in the Book of Mormon, clearly illustrates this. See John W. Welch, *The Sermon at the Temple and the Sermon on the Mount: A Latter-day Saint Approach* (Salt Lake City: Deseret Book; Provo, Utah: Foundation for Ancient Research and Mormon Studies, 1990).

23. Angel Sáenz-Badillos, *A History of the Hebrew Language,* trans. John Elwolde (Cambridge: Cambridge University Press, 1996), 166–71.

Hebrew, which is actually Aramaic, such as John 19:17. This makes it possible that the Hebrew inscription over Jesus' head on the cross could have been written in Aramaic (see Luke 23:38 and John 19:20). However, Jesus lived in a world where Hebrew and Aramaic existed side by side and served as constant influences on one another, so a simple inscription in either language was likely to be readable in the other.[24]

Beyond the Semitic languages were the languages of imperial control. The language of the Roman Empire was Latin, but in the eastern part of the empire, most official empire business was conducted in Greek.[25] It might have been possible to hear Latin at the Antonia Fortress (although there is good evidence that the "Roman" soldiers in Judea were Samaritans or other auxiliaries and thus not Latin speakers)[26] or in the legionary camps after the Jewish revolt. But even there, one could easily find someone who knew some Greek. Latin was obviously the native language of the Roman procurators and prefects who governed the province, but like all upper-class Romans, they would have been tutored in Greek. During the Roman period, Greek (and its attendant cultural associations) was the language of commerce and communication between the various parts of the eastern Roman Empire. This was the language that Paul spoke on his missionary journeys and was the idiom of his epistles. It is likely that some of the other Apostles knew some Greek, and there is even some evidence that Jesus himself knew Greek, as his interview with Pilate seems to indicate.[27] Although the earliest

---

24. More complex inscriptions would require more advanced knowledge, but "Jesus of Nazareth, King of the Jews," would be very similar in both Hebrew and Aramaic.

25. The existence of Greek as a language of commerce, and therefore the existence of a Jewish knowledge of Greek, is not a new argument. See Saul Lieberman, *Greek in Jewish Palestine* (New York: Jewish Theological Seminary of America, 1994), 1–4. For a more recent discussion of this point from the perspective of rabbinics, see also Daniel Sperber, "Rabbinic Knowledge of Greek," in *The Literature of the Sages, Second Part: Midrash and Targum, Liturgy, Poetry, Mysticism, Contracts, Inscriptions, Ancient Science, and the Languages of Rabbinic Literature,* ed. Shmuel Safrai and others (Assen, Neth.: Royal Van Gorcum; Minneapolis, Minn.: Fortress Press, 2006), 627–40.

26. See Emil Schürer, *A History of the Jewish People in the Time of Jesus Christ,* rev. and ed. Geza Vermes and Fergus Millar, 3 vols. (Edinburgh: T. & T. Clark, 1973–87), 1:363–66.

27. It is possible that Jesus spoke through an interpreter, but the Gospel accounts give no indication of this. See the discussion in G. Scott Gleaves, *Did Jesus Speak Greek: The Emerging Evidence of Greek Dominance in First-Century Palestine* (Eugene, Ore.: Pickwick Publications, 2015). In the BYU New Testament Commentary series, see S. Kent Brown, *The Testimony of Luke* (Provo, Utah: BYU Studies, 2015), 26–27, 159, 1055. See also Sáenz-Badillos, *History of the Hebrew Language,* 167–68. It should be noted that if there were any Christian texts written in Hebrew or Aramaic, as Papias famously claimed for the Gospel of Matthew, they have not survived, even in fragments, to the present age.

converts to Christianity would have likely had the strongest background in Aramaic (and, to a lesser extent, Hebrew), Greek carried the day and was the language of missionary work and New Testament writings.

Varieties of Judaism

Judaism was a complex system, or series of systems, during the period immediately preceding and following the rise of Christianity. Some scholars, such as Jacob Neusner, have suggested that instead of saying "Judaism," it is more correct to describe the ancient situation as "Judaisms."[28] Jews living around the time of Jesus Christ divided themselves into various parties or groups (what Josephus, in a probable attempt to make them understandable to his Greek-speaking audience, called "philosophies"), which were essentially independent and different forms of Judaism. The names of some of these parties, such as the Pharisees and the Sadducees, are very familiar to readers of the New Testament. In many cases, their appearance and general description in the New Testament is supported by descriptions and portrayals in other places. Other groups, such as the Essenes or the Therapeutae, are more obscure to the present-day reader. These parties did not seem to affect the authors and editors of the New Testament as directly, so they are not included. Despite their differences, these groups shared enough similar beliefs that New Testament scholar E. P. Sanders postulated the existence of a "common Judaism."[29]

Probably the most important of these Jewish groups for the New Testament and later Judaism is the Pharisees. The name is usually understood as a Greek transliteration of the Hebrew term *perushim,*[30] from a root that indicates separateness.[31] In his *Jewish Antiquities,* the Jewish historian

---

28. See Jacob Neusner, William Scott Green, and Ernest S. Frerichs, eds., *Judaisms and Their Messiahs at the Turn of the Christian Era* (Cambridge: Cambridge University Press, 1988), xi. Against this point, see Daniel Boyarin, "Beyond Judaisms: Meṭaṭron and the Divine Polymorphy of Ancient Judaism," *Journal for the Study of Judaism* 41 (2010): 323–65.

29. This includes the centrality of the law of Moses. See E. P. Sanders, *Jewish Law from Jesus to the Mishnah: Five Studies* (London: SCM Press; Philadelphia: Trinity Press International, 1990), 327–28. For an important corrective against some of Sanders's claims, see the review essay by Martin Hengel and Roland Deines, "E. P. Sanders' 'Common Judaism,' Jesus, and the Pharisees," *Journal of Theological Studies* 46, no. 1 (1995): 1–70.

30. It appears as such in rabbinic literature. See Marcus Jastrow, comp., *A Dictionary of the Targumim, the Talmud Babli and Yerushalmi, and the Midrashic Literature,* 2 vols. (New York: Pardes Publishing House, 1950), 2:1222.

31. On this point, see A. I. Baumgarten, "The Name of the Pharisees," *Journal of Biblical Literature* 102, no. 3 (1983): 411–28. Baumgarten suggests that it should be read instead as *paroshim,* "the specifiers." The Semitic root is the same in either case.

Josephus describes the Pharisees as living an austere life, respecting elders, believing in a doctrine of free will, and believing in the persistence of the soul[32] after death (*Antiquities* 18.1.3). He goes on to suggest that the Pharisees were the most influential among the Jewish people. The Gospels, especially the Gospel of Matthew, paint the Pharisees as being opposed to Jesus. But of all the Jewish parties, the Pharisees appear to have the closest beliefs to the earliest Christians, as may be seen in the conversion of several known Pharisees to nascent Christianity, the most famous of these being Paul.[33] This closeness suggests that some of the recorded difficulties the Pharisees found with Christ were a result of boundary maintenance, or the practice of creating and overemphasizing boundaries that were not part of the actual law of Moses; they focused chiefly on food laws regarding preservation and preparation. In addition to the Pharisees presentation in Josephus's writings and the New Testament, they are generally seen as the intellectual ancestors of the sages of the rabbinic movement, although there were some key differences in practice and scriptural interpretation.[34]

The Sadducees are the second of the Jewish parties that are most familiar to New Testament readers. This is in part because of the role they played in the judicial system of Judea, including the trial and Crucifixion of Jesus.[35] Their name is generally understood as deriving in some way from the Hebrew name Zadok, the high priest in the days of Solomon and the progenitor of the priestly line.[36] Josephus informs his readers that the Sadducees believe in only the law of Moses as it is written and that the soul dies along with the

32. Josephus uses ψυχή (*psychē*) here.

33. Paul calls himself a Pharisee in Philippians 3:5. Nicodemus, who comes to Jesus by night in John 3 and assists Joseph of Arimathea with the preparation of Jesus' body in John 19:39, is identified as a Pharisee in John 3:1. Acts 15:5 suggests that there were enough believers who still identified as Pharisees that they could be identified as a block.

34. This position is well laid out in Shaye J. D. Cohen, "The Significance of Yavneh: Pharisees, the Rabbis, and the End of Jewish Sectarianism," *Hebrew Union College Annual* 55 (1984): 27–53. The connection between the Pharisees and the rabbinic sages has led to unfortunate instances of anti-Semitic sentiment, as the Gospel polemics against the Pharisees are applied first to rabbinic Judaism and then to later Jews.

35. John W. Welch points out that because the Sadducees were likely in control of the Sanhedrin, this means that using rabbinic laws to determine the legality of the trial of Jesus is difficult at best. See John W. Welch, "Latter-day Saint Reflections on the Trial and Death of Jesus," *Clark Memorandum* (Fall 2000): 2–13.

36. For Zadok during the reign of David and Solomon, see 2 Samuel 8:17; 15:24–29; and 1 Kings 1. For his position as the progenitor of the priests who formed an integral part of the eschatological temple, see Ezekiel 43:19; 44:15; 48:10–12.

body.[37] According to Acts 23:5–9, Paul is able to escape a legal judgment by turning the Sadducees in the court against the Pharisees on the topic of the resurrection and the immortality of the soul. Josephus suggests that the Pharisees were the more powerful group, so the Sadducees kept their distinctive opinions to themselves when in formal, elevated positions. (Josephus claims to be a Pharisee himself, and this may have influenced his portrayal of this position.)[38] As portrayed in both Josephus's writings and the New Testament, the Sadducees were largely made up of the priestly elite. The "chief priests," referenced especially in the arrest and trial of Jesus, were likely members of the Sadducean party.

The third group, who Josephus called the Essenes, do not explicitly appear in the New Testament, although some scholars have postulated their connection with early Christianity. After the spectacular discovery of the Dead Sea Scrolls, the community associated with that site has been identified with the Essenes. According to Josephus, Essenes were sufficiently separate from the rest of Judaism because they believed the Jerusalem Temple was spiritually fallen. As a result, they did not take part in the Temple sacrifices, although they would send offerings. According to Josephus, a certain subclass of the Essenes lived in celibate communities apart from other Jews.[39] Like the Essenes, the Qumran community also believed that the Jerusalem Temple was fallen and gathered in separatist communities. The similarities between the Qumran sect and the Essenes described by Josephus point most scholars to the consensus that they are the same group.[40] The Qumran community called themselves the "sons of

---

37. Josephus, *Antiquities* 18.1.4. As strange as this idea could seem to Latter-day Saint readers, this belief is in keeping with the general trend in the Hebrew Bible, especially with the preference the Sadducees gave to the written law of Moses. There are very few verses in our current Old Testament, and almost none in the first five books of the Bible, that can be understood as referring to an afterlife.

38. Josephus, *Life* 10–12. His self-identification has been challenged by scholars. See Steve Mason, *Flavius Josephus on the Pharisees: A Composition-Critical Study* (Leiden, Neth.: Brill, 1991).

39. In his *The Contemplative Life,* Philo of Alexandria describes a group called the Therapeutae. This group also lived in largely celibate communities dedicated to serving God. This has led some to connect Philo's Therapeutae with Josephus's Essenes. Although this is probably a step too far, it is not too much to say that these groups both stemmed from a similar impulse in the Second Temple Jewish mindset.

40. The arguments for this are laid out in Albert Baumgarten, "Who Cares and Why Does It Matter? Qumran and the Essenes, Once Again!," *Dead Sea Discoveries* 11, no. 2 (2004): 174–90. Like most scholarly theories, it is not monolithic. Magen Broshi has recently written a response to Baumgarten's argument, laying out the difficulties

Zadok," suggesting a connection with the Sadducees or at least an appeal to a similar ideology and history.[41] Although the Essenes and the Qumran people do not have the same immediate connection to the New Testament as the Sadducees and the Pharisees, the *War Scroll* from Caves 1 and 4 near the Dead Sea illustrate the apocalyptic and utopian impulse in first-century Judaism, an impulse with strong connections to nascent Christianity.

In addition to the three groups, Josephus mentions the Fourth Philosophy; it is the subject of much debate, not the least because he does not even give it a name, although he does mention the founder. Josephus suggests that, in terms of practices and beliefs, followers of the Fourth Philosophy are in line with the Pharisees. He also suggests that they are revolutionaries who will have no king besides God. The Fourth Philosophy came into prominence during the Jewish revolt of AD 66–70. The Zealots, with whom Jesus' disciple Simon Zelotes was apparently associated, can perhaps be connected to this group.[42] The name "Zealot" comes from the story of Phinehas in Numbers 25, who rescued Israel through a violent attack and was commended for his zeal in verse 11. It is unclear from both Josephus and the New Testament how organized and monolithic the revolutionary impulse and the Fourth Philosophy movement were among the Jews. The lack of large groups of revolutionaries suggests that the movement was not widespread. What is clear from the various sources is that, although Jews did not organize against the Romans, there was an undercurrent of revolutionary teaching and thinking in the Judaism of the early Roman Empire. The presence of an apparent Zealot among Jesus' closest followers suggests that revolutionary ideas were also present in earliest Christianity, although Jesus' own teachings put a very different spin on what was intended by the revolution.

For Latter-day Saints used to thinking in terms of the Restoration and the "only true and living Church" (D&C 1:30), the multiplicity of approaches to

---

with connecting the Essenes with the Qumran Community. See "Essenes at Qumran? A Rejoinder to Albert Baumgarten," *Dead Sea Discoveries* 14, no. 1 (2007): 25–33.

41. Lawrence H. Schiffman, *The Eschatological Community of the Dead Sea Scrolls: A Study of the Rule of the Congregation* (Atlanta: Scholars Press, 1989), 12, 69.

42. He is called Simon the Canaanite in Mark 3:18 and Matthew 10:4. The Greek here is Καναναῖος, which is likely to be read as "Cananean" instead of "Canaanite." This does not, therefore, connect Simon to the ancient nation of the Canaanites, making him a non-Israelite. Instead, the term is to be connected with Hebrew/Aramaic *qana,* which means "to be jealous" or "zealous." This name then becomes a transliteration of the Aramaic equivalent of Zelotes, marking Simon as a part of this group of revolutionaries.

Judaism can seem strange. This is especially true in light of the fact that, although each division within Judaism had diverse ideas about the nature of God and the law, they were broadly united in their Jewish identity and had more in common with one another than they did with the religious systems of non-Jews described in the next section. They were united in their adherence to the law of Moses and the Jerusalem Temple. Jesus' superiority to the Temple and the law of Moses, as laid out in the New Testament, meant that the earliest Christians had an ambiguous relationship with the foundational elements of Judaism, but the fact remains that they still had a relationship with them.

Religious Experience in the Roman Empire

As we look at the world of ancient religion and the New Testament, it is important to note that the term "religion," as applied to that time, suggested far more than one set of beliefs and practices. Within the ancient world, there are a wide variety of activities that scholars have identified as "religion." Many of these activities were part and parcel with the social and political life of those living in the orbit of Roman power. There were mystery cults alongside official civic cults. Magicians and itinerant street philosophers plied their wares to the mixed populace of a Hellenized world. Gods from all over the Mediterranean were worshiped side by side—Isis and Aphrodite, Jupiter and Baalshamin.[43] It was into this world of religious pluralism and practice that the promised Messiah of Judaism came and the New Testament was produced.

In fact, one of the primary features of "religion" within the Roman world was not only its variety but also the fact that this variety took place within a single system. In his very useful introduction to religion in the Roman Empire, James B. Rives notes, "The diversity of religion in the Roman world was not that of separate and distinct 'religions,' each with its own set of core beliefs and principles and its particular scriptures, clergy, shrines, rituals, and customs. . . . [T]he coexistence of religious conceptions and practices that would seem incompatible to people used to the idea of 'a religion' was apparently taken for granted in the Roman Empire."[44] This variety allowed

43. Susanne Erbelding, "Imperium der Götter: Isis—Mithras—Christus. Kulte und Religionen im Römischen Reich," *Antike Welt*, no. 6 (2013): 33–40.

44. James B. Rives, *Religion in the Roman Empire* (Oxford: Blackwell Publishing, 2007), 5.

for a number of different, but related, practices to flourish in the empire, often side by side. Thus an ordinary citizen of the Roman Empire could expect to sacrifice to the local god of the city, to attend a festival in the honor of the divinized emperor, and perhaps to be a member of a mystery cult. None of these things would have been seen as parts of separate religious systems.

Judaism and then Christianity were, in many ways, exceptions to these observations. Because of the injunction against the creation of images and the worship of gods besides the God of Israel in Exodus 20:3–5, Judaism could not and would not fully integrate with non-Jewish religious practice. However, Judaism in the Second Temple period still existed in a Roman world and so shared with the surrounding world their notions of "religion" and ritual practice. Christianity also inherited from Judaism the covenant concern with worshiping false gods. Because it was a missionary religion that drew its new converts from both Jewish and non-Jewish backgrounds, early Christianity used elements or vocabulary from the world in order to make its point, whether in Paul's or Jesus' use of "mystery" or in specific quotations from Greek or Roman poets. Thus, even while rejecting the Greco-Roman plurality of gods and tolerance of practice, Judaism and early Christianity remained part of the ancient religious world.

Although viewed as part of a single spectrum, ancient religion may be thought of in several categories, such as the ancient customary cults, the Roman imperial cult, and the mystery cults. There is a considerable amount of overlap to these categories, but they provide useful spaces for modern thinkers to understand the variety of ancient religious expression. The customary cults were the everyday cults dedicated to the gods worshiped in various cities and communities in the Roman world. The priesthood of these cults was often hereditary and part-time, and the rites and rituals were handed down from time immemorial. The imperial cults represented honors given to reigning and former emperors and were an important part of the social and cultural notions of rulership in especially the Greek east (where most of the New Testament has its formation and context).[45] Mystery cults were special, often secret, ritual associations that

45. For a general overview, see Zsuzsanna Várhelyi, "Imperial Cult, Roman," in *The Oxford Encyclopedia of Ancient Greece and Rome*, ed. Michael Gagarin (Oxford: Oxford University Press, 2010), https://www.oxfordreference.com/display/10.1093/acref/9780195170726.001.0001/acref-9780195170726-e-619. For a discussion of the

promised esoteric doctrines and teachings to their adherents, both in this life and the life to come. One, the Cult of Mithras, was actually a rival to Christianity for members among certain segments of Roman society.[46] We should again underscore that the average citizen in a Roman city would take part in any or all of these over the course of his or her life. This is partly why Judaism and later Christianity were viewed as antisocial and insular by their polytheistic neighbors.[47] They partook of a particularism that simply did not make sense in the Greco-Roman worldview.

The plurality of religious practices in the ancient Roman world points to an important difference in ancient religious thought about how religion is described. We often use words like "faith" or "belief" to describe religion, while the ancient world was much more likely to describe the ritual practices associated with the worship of a given god. Part of this development is visible in the New Testament itself, of course, but much of this comes from later Christian religious discourse. Because of this, when looking at the variety of religious experiences in the ancient world, it is helpful to note that they would have been understood and characterized as experiences. In both Judaism and Roman religion, the primary words used for describing religious practices are words of action and doing—not words associated with faith and belief.

Of the three broad categories in the Greco-Roman religious spectrum, the local cults were the most ancient and were largely assumed as part of the general cultural world.[48] These local cults were the traditional practices associated with the various gods, as understood by their communities. In the eastern part of the Roman Empire, which was often made up of Hellenized cities, the original ancient deities were often understood and referred to by their Greek names and worshiped in a somewhat syncretic fashion. The most famous example of this from the New Testament is Ephesian Artemis, called Diana in the King James Version of Acts 19:24–35.

---

imperial cult in the Greek east, see S. R. F. Price, *Rituals and Power: The Roman Imperial Cult in Asia Minor* (Cambridge: Cambridge University Press, 1984).

46. There is a nice overview in Ramsay MacMullen, *Paganism in the Roman Empire* (New Haven, Conn.: Yale University Press, 1981), 122–27. For a more in-depth introduction, see Manfred Clauss, *The Roman Cult of Mithras: The God and His Mysteries,* trans. Richard Gordon (New York: Routledge, 2001).

47. Peter Schäfer, *Judeophobia: Attitudes toward the Jews in the Ancient World* (Cambridge, Mass.: Harvard University Press, 1998).

48. See Avram Richard Shannon, "Other Peoples' Rituals: Tannaitic Perspectives on Graeco-Roman Ritual" (PhD diss., The Ohio State University, 2015), 297–326.

Greek Artemis was a goddess of the hunt and was considered by her worshipers to be a virgin goddess.[49] In contrast, the Artemis worshiped in Ephesus and the rest of Asia Minor was a mother goddess associated with animals and fertility.[50] The ancients understood these syncretic gods variously as aspects of the same god or goddess or as different gods worshiped under the same name.

As the example of Ephesian Artemis illustrates, the rituals of each cult tended to center on one individual temple and included the idea that the associated deity's power rested within that place. Like the surrounding Greco-Roman world, Judaism had a strong locative element, with the Temple being the center of their world and the place where God himself was said to live. According to the Tanhuma, a late antiquity collection of Jewish Midrashic materials, the land of Israel is the center of the world, Jerusalem is the center of the land of Israel, the Temple is the center of Jerusalem, and the Foundation Stone is the center of the Temple.[51] Although relatively late in regards to the Judaism of the New Testament, there are similar notions of the centrality of Jerusalem and the Jerusalem Temple in the New Testament itself, such as the assertion in Matthew 5:35 that "it is the city of the great King." In ancient Mediterranean religion, place was one of the most important things (see, for example, "the place" in Luke 22:40).[52]

As with Judaism, the worship practices of a local cult could spread, and occasionally, a cult or practice could develop into a Panhellenic cult that was honored and practiced all across the Greek or Roman world. The cult of Apollo and the Oracle at Delphi forms one such example.[53] Apollo was considered by the ancient Greeks to be the god of prophecy, and his priestess at Delphi was able to answer questions for cities and individuals throughout the Greek-speaking world.[54] The influence of this Panhellenic cult was even

---

49. "Homeric Hymn to Aphrodite," 17–19.

50. See the discussion of this goddess's appearance in the New Testament and a picture of a statue of Ephesian Artemis in Richard Neitzel Holtzapfel, Eric D. Huntsman, and Thomas A. Wayment, *Jesus Christ and the World of the New Testament: An Illustrated Reference for Latter-day Saints* (Salt Lake City: Deseret Book, 2006), 169.

51. Tanhuma, *Qedoshim* 10.

52. For more information on this point broadly and an explanation of some difficulties with it, see Jonathan Z. Smith, *To Take Place: Toward Theory in Ritual* (Chicago: University of Chicago Press, 1992). Smith notes that Christianity changes and challenges this notion, making ritual particularly portable. Smith, *To Take Place,* 117.

53. Jon D. Mikalson, *Ancient Greek Religion,* 2nd ed. (Oxford: Wiley-Blackwell, 2010), 92–102.

54. Jennifer Larson, *Ancient Greek Cults: A Guide* (New York: Routledge, 2007), 93–94.

felt in nonofficial capacities. According to Acts, Paul encounters a woman who is able to prophesy. In the King James Version, the girl is "possessed with a spirit of divination" (Acts 16:16). The Greek for "spirit of divination" is *pneuma pythona,* a "Pythian spirit." The girl's ability to prophesy, even in the hostile version, is characterized in the New Testament as being related to Apollos Pythios and the Oracle at Delphi. It should be noted, however, in the case of both the Jerusalem Temple and the worship of Apollo Pythios at Delphi, that even as they spread, these Panhellenic cults remained strongly centered in their associated place. For example, the destruction of the Jerusalem Temple as a center point would have far-reaching effects on how later Judaism and Christianity would develop.[55]

Although still rooted in their place of origin, Panhellenic and local cults began forming more moveable ideologies and practices. This includes Christianity's notion that the believers in Christ became the temple of God. This is seen in 1 Corinthians 3:16–17 and Ephesians 2:21. It achieves what is probably its fullest expression in the apocryphal *Epistle of Barnabas* 16:1–10. There, the physical temple in Jerusalem was rejected in favor of a temple made of redeemed humanity. Judaism, as exemplified by the rabbinic sages, continued to emphasize the Temple even after its destruction and created a system rooted in the memory of a standing temple, even as they moved beyond the Temple's specific institutions and location.[56]

Mystery cults were voluntary associations that claimed to give their initiates special knowledge or a superior position in the afterlife. Sometimes, like the cults of Mithras and Isis, they were adaptations of non-Greek and non-Roman cultic systems.[57] Other mysteries, like the famous Eleusinian Mysteries, were thoroughly Greek in their history and outlook, having grown up on Greek soil.[58] What these systems held in common was a claim to special knowledge that could only be given to those who were ritually

---

55. Titus, the Roman general in charge of the siege of Jerusalem and ultimately responsible for the destruction of the Temple, has sometimes waggishly been called the greatest religious reformer in history because of his profound effects on Judaism and Christianity.

56. Jacob Neusner's formulation of this point has become classic. See Jacob Neusner, "Map without Territory: Mishnah's System of Sacrifice and Sanctuary," *History of Religions* 19, no. 2 (1979): 103–27. More recently, Naftali Cohn has shown the ways in which the sages of the Mishnah explicitly used memory of the Temple and temple rituals to build and validate their authority within and over Judaism. Naftali S. Cohn, *The Memory of the Temple and the Making of the Rabbis* (Philadelphia: University of Pennsylvania, 2013).

57. They appear, however, to be adaptations and not explicit continuities. For example, Clauss argues there is not a strong connection between Persian Mitra and Roman Mithras. See Clauss, *Roman Cult of Mithras,* 3–8.

58. Larson, *Ancient Greek Cults,* 73–76.

prepared. This creates some difficulties for modern students of these cults because this special knowledge was guarded as a secret, and many of those secrets still remain uncovered or unknown.[59] The secret rites inducted people into the presence of the deity who was the mystery's patron. Hence, the New Testament usage of the word "mystery" should probably be understood, at least at some level, in continuity with the broader Greek and Roman usage of the term.

When explaining the parables to his disciples, Jesus Christ tells them, "It is given unto you to know the mysteries of the kingdom of heaven, but to them it is not given" (Matt. 13:11). Here Jesus deploys "mystery" in the sense of some kind of knowledge that is reserved for those who are spiritually in tune (in this case, the disciples). In addition to the Greco-Roman conceptions that feed into the Greek word, there are also likely connections with Jewish and Hebrew or Aramaic usage of the word *raz*, which means "secret" or "mystery." Thus one interpretation of this parable is that some of Jesus' own teachings were not intended for all audiences. It also may have had a connection to knowledge meant to be protected and kept secret and sacred.

For Latter-day Saints, this has strong connections to certain elements of modern temple worship. This is not to say that every time Jesus or the New Testament authors employ the word "mystery" they are specifically alluding to the ceremonies and doctrines practiced in the temples of the Church of Jesus Christ today. However, the idea of truths that are hidden from the world at large because of their importance and sacredness is a notion that resonates with Latter-day Saints today. Many take comfort from Jesus' teachings in the Sermon on the Mount: "Give not that which is holy unto the dogs, neither cast ye your pearls before swine, lest they trample them under their feet, and turn again and rend you" (Matt. 7:6). The ancient world was one where the religious experience was divided between those who knew and those who did not. This is one place where modern Saints find themselves in continuity with the inhabitants of Roman Judea. This is true even when the specific mystery has a different referent in ancient versus modern Christianity, let alone among Judaism, Christianity, and the various polytheistic religions of the ancient world.

At the other end of the spectrum from the ancient "local" cults was the imperial cult, although it is important to remember that we are, even here, still dealing with a spectrum. For example, there was no such thing as the imperial cult as one entity. It was, instead, a series of local honors offered

59. Nagy, "Fire Ritual of the Iguvine Tables," 151–58.

to the emperor and was never centralized or controlled by the emperor.[60] In some ways, this practice was just as strongly local as the local cults discussed above. The local expressions of the imperial cult were viewed and understood as recent innovations and were usually framed as spontaneously arising from a given city's appreciation for the emperor.

Within the Roman world, the primary method of religious expression was sacrifice. This was true in Greco-Roman religions, it was true in native cults in Syria and the Near East, and it was true in Judaism. In the New Testament, the prevalence of sacrifice is presumed, both by the Jerusalem Council (Acts 15:29) and by Paul's specific advice to the Corinthian Saints (1 Cor. 10:16–21). In many ways, one of the goals of the Epistle to the Hebrews is to work through the connection between animal sacrifice in the Jerusalem Temple and Christ's sacrifice. Because sacrifice was so important in both Roman and Jewish ritual practice, it is important for modern readers of the New Testament to allow for the centrality of this ancient practice rather than impose more modern notions of religious expression.

Gender Dynamics

When dealing with the question of gender and gender roles in the world surrounding the New Testament, it is especially important to remember the observation of novelist L. P. Hartley: "The past is a foreign country: they do things differently there."[61] The status of especially women was, in many ways, strongly curtailed in the ancient world. The scriptures themselves are largely written by men from a male point of view and are generally male facing. This can sometimes obscure the female perspective. It would, on the one hand, be a mistake to downplay the importance of figures like Mary, Martha, Mary Magdalene, and Mary, the mother of Jesus, within the scriptural narrative of the New Testament. On the other hand, it would be a disservice to suggest that the prevalence of these particular women somehow covers the fact that the New Testament is largely unconcerned with the female experience. The writings of Paul, in particular, have elements that have been used shamefully in the past to explain or justify the oppression or ill-treatment of women. It is, therefore, especially important when discussing gender roles and women to keep in mind the cultural background informing the New Testament authors and editors in order to allow us to be "more wise" than they had been (see

60. Karl Galinsky, "The Cult of the Roman Emperor: Uniter or Divider?," in *Rome and Religion: A Cross-Disciplinary Dialogue on the Imperial Cult,* ed. Jeffrey Brodd and Jonathan L. Reed (Atlanta: Society of Biblical Literature, 2011), 1–21; Price, *Rituals and Power,* 53.

61. L. P. Hartley, *The Go-Between* (London: Hamish Hamilton, 1953), 9.

Morm. 9:31). Latter-day Saints do not believe that the scriptures are without error,[62] and this can be a place for discussion and improvement.

Generally speaking, women were not property in the Mediterranean world that served as the cradle for Christianity, but there were elements of their lives that were treated as part of property law, especially their reproductive capability.[63] The New Testament is, in many ways, the result of a hybrid Jewish and Greco-Roman world, and so it is helpful to see how these two cultures understood and legislated about women and women's roles. It is also worth noting the ways in which the New Testament is in continuity with those ideas as well as the ways that it rejects them.

Marriage is one way that society expresses notions of gender and gender roles. Michael L. Satlow wrote a book on Jewish marriage in antiquity, drawing mostly on rabbinic evidence with some reference to Second Temple Jewish literature.[64] In regard to the relationship between Jewish and non-Jewish conceptions of marriage and gender, Satlow asserts, "*There is nothing essentially Jewish about 'Jewish' marriage in antiquity.*"[65] He suggests that ancient Jews living in Judea were influenced by Greco-Roman ideas of marriage, especially Stoic ones. These ideas held that marriage was a natural state established by the gods and that a person's primary purpose was to set up a household and have children.[66]

The New Testament seems to continue this idea and contains elements of the appeal to the "natural" and therefore God-given character of marriage, but the text also dismisses the idea of a household as the only ideal. When asked about divorce, Jesus responds by appealing to the story of the creation of Adam and Eve—a story that does not play very much into marriage in the Hebrew Bible but appears extensively in Second Temple sources.[67] In fact, Jesus ends his teachings on marriage with the statement "What . . . God hath joined together, let not man put asunder" (Matt. 19:6). The assumption behind this teaching is that God created marriage with Adam and Eve, and

---

62. On this point, see Jeffrey R. Holland, "My Words . . . Never Cease," *Ensign* 38, no. 5 (May 2008): 91–94; see also the study by Joshua M. Matson in the present volume titled "Instructed in the Way of the Lord."

63. There is an excellent discussion on this point of rabbinic law in Judith Romney Wegner, *Chattel or Person: The Status of Women in the Mishnah* (Oxford: Oxford University Press, 1992).

64. Michael L. Satlow, *Jewish Marriage in Antiquity* (Princeton, N.J.: Princeton University Press, 2001).

65. Satlow, *Jewish Marriage in Antiquity,* xvi, emphasis in original.

66. Satlow, *Jewish Marriage in Antiquity,* 11–13. He contrasts this with the Babylonian perspective, which seems to have seen marriage as being about preserving sexual continence.

67. Satlow, *Jewish Marriage in Antiquity,* 190.

marriage is therefore a "natural" state. On the other hand, Jesus suggests that following him and his order supersedes the household with its attendant domestic responsibilities: "Think not that I am come to send peace on earth: I came not to send peace, but a sword. For I am come to set a man at variance against his father, and the daughter against her mother, and the daughter in law against her mother in law. And a man's foes shall be they of his own household" (Matt. 10:34–36). Jesus is paraphrasing Micah 7:6 here. Jesus' reference to the household is very likely significant in light of the prevailing ideology of marriage being primarily concerned with the establishment of a household, as laid out by Satlow. We see that Jesus allows for his surrounding culture but rejects some of its ideas and ideologies.

The strongest rejection of the ancient notions of gender (and class) in the New Testament is found in Galatians 3:28, where Paul asserts, "There is neither Jew nor Greek, there is neither bond nor free, there is neither male nor female: for ye are all one in Christ Jesus." The breaking down of traditional social orders, including gender roles, is something that is visible in both Paul's and Jesus' teachings. We should note, however, that Ephesians also contains a statement that seems to place women within their traditional marriage role of being subservient: "Wives, submit yourselves unto your own husbands, as unto to the Lord" (Eph. 5:22). This is followed by an explanation comparing the wife to the Church and the husband to Jesus, suggesting that a similar relationship should exist between husbands and wives. The Greek word translated as "submit" does appear in the best manuscripts. This is still a problem, since verse 22 actually has *no* verb, and so something must be added to make sense of the verse. Something like "submit" seems to make the best sense, distasteful as it is to current sensibilities, especially based on the presence of the Greek verb for "submit" in verse 21.

Among the intriguing aspects of gender in the ancient Roman world are questions about family, celibacy, and the nature of man- and womanhood. In keeping with its often eschatological approach, in which the kingdom of God was seen as imminent, the New Testament seems to appeal to a certain kind of celibacy—something that makes Latter-day Saints occasionally uncomfortable. This is, once again, a place to remember to not impose modern notions or expectations on ancient Christians and believers in Jesus. Contrary to how Latter-day Saints sometimes speak, later Christian notions of the importance and glorification of celibacy derive from statements that are presented in the New Testament as we have it.

In Matthew 19:3–9, Jesus was involved in a controversy with the Pharisees over the appropriateness of divorce (according to rabbinic sources, this was a moving concern of the Pharisaic schools in Jesus' day).[68] Jesus very famously says that divorce was not approved by God, and that divorce for any cause is invalid, with the exception of adultery. He does so by appealing to the creation and marriage of Adam and Eve discussed above.

His disciples are amazed by what they perceive as the strictness of Jesus' pronouncement and suggest that it is better for people not to marry at all. Jesus' response is somewhat ambiguous and difficult to understand, a fact that Jesus is aware of, since he prefaces his statement by saying, "All men cannot receive this saying, save they to whom it is given" (Matt. 19:11). He then proceeds to talk about eunuchs, using the Greek word from which the English word derives:[69] "For there are some eunuchs, which were so born from their mother's womb: and there are some eunuchs which were made eunuchs of men: and there be eunuchs, which have made themselves eunuchs for the kingdom of heaven's sake. He that is able to receive it, let him receive it" (Matt. 19:12). The base lexical meaning of this Greek term, as in English, refers to castrated males. Jesus is not, however, necessarily referring to eunuchs in the solely technical sense. In fact, the context of the disciples' questions seems to indicate that marriage could be the topic here, so Jesus may be talking about a voluntary state of celibacy that some adopted for the purpose of the kingdom of heaven, as in modern missionary service.

For Latter-day Saints, some of these teachings are very difficult, especially in light of the revelation about the eternal nature of the marriage covenant. Eternal marriage is one of the distinctive doctrines of the Restoration, and accordingly, Latter-day Saints would like to see eternal marriage in all ages of history. A clear example of this may be seen in the writings of Elder Bruce R. McConkie. For example, speaking of Paul's perspective on marriage, Elder McConkie suggests, "Knowing what he did about the doctrine of celestial marriage and exaltation, it is unthinkable that he would have counseled against marriage, except in some peculiar circumstance. There might be cases today in which individuals should not marry, but it is not the general rule, and the principle of not marrying is not the doctrine of the Church now any more than it was in his day."[70] One of Elder McConkie's assumptions is that Paul knew the same doctrine

68. See *Mishnah Gittin* 9:9–10, in Herbert Danby, *The Mishnah: Translated from the Hebrew with Introduction and Brief Explanatory Notes* (Peabody, Mass.: Hendrickson, 2011), 320–21.

69. Εὐνοῦχοι (*eunouchoi*).

70. Bruce R. McConkie, *Mormon Doctrine,* 2nd ed. (Salt Lake City: Bookcraft, 1966), 120.

of celestial marriage and exaltation as taught in the Church today.[71] This assumption does not necessarily follow. In fact, speaking through Joseph Smith on the ordinances of the temple, God told the Church in 1841, "And verily I say unto you, let this house be built unto my name, that I may reveal mine ordinances therein unto my people; For I deign to reveal unto my church things which have been kept hid from before the foundation of the world, things that pertain to the dispensation of the fulness of times" (D&C 124:40–41). Thus we cannot assume that the ancient New Testament authors fully understood the doctrine of eternal marriage.

As seen above, notions of marriage were different in the ancient world than they are in modern context. It is important for Latter-day Saints to remember that the relatively modern buzzword of "traditional marriage" is not the same as our doctrine of celestial marriage. Joseph Smith's revelations about eternal marriage, and especially plural marriage, flew in the face of ideas of traditional marriage.[72] In many ways this is a reminder to read the scriptures in the manner suggested by Brigham Young—as though we are in the shoes of the ancient authors.[73] This includes not assuming they approached things the same way that we do in the modern age.

Slavery

Slavery is another topic that is distasteful to modern readers, but it was a vital part of how the ancient world existed and understood itself.[74] It even finds expression in the New Testament, as Paul often refers to himself as a "slave" to Jesus Christ. Although English maintains a semantic distinction between "servant" and "slave," the Greek of the New Testament does not do so. It is also useful to note that the most distinctive feature of especially American

71. Elder McConkie was, of course, very influential on a generation of Latter-day Saint thinking. See Kent R. Brooks, "Paul's Inspired Teachings on Marriage," in *Go Ye into All the World: Messages of the New Testament Apostles, 31st Annual Sidney B. Sperry Symposium* (Salt Lake City: Deseret Book, 2002), 75–97. Brooks's article is essentially an articulation of the belief that Paul's teachings on marriage were in harmony with and, in fact, identical to modern teachings of the Church.

72. "Plural Marriage in Kirtland and Nauvoo," Gospel Topics Essays, The Church of Jesus Christ of Latter-day Saints, accessed March 29, 2021, https://www.churchofjesuschrist.org/study/manual/gospel-topics/plural-marriage-in-kirtland-and-nauvoo?lang=eng.

73. John A. Widstoe, comp., *Discourses of Brigham Young* (Salt Lake City: Deseret Book, 1954), 128.

74. For a disturbing but informative discussion of the place that slavery and images of Roman slavery have in the American imagination, see Ricardo Apostol, "Revenge/Porn: *Django Unchained,* Terence's *Eunuchus,* and the Role of Roman Slavery in the American Imagination," *Arion: A Journal of the Humanities and the Classics* 23, no. 1 (2015): 91–114.

slavery—race and skin color—was not part of the ancient conception of slavery.[75] This should especially encourage us to be careful to look at notions within their original social and societal contexts.

As with many things in the ancient world, the situation of slaves in the New Testament is a result of two worlds: a Greco-Roman one, based on the surrounding culture and laws, and a Jewish one, based on interpretations of laws found in the Hebrew Bible. There were similarities in the two legal worlds, such that the types of slavery in both systems more resemble each other than they resemble historical American chattel slavery. There are also clear differences. Understanding the New Testament position on slavery requires acknowledgment of the influence of both these legal worlds. In some ways, the first and most important thing to reiterate on this point is that slavery was legal and expected in both the Roman *and* the Jewish systems. Biblical law (which served as the basis for later Jewish law) presumed the existence of slaves. There was no universal manumission mandated by the law of Moses.[76]

The Hebrew Bible has in-depth laws about the disposition of slaves and outlines rules governing the care and acquisition of slaves. Exodus 21:2–6 is typical:

> If thou buy an Hebrew servant,[77] six years he shall serve: and in the seventh he shall go out free for nothing. If he came in by himself, he shall go out by himself: if he were married, then his wife shall go out with him. If his master have given him a wife, and she have born him sons or daughters; the wife and her children shall be her master's, and he shall go out by himself. And if the servant shall plainly say, I love my master, my wife, and my children; I will not go out free: Then his master shall bring him unto the judges;[78] he shall also bring him to the door, or unto the door post; and his master shall bore his ear through with an awl; and he shall serve him for ever.

This section illustrates a number of important points about ancient slavery, many of which were current in the hybrid Jewish and Roman environment

75. Keith R. Bradley, "Roman Slavery and Roman Law," *Historical Reflections/Réflexions Historique* 15, no. 3 (1988): 477–78.

76. This point would, of course, be used to justify slavery into the early modern period. This serves as an unfortunate reminder of the importance to constantly think about how we read scripture and to recognize that scriptural interpretation matters.

77. Other translations have "slave" here.

78. These are often understood to be the judges, as seen in the KJV of Exodus 21:6. It can also be translated as "God." The Hebrew here is *Elohim*, אלוהים.

that served as the matrix for the New Testament. There are several telling things that can be inferred from this law.

The first is to recognize that Exodus is making a clear distinction between an Israelite slave and a non-Israelite slave. In this section, there is no specific mention of non-Israelite slaves, but the specification of Israelite slaves implies the existence of non-Israelite slaves. The fact that Israelite slaves were set free in the seventh year indicates that non-Israelite slaves had no such protection. Leviticus 25:44–46, speaking on the Sabbatical and Jubilee years, addresses this point specifically:

> Both thy bondmen, and thy bondmaids, which thou shalt have, shall be of the heathen that are round about you; of them shall ye buy bondmen and bondmaids. Moreover of the children of the strangers that do sojourn among you, of them shall ye buy, and of their families that are with you, which they begat in your land: and they shall be your possession. And ye shall take them as an inheritance for your children after you, to inherit them for a possession; they shall be your bondmen for ever: but over your brethren the children of Israel, ye shall not rule one over another with rigour.

Leviticus thus explicitly notes that while Israelites go free in the Sabbatical year (Leviticus actually differs from Exodus in allowing Israelites to be enslaved), non-Israelites do not go free. We note that although the rule for non-Israelite slaves features an imperative in the King James Version, it is in the imperfect tense, which can have, as with the English future tense, an imperative meaning. It does not, however, need to be read that way. It could simply be read as a permissive, forbidding the Israelites to take Israelite slaves but allowing them non-Israelite slaves without expressly approving of the practice. On the other hand, Leviticus 25:46 seems to suggest a favorable perspective on the possession and retention of non-Israelite slaves.

In addition, although the slave himself was able to leave a free man (and this seems to have been a basic right of Israelites or Jews enslaved to other Jews), if a master gave him a wife and she had any children, those children were the property of the master.[79] This indicates, incidentally, that one of the things owned under the law of Moses was a female slave's reproductive abilities.[80]

---

79. It is unclear in the law of Moses whether these child slaves had any right or ability to go free.

80. Paul V. Flesher, *Oxen, Women, or Citizens? Slaves in the System of the Mishnah* (Atlanta: Scholars Press, 1988), 17; see also Wegner, *Chattel or Person,* 19.

The biblical book of Deuteronomy contains a nuance on this idea. In the version of the Ten Commandments preserved in that book, the law of the Sabbath had a different reason given from the version in Exodus:

> Keep the sabbath day to sanctify it, as the Lord thy God hath commanded thee. Six days thou shalt labour, and do all thy work: But the seventh day is the sabbath of the Lord thy God: in it thou shalt not do any work, thou, nor thy son, nor thy daughter, nor thy manservant, nor thy maidservant, nor thine ox, nor thine ass, nor any of thy cattle, nor thy stranger that is within thy gates; that thy manservant and thy maidservant may rest as well as thou. And remember that thou wast a servant in the land of Egypt, and that the Lord thy God brought thee out thence through a mighty hand and by a stretched out arm: therefore the Lord thy God commanded thee to keep the sabbath day. Honour thy father and thy mother, as the Lord thy God hath commanded thee; that thy days may be prolonged, and that it may go well with thee, in the land which the Lord thy God giveth thee. (Deut. 5:12–15)

In this passage, the Lord commanded Israel to not work on the Sabbath, in part to prevent their slaves from working on the Sabbath. Israel was to remember their own status as slaves in the land of Egypt before being rescued by God.

In all these discussions, part of the difficulty is understanding which statements have legal weight and which are primarily intended as ideological statements. A similar difficulty exists in discussing Roman slavery.[81] Under the Roman system, a person could become a slave by being born to a female slave or by being captured in war. Those who held Roman citizenship could also sell themselves or their children into slavery.[82] One of the features that characterized Roman cultural and legal engagement with slavery was fear of both individual and generalized slave rebellion. The historical fact of various slave rebellions, including the famous Spartacus rebellion of 73–71 BC, fueled this fear. Tacitus speaks of an example wherein a slave murdered his master, and all the master's slaves were crucified according to the law. There was some discussion of this in the Senate, but the majority voted to uphold the law, since it was the only way to be safe from the large Roman slave population.[83] The ideology about Roman slavery was

81. Bradley, "Roman Slavery and Roman Law," 482.

82. *Digest* 1.5.1, quoted in Bradley, "Roman Slavery and Roman Law," 482. Note the similarity with the Israelite law in that slave status is acquired from the mother.

83. This incident is discussed in Keith Hopkins, "Novel Evidence for Roman Slavery," *Past and Present*, no. 138 (1993): 3–27.

predicated on these notions of fear and the distrust of slaves.[84] It is in this context that the New Testament position on slaves and slavery needs to be understood.

As with women, the New Testament position on slaves is a result of Christian revolutionary teachings coupled with support and reification of the existing social order. Ephesians contains what is probably the most complete example of this:

> Servants, be obedient to them that are your masters according to the flesh, with fear and trembling, in singleness of your heart, as unto Christ; Not with eyeservice, as menpleasers; but as the servants of Christ, doing the will of God[85] from the heart; With good will doing service, as to the Lord, and not to men: Knowing that whatsoever good thing any man doeth, the same shall he receive of the Lord, whether he be bond or free. And, ye masters, do the same things unto them, forbearing threatening: knowing that your Master also is in heaven; neither is there respect of persons with him. (Eph. 6:5–9)

Christianity, therefore, represents an attempt to strike a middle road between its message of universal freedom for humanity through Jesus Christ and the recognition of the realities of living within in a world where slaveholding was common and expected. Ephesians attempts to put the regular social order in the terms of humanity's relationship to God and his demand that all human interactions be suffused with goodwill.

Although slavery remains unacceptable today, it was a fact of life in the world of the New Testament, being a feature of both Roman and Jewish law. Although biblical law assumed a world without the fear of slave rebellions that featured prominently in the Roman sources, it still assumed slavery. The New Testament authors deal with slavery in ways that were revolutionary in their spreading of the gospel message of salvation to both slaves and masters, but they do not condemn slavery as an institution. Given the charged political nature of slavery and the distrust of the Christian system, this was likely good sense because it allowed for the spread of the Christian message free from accusations of fomenting slave rebellion.

The experience of the primitive Church and the delicacy involved in navigating social expectation are mirrored by the experience of the restored Church. Antebellum America, which served as the matrix for the Restoration, was, of course, highly racialized, as well as a country where slavery was largely legal and heavily debated. Like early Christian discourse,

84. Hopkins, "Novel Evidence for Roman Slavery," 5.

85. This is the same Greek word *kyrios* translated as "masters" in the first sentence.

Latter-day Saint discourse about slavery was at once coming from its surrounding culture and its opposing scripture.[86] The Book of Mormon contains the bold statement that "[the Lord] inviteth them all to come unto him and partake of his goodness; and he denieth none that come unto him, black and white, bond and free, male and female; and he remembereth the heathen; and all are alike unto God, both Jew and Gentile" (2 Ne. 26:33). This statement, along with others, illustrates the ideological background of the earliest Latter-day Saint experiences with notions of race and color.

Conclusion

Nephi reminds us that the Lord speaks to people "according to their language, unto their understanding" (2 Ne. 31:3). This process of speaking according to the understanding of the people is evident in the New Testament. The authors and audiences of the various New Testament books were part of their cultural world, even as they sought to transcend it through the gospel and teachings of Jesus Christ. Understanding the contexts in which the New Testament authors and their audiences lived can help us to better understand the New Testament and further apply its teachings to our lives.

86. See W. Paul Reeve, *Religion of a Different Color: Race and the Mormon Struggle for Whiteness* (Oxford: Oxford University Press, 2015).

New Testament Authorship

John Gee

Authorship in the ancient world implies authors. Someone had to write a work. Here we will look at what is known about the authors of the New Testament in light of the ancient processes of authorship. Many ancient authors did not attach their names to their written works. Letters were an exception to this practice. Most ancient letters give the name of the sender and the recipient, as it was necessary for the messenger to identify the recipient and for the recipient to know who the message was from. Hebrews and 1 John are the only letters that do not follow this pattern. Most of the New Testament is comprised of letters.

Composition

Documents in the ancient world were authored in a number of ways.[1] Some, such as letters, were usually dictated to scribes. The scribe might append a note to the document: "I wrote it on his behalf since he did not know letters."[2] "I wrote on his behalf, being requested to because of his cumbersome writing although he wrote his name."[3] The Epistle to the Romans was written this way: "I, Tertius, who wrote this letter, greet you in the Lord."[4] Letters could also be written by individuals: "A copy of this document was

1. For this discussion, I have cited papyri by their standard papyrological abbreviations. John F. Oates and William H. Willis, eds., "Checklist of Editions of Greek, Latin, Demotic, and Coptic Papyri, Ostraca, and Tables," Papyri.info, accessed November 1, 2023, https://papyri.info/docs/checklist.

2. Analpap. 30.41 15 (AD 103): ἔγραψα̣ ὑπ(ὲρ) αὐτοῦ μὴ εἰ̣δ(ότος) γρ̣[ά(μματα)]. Compare BASP 53.95.1 21 (20 BC); BGU 1.189 12–14 (AD 7); BGU 2.636 31–33 (AD 20); P. Hamb. 3.218 23 (AD 29–30); BGU 1.190 15–16 (AD 81–96); BGU 1.183 30–33, 46–47 (AD 85); BGU 2.526 36–41 (AD 86); BGU 1.350 23–24 (AD 98–117); BGU 2.538 35–36 (AD 100); AfP 61.328.3 6–8 (AD 102); BGU 2.600 7–8 (AD 120–140); BGU 1.87 32 (AD 144).

3. BGU 1.69 19–21 (AD 120): ἔ[γ]ραψα ὑπὲρ α[ὐ]τοῦ ἐρωτηθὶς(*) διὰ τὸ βρα[δ]ύτερα(*) αὐτὸν γράφιν(*) αὐτο γράφοντος [τὸ ὄ]νομα(*). Compare BGU 2.543 16–17 (27 BC).

4. Rom. 16:22. All translations are author's own.

written by me. . . . I wrote most of it."[5] Some of Paul's letters were written by him: "I, Paul, wrote this with my own hand."[6] "You see what a long letter I have written to you with my own hand."[7] To others he appended a note in his own hand: "The greeting of Paul by my own hand."[8] Letters were sent via messengers: "I have written you another letter. . . . My brother, I sent Isidore for this reason."[9] Many of the New Testament writings follow the same pattern.[10] Other writings were taken from lectures in shorthand by stenographers, transcribed, and then edited.[11] Various writings, such as letters, were gathered into collections.[12]

Writing books was usually farmed out to professional scribes: "Send to us about the scrolls that you have finished."[13] Collections of texts were stored (for example, "the books of the registers in the library in Patrikos"[14]) and might be copied there (for example, "likewise, the copies to the library of the places as I ordered"[15]) or sent out ("Because Serapion will have the scribal office, which he previously had, on behalf of which I previously written, you did well to deliver to him promptly the books of the registers"[16]). Books were often loaned out: "I have returned the box and the books through Heraklates as you wrote."[17]

While most preserved letters are between individuals, letters to groups of individuals have also survived. In cases of letters addressed to groups, the

---

5. BGU 1.300 12–14 (AD 148): τ[ὸ] χειρόγραφον τοῦτο δισσὸν γραφὲν ὑπ' ἐμοῦ . . . ἔγραψα τὰ πλ[εῖσ]τα.

6. Philem. 1:19.

7. Gal. 6:11.

8. 1 Cor. 16:21; see also Col. 4:18 and 2 Thes. 3:17.

9. BGU 1.249 3–6 (AD 75–76): καὶ δι' ἑτ[έρας ἐπι]στολῆς ἔγραψά σοι, . . . ἄδελφέ μου, Ἰσίδωρον ἔπεμψα τούτου εἵνε[κα]. Compare BGU 2.595 11–13 (AD 70–80).

10. Eph. 6:21–22; Col. 4:7–9; Titus 3:12–13; 1 Pet. 5:12.

11. Lincoln H. Blumell, with T. W. Mackay and Gregg Schwendner, eds., *Didymus the Blind's Commentary on Psalms 26:10–29:2 and 36:1–3 (P. BYU I)* (Turnhout, Belg.: Brepols, 2019), 12–14.

12. Pliny, *Epistles* 1.1.1.

13. P.Oxy. 2.296 6–7: πέμψον ἡμεῖν περὶ τῶν βιβλίον ἧ ἐξήρτισας.

14. BGU 3.981 9–10 (AD 79): [τ]ὴν [ἐ]μ(*) Πατρικοῖς βιβλιοθήκ(ην) [τὰ τῆς τάξεως] βιβλία.

15. BGU 3.981 10–11: ὁμ[ο]ίως δὲ καὶ εἰς τὴν ἐπὶ τόπων [βιβλιοθήκην] τὰ ἀντίγραφα ὡς ἐκελεύσθη.

16. BGU 4.1096 2–8 (AD 38): ἐπεὶ Σαραπίων[α] ἔσχον γραμματέα, ὃν πρότερον εἶχον, ὑπὲρ οὗ [κ]αὶ ἄλλοτέ σοι ἔγραψα, εὖ ποιήσεις παραδοὺς αὐτῷτὰ τῆς τάξεως βυβλία ἐξαυτῆς.

17. P.Oxy. 8.1153 3–4 (AD 1–99): [ἐ]κομισάμην διὰ Ἡρακλᾶτος τὰς κίστας, [σὺν] τοῖς βιβλίοις, ὡς γράφεις.

author identified himself by his title and office.[18] In contrast, letters to individuals only exceptionally identified the author's title.[19] If anything, letters were liable to identify the individual to whom they are directed rather than the individual who sent them. New Testament letters conform to this pattern.

Most letters that survive from the ancient world are not forgeries. The question is whether any of the New Testament books are forgeries—that is, books that were not actually written by the authors to whom they were attributed. Most of the debate over the authorship of books in the New Testament seems to have started in the late second century.[20]

We should look at authorship disputes in the history of the first centuries of Christianity. At the end of the first century, the church was suffering from a leadership crisis when the young (νέοι, *neoi*), ambitious (ζ-λος, *zēlos*), and foolish (ἄφρονες, *aphrones*) were stirred up (ἐπηγέρθησαν, *epēgerthēsan*) to rebellion (στάσις, *stasis*) against the honored (ἐνδόξους, *endoxous*) and wise (φρονίσμους, *phronismous*) leaders of the church[21] because they wanted to be in charge (φιλοπρωτεύων, *philoprōteuōn*).[22] They anonymously turned over the church leaders to the Romans for execution[23] and refused to be governed by church leaders in a supervisory capacity.[24]

At the beginning of the second century, the church struggled with those who said that Jesus did not actually suffer.[25] In addition, the existence of those who would only believe something in writing[26] made certain leaders reluctant to pass on oral traditions.[27] Thus, in the second century, there was a widespread fabrication of that oral tradition, with writings claiming to be the secrets that Jesus gave to his apostles after his Resurrection.[28] While

18. P.Lond. 6.1912; P.Gen. 2.1.10; P.Oxy. 42.3020; P.Vind.Worp 12.

19. For an exception, see P.Soter. 28.

20. Edmon L. Gallagher and John D. Meade, *The Biblical Canon Lists from Early Christianity: Texts and Analysis* (Oxford: Oxford University Press, 2017), 41–44.

21. 1 Clement 3:2–3; Ignatius, *Epistle to the Magnesians* 3:1.

22. 3 John 1:9. Compare Irenaeus, *Against Heresies* 1.28.1.

23. Pliny, *Epistles* 10.96.5; Ignatius, *Epistle to the Ephesians* 1:2; 12:1; 21:2; Ignatius, *Epistle to the Trallians* 10:1; Ignatius, *Epistle to the Romans* 1:1; 4:1–5:3; 7:1–2; Ignatius, *Epistle to the Smyrnaeans* 4:2; 11:1; Eusebius, *History of the Church* 3.19–20, 3.32.

24. 3 John 1:9; Ignatius, *Epistle to the Ephesians* 3:1–4:2; 7:1; 9:1; Ignatius, *Epistle to the Magnesians* 2:1; 6:1; 13:2; Ignatius, *Epistle to the Trallians* 2:1–2; 3:1; 7:1; 13:2; Ignatius, *Epistle to the Philadelphians* 7:1–2; Ignatius, *Epistle to the Smyrnaeans* 8:1–2.

25. Ignatius, *Epistle to the Trallians* 10:1; Ignatius, *Epistle to the Smyrnaeans* 1:1–3:3.

26. Ignatius, *Epistle to the Philadelphians* 8:2.

27. Ignatius, *Epistle to the Trallians* 5:1–2.

28. *Apocryphon of John*; *Sophia Jesu Christi*; *1 Jeu*; *2 Jeu*; *Pistis Sophia*. See also John Gee, "The Apocryphal Acts of Jesus," *Interpreter: A Journal of Latter-day Saint Faith and Scholarship* 2 (2012): 182–86.

the practice of citing revelation was used in the second century,[29] by the third century, it had largely disappeared.[30] Starting in the second century, there were also numerous forgeries created[31] to fill the community's desire for instructions in writing, particularly about the founding generation of the church. During the second century, there were also widespread accusations that various Christian groups altered the text of their scriptures.[32] The presence of forgeries set the stage for questioning the authorship of older scriptural texts, which began in the third century. For example, Tertullian claimed that Hebrews was written by Barnabas and considered the *Shepherd of Hermas* to be a forgery,[33] although it was quite popular in the early church.[34] In the fourth century, Eusebius questioned the authorship of Hebrews[35] and Revelation[36] and the authenticity of James, 2 Peter, 2 John, 3 John, and Jude.[37] (The authenticity of these was not questioned in earlier times.) He also questioned the authenticity of *2 Clement* and other works attributed to Clement.[38]

In the fourth century, after so many accusations of forged books, writers like Eusebius used the citation of works by the earlier Christians as an indication of authenticity.[39] This approach has much to commend it but puts certain books at a disadvantage. Smaller works are less likely to be cited than larger works, if for no other reason than that there is less to cite. There are, in fact, fewer citations of the smaller books among the early Christian authors. It was also easier to forge a smaller book. It is thus unsurprising that most of the books whose authenticity was disputed by Eusebius and others in the fourth century are shorter in length. The reason

29. *Shepherd of Hermas* 1:2.

30. Tertullian, *On Modesty* 21–22.

31. Tertullian, *On Baptism* 17.

32. Justin Martyr, *Dialogue with Trypho* 73; Irenaeus, *Against Heresies* 1.8.1; 1.27.2, 4; 3.2.1; 5.30.1; Tertullian, *Against Marcion* 4.2; Tertullian, *On Baptism* 1.17; Tertullian, *Prescription against Heresies* 17, 18, 38; John Gee, "The Corruption of Scripture in Early Christianity," in *Early Christians in Disarray: Contemporary LDS Perspectives on the Christian Apostasty,* ed. Noel B. Reynolds (Provo, Utah: Foundation for Ancient Research and Mormon Studies, 2005), 165–72.

33. Tertullian, *On Modesty* 20.

34. P.Mich. 1.30; P.Oxy. 1.5; 3.404; 9.1172; 13.1599; 15.1783; 15.1828; 50.3526; 50.3527; 50.3528; 69.4705; 69.4706; 69.4707, all second through fourth century.

35. Eusebius, *History of the Church* 3.38.

36. Eusebius, *History of the Church* 3.39; but see 3.25.4.

37. Eusebius, *History of the Church* 3.25.

38. Eusebius, *History of the Church* 3.38.

39. Eusebius, *History of the Church* 3.3.

that Eusebius doubted the authenticity of James and Jude is because they were not quoted much by early authors.[40]

The earliest preserved collections of New Testament books are Chester Beatty Papyrus I ($\mathfrak{P}^{45}$) and II ($\mathfrak{P}^{46}$), both dating to AD 200–250, only about 150 years after the books of the New Testament were written. By the second century, a number of scriptural forgeries, such as the *Gospel of the Hebrews,*[41] the *Gospel of Peter,*[42] and the *Gospel of Judas,* were already said to be circulating. So those who collected the various New Testament books into collections seem to have had forgeries available to include if they wished to, but they apparently chose not to, showing some discrimination between genuine and forged documents in the selection process. The ancient manuscript tradition preserves attributions of the various books, and these attributions are consistent. This observation is important in establishing the authorship of these texts.

Evidence for the Authorship of Individual New Testament Books

The earliest evidence for authorship of the various New Testament books can be summarized as follows:

Matthew

Earliest quotation as authoritative scripture: mid-first century (*Didache*).[43]

Earliest identification of author: In the second century, Papias said that Matthew wrote a Gospel in Hebrew.[44] As a tax collector, Matthew would have had to be literate in Greek, and the translation would have taken place before the mid-first century. At the end of the second century, Irenaeus attributed the Gospel to Matthew.[45] The manuscripts identify the author of this work as Matthew as early as the fourth century.[46]

By the beginning of the second century, it was the most frequently quoted book from the New Testament.[47]

---

40. Eusebius, *History of the Church* 2.23.

41. Eusebius, *History of the Church* 3.25, 27.

42. P.Oxy. 60.4009 (second century AD). See also Thomas A. Wayment, *The Text of the New Testament Apocrypha (100–400 CE)* (New York: Bloomsbury, 2013), 49.

43. Matt. 6:9–13, quoted in *Didache* 8:2; Matt. 7:6, quoted in *Didache* 9:5.

44. Papias, fragment 6; Eusebius, *History of the Church* 3.39.16.

45. Irenaeus, *Against Heresies* 3.1.1; Eusebius, *History of the Church* 5.8.2.

46. Codex Sinaiticus, running header, Q74-f.1r through Q76-f.2r.

47. Ignatius, *Epistle to the Ephesians* 14:2; 17:1; 19:2; Ignatius, *Epistle to the Magnesians* 9:3; Ignatius, *Epistle to the Trallians* 11:1; Ignatius, *Epistle to the Romans* 6:1; Ignatius,

Mark

Earliest quotation as authoritative scripture: beginning of the second century (Clement).[48]

Earliest identification of author: In the second century, Papias said that Mark wrote a Gospel based on Peter's preaching.[49] At the end of the second century, Irenaeus attributed the Gospel to Mark.[50] The manuscripts identify the author of this work as Mark as early as the fourth century.[51]

Luke

Earliest quotation as authoritative scripture: beginning of the second century (Clement, Polycarp).[52]

Earliest identification of author: At the end of the second century, Irenaeus attributed the Gospel to Luke.[53] The manuscripts identify the author of this work as Luke as early as the fourth century.[54]

John

Earliest quotation as authoritative scripture: beginning of the second century (Ignatius).[55]

Earliest identification of author: At the end of the second century, Irenaeus attributed the Gospel to John.[56] The manuscripts identify the author of this work as John as early as the third century.[57]

Epistle to the Philadelphians 3:1; Ignatius, *Epistle to the Smyrnaeans* 1:1; 6:1; Ignatius, *Epistle to Polycarp* 1:3; 2:2; 3:2; *1 Clement* 13:2; 46:8; Polycarp, *Epistle to the Philippians* 2:3; 7:2; *Barnabas* 4:14; 5:9; 7:3; 12:10; *2 Clement* 2:4; 4:2; 6:2; 9:11.

48. Mark 9:42, quoted in *1 Clement* 46:8; Andreas Lindemann, "The Apostolic Fathers and the Synoptic Problem," in *New Studies in the Synoptic Problem: Oxford Conference April 2008; Essays in Honour of Christopher M. Tuckett,* ed. P. Foster and others (Leuven, Belg.: Uitgeverij Peeters, 2011), 693–94.

49. Papias, fragment 6; Eusebius, *History of the Church* 3.39.14–15.

50. Irenaeus, *Against Heresies* 3.1.1; Eusebius, *History of the Church* 5.8.3.

51. Codex Sinaiticus, running header, Q76.f2v through Q77-f.5r, plus colophon: ευαγγελλι ο ν κατα μαρκ ο ν.

52. Luke 6:31, 37–38, quoted in *1 Clement* 13:2. Luke 6:37, 20, quoted in Polycarp, *Epistle to the Philippians* 2:3.

53. Irenaeus, *Against Heresies* 3.1.1; Eusebius, *History of the Church* 5.8.3.

54. Codex Sinaiticus, running header, Q77-f.5r through Q79-f.7v, plus colophon: ε υαγγ ε λλι ο ν κατα λ ο υκαν.

55. John 3:8, quoted in Ignatius, *Epistle to the Philadelphians* 7:1.

56. Irenaeus, *Against Heresies* 3.1.1; 3.22.5; Eusebius, *History of the Church* 3.23.3; 5.8.4.

57. P.Bodm. II, XIV, XV; See also Codex Sinaiticus, running header, Q80-f.1r through Q81-f.6r, plus colophon: ευαγγ ε λλι ο ν κατα ιωαννην.

Acts

Earliest quotation as authoritative scripture: beginning of the second century (Polycarp).[58]

Earliest identification of author: By the end of the second century, Luke is clearly indicated as the author of Acts.[59]

Romans

Earliest quotation as authoritative scripture: beginning of the second century (Ignatius).[60]

Earliest identification of author: At the beginning of the third century, Tertullian attributed this epistle to Paul.[61] The manuscripts identify the author of this work as Paul as early as the fourth century.[62]

1 Corinthians

Earliest quotation as authoritative scripture: beginning of the second century (Ignatius, Clement, Polycarp).[63]

Earliest identification of author: At the beginning of the third century, Tertullian attributed this epistle to Paul.[64] The manuscripts identify the author of this work as Paul as early as the third century.[65]

A further note: At the beginning of the second century, the First Epistle to the Corinthians cited as authoritative scripture was the second most popular book in the New Testament.[66]

---

58. Acts 2:24, quoted in Polycarp, *Epistle to the Philippians* 1:2.

59. Irenaeus, *Against Heresies* 3.14.1.

60. Rom. 1:3, quoted in Ignatius, *Epistle to the Smyrnaeans* 1:1; Rom. 9:5, quoted in *1 Clement* 32:2; Rom. 1:32, quoted in *1 Clement* 35:5; Rom. 12:17, quoted in Polycarp, *Epistle to the Philippians* 6:2.

61. Tertullian, *Against Marcion* 5.13–14.

62. Codex Sinaiticus, Q82-f.1r.

63. 1 Cor. 6:9–10, quoted in Ignatius, *Epistle to the Ephesians* 16:1; 1 Cor. 1:18, 20, quoted in Ignatius, *Epistle to the Ephesians* 18:1; 1 Cor. 4:4, quoted in Ignatius, *Epistle to the Romans* 5:1; 1 Cor. 15:8–9, quoted in Ignatius, *Epistle to the Romans* 9:2; 1 Cor. 2:9, quoted in *1 Clement* 34:8; 1 Cor. 6:9–10, quoted in Polycarp, *Epistle to the Philippians* 5:3.

64. Tertullian, *Against Marcion* 5.5–10.

65. P.Panop.Beatty II f.38v. See also Codex Sinaiticus, Q82-f.7v.

66. Ignatius, *Epistle to the Ephesians* 16:1; 18:1; Ignatius, *Epistle to the Trallians* 12:3; Ignatius, *Epistle to the Romans* 4:3; 5:1; 9:2; Ignatius, *Epistle to the Philadelphians* 3:3; *1 Clement* 34:8; 37:5; 47:3; 49:5; Polycarp, *Epistle to the Philippians* 5:3; 9:2; *2 Clement* 9:7; *Epistle to Diognetus* 5:15.

2 Corinthians

Earliest quotation as authoritative scripture: beginning of the second century (Polycarp).[67]

Earliest identification of author: Tertullian identified the author of this epistle as Paul at the beginning of the third century.[68] The manuscripts identify the author of this work as Paul as early as the third century.[69]

Galatians

Earliest quotation as authoritative scripture: beginning of the second century (Polycarp).[70]

Earliest identification of author: At the beginning of the third century, Tertullian identified the author of this epistle as Paul.[71] The manuscripts identify the author of this work as Paul as early as the third century.[72]

Ephesians

Earliest quotation as authoritative scripture: beginning of the second century (Polycarp).[73]

Earliest identification of author: Tertullian attributed this epistle to Paul at the beginning of the third century.[74] The manuscripts identify the author of this work as Paul as early as the third century.[75]

Philippians

Earliest quotation as authoritative scripture: beginning of the second century (Polycarp).[76]

---

67. 2 Cor. 8:21, quoted in Polycarp, *Epistle to the Philippians* 6:1; 2 Cor. 4:12, quoted in Mathetes, *Epistle to Diognetus* 5.

68. Tertullian, *Against Marcion* 5.11–12.

69. P.Panop.Beatty II f.61f. See also Codex Sinaiticus, Q83-f.6r.

70. Gal. 4:26, quoted in Polycarp, *Epistle to the Philippians* 3:3; Gal. 5:17, quoted in Polycarp, *Epistle to the Philippians* 5:3; Gal. 6:7, quoted in Polycarp, *Epistle to the Philippians* 5:1.

71. Tertullian, *Against Marcion* 5.2–4.

72. P.Panop.Beatty II f. 81r. See also Codex Sinaiticus, Q84-f.2v.

73. Eph. 2:8–9, quoted in Polycarp, *Epistle to the Philippians* 1:3; Eph. 4:26, quoted in Polycarp, *Epistle to the Philippians* 12:1.

74. Tertullian, *Against Marcion* 5.17–18.

75. P.Panop.Beatty II f.75r. See also Codex Sinaiticus, Q84-f.4v.

76. Philip. 2:16, quoted in Polycarp, *Epistle to the Philippians* 9:2.

Earliest identification of author: Tertullian attributed this letter to Paul in the beginning of the third century.[77] The manuscripts identify Paul as the author of this work as early as the third century.[78]

Colossians

Earliest quotation as authoritative scripture: end of the second century (Irenaeus).[79]

Earliest identification of author: Tertullian attributed this work to Paul in the beginning of the third century.[80] The manuscripts identify Paul as the author of this work as early as the third century.[81]

1 Thessalonians

Earliest quotation as authoritative scripture: end of the second century (Irenaeus).[82]

Earliest identification of author: At the beginning of the third century, Tertullian attributed this epistle to Paul.[83] The manuscripts identify Paul as the author of this work as early as the third century.[84]

2 Thessalonians

Earliest quotation as authoritative scripture: beginning of the second century (Polycarp).[85]

Earliest identification of author: In the beginning of the third century, Tertullian attributed this epistle to Paul.[86] The manuscripts identify Paul as the author of this work as early as the fourth century.[87]

77. Tertullian, *Against Marcion* 5.20.
78. P.Panop.Beatty II f.86r. See also Codex Sinaiticus, Q84-f.7r.
79. Col. 1:14, quoted in Irenaeus, *Against Heresies* 5.2.2.
80. Tertullian, *Against Marcion* 5.19.
81. P.Panop.Beatty II f.90r. See also Codex Sinaiticus, Q84-f.8v.
82. 1 Thes. 5:23, quoted in Irenaeus, *Against Heresies* 5.6.1.
83. Tertullian, *Against Marcion* 5.15.
84. P.Panop.Beatty II f.94r. See also Codex Sinaiticus, Q85-f.2v.
85. 2 Thes. 3:15, quoted in Polycarp, *Epistle to the Philippians* 11:3.
86. Tertullian, *Against Marcion* 5.16.
87. Codex Sinaiticus, Q85-f.4r.

1 Timothy

Earliest quotation as authoritative scripture: beginning of the second century.[88]

Earliest identification of author: Tertullian, at the beginning of the third century, attributed this epistle to Paul.[89] The manuscripts identify the author of this work as Paul as early as the fourth century.[90]

2 Timothy

Earliest quotation as authoritative scripture: beginning of the second century (Polycarp).[91]

Earliest identification of author: At the beginning of the third century, Tertullian identified the author of this epistle as Paul.[92] The manuscripts identify the author of this work as Paul as early as the fourth century.[93]

Titus

Earliest quotation as authoritative scripture: end of the second century (Irenaeus).[94]

Earliest identification of author: Tertullian, at the beginning of the third century, attributed this letter to Paul.[95] The manuscripts identify the author of this work as Paul as early as the fourth century.[96]

Philemon

Earliest quotation as authoritative scripture: beginning of the third century (Tertullian, mentioned but not quoted).[97]

Earliest identification of author: Tertullian identified this as an epistle of Paul in the early third century.[98] The manuscripts identify the author of Philemon as Paul as early as the fourth century.[99]

---

88. 1 Tim. 6:7, 10, quoted in Polycarp, *Epistle to the Philippians* 4:1.
89. Tertullian, *Against Marcion* 5.21.
90. Codex Sinaiticus, Q86-f.2r.
91. 2 Tim. 4:10, quoted in Polycarp, *Epistle to the Philippians* 9:2.
92. Tertullian, *Against Marcion* 5.21.
93. Codex Sinaiticus, Q86-f.3v.
94. Titus 3:10, quoted in Irenaeus, *Against Heresies* 1.16.3.
95. Tertullian, *Against Marcion* 5.21.
96. Codex Sinaiticus, Q86-f.5r.
97. Tertullian, *Against Marcion* 5.21.
98. Tertullian, *Against Marcion* 5.21.1.
99. Codex Sinaiticus, Q86-f.5v.

Hebrews

Earliest quotation as authoritative scripture: beginning of the second century (Clement).[100]

Earliest identification of author: The authorship of Hebrews is probably the most complicated of any New Testament book. In the third-century manuscript named Chester Beatty Papyrus II, Hebrews is placed among the Epistles of Paul between Romans and 1 Corinthians,[101] indicating that, by at least the early third century, it was attributed to Paul. In codices containing the Pauline Epistles, the Epistles are generally ordered according to length. Placement of Hebrews in the manuscripts reflects the opinion of the scribes who compiled or wrote the codex about who wrote Hebrews. The third-century codex places Hebrews among the letters of Paul; starting in the fourth century, Hebrews is moved out of the rest of the Pauline corpus. Eusebius claimed that Hebrews was disputed because the church in Rome disputed its Pauline authorship.[102] The Latin-speaking branch of Christianity seems to have disputed Paul's authorship. The third-century Latin church father Tertullian claimed that Barnabas wrote Hebrews, not Paul.[103] In the third century, the native Greek-speaking Origen cited this Epistle as being authored by Paul, though he noted that the Greek is more polished than it is in Paul's other letters. He also cited those who thought that Luke or perhaps Clement authored it but admitted that he could not solve the authorship issue.[104] The manuscripts reflect the change in opinion among Christian thought leaders about the authorship.

James

Earliest quotation as authoritative scripture: mid-second century (Justin Martyr).[105]

Earliest identification of author: The manuscripts identify the author of this work as James (Jacob) as early as the fourth century.[106] Which James—James the brother of John or James the brother of Jesus—is not specified.

---

100. Heb. 1:3–4, 5, 7, 13, quoted in *1 Clement* 36:2, 4, 3, 5, respectively.
101. P.Panop.Beatty II f.21r through f.38v.
102. Eusebius, *History of the Church* 3.3.
103. Tertullian, *On Modesty* 20.
104. Eusebius, *History of the Church* 6.25.11–14.
105. James 5:12, quoted in Justin Martyr, *Apology* 1.16.5.
106. Codex Sinaiticus, Q89-f.1v, Q89-f.2v.

1 Peter

Earliest quotation as authoritative scripture: beginning of the second century (Ignatius, Clement, Polycarp).[107] Papias was also citing from 1 Peter in the early second century.[108]

Earliest identification of author: The manuscripts identify the author of this work as Peter as early as the fourth century.[109]

Other notes: By the beginning of the second century, the First Epistle of Peter was the third most popular book in the New Testament at the time.[110] Because its frequent citation in the early second century is disproportionate to its size, it seems to have been seen as supremely authoritative, which is consistent with the letter being authored by Peter.

2 Peter

Earliest quotation as authoritative scripture: end of the second century (Irenaeus).[111]

Earliest identification of author: The manuscripts identify Peter as the author of this work as early as the fourth century.[112]

1 John

Earliest quotation as authoritative scripture: beginning of the second century (Polycarp).[113] Papias was also citing from 1 John in the early second century.[114]

Earliest identification of author: The Muratorian Fragment, which is a Latin list of authoritative texts dated as early as the second century, clearly

---

107. 1 Pet. 2:5, quoted in Ignatius, *Epistle to the Ephesians* 9:4; 1 Pet. 4:8, quoted in *1 Clement* 49:5 and *2 Clement* 16:4; 1 Pet. 1:8, quoted in Polycarp, *Epistle to the Philippians* 1:3; 1 Pet. 1:13, 21, 22, quoted in 2:1–2; 1 Pet. 2:11, quoted in 5:3; 1 Pet. 4:7, quoted in 7:2; 1 Pet. 2:24, quoted in 8:1; 1 Pet. 2:17, quoted in 10:2; 1 Pet. 4:4, quoted in *2 Clement* 16:4.

108. Papias, fragment 6, in Eusebius, *History of the Church* 3.39.16.

109. Codex Sinaiticus, Q89-f.3r, Q89-f.5r.

110. See Ignatius, *Epistle to the Ephesians* 5:3; *1 Clement* 49:5; Polycarp, *Epistle to the Philippians* 1:3; 2:1–2; 5:3; 7:2; 8:1; 10:2; *2 Clement* 16:4.

111. Irenaeus, *Against Heresies* 5.23.2.

112. Codex Sinaiticus, Q89-f.5r, Q89-f.6r.

113. 1 John 4:2–3, quoted in Polycarp, *Epistle to the Philippians* 7:1.

114. Papias, fragment 6, in Eusebius, *History of the Church* 3.25.2.

identifies John as the author of the Epistle.[115] Other manuscripts identify John as the author of this work as early as the fourth century.[116]

2 John

Earliest quotation as authoritative scripture: beginning of the second century (Polycarp).[117]

Earliest identification of author: The manuscripts identify John as the author of this work as early as the fourth century.[118]

3 John

Earliest quotation as authoritative scripture: fourth century (Pseudo-Clementines).[119]

Earliest identification of author: In the middle of the third century, Eusebius mentioned this epistle and attributed it to John but added that some individuals doubted the attribution.[120] The manuscripts identify the author of 3 John as John as early as the fourth century.[121]

Jude

Earliest quotation as authoritative scripture: End of the second century (Tertullian).[122]

Earliest identification of author: The author of this work is identified as Jude in the manuscripts as early as the fourth century.[123]

Revelation

Earliest quotation as authoritative scripture: Mid-second century (Justin Martyr).[124]

---

115. Muratorian Fragment 26–32. See discussion on this fragment and its dating in Gallagher and Meade, *Biblical Canon Lists from Early Christianity*, 175–79.

116. Codex Sinaiticus, Q89-f.8r.

117. 2 John 1:7, quoted in Polycarp, *Epistle to the Philippians* 7:1.

118. Codex Sinaiticus, Q89-f.8v.

119. 3 John 1:8, quoted in *Clementine Homilies* 17.19.

120. Eusebius, *Church History* 6.25.10.

121. Codex Sinaiticus, Q89-f.8v.

122. Jude 1:14–15, quoted in Tertullian, *On the Apparel of Women* 1.3.

123. Codex Sinaiticus, Q89-f.8v, Q90-f.1r.

124. Rev. 20:2, quoted in Justin Martyr, *Dialogue with Trypho* 81.4.

Earliest identification of author: In the second century, Justin Martyr attributed Revelation to John.[125] The manuscripts identify the author of this work as John as early as the fourth century.[126]

Counterarguments

Noting the struggles within the second-century church over authority, the role of prophecy, and the content of scripture, one might argue that we are simply seeing the choices of the victors, which may not have anything to do with authenticity. Orthodox writers, however, were not the only ones to quote from the New Testament. For example, in the Nag Hammadi library, there are quotations of all the books of the New Testament except Philemon and 3 John,[127] the two shortest books. Again, the shorter books are the least likely to be quoted.[128] Still, the fact that the canonical works were quoted shows that the New Testament, at least parts of it, were still considered somewhat normative even among unorthodox believers. The Gnostics had a more limited range of works than is represented in the Nag Hammadi library,[129] but they still managed to quote from or refer to Matthew,[130] Mark,[131] Luke,[132] John,[133] Romans,[134] 1 Corinthians,[135] 2 Corinthians,[136] Ephesians,[137] Philippians,[138] Colossians,[139] 1 Timothy,[140] 2 Timothy,[141] Hebrews,[142] 1 Peter,[143]

---

125. Justin Martyr, *Dialogue with Trypho* 81.4.

126. Codex Sinaiticus, Q90-f.1v; Q91-f.2r.

127. Craig A. Evans, Robert L. Webb, and Richard A. Wiebe, *Nag Hammadi Texts and the Bible: A Synopsis and Index* (Leiden, Neth.: E. J. Brill, 1993), 482–541.

128. Noted in Tertullian, *Against Marcion* 5.21.

129. These are the *Apocryphon of John, Zostrianos, Allogenes* (the Foreigner), and the book of Zoroaster. For a discussion, see David Brakke, *The Gnostics: Myth, Ritual, and Diversity in Early Christianity* (Cambridge, Mass.: Harvard University Press, 2010), 29–51.

130. *Apocryphon of John* II 2.9–14; 27.21–30.

131. *Apocryphon of John* II 27.21–30.

132. *Apocryphon of John* II 27.21–30.

133. *Apocryphon of John* II 4.21–24; 6.15–18; 27.11–14.

134. *Apocryphon of John* II 28.26–29; 30.4–7.

135. *Apocryphon of John* II 7.25–26; 13.8–13; 26.3–7.

136. *Apocryphon of John* II 28.26–29.

137. *Apocryphon of John* II 7.25–29; 30.7–11; 31.5–6.

138. *Apocryphon of John* II 2.4–5; 7.27–29.

139. *Apocryphon of John* II 7.25–26; 14.21–24.

140. *Apocryphon of John* II 2.29–32; 26.3–7.

141. *Apocryphon of John* II 26.3–7.

142. *Apocryphon of John* II 7.25–26.

143. *Apocryphon of John* II 7.25–26.

and Revelation.[144] Thus, the New Testament books served not only as source material for orthodox believers but for their opponents as well.

Conclusions

Most of the books in the New Testament were already considered authoritative by the second century. Questions about authorship did not arise until the third century. Before that time, the authorship of New Testament books was not questioned. In general, the Brigham Young University New Testament Commentary series will follow the early Christians on the matter of authorship.

144. *Apocryphon of John* II 2.16–19; 4.21–24.

Digging into the Synoptic Gospels

How Matthew, Mark, and Luke Fit Together

Brent J. Schmidt

A teacher or student sits down and reads the Gospel of Matthew. After reading Matthew's supernal narrative, that same teacher or student begins to read the Gospel of Mark. Soon, the reader notices something odd about the two narratives. "A lot of this material is familiar," the reader remarks. At last, the individual arrives at Luke's Gospel. After passing through the first two chapters, which are unique to Luke, the reader declares, "This is the same story!" Exactly. It does not require a lot of concentration to quickly grasp that these three Gospel accounts are connected to each other in some fashion because they share many narratives, or what scholars call pericopes. The questions are: What is the nature of that connection? Did the Gospel writers borrow from each other? Did they draw from a common reservoir of information about Jesus' life and ministry? Let us take a brief look to see the possibilities.

Matthew, Mark, and Luke wrote to different audiences and, rested their work on their individual perspectives. These synoptic Gospels (Greek "viewing [things] together")[1] contain remarkable similarities between their portrayals of chronology, content, and even quotations from Jesus, especially when compared to the unique Gospel of John. Considering the striking parallels between these three synoptic Gospels, students have long questioned what literary relationship existed between them when they were composed.

Unfortunately, during the last two-plus centuries, no consensus has emerged as to what this relationship was. Although scholars have proposed many theories about this intriguing intertextual relationship, their inability

1. Alan Taylor Farnes, "The Synoptic Gospels: Matthew, Mark, and Luke," in *New Testament History, Culture, and Society: A Background to the Texts of the New Testament,* ed. Lincoln H. Blumell (Provo, Utah: Religious Studies Center, Brigham Young University; Salt Lake City: Deseret Book, 2019), 290–303.

to satisfactorily answer the synoptic question has often become a point of considerable contention. This creates a related pressing problem in New Testament studies of exactly who Jesus was, since his identity is bound most closely to the earliest of the Gospel accounts. One scholar called the synoptic problem "the most fascinating literary enigma of all time."[2] Answers to this enigma could provide clarity about many biblical details as well as potentially provide more information about Jesus, his ministry, his earliest disciples, and the organization of his followers.

The synoptic question has at times introduced a crisis of faith for the studious believer, especially those traditional Protestants who see the Bible as authoritative and absolute. Appealing to "scripture alone" (*sola scriptura*) seems insufficient because it is incomplete. Unbelievers who challenge Jesus' historicity commonly assert that all the synoptic Gospels are unreliable because they are all written very late.[3] While at times admittedly perplexing, the synoptic problem does not present significant obstacles for Latter-day Saints because of the Restoration. In addition to the text of the New Testament, members find faith-affirming details about Jesus' character and ministry from the scriptures of the Restoration, modern prophets, and—most importantly—continuing revelation. Therefore, a final resolution to the synoptic problem is unnecessary for a Latter-day Saint to be confident regarding the basic realities of Jesus' nature, life, mission, and sacrifice.

For example, Latter-day Saints are blessed with a second witness of the general accuracy of the Sermon on the Mount discourse as recorded in the Gospel of Matthew 5–7. In the Book of Mormon, Jesus, as a resurrected being, faithfully rehearses most of this text. As further evidence, some of the forty-day literature, which consists of apocryphal documents that describe what Jesus taught for the forty days between his Resurrection and his Ascension (Acts 1:3), offers intriguing sources to explore.[4] With a second written witness, apocryphal clues, and modern revelation,

---

2. Mark Goodacre, *The Synoptic Problem: A Way through the Maze* (New York: Sheffield Academic Press, 2001), 32.

3. Raphael Lataster, *Questioning the Historicity of Jesus: Why a Philosophical Analysis Elucidates the Historical Discourse* (Leiden, Neth.: Brill, 2019), 34. See a critique in John Gee's review, "The Implications of Some Standard Assumptions of New Testament Scholars: Responding to a Modern Anti-Christ," *Interpreter: A Journal of Latter-day Saint Faith and Scholarship* 46 (2021): 15–32.

4. Richard Lloyd Anderson, "Imitation Gospels and Christ's Book of Mormon Ministry," in *Apocryphal Writings and the Latter-day Saints,* ed. C. Wilfred Griggs (Provo, Utah: Religious Studies Center, Brigham Young University, 1986), 53–107.

members of The Church of Jesus Christ of Latter-day Saints can affirm the accuracy of the Sermon on the Mount and use it as a reliable witness to sustain their faith in Christ and his teachings.

Modern disciples should not be jarred when these synoptic texts often contradict each other regarding less-than-noteworthy details of Jesus' mortal ministry. In fact, Joseph Smith remarkably titled some of the synoptic Gospels as the "Testimony of Matthew" or the "Testimony of John." This is precisely the language the Lord uses when referring to John's Gospel in a revelation to Joseph Smith as "the testimony of John,"[5] demonstrating that differences found in the Gospels can be attributed to individual perspective, just as one person's recollection of a spiritual event will differ from the recollection of another who shares that same event. In contrast, the additions of the term "gospel" to the titles of later medieval Bible manuscripts, which form the origin of the Gospel of Matthew, Mark, and Luke, may subtly convey an erroneous sense of authority and uniformity present in the words *sola scriptura*.

To illustrate, the earliest Greek manuscripts only contain the phrase "according to" Matthew, Mark, or Luke, suggesting that these writers were only presenting their point of view and their testimony about Jesus' life and ministry. It is very likely that the "Gospel of" headings were not added until the second century AD "on a basis to which we no longer have access."[6] Joseph Smith's insight about the nature of the synoptics and John as "testimonies" suggests that similarities or differences between them over details should not undercut one's confidence in the factuality of the narratives.

Matthean Priority

What chronological order were these synoptic Gospels written in? The answer is still heavily debated. Ancient extrabiblical sources hold that, first, Matthew produced a work in Aramaic on the life of the Savior.[7] If this is correct, Matthew's work likely consisted of notes on important events such as the Sermon on the Mount, which assumption is the reason many scholars consider that

5. D&C 88:3; also see D&C 88:141.

6. John Nolland, *The Gospel of Matthew: A Commentary on the Greek Text* (Grand Rapids, Mich.: Eerdmans, 2005), 2.

7. See Papias's notation in Eusebius, *Ecclesiastical History* 3.39.16. Some scholars have challenged Eusebius's source, which they considered legendary and doubtful. However, Eusebius and Augustine also accepted this source tradition of an early Aramaic work about Jesus by Matthew. These fourth-century Christians likely had more information about the beginnings of the New Testament than is available today.

Matthew's Gospel was written first. These purported notes probably included Jesus' invitation to enter into his new temple-centered covenant, as found in the Sermon on the Mount text,[8] and an outline of some of Jesus' other teachings in Aramaic. Linguistic evidence from Paul in 1 and 2 Thessalonians (dated to no later than AD 52) seemingly imitates Matthew's eschatological teachings, metaphors, similes, and keywords found in Matthew 23–25.[9] Further, quotations by early church fathers contain many verbal echoes of Matthew's Gospel and thereby provide subtle evidence that his Gospel was written first.[10] Finally, the *Didache,* an early Christian document dated by some to the first century, refers to "the gospel."[11] The gospel quoted therein contains Jesus' teachings found in Matthew 6:9–13[12] and 7:6,[13] not from the Gospels of Luke or Mark. An early form of Matthew's Gospel must then predate the *Didache* and thus must date sometime before Acts 15 at the latest, which puts its composition before the Gospel of Mark. It also "preserves the injunction of Jesus to his apostles not to preach to the Gentiles [Matt. 10:5–6]. Such prohibitions are absent from Luke and Mark, which were written after the permission to preach to the Gentiles. Thus, Matthew must have been written before the prohibition was lifted in Acts 9–10. This detail would place the writing of Matthew's initial draft within a few years of the resurrection."[14]

Mark may have utilized Matthew's Aramaic notes, Peter's recollections, testimonies of other disciples, first-hand accounts of Jesus' family members, and other oral material in his Greek Gospel (most likely composed in the AD 60s).[15] Later, probably making use of his own early Aramaic material

---

8. John W. Welch, "Echoes from the Sermon on the Mount," in *The Sermon on the Mount in Latter-day Scripture,* ed. Gaye Strathearn, Thomas A. Wayment, and Daniel L. Belnap (Provo, Utah: Religious Studies Center, Brigham Young University; Salt Lake City: Deseret Book, 2010), 312–40.

9. Bernard Orchard and Harold Riley, *The Order of the Synoptics: Why Three Synoptic Gospels?* (Macon, Ga.: Mercer University Press, 1987), 38–39, 118–20; Peter LP Simpson, *The Authenticity of the Gospels* (Nashville: HarperCollins Christian, 2019), 64.

10. Orchard and Riley, *Order of the Synoptics,* 118–22; Simpson, *Authenticity of the Gospels,* 64.

11. *Didache* 8.2, 15.3, 4; Robert A. Kraft, "Didache," in *The Anchor Bible Dictionary,* ed. David Noel Freedman, 6 vols. (New York: Doubleday, 1992), 2:197–98. I am indebted to John Gee for the argument found in "Implications."

12. *Didache* 8.2.

13. *Didache* 9.5.

14. Gee, "Implications," 29.

15. Julie M. Smith, *The Gospel according to Mark,* New Testament Commentary (Provo: BYU Studies, 2018), 850–51; Martin Mosse, *The Three Gospels: New Testament History Introduced by the Synoptic Problem* (Colorado Springs, Colo.: Paternoster, 2007), 116–22.

and Mark's completed Greek Gospel, Matthew seems to have written his own lengthy Greek Gospel (which most scholars date to around the time of the fall of the Jerusalem temple in c. AD 70), borrowing and tweaking Mark's earlier writing in many places. Luke's later Gospel, written before AD 80, may have drawn from Matthew's and Mark's writing, while also incorporating oral witnesses, as he plainly noted in Luke 1:1–3.[16]

Augustine of Hippo (AD 354–430) probably came to his conclusion of Matthaean priority because it traditionally was accepted in his era as the first Gospel among the New Testament accounts. Augustine believed that Matthew had personally witnessed Jesus' ministry, which made his Gospel more valid for learning and preaching.[17] He likewise asserted that Mark, whom he believed was not an original disciple, only expanded on Matthew's Aramaic writing when he composed his short Gospel in Greek.[18] Augustine may have had information about some of these authorial details that unfortunately are now lost, if they ever existed. There are many examples of Mark expanding Matthew's short periscopes—a phenomenon that needs explanation—that possibly rest on original Aramaic notes.[19] It is likely that these Aramaic original notes and outlines, if they existed, would have been memorized by many in the early community, whose members were mostly illiterate. Such an act would have formed an oral tradition that tied directly back to Jesus' ministry, thus providing a common template for the Greek synoptic Gospels.

Additional evidence for Matthean priority is found in the Muratorian Canon, a Latin list of books considered canonical in about AD 180. It lists the traditional composition order of the Gospels as Matthew, Mark, Luke, and John.[20] This is the order of authorship found in the earliest Greek manuscripts of the New Testament and in the writings of Irenaeus and Origen, an order that was accepted until the early nineteenth century.[21]

---

16. S. Kent Brown, *The Testimony of Luke,* Brigham Young University New Testament Commentary (Provo: BYU Studies, 2015), 52, 55; Mosse, *Three Gospels,* 274.

17. Augustine, *De Consensu Evangelistarum* 1.3: "Qui secuti dominum in carne praesentem dicentem audierunt facientemque viderunt atque ex ejus ore ad evangelizandum missi sunt."

18. Augustine, *De Consensu Evangelistarum* 1.4: "Marcus eum subsecutus tamquam pedisequus et breviator ejus videtur."

19. One famous example is Matt. 8:2–3 and Mark 1:40–42.

20. R. T. France, *Matthew: Evangelist and Teacher* (Grand Rapids, Mich.: Academie Books, 1989), 13.

21. France, *Matthew: Evangelist and Teacher,* 13, 27.

Markan Priority

Although some early Christian writers believed that Matthew's Aramaic work about Jesus' ministry was the first composed,[22] many scholars find evidence that the extant Greek Gospels of Matthew and Luke utilized Mark's Greek Gospel as their main source. The Gospel of Mark reveals the least acquaintance with the Roman conflict in Palestine in AD 66–70, from which many scholars conclude that Mark was written prior to that conflict and the other synoptic Gospels were written afterward. This theory is called "Markan priority."[23] Some scholars have demonstrated that Matthew's Greek Gospel text contains ninety percent of Mark, much of it verbatim.[24] In fact, Mark has only about fifty unique verses.[25] Matthew utilized 600 of Mark's 660 verses, streamlining and enriching Mark's narrative with dialogue.[26] If Mark had written his shorter Gospel after Matthew, as the accounts stand, he would have preserved almost nothing new. Thus most scholars hold that Matthew produced a revision of Mark's Gospel and included additional material.[27]

Moreover, many scholars generally believe that, in addition to following Mark's Gospel, both Matthew and Luke utilized an oral tradition or written document that has not survived, commonly referred to as "Q" (from the German *Quelle,* meaning "source"), to write their Gospels. This Q theory asserts that Matthew and Luke expanded Mark's Gospel with additional material from this hypothetical Q source. According to this generally accepted theory, there were about two hundred verses common to Matthew and Luke that formed the entirety of this purported document.[28]

---

22. Eusebius, *Ecclesiastical History* 3.39.16.

23. Luke Timothy Johnson, *The Writings of the New Testament: An Interpretation,* rev. ed. (Minneapolis: Fortress Press, 1999), 144; Paul J. Achtemeier, "Mark, Gospel of," in Freedman, *Anchor Bible Dictionary,* 4:154.

24. Donald A. Hagner, *Matthew 1–13,* Word Biblical Commentary, vol. 33A (Dallas: Word Books, 1993), xlvii.

25. W. F. Albright and C. S. Mann, *Matthew,* The Anchor Bible (Garden City, N.Y.: Doubleday, 1971), xl.

26. Barbara E. Reid, *The Gospel According to Matthew* (Collegeville, Minn.: Liturgical Press, 2005), 8.

27. Daniel J. Harrington, *The Gospel of Matthew,* vol. 1 of Sacra Pagina (Collegeville, Minn.: Liturgical Press, 1991), 5–6.

28. Albright and Mann, *Matthew,* xliii; C. G. Montefiore counted about 230 Q verses that both Matthew and Luke share. See "Introduction," in *The Synoptic Gospels,* ed. C. G. Montefiore, vol. 1 2nd ed. (New York: Ktav Publishing House, 1968), lxii.

This document or reconstructed Q begins with the ministry of John the Baptist, describes Jesus' baptism, and ends before Jesus' death.[29] The fact that the central aspects of Christ's death and Resurrection are missing from this theoretical source stands in stark contrast with Tacitus, a Roman historian with no ties to Christianity, who referred to key points of Jesus' death. This observation suggests that Q was incomplete, if it ever existed.[30] Nevertheless, Q may represent the earliest Christians' remembrances of Jesus' preserved words and deeds that spoke to their needs (for example, solutions to poverty, social ostracism, family challenges, or oppressive officials).

While Matthew's Greek work as it has been preserved runs parallel to the other synoptic Gospels of Mark and Luke in many respects, there are major divergences that point to Matthew drawing on earlier notes or from other oral or written materials usually known as "M."[31] Certainly,

> Matthew includes some of the most exclusive texts in all of the Gospels. Only he inserts Jesus' sayings in 10:5–6 and 15:24 about Jesus and his disciples going only to the lost sheep of the house of Israel. Only he anticipates a perennially incomplete Jewish mission (10:23). On the other hand, Matthew just as uniquely presents some of the most inclusive texts imaginable. Only he has Gentile Magi come and worship the Christ child (2:1–12). Only he speaks of Israel being judged and replaced by a new "people" (21:43). Only he includes the Great Commission, in which Jesus sends his followers to make disciples from every ethnic group on the face of the globe (28:19).[32]

In like manner, Luke's narrative of Christ's extended family and birth demonstrates his utilization of other source material known as "L."[33] Luke's unique material, or L, includes the parable of the good Samaritan (10:25–37), the story of Martha and Mary attending to Jesus (10:38–42), the parables of the prodigal son (15:11–32) and the unjust judge (18:1–8), and the risen Christ's journeying with the two travelers to Emmaus (24:13–35).

---

29. Albright and Mann, *Matthew,* xliii; Mosse, *Three Gospels,* 96.

30. Tacitus, *Annals* 15.44; Mosse, *Three Gospels,* 96.

31. M. Eugene Boring, "The Gospel of Matthew: Introduction, Commentary, and Reflections," in *The New Interpreter's Bible,* vol. 8 (Nashville: Abingdon Press, 1995), 91–92; Nolland, *Gospel of Matthew,* 7; Curtis Mitch and Edward Sri, *The Gospel of Matthew* (Grand Rapids: Baker Academic, 2010), 22; Floyd V. Filson, *A Commentary on the Gospel According to St. Matthew* (London: Adam & Charles Black, 1960), 9–10, 18.

32. Craig L. Blomberg, *Matthew,* vol. 22 of The New American Commentary (Nashville: Broadman Press, 1992), 26.

33. Johnson, *Writings of the New Testament,* 138–39.

It should be noted that Eusebius, an early fourth-century historian (AD 263–339), provides evidence based on quotes from Papias that show Mark's authorship of the first Greek Gospel. Papias is said to have heard the Apostle John himself and was an associate of Polycarp of Smyrna (c. AD 69–135), a disciple of the Apostle John.[34] Eusebius wrote that Mark, who he believed was a later disciple and long served as Peter's interpreter, set down in writing Peter's oral stories about Jesus after Peter's death.[35] Because Peter was one of Jesus' Apostles, Mark's Gospel essentially contained Peter's witness, an observation borne out in Mark's large number of accounts that feature Peter. Eusebius seems to suggest that Mark wrote his Greek Gospel first, and because his work carried the authority of Peter, other Gospel writers drew from and quoted it.

Ancient oral histories were commonly passed down from generation to generation and were highly regarded. As a general practice, only much later were they written down.[36] The importance of developing one's memory for many ancient elites led to the notion that word-of-mouth accounts were often considered more accurate than written sources. Papias admitted that he preferred oral communications about Jesus rather than written ones. According to Eusebius, Papias said, "I did not suppose that information from books would help me so much as the word of a living and surviving voice."[37]

Character of the Sources

Understanding first-century realities of how the ancients used and quoted sources is helpful in comprehending why there is no academic consensus about a solution to the synoptic problem. As previously mentioned, ancient cultures placed a lot of weight on oral tradition, often considering a personal account passed on through word of mouth to be more accurate than written sources. One scripture-based solution to the relationship

34. Irenaeus, *Against Heresies* 5.33.4; Eusebius, *Ecclesiastical History* 3.39.1.

35. Eusebius, *Ecclesiastical History* 3.39.15. Eusebius quoted the somewhat legendary second-century bishop Papias, who was quoting John the Elder.

36. Good examples of this phenomenon are Homer's *Iliad* and *Odyssey* as well as Plutarch's biographies in New Testament times.

37. Eusebius, *Ecclesiastical History* 3.39.4; quoted in Lee Martin McDonald, *The Formation of the Biblical Canon,* vol. 2 (New York: Bloomsbury, 2017), 8. The quotation is from Eusebius, *The Ecclesiastical History,* trans. Kirsopp Lake, 2 vols. (London: William Heinemann, 1928), 1:293.

between the synoptic Gospels is found in Luke. According to the King James Version of Luke 1:1–3, Luke wrote to Theophilus, likely a Roman official, that he had carefully consulted "those things which are most surely believed among us, even as they delivered them unto us, which from the beginning were eyewitnesses, and ministers of the word." To clarify, the Greek arrangement of this sentence makes it clear that those who "delivered . . . [the stories about Jesus] unto us [were the] . . . eyewitnesses, and ministers." Who were these witnesses that Luke's testimony mentioned? Can Luke's claim be trusted? Did Luke interview Peter, James, John, and some of the women who had experiences with Jesus during his ministry?[38] Was Mary, Jesus' mother, one of these witnesses? It is likely that she was. But why would Luke not specifically mention her? Responsible ancient historians often cited their oral sources, but not all did.

Concerning Luke's report of Jesus' birth, he does not specifically mention Mary in this passage, although she certainly would have been the best eyewitness of special and unique events that occurred before her son's birth. Although Luke certainly mentions Mary's faithfulness, he places particular emphasis on the special circumstances surrounding Jesus' birth and the beginning of his ministry. It is important to remember that in antiquity men and women had specific and rigid gender roles. Women had indoor duties, and men had outdoor responsibilities. These Mediterranean societies were patriarchal in public, but women dictated the domestic sphere of life. While fame was considered proper for men's out-of-house responsibilities, it was generally deemed improper for women's domestic roles. Ancient women's names are usually mentioned as sparingly as possible to bring them honor. Being commonly talked about by men was consistently considered to be dishonorable.[39] Luke must have been influenced by these gender conventions that were commonly held throughout the Mediterranean world. Though he sometimes described

---

38. Joseph, Jesus' stepfather, is already off the stage during Jesus' ministry. We know that Luke went to Jerusalem with Paul on the Apostle's last trip to the city where he was arrested because of the "we" passage (Acts 21:15–18); hence, that trip would have allowed Luke to meet and interview those followers of Jesus who still resided in the city, very likely Mary among them. Brown, *Testimony of Luke,* 20–22.

39. This is certainly a complex topic. One seminal text that social historians often consider to reflect Mediterranean attitudes is the popular fifth-century BC Athenian politician Pericles's funeral oration, which casually mentioned that a woman's reputation is great whose fame for good or ill was least discussed by males. See Thucydides, *History* 2.45.2.

how Jesus lovingly transcended these gender roles, Luke did not identify his sources, many of whom must have been women. Because he kept silent about the origin of certain accounts in his Gospel, he shut out details that would have provided answers to the synoptic question.

Ancients held many different assumptions about historical resources that make it especially difficult to answer modern questions about those sources. Unfortunately, fragmentary and incomplete quotations of Papias and questionable assertions of Eusebius and Augustine, while very limited by modern standards, are the best and only extant ancient sources that touch on the origins of synoptic Gospel authorship. Their writings are not as early as we would need in order to conclusively answer the synoptic question, but their witnesses support the most likely scenario: Matthew probably composed notes and outlines of Jesus' teachings in Aramaic, including the Sermon on the Mount; Mark was the first to write a lengthy Greek Gospel seemingly dependent on some of Matthew's notes, on Peter's witness, and on many other oral witnesses and traditions; and later, Matthew and Luke composed their Gospels as we now know them based on all the writings, first-hand accounts, and oral remembrances that were available at the time.

In sum, for Latter-day Saints, it is extremely helpful to remember that these synoptic Gospels are truly testimonies, with each Gospel being written for a specific Jewish or Gentile audience. As testimonies, they present basic facts of Jesus' ministry that fit together nicely. Although these testimonies are often in agreement about specific items, in other instances they may be contradictory about certain details. Their agreement or disagreement about certain aspects of Jesus' ministry does not detract from their grand purpose in teaching that Jesus is the Messiah or Christ. John's later testimony cemented the most important details of Jesus' suffering, death, and Resurrection as described by the synoptic Gospels in varying ways.

Embracing Paul's Epistles

An Introduction to Questions of Authorship

Brent J. Schmidt

When stepping into the world of Paul's letters, teachers and students find themselves inside a multitude of principles and doctrines taught by the Apostle while, under divine nudging, he moved across the northern Mediterranean world. For English readers, except for a few well-known and oft-quoted passages, part of the problem in understanding Paul's expressions lies in the King James Version of the Bible that was published more than four hundred years ago. But let us not fall into discouragement when trying to grasp the ideas of a very smart and faithful servant of Jesus Christ. With persistence, we can view clearly Paul's portrait of the celestial harmony and personal responsibility that emerges from Christ's grace, which the Father bestows upon the faithful as both a free and reciprocal gift, inviting a covenant relationship.

It is a matter of historical record that Paul wrote many letters to individuals and Christian communities to address their needs and doctrinal questions, to provide encouragement, and to admonish them to repent and follow Christ. These Epistles, containing as they do only Paul's side of all the communication that passed between him and these individuals and groups, often make his intended meaning notoriously difficult to ascertain (see 2 Pet. 3:15–16). It seems that the Epistles Paul wrote to one individual Christian community or another, although inspired, were not necessarily binding for the entire emerging Christian community in the Mediterranean region. In a different vein, the presence of letters assigned to Paul in the New Testament, especially those letters that are disputed as coming from him, sets up the question of whether a letter possibly written by an admirer of Paul, even if now in the New Testament canon, is as valuable as one written by a person possessing the apostolic authority he did. If and when we can responsibly embrace the point of view that Paul was the author of a certain letter, or even that an Epistle was written under his direction, that letter then carries the weight of an Apostle commissioned by Jesus Christ himself. In this way, the gap between an admirer's letter that has made its way into the New Testament and letters from the Apostle himself is more than minimal. It becomes enormously significant.

The thirteen Epistles ascribed to Paul, in time, became part of the scriptural canon established by Athanasius (AD 296–373).[1] As the bishop of Alexandria, Athanasius organized Paul's Epistles based on the descending length of the original Greek text, beginning with Romans and ending with Philemon.[2] However, the actual chronological order of the books in the late AD 40s and into the 50s probably was 1 Thessalonians, Galatians, 1 and 2 Corinthians, Philemon, Philippians, and Romans.[3] Today, with the exception of an academic group who holds that Paul wrote only four surviving letters (Romans, 1 and 2 Corinthians, and Galatians), most scholars consider the letters listed above to be the work of Paul himself. That is not the case with the rest of the Epistles traditionally identified with Paul. Scholars are more or less evenly divided about whether or not Paul authored Colossians and 2 Thessalonians, while most scholars consider Ephesians and the pastoral Epistles of 1 Timothy, 2 Timothy, and Titus to be pseudepigraphical (Greek for "written down as an imitation or falsely").[4] Hebrews was not attributed to Paul in the earliest manuscripts, and today it is not considered Pauline, as the recently published volume in the BYU New Testament

1. Athanasius, *Festal Letter* 39.5, in *Nicene and Post-Nicene Fathers of the Christian Church,* 2nd ser., ed. Philip Schaff and Henry Wace, 14 vols. (Grand Rapids, Mich.: Eerdmans, 1994), 4:552. See also Athanasius, *Letter* 39.18; for a discussion, see Bronwen Neil, "Towards Defining a Christian Culture: The Christian Transformation of Classical Literature" in *The Cambridge History of Christianity: Volume 2, Constantine to* c. *600,* ed. Augustine Casiday and Frederick W. Norris (Cambridge: Cambridge University Press, 2007), 318. David Brakke, "Canon Formation and Social Conflict in Fourth-Century Egypt: Athanasius of Alexandria's Thirty-Ninth *Festal Letter,*" *Harvard Theological Review* 87, no. 4 (1994): 395–419. Brakke argues that there were a number of forces—social, political, and ecclesiastical—pushing Athanasius to make up his list of accepted books and to effectively close the canon against his rivals. For a general discussion of canon, see Edmon L. Gallagher and John D. Meade, *The Biblical Canon Lists from Early Christianity: Texts and Analysis* (New York: Oxford University Press, 2017).

2. David Trobisch, *Paul's Letter Collection: Tracing the Origins* (Minneapolis: Fortress, 1994), 1–27.

3. Arthur J. Dewey and others, trans., introduction to *The Authentic Letters of Paul: A New Reading of Paul's Rhetoric and Meaning* (Salem, Ore.: Polebridge Press, 2010).

4. S. Kent Brown, *The Epistle to the Ephesians,* BYU New Testament Commentary (Provo, Utah: BYU Studies, 2023), 2–15, argues for Paul as author chiefly because of the quiet historical situation mirrored in the letter—no troubles with Roman authorities and no apostasy within the Church, characteristics that bedeviled Christianity in the late first and early second centuries.

Commentary concludes.[5] Its authorship will not be discussed in this essay.[6] In its simplest sense, the term "pseudepigraphical,"[7] as understood in academia, only means that scholars believe that a work was written by someone other than Paul. When judging authenticity, scholars generally consider the writing style, the theology, and the general themes of the seven authentic Epistles to be similar, while the other Epistles seem quite different, and therefore many scholars reject them as written by the Apostle.

Again, the term "pseudepigraphical," which has often been used to categorize the above-mentioned six Epistles, does not mean they are false or erroneous but only that they were written by someone other than Paul. They could, however, still bear his imprint. An unnamed secretary, who was authorized by him, may have composed them under his direction—and thus they would still be authoritative. On the other hand, the term also applies to documents that were written much later by someone other than the assumed author and were designed to corrupt Christian doctrine or to gain more readers and fame and to make money. Does it matter whether an Apostle of the Lord Jesus Christ like Paul wrote a text or some other faithful Church member wrote it, someone like a modern stake president, who did not wear the apostolic mantle but followed the Apostles and may have even written down their words as closely as he or she could remember? In response, the term "pseudepigraphical" is not definitive enough to be helpful for Latter-day Saints to indicate the authority (or lack of authority) behind a given New Testament work.[8]

Concerning whether Paul wrote the six Epistles in question, from a Latter-day Saint point of view, prophets have frequently used spokesmen and scribes to do God's work. For example, we think of Baruch, Jeremiah's scribe, and Tertius, the penman for Paul (see Jer. 36:1–4 and Rom. 16:22). What is most important to know is not so much who the original author was but whether the resulting Epistle was composed under the influence of revelation and the Holy Ghost. We accept "the Bible to be the word of God as far as it is translated [or transmitted] correctly" (A of F 1:8), and so these writings were inspired. Therefore, as far as the Church is concerned, these six Epistles are legitimate and authoritative.

5. See Richard D. Draper and Michael D. Rhodes, *Epistle to the Hebrews,* Brigham Young University New Testament Commentary (Provo, Utah: BYU Studies, 2021), 4–11.

6. Some codices place Hebrews among the Pauline Epistles, and for this reason it was later considered by many during the Middle Ages to have been authored by Paul.

7. "Pseudepigraphical" is synonymous with "pseudepigraphal."

8. See "Bible Dictionary," in the Holy Bible published by The Church of Jesus Christ of Latter-day Saints (1979), s.v. "Pseudepigrapha."

This position stands in contrast to scholars who have argued that these Epistles were actually written by Paul's disciples a generation or two after the Apostle's death. According to these scholars, these pseudepigraphical letters became part of the Christian corpus of scripture because they were subsequently accepted by Jesus' followers to be in general accord with Pauline ideas. Such individuals also believe that they are not necessarily binding on the Christian community today.[9] However, late first- and early second-century Christians attributed these six letters to Paul and therefore accepted them as binding.

The modern unwillingness to accept them as Pauline is partly due to theological bias. Particularly, most Protestant biblical scholars have commonly believed that a church organization did not develop until after Paul's death. They have therefore traditionally considered Ephesians and the pastoral Epistles to have been written much later by individuals motivated to justify the existence of Christian churches and doctrines present in early Catholic tradition.[10]

Like some New Testament scholars today, Martin Luther had no scruples about ranking different books of the Bible as more or less valuable depending on whether they evidenced his defining message of grace and justification by faith (*sola gratia* and *sola fide*). He liked certain Pauline works, such as Romans and Galatians, because they contained proof texts that were central to his theology.[11] Matching this same bias, a current group of scholars believe some of the letters that they judge to be pseudepigraphical have a softer tone than that of the alleged radical Paul, who, in their view, preached free grace and justification by faith. Thus they consider them as not written by Paul and, hence, as less authoritative. In many ways, modern scholars, like Luther, may have not recognized or controlled their biases. They may have categorized the Epistles as authentic or questionable based on their preconceived notions about the teachings of Jesus' followers, the meaning of Paul's writings, and how closely a particular letter fits with their current theologies of faith, justification, and grace. Nevertheless, all six Epistles, including Hebrews, became part of the biblical canon beginning in the late fourth century.

---

9. See John Gee's article in this volume, "New Testament Authorship."

10. For a sample of how 2 Thessalonians and the pastoral Epistles are treated as late efforts to adjust Christian life to the realities of the second century AD rather than to the expectation of the imminent Second Coming of Christ, see Helmut Koester, *History and Literature of Early Christianity,* Introduction to the New Testament, 2 vols. (Philadelphia: Fortress, 1982), 2:241–46, 297–305.

11. Diarmaid MacCulloch, *The Reformation* (New York: Penguin Books, 2005), 134.

Paul's Epistles were popularly circulated and read aloud among various churches (Col. 4:16; 1 Thes. 5:27). Peter noted that Paul composed these letters in wisdom, but Peter or his scribe asserted that the meanings of these Epistles were changed and twisted, knowingly or unknowingly, by the unlearned "unto their own destruction" (2 Pet. 3:15–16). In other words, even in very early times, just like today, some Christians did not understand the supposedly straightforward meanings of Paul's Epistles, and they were spiritually harmed because of their occasional willful ignorance. Misunderstanding these Epistles had serious spiritual consequences during the Apostasy because many interpreted them to validate such false doctrines as the total depravity of man, cheap grace, easy faith, predestination, determinism negating moral agency, indulgences, and many similar teachings and practices.

Latter-day Saints believe the Bible, except for the Song of Solomon, bears the inspiration of God when rendered faithfully into a modern tongue. The translation of the Bible is, in fact, of equal concern for Latter-day Saints as its authorship. Joseph Smith believed "the Bible as it read when it came from the pen of the original writers."[12] However, he also taught that the Bible had been twisted and changed by "ignorant translators, careless transcribers, or designing and corrupt priests [who] have committed many errors."[13] Much of the doctrinal uncertainty of the Bible stems from incorrectly and anachronistically interpreting Paul's Epistles to support such theological beliefs as those promoted by Augustine and Luther.

For example, in the first century, faith (*pistis* in ancient Greek) was associated with gaining knowledge, making covenants, becoming faithful, and maintaining relationships with God and fellow humans through the patron-client system.[14] That is to say, in this ancient Mediterranean system of vertical reciprocity known as *charis,* "grace," a powerful patron would provide gifts to a lowly client to increase his reputation in society. Upon

---

12. "History, 1838–1856, Volume E-1 [1 July 1843–30 April 1844]," 1755, Joseph Smith Papers, accessed June 26, 2023, https://www.josephsmithpapers.org/paper-summary/history-1838-1856-volume-e-1-1-july-1843-30-april-1844/127. "From sundry revelations which had been received, it was apparent that many important points, touching the salvation of man, had been taken from the Bible, or lost before it was compiled." "History, 1838–1856, Volume A-1 [23 December 1805–30 August 1834]," 183, Joseph Smith Papers, accessed June 26, 2023, https://www.josephsmithpapers.org/paper-summary/history-1838-1856-volume-a-1-23-december-1805-30-august-1834/189.

13. "History, 1838–1856, Volume E-1," 1755.

14. For all the evidence about these controversial points about faith, see my work *Relational Faith: The Transformation and Restoration of* Pistis *as Knowledge, Trust, Confidence, and Covenantal Faithfulness* (Provo, Utah: BYU Studies, 2022).

accepting the patron's generous gifts, this client was then obligated to support and reciprocate the patron in whatever way the lower-ranking person might be able. This *charis* convention of gift exchange thereby formed a social and political alliance, similar to how most social organizations work today. Of course, the client could never fully repay the patron for his obliging *charis* gift, known in anthropology and sociology as vertical reciprocity. Almost without exception, the humble client sought to give something in return to his generous patron. Significantly, this patron-client system of *charis* connected Paul's ancient Mediterranean world together, and Paul utilized this convention to explain to early Gentile Christian communities how God the Father's *charis* obligated his children to form and develop a relationship with him through making and keeping covenants, thus undercutting the conventional and traditional Protestant belief of easy grace and salvation by faith alone (*sola gratia* and *sola fide*).

However, beginning with Augustine (AD 356–430) and because of the widespread influence of Neoplatonism, faith became a mystical, emotional, and inner experience that God enigmatically granted by ephemeral grace to some who were mysteriously and unexpectedly predestined to receive salvation. The Roman world of the fifth century AD was politically collapsing and no longer associated *charis* with covenantal relationships of the client-patron system. Augustine and many others twisted the active, relational covenant nuances of faith into the "Rule of Faith," which eventually meant possessing only a mental ascent to or a mental belief in the creeds and doctrines of the orthodox tradition. Augustine also misunderstood Paul's use of *charis* when he asserted that it was a no-strings-attached, unconditional, free gift.[15] These ideas were all based on Augustine's own innovative interpretations of the Pauline Epistles that he chose to feature largely because of Neoplatonic philosophical ideas that he had embraced. However, grace in the first century implied receiving all the gifts of God, especially Christ's Atonement, and then reciprocating with God by making covenants with him as a partnership of discipleship within the patron-client relationship. This relationship was anciently strengthened by means of loyal devotion to God the Father and cultivating discipleship, as it also is today.

What some consider to be the "authentic" Pauline Epistles have also served to justify other later doctrinal errors, including but not limited to original sin, infant baptism, limited atonement, assured salvation of believers, irresistible

15. Brent J. Schmidt, *Relational Grace: The Reciprocal and Binding Covenant of* Charis (Provo, Utah: BYU Studies, 2015), 130–34.

grace, justification by faith alone, the wickedness of the Fall, and Adam's alleged sin.[16] As already noted, Joseph Smith pointed out that "from sundry revelations which had been received, it was apparent that many points touching the salvation of men, had been taken from the Bible, or lost before it was compiled."[17] It is certainly possible that some of these Pauline Epistles had suffered from copying and recopying even before Augustine and then Luther received and misinterpreted them. It is likely that 1 Nephi 13–14 pointed to some in the Hellenistic and later medieval church as possible culprits for introducing changes in how people understood scripture.[18] Whatever the character of the original New Testament text was, 1 Nephi 13:26 notes that many plain and precious parts and covenants of the gospel were taken out, and that very possibility includes the Pauline Epistles through their transmission, misinterpretation, and mistranslation.[19]

Even allowing for mistakes and deviations in his letters, Paul's Epistles can still be supernal in establishing doctrines of the gospel of Jesus Christ, especially when translated and read in light of their first-century context and illuminated by the Restoration. Paul taught doctrines and principles to his readers that were often neglected in Christian historical thought and were not comprehensible until the Restoration, such as his teachings about the Fall (Rom. 5), the Atonement (Rom. 5; 1 Cor. 15; etc.), baptism for the dead (1 Cor. 15:29), charity (1 Cor. 13), gifts of the Spirit (1 Cor. 12), the holiness of one's body (1 Cor. 3:16; 6:15, 19), and the essential character and meaning of baptism (Rom. 6). Despite the idea that New Testament texts were changed according to the doctrinal biases promoted at the time, the Book of Mormon and other Restoration scripture, including the Joseph Smith Translation of the Bible and other teachings of modern prophets, can restore correct doctrine that was lost or made unclear in Paul's Epistles.

16. Many of these doctrines were expressed most famously by Calvin's followers as TULIP at the second council of Dort (1618–1619). Perseverance of the saints means an individual cannot fall from God's grace once he or she has been unexpectedly saved by a deterministic, all-powerful God through a passive-emotional experience.

17. "History, 1838–1856, Volume A-1," 183.

18. Stephen E. Robinson, "Nephi's 'Great and Abominable Church,'" *Journal of Book of Mormon Studies* 7, no. 1 (1998): 32–39.

19. See John Gee's study "Textual Criticism: How Scholars Attempt a Restoration of All Things Textual" in this volume.

Textual Criticism

How Scholars Attempt a Restoration of All Things Textual

John Gee

The copying of manuscripts is a human activity. Humans make mistakes. The longer the manuscript, the more mistakes. Thus, no two of the more than 5,600 complete or partial manuscripts of the New Testament are identical.[1] Textual criticism is the discipline that deals with variations in the text. "It has sometimes been said that textual criticism is the crown and summit of all scholarship. This is not evidently or necessarily true; but it is true that the qualities which make a critic, whether they are thus transcendent or no, are rare, and that a good critic is a much less common thing than for instance a good grammarian."[2]

Textual criticism can be used for many different things. For example, it can study the errors that scribes made to determine scribal habits. Although scribes may each have had their own habits, many of these habits fell into general scribal tendencies. Textual criticism can also be used to group similar textual variations together. Going further, establishing relationships between manuscripts or groups of manuscripts allows the construction of a stemma of those relationships, which can allow one to reconstruct which manuscripts might be closer to the original. In theory, one can use textual criticism to reconstruct the original reading of the text, but this is the case only if the original reading has survived. Scholars know this, and they sometimes conjecture readings that they think are original

1. Daniel B. Wallace, "Lost in Transmission: How Badly Did the Scribes Corrupt the New Testament Text?," in *Revisiting the Corruption of the New Testament: Manuscript, Patristic, and Apocryphal Evidence,* ed. Daniel B. Wallace (Grand Rapids, Mich.: Kregel, 2011), 27.

2. A. E. Housman, "The Application of Thought to Textual Criticism," *Proceedings of the Classical Association* 18 (1922): 69.

but did not survive. Conjectured readings, however, "should have no place in a Greek New Testament text."[3] While many of these conjectures are reasonable, they are also speculative, and there is no empirical way of verifying whether the guess is accurate. The danger of the conjectural reading is that we may be rewriting the text to say what we want it to say rather than what it actually said. The more cautious, responsible approach is to limit ourselves to readings that are attested in the manuscripts, not because they are perfect but because, as mere scholars, we should not trust ourselves to rewrite them.

It is precisely the ability of scholars to rewrite the text that leads cautious and alert individuals to suspect that there is something fishy about textual criticism and that textual critics cannot be trusted. They note that "any attempt to analyse good or bad readings in a Greek New Testament is both selective and subjective."[4] Therefore, they think that, when it comes to textual criticism, "the sins committed by biblical scholars in connection with the Greek N[ew] T[estament] are far too numerous."[5] Some suspect that textual critics, rather than restoring the original text, are merely manipulating it for personal or theological ends: "New Testament textual criticism from the time of Erasmus onward has been detrimental to Christian virtues. It has turned out to be a breeding ground of *rabies theologorum*. It should be abolished for ethical reasons. Fortunately, even comprehensive NT commentaries do care very little for textual criticism anyhow."[6]

Latter-day Saints should have other reasons for being interested in textual variants[7] since prophets have stated that parts of the Bible have been

---

3. J. K. Elliott, "The United Bible Societies Greek New Testament: An Evaluation," *Novum Testamentum* 15, no. 4 (1973): 291, https://doi.org/10.2307/1560267.

4. Elliott, "United Bible Societies Greek New Testament," 294.

5. Rykle Borger, "Remarks of an Outsider about Bauer's Wörterbuch, BAGD, BDAG, and Their Textual Basis," in *Biblical Greek Language and Lexicography: Essays in Honor of Frederick W. Danker,* ed. Bernard A. Taylor and others (Grand Rapids, Mich.: William B. Eerdmans, 2004), 47.

6. Borger, "Remarks of an Outsider," 47.

7. Previous treatments of textual criticism by Latter-day Saints include Thomas A. Wayment, "Textual Criticism and the New Testament," in *New Testament History, Culture, and Society: A Background to the Texts of the New Testament,* ed. Lincoln H. Blumell (Provo, Utah: Religious Studies Center, Brigham Young University; Salt Lake City: Deseret Book, 2019), 659–71; John Gee, "Textual Criticism and Textual Corruption in Coffin Texts 131–142," in *Proceedings of the Tenth International Congress of Egyptologists,*

corrupted. Joseph Smith is famously reputed to have stated, "I believe the Bible as it read when it came from the pen of the original writers. Ignorant translators, careless transcribers, or designing and corrupt priests have committed many errors."[8] Textual criticism bears this out.

Manuscript variation can be deliberate or accidental. Accidental variation is usually called scribal error. Deliberate variation is editorial work by the scribe. Determining whether variation is accidental or deliberate is often difficult because it requires ascertaining the intentions of the scribe. Unless it can be argued otherwise, one generally assumes that the change in the text is accidental—especially if it fits in a known category of accidental mistakes.

This survey will not cover even a fraction of the textual changes in the New Testament. As one textual critic put it: "The best estimate is that there are between 300,000 and 400,000 textual variants among the manuscripts,"[9]

---

ed. P. Kousoulis and N. Lazarides (Leuven, Belg.: Peeters, 2015), 1345–50; Lincoln H. Blumell, "Luke 22:43–44: An Anti-Docetic Interpolation or an Apologetic Omission?," *TC: A Journal of Biblical Textual Criticism* 19 (2014): 1–35; Thomas A. Wayment, "P. Oxy. 2383 ($\mathfrak{P}^{69}$) One More Time," *Novum Testamentum* 54, no. 3 (2012): 288–92; Lincoln H. Blumell, "The Text of the New Testament," in *The King James Bible and the Restoration,* ed. Kent P. Jackson (Provo, Utah: BYU Religious Studies Center; Salt Lake City: Deseret Book, 2011), 61–74; Thomas A. Wayment, "A New Transcription of P. Oxy. 2383 ($\mathfrak{P}^{69}$)," *Novum Testamentum* 50 (2008): 351–57; Carl W. Griffin and Frank F. Judd Jr., "Principles of New Testament Textual Criticism," in *How the New Testament Came to Be,* ed. Kent P. Jackson and Frank F. Judd Jr. (Provo, Utah: BYU Religious Studies Center; Salt Lake City: Deseret Book, 2006), 78–92; Carol F. Ellertson, "New Testament Manuscripts, Textual Families, and Variants," in Jackson and Judd, *How the New Testament Came to Be,* 93–108; John Gee, "The Corruption of Scripture in Early Christianity," in *Early Christians in Disarray: Contemporary LDS Perspectives on the Christian Apostasy,* ed. Noel B. Reynolds (Provo, Utah: Foundation for Ancient Research and Mormon Studies, 2005), 163–204; and Thomas A. Wayment, "Two Textual Variants from the Freer Pauline Codex (I)," *Journal of Biblical Literature* 123, no. 4 (2004): 737–40.

8. *Teachings of the Prophet Joseph Smith,* sel. and arr. Joseph Fielding Smith (Salt Lake City: Deseret Book, 1976), 327. Though familiar, the quotation may not be fully accurate. The only contemporary report of this sermon, from Joseph Smith's journal kept by Willard Richards reads: "I believe the bible, as it ought to be, as it came from the pen of the original writers." See Andrew F. Ehat and Lyndon W. Cook, eds., *The Words of Joseph Smith: The Contemporary Accounts of the Nauvoo Discourses of the Prophet Joseph* (Provo, Utah: Religious Studies Center, 1980), 256; Andrew H. Hedges, Alex D. Smith, and Brent M. Rogers, eds., *Journals: Volume 3: May 1843–June 1844,* Joseph Smith Papers (Salt Lake City: Church Historian's Press, 2015), 113. The sense of the two versions remains essentially the same.

9. Wallace, "Lost in Transmission," 26, 20.

of which about 10,000 appear in the better critical editions.[10] This study will attempt to cover all the major categories of textual changes. It will also provide real examples of textual corruption that make a difference in how the text was read and thus understood. It will also identify places where one can argue that plain and precious things have been lost from the traditional text.

Frequency of Scribal Errors

To get an idea about the frequency of scribal errors, consider a literary text that is not part of the New Testament. Looking at places where the scribe catches his mistake and corrects it (also called corrections *in scribendo*) gives some idea of the frequency of mistakes if we assume that the scribe is likely to catch his mistakes. As an illustration, for the *Gospel of Thomas* and the *Gospel of Philip* in Nag Hammadi Codex II,[11] we have the following chart of the number of errors per page:

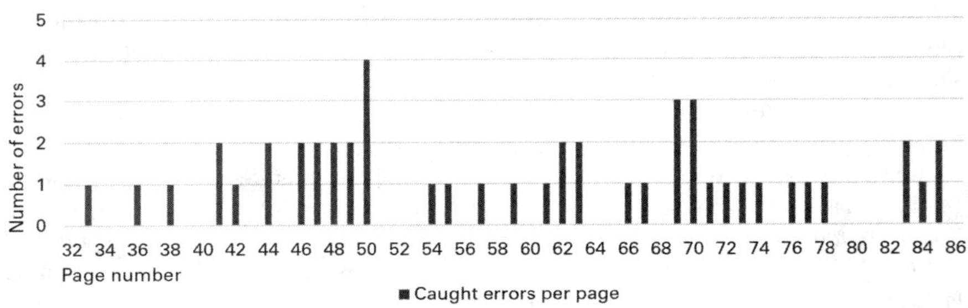

As is clear from the chart, one expects the scribe to have caught an error roughly every other pag,e but as time goes by, more mistakes were made. After the beginning of a new book (at p. 51 and p. 86), there is a huge drop in the number of mistakes caught. Presumably the scribe would have taken a rest at the end of the book, and when he started again, he was fresh and thus making fewer errors. Over the course of fifty-five pages, the scribe made forty-six mistakes, for an average of slightly less than one per page. These, of course, are only the errors that the scribe caught and corrected.

10. Elliott, "United Bible Societies Greek New Testament," 279.

11. The edition of the *Gospel of Thomas* and the *Gospel of Philip* in *Nag Hammadi Codex II,2–7,* vol. 1, ed. Bentley Layton (Leiden, Neth.: E. J. Brill, 1989), lists the *in scribendo* errors in the footnotes.

By comparison, in early New Testament manuscripts, the error rate ranges between 1.0 and 7.9 per hundred words,[12] with a mean of 4.2 and a median of 4.9. This means that scribes made a mistake on average every twenty to twenty-five words. Even the most highly trained scribes typically made one mistake every hundred words, while an average scribe made four times as many errors and a poor scribe made significantly more errors. These examples deal with honest, well-meaning individuals—most New Testament scribes fit that category—not those who deliberately altered the text. There were some of those too.

Types of Scribal Errors

Scribal errors fall into general categories, including orthographic and grammatical errors, linguistic updating, omissions, additions, harmonization, and doctrinal adjustments. We will examine these one at a time.

Orthographic Errors

Biblical manuscripts, like other ancient documents, often contain spelling errors. Text editions, even critical editions, almost always correct these spelling errors, making them invisible to the modern reader.[13] Consequently, most discussions of textual criticism ignore orthographic variants.[14]

Many of the orthographic variants come from sound shifts, which indicate changes in how a letter is pronounced.[15] Common sound shifts can be tracked over time.[16] The following table illustrates orthographic variations over time by displaying the number of spelling errors caused by particular sound shifts[17]

---

12. James R. Royse, *Scribal Habits in Early Greek New Testament Papyri* (Atlanta: Society of Biblical Literature, 2008), 123, 263, 373, 495, 579, 656.

13. Royse, *Scribal Habits in Early Greek New Testament Papyri,* 80.

14. Elliott, "United Bible Societies Greek New Testament," 280.

15. Royse, *Scribal Habits in Early Greek New Testament Papyri,* 79–81.

16. Francis Thomas Gignac, *A Grammar of the Greek Papyri of the Roman and Byzantine Periods,* 2 vols. (Milan: Istituto Editoriale Cisalpino - La Goliardica, 1981), 1:183–294.

17. We are tracking only vowel shifts. Vowel shifts occurring only once are not given in the table. These include η → α (fifth century AD); η → αι (fourth century AD); η → υ (fourth century AD); ι → α (first century BC); ο → ε (first century BC); ο → οι (fourth century BC); ο → ου (fourth century AD); ο → ωι (first century AD); ου → η (fifth century AD); ου → υ (fifth century AD); ου → ωι (first century BC); υι → υ (first century BC); ω → ωο (first century AD); ωι → ω (first century BC). With only one attested change in a passage, it is hard to argue that this is a shift and not some other sort of error.

found in twenty random papyri from each century.[18] Although this particular random sample does not include all sound shifts, it does demonstrate the range of shifts and how they changed over time. (Bolded rows highlight sound shifts that survive in modern Greek.)

18. The papyri were:

Fourth century BC: UPZ 1.1; Defixionem tabellae 100, 102, 103, 158. (Because of the limited number of surviving papyri from this time period, this century has fewer than twenty papyri in the sample.)

Third century BC: BGU 6.1283; 10.1996; Chr. Mitt. 28; Chr. Wilck. 223; CPR 10.47; 18.19; 18.28; O. Bodl. 1.21; O. Leid. 4; O. Theb. 7; O. Theb. Taxes 2.23; P. Cair. Zen. 1.59002; 1.59016; P. Hamb. 1.106; 4.239; P. Heid. 6.385; 7.390; P. Lond. 7.2022; P. Strasb. 7.622; UPZ 2.159.

Second century BC: BGU 6.1285; O. Bodl. 1.153; O. Cair. 39; O. Leid. 1; O. Wilck. 338; P. Amh. 2.32r; P. Dion. 10; P. Erasm. 2.51a; P. Heid. 3.232; P. Koeln. 9.365; P. Monts. Roca. 4.77; P. Ryl. 4.572; P. Tebt. 1.26; 4.1142; 3.2.871; 3.2.1044; P. Yale 1.42; SB 6.9367; 18.14023; Stud. Pal. 4.1.

First century BC: BGU 4.1122; 4.1208; 8.1872; 8.1778; 16.2582; JJP 44.104.1; O. Bodl. 1.217; O. Edfou. 3.368; O. Mich. 2.760; O. Wilck. 326; P. Bingen. 45; P. Herc. 19.698; P. Herc. 1602; P. Koeln 1.51; P. Oxy. 4.743; 7.1061; P. Ryl. 4.579; P. Wash. Univ. 1.11; SB 6.9612; 24.16073.

First century AD: BGU 4.1078; 11.2097; CdE 85.241; O. Berenike 1.23; O. Berl. 29; O. Bodl. 2.1181; O. Did. 360; O. Heid. 156; O. Petr. Mus. 162; O. Wilb. 29; O. Wilck. 1374; P. Fay. 111; P. Lond. 2.259; P. Mich. 12.635; P. Oxy. 9.1188; 73.4953; P. Princ. 2.23; P. Turner 18; SB 5.8034; 20.14285.

Second century AD: BGU 3.852; 20.2863; O. Claud. 1.169; O. Edfou 1.154; O. Ont. Mus. 1.15; O. Wilck. 196; P. Alex. Giss. 4; P. Brem. 48; P. Fam. Tebt. 9; P. Kar. Goodsp. 38; P. Mil. Vogl. 2.98; P. Oxy. 3.496; 7.1032; 47.3328; P. Sarap. 2; PSI 1.101; 17.1698; SB 14.11577; 16.12743; 20.14111.

Third century AD: BGU 4.1030; CPR 1.95; O. Did. 29; O. Mich. 1.417; P. Cair. Isid. 62; P. Flor. 1.47a; P. Grenf. 2.69; P. Harrauer 35; P. Lond. 3.1164c; P. Oxy. 14.1631; 14.1713; 34.2709; 43.3131; 70.4775r; P. Rein. 2.91; P. Tebt. 2.334; PSI 14.1417; SB 1.5467; 12.10884; 24.15987.

Fourth century AD: CPR 17A.17a dupl.; O. Mich. 1.214; O. Stras. 1.168; P. Abinn. 3; P. Ant. 2.89; P. Cair. Isid. 126; P. Coll. Youtie 2.83; P. Herm. 7; P. Lips 1.20; P. Mich. 12.636rp dupl.; P. Oxy. 1.41; 31.2571; 54.3756; 67.4604; P. Rein. 2.92; P. Select. 18; PSI 3.201; SB 14.11592; 18.13913; 22.15840.

Fifth century AD: BGU 12.2162; CPR 10.110; JJP 38.56; MPER n.s. 13.10; O. Oasis. Sarm. 6; P. Bad. 4.91a; P. Herm. 69; P. Köln Gr. 14.587; P. Muench 1.15; P. Oxy. 8.1122; 16.1957; 63.4393; 68.4697; 82.5327; P. Rein. Cent. 95; P. Select 8; P. Wisc. 1.10; PSI 6.689a; SB 18.13620; 28.17196.

Shift	4th c. BC	3rd c. BC	2nd c. BC	1st c. BC	1st c. AD	2nd c. AD	3rd c. AD	4th c. AD	5th c. AD
α → ε				2			1	1	
α → ο						1		2	
αι → α	1	2							
αι → ε				**1**	**3**	**1**	**8**	**9**	**4**
αυ → α				1	1			4	1
ε → α						2	2	7	
ε → αι						**1**	**7**	**35**	**3**
ε → ει			1	1					
ε → η	1						1	1	1
ε → ι	1				1				
ε → ο			1			1		1	
ει → ε			1	2	1	1			
ει → η			2	3	2		1	4	
ει → ι			**9**	**35**	**23**	**7**	**38**	**73**	**24**
η → ε							3	2	
η → ει			5	1				1	
η → ηι			1	2	2	5			
η → ι					1			2	
η → ω						1			
ηι → η				3					
ι → ε				1		1			2
ι → ει			**3**	**12**	**18**	**14**	**22**	**7**	**10**
ι → υ				2					
ο → α						1	2	1	
ο → ω					**8**	**4**	**16**	**4**	**6**
οι → αι								3	2
οι → ο		1	1	2	1				
οι → υ					5		4	2	1
ου → ο	5		2	1		1		1	
ου → ω				1		1		6	
υ → η								2	
υ → οι								1	
υ → ου					1		2		1
υι → ει									1
ω → ο		**1**	**3**	**5**	**19**	**6**	**9**	**9**	**2**
ω → ου						1	2	5	1
ω → ωι		1	6	5	6	2			

It is important to recognize that some of these sound shifts (like ει ↔ ι and ο ↔ ω) took place before the New Testament was written.[19] We cannot expect that the New Testament authors wrote their works in correct classical orthography. Later copyists would have corrected the orthography and therefore edited the manuscripts they were copying. The unevenness of the spelling errors in the manuscripts indicates that virtually all scribes acted as editors of the texts that they copied—not just as copyists.

While spelling errors from a shift in pronunciation might indicate scribes taking dictation as someone read the text,[20] it can also be caused by subvocalization—where a scribe sounds out the words in his mind.[21] In the ancient world, reading was almost always done aloud.[22] Augustine relates that Ambrose of Milan was an exception: "But when he was reading, his eye used to be guided through the pages, and his heart used to search out the meaning, but his voice and tongue were immobile."[23] Although subvocalization likely occurred, the most common ancient practice was for scribes to read the words aloud while copying.

Other sound shifts came after the New Testament was written. These sound shifts can create textual variants. For example, in Matthew 24:7, the standard printed text has καὶ ἔσονται λιμοὶ καὶ λοιμοὶ καὶ σεισμοὶ κατὰ τόπους, "and there will be famines and plagues and earthquakes in places." By the second century, λιμοὶ (*limoi*) and λοιμοὶ (*loimoi*) were pronounced identically.[24] The fourth-century Codex Vaticanus collapsed these two words to one word: λιμοὶ (*limoi*), "famines." Patristic Greek drops the term λιμὸς (*limos*), "famine," and keeps λοιμὸς (*loimos*), "plague," but changes the gender to feminine: λοίμη (*loimē*), "plague."[25] Because the scribes could not distinguish "famine" from "plague" in pronunciation, the scripture was simplified. In this case, the earlier manuscripts do not preserve the more accurate reading.

---

19. See also R. Whitney Tucker, "Chronology of Greek Sound Changes," *American Journal of Philology* 90, no. 1 (1969): 36–47, with a slightly different chronology.

20. Royse, *Scribal Habits in Early Greek New Testament Papyri,* 83.

21. William A. Johnson, *Bookrolls and Scribes in Oxyrhynchus* (Toronto: University of Toronto Press, 2004), 39–40.

22. Royse, *Scribal Habits in Early Greek New Testament Papyri,* 84.

23. Augustine, *Confessions* 6.3: *sed cum legebat, oculi ducebantur per paginas et cor intellectum rimabatur, vox autem et lingua quiescebant.* All translations are the author's own unless otherwise noted.

24. Gignac, *Grammar of the Greek Papyri,* 1:271–72.

25. G. W. H. Lampe, ed., *A Patristic Greek Lexicon* (Oxford: Clarendon Press, 1961), 811.

The sporadically attested sound shift ου → ω[26] might be the cause of a textual variant in Matthew 25:1, where εἰς ὑπάντησιν τοῦ νυμφίου (*nymphiou*), "to the meeting of the groom," becomes εἰς ὑπάντησιν τῷ νυμφίῳ (*nymphiō*), "to meeting the groom," in the fifth-century Codex Ephraemi Rescriptus. Another explanation is that while the verb ὑπαντάω (*hypantaō*) normally takes the dative (such as Matt. 8:28), it can also take the genitive,[27] and the scribe may have corrected the text to the more common dative usage. Thus, this might be an example of a grammatical error.

One of the clearest instances where the orthography presents a problem is with the personal pronouns. By the first century AD, η (*eta*) was being written for υ (*upsilon*), and by the end of the first century υ (*upsilon*) was written for η (*eta*).[28] There was a complete confusion of the two letters. This means that the first- and second-person plural personal pronouns ("we" and "you") were pronounced identically. Eventually, a new form of the second-person plural pronouns was introduced, and it has survived into modern Greek.[29] These errors permeate the places in the New Testament where these pronouns are used most often: the Epistles. The identical pronunciation happens in all grammatical cases, and it can significantly change or confuse the meaning. Context does not always determine the correct pronoun easily. According to 2 Corinthians 6:16, are "we" the temple of the living God or are "you"? Confusion in the manuscripts appears in the following places:

- Nominative (ἡμεῖς / ὑμεῖς [*hēmeis*, "we" / *humeis*, "you"]): 2 Corinthians 6:16; Galatians 4:28.
- Genitive (ἡμῶν / ὑμῶν [*hēmōn*, "of us" / *hymōn*, "of you"]): John 8:54; Acts 3:22, 25; 19:37; 28:25; Romans 14:12, 16; 1 Corinthians 15:14; 2 Corinthians 1:11; 3:2; 8:7; Galatians 4:6; Colossians 1:7; 2 Timothy 4:22; Hebrews 9:14; 1 Peter 2:21; 1 John 1:4; 2 John 1:12; Jude 1:3; Revelation 2:23.

---

26. Gignac, *Grammar of the Greek Papyri*, 1:208–9.

27. Henry George Liddell, Robert Scott, Henry Stuart Jones, and Roderick McKenzie, comps., *A Greek-English Lexicon* (Oxford: Clarendon Press, 1968), 1852.

28. Gignac, *Grammar of the Greek Papyri*, 1:262–65.

29. The forms are nominative ἐσεῖς, genitive ἐσᾶς/σάς, accusative ἐσᾶς/σάς. The form is attested as early as the ninth-century *Life of Saint George*; see Johannes B. Aufhauser, *Das Drachenwunder des Heiligen Georg in der grieschischen und lateinischen Überlieferung* (Leipzig, Ger.: B. G. Teubner, 1911), 136 line 22. These forms are entrenched in the works of the tenth-century emperor Constantine VII Porphyrogenitus; see E. A. Sophocles, "A Glossary of Later and Byzantine Greek," *Memoirs of the American Academy of Arts and Sciences* 7 (1860): 88.

- Dative (ἡμῖν / ὑμῖν [*hēmin*, "to us" / *hymin*, "to you"]): John 6:27; 11:50; Acts 7:38; 13:26; 15:7; 16:17; 2 Corinthians 8:7; Ephesians 4:32; 6:12; Philemon 1:6; Hebrews 13:21; 1 Peter 2:21; 1 John 2:25.
- Accusative (ἡμᾶς / ὑμᾶς [hēmas, "us" / *hymas*, "you"]): Romans 13:11; 15:7; 1 Corinthians 7:15; Ephesians 5:2; Colossians 1:12; 2:13; 1 Peter 3:18; 2 Peter 3:11.

Similar variation in derived forms appears in Luke 16:12 (ἡμέτερον / ὑμέτερον [*hēmeteron*, "our own" / *hymeteron*, "your own"]) and Acts 27:34 (ἡμετέρας / ὑμετέρας [*hēmeteras* / *hymeteras*]).

Although orthographic variants are usually ignored by textual editions, they can make a big difference in how the text is understood.

Grammatical Errors

Few of the New Testament authors were native Greek speakers. Luke seems to have been one, but he may have been the only one. Even Paul, who grew up in Tarsus, which at least was a Greek area, does not seem to have been a native speaker. The Christian scholar Origen, himself a native speaker, commented on how bad Paul's Greek was.[30] Even Luke wrote in Koine Greek and not good classical Greek. The New Testament writers wrote in the best Greek that they knew, but their grammar was not always perfect—a fact that bothered some later native speakers.

Certain copyists insisted on fixing the bad Greek of the New Testament writers. In James 3:3, the fourth-century Codex Sinaiticus has εις το πιθεσ'θ'αι αυτους ημιν (*eis to pithesthai autous hēmin*). The fourth-century Codex Vaticanus has εις το πειθεσθαι αυτ'ο'υ'ς' ημιν (*eis to peithesthai autous hēmin*). The fifth-century Codex Alexandrinus has προς το πειθεσθαι ημιν αυτους (*pros to peithesthai hemin autous*), all of which translate as "that you may obey us." Normally in classical Greek, the dative, or indirect object, precedes the accusative, the direct object. The opposite is true of Hebrew. The earlier manuscripts preserve the original unusual order in James. Codex Alexandrinus (as is somewhat typical of this manuscript) transposes the words to make it fit normal Greek syntax.

Linguistic Updating

Over time, as manuscripts were copied, archaic or obsolete passages would sometimes be updated to reflect the most current language. This phenomenon is better known from the Hebrew Bible. For example, in Genesis 12:15,

30. Eusebius, *Ecclesiastical History* 6.25.11.

the Masoretic text has ותקח האשה בית פרעה "and the woman was taken (to) the house of Pharaoh" where the preposition "to" is missing, though the earlier form of Hebrew did not require it. The Samaritan Pentateuch, an older manuscript, has ותקח האשה ביתה פרעה "and the woman was taken to the house of Pharaoh."

The Samaritan Pentateuch preserved the locative "he" in construct for the noun "house," a linguistic phenomenon that only occurs in preexilic Hebrew texts.[31] The Masoretic text has dropped this archaic feature and linguistically updated the text. In this particular instance, the change makes no difference in the translation.

Linguistic updating applies to all textual versions and is not necessarily uniform across all versions. For example, in some places, the Dead Sea Scrolls may preserve an older form, while in a different place in the same book, the much later Masoretic text may preserve the same older form.

Linguistic updating or correction also occurs in the New Testament. In Matthew 27:5, the reading variants deal with whether Judas threw the money ἐν τῷ ναῷ (*en tō naō* [dative]) or εἰς τὸν ναὸν (*eis ton naon* [accusative]); both translate as "into the temple." The fourth-century manuscripts (Sinaiticus and Vaticanus) read εἰς τὸν ναὸν, and the fifth-century manuscripts (Alexandrinus and Ephraemi) read ἐν τῷ ναῷ. The older Greek form was to use ἐν + dative to indicate motion toward a place.[32] By the time the New Testament was being written, this expression began to be replaced by εἰς + accusative.[33] In this example, the earlier manuscripts, which are still about three centuries after the original account was written, do not attest the linguistically earlier reading.

The famous passage in James 1:5 reads in English, "Let him ask of God who giveth to all men liberally and upbraideth not." The fourth-century Codex Sinaiticus has αιτιτω παρα του διδοντος ΘΥ πασιν απλως και μη ονιδιζοντο'ς'. The fourth-century Codex Vaticanus has αιτειτω παρα του διδοντος ΘΥ πασιν απλως και μη ονειδιζοντος. The fifth-century Codex Alexandrinus, however, has αιτειτω παρα του ΘΥ του διδο(ν)τος πασιν απλως και μη ονιδιζοντος.

31. Ronald Hendel and Jan Joosten, *How Old Is the Hebrew Bible? A Linguistic, Textual, and Historical Study* (New Haven, Conn.: Yale University Press, 2018), 44–45, 54, 67–68, 83.

32. Herbert Weir Smyth, *Greek Grammar* (Cambridge, Mass.: Harvard University Press, 1920), 351–52, §1536.

33. Robert Browning, *Medieval and Modern Greek* (London: Hutchinson University Library, 1969), 42.

All these versions would be translated the same way in English because English cannot follow the flexible syntax of Greek. In classical Greek, it was common to place the attributive participle (διδόντος [*didontos*], "giving") before the noun (θεοῦ [*theou*], "of God") and, separated from its adjuncts, the words that modify it (πᾶσιν ἁπλῶς [*pasin haplōs*], "to all sincerely").[34] In Koine Greek, this was more unusual and awkward, and so it most often included the adjuncts with the participle between the article and the noun.[35] Starting in the second century AD, it was more common to place the participle with its adjuncts after the noun it modifies,[36] which is the order followed in Codex Alexandrinus. Though this syntactic difference is invisible in translation, it is still an indication of linguistic updating.

Omissions and Additions

When comparing two manuscripts wherein one has material that the other does not, what looks like an addition from the view of one manuscript will look like an omission from the view of the other manuscript. Which reading is correct? This may not be obvious for any given reading.

It might be helpful to know the relative frequency of additions to omissions. Which mistake was more common? Most textual editors assume that additions were more frequent than omissions. But the method employed for the most part by editors over the last hundred years from Tischendorf and Hort to the 2012 Greek New Testament issued by the United Bible Societies has been to apply "two simple rules: A. Follow the Alexandrian uncials (principally א B and the early papyri); B. When in doubt, select the shorter reading."[37] This is normally formulated as a rule (in Latin): *lectio brevior potior,* "the shorter reading is to be preferred." This rule assumes that additions are more common than omissions.

Although this rule is widely held, many have questioned it. Unfortunately, there have been few empirical tests of the proposition. This occurs in part because most text critics come from the humanities and thus tend

34. Smyth, *Greek Grammar,* 294, §1166.

35. Friedrich Blass and Albert Debrunner, *A Greek Grammar of the New Testament and Other Early Christian Literature,* trans. Robert W. Funk (Chicago: University of Chicago Press, 1961), 250–51, §474(5a).

36. P. Oxy. 2.237 17 (AD 186); SB 14.12037 10–11 (second century AD); P. Oxy. 6.937 29–30 (third century AD).

37. J. M. Ross, "Some Unnoticed Points in the Text of the New Testament," *Novum Testamentum* 25, no. 1 (1983): 59, https://doi.org/10.2307/1560482.

to have an aversion to mathematics. Another reason comes from an analogy put forth by the most readable textual critic A. E. Housman:

> [Textual criticism] is not susceptible of hard-and-fast rules. It would be much easier if it were; and that is why people try to pretend that it is, or at least behave as if they thought so. Of course you can have hard-and-fast rules if you like, but then you will have false rules, and they will lead you wrong; because their simplicity will render them inapplicable to problems which are not simple, but complicated by the play of personality. A textual critic engaged upon his business is not at all like Newton investigating the motions of the planets: he is much more like a dog hunting for fleas. If a dog hunted for fleas on mathematic principles, basing his researches on statistics of area and population, he would never catch a flea except by accident. They require to be treated as individuals; and every problem which presents itself to the textual critic must be regarded as possibly unique.[38]

We need to make a distinction between individual problems in any particular passage, which should be treated on an individual level, and general (rather than hard-and-fast) rules that should correspond to the empirical reality for entire texts.

How frequent are omissions? One method proposed for measuring the changes is to look at the singular readings of a manuscript. Singular readings are readings in one manuscript that are not found in other manuscripts. They are thus less indicative of a general trend in the text and more indicative of the idiosyncrasies for that particular manuscript. One can only talk about singular readings where there are a large number of manuscripts, like the books of the Bible or the works of Homer. Most ancient works have a handful of manuscripts at most, and so singular readings cannot be an issue.

On the one hand, singular readings can show characteristics of one particular scribe; on the other hand, if multiple scribes coincidentally make the same mistake, then the reading is no longer singular; consequently, looking at singular readings will not identify the scribe's error. Looking at New Testament papyrus manuscripts, we notice that, of the singular readings in $\mathfrak{P}^{45}$, 28.6 percent are omissions.[39] Many of these are of more than one word. Of the singular readings in $\mathfrak{P}^{46}$, 35.6 percent are omissions.[40] Many of these are of more than one word. Depending on how they are counted,

38. Housman, "Application of Thought to Textual Criticism," 68–69.
39. Royse, *Scribal Habits of Early Greek New Testament Papyri*, 131.
40. Royse, *Scribal Habits of Early Greek New Testament Papyri*, 270.

either 28.3 percent or 30.2 percent of singular readings in $\mathfrak{P}^{47}$ are omissions.[41] In $\mathfrak{P}^{66}$, 18.3 percent of the singular readings are omissions, but this is after later correctors restored many omitted phrases, words, and parts of words.[42] Of the singular readings in manuscript $\mathfrak{P}^{72}$, 29.7 percent are omissions.[43] In manuscript $\mathfrak{P}^{75}$, 32.1 percent of the singular readings are omissions.[44] In manuscript $\mathfrak{P}^{127}$, 30.5 percent of the singular readings are omissions.[45] Thus the attested range of omissions among singular readings in early New Testament papyrus manuscripts is between 18.3 percent and 35.6 percent. By itself, this observation is incomplete.

How frequent were additions to the text? Of the singular readings in $\mathfrak{P}^{45}$, 13.8 percent are the result of addition; all but four are a single word.[46] Of the singular readings in $\mathfrak{P}^{46}$, 11.5 percent are additions; only two additions are two words rather than one word.[47] Among singular readings in $\mathfrak{P}^{47}$, 11.3 percent or 13.2 percent are additions. Of the additions, the only one more than a single word is a dittography.[48] In $\mathfrak{P}^{66}$, between 13.8 percent and 15.6 percent of the singular readings are additions.[49] Only three of them are two words long; the rest are a single word. Of the singular readings in manuscript $\mathfrak{P}^{72}$, 18.9 percent are additions.[50] These additions are only one word, with one exception that adds four. In manuscript $\mathfrak{P}^{75}$, 10.4 percent of the singular readings are additions.[51] In manuscript $\mathfrak{P}^{127}$, 17.2 percent of the singular readings are additions.[52] Hence, additions account for between 10.4 percent and 18.9 percent of the singular readings. On average they occur about half as often as omissions.

If one pools the manuscripts together and drops the ambiguous cases, then 43.1 percent of the singular readings are omissions and 13.0 percent are additions, which means that there are 3.3 times as many omissions as additions among singular readings.

---

41. Royse, *Scribal Habits of Early Greek New Testament Papyri,* 376.
42. Royse, *Scribal Habits of Early Greek New Testament Papyri,* 511.
43. Royse, *Scribal Habits of Early Greek New Testament Papyri,* 586.
44. Royse, *Scribal Habits of Early Greek New Testament Papyri,* 662.
45. Alan Taylor Farnes, *Simply Come Copying* (Tübingen, Ger.: Mohr Siebeck, 2019), 59–60.
46. Royse, *Scribal Habits of Early Greek New Testament Papyri,* 125.
47. Royse, *Scribal Habits of Early Greek New Testament Papyri,* 267–69.
48. Royse, *Scribal Habits of Early Greek New Testament Papyri,* 374–76.
49. Royse, *Scribal Habits of Early Greek New Testament Papyri,* 505.
50. Royse, *Scribal Habits of Early Greek New Testament Papyri,* 582.
51. Royse, *Scribal Habits of Early Greek New Testament Papyri,* 660.
52. Farnes, *Simply Come Copying,* 59.

Another way to look at the problem is to look at errors that the scribe corrected while copying—corrections *in scribendo,* as they are termed in Latin. In the same set of manuscripts,[53] omissions account for 32.0 percent of the corrections *in scribendo,* while additions account for 12.5 percent of the corrections *in scribendo.* Of these corrections, omissions are 2.6 times as frequent as additions. One can also look at corrections by later hands, which were presumably comparing the manuscript with others. This yields 27.8 percent of the errors being omissions and 0 percent additions.[54] By various ways of checking for errors, omissions are 2.6 to 3.3 times as likely as additions. J. M. Ross stated, "It usually requires more effort to add than to omit, so that mere carelessness would tend to shorten rather than enlarge the text."[55]

After examining the evidence, James R. Royse asked "how earlier scholars could have formulated a rule that so clearly—as it turns out—goes against the scribal activity evidenced in our papyri."[56] He answers his question, in part, as follows:

> The frequency with which scholars such as Hort and Metzger appeal to the preference for the shorter reading is doubtless in part due to the ease and objectivity of its application. Whether a particular reading fits the style of the author, is grammatically smoother, follows Semitic idiom, or is theologically more acceptable, is usually very much a matter of debate, and reaching any decision on such issues would involve the weighing of a great deal of evidence. But deciding whether one reading is shorter than another is, at least usually, a perfectly straightforward task. It is therefore convenient to reduce textual questions to questions of length, and then to decide accordingly.[57]

While this does not mean that there are no additions to the text, omissions are significantly more likely to occur than additions, so textual critics should not rely on a rule that gives them the wrong answer the majority of the time.

Omissions. The most common scribal mistake is to drop something, such as a letter, a word, or a phrase. The technical term for this mistake is *haplography.* Most omissions are accidental, but some are intentional:

53. Royse, *Scribal Habits of Early Greek New Testament Papyri,* 115–16, 225–27, 365–67, 422–43, 560–69, 632–40.

54. Royse, *Scribal Habits of Early Greek New Testament Papyri,* 118, 235–42, 569–70.

55. Ross, "Some Unnoticed Points in the Text of the New Testament," 60.

56. Royse, *Scribal Habits of Early Greek New Testament Papyri,* 705.

57. Royse, *Scribal Habits of Early Greek New Testament Papyri,* 711.

"A scribe may have omitted material which he deemed to be superfluous, harsh or contrary to pious, liturgical usage or ascetical practice."[58]

Dropping a letter is a frequent occurrence that is mostly obvious and readily detectable by comparing one manuscript to another. Sometimes, however, the word missing a letter is also a word and may make sense on its own. In 1 John 5:10, the text reads: ὁ πιστεύων εἰς τὸν υἱὸν τοῦ θεοῦ ἔχει τὴν μαρτυρίαν ἐν ἑαυτῷ (*en heautō*, "within himself" [last two words]), "He who believes in the Son of God has the testimony within himself." A number of later manuscripts drop a single letter, giving ὁ πιστεύων εἰς τὸν υἱὸν τοῦ θεοῦ ἔχει τὴν μαρτυρίαν ἐν αὐτῷ (*en auto,* "in him" [last two words]), "He who believes in the Son of God has the testimony in him." By dropping a single letter, the pronoun changes its referent from the believer to the Son of God—no small change in meaning.

An example of dropping a word is found in Romans 9:31–32. Most manuscripts have Ἰσραὴλ δὲ διώκων νόμον δικαιοσύνης εἰς νόμον οὐκ ἔφθασεν δικαιοσύνης. διὰ τί; ὅτι οὐκ ἐκ πίστεως ἀλλ' ὡς ἐξ ἔργων νόμου· "When Israel pursued the law of righteousness in the law, they did not obtain righteousness. Why? Because it was not from faith but from the works of the law." Several manuscripts drop the last word νόμου (*nomou*), "of the law." Paul otherwise uses the phrase ἔργων νόμου, "works of the law."[59] The scribe of Codex Sinaiticus omitted the word νόμου as one of three omissions in as many lines of text.[60]

An example of dropping a phrase is Matthew 28:7. Where most manuscripts have Ἠγέρθη ἀπὸ τῶν νεκρῶν (*Ēgerthē apo tōn nekrōn*), "he is raised from the dead," the late fifth-century Codex Bezae Cantabrigiensis (D) has simply Ἠγέρθη (*Ēgerthē*), "he is raised."

Sometimes an entire verse or more might be dropped from the text. The following verses are missing in some manuscripts of the New Testament: Matthew 9:34; 12:47; 17:21; 18:11; 21:44; 23:14; Mark 7:16; 9:44; 11:26; 16:9–20; Luke 5:39; 12:21; 17:35; 19:25; 22:17–20, 43–44; 23:17; 24:12, 40; John 5:4; 7:53–8:11; 12:7–8; 14:14; Acts 8:37; 15:34; 24:6–8; 28:29; Romans 16:24–27; 1 Corinthians 14:34–35; and 1 John 5:7–8. Whether these are omissions or additions in each case must be determined on an individual basis. The basic scribal tendency, however, was to leave things out.

---

58. Elliott, "United Bible Societies Greek New Testament," 297.

59. Rom. 3:20, 28; Gal. 2:16.

60. This is clear in the photographs. *Codex Sinaiticus* (London: British Library, 2010), Q82-f.4v.

Special categories of omission are those cases where the scribe's eye slips from the beginning of a word that either looks similar (*homoioarchteon*) or is identical (*homoarchteon*) to another word slightly later in the text, or where the scribe's eye slips from the end of a word that looks similar (*homoioteleuton*) or identical (*homoteleuton*) to another word slightly later in the text. It is easier to argue that these cases are examples of omission. Simply dropping something from the text without explanation, however, is much more common than all of these special cases put together.

An example of homoarchteon is in Matthew 27:40. While most of the manuscripts have σῶσον σεαυτόν, εἰ υἱὸς εἶ τοῦ θεοῦ, καὶ κατάβηθι ἀπὸ τοῦ σταυροῦ, "Save yourself, if you are the son of God, and come down from the cross," in some manuscripts the scribe's eye has slipped from the κα (*ka*) in καὶ (*kai*) to the κα (*ka*) in κατάβηθι (*katabēthi*). Thus the intervening material—in this case the word καὶ (*kai*), "and"—has been omitted.

Another example of homoarchteon is in Matthew 23:14. Several early manuscripts are missing this verse entirely. The verse is in a series of statements that all begin with οὐαὶ ὑμῖν γραμματεῖς και φαρισαῖοι ὑποκριταί, "Woe to you, bureaucrats and Pharisees, hypocrites!" Though the verse is missing from the fourth-century manuscripts, it does appear in the fifth-century Freer Codex as well as some later manuscripts.

One example of homoioteleuton is in 1 Corinthians 1:14, where Paul says, εὐχαριστῶ τῷ θεῷ ὅτι οὐδένα ὑμῶν ἐβάπτισα εἰ μὴ Κρίσπον καὶ Γάϊον, "I thank God that I baptized none of you except Cripsus and Gaius." The phrase τῷ θεῷ (*tō theō*) has dropped out because of homoioteleuton. The sequence of letters in early manuscripts would have looked something like ΕΥΧΑΡΙΣΤΩΤΩΘΩΟΤΙ, and the scribe's eye would have slipped from the first to the third omega (Ω) in the string, omitting everything in between. The normal syntax for εὐχαριστῶ (*eucharistō*) is to have the entity thanked in the dative case,[61] which argues for including the missing expression.

An example that could be either homoarchteon or homoteleuton is the passage in 1 Corinthians 15:54. The text reads, ὅταν δὲ τὸ ***φθαρτὸν τοῦτο ἐνδύσηται ἀφθαρσίαν καὶ τὸ*** θνητὸν τοῦτο ἐνδύσηται ἀθανασίαν, "when this corruption is clothed in incorruption and this mortal is clothed in

61. For example, BGU 2.531 7 (first century AD); BGU 3.843 9 (first–second century AD); BGU 1.180 23–24 (second century AD); Chr.Wilck. 480 6 (second century); BGU 3.816.v3–12 (third century AD); CPR 7.15 21 (fourth century AD); BGU 3.798 6 (fourth–seventh century AD).

immortality." The scribe's eye skipped from one definite article (τό [*to*], "the") to the next and consequently omitted the entire bolded phrase (*to phtharton touto endysētai aphtharsian kai to*).

Additions. Deletions were more likely to be caused by scribal carelessness or sloppiness, but scribes also added to the text as well. This sort of mistake could have been accidental as well as deliberate.

Possibly the most common accidental addition is called *dittography*—the repetition of words. This is particularly frequent at the end of a line or page where the last word or words will be repeated at the beginning of the next line or page. For example, in John 1:27, in Papyrus Bodmer II (𝔓[66]), the scribe wrote τον at the end of the line and repeated it at the beginning of the next line.[62]

There are deliberate additions as well. One common addition in the New Testament manuscripts is the addition of the word ἀμήν, "Amen," at the end of New Testament books. This first appeared in the third century AD, but in most cases does not appear at the end of the earliest manuscript or manuscripts.

New Testament Work	Earliest Manuscript Ending without ἀμήν	Earliest Manuscript Ending with ἀμήν
Matthew	ℵ, B, 4th century	A, 5th century
Mark	A, 5th century	C, 5th century
Luke	𝔓[75], 3rd century	B, 4th century
John	ℵ, 4th century	C, 5th century
Acts	ℵ, 4th century	Ψ, 8th century
Romans	𝔓[46], 3rd century	𝔓[46], 3rd century
1 Corinthians	ℵ, B, 4th century	ℵ, 4th century
2 Corinthians	𝔓[46], 3rd century	ℵ, 4th century
Galatians	𝔓[46], 3rd century	𝔓[46], 3rd century
Ephesians	𝔓[46], 3rd century	ℵ, 4th century
Philippians	𝔓[46], 3rd century	𝔓[46], 3rd century
Colossians	ℵ, 4th century	ℵ, 4th century
1 Thessalonians	ℵ, B, 4th century	ℵ, 4th century
2 Thessalonians	ℵ, B, 4th century	ℵ, 4th century
1 Timothy	ℵ, 4th century	ℵ, 4th century
2 Timothy	ℵ, 4th century	ℵ, 4th century

62. Victor Martin, *Papyrus Bodmer II* (Cologny-Genève, Switz.: Bibliotheca Bodmeriana, 1956), 39; Royse, *Scribal Habits of Early Greek New Testament Papyri,* 441.

New Testament Work	Earliest Manuscript Ending without ἀμήν	Earliest Manuscript Ending with ἀμήν
Titus	א, 4th century	א, 4th century
Philemon	א, 4th century	א, 4th century
Hebrews	𝔓46, 3rd century	א, 4th century
James	א, B, 4th century	1505, 11th century
1 Peter	א, B, 4th century	א, 4th century
2 Peter	𝔓72, א, B, 4th century	𝔓72, א, 4th century
1 John	א, B, 4th century	P, 6th century
2 John	א, B, 4th century	1758, 13th century
3 John	א, B, 4th century	L, 8th century
Jude	א, B, 4th century	א, B, 4th century
Revelation	א, 4th century	א, 4th century

Histories, biographies, literary texts, and letters did not end with ἀμήν, but liturgical readings did. Since the reading of scriptures had been a part of worship in Jewish synagogues,[63] the Christians continued the practice; reading scripture (the apostles and prophets) as part of the Christian worship service is attested by the second century.[64] The office of lector (ἀναγνωστής)—someone who read (or chanted) the scriptures during worship services—is attested as early as the early third century.[65] The precise readings generally rotated but were not fixed.[66] The large codices, like Sinaiticus, Vaticanus, and Alexandrinus, were deluxe editions created to serve as Bibles to be read in church services. The (mostly later) additions of ἀμήν at the end of the work in a manuscript served a liturgical purpose and seems unlikely to have been part of the original texts, which were not initially written for liturgical purposes.

As an aside, it is worth noting that lectors had another significant impact on New Testament manuscripts. Greek documents were written either in a literary hand, with the letters carefully and distinctly written, or in a documentary hand, which was more quickly written and more cursive,

63. Luke 4:16–21.

64. Justin Martyr, *Apology* 1.67.

65. Tertullian, *Prescription against Heretics* 41. There is some ambiguity about this term in papyri; see Malcolm Choat, *Belief and Cult in Fourth-Century Papyri* (Turnhout, Belg.: Brepolis, 2006), 60.

66. Ágnes T. Mihálykó, *The Christian Liturgical Papyri: An Introduction* (Tübingen, Ger.: Mohr Siebeck, 2019), 56–57.

with letters ligatured together. Using lectors, who were not necessarily professional scribes, to read scriptural texts as part of the liturgy required that those scriptural texts be written in the more distinct, and significantly more expensive, literary hand,[67] which is why more of the early Greek New Testament manuscripts are in uncial hands.

Another intentional addition to the text is in the Sermon on the Mount. In Matthew 5:22, Jesus says, πᾶς ὁ ὀργιζόμενος τῷ ἀδελφῷ αὐτοῦ ἔνοχος ἔσται τῇ κρίσει· "Anyone who is angry with his brother will be guilty in the judgment." The variants in the manuscripts also have πᾶς ὁ ὀργιζόμενος τῷ ἀδελφῷ αὐτοῦ ***εἰκῇ*** ἔνοχος ἔσται τῇ κρίσει· "Anyone who is angry with his brother ***without a reason*** [εἰκῇ, *eikē*] will be guilty in the judgment." This other reading is known as early as the second century. Near the end of the second century, Irenaeus wrote that "the teaching of the Lord" (*ex Domini doctrina*) was that "not only one who slew, would it be the cause of his damnation, but also one who was angry with his brother ***without a cause***" (*et non solum qui occidit, reus erit occisionis ad damnationem, sed et qui irascitur* **sine causa** *fratri suo*).[68] However, Irenaeus's contemporary Origen claimed that some manuscripts had improperly added the term.[69] The earliest manuscript of this passage, the late second-century[70] $\mathfrak{P}^{64/67}$, does not have this reading, but most of the rest of the manuscripts do. Someone who is angry can always seem to come up with a reason why they are angry. The purpose of the change, which seems intentional, was "to soften the rigor of the precept."[71] (The Book of Mormon parallel text in 3 Nephi 12:22 also does not have "without a cause.") This argues that this single Greek word, which significantly changes the intent and meaning of the passage, was a later addition.

---

67. Roger S. Bagnall, *Early Christian Books in Egypt* (Princeton, N.J.: Princeton University Press, 2009), 50–69, especially 57. A literary hand would have cost more than three times what a documentary hand would.

68. Irenaeus, *Against Heresies* 2.32.1, emphasis added.

69. Ronald E. Heine, *The Commentaries of Origen and Jerome on St. Paul's Epistle to the Ephesians* (New York: Oxford University Press, 2002), 205.

70. Manuscript dates in the standard editions often are at variance with papyrological dates; see Pasquale Orsini and Willy Clarysse, "Early New Testament Manuscripts and Their Dates: A Critique of Theological Palaeography," *Ephemerides Theologicae Lovanienses* 88, no. 4 (2012): 443–74. I follow Orsini's and Clarysse's dates here.

71. Bruce M. Metzger, *A Textual Commentary on the Greek New Testament* (London: United Bible Societies, 1971), 13; Roger L. Omanson, *A Textual Guide to the Greek New Testament* (Stuttgart, Ger.: Deutsche Bibelgesellschaft, 2006), 6.

Harmonization

Though a couple of Gospel writers based their work on previous accounts, each wrote his own book. Later copyists sometimes harmonized the separate Gospel accounts by bringing phrases from one account to another so that each Gospel provides a similar story or meaning. Part of this harmonizing tendency came from the repetitive hearing of scripture as part of the liturgy read by the lector every week. Some harmonizing also resulted from individual study.[72] Part of it stemmed from the frequent early Christian practice of memorizing entire books of scripture.[73] Memorization of lengthy passages of the Iliad and Odyssey and textbooks as part of an ancient Greek education was not unusual.[74] The Christians just had a different set of books that they memorized. But this memorization could interfere with copying the text. For instance, in Matthew's account of events in the Garden of Gethsemane, two manuscripts, one from the fifth century (C) and one from the sixth (Φ), added Luke 22:43–44 after Matthew 26:39. The fifth-century manuscript added it into the margin. Other manuscripts were influenced by the liturgy or memorization in harmonizing the passage.[75]

Doctrinal Adjustments

Sometimes the text of the New Testament was adjusted to reflect changes in teachings of the early Christian Church. An example of this is found in John 1:18. The early Greek manuscript readings, organized roughly chronologically, are as follows:

- P. Bodmer II (𝔓[66], AD 200–250): θν ουδεις εωρακεν πωποται μ̣ονογενης θς ο ων εις τον κολπον τ[ου] πρς εκινος εξηγησατο, "No one has ever seen

---

72. ⲙⲉⲗⲉⲧⲉ ⲛ̄ⲛ̣[ⲉⲕ]ⲯⲁⲗⲙⲟⲥ ⲉⲓⲧⲉ ⲛ̄ⲟⲩⲓⲁⲛⲓⲛ ⲉⲓⲧⲉ ⲛ̄ⲣⲙ̄ⲛ̄ⲕⲏⲙⲉ ϩⲟⲟⲩ <ⲛⲓⲙ>, "Study your Psalms every day whether in Greek or in Coptic." P. Kell. Copt. 19 13–14, in Iain Gardner, Anthony Alcock, and Wolf-Peter Funk, eds., *Coptic Documentary Texts from Kellis,* vol. 1 (Oxford: Oxbow Books, 1999), 157.

73. Apa Panoute, *The Life of Apa Onnophrios, the Anchorite,* fol. 2a, in E. A. Wallis Budge, *Coptic Martyrdoms etc. in the Dialect of Upper Egypt* (London: British Museum, 1914), 206.

74. Xenophon, *Symposium* 3.5: ὁ πατὴρ ὁ ἐπιμελούμενος ὅπως ἀνὴρ ἀγαθὸς γενοίμην ἠνάγκασέ με πάντα τὰ Ὁμήρου ἔπη μαθεῖν· καὶ νῦν δυναίμην ἂν Ἰλιάδα ὅλην καὶ Ὀδύσσειαν ἀπὸ στόματος εἰπεῖν. Raffaella Cribiore, *Gymnastics of the Mind: Greek Education in Hellenistic and Roman Egypt* (Princeton, N.J.: Princeton University Press, 2001), 213.

75. Blumell, "Luke 22:43–44: An Anti-Docetic Interpolation or an Apologetic Omission?," 7.

God; an only-begotten God, who is in the bosom of the Father, he has explained him."

- P. Bodmer XV (𝔓[75], AD 200–250): θν ουδεις πωποτε εορακεν ο μονογενης θς ο ων εις τον κολπον του πατρος εκεινος εξηγησατο, "No one has ever seen God; the only-begotten God, who is in the bosom of the Father, he has explained him."
- Codex Sinaiticus (א, AD 300–400): θν ουδεις εωρακεν πωποτε 'ο' μ'ο'νογενης θς 'ο ων' ει'ς' τ'ο(ν)' κολπον του πατρος εκεινος εξηγησατο, "No one has ever seen God; the only-begotten God, who is in the bosom of the Father, he has explained him."
- Codex Vaticanus (B, AD 300–400): θν ουδεις εορακεν πωποτε μον'ο'γενης θς ο ων εις τον κολπον του πατρος εκεινος εξηγησατο, "No one has ever seen God; an only-begotten God, who is in the bosom of the Father, he has explained him."
- Codex Alexandrinus (A, AD 400–500): θν ουδεις εωρακεν πωποτε ο μονογενης υιος ο ων εις τον κολπον του πρς εκεινος εξηγησατο, "No one has ever seen God; the only-begotten son, who is in the bosom of the Father, he has explained him."
- Codex Ephraemi Rescriptus (C, AD 400–500): θν ουδεις εωρακεν πωποτε ο μονογενης θς 'σ̣ε̣'[76] ο ων εις τον κολπον του πρς εκεινος εξηγησατο, "No one has ever seen God; the only-begotten God, who is in the bosom of the Father, he has explained you."

The key issue is whether to read μονογενὴς θς (*monogenēs theos*), "only-begotten God," or μονογενὴς υἱὸς (*monogenēs huios*), "only-begotten son." The presence or absence of the definite article, the placement of the adverb, and the spelling are minor issues. Codex Sinaiticus, as is common, drops multiple words in this passage that a later scribe had to insert as corrections. The Byzantine text (the text based on manuscripts from the Byzantine period), like Alexandrinus, has μονογενὴς υἱὸς (*monogenēs huios*), "only-begotten son." John elsewhere used the expression "only-begotten son" in the accusative (τὸν υἱὸν τὸν μονογενῆ, *ton huion ton monogenē*; John 3:16) and the genitive (τοῦ μονογενοῦς υἱοῦ τοῦ θεοῦ, *tou monogenous huiou tou theou*; John 3:18).

Conjecturally, we could hypothesize that the text originally read ὁ μονογενὴς υἱὸς τοῦ θεοῦ (*ho monogenēs hiouos tou theou*), "the only-begotten son of God," which matches John's usage in John 3:18, and this conjectural reading has support, not in a New Testament manuscript but in

76. The corrector is supposed to have corrected this to υιος, but I cannot see it in the photographs.

early quotations of the passage. Clement of Alexandria paraphrases the passage and gives ὁ μονογενὴς υἱὸς θεὸς (*ho monogenēs hiuos theos*), "the only-begotten son and God," in one place[77] and υἱὸς μονογενὴς (*hiuos monogenēs*), "only-begotten son," in another place.[78] Clement's contemporary Irenaeus quotes this passage twice, though the work survives only in a Latin translation. The quotes differ slightly:

> *Deum enim, inquit, nemo vidit unquam, nisi unigenitus Filius Dei, qui est in sinu Patris, ipse enarravit.* "For, he said, no one has ever seen God, unless the only-begotten son of God, who is in the bosom of the Father, has declared him."[79]

> *Deum nemo vidit unquam, nisi unigenitus Filius, qui est in sinu Patris, ipse enarravit.* "No one has ever seen God, unless the only-begotten son, who is in the bosom of the Father, has declared him."[80]

The intrusive words introducing the quotation in the first passage can be ignored. Half of the second-century quotations have "son" and half have "son of God." The presence of "son" in the quotations and the later manuscripts compared to its absence in the earlier manuscripts argues that the earlier manuscripts have dropped the word. The presence of "God" in half of the early quotations and all of the manuscripts argues that "only-begotten son of God" was the probable earliest reading.

The most significant difference in Irenaeus, however, is the addition of *nisi*, "except, unless," which is the equivalent of Greek ἐὰν μὴ (*ean mē*) or εἰ μὴ (*ei mē*). The expression ἐὰν μὴ (*ean mē*) appears seventeen other times in John.[81] The expression εἰ μὴ (*ei mē*) appears fourteen other times in John.[82] Either expression would be the equivalent of the Latin, and since they both appear approximately the same number of times, it would be difficult to tell which one John might prefer simply based on frequency. But John prefers to use εἰ μὴ (*ei mē*) before a noun, a prepositional phrase, or a phrase containing the verb εἰμί (*eimi*) "to be," and he prefers to use ἐὰν μὴ (*ean mē*) before verbal phrases. Since this is a verbal phrase, the retroversion from the Latin would be ἐὰν μὴ (*ean mē*). This reading in Irenaeus predates any

---

77. Clement of Alexandria, *Who Is the Rich Man Who Is Saved?* 37.

78. Clement of Alexandria, *Stromata* 1.26.

79. Irenaeus, *Against the Heresies* 3.11.6.

80. Irenaeus, *Against the Heresies* 4.20.6.

81. John 3:2, 3, 5, 27; 4:48; 5:19; 6:44, 53, 65; 7:51; 8:24; 12:24; 13:8; 15:4 (twice), 6; 16:7; 20:25.

82. John 3:13; 6:22, 46; 9:33; 10:10; 13:10; 14:2, 6, 11; 15:22; 17:12; 18:30; 19:11, 15.

of the surviving manuscripts by about half a century. (The Joseph Smith Translation also has "except" here but with additional changes.[83] Retroverted into Greek, the Joseph Smith Translation "no man hath seen God at any time, except he hath borne record of the Son" would read θεὸν οὐδεὶς ἑώρακεν πώποτε· ἐὰν [or εἰ] μὴ τὸν μονογενῆ υἱὸν ἐκεῖνος ἐξηγήσατο.)

The reading μονογενης θς (*monogenēs theos*), "only-begotten God," was used by Gnostics (and others)[84] for whom μονογενής (*monogenēs*), "only-begotten," was a term for the first emanation of the invisible (or unseeable) Spirit, who is God or the first being.[85] The Gnostics seem to have supported their stance with this scripture. On the other hand, μονογενης υιος (*monogenēs hiuos*), "only-begotten son," reflects the wording in the Nicaean Creed, which either could have been pulled from the other usage in John—such as from John 3:16, 18—or through access to a pre-Gnostic manuscript. Either reading could, in fact, support either doctrinal stance, but particular readings more strongly support particular stances.

Only one, and one of the latest, of the pre-sixth-century manuscripts reads υιος (*hiuos*), "son," agreeing with the second-century quotations; the rest read θς (*theos*), "God." The later reading ("son") looks to have been doctrinally adjusted—away from a reading that would support Gnostics to one that would support the Nicaean Creed.

The passage has been doctrinally adjusted twice: First, the Gnostics in the second century dropped ἐὰν μὴ (*ean mē*) to eliminate the possibility of man ever seeing God, and they dropped υἱός (*hiuos*) because they believed that μονογενής (*monogenēs*) was an emanation of God and not his son. Making these changes made the text accord with their doctrine. The second time, the orthodox changed "only-begotten God" to "only-begotten son" to make the scriptural text conform with the Nicaean Creed, but since Nicaean Christianity shared the Neoplatonic presuppositions about no human being having direct access to God, there was no incentive to restore an "except" had one been known. The Joseph Smith Translation here is arguably closer to the original reading than the current editions of the Greek New Testament.

---

83. Joseph Smith Translation, New Testament Manuscript 2, in *Joseph Smith's New Translation of the Bible: Original Manuscripts,* ed. Scott H. Faulring, Kent P. Jackson, and Robert J. Matthews (Provo, Utah: Religious Studies Center, Brigham Young University, 2004), 443.

84. *Valentinian Exposition,* Nag Hammadi Codex XI 24.31–39; 25.20–22; 40.30–34.

85. Irenaeus, *Against Heresies* 1.1.1–2; 2.1, 4, 5; 12.1; 2.17.11; 3.11.1; Tertullian, *Against the Valentinians* 7.1; 10.1; 11.1; Hippolytus, *Refutation of All Heresies* 6.33.2; *Apocryphon of John* III.9.15–19; *Gospel of the Egyptians* III.68.10–69.5.

Another example of doctrinal adjustment comes from modern times. Galatians 5:19–21 lists the various works of the flesh. The list starts with μοιχεία, πορνεία, ἀκαθαρσία, ἀσέλγεια, "adultery, immorality, uncleanness, licentiousness." Three of the four manuscripts before the sixth century dropped the first term μοιχεία, "adultery," though one of the manuscripts is well-known for dropping things out, and a corrector has added it. Though the words have similar endings, *homoteleuton* would skip from the first term to a later term. This is simply a dropping of the variants. Some of the manuscripts give this as a list with each word on a separate line. In this case, the doctrinal adjustment is modern, not ancient. One major modern critical edition dropped μοιχεία, "adultery," without even noting that there was a textual variant.[86]

Plain and Precious Things

Latter-day Saints have an interest in textual criticism because of Nephi's prophecy that people will "have taken away from the gospel of the Lamb many parts which are plain and most precious; and also many covenants of the Lord have they taken away" (1 Ne. 13:26). While Latter-day Saints often refer to the taking away of plain and precious things in a general way, specific instances of removal of plain and precious things or of covenants are rarely mentioned. This vagueness does not serve us well in responding to assertions that "viable textual variants that disturb cardinal doctrines found in the NT have not yet been produced."[87] Examination of some specific examples of changes in the biblical text can help clarify the processes by which plain and precious things were removed. Although many plain and precious things were removed by changing the definitions of words,[88] here we will highlight plain and precious things removed that are accompanied or caused by changes to the text.

Teachings on Divorce

The Mishnah noted a controversy between the "Galilean heretic" (presumably Jesus) and the Pharisees over divorce.[89] The Gospel of Matthew recorded an account about the controversy, but what exactly Jesus taught

86. *The Greek New Testament,* 3rd ed. (Stuttgart, Ger.: United Bible Societies, 1975), 660. For a critical assessment of the edition, see Borger, "Remarks of an Outsider," 35–40.
87. Wallace, "Lost in Transmission," 55.
88. See Gee, "Corruption of Scripture in Early Christianity," 177–88.
89. *Mishnah Yadayim* 4.8.

is a problem. The two earliest manuscripts differ about what Jesus said in Matthew 19:9.

The fourth-century Codex Sinaiticus has the following:

> λεγω δε ϋμιν οτι ος εαν απολυση̣ τη(ν) γυν[[ε]]'αι'κα αυτου μη επι πορνια και γαμηση̣ αλλην μοιχατε, "I say to you that whosoever divorces his wife except for immorality and marries another commits adultery."

Codex Vaticanus, also from the fourth century, has the following:

> λεγω δε ϋμιν ος αν απ'ο'λυση την γυναικα αυτ'ο'υ παρεκτος λογου πορ'νει'ας ποιει αυτην μοιχ'ου'θηναι και ο απολελυ'με'νην γαμησας μοιχατ'αι', "I say to you that whosoever divorces his wife except for reason of immorality causes her to commit adultery and whoever marries a woman who is divorced commits adultery."

Here the earliest manuscripts of the text have completely different readings. One has the divorced man who remarries committing adultery, and the other has the divorced woman and any future husband committing adultery. Later manuscripts have readings that differ even from these. The variants cannot be accounted for by typical scribal error. The text of Matthew 19:9 clearly has been deliberately altered. Either one or both readings have substantially altered Jesus' words, and it is not clear that any manuscript preserves what Jesus said. Although textual criticism enables us to locate the textual tampering, it does not necessarily enable us by itself to determine which reading is correct.

The Ending of Mark's Gospel

Perhaps the most significant omission is the ending of Mark's Gospel. There are four basic endings of Mark:[90]

1. The standard ending preserved in the Textus Receptus, the traditional text used in the Greek Orthodox Church. These verses are attested as early as the fifth century in Codex Alexandrinus. Also, the vocabulary from them was used by Justin Martyr in the second century.[91]
2. An expanded form of the traditional ending preserved in one Greek manuscript, the fifth-century Freer Codex in Washington.
3. A version that adds an extra verse as a preface after verse 8.
4. An abbreviated ending that is missing the last twelve verses (Mark 16:9–20). This ending is attested in the two fourth-century codices (Sinaiticus [א] and Vaticanus [B]) and in other later manuscripts.

90. Metzger, *Textual Commentary on the Greek New Testament,* 122–26.

91. Justin Martyr, *Apology* 1.45.

One complicating factor is that the last verse before the disputed verses ends abruptly with the sentence ἐφοβοῦντο γάρ, "for they were afraid" (Mark 16:8). There are two problems with this sentence. First, although the enclitic particle γάρ, "for," used as a conjunction regularly comes second in a sentence,[92] it typically does not end a sentence. Second, the middle/passive form of φοβέω, "to fear," is typically followed by an object, a prepositional phrase, a relative clause, or an articular infinitive indicating what was feared.[93] Both words anticipate at least a following word or phrase; they indicate that the sentence is incomplete. This is a clear indication that the abbreviated ending is not the original ending of Mark. On the other hand, the connection to the following verses has been characterized as "awkward."[94] That said, we do not know what the women feared—another pointer to an omission.

The codex—individual sheets gathered together and bound on one side like modern books—was introduced in the late first century,[95] and a large portion of the early codices are Christian in content.[96] Even in the third century, the normal book was still a scroll or book roll rather than a codex.[97] The handwriting on codices is "often of an informal and workaday type, fairly quickly written, serviceable rather than beautiful, of value to a man interested in the content of what he is reading rather than its presentation. . . . These give the impression of being 'utility' books; margins are small, lines usually long."[98]

If we presume a manuscript of Mark being written in a codex, as early manuscripts of Mark invariably were, then it is easy to suppose the loss of the last page since the outer pages of a codex are the most likely to suffer damage. Thus some suppose that "the Gospel accidentally lost its last leaf before it was multiplied by transcription," and the shorter ending is merely "the earliest ascertainable form of the Gospel of Mark,"[99] not the original

---

92. Smyth, *Greek Grammar,* 637–38, §2803.

93. Liddell, Scott, Jones, and McKenzie, *Greek-English Lexicon,* 1946.

94. Metzger, *Textual Commentary on the Greek New Testament,* 125.

95. Larry W. Hurtado, *The Earliest Christian Artifacts: Manuscripts and Christian Origins* (Grand Rapids, Mich.: William B. Eerdmans, 2006), 50–51; Bagnall, *Early Christian Books in Egypt,* 72.

96. Eric G. Turner, *The Typology of the Early Codex* (Philadelphia: University of Pennsylvania Press, 1977), 37; Hurtado, *Earliest Christian Artifacts,* 43–93; Bagnall, *Early Christian Books in Egypt,* 72–73.

97. Bagnall, *Early Christian Books in Egypt,* 71; Johnson, *Bookrolls and Scribes in Oxyrhynchus,* 231–48.

98. Turner, *The Typology of the Early Codex,* 37.

99. Metzger, *A Textual Commentary on the Greek New Testament,* 126.

form of Mark's record. This would account for the manuscripts that lack the last twelve verses. If the original ending of Mark's Gospel went completely missing, one might propose that the longer ending was simply a later scribe writing what he thought should have been there.

On the other hand, part of the standard ending is quoted by Justin Martyr in the second century. Justin wrote, τὸ οὖν εἰρημένον 'Ράβδον δυνάμεως ἐξαποστελεῖ σοι ἐξ 'Ιερουσαλὴμ προαγγελτικὸν ***τοῦ λόγου*** τοῦ ἰσχυροῦ, ὃν ἀπὸ 'Ιερουσαλὴμ οἱ ἀπόστολοι αὐτοῦ ***ἐξελθόντες πανταχοῦ ἐκήρυξαν***, "What he says, 'he shall send you the rod of power from Jerusalem,' is the foretelling of ***the*** mighty ***word*** which his apostles ***who came forth*** from Jerusalem, ***preached everywhere***,"[100] which parallels Mark 16:20: ἐκεῖνοι δὲ ***ἐξελθόντες ἐκήρυξαν πανταχοῦ***, τοῦ κυρίου συνεργοῦντος καὶ ***τὸν λόγον*** βεβαιοῦντος διὰ τῶν ἐπακολουθούντων σημείων, "Then ***going forth, they preached everywhere***, while the Lord worked with them and ***the word*** was made sure by the signs that followed." Hence, Justin quoted from the longer ending of Mark about two centuries before any preserved manuscript of Mark's Gospel.

Irenaeus, from slightly later in the second century, also knows the longer ending of Mark. Irenaeus states, *et contulit credentibus in se super serpentes et corpions calcare, et super omnem virtutem inimici*, "and he conferred those who believed in him to tread on snakes and scorpions, and over all the power of the enemy,"[101] which quotes Mark 16:17–18.[102] Later, Irenaeus not only quotes Mark 16:19 but attributes it to Mark: *In fine autem Evangelii ait Marcus: 'Et quidem Dominus Jesus, postquam locutus est eis, receptus est in coelos, et sedet ad dexteram Dei;' confirmans qnod a Propheta dictum est*, "At the end of his Gospel, Mark says: 'And after the Lord Jesus had spoken to them, he was received into heaven, and sat on the right hand of God.'"[103] Again, this quotation came at least a century before any preserved manuscripts with the ending of Mark.

If the longer standard ending is attested three centuries before the manuscripts, how do we account for the incompleteness of Mark 16:8? Just as manuscripts can lose leaves, they can also lose portions of leaves. But this would imply that different manuscripts of Mark ended the line at the same place. Some evidence exists that scribes copied line by line,[104] and those

100. Justin Martyr, *Apology* 1.45.

101. Irenaeus, *Against Heresies* 2.20.3.

102. The quotation of Jesus in Mark 16:15–18 is also quoted in Mormon 9:22–24 and ascribed to the Resurrected Jesus, as Mark's passage is.

103. Irenaeus, *Against Heresies* 3.10.5.

104. Johnson, *Bookrolls and Scribes in Oxyrhynchus*, 39–49.

that did so tried to preserve line lengths. "Anyone who has studied the literary papyri will be familiar with scribes' constant efforts to adjust the horizontal spacing of a prose text to regularize the right margin."[105] This is also a characteristic of the earliest intact codices that include Mark: Sinaiticus (א), Vaticanus (B), and Alexandrinus (A).

In sum, the longer, standard ending of Mark is attested earlier than the manuscripts that are missing the ending. In this light, it should be retained as the superior reading. The shorter ending of Mark is missing the Resurrection of Jesus. Obviously, the removal of Mark's testimony of the Resurrection and the missionary charge to the eleven Apostles must be counted as plain and precious things that were lost.

The Blood of the Covenant

One of the curiosities of the Gospels is that, except for the prophecy in Luke 1:72 ("To perform the mercy promised to our fathers, and to remember his holy covenant"), the Greek word for "covenant" only appears once in each of the synoptic Gospels during the introduction of the sacrament, but the word is not translated into English that way. The familiar King James Version of the passage in Matthew's Gospel when Jesus blessed the wine is as follows:

> And he took the cup, and gave thanks, and gave it to them, saying, Drink ye all of it; For this is my blood of the new ***testament,*** which is shed for many for the remission of sins. (Matt. 26:27–28)

In the King James Version, we read nothing about covenants. This is an artifact of this particular translation. There is a reason that Latter-day Saints have as an article of faith that declares, "We believe the Bible to be the word of God as far as it is translated correctly" (A of F 1:8). The standard Greek for this passage is:

> καὶ λαβὼν τὸ ποτήριον καὶ εὐχαριστήσας ἔδωκεν αὐτοῖς λέγων, Πίετε ἐξ αὐτοῦ πάντες, τοῦτο γάρ ἐστιν τὸ αἷμά μου τῆς καινῆς ***διαθήκης*** τὸ περὶ πολλῶν ἐκχυννόμενον εἰς ἄφεσιν ἁμαρτιῶν. (Matt. 26:27–28)

One of the things to notice in the Greek is that πάντες, "all," is in the nominative case and therefore refers to the subject. The translation means that all of the disciples should drink rather than that the disciples should drink all of the cup. As it stands, the King James Version is somewhat ambiguous.

105. Johnson, *Bookrolls and Scribes in Oxyrhynchus,* 40.

The Greek text does mention the word for “covenant,” διαθήκης, but its occurrences present a number of textual variants. We will arrange those that date before the seventh century, more or less in chronological order by manuscript:

𝔓^{37} (third century):[106]	τοῦτο γάρ ἐστιν τὸ αἷμά μου τῆς διαθήκης
א (fourth century):	τουτο γαρ εστιν τ‛ο′ αιμα μου της διαθηκης
B (fourth century):	τουτο γαρ ε‛στι(ν)′ το αιμα μου της διαθ‛η′κης
A (fifth century):	τουτο γαρ εστιν το αιμα μου το της καινης διαθηκης
C (fifth century):	τοῦτο γάρ ἐστιν τὸ αἷμά μου τὸ τῆς καινῆς διαθήκης
D (fifth century):	τοῦτο γάρ ἐστιν τὸ αἷμά μου τῆς καινῆς διαθήκης
W (fifth century):	τοῦτο γάρ ἐστιν τὸ αἷμά μου τὸ τῆς καινῆς διαθήκης
Z (sixth century):	τοῦτο γάρ ἐστιν τὸ αἷμά μου τῆς διαθήκης

There are two variants. One reads, “for this is my blood of the covenant,” and the other reads, “for this is my blood of the new covenant.” The fourth-century manuscripts differ from the fifth-century manuscripts because the fifth-century manuscripts have the word καινῆς (*kaines*), “new,” whereas the fourth-century manuscripts do not. (Some also add the word τὸ [*to*], “the,” but that does not change the meaning and disappears in translation.) We need to decide between a reading that translates as “for this is my blood of the covenant” and one that can be rendered “for this is my blood of the new covenant.” How do we judge the correct reading?

On the one hand, we could look at the dates of the manuscripts and decide that the early ones had the original and καινῆς, “new,” was added in the fifth century. On the other hand, we might suspect the scribal tendencies that characterize the various manuscripts. The papyrus 𝔓^{37} is a single leaf of an unknown codex that was purchased in Cairo in 1924. Codex Sinaiticus (א) is a large deluxe codex made to be read in large churches; it ended up in a monastery in Sinai. Codex Vaticanus (B) is also a large deluxe codex made to be read in large churches; it ended up in the Vatican Library.

---

106. The dating for this particular papyrus has been changed since many of the standard reference works have been written. The new papyrological date is the second half of the third century. See Orsini and Clarysse, “Early New Testament Manuscripts and Their Dates,” 443–74.

Manuscripts ℵ and B are notorious for dropping things out.[107] Based on that information, we might conclude that the eye of the scribe slipped from the end of τῆς to the end of καινῆς and so omitted the word, which is preserved in later manuscripts from a better textual tradition.[108] Whether "new" was added in the fifth century or whether the scribe accidentally omitted the word in the fourth century are both valid lines of argument that lead to contradictory conclusions.

A careless attempt to apply 1 Nephi 13 to the case might assume that, since plain and precious things were taken out of the Bible, we should assume that text has been removed, and we should therefore follow the longer reading. But the King James Version already follows that reading, so nothing would have actually been lost in this case.

An Old Testament Quotation. At this point, we might notice something that helps to break the deadlock. Jesus was not just making a statement; he was altering a quotation of the Old Testament, a part of the Passover story that he was commemorating with his Apostles. The passage is from Exodus, which reads in Greek ἰδοὺ τὸ αἷμα τῆς διαθήκης, "Behold, the blood of the covenant" (Ex. 24:8).

There are two contexts for this quotation that need to be understood. The first of these is the context in which Jesus quoted it. Jesus quoted the passage during his Last Supper, a Passover meal with his Apostles. The Passover is a yearly commemoration of the Exodus of the children of Israel from Egypt.

The second context is the context for when it was originally uttered. The quotation occurred as part of a covenant ceremony. After Israel left Egypt and went to Sinai, where God uttered the ten commandments (Ex. 20) and gave the law (Ex. 21–23), Moses recited the judgments (Ex. 24:3). He then wrote them down and built an altar (Ex. 24:4). He next offered burnt offerings and peace offerings (Ex. 24:5), saving the blood (Ex. 24:6). Part of the blood was sprinkled on the altar (Ex. 24:6), which was typical for both burnt offerings (Lev. 1:5, 11) and peace offerings (Lev. 3:2, 8, 13). Moses then read the book of the covenant to the people, who accepted the terms of the covenant (Ex. 24:7). Next, Moses sprinkled the people with the blood saying, "This is the blood of the covenant" (Ex. 24:8). Then Moses, the chief priests,

107. Ross, "Some Unnoticed Points in the Text of the New Testament," 59–60.

108. Others think that "if it had been present originally, there is no good reason why anyone would have deleted it." Metzger, *Textual Commentary on the Greek New Testament,* 64. The exact same verbiage (with only one change) appears in Omanson, *Textual Guide to the Greek New Testament,* 46.

and seventy of the elders of Israel saw God and had a meal in his presence (Ex. 24:9–11). After that, Moses ascended to the mountain for forty days to receive the tablets of stone (Ex. 24:12–18). The quotation Jesus uttered was a sign marking those who had officially entered into the covenant.

Intriguingly, the verse quoted also exhibits a significant textual variant, but this variant does not appear in the standard published critical text of the Hebrew Bible.[109] The earliest Hebrew manuscript of Exodus 24, the tattered manuscript labelled 4QpaleoExod^{m} (= 4Q22) from the Dead Sea Scrolls, has only three words from the passage, but enough exists to see that it reads differently from the standard or Masoretic Hebrew text.[110] Targum Onqelos, which dates to the last half of the first century or early second century AD,[111] features a phrase that does not appear in the Hebrew text (here italicized), specifying that "Moses took the blood and sprinkled it on *the altar for an atonement for* the people."[112] Is this difference in the text an addition or an omission? *Targum Onqelos* has a "tendency to remain close to the Hebrew text—at least in regard to the number of words—in comparison to the more expansive Palestinian Targums."[113]

A common feature in the Targums—translations of the Hebrew scriptures into Aramaic that often exhibit explanatory interpretations—stems from the desire to avoid "anthropomorphizing God, that is, giving God human attributes like voice, feelings, limbs, and . . . a spirit. They even avoid the impression that God engages in direct action, in the way a person would, and designed a variety of ways to recast passages in the Hebrew text that do this."[114] The avoidance of anthropomorphisms usually results in expanding the text. The Targums also add text "to make the translated

---

109. There is no indication of this textual variant in K. Elliger and W. Rudolph, eds., *Biblia Hebraica Stuttgartensia* (Stuttgart, Ger.: Deutsche Bibelsgesellschaft, 1977), 125.

110. Eugene Ulrich, ed., *The Biblical Qumran Scrolls: Transcriptions and Textual Variants* (Leiden, Neth.: Brill, 2013), 1:85: [...]נשמע ו[...] הברית[...]האלה. A fifteenth-century AD manuscript of the Septuagint now in the Bibliothèque Nationale in Paris contains a long paraphrase that adds εραντισεν αυτους εκ του αιματος του εν τω κρατηρι, "he sprinkled them with the blood that was in the basin," but because this comes so late and is otherwise unattested, it seems unlikely to be genuine. Bibl. Nat. Gr. 17A, dated 1439. See John William Wevers, ed., *Exodus* (Göttingen, Ger.: Vandenhoeck und Ruprecht, 1991), 9, 278.

111. Paul V. M. Flesher and Bruce Chilton, *The Targums: A Critical Introduction* (Waco, Tex.: Baylor University Press, 2011), 155.

112. ונסיב משה ית דמא וזרק על מדבחא לכפרא על עמא in Alexander Sperber, *The Bible in Aramaic* (Leiden, Neth.: E. J. Brill, 2004), 1:130.

113. Flesher and Chilton, *Targums,* 111.

114. Flesher and Chilton, *Targums,* 21.

material intelligible."[115] It is difficult, though, to see how the kind of addition in Exodus 24:8 necessarily makes the text more intelligible. The standard scriptural passages about sprinkling blood on the altar (Lev. 1:5, 11; 3:2, 8, 13) do not state that their purpose was atonement, so it is almost impossible to explain the addition as some sort of harmonization of the covenant ceremony with expectations from the law of Moses. On the other hand, the prepositions translated as "on" and "for" are the same preposition. Hence the similarity of initial letters of the additional phrase in the Targum with the expression following it is the sign of a copyist's slip of the eye from the earlier to the later phrase—a classic homoarchteon. So the Targum's addition about the altar and the atonement might be a correct translation of an original phrase that has been accidentally dropped from the standard Hebrew text.

The passage in Exodus is significant because it comes from the ceremony at Mount Sinai when Israel formally accepted the covenant. "The acceptance of the commandments at the covenant at Sinai has served for all succeeding generations as the model for entry into the covenant."[116] Jesus modified the quotation by adding the word μου, "my," to the phrase so that it says "my blood" (Matt. 26:28). During the Last Supper, Jesus looked back to the Passover and the covenant at Sinai and introduced his Apostles to *his* covenant as distinct from the covenant at Sinai. The parallel is strengthened by the larger context because Jesus says that his blood is ἐκχυννόμενον, "poured out" (Matt. 26:28), while the Septuagint Exodus version uses a verb from the same root to note that the blood is προσέχεεν, "poured out" (King James "sprinkled"), on the altar (Ex. 24:6).

The fact that Jesus was referring to a part of the Passover story argues that the original wording was closer to the Old Testament and that the change was added in the fifth century. This conclusion will become clearer later on.

Parallel Versions. The parallel version to the Matthew verse found in Mark 14:24 also has similar textual corruption apparent in the manuscripts. Again, those manuscripts dating before the seventh century will be listed roughly in chronological order, and the spelling has been normalized so only the changes in wording are different:

115. Flesher and Chilton, *Targums*, 379.

116. Menachem Finkelstein, *Conversion: Halakhah and Practice* (Ramat-Gan, Israel: Bar-Ilan University Press, 2006), 43.

א (fourth century):	Τοῦτό ἐστιν τὸ αἷμά μου τῆς διαθήκης
B (fourth century):	Τοῦτό ἐστιν τὸ αἷμά μου τῆς διαθήκης
A (fifth century):	Τοῦτό ἐστιν τὸ αἷμά μου τὸ τῆς καινῆς διαθήκης
C (fifth century):	Τοῦτό ἐστιν τὸ αἷμά μου τῆς διαθήκης
D (fifth century):	Τοῦτό ἐστιν τὸ αἷμά μου [[τὸ]] τῆς διαθήκης
W (fifth century):	Τοῦτό ἐστιν τὸ αἷμά μου τὸ τῆς διαθήκης

The choice of manuscript variant is between "this is my blood of the covenant" and "this is my blood of the new covenant." The Greek of the phrase is the same in Matthew and Mark, with the exception that Matthew adds γάρ, "for." Almost all of the manuscripts are the same, but only one of them (A) adds the term καινῆς, "new." Many of the manuscripts that had the addition in Matthew do not have it in Mark. One of them corrects the addition of τὸ, "the," which suggests that it should not be there. The manuscript witnesses here make it seem as though καινῆς, "new," was added to Jesus' words in both Matthew and Mark in manuscript A.

Luke differs from Matthew and Mark in his version of what Jesus says when he presented the cup:[117] τοῦτο τὸ ποτήριον ἡ καινὴ διαθήκη ἐν τῷ αἵματί μου, "This cup is the new covenant by means of my blood" (Luke 22:20). There are manuscript variations in the order of verses or even whether this verse was included, but not in the wording of this particular passage (when it is included). We have no manuscript that would indicate other than Luke's wording.

We possess one other reference to wording spoken over the cup and that comes from Paul.[118] Paul gives the words as τοῦτο τὸ ποτήριον ἡ καινὴ διαθήκη ἐστὶν ἐν τῷ ἐμῷ αἵματι (1 Cor. 11:25), which is identical to the wording of Luke, except that the verb ἐστὶν, "to be," is made explicit. There are textual variants that give the last words of the phrase as τῷ αἵματι μου, "my blood," but the difference is one that disappears in translation. Luke and Paul have basically identical wording on this subject. Since Luke and Paul were companions in their travels,[119] their identical wording makes sense.

117. S. Kent Brown, *The Testimony of Luke* (Provo, Utah: BYU Studies, 2015), 996–1000.

118. Most scholars claim that Paul is the earliest source. I reject this claim because I date Matthew much earlier than the Pauline corpus. For my arguments on dating, see John Gee, "The Implications of Some Standard Assumptions of New Testament Scholars: Responding to a Modern Anti-Christ," *Interpreter: A Journal of Latter-day Saint Faith and Scholarship* 46 (2021): 26–30.

119. Col. 4:14; 2 Tim. 4:11; compare the "we" passages in Acts where it is evident that Luke, the author of Acts, was traveling with Paul (see Acts 16:10–17; 20:5–21:18; 27:1–28:16).

The situation as I would reconstruct the manuscript history is as follows: Matthew was one of Jesus' Apostles. He was present at the Last Supper and, as an eyewitness, "ordered the accounts."[120] Mark was a companion of Peter, who, as an Apostle, was also present at the Last Supper, and wrote his account "as much as he remembered."[121] Though there is some disagreement about whether Matthew or Mark comes first and who used whose account,[122] both come before Luke. Matthew and Mark understood the reference that Jesus made to the founding of the covenant from the Passover story and used the Septuagint (the ancient Greek translation of the Old Testament) wording of the passage in composing their Greek versions. Their versions do not include the word καινῆς, "new." A number of years later, when Paul wrote his letter to Corinth (AD 57), he stressed the difference between the covenant of Moses, which requires circumcision, and the covenant of Christ, which does not. He emphasized that Christ's covenant is new and thus deliberately includes the word καινὴ, "new." Luke, writing his Gospel later (after AD 53), compiled from those who had undertaken the task before him—like Matthew and Mark (Luke 1:1)—and from his own interviews with those who had been present (Luke 1:2). He followed the wording of his companion Paul and so also included the word καινὴ, "new."

For many years, the copies of the Gospels were copied by later scribes who preserved the wording of the various versions as they were. In the fifth century, however, the scribes started to harmonize the different readings.[123] Rather than recast the sentences, they simply took the word καινὴ from Luke and applied it to Matthew and, somewhat inconsistently, to Mark.

This reconstruction is hypothetical and speculative but explains the evidence as we have it. The actions taken seem innocent enough, but the impact over time served to take away the idea of covenant. How this happened is an interesting story and not hypothetical.

---

120. Papias, fragment 4, in Eusebius, *Ecclesiastical History* 3.39.16.

121. Papias, fragment 4, in Eusebius, *Ecclesiastical History* 3.39.15.

122. I date Matthew before Mark and both before about AD 52. Gee, "Implications of Some Standard Assumptions of New Testament Scholars," 26–30.

123. For a discussion of harmonization, see Metzger, *Textual Commentary on the Greek New Testament,* xvi; Omanson, *Textual Guide to the Greek New Testament,* 18*–19*; Michael W. Holmes, "The Text of the Matthean Divorce Passages: A Comment on the Appeal to Harmonization in Textual Decisions," *Journal of Biblical Literature* 109, no. 4 (1990): 651–52; Cambry G. Pardee, *Scribal Harmonization in Greek Manuscripts of the Synoptic Gospels from the Second to the Fifth Century* (PhD diss., Loyola University Chicago, 2016).

Taking Away the Covenant. During the first century, the emphasis of Paul and those who were close to him was on the covenant of Christ as a new covenant in opposition to the covenant of Moses. The first Christians believed they entered into a new covenant that Jesus had introduced. For example, Paul tells the Saints in Corinth: "God . . . also hath made us able servants of the new covenant [διακόνους καινῆς διαθήκης]; not of the letter, but of the spirit: for the letter killeth, but the spirit giveth life" (2 Cor. 3:5–6, translation from KJV adjusted). This understanding was based on both the teachings of Jesus and the words of Jeremiah:

> Behold, the days come, saith the Lord, when I will make a new covenant [διαθήκην καινήν] with the house of Israel and with the house of Judah: Not according to the covenant that I made with their fathers in the day when I took them by the hand to lead them out of the land of Egypt; because they continued not in my covenant, and I regarded them not, saith the Lord. For this is the covenant that I will make with the house of Israel after those days, saith the Lord; I will put my laws into their mind, and write them in their hearts: and I will be to them a God, and they shall be to me a people. (Heb. 8:8–10, KJV, quoting Jer. 31:31–33)

Jesus became "the mediator of the new covenant [διαθήκης καινῆς], that by means of death, for the redemption of the transgressions that were under the first covenant, they which are called might receive the promise of eternal inheritance" (Heb. 9:15, translation from KJV adjusted). The New Testament, as a collection, did not yet exist, and translations rendering the phrase as "new testament," as if characteristic of New Testament times, are anachronistic.

Understanding the sacrament of the Lord's Supper as a covenant was already disappearing by the end of the second century. At the beginning of the second century, Clement of Rome reminded the quarreling Saints at Corinth that the sacrament was supposed to unify them.[124] Ignatius, writing around the same time, talked to the Saints at Rome about how his desire to partake of the sacrament exceeded his desire for other food or the pleasures of life but did not explain why this was so.[125] He did note to the Saints in Philadelphia that there was only one Eucharist, or sacrament of the Lord's Supper, and that it should unify the Saints.[126] He issued this warning immediately after warning them that there were schismatics with strange opinions

124. *1 Clement* 46.
125. Ignatius, *Epistle to the Romans* 7.
126. Ignatius, *Epistle to the Philadelphians* 4.

in the church.[127] To the Saints in Smyrna, he observed that those who were introducing dangerous errors avoided even partaking of the Eucharist and joining in prayer because they did not really believe in Christ.[128] Pliny noted that for the Christians he talked to at the beginning of the second century, baptism was an oath and covenant (*sacramento*), but the sacrament of the Lord's Supper was simply "an ordinary and harmless meal" (*cibum, promiscuum tamen et innoxium*).[129] For Justin Martyr, in the middle of the second century, the emphasis was that only those who truly believed and had been baptized could receive the sacrament of the Lord's Supper.[130] Justin presents baptism as being for the washing away of sins[131] and the sacrament for eating and drinking the flesh and blood of the Savior for salvation.[132]

Other trends in second-century Christianity did away with the sacrament of the Lord's Supper altogether. The *Gospel of Judas* has Jesus mocking (ⲥⲱⲃⲉ) the Lord's Supper as a "misunderstanding" (ⲙⲛⲧⲁⲑⲏⲧ) and only the foolish orthodox thought that "this is what is right" (ⲡ[ⲉ] ⲡⲉⲧⲉⲥϣⲉ).[133] The fact that the *Gospel of Judas* was circulating before the end of the second century (Irenaeus refers to it)[134] indicates that, for certain second-century Christians, the sacrament of the Lord's Supper was something they wanted to get rid of. If it was only an innocuous meal, what did it matter if it was kept?

Irenaeus, writing at the end of the second century, understood that at the Last Supper Jesus "admitted that [the cup] was his blood and taught that it was a new offering of the new covenant, which the church received from the apostles and offered to God in all the world."[135] The sacrament became a sacrifice offered to God as part of the new covenant rather than the covenant itself. For Irenaeus, the purpose of the ordinance was "the inheritance of the earth in which the new fruit of the vine is drunk, and the physical resurrection of His disciples."[136] Irenaeus was referring to Jesus' promise "to drink from the fruit of the vine with His disciples" in

---

127. Ignatius, *Epistle to the Philadelphians* 3.

128. Ignatius, *Epistle to the Smyrnaeans* 7.

129. Pliny, *Letters* 10.96.7.

130. Justin Martyr, *Apology* 1.66.

131. Justin Martyr, *Apology* 1.61, 66.

132. Justin Martyr, *Apology* 1.66.

133. *Gospel of Judas* 33.26–35.2.

134. Irenaeus, *Against Heresies* 1.31.1.

135. Irenaeus, *Against Heresies* 4.17.5: *suum sanguinem confessus est et novi testamenti novam docuit oblationem; quam ecclesia ab apostolic accipiens in universe mundo offert Deo.*

136. Irenaeus, *Against Heresies* 5.33.1; compare 5.2.2.

the kingdom of heaven.[137] Clement of Alexandria, writing an instruction manual for new Christians around the same time, claimed that "to drink the blood of Jesus is to partake of the Lord's incorruption."[138] It was a "mixture of the old law and the new word," a gateway to the Resurrection.[139] But when Clement quoted the words of Jesus from Matthew, he dropped words about the covenant altogether.[140] The sacrament of the Lord's Supper was no longer a covenant.

Clement of Alexandria also argued that "God is the cause of all good things, but of some foremost, as of the old and new (νέας) covenant [or "Old and New Testament"] and of others subsequently, as of philosophy."[141] Written at the end of the second century, it is difficult to tell from this passage whether Clement employed the term "covenant" to refer to covenants or to scriptural texts. That he means the latter is shown by a passage later in the work, where Clement argued that something is to be believed because "it is preached and said through the Old and through the New Testament [νέας διαθήκης]" immediately before quoting the Gospel of John and the Psalms.[142] Clement's pupil, Origen, was probably the first to employ the precise phrase καινὴ διαθήκη, "new covenant/new testament," in reference to the New Testament by the Greek phrase after which it would forever be known.[143]

Thus, while the early Christian understanding of the sacrament was changing, the meaning of the phrase καινὴ διαθήκη changed from the new covenant with Israel initiated by Jesus to the New Testament as a record of the new covenant to a term for a book of scripture. This contributed to the loss of the understanding of covenant. The change in the meaning of the term preceded the harmonization that further corrupted the plain meaning of the text.

The Blood of Christ

Luke's account of the Garden of Gethsemane contains two verses (Luke 22:43–44) that have been the subject of much dispute:[144] ὤφθη δὲ αὐτῷ ἄγγελος

---

137. Irenaeus, *Against Heresies* 5.33.1.

138. Clement of Alexandria, *Paedogogus* 2.2.19.4.

139. Clement of Alexandria, *Paedogogus* 2.2.29.1.

140. Clement of Alexandria, *Paedogogus* 2.2.32.2: Τοῦτό μού ἐστιν τὸ αἷμα.

141. Clement of Alexandria, *Stromata* 1.5.28.1.

142. Clement of Alexandria, *Stromata* 5.13.85.1.

143. Origen, *Commentary on John* 10.18.

144. Blumell, "Luke 22:43–44: An Anti-Docetic Interpolation or an Apologetic Omission?," 1–35. This analysis follows Blumell's argument. Note also the claim by Elliott, "United Bible Societies Greek New Testament," 297: "Luke xxii 43–44 is more likely to

ἀπ' οὐρανοῦ ἐνισχύων αὐτόν. καὶ γενόμενος ἐν ἀγωνίᾳ ἐκτενέστερον προσηύχετο· καὶ ἐγένετο ὁ ἱδρὼς αὐτοῦ ὡσεὶ θρόμβοι αἵματος καταβαίνοντες ἐπὶ τὴν γῆν, "Then an angel from heaven appeared to him strengthening him. And being in the most intense agony, he continued to pray, and his sweat became as if drops of blood falling to the ground." The second-century Christian author Justin Martyr knew of this passage.[145] The earliest manuscript containing Luke's account of Gethsemane, which is the late second-century manuscript 0171 (= PSI 2.124 + PSI 1.2), though fragmentary, contains the end of the account: . . . θρο(μ)[βοι αιματο]ς κ̣α̣τ̣[α]βαι[νοντες ε]π̣ι την γην. This clearly shows that the account was known in the earliest manuscript in existence for Luke 22:44 and was part of the account in the second century. Irenaeus, writing at the end of the second century, also said that Jesus "sweat great drops of blood."[146]

In the second century, however, intellectuals began to criticize Christ and Christianity. The second-century author Celsus specifically attacked the account of Jesus in the Garden of Gethsemane because Jesus "shrieked and howled and prayed to avoid the fear of destruction" and did not act as befitting a god.[147] The third-century critic of Christianity Porphyry claimed that Jesus' actions in the Garden of Gethsemane "were not worthy of a son of God, or even of a wise man who scorned death."[148] Third-century Christian authors like Tertullian were somewhat embarrassed about the Gethsemane account.[149] During the late fourth century, Ambrose also noted that Christians were bothered by Christ's actions in Gethsemane

---

have been omitted by scribes who found the theological content offensive, rather than be a conscious addition by scribes."

145. Justin Martyr, *Dialogue with Trypho* 103: ἐν γὰρ τοῖς ἀπομνημονεύμασιν, ἅ φημι ὑπὸ τῶν ἀποστόλων αὐτοῦ καὶ τῶν ἐκείνοις παρακολουθησάντων συντετάχθαι, ⟨γέγραπται⟩ ὅτι ἱδρὼς ὡσεὶ θρόμβοι κατεχεῖτο, αὐτοῦ εὐχομένου καὶ λέγοντος· ⟨Πάτερ,⟩ παρελθέτω, εἰ δυνατόν, τὸ ποτήριον τοῦτο· "For in the memoires, which I say were composed by his apostles and those who followed them, it is written that his sweat fell down like drops of blood while he was praying and saying: 'Father, if it is possible, let this cup pass.'"

146. Irenaeus, *Against the Heresies* 3.22.2: *sudasset globos sanguinis* / ἵδρωσε θρόμβους αἵματος.

147. Origen, *Contra Celsum* 2.24, 33: τί οὖν ποτνιᾶται καὶ ὀδύρεται καὶ τὸν τοῦ ὀλέθρου φόβον εὔχεται παραδραμεῖν. . . . τί δὲ καὶ γενναῖον ἔδρασεν οἷον θεός, καταφρονῶν ἀνθρώπων καὶ διαγελῶν καὶ παίζων τὸ συμβαῖνον ὁ Ἰησοῦς.

148. Porphyry, fragment 62: καὶ αὐτὸς ἀγωνιῶν καὶ τῇ προσδοκίᾳ τῶν δεινῶν ἐπαγρυπνῶν καὶ δι' εὐχῆς παρακαλῶν τὸ πάθος ⌈αὐτῷ⌉ παρελθεῖν λέγων τοῖς γνωρίμοις . . . ταῦτα γὰρ οὐκ ἄξια παιδὸς Θεοῦ τὰ ῥήματα, ἀλλ' οὐδ' ἀνθρώπου σοφοῦ θανάτου καταφρονοῦντος.

149. Tertullian, *On Flight in Persecution* 8.

because it did not match Roman or stoic ideals of facing death.[150] The fourth-century author Epiphanius of Salamis wrote that Luke 22:44 "is in the Gospel of Luke, in uncorrected manuscripts, and it is used according to the testimony of saint Irenaeus against the heretics who say that Christ only appeared to be present. But the orthodox, being afraid and not understanding the purpose and power, removed the saying: 'being in agony, he sweat, and his sweat became great drops of blood, and an angel appeared strengthening him.'"[151] Thus third-century manuscripts ($\mathfrak{P}^{69\text{vid}}$, $\mathfrak{P}^{75}$) and one fourth-century manuscript (B) omit the passage, though the fourth-century Codex Sinaiticus (א) includes it.

Consequently, the passage about Jesus sweating great drops of blood in Gethsemane was attacked by opponents of Christianity, and in a sheepish response, orthodox Christians removed it from their scriptures because they were embarrassed by it. This is a section that Latter-day Saints would regard as plain and precious.

Conclusions

A wide variety of changes and corruptions can occur in an ancient text. With hundreds of exemplars, the New Testament manuscripts attest most of these corruptions. Textual criticism is used to evaluate these corruptions and can sometimes point to the original reading if that reading survives in the manuscripts. In some cases, however, textual criticism alone cannot restore the ancient reading. In other cases, it can point to plain and precious teachings that have been lost, at least at some point in time. We should also realize that the removal of plain and precious teachings can be an ongoing process and that sometimes it is the very textual critics who are trying to recover the text who may be inadvertently guilty of corrupting it.

---

150. Ambrose, *Commentary on Luke* 10.56: "*Haerent plerique hoc loco, qui tristitiam salutaris ad argumentum inolitae potius a principio quam susceptae ad tempus infirmitatis inclinant et naturalis sensum cupiunt detorquere sententiae.*"

151. Epiphanius, *Against the Heresies* 31.4–5: κεῖται ἐν τῷ κατὰ Λουκᾶν εὐαγγελίῳ ἐν τοῖς ἀδιορθώτοις ἀντιγράφοις,—καὶ κέχρηται τῇ μαρτυρίᾳ ὁ ἅγιος Εἰρηναῖος ἐν τῷ κατὰ αἱρέσεων πρὸς τοὺς δοκήσει τὸν Χριστὸν πεφηνέναι λέγοντας, ὀρθόδοξοι δὲ ἀφείλαντο τὸ ῥητόν, φοβηθέντες καὶ μὴ νοήσαντες αὐτοῦ τὸ τέλος καὶ τὸ ἰσχυρότατον—καὶ «γενόμενος ἐν ἀγωνίᾳ ἵδρωσε, καὶ ἐγένετο ὁ ἱδρὼς αὐτοῦ ὡς θρόμβοι αἵματος, καὶ ὤφθη ἄγγελος ἐνισχύων αὐτόν».

Educating the Ancient Saints about Christ

S. Kent Brown

Character of the Audiences

In the first chapter of his book *Christianizing the Roman Empire,* Ramsay MacMullen, emeritus Yale professor of history and classics, points out what seems to be obvious—namely, that "from the very beginning, Jesus' disciples followed him instantly, without instruction." During following years, he continues, "new adherents, by supernatural actions, were won to instantaneous belief, or trust."[1] None, it seems, required any doctrinal teaching before becoming followers of Jesus.

In his effort to support these observations, MacMullen turns to ancient sources. He cites two among many, one Christian and one pagan, about two centuries apart. The Christian source derives from the *Religious History* of Theodoret, the controversial bishop of Cyrrhus in Syria (died c. AD 466). Theodoret wrote about the miraculous conversion of hundreds of Bedouin who traveled to a pillar of stone some "forty miles east of Antioch" to see a certain Symeon who lived on its top.[2] The pagan source is from "a votive stele put up in a Saturn-shrine twenty miles from Carthage in A.D. 238." The Saturn worship, led by a visionary priest, miraculously secured good health for devotees. MacMullen concludes that "for both the Christian and the non-Christian, in such scenes [that produced miracles] the essential and, so far as we can tell, the only thing believed in was some supernatural power to bestow benefits."[3] Simple and to the point.

---

1. Ramsay MacMullen, *Christianizing the Roman Empire, A.D. 100–400* (New Haven, Conn.: Yale University Press, 1984), 4.

2. MacMullen, *Christianizing the Roman Empire,* 1–2; Theodoret, *Religious History* 26.13–14, in *A History of the Monks of Syria by Theodoret of Cyrrhus,* translated with an introduction and notes by R. M. Price, Cistercian Studies Series, vol. 88 (Trappist, Ken.: Liturgical Press, 1985), 166–67, https://www.scribd.com/doc/142038526/A-History-of-the-Monks-of-Syria-Theodoret-of-Cyrrhus-2008-OCR.

3. MacMullen, *Christianizing the Roman Empire,* 4.

To cement this conclusion into place, he turns to the religiosity of people living in Saxony and nearby regions of Germany around AD 1600, a much later period that, in his assembling of evidence, sheds relevant light on the first and second centuries AD. In those European areas, after a person discounts "the upper-class circles, . . . the vast bulk of the population are found to have been largely or totally ignorant of the simplest matters of doctrine, rarely or never attending church."[4] MacMullen's general conclusion is that the religious masses are almost totally ignorant of the basic teachings of their faith, especially those who came to their belief through an unusual or miraculous experience.

However, I judge that the earliest Christians were different. How so? A review of the New Testament and early Christian literature shows that Christian church leaders felt responsible for instructing their fellow church members on how to follow Christ as their spiritual model. In its own way, education about how to live in this fashion was more important than embracing miracles.

To be sure, the kinds of miraculous occurrences described by Theodoret in the eastern Mediterranean and documented by the stele at the Saturn shrine in North Africa find similar exemplars in the ministries of Jesus and the Apostle Paul, wherein uncounted, unnamed people were healed and received relief because of the divine powers entrusted to these two men and other associates. Even so, early followers doubtless embraced some sort of belief in what Jesus and Paul taught.

In Jesus' case, two scenes present themselves. In one, at the end of a Sabbath day in Capernaum, "when the sun was setting, all they that had any sick with divers diseases brought them unto [Jesus]; and he laid his hands on every one of them, and healed them" (Luke 4:40). A few days or weeks later, after Jesus had chosen and announced the Twelve, he uttered his landmark Sermon on the Plain at a nearby location. As he moved among the gathered crowd, who "came to hear him, and to be healed of their diseases; . . . the whole multitude [surged and] sought to touch him: for there went virtue ["power," Greek singular *dynamis*] out of him, and healed them all" (Luke 6:17, 19). The recipients of Jesus' healing powers were surely grateful for the relief from disease and other afflictions. But months later, recalling the healings at Capernaum at the end of a Sabbath day, Jesus leveled criticism: the healing experiences did not lead to true commitment.

4. MacMullen, *Christianizing the Roman Empire*, 5.

Why? Jesus uncovered the reasons when he began "to upbraid the cities wherein most of his mighty works [Greek plural *dynameis*] were done, because they repented not." Specifically, Jesus condemned the town of Capernaum and its inhabitants: "Thou, Capernaum, which art exalted unto heaven, shalt be brought down to hell: for if the mighty works, which have been done in thee, had been done in Sodom, it would have remained until this day" (Matt. 11:20, 23). Plainly, Jesus hoped that those who had received his healing would respond to his message with faith and repentance.

In a second instance, we see Jesus descending from Nazareth to Capernaum and attending a synagogue service on the Sabbath. In the building, "there was a man, which had a spirit of an unclean devil." At a certain point, Jesus "rebuked" the devil and forced him out of the man. Naturally, the crowd was "all amazed" (Luke 4:31–36). In that crowd were certainly Peter and his brother Andrew, into whose home Jesus was invited following the service. There is good reason to suppose that the future Apostles James and John, and possibly Levi, were also in the synagogue that morning and witnessed the exorcism. Why? Because Mark records that, after the service, in a group that included Jesus, "they entered into the house of Simon and Andrew, with James and John," where they found the mother of Peter's wife lying "sick of a fever." In that home, Jesus "took her by the hand, and lifted her up; and immediately the fever left her" (Mark 1:29–31). At this moment, at least four of Jesus' future Apostles had witnessed two miracles in one morning, the first in the synagogue and the second in the home. To be sure, we do not know whether Levi saw either of the miracles, but he surely would have heard about them soon enough. But that is not the whole story.

The action continues a day or two later on the nearby shore of the Sea of Galilee. Although MacMullen claims that the wider group of disciples followed Jesus without knowing his teachings, we soon see that MacMullen's observation needs refining. As Jesus was pressed by people on the shoreline "to hear the word of God," he spotted "two ships standing by the lake." Jesus climbed "into one of the ships, which was Simon's, and prayed that he would thrust out a little from the land." At that point, Jesus "sat down, and taught the people out of the ship" (Luke 5:1–3). Although we possess nothing of what Jesus said on that occasion, it is important to notice that Simon Peter and his brother Andrew heard Jesus' sermon while working with their nets and sitting in the boat next to him. Judging from what Jesus said to gatherings on other occasions, we understand that they and the members of the crowd now knew something of his message and his expectations for believers. Further, it is reasonable to believe that James and John were part of the listening crowd that day because they were nearby when a net erupted with an overwhelming catch of fish. Hence, although they had already witnessed miracles, these men were not uninformed when Jesus called them to "catch men" (Luke 5:6–10).

Besides this scene, it is also reasonable to think that one or more of these men had heard John the Baptist declare Jesus to be "the Lamb of God, which taketh away the sin of the world" (John 1:29). After all, Andrew was an early disciple of John and introduced his brother Simon Peter to Jesus (see John 1:40–42). Later, Andrew and another disciple of John spent an entire Sabbath with Jesus. One can only imagine what the conversation was like. Because Jesus always guided discussions, Andrew and his friend would have likely come away from their experience with a grasp of Jesus' teachings, even if rather elementary (see John 1:35–39).

In Paul's case, we read that he resided in Ephesus for "two years; so that all they which dwelt in Asia heard the word of the Lord Jesus, both Jews and Greeks." Moreover, we learn that "God wrought special miracles by the hands of Paul." What were those miracles? Some were "so that from his body were brought unto the sick handkerchiefs or aprons, and the diseases departed from them, and the evil spirits went out of them" (Acts 19:10–12). We are not informed whether the recipients of these stunning powers were Christians or outsiders who had simply heard of miracles wrought by him and were seeking relief. Notably, many would soon turn away from him and his message. Such occurrences are documented by his own words.

First, we turn to Paul's Epistle to the Galatians, a letter written c. AD 48. In a tough response to Christians residing in central Asia Minor who had turned away from his message of peace and grace to one of laws and confining guidelines, he seethed, "I marvel that ye are so soon removed from him that called you into the grace of Christ unto another gospel." He had more to say. He knew that "there be some that trouble you, and would pervert the gospel of Christ." Now he almost shouted, "Though we, or an angel from heaven, preach any other gospel unto you than that which we have preached unto you, let him be accursed." Trying to control his rage, he repeated his earlier words for emphasis: "If any man preach any other gospel unto you than that ye have received, let him be accursed" (Gal. 1:6–9). What is the clear, vivid message? Galatians, written before AD 50, paints a scene filled with dark, clanging colors that portray Church members turning away from principles and doctrines that Paul had taught them, leading him to question whether he had "bestowed upon [them] labour in vain" and to wonder who "did hinder [them] that [they] should not obey the truth?" (Gal. 4:11; 5:7).[5]

Turning to 1 Corinthians, written very possibly in AD 55 while Paul was still residing in Ephesus,[6] we find Paul writing about facing "many adversaries" (1 Cor. 16:8–9). Not long afterward, in a second letter to Corinth, he made a disturbing reference to "our trouble which came to us in Asia, . . . insomuch that we despaired even of life" (2 Cor. 1:8).[7] A few months later, from a ship taking him toward Jerusalem, Paul disembarked at Miletus and requested that "the elders of the church" in Ephesus join him there (Acts 20:15–17). After Church leaders and others finally reached him, likely after three days' journey, Paul gave to them a farewell speech. On that occasion, he begged those present that they "take heed therefore unto yourselves, and to all the flock." He then surprised his Ephesian friends by warning "that after my departing shall grievous wolves enter in among you, not sparing the flock." Worse than these outsiders, he intoned, "of your own selves shall men arise, speaking perverse things, to draw away disciples after them" (Acts 20:28–30).

What becomes clear is that Paul, the first Christian author and one of the first missionaries, was fighting a battle of retreat. Converts turned away from his message even while he lived. This circumstance appears surprising to Paul because he had set up a means to keep people on track. Besides the weekly remaking of covenants when partaking of the Eucharist, or sacrament, Paul consistently reviewed scriptures and church teachings with them.

We catch a first glimpse of this arrangement when Paul discussed the relative value of speaking in tongues and prophesying during church services in 1 Corinthians 14. Behind this chapter's long discussion is the fact that the earliest Christians instructed each other. Of course, it is uncertain how much time was devoted to discussing scripture and to talking about the distinctive features of their faith. Writing more than a century later, in his *First Apology,* Justin Martyr noted in passing that the reading and

---

5. Jerome Murphy-O'Connor, *Paul: A Critical Life* (New York: Oxford University Press, 1996), 199; see the helpful study on Galatians by George A. Horton Jr., "Concern, Correction, and Counsel for Converts," in *Studies in Scripture: Volume Six, Acts to Revelation,* ed. Robert L. Millet (Salt Lake City: Deseret Book, 1987), 83–106.

6. Frederick Fyvie Bruce, *Paul: Apostle of the Heart Set Free* (Grand Rapids, Mich.: William B. Eerdmans, 1977), 273, 475.

7. For a helpful review of the Corinthian correspondence, see David R. Seely, "'Is Christ Divided?' Unity of the Saints through Charity," in Millet, *Studies in Scripture: Volume Six,* 57–82.

discussing of scripture took place "as long as time permits."[8] But we don't know whether this was so in Paul's earlier era.

However, we do know that the unique message of the Atonement was an essential part of their education. For instance, Paul wrote, "I delivered unto you *first of all* that which I also received, how that Christ died for our sins according to the scriptures" (1 Cor. 15:3, emphasis added; see also 1 Cor. 11:23–29). This was his message and the message of other missionaries (see Rom. 16:25; 1 Cor. 15:12–20). From this, we can conclude that Church members were not like the pagan masses, who, for worship, merely "called upon the gods . . . and with incense and wine made obeisance to [the Roman emperor's] statue."[9] Worship for Christians included receiving a reservoir of truth about Jesus Christ's Atonement that led them not just to a broad understanding but more precisely—to faith in Christ (see 1 Cor. 2:4–5).[10] In all of their worship, they were not to be "contentious," for which "we have no such custom, neither the churches of God"; indeed, they were to avoid sparking "divisions" inside their congregations (1 Cor. 11:16, 18–19).

That such instruction within Christian worship continued to be the norm is evident from both later Christian and Roman sources. The *Didache,* also known as *The Teaching of the Twelve Apostles,* was composed perhaps as early as AD 100 and perhaps as late as AD 150.[11] It came to serve as a handbook-like manual on church morals and procedure. Mirroring the presence of teachers, both resident and itinerant, we read, "Whosoever, therefore, cometh and teacheth you all these things that have been said before [as summarized in the *Didache*], receive him." In addition, if an instructor "teach so as to increase righteousness and the knowledge of the Lord, receive him as the Lord" (*Didache* 11:1–2). Importantly, the teaching in the church embraced practical matters too. For example, an unemployed person was "not [to] live with you idle" (*Didache* 12:4). When a "wayfarer" arrived among them, believers were to "assist him as far as ye are able" (*Didache* 12:2).[12] And so it went.

---

8. Justin Martyr, *First Apology* 67, in *The Ante-Nicene Fathers: The Writings of the Fathers down to A.D. 325,* ed. Alexander Roberts and James Donaldson, 10 vols. (New York: Charles Scribner's Sons, 1926), 1:186 (hereafter cited as *ANF*).

9. Pliny, *Letters* 10.96.5; the translation is that of Patrick Gerard Walsh, *Pliny the Younger: Complete Letters* (New York: Oxford University Press, 2006), 278.

10. Gerhard Kittel and Gerhard Friedrich, *Theological Dictionary of the New Testament,* 10 vols. (Grand Rapids, Mich.: William B. Eerdmans, 1964–74), 3:712, 715–16.

11. Johannes Quasten, *Patrology,* 3 vols. (repr., Utrecht, Neth.: Spectrum Publishers, 1975), 1:36–37. Vol. 4 published by Christian Classics, Westminster, Md., 1988.

12. *ANF,* 7:381.

The practice of instruction in Christian congregations is made certain in the middle of the second century by Justin Martyr, who was born in Samaria c. AD 114 and spent his career in Rome until his death c. AD 165. In his *First Apology,* written during the reign of the emperor Antoninus Pius (AD 137–61), he made another simple reference to instruction in the church. After describing the Eucharist, or sacrament, he then affirmed that "we afterwards [in our meetings] continually remind each other of these things." Further, "on the day called Sunday, all who live in cities or in the country gather together to one place, and the memoirs of the apostles or the writings of the prophets are read." Thereafter, "the president verbally instructs, and exhorts to the imitation of these good things." In a generous act, to "those who are absent" from the weekly church service and are thus not able to partake of the sacrament, or Eucharist, "a portion [of the sacrament] is sent by the deacons."[13]

Predating Justin's *First Apology,* and possibly the *Didache,* stands the important letter of Pliny the Younger, the Roman governor of Bithynia-Pontus in northern Asia Minor (AD 109–111), in which he details to Emperor Trajan how he dealt with Christians who embraced "a debased and boundless superstition."[14] His letter dates to the autumn of AD 110[15] and frames the earliest non-Christian description of Christian beliefs and practices. From his interviews with lapsed believers, Pliny learned that "at dawn on a fixed day" (Sunday), Christians assembled "to sing a hymn antiphonally to Christ as God." During the service, they bound "themselves by an oath, not for the commission of some crime, but to avoid acts of theft, brigandage, and adultery, [and] not to break their word."[16] Among the "elements to be distinguished in the regular occasions of the church," we find "the meeting for instruction by preaching and reading, diversified by prayer and singing."[17]

From what we have reviewed thus far, we behold the early Christians as more than an uninformed mass of people with simple, basic beliefs. On the contrary, through the Gospels and through Paul's first correspondence with Church members in Corinth, we see faith in Christ resting on a Spirit-centered teaching rather than on the enticing character of miracles. We also see a conscious effort among believers to educate themselves and each

13. Justin Martyr, *First Apology* 67, in *ANF,* 1:185–86.

14. Pliny, *Letters* 10.96.8; the translation is by Walsh, *Pliny the Younger,* 279.

15. Adrian Nicholas Sherwin-White, *The Letters of Pliny: A Historical and Social Commentary,* cor. ed. (New York: Oxford University Press, 1985), 693.

16. Pliny, *Letters* 10.96.7; the translation is by Walsh, *Pliny the Younger,* 278–79.

17. Sherwin-White, *Letters of Pliny,* 702.

other about the important principles and doctrines linked to Jesus and his Atonement. By instruction, these people came to constitute informed converts as documented in the New Testament, no matter their ethnic or social backgrounds and living conditions.

Who Were the Audiences?

The Letters in the Book of Revelation

Most New Testament letters name their audiences, but not all. In the book of Revelation, written about AD 95, we possess seven letters given to churches in western Asia Minor (see Rev. 1:4; 2–3). Addressed to congregations within an area stretching 100 miles from Pergamum in the north to Ephesus in the south, as well as 130 miles inland and eastward to Laodicea,[18] the letters show that the main challenges for these church members were persecution and apostasy.[19] One puzzle is why the churches at Colossae and Hierapolis, which were located near Laodicea, were not included in the seven letters. Possibly, the number of believers in these two cities were small when Revelation was composed, or the church members in the two cities were thought of as included within the circle of Laodicea.

The book of Revelation reflects the dire consequences of persecution against church members in the seven congregations. Beginning in the years under Emperor Domitian (AD 81–96), Christians were caught by the faith-challenging requirement to offer sacrifice to the deified Roman emperor. Penalties for noncompliance could bring exile, a fine, or even death. Christians felt like they could not offer sacrifice to the emperor and also worship Christ. We learn of a man named Antipas from Pergamum in western Asia Minor, who paid the ultimate penalty of death for his faith in Christ (see Rev. 2:10, 13). Moreover, to underscore the reality of persecution, we observe that the book of Revelation was written by John on the island of Patmos after Roman authorities exiled him there because of his refusal to worship Domitian (see Rev. 1:9). Holding onto one's belief in this era was unsettling and could be costly—even deadly.

---

18. Tim Cornell and John Matthews, *Atlas of the Roman World* (New York: Equinox, 1982), 150–51; Yohanan Aharoni and others, *The Carta Bible Atlas*, 4th ed. (Jerusalem: Carta, 2002), nos. 270, 271.

19. As an interesting detail, decades earlier, about AD 50 during his second missionary journey, the Apostle Paul met and baptized "Lydia, a seller of purple," who had grown up in "the city of Thyatira," one of the seven Christian centers addressed by the Lord in Revelation (see Acts 16:14–15 and Rev. 2:18–29).

Further, the book of Revelation also exposes the inner turmoil of apostasy, even heresy, among the seven congregations in the days of its composition.[20] For example, in Revelation we read about traveling teachers in Ephesus, the Apostle Paul's old stomping ground (see Acts 19:1–20:1), "which say they are apostles, and are not." Church members in Ephesus had "tried" or tested the claims of these itinerant preachers and "found them liars" (Rev. 2:2). These people were not claiming to be among the Twelve but were saying that they were authorized teachers of the gospel message.[21] Then we hear about "the Nicolaitans, which I [the Lord] also hate" (Rev. 2:6, 15). Evidently, these people were antinomians, who believed that because Jesus had freed his followers from the law and its requirements, it was necessary to participate in all lawless and licentious acts in order to be able to surmount worldly temptations.[22]

The Letters of Paul

Some of Paul's letters have led to questions about whether he was their author. Speaking generally, all scholars accept only four as certainly from him—Romans, the two Corinthian letters, and Galatians. Beyond these four, scholars part ways. In general, the most radical scholars believe that Paul wrote only the four and customarily assign the others to unknown authors, usually disciples of Paul. Traditional scholars, although admitting that problems adhere to certain letters, hold that all the epistles ascribed to Paul since antiquity were written or dictated by him.[23] A third group generally accepts Paul's authorship of all the letters assigned to him except the pastoral Epistles (the two letters to Timothy and the one to Titus) and the Epistle to the Hebrews. Since the second century and until modern times, it was acknowledged that all the letters ascribed to Paul were sent to the congregations and individuals whom we know from our copies of the New Testament,

---

20. William H. C. Frend, *The Rise of Christianity* (Philadelphia: Fortress Press, 1984), 128, 137–38.

21. Richard D. Draper and Michael D. Rhodes, *The Revelation of John the Apostle,* Brigham Young University New Testament Commentary (Provo, Utah: BYU Studies, 2016), 124.

22. Draper and Rhodes, *Revelation of John the Apostle,* 126. Consult the helpful summary of the book of Revelation by Gerald N. Lund, "'Things Which Must Shortly Come to Pass,'" in Millet, *Studies in Scripture: Volume Six,* 256–75.

23. For well-thought-out approaches to the traditional view, see Sidney B. Sperry, *Paul's Life and Letters* (Salt Lake City: Bookcraft, 1955); and Richard Lloyd Anderson, *Understanding Paul* (Salt Lake City: Deseret Book, 1983).

including the Epistle to the Ephesians, whose phrase "at Ephesus" is missing from the earliest manuscript of his letter as well as from other important texts (Eph. 1:1).[24] Only the traditional scholars still hold to this viewpoint.

Broadly speaking and adopting the traditional view of Paul's Epistles for the moment, most of his surviving letters were written to congregations gathered in certain cities (for example, Romans) or to groups of believers spread across a large definable area (for example, Galatians). Only four were written to individuals: the short Epistle to Philemon and the three pieces of correspondence to Timothy and Titus. In the case of Philemon, the letter was carried by Onesimus to Colossae, where Epaphras was a church leader with whom Paul had spent difficult days (see Philem. 1:10, 12, 23, and Col. 4:9, 12–13).[25] The two Epistles to Timothy were presumably sent to Timothy at Ephesus (see 1 Tim. 1:3 and 2 Tim. 1:18), and the letter to Titus apparently reached him on the island of Crete (see Titus 1:5).[26]

The Epistle to the Hebrews reveals a group of recipients that differs from all others, except perhaps the audiences of the Gospel of Matthew, the Epistle of James, and the book of Revelation. The teacher of Clement of Alexandria, Pantaenus, who became the first head of the famous catechetical school in Alexandria, knew this letter as "To the Hebrews."[27] The Epistle, almost a treatise, addresses Jewish Christians who had a high regard for Moses (see Heb. 3:1–6) and a background in temple liturgy (see Heb. 6:19–7:28). This observation is confirmed by the publication of the fragmentary *Commentary on Melchizedek* from the Dead Sea Scrolls found in Cave 11 (11Q13 [11QMelch]).[28] In that text, written in Hebrew and composed before the Epistle to the Hebrews was written, the Palestinian Jewish

---

24. Markus Barth, *Ephesians: Introduction, Translation, and Commentary,* vol. 34 of The Anchor Bible, 2 vols., fifth printing (Garden City, N.Y.: Doubleday, 1981), 11, 67; Thomas M. Winger, *Ephesians,* Concordia Commentary: A Theological Exposition of Sacred Scripture (St. Louis: Concordia Publishing House, 2015), 77–83.

25. For a helpful discussion of Philemon, consult David R. Seely, "From Unprofitable Servant to Beloved Brother in Christ," in Millet, *Studies in Scripture: Volume Six,* 165–77.

26. On the pastoral Epistles, see the study of Bruce A. Van Orden, "The Pastoral Epistles," in Millet, *Studies in Scripture: Volume Six,* 178–91.

27. Eusebius, *Ecclesiastical History* 5.11.4 (Pantaenus is called "the last" in Clement's quoted list); 6.14.4 (called "the blessed elder," who claimed the letter was written by Paul "to the Hebrews"). See Hugh Jackson Lawlor and John Ernest Leonard Oulton, *Eusebius, Bishop of Caesarea: The Ecclesiastical History and the Martyrs of Palestine,* 2 vols. (repr., London: SPCK, 1954), 1:156, 189; 2:166, 198–99; Quasten, *Patrology* 2:4–5.

28. See Florentino García Martínez, *The Dead Sea Scrolls Translated: The Qumran Texts in English,* 2nd ed. (Leiden, Neth.: E. J. Brill; Grand Rapids, Mich.: William B. Eerdmans, 1996), 139–40.

author ascribes to Melchizedek the same characteristics that Hebrews assigns to Jesus. "Melchizedek is presented as a heavenly Redemption figure who will execute divine judgment and salvation. . . . The heavenly Son of God of Hebrews 7, who rules above all heavenly and earthly powers, and lives forever to make intercession for those who put their trust in him, has his counterpart now in the heavenly Melchizedek at Qumran."[29] This is not all. The Melchizedek text brings together important "Old Testament passages centering in Isaiah 61 and the jubilee-year text in Leviticus 25" as well as other passages, chiefly from the Psalms, that "contemporized Old Testament texts" in an expectation of Melchizedek's role in the salvation drama that was about to unfold.[30] We meet exactly the same style of reflection and commentary on key Old Testament passages discussed in Hebrews 1, which mostly quote from Psalms except the quotation from 2 Samuel 7:14 in Hebrews 1:5. It is evident, therefore, that the letter to the Hebrews consisted of a general circular aimed at Christianized Jews.[31]

The Seven Catholic Epistles

The letters not associated with the Apostle Paul, called the Catholic Epistles by Christian authors of the third and fourth centuries,[32] present intriguing scenarios in the nascent church. The letter from James, whose author was possibly the younger brother of Jesus, was aimed at an audience that is named "the twelve tribes which are scattered abroad" (James 1:1). If, in fact, this James was the Epistle's author, its composition predated AD 62, when James was stoned to death in Jerusalem.[33] Owing to its very Jewish character, the letter seems to be composed mainly for Jewish Christian members of the Church. As we have already noticed, the letter joins the Gospel of Matthew, the Epistle to the Hebrews, and the book of Revelation as the most Jewish books in the New Testament. As an example, James

---

29. James A. Sanders, "Cave 11 Surprises and the Question of Canon," in *New Directions in Biblical Archaeology,* ed. David Noel Freedman and Jonas C. Greenfield (Garden City, N.Y.: Doubleday, 1969), 102.

30. Sanders, "Cave 11 Surprises and the Question of Canon," 102; see also Michael O. Wise, Martin G. Abegg Jr., and Edward M. Cook, *The Dead Sea Scrolls: A New Translation* (San Francisco: HarperOne, 2005), 590–91.

31. Consult the helpful study by Joseph F. McConkie, "Jesus Christ, Symbolism, and Salvation," in Millet, *Studies in Scripture: Volume Six*, 192–206.

32. Werner Georg Kümmel, *Introduction to the New Testament,* trans. A. J. Mattill Jr., 14th rev. ed. (Nashville: Abingdon Press, 1966), 283.

33. Josephus, *Antiquities of the Jews* 20.9.1 (§200).

writes the term "synagogue" in a place where we expect a pointer to the church (KJV translated the Greek *synagogē* as "assembly" in James 2:2). In its substance, "it is an interpretation of the Old Testament law and the Sermon on the Mount in the light of the Christian Gospel."[34] Historically, it remained among the disputed works into the medieval period, being famously rejected by Martin Luther as nonapostolic and as countering the Apostle Paul's teaching.[35] Perhaps ironically, the Epistle of James became the main springboard for the Restoration of the gospel after Joseph Smith read the lines in James 1:5–6 (see JS–H 1:11–13).

The two letters from Peter offer contrasting contents. First Peter is addressed to Church members, whom he calls "strangers," in central and northern Asia Minor—"throughout Pontus, Galatia, Cappadocia, Asia, and Bithynia" (1 Pet. 1:1). Second Peter is written more generally "to them that have obtained like precious faith with us" (2 Pet. 1:1). The intended recipients may have been the same. One of 1 Peter's dominant themes is "suffering" because of persecution (1 Pet. 3:14; 4:12, 19; 5:9). We are not to "be troubled" by afflictions, he wrote, because Christ suffered, "leaving us an example" (1 Pet. 2:21; 3:14; see also 1 Pet. 1:11; 2:23; 5:1).[36] In my opinion, the first letter's treasury holds some of the most sublime doctrines in the New Testament. In mild contrast, 2 Peter sends out a warning about apostasy creeping into Christian ranks. Specifically, this condition is to come in the form of "false prophets" and "false teachers among you, who privily shall bring in damnable heresies." Peter worried that people would believe the heretics when he said, "Many shall follow their pernicious ways" (2 Pet. 2:1–2). But this is only part of the story. Evidently, among some congregations, these people had already arrived and enjoyed full fellowship. Calling them "blemishes," Peter wrote that they had come "with their own deceivings while they feast with you" (2 Pet. 2:13). The music had gone out of tune. That said, 2 Peter includes a few passages well known to Latter-day Saints; to wit, "Be partakers of the divine nature" (2 Pet. 1:4), "Make your

34. Henry Clarence Thiessen, *Introduction to the New Testament* (Grand Rapids, Mich.: William B. Eerdmans, 1943), 272.

35. Kümmel, *Introduction to the New Testament,* 285. A helpful summary is that of Larry E. Dahl, "A String of Gospel Pearls," in Millet, *Studies in Scripture: Volume Six,* 207–24.

36. Frank F. Judd Jr., "The Case for Petrine Authorship of 1 Peter," in *The Ministry of Peter, the Chief Apostle,* 43rd Annual Brigham Young University Sidney B. Sperry Symposium, ed. Frank F. Judd Jr., Eric D. Huntsman, and Shon D. Hopkin (Provo, Utah: BYU Religious Studies Center, 2014), 247–65.

calling and election sure" (2 Pet. 1:10), "No prophecy of the scripture is of any private interpretation" (2 Pet. 1:20), and "The day of the Lord will come as a thief in the night" (2 Pet. 3:10).[37]

If we can assign a location to the three letters of John, they fit in western Asia Minor. John was last active in that region during his mortal life. In the book of Revelation, the letters to the seven churches of the Roman province of Asia clearly tie John's late ministry to that area (see Rev. 2–3). Like 2 Peter, the three Epistles of John also exhibit the growing, worrisome threats of apostasy underlined in that letter. And like Peter's correspondence, John's letters reflect the Christian situation in Asia Minor. For example, we learn about "many antichrists" (1 John 2:18), "many false prophets" (1 John 4:1), and "many deceivers . . . who confess not that Jesus Christ is come in the flesh" (2 John 1:7; see also 1 John 4:3). Plainly, a form of docetism—a doctrine that Jesus had not come in the flesh but only seemed to do so—had invaded the churches in ancient Turkey (see 1 John 4:2–3 and 2 John 1:7). What is more, we find certain Church leaders refused to receive apostolic representatives (see 3 John 1:9–10).[38]

The Epistle of Jude offers the intriguing possibility of another letter from a brother of Jesus, for he calls himself "the servant of Jesus Christ, and brother of James" (Jude 1:1). Several Judes or Judases are known from scripture, of course. But his link to James opens the door to a relationship to Jesus, an older brother (see Matt. 13:55 and Mark 6:3). This Jude characterized his audience as "them that are sanctified by God the Father, and preserved in Jesus Christ" (Jude 1:1). Even in this light, we cannot determine the letter's destination. The best possibility consists of believers in ancient Palestine, which included Galilee since Jude's family continued to reside there. According to Hegesippus, an early Christian author of the second century AD, Emperor Domitian set in motion a dragnet to find descendants of King David and destroy them as threats to the Roman

---

37. See the helpful summary in Monte S. Nyman, "The Sublime Epistles of Peter," in Millet, *Studies in Scripture: Volume Six*, 225–35; also consult John W. Welch and Brent J. Schmidt, "Reading 2 Peter as a Farewell Text," in Judd, Huntsman, and Hopkin, *Ministry of Peter, the Chief Apostle*, 317–35.

38. Walter Bauer, *Orthodoxy and Heresy in Earliest Christianity*, ed. Robert Kraft and Gerhard Krodel (Philadelphia: Fortress Press, 1971), 91–94, argues that John's Epistles mirror a struggle between "orthodox" and "heretical" Christians for control of the congregations in Asia Minor with, in some cases, the "orthodox" withdrawing from the so-called heretics because the latter formed the majority of certain congregations. Also consult the helpful summary by Thomas W. Mackay, "The Epistles of John," in Millet, *Studies in Scripture: Volume Six*, 236–43.

government. Caught in the net were two grandsons of Jude who appeared before Domitian as farmers of small plots of ground, likely in Galilee where Jude's family possibly owned property since the days of Mary and Joseph. Deeming them to be no threat, the emperor dismissed them.[39] In his letter, Jude warned against false teachers, "certain men [who] crept in unawares, who were . . . ungodly men, turning the grace of our God into lasciviousness, and denying . . . our Lord Jesus Christ" (Jude 1:4). In both its tenor and content, the Epistle resembles 2 Peter, which must have served as a model for Jude's letter.[40]

The Gospels and the Book of Acts

Among the Gospels, only Luke spells out his audience—an individual who was a ranking Roman official named Theophilus (see Luke 1:3 and Acts 1:1). To determine the readerships of the other Gospels, one must look for clues inside their narratives.

The genealogy that opens Matthew's story about Jesus is one that especially Jewish readers would have appreciated (see Matt. 1:1–17) because it hinges on the names of David and Abraham (Matt. 1:1). In addition, students of Matthew's Gospel have long noticed his clear objective to place Jesus' ministry within the framework of Old Testament prophecy fulfilled. Before chapter 1 ends, we read the fulfillment of Isaiah's prophecy about a virgin giving birth to a son named Emmanuel: "Now all this was done, that it might be fulfilled which was spoken of the Lord by the prophet [Isaiah]" (Matt. 1:22; see Isa. 7:14). Matthew repeats similar wording another ten times in connection with crucial moments in Jesus' life and ministry (see Matt. 2:15, 17, 23; 8:17; 12:17; etc.). Even Jesus referred to fulfilling prophecy at the time of his arrest, asking Peter, who had just assaulted the high priest's servant by cutting off his ear, "How then shall the scriptures be fulfilled [about Jesus' suffering], that thus it must be?" (Matt. 26:54).

Furthermore, scholars have found that the teachings of Jesus recorded by Matthew are divided into five parts, likely in imitation of the five books of Moses in the Old Testament. Each part is separated by an expression like "And it came to pass, when Jesus had ended these sayings" (Matt. 7:28; see also Matt. 11:1; 13:53; 19:1; 26:1). The lesson is that Jesus is the new

39. Eusebius, *Ecclesiastical History* 3.19–20.

40. See the helpful study by Catherine Thomas, "Refuge in God's Love," in Millet, *Studies in Scripture: Volume Six,* 244–55.

lawgiver, replacing the prophet Moses. Although we could point to other Jewish features, such as the emphasis on Jesus as the new Davidic king, these examples suffice to make the case that Matthew was writing to fellow Jews.[41] It is almost as if Matthew was responding to questions from Jewish acquaintances who asked, "Well, if Jesus was the Messiah, why did I not see him in that light?"

Mark's Gospel, in the view of most New Testament scholars, holds pride of place as the first Gospel written, from which the other three authors derived much of their inspiration and material about Jesus. And why did they follow his lead? Likely because Mark was reproducing accounts of the chief Apostle Peter, and that fact carried weight.[42] In this connection, Papias, an early Christian author who was active between AD 120 and 140 and whose writings are preserved only in part through short quotations from later authors, reported that Mark was the interpreter of Peter during the years before Peter's death in Rome c. AD 64 when the emperor Nero's persecution of Christians roared to life (see a possible reference to Mark in "Marcus my son" at 1 Pet. 5:13). Mark was evidently the same as John Mark, whose mother owned a home in Jerusalem where believers used to gather. It was this Mark who accompanied Paul on his first missionary journey (see Acts 12:12, 25; 13:5). According to Papias, Mark was himself not an original disciple of Jesus and hence his Gospel consisted of "all that he recalled of what" Peter had said, working hard "not to omit anything of what he heard." [43] Knowing that Mark recorded what Peter taught gives us insight into Mark's audience.

In addition, when Mark recorded Jesus' prophecy of the fall of Jerusalem, his Gospel shows no knowledge of the fateful events of AD 70 when the city succumbed to the Roman army (they would have been easy to insert in some form). We can conclude that Mark must have written his Gospel before the end of AD 69. Further, when Mark accompanied Peter to Rome, he likely witnessed the fury of Nero's persecution and its deadly aftermath. Because Mark presented "the Christ who continues to speak

---

41. Robert L. Millet, "The Testimony of Matthew," in *Studies in Scripture: Volume Five, The Gospels,* ed. Kent P. Jackson and Robert L. Millet (Salt Lake City: Deseret Book, 1986), 47–57.

42. Eric D. Huntsman, "The Petrine *Kērygma* and the Gospel according to Mark," in Judd, Huntsman, and Hopkin, *Ministry of Peter, the Chief Apostle,* 170–71.

43. Eusebius, *Ecclesiastical History* 3.39.15 records that Peter "used to adapt his instructions to the needs [of the moment]."

and act meaningfully in the context of crisis,"[44] and because his record exhibits Latinisms that are characteristic of the Roman Empire,[45] the best candidate for the place of composition is Rome. With this in mind, Mark's Gospel was likely written for Gentile Christians whom he had met on his journeys with Peter and who resided in the broader Roman Empire, but especially in Italy.[46]

The Gospel of Luke and the book of Acts likely have the same audience because the same author wrote them.[47] This observation is made firm in the dedication of the two volumes to a certain Theophilus (see Luke 1:3 and Acts 1:1). This man may well have sponsored Luke's task to write an account of the growth of the gospel message from a backwater area in tiny Galilee to a major institution that spread its influence to Rome, the capital city of a vast empire. We judge that Theophilus was a ranking Roman official because of the words Luke assigns to him: "most excellent," a title that shows up elsewhere in Acts for other Roman dignitaries (see Acts 23:26; 24:3; 26:25). As a second- or third-generation believer, Luke was not one of the original "eyewitnesses and ministers of the word" (Luke 1:2). As a Gentile and an occasional companion to Paul, the Apostle to the Gentiles (see Col. 4:14 and 2 Tim. 4:11), Luke's intent was to tell the story of Jesus and his disciples to a Gentile audience. This is evident not only in Luke's dedication of his two volumes to the Gentile man Theophilus but also in his excellent Greek style and in his portrayal of Jews who fought the Christian faith in a very bad light (see Acts 13:44–50; 14:1–5, 19; 17:5–13; 18:12–17; 21:26–31). To fit with his interest in the gospel spreading to the Gentiles, he knowingly added the account of the call and mission of the Seventy, whose specific assignment was to preach to Gentiles (see Luke 10:1–12, 17–20 and D&C 107:25).[48]

---

44. William L. Lane, *The Gospel according to Mark: The English Text with Introduction, Exposition and Notes* (Grand Rapids, Mich.: William B. Eerdmans, 1974), 25.

45. Friedrich Blass and Albert Debrunner, *A Greek Grammar of the New Testament and Other Early Christian Literature,* trans. Robert W. Funk (Chicago: University of Chicago Press, 1961), §5; Martin Hengel, *Studies in the Gospel of Mark,* trans. John Bowden (Philadelphia: Fortress Press, 1985), 29, 137, n. 161.

46. Hengel, *Studies in the Gospel of Mark,* 29; for a helpful study, see S. Kent Brown, "The Testimony of Mark," in Jackson and Millet, *Studies in Scripture: Volume Five,* 61–87; for Mark's composition, see Lane, *Gospel according to Mark,* 7–25; and for the Gospel in general, consult Julie M. Smith, *The Gospel according to Mark,* Brigham Young University New Testament Commentary (Provo, Utah: BYU Studies, 2018).

47. For a helpful summary, see Richard Lloyd Anderson, "The Testimony of Luke," in Jackson and Millet, *Studies in Scripture: Volume Five,* 88–108.

48. S. Kent Brown, *The Testimony of Luke,* Brigham Young University New Testament Commentary (Provo, Utah: BYU Studies, 2015), 507–16, 520–24.

John's Gospel begins with a bang: "In the beginning," a clear imitation of the opening of the first book of scripture in the Old Testament. This opening points to one of John's audiences: Jewish Christians. His Gospel does not seem to be for the uninitiated but rather for those already in the Christian fold. John knew Jewish law and expressed items from it in different contexts (see John 2:6; 18:28; 19:31). He also knew Old Testament scripture (see John 12:38–40; 13:18; 15:25; etc.). In addition, the text shows John's acquaintance with Gentile ways, leading us to conclude that his audience also included Gentile Christians. For instance, the concern with the *logos,* or the "word," exhibits ties to Stoic thought (see John 1:1, 9, 11; etc.). And Jesus' statements about eating his flesh and drinking his blood form links to the mystery religions of the Greco-Roman world (see John 6:51–57). Naturally, John frames such elements so that they are understood within the life and ministry of Jesus, not a philosophical system or mystery religion.[49]

John's purpose appears to have been *paraenesis,* or "teaching." That is, his intent was to introduce his readers to a deeper, richer understanding of who Jesus was and is and how his Atonement has made a difference for all.[50] John's narratives of the wedding at Cana, Jesus' meeting of the Samaritan woman at Jacob's well, Jesus' raising of Lazarus, and other accounts have touched the lives of millions of Christian believers throughout the centuries and will continue to do so. John himself set out his objective when he wrote about his narrative: "These [stories] are written, that ye might believe that Jesus is the Christ, the Son of God; and that believing ye might have life through his name" (John 20:31).

For Further Reading

Jackson, Kent P., and Robert L. Millet, eds. *Studies in Scripture: Volume Five, The Gospels.* Salt Lake City: Deseret Book, 1986.

Millet, Robert L., ed. *Studies in Scripture: Volume Six, Acts to Revelation.* Salt Lake City: Deseret Book, 1987.

49. C. Kingsley Barrett, *The Gospel according to St John: An Introduction with Commentary and Notes on the Greek Text* (London: SPCK, 1955), 28–33; Leon Morris, *The Gospel according to John: The English Text with Introduction, Exposition and Notes* (Grand Rapids, Mich.: William B. Eerdmans, 1971), 60–64.

50. For a helpful summary of the first half of John's Gospel, see C. Wilfred Griggs, "The Testimony of John," in Jackson and Millet, *Studies in Scripture, Volume Five,* 109–26.

Collections

Making Sense of the Greek Manuscripts and Later English Translations

Eric D. Huntsman

Despite the long dominance of the King James Version (KJV) in the English-speaking world, three factors have led to efforts to produce new Bible translations. First, English, like all languages, continues to change, and despite the beautiful cadences and expressions of the King James Bible, its archaic forms and word uses have become increasingly difficult for many modern readers. Second, scholars' understanding of and facility with biblical Hebrew and Greek continues to improve, particularly in the areas of lexicography (word usage) and grammar. Third, and most important for this discussion of the Greek New Testament, the discovery of older manuscripts than those used by Erasmus (1469–1536) and his successors has required a reexamination of many passages.[1]

The Codex Alexandrinus (A), an early fourth-century uncial manuscript of the Gospels, was presented to Charles I of England in 1627. Like the much later manuscripts used by Erasmus, Stephanus, and Beza, it provides a very early witness of a Byzantine text type that generally offers to readers smooth and uncomplicated readings. Such manuscripts formed the basis of the so-called Textus Receptus, or "received text," which was an edited cluster of medieval manuscripts that underlay important translations into European languages, including English.

However, in the fifth edition (1657) of his Polyglot Bible, Brian Walton first published a collection of variant readings that included manuscripts outside of the Byzantine family.[2] Then in 1719, Edward Wells (1667–1727)

1. Bruce M. Metzger, *The New Testament: Its Background, Growth, and Content,* 2nd ed. (Nashville: Abington Press, 1983), 284–86.

2. Brian Walton, *Biblia Sacra Polyglotta, complectentia Textus Originalis* . . . (London: Thomas Roycroft, 1657); see the discussion of Bruce M. Metzger and Bart D. Ehrman, *Text of the New Testament,* 4th ed. (New York: Oxford University Press, 2005), 153.

published an edition relying upon more ancient manuscripts than those upon which the Textus Receptus had been based; when published, Wells's edition differed 210 times from the Elzevir text, upon which the KJV was largely based.[3] Relying solely upon earlier uncial manuscripts, Karl Lachmann (1793–1851) produced a text in 1831 that varied significantly from the Textus Receptus. Nevertheless, Lachmann confidently claimed that his edition reflected the New Testament as it had existed in the fourth century.[4] The greatest changes, however, occurred with Constantin von Tischendorf's 1844 discovery of Codex Sinaiticus (א), a complete uncial manuscript dating to the third quarter of the fourth century, and with his examination of the Codex Vaticanus (B), another fourth-century uncial that had been in the Vatican library since the late fifteenth century but had not been widely consulted. These two codices represent important examples of the Alexandrian textual family, a generally shorter, often more abrupt family that differed significantly from the manuscripts used in most previously printed editions of the Greek New Testament.[5]

In 1881, Brooke Westcott and Fenton Hort proposed that the Alexandrian text type, which is generally shorter and lacks the kind of refinements in style and grammar that suggest later textual developments, must be the closest to the original autographs.[6] The edition of the Greek text of the New Testament that Westcott and Hort produced in that year is a good example of a so-called "eclectic text," which draws its readings critically from a great number of different manuscripts.[7]

The year 1881 also witnessed the start of the English Revised Version (ERV) of the KJV, which had been commissioned by the Anglican Church in the Convention of Canterbury in 1870 and was completed and published in 1885.[8] Basing its Greek text upon the editions of Tregelles, Tischendorf,

---

3. Metzger and Ehrman, *Text of the New Testament,* 155.

4. Karl Lachmann, *Novum Testamentum Græce, ex recensione Caroli Lachmanni* (Berlin, 1831); Metzger and Ehrman, *Text of the New Testament,* 170–71; Comfort, *Essential Guide to Bible Versions,* 149–50.

5. Metzger and Ehrman, *Text of the New Testament,* 62–65, 172–73; Comfort, *Essential Guide to Bible Versions,* 75–77, 78–80, 149–50.

6. Metzger and Ehrman, *Text of the New Testament,* 174–79, 312–13; Comfort, *Essential Guide to Bible Versions,* 150–51.

7. Brooke Foss Westcott and Fenton John Anthony Hort, *The New Testament in the Original Greek* (New York: Harper and Brothers, 1881).

8. C. J. Ellicott and others, eds., *The New Testament of our Lord and Saviour Jesus Christ, Translated out of the Greek: Being the Version Set Forth A.D. 1611, Compared with the Most Ancient Authorities and Revised, A.D. 1881* (Oxford: Oxford University Press, 1881).

and Westcott and Hort,[9] the translation committee made thousands of changes. Intended as a revision, not a retranslation, of the KJV, the result was nonetheless characterized as "strong in Greek, weak in English."[10] Members of the American committee that had worked with the ERV published the American Standard Version (ASV) in 1901.[11] While putting into practice some of the preferences of the American Committee that had not been accepted by the English committee, the ASV likewise sought for literal renderings of what were regarded as more trustworthy texts that privileged the tradition represented by Sinaiticus (א) and Vaticanus (B). Consequently, both the ERV and the ASV lacked, queried, or relegated to marginal notes some well-known and cherished passages, such as the doxology ending the Lord's Prayer (Matt. 6:13) and the long ending of Mark (Mark 16:9–20), that did not appear in many of the older manuscripts.[12]

Such substantive changes, perhaps more than changes in wording to reflect more contemporary usage, aroused the anger of more conservative biblical scholars. Foremost among these was John W. Burgon (1813–1888), who maintained that God had superintended the survival of the most accurate manuscripts, thereby guaranteeing that those used by Erasmus and his successors were the most correct.[13] The arguments of Burgon and other conservatives were largely adopted by J. Reuben Clark (1871–1961), longtime member of the First Presidency of the Church, who was particularly concerned by the publication of the Revised Standard Version of 1952 (RSV).[14]

---

9. Edwin Palmer, ed., *Η ΚΑΙΝΗ ΔΙΑΘΗΚΗ. The Greek Testament with the Readings Adopted by the Revisers of the Authorised Version* (Oxford: Clarendon Press, 1881).

10. Charles Haddon Spurgeon, as quoted in Metzger, *New Testament: Its Background,* 288; Comfort, *Essential Guide to Bible Versions,* 162.

11. Philip Schaff and others, eds., *The Holy Bible, Containing the Old and New Testaments, Translated out of the Original Tongues, Being the Version Set Forth A.D. 1611, Compared with the Most Ancient Authorities and Revised A.D. 1881–1885, Newly Edited by the American Revision Committee A.D. 1901,* standard ed. (New York: Thomas Nelson and Sons, 1901).

12. Metzger and Ehrman, *Text of the New Testament,* 322–27; Comfort, *Essential Guide to Bible Versions,* 162–65.

13. John William Burgon, *The Revision Revised* (London: John Murray, 1883); John William Burgon and Edward Miller, eds., *The Traditional Text of the Holy Gospels Vindicated and Established* (London: George Bell and Sons, 1896); John William Burgon, *The Causes of the Corruption of the Traditional Text of the Holy Gospels, Being the Sequel to "The Traditional Text of the Holy Gospels,"* ed. Edward Miller (London: George Bell and Sons, 1896). See the discussion of Metzger and Ehrman, *Text of the New Testament,* 181–82.

14. *The Holy Bible, Revised Standard Version. Containing the Old and New Testaments, Translated from the Original Tongues; Being the Version Set Forth A.D. 1611, Revised*

This edition—seen as a continuing revision of the 1611 KJV, the 1885 ERV, and the 1901 ASV—was based largely on the 1927 eclectic Greek text of Erwin Nestle, but it sought also to take into account several recently discovered New Testament papyri, which provided an earlier witness than the manuscripts previously used in the preparation of Greek editions. Although the RSV and its successors soon became the standard text for many "mainline" Protestant denominations, it was not received well by conservative Christians,[15] including President Clark.

Although President Clark made it clear that he was not a linguist or textual scholar and that his opinions were his own,[16] his exhaustive research, thorough argumentation, and prestige helped reinforce the KJV's position as the official English Bible of the Church.[17] President Clark exhibited an understandable preference for the literary excellence of the KJV,[18] but he was more concerned about the changes in substance over form that occurred when new translations were based on critical Greek editions rather than the Textus Receptus. In addition to the arguments of Burgon and others against the Alexandrian and in support of the Byzantine textual family, President Clark's 1956 *Why the King James Version* raised concerns over word choices, omissions, and other differences and implications of such changes for the nature of Christ.[19] In particular, President Clark understandably worried that Sinaiticus (א) and Vaticanus (B), having been presumably prepared in Egypt during the great theological controversies of the fourth century, might have differed because of heretical attempts to deny or reduce the divinity of Christ.[20] A fuller understanding of Arianism and additional textual discoveries require some modification of President

---

A.D. 1881–1885 and A.D. 1901; Compared with the Most Ancient Authorities and Revised A.D. 1952 (New York: Thomas Nelson, 1952; 2nd ed. 1971).

15. Comfort, *Essential Guide to Bible Versions,* 165–70.

16. J. Reuben Clark Jr., *Why the King James Version* (Salt Lake City: Deseret Book, 1956), 200.

17. Philip L. Barlow, "Why the King James Version?: From the Common to the Official Bible of Mormonism," *Dialogue* 22, no. 2 (Summer 1989): 24–36, rev. and exp. in Philip L. Barlow, *Mormons and the Bible* (Oxford: Oxford University Press, 1991), 158–74.

18. "Could any language be too great, too elegant, too beautiful, too majestic, too divine-like to record the doings and sayings of Jesus of Nazareth, the Christ?" Clark, *Why the King James Version,* 355.

19. Clark, *Why the King James Version,* 194–226, 243–51, 306–50, 395–417. Many of these arguments were proposed earlier in his April 1954 general conference address "Our Bible," reprinted in *J. Reuben Clark: Selected Papers,* ed. David H. Yarn (Provo, Utah: Brigham Young University Press, 1984), 77–94.

20. Clark, "Our Bible," 79–80; Clark, *Why the King James Version,* 27.

Clark's position,[21] but his concerns for the devotional associations of the KJV for Latter-day Saints, the harmony of KJV renderings with modern scripture and the Joseph Smith Translation (JST), and the doctrinal implications of new translations and textual changes retain considerable validity.

Indeed, despite earlier ambivalence about the KJV,[22] the traditional version has become and remains the official English version of the Bible used by The Church of Jesus Christ of Latter-day Saints. Having one official version has not only allowed for standardization in Church publications and sermons[23] but also provides for unity and a common spiritual experience with the text among members sharing a common faith.[24] Although many other reasons have been given regarding the importance of the KJV's status,[25] per-

---

21. Rather than denying godhood to Christ or proposing that the Father had created the Son out of nothing, Arianism actually emphasized the individuality of the Father and the Son, subordinating the Son to the Father and maintaining his special role as the only "begotten, not made," a position more amenable to Restoration theology than post-Nicean creedal orthodoxy. Nathan A. Jacobs, "The Begotten-Not-Made Distinction in Eastern Pro-Nicenes," *Religious Studies* 55, no. 4 (2019): 503–35.

In 1955–56, M. Martin Bodmer purchased a number of significant papyri in Cairo. Two of them, $\mathfrak{P}^{66}$ and $\mathfrak{P}^{75}$, date to the late second century and provide witnesses to the early Alexandrian family that far antedate the Arian controversy. $\mathfrak{P}^{66}$ (P.Bodm. II), a codex of John published in 1956 by Victor Martin, contains both Alexandrian and Western elements. $\mathfrak{P}^{75}$ (P.Bodm. XIV–XV), a codex of Luke and John published by Martin and Rodolphe Kasser in 1961, is very similar to Vaticanus (B).

22. Barlow, *Mormons and the Bible,* 148–58, notes the openness of Joseph Smith and Brigham Young to the possibility of other English translations, although they and Latter-day Saints took the KJV for granted until the advent of higher biblical criticism.

23. D. Kelly Ogden, "Bible: King James Version," in *Encyclopedia of Mormonism,* ed. Daniel H. Ludlow, 4 vols. (New York: Macmillan, 1992), 1:109.

24. Even Barlow, who otherwise argues against scholarly grounds against continued or at least exclusive use of the KJV, observes, "Yet if arguments marshaled for the King James Bible are contested by the standards of modern scholarship, Mormonism's KJV loyalties are understandable on religious grounds. . . . The insistence on some one linguistic style for its sacred texts by any religious body is motivated in part by the concern to find or preserve prose as satisfying to the worshipper as to the scholar (or sometimes even over and against the scholar). Language has for ages been viewed as embodying elements of the sacred; it follows that a yearning for the 'highest' language will often accompany what believers feel are receptions of divine communications. At least at the unconscious level, the quest is often as much for a sense of the numinous, a sense of holiness and mystery and divinity and dignity, as for the mere content of a given passage." Barlow, *Mormons and the Bible,* 178.

25. Joseph Fielding McConkie, "Modern Revelation: A Window to the Past," in *"To Be Learned Is Good If . . . ,"* ed. Robert L. Millet (Salt Lake City: Bookcraft, 1987), 126; Franklin S. Gonzales, "I Have a Question: With So Many English Translations of the Bible That Are Easy to Read, Why Does the Church Still Use the King James Version?," *Ensign* 17 (June 1987): 23–25; Barlow, *Mormons and the Bible,* 175–78.

haps the most important is the fact that the KJV was the common English translation at the time of Joseph Smith, leading the Prophet to echo its phraseology in his translation of the Book of Mormon, in his own recorded revelations, and in his own inspired revision of the Bible, the Joseph Smith Translation.[26] The continuity of the language of the standard works of the Church makes it easier for students of the scriptures to see connections and recognize literary and doctrinal parallels.[27]

While not replacing the KJV in Latter-day Saint usage, translations since the RSV can nonetheless serve a valuable role to supplement study of the Bible, particularly the New Testament. The most prominent of these, employing modern but not colloquial English, can help readers unravel some difficult passages in the KJV where archaic English diction and changed usage make understanding difficult. Furthermore, many of these translations incorporate or note textual issues raised by the discovery of additional manuscripts and the changing state of textual criticism, although one must be aware that the majority of opinions about current scholarship are far from conclusive.

The first of these translations was a conservative response to the RSV. In 1971, evangelical scholars of the Lockman Foundation produced the New American Standard Bible of 1971 (NASB),[28] a very conservative translation that sought for a word-for-word rendering of the Hebrew and Greek and chose to retain in brackets passages that the ASV and RSV had omitted, while noting that they did not appear in some ancient manuscripts.[29] Notable among its conservative tendencies was the NASB's practice prior to its 1995 revision of using the traditional Elizabethan pronouns "thou," "thee," and "thine" "in the language of prayer when addressing Deity."[30]

---

26. Bruce R. McConkie illustrated this point by writing, "[The KJV] Bible came into being to prepare the way for the translation of the Book of Mormon and to set a literary pattern and standard for the revelations in the Doctrine and Covenants." Bruce R. McConkie, "The Bible, a Sealed Book," in *Teaching Seminary: Preservice Readings* (Salt Lake City: The Church of Jesus Christ of Latter-day Saints, 2021), accessed September 18, 2023, https://www.churchofjesuschrist.org/study/manual/teaching-seminary-preservice-readings-religion-370-471-and-475/the-bible-a-sealed-book.

27. Ogden, "Bible: King James Version," 109.

28. Reuben A. Olson and others, eds., *New American Standard Bible* (La Habra, Calif.: Foundation Press Publications, 1971; updated ed., Anaheim, Calif.: Foundation Publications, 1995).

29. Comfort, *Essential Guide to Bible Versions,* 171–72.

30. Reuben A. Olson and others, *New American Standard Bible: New Testament* (La Habra, Calif.: Foundation Press, 1963), foreword.

The New International Version of 1978 (NIV) was a fresh translation, rather than a further revision, of the Bible in English.[31] Although its New Testament is based on the critical Greek text of the United Bible Societies' 1966 edition of the Greek New Testament, it nonetheless chose to agree with the Textus Receptus in many significant passages. Seeking to retain modern but familiar readings for well-known and important passages, the NIV received widespread acceptance, outselling the KJV in 1987.[32]

The most conservative response was the New King James Version of 1982 (NKJV).[33] Its translation is for the most part modern, although it preserves many familiar wordings and patterns. Most significantly, the NKJV remained absolutely faithful to the Textus Receptus for the New Testament, although it noted places where it diverged from critical eclectic texts or from the so-called "Majority Text," an edition of the Greek text that draws its readings primarily from the Byzantine text family, since the majority of extant manuscripts come from this group.[34]

Other important translations include the 1986 New Jerusalem Bible (NJB)[35] and the 1990 New Revised Standard Version (NRSV).[36] The NJB is an updated version of the Jerusalem Bible printed in England in 1966 as an English companion to the French *La Bible de Jérusalem*. Both of these were translated at the Dominican Biblical School of Jerusalem and were the first Roman Catholic Bibles translated directly from Hebrew and Greek rather than the Latin Vulgate. Although the NJB was more accurate than its predecessor, its decision to use more gender-inclusive language made it less traditional. Roman Catholic doctrine did not noticeably affect the translation, but while employing critical texts, the translators often opted for readings from the Western text family, which is the one most attested in the writings of early Latin church fathers.[37]

---

31. Edwin H. Palmer and others, eds., *The Holy Bible, New International Version: Containing the Old Testament and the New Testament* (Grand Rapids, Mich.: Zondervan, 1978; rev. ed. 1984).

32. Comfort, *Essential Guide to Bible Versions*, 189–92; see also Metzger, *New Testament: Its Background*, 292.

33. Arthur Farstad, ed., *Holy Bible: The New King James Version: Containing the Old and New Testaments* (Nashville: Thomas Nelson, 1982).

34. Comfort, *Essential Guide to Bible Versions*, 152–55, 173–74; Metzger, *New Testament: Its Background*, 292.

35. Henry Wansbrough, ed., *The New Jerusalem Bible* (New York: Doubleday, 1985).

36. Bruce M. Metzger and others, eds., *The New Revised Standard Version* (New York: Oxford University Press, 1990).

37. Comfort, *Essential Guide to Bible Versions*, 186–87, 192–93.

The NRSV is a further modernization of the RSV that likewise follows the principle of gender inclusiveness. This revision most closely follows a recent version of the critical texts of the Greek New Testament, the twenty-sixth edition of the Nestle-Aland text or the third edition by the United Bible Societies.[38] Consequently, its translation often differs substantially from the KJV and the NKJV, which were based on the Textus Receptus. Like the RSV before it, the NRSV is often accused of "reading out" Christian allusions in the Old Testament in its translation.[39]

When assessing different translations for use as study aids, two important factors must be considered: the translation methodology followed and the theological or philosophical biases of the translators. Two different translation methodologies are (1) formal equivalence (word-for-word), which stresses a faithful rendering of the meaning of Hebrew and Greek words into the new language, and (2) dynamic equivalence (thought-for-thought), which seeks to recreate for its readers the effect the text had on its original audience. A good translation must be both reliable and readable and so, to a certain extent, must contain elements of both formal and dynamic equivalence.[40]

However, the overriding concern should be reliability, especially if difficulty in reading can be overcome with sufficient study aids.[41] True formal equivalence is obtained only by an interlinear translation. The most strictly literal, but readable, translation is the NASB, but the KJV, NKJV, and RSV are also literal. The NRSV can be judged as literal with some freedom to be idiomatic, whereas the NIV and the NJB tend to be towards the middle of the spectrum. An example of a very dynamically equivalent translation is Today's English Version, sometimes known as the "Good News Bible" for its colloquial style.[42]

---

38. Kurt Aland, Eberhard Nestle, and others, eds., *Novum Testamentum Graece,* 26th ed. (Stuttgart: Deutsche Bibelgesellschaft, 1979); Kurt Aland and others, *The Greek New Testament* (Stuttgart: United Bible Societies, 1966; 2nd ed. 1968; 3rd ed. 1975).

39. Comfort, *Essential Guide to Bible Versions,* 174–76.

40. See Comfort, *Essential Guide to Bible Versions,* 103–8; and Robert W. Milliman, "Translation Theory and Twentieth-Century Versions," in *One Bible Only? Examining Exclusive Claims for the King James Bible,* ed. Roy E. Beacham and Kevin T. Bauder (Grand Rapids, Mich.: Kregel, 2001), 134–43.

41. This is essentially the position of J. Reuben Clark, who allowed the difficulties of reading the KJV but thought that "a little work with a reference book . . . could overcome this small obstacle." See Barlow, "Why the King James Version," 32.

42. Comfort, *Essential Guide to Bible Versions,* 234–35; Milliman, "Translation Theory and Twentieth Century Versions," 143–47.

A translation's position on the continuum between formal and dynamic equivalence, however, is not enough. Evangelical scholars who were quite conservative on doctrinal issues produced both the NASB and NIV, whereas the decidedly more liberal NRSV falls between the NASB and NIV in terms of formal equivalence. The bias of translators can often be discerned in the book introductions and the notes of study Bibles. In the actual translation, one litmus test for evangelical Christians has often been whether a translation renders the Hebrew *ʾalmah* of Isaiah 7:14 as "virgin" or "young woman." As another example, in considering eight disputed New Testament passages that could refer to Jesus as "God," Barlow found that the KJV did so four times; the RSV, the predecessor of the NRSV, did so four times; and the NIV did so seven out of eight times. By contrast, the New World Translation, sponsored by the Jehovah's Witnesses, did not render any of these passages as affirming Jesus' divinity.[43] Determining doctrinal biases is not always easy.

Despite significant differences in the actual translations of the New Testament, the greatest differences stem from the underlying Greek texts that these translations use. In reality, the doctrinal impact that these differences make is minimal. Metzger has noted, "The overwhelming majority of such variant readings involve inconsequential details. . . . In any event, no doctrine of Christian faith depends solely upon a passage that is textually uncertain."[44] Nevertheless, the ongoing development of textual criticism will continue to have an important impact on the study and translation of the New Testament.

As President Clark once expressed, he hoped that continued work in this area "will somehow provoke . . . the desire and determination to go over the manuscripts and furnish us, under the direction and influence of the Holy Ghost, a translation of the New Testament that will give us an accurate translation that shall be pregnant with the great principles of the Restored Gospel."[45] Consequently, Latter-day Saints have an interest to work on our own translation to help support our study of the New Testament—a translation that prefers a relatively high degree of formal equivalence, aims for high tone in translation that maintains long-held spiritual associations with the text, bears in mind doctrinal implications, and maintains resonance with the other standard works.

---

43. Barlow, "Why the King James Version," 39–40.
44. Metzger, *New Testament: Its Background*, 281.
45. Clark, *Why the King James Version*, viii–ix.

Why the Earliest New Testament Manuscripts May Not Be the Best

John F. Hall

Problems in the textual transmission of the Bible have been recognized since the earliest days of the Church. When the Angel Moroni first appeared to the Prophet Joseph Smith, he is described as reciting the last chapter of Malachi but quoting several verses differently from the text contained in the King James Version (see JS–H 1:36–39). Portions of Isaiah and of the New Testament book of Acts were, however, cited exactly as formulated in the King James text (see JS–H 1:40). That some sections of the biblical text are accurate, while others have been corrupted, we accept as a doctrinal tenet articulated by the Prophet Joseph Smith in the eighth Article of Faith. The Prophet provides further insight into the matter in his statement "I believe the bible as it read when it came from the pen of the original writers; ignorant translators, careless transcribers, or designing or corrupt priests have committed many errors."[1] Implicit in this teaching is the suggestion that the older the text, the closer the text may be to its original form and the less likely it is to have fallen prey to ignorant translators or careless transcribers.

In this case, as in so many other areas, the Prophet Joseph saw far beyond the scholars of his own day. Since that time, an entire field of scholarship has arisen to establish as accurately as possible the correct form of ancient texts. We use textual criticism, or the careful comparison of ancient texts, when several surviving manuscripts preserve different readings among themselves. Whether considering manuscripts of the Bible or other manuscripts from the ancient Mediterranean world, the fundamental principle

1. "History, 1838–1856, Volume E-1 [1 July 1843–30 April 1844]," 1755, Joseph Smith Papers, accessed July 27, 2022, https://www.josephsmithpapers.org/paper-summary/history-1838-1856-volume-e-1-1-july-1843-30-april-1844/127.

of the textual critic is to give greater credence to the older manuscripts of any particular text.

Through the textual criticism of variant manuscripts, a standardization of many ancient texts, especially those of Greek or Roman origin, occurred in the late nineteenth and early twentieth centuries. Such Greek and Latin texts enjoy wide acceptance among classicists and comprise a relatively stable and unchanging body of literature taught in secondary schools and universities. Most surviving Greek and Latin classics were composed before the time of the New Testament. When the manuscripts of the Greek and Latin classics are compared with surviving New Testament manuscripts, we see quickly that there are controversies about certain sections of the New Testament because of the differences among them. Many present ambiguous passages do not accord with our understanding of gospel principles, thus affirming the statements of the Prophet Joseph Smith that pertain to the New Testament text.

The Manuscripts of the Greek and Latin Classics

Before the invention of printing, the propagation of literary works was a laborious process. Scribes copied a text by hand onto either papyrus scrolls or page-like pieces of parchment and then usually sewed them together to form a codex—the forerunner of the modern book. In comparison to modern printing, the fact that scribes produced very few written volumes through this process explains in part the scarcity of surviving texts. Moreover, the observation that hand copying was subject to easy error explains the wide variation demonstrated when a number of manuscripts survive. When such manuscripts date from a time much later than the original date of composition, human errors occur more frequently, and there are even wider variations among manuscripts.

With the calamitous fall of the Roman Empire, many manuscripts of classical compositions were destroyed. Moreover, during preceding decades in certain areas of the empire, postapostasy Christians sometimes sought to destroy works written by non-Christians, including many written by the great thinkers of Greco-Roman antiquity. Perhaps for these reasons, manuscripts of classical works are of late date. Few date back to antiquity; most copies derive from the late medieval era or the Renaissance, either possessed by Christian monasteries or preserved in the Arabic world, where the study of Greek and Latin classics was encouraged.[2] For example, the

2. M. van Esbroeck, "Arabic Language and Literature," in *Encyclopedia of the Early Church*, ed. Angelo Di Berardino, trans. Adrian Walford (New York: Oxford University Press, 1992), 1:65–66.

oldest manuscripts of the fifth-century BC Athenian tragedians, Aeschylus and Euripides, go back to the eleventh century, more than fifteen hundred years after the original composition of the works! The histories of their Athenian contemporaries, Thucydides and Xenophon, are preserved by only a few manuscripts; the earliest manuscript of the former's work dates to the tenth century AD, while the earliest codices of the latter are from the fourteenth century. The Boeotian poet Hesiod, who wrote the *Theogony* around 700 BC, did not have a near-complete text until the end of the thirteenth century. Thus the *Theogony*'s text is formulated from copies made almost two thousand years after the original composition![3]

The works and authors cited constitute only a sampling of Greek authors and texts, though they are representative of situations repeated in the case of almost every Greek author and surviving work. Even Homer, the earliest and perhaps most important Greek writer, fared no better. His widespread popularity and the use of his work as a basic school text required many copies of Homer's *Iliad* and *Odyssey.* Accordingly, the chances for surviving manuscript copies should have increased. Nevertheless, despite a few fragments that date from the first century AD, the first near-complete texts of Homer are twelfth- and thirteenth-century manuscripts. As a result, Homeric texts are based on copies that are twenty-one hundred years removed from the author!

Roman authors were almost as poorly preserved as their Greek predecessors. However, since Latin remained the language of much of Europe during the Middle Ages, it could be expected that Latin works would be better preserved and have texts based on manuscripts of earlier provenance. Indeed, most Roman manuscripts are only a thousand years removed from their time of composition. The earliest manuscripts of Caesar, Cicero, Catullus, Horace, Ovid, and Seneca all date from the ninth century AD. Two very popular Roman authors, even among Christian audiences, were Vergil and Livy. Their works were preserved in copies made only a few centuries later. A manuscript preserving large parts of Livy's work dates to the fifth century AD, and two manuscripts of Vergil's date to the fourth century AD, barely three hundred years after the composition of Vergil's poetry. Compared to the dates of other classical works, the manuscripts of Vergil and Livy are amazingly early.

3. M. L. West, "The Medieval and Renaissance Manuscripts of Hesiod's *Theogony*," *The Classical Quarterly* 14, no. 2 (November 1964): 165–89, https://doi.org/10.1017/S0009838800023739.

The texts of classical authors as established through the manuscript tradition are generally accepted as accurate. For most works, a sufficient number of manuscripts survive to allow comparison to the accepted version of a text. Occasionally, the text of a work may derive from only a single manuscript. For example, extant portions of the first six books of the eminent Roman historian Tacitus's *Annales* are preserved in a single ninth-century manuscript. The incomplete text by first-century historian Velleius Paterculus, who chronicled the reign of the emperor Tiberius, was copied in the seventeenth century from a manuscript that was subsequently lost and no longer exists. Despite the scant documentation for these texts, and with little debate or discussion, they are nevertheless accepted at face value and widely used as authoritative historical sources for the period.

The Manuscripts of the New Testament

There are three kinds of New Testament documents: papyrus fragments or manuscripts; parchment manuscripts written in Greek capital letters called "uncials," the standard transcription format of ancient times; and later manuscripts transcribed in the smaller hand and lowercase characters customarily used in late antique or medieval Greek manuscripts, named "minuscules."[4] Of these three types of New Testament Greek documents, there survive in whole or in part well over five thousand New Testament manuscripts, and these do not include manuscripts written in other languages such as Armenian, Latin, Coptic, Ethiopian, and more. By comparison to Homer, a classical author for whom a large number of manuscript copies or papyrus fragments survive, the New Testament documents are far more numerous than Homer's 1,569 pieces of papyri and 188 uncial manuscripts that survive to attest his work.[5] So numerous are New Testament manuscripts that one scholar exclaimed, "The textual critic of the New Testament is embarrassed by the wealth of material."[6]

---

4. Bruce M. Metzger and Bart D. Ehrman, *The Text of the New Testament: Its Transmission, Corruption, and Restoration,* 4th ed. (New York: Oxford University Press, 2005), 16–31.

5. Clay Jones, "The Bibliographical Test Updated," Christian Research Institute, updated April 12, 2023, https://www.equip.org/articles/the-bibliographical-test-updated/; Eldon Jay Epp, "Textual Criticism: New Testament," in *The Anchor Bible Dictionary,* ed. David Noel Freedman, 6 vols. (New York: Doubleday, 1992), 6:420–23; Bart D. Ehrman, *The Textual Reliability of the New Testament: Bart D. Ehrman and Daniel B. Wallace in Dialogue,* ed. Robert B. Stewart (Minneapolis: Fortress, 2011), 19; Josh McDowell, *The New Evidence That Demands a Verdict* (Nashville: Thomas Nelson, 1999), 38.

6. Metzger and Ehrman, *Text of the New Testament,* 47–51.

In current scholarly study of the New Testament text, considered most authoritative are several lengthy papyrus documents of surprisingly early date that preserve large tracts of both Gospels and Epistles. These papyri were acquired during the 1930s in the British collection of Chester Beatty and during the 1950s in the Swiss collection of Martin Bodmer. The Chester Beatty papyri include three very old copies of parts from the New Testament. A papyrus ($\mathfrak{P}^{45}$) codex (in book form), preserving thirty leaves of the Gospels and the book of Acts (size 10 inches by 8 inches), dates to around AD 200–250, less than a century and a half to two centuries after the original writing of these books. Of even earlier date is a papyrus ($\mathfrak{P}^{46}$) of eighty-six extant leaves (size 11 inches by 6½ inches) that preserves ten Pauline letters. Also of similar date is a papyrus ($\mathfrak{P}^{47}$) containing ten leaves from the book of Revelation. Most phenomenal, however, is a small papyrus fragment of the Gospel of John ($\mathfrak{P}^{52}$) that has been dated to approximately AD 100 and, depending on the dating of John's actual writing of the Gospel, is possibly only a scant few decades removed from the composition of John's original text.[7]

The Bodmer papyri are also of pristine date. A more complete copy of the Gospel of John, the Bodmer Papyrus II ($\mathfrak{P}^{66}$), is preserved in this papyrus codex of 104 pages (size 6 inches by 5½ inches) that dates from AD 200. Similarly, a single-quire codex of the Gospel of Luke and the Gospel of John ($\mathfrak{P}^{75}$) was transcribed perhaps as early as AD 175. That copies of portions of the New Testament survive from a period so near the time of their original composition becomes all the more remarkable considering the long centuries between the composition of classical texts and their earliest surviving manuscripts.[8] Metzger observed that "the time between the composition of the books of the New Testament and the earliest extant copies is relatively brief. Instead of a lapse of a millennium or more, as is the case of not a few classical authors, several New Testament papyri exist that were copied within a century or so after the composition of the original documents."[9]

With confirmation of ancient papyri that are so little removed from the time of the author's writing, why do we not place greater credence in the text of the New Testament as it exists? Indeed, classicists have considerable confidence in the texts of the classics even when they are constructed from manuscripts

7. Metzger and Ehrman, *Text of the New Testament,* 54–56.
8. Metzger and Ehrman, *Text of the New Testament,* 52–59.
9. Metzger and Ehrman, *Text of the New Testament,* 51.

that are one and, in some cases, two millennia removed from the composition of the original texts. With regard to the present New Testament text, we can, in fact, trust that many portions of the text are transmitted, transcribed, and translated correctly. However, we must also remain cognizant of problematic passages and remember that the papyri enumerated above have come to the attention of the textual critic only recently. The complete versions of the New Testament in use by disparate Christian sects and in various languages derive not from pristine papyri but from parchment manuscripts of later date, some fraught with textual problems.

The most important manuscripts of the New Testament date to the fourth and fifth centuries AD. Fourth-century uncial manuscripts may belong to the fifty New Testament copies commissioned by the emperor Constantine in AD 331. The most important of these manuscripts, the Codex Sinaiticus (א), was discovered in 1844 in the Sinai monastery of St. Catherine and later presented to Czar Alexander II of Russia, who was instrumental in securing its release from the orthodox monastery. After the Russian revolution, the communists sold the text to the British Museum, where it resides at present. It is the only complete manuscript copy of the entire New Testament that dates from the fourth or fifth century.

Although not as complete as the Codex Sinaiticus, the Codex Vaticanus (B) is just as old. In all likelihood, it was also one of the Constantinian manuscripts, though because of certain deficiencies it may have not been accepted among the fifty manuscripts.[10] It has been housed in the Vatican library since before the first catalogue of its holdings was made in the fourteenth century and may have been in the possession of the church at Rome since the manuscript's production in the fourth century. Indeed, when St. Jerome translated scriptures into the Latin Vulgate late in the fourth century, it is possible he consulted the Codex Vaticanus (B) among others.

Other important uncial manuscripts are the Codex Alexandrinus (A) and the Codex Ephraemi (C), both of fifth-century provenance. The Codex Bezae (D^{ea}) is another fifth-century manuscript that offers not only the text of the original Greek New Testament but also a Latin translation. The bilingual text is arranged so that Greek and Latin face one another on opposite pages. The manuscript was given to Cambridge University in 1581 by its namesake, Theodore Beza, successor to John Calvin as the Protestant leader in Geneva.

---

10. Metzger and Ehrman, *Text of the New Testament,* 15–16, 62–86.

While several fifth-century "Old Latin" or Syriac translations of the Greek New Testament exist, all other original Greek manuscripts of the New Testament are of later date. It is difficult to say which, if any, of these hundreds of later texts, with their unknown corruptions or deficiencies, may have influenced late-Renaissance scholars translating the New Testament into the vernaculars of their respective nations or churches. Certainly, Jerome's Latin Vulgate, widely used and familiar to most scholars of that time, would have influenced many of these translations, including the King James Version.[11] In the King James Version, it is likely that Greek New Testament codices known to have been in England at the time would certainly have been consulted. These include the previously noted Codex Bezae of fifth-century provenance as well as the sixth-century Codex Laudianus (E^a) in the possession of Oxford University. The consultation of these earlier Greek manuscripts may lend greater credence to the King James text, but even a cursory reading and comparison of the Greek and Latin versions of the New Testament unsurprisingly demonstrates the heavy reliance of King James translators on the Latin Vulgate.

The very real antiquity of many New Testament manuscripts in the original Greek provides clear evidence that much of the New Testament text may be quite sound. Similarly, textual departures from early texts, as manifest in later texts, corroborate the Prophet Joseph's admonition about textual mistakes occasioned by either careless transcribers or by priestly scribes, who sought to emend texts they were copying to accord with doctrinal principles of the churches during their time and place—doctrines that had departed, in some instances, far from the New Testament authors' original intent and teachings.

11. Metzger and Ehrman, *Text of the New Testament,* 94–126.

The Open Canon and the Modern Reader

Tom R. Roberts

The sense of the terms "canon" and "canonical" can be readily understood. They derive from the Greek word *kanōn* (κανών), which comes from the Semitic term *kanē,* and bear the sense of a reed or corn stalk that has been notched for the purpose of measuring an item's length. It was a simple step to make *kanōn* metaphorical and apply it to the notion of a standard or norm, whether in art, music, literature, or even human behavior. By the New Testament era, the standards for measuring scriptural texts were very diverse and all centered on the Old Testament, as is evident from the coexistence of the Samaritan Pentateuch, the proto-Masoretic Hebrew Bible, the Dead Sea Scrolls, and the Septuagint. As time went on, certain Christians saw value in gathering the letters of Paul into a corpus that would offer guidance both for church organization and for personal belief and morality. To these letters were added, over time, the Gospels, the book of Acts, and other distinctively Christian texts.

In the debates of the second century, diverse groups, especially the Gnostics, put forward differing views of what should go into the Christian canon. Church councils made decisions about the written works of heretical groups and chose to discard documents they considered noncanonical once the canon in the West was closed. This controversy about the Apocryphal documents lasted until the Council of Trent in 1566. Some of these works survived into modern times.[1] We now turn to the main issues that affect an open canon—a canon that can be expanded by new revelation.

1. See the essay "The Rise of Canonical and Apocryphal Literature" by S. Kent Brown and David J. Larsen in this volume.

Closed versus Open Canon

Whether a canon is still open or closed has caused a great deal of controversy over many centuries. But what is a canon? It has been defined as a measuring rod whereby teachings accepted by a faith community are compared to previously revealed information to determine whether the same authoritative value can be placed upon a new body of revelation.[2] As we have seen, the Christian connotation of the term "canon" denotes "reed" (Greek *kanōn*) and points to a measuring rod, to standards, or to a general list or catalogue. Athanasius, bishop of Alexandria (died May 2, 373), first used the term to designate scripture. The practice of canonization stems from the Old Testament lists that were in flux until the apparent stabilization at the Council of Jamnia (c. AD 90).[3]

In Hebrew custom, defiled hands were forbidden to touch the Torah (*kaneh*), without a ceremonial washing. Therefore, Gentiles were considered unworthy of such a task. Despite such tradition, the pre-Christian *Letter of Aristeas* offers a somewhat fanciful account of the Old Testament translation from Hebrew into Greek being created because a need had arisen among Greek-speaking Jews in Egypt for a Greek copy of the scriptures. Thereafter, the Greek translation of the Old Testament obtained a status for community worship and public reading.[4] Translating the Hebrew scriptures into Greek opened the door to understanding concepts like salvation, sacrifice, and divine deliverance in very different ways. The Hebrew words to form these concepts did not have a direct translation into Greek, so Jews had to find new ways to explain their views. This began the Greek influence on Semitic beliefs. Roger Beckwith captures this conundrum very succinctly: "If, however, Hellenistic Judaism was influenced by Semitic Palestine, the converse is also true: that Palestinian Judaism was

---

2. Harry V. Gamble, "Canon: New Testament," in *The Anchor Bible Dictionary,* ed. David Noel Freedman, 6 vols. (New York: Doubleday, 1992), 1:852–61.

3. For the importance of the Jewish gathering at Jamnia, see Lee Martin McDonald, *The Formation of the Christian Biblical Canon* (Nashville: Abingdon Press, 1988), 60–66; and Jack P. Lewis, "Jamnia Revisited," in *The Canon Debate,* ed. Lee Martin McDonald and James A. Sanders (Peabody, Mass.: Hendrickson Publishers, 2002), 146–62.

4. James Hastings, ed., *Dictionary of the Bible,* rev. ed. by Frederick C. Grant and Harold Henry Rowley (New York: Charles Scribner's Sons, 1963), s.v. "canon of the Old Testament," 121–23; R. Glenn Wooden, "The Role of 'the Septuagint' in the Formation of the Biblical Canons," in *Exploring the Origins of the Bible: Canon Formation in Historical, Literary, and Theological Perspective,* ed. Craig A. Evans and Emmanuel Tov (Grand Rapids, Mich.: Baker Publishing Group, 2008), 129–46.

influenced by the Hellenistic world, and much more deeply than used to be supposed."[5]

During this time of translation into Greek, students of the canon argued that when a point of corruption entered the canonical process, the original purpose of the text was altered. For example, when someone in authority made a change that did not mirror the intent of the scripture, future readers of that scripture would understand it differently. Others will suggest that there was a canonical cycle after the moment of corruption that resulted in a fall into apostasy, thus moving the canonizing process into a reconstruction-and-rebirth cycle where canonical teachings were reintroduced in the light of new revelation. For example,

> the People of Judah and Israel, thus restored to their territory and to the worship of their God, ruled by a Davidic monarch rather than by foreigners, their land renewed and their cities rebuilt, are now ready for the renewal of the covenant. The covenant is "not like the covenant I made with their forefathers, when I took them by the hand to lead them out of Egypt" (Jer. 31:31). Here, for the first time, the idea of covenant in oracles of restoration is linked with reenlandisement and the reunification of Israel. The radical newness of the covenant is emphasized by its contrast with the Sinaitic covenant: whereas the former covenant was written on tablets of stone, the new covenant would reside in the hearts of the participants in a "redeemed society"; it would be "formulated on the basis of individuals who responded to the free expression of divine love."[6]

Traditional interpreters maintain that Israel's canon was produced by historical readings and the gathering of books in the Great Synagogue, where the canon was closed and took its final form consisting of three divisions: Law, Prophets, and Writings.[7] These modern form critics feel there was a final editing that resulted in the finished canonical shaping of the text in the days of Ezra, who served as chief editor over the redacting process. Other critics generally do not believe the canon was ever closed, due to the shaping of the scriptures from varied sources, such as the Septuagint, the Dead Sea Scrolls, and the Samaritan Pentateuch, all of which were not edited in

---

5. Roger Beckwith, *The Old Testament Canon of the New Testament Church and Its Background in Early Judaism* (Grand Rapids, Mich.: William B. Eerdmans, 1985), 31.

6. Stephen D. Ricks, "The Prophetic Literality of Tribal Reconstruction," in *Israel's Apostasy and Restoration; Essays in Honor of Roland K. Harrison,* ed. Avraham Gileadi (Grand Rapids, Mich.: Baker Book House, 1988), 278–79.

7. Frederick Fyvie Bruce, *The Canon of Scripture* (Downers Grove, Ill.: Intervarsity Press, 1988), 17–32.

the Great Synagogue. In addition, the same critics do not accept that the Great Synagogue closed the canonical process, because if it did, their process would not have been obscured. One critic explains,

> It is clear from the sketch of the process that particular editors, religious groups, and even political parties were involved. At times one can describe these groups historically or sociologically, such as the reforming Deuteronomic party of Jerusalem, or the editors associated with Hezekiah's court (Prov 25.1). But basic to the canonical process is that those responsible for the actual editing of the text did their best to obscure their own identity. Thus the actual process by which the text was reworked lies in almost total obscurity.[8]

In this light, today's canon can be considered to be an ongoing process (if one holds to an open canonical stance), which extends into the writings of modern churches and local synods. Our contemporary challenge is to evaluate the canonical issues of the past and revisit those issues with modern textual discoveries in mind to see whether the assumptions of open and closed canonical systems can be applied to today's study of text, canon, and tradition. Modern canonical critics advance the implications of a self-authenticating canon based on the mutual reinforcement of continuing and reoccurring narratives and literary structures that are contained within the internal evidence of the text. They even claim the literary structural subunits lead to larger units on a superstructural level, which results in larger parallelisms and poetic patterns. Therefore, the internal structure of the text can point to authenticity by the establishment of the literary prose or style of the writer or editor. In the case of the Bible, this same principle can be broadened beyond a particular book and applied to a group of books or a corpus.

Open canon critics do not usually explore the diversity in the canon but try to create harmonious explanations despite tensions and differences contained within the texts themselves. This diversity, in their view, is not one of tension between the origins and associated concerns about any particular biblical document, but they believe diverse opinions arise from the differences of emphasis as one moves from one book of scripture to another. For example, the synoptic tradition within the corpus of the New Testament has a view of Christ's life and ministry that is roughly shared by the synoptic writers. The proposed "Q" (from *Quelle,* "source") hypothesis may be the source of those traditions.

---

8. Brevard S. Childs, *Introduction to the Old Testament as Scripture* (Philadelphia: Fortress Press, 1979), 78.

Resting on a different calendrical scheme for the Passover that became accepted in the canonizing process, the Gospel of John thematically reinterprets Jesus as the Passover Lamb and reorganizes the data to center around Jesus' identity as the great "I Am."[9] John is using Jesus as the communities' personal Passover to show his identity. According to Clement of Alexandria (c. AD 200), John was a mystic heavily trained in the allegorical method of interpreting the text. Eusebius[10] reiterates the same connotation.

In a similar vein, rabbis and mystical teachers taught different aspects of their message in public than they did in private tutorials—an attempt to lead disciples to a different, deeper grasp of the sacred matters that we find in John's Gospel. Jesus himself did this too. For example, Matthew 13:10–23 included the mystical teachings of Jesus directed to the disciples. As Jesus said in verse 16, "But blessed are your eyes, for they see: and your ears, for they hear." This blessing Jesus issued as a rabbi was to demonstrate that his disciples understood his parabolic teaching. This act framed how Jesus' followers would understand and pass on his words. As Michael Kruger said in more formal language, "The canon is not something to be judged as much as it is the thing that does the judging. When this attribute of the canon is appreciated, once again, we can see how the canon is not so much shaped by the community of faith, but a means of shaping the community of faith."[11]

A question here is, Where does the authority lie in the canonical process?[12] That is to say, who chose the works that would become scripture, such as the Gospels? The lofty view of inerrant inspiration assumes that the authority figure has clear, direct communication with God. The human participant or author is little more than a mechanical scribe for God's words. This heavenly dictation would naturally carry with it the authority of God's words. However, if God's Spirit moved through the community and inspired members to require that books be read publicly by the Old Testament priesthood

---

9. Colleen M. Conway, "John, Gospel of," in *The New Interpreter's Dictionary of the Bible*, 5 vols., ed. Katherine Doob Sakenfield (Nashville: Abingdon Press, 2008), 3:357–58, for a discussion of "Jesus as incarnate logos [word]."

10. John R. Dummelow, ed., *A Commentary on the Holy Bible by Various Writers* (New York: Macmillan, 1933), 770.

11. Michael J. Kruger, *Canon Revisited: Establishing the Origins and Authority of the New Testament Books* (Wheaton, Ill.: Crossway, 2012), 131.

12. The authority in the canonical process frequently began with the author or editor said to be the creator of the sacred text, whether Jewish, Hellenistic, or Christian. This circumstance would apply equally to works attributed to David, Aristotle, or Paul. See Jed Wyrick, *The Ascension of Authorship: Attribution and Canon Formation in Jewish, Hellenistic, and Christian Traditions* (Cambridge, Mass.: Harvard University Department of Comparative Literature, 2004), 1–19, 382–97.

because of the books' authority and instructional value, the community influenced the canonical shape, which influenced the growth of the revelation. We see this in the reading of sacred texts under Ezra's direction and the following rehearsal of God's sacred acts undertaken in the distant past (Neh. 8:13–9:38). Hence, Israel both shaped the canon and was shaped by the canonical process—an adjustment to Kruger's viewpoint above.

The Eastern Orthodox Church has never accepted inspiration through heavenly dictation. Eastern churches maintain that the Holy Spirit inspired the writers, who were full of human shortcomings and limitations of understanding based on their personal and intellectual backgrounds. Therefore, in their view, "the Bible is the inspired word of God in terms of content rather than style, grammar, history, or frame."[13]

After the Writings and the Prophets, or *Haf Tarah,* were added as scripture, the term "law," or *Torah,* did not mean the first five books of the decalogue only but grew to encompass the entire codification of God's revelation in rabbinic Judaism.[14] So anything that was accepted as scripture could present lawful instruction and ethics to guide one's conduct. By the time of the early Church, the Law and the Prophets were regarded as scripture in the general sense of the term, as shown in Luke 24:44.

One constant motif in Old Testament literature was that God was both Savior and Judge as well as judgmental and prophetic. Israel in exile needed hope and *l'chayim,* "life" (see Gen. 45:5; Ezra 9:8–9). By this time, with occasional exceptions, the resurrection had burned itself forever into the collective memory of Judaism. Torah was for sustaining life and, in the final analysis, was the authority that gave meaning to the canon.[15] In the Hebrew frame of reference, life demonstrated reality not only for God in the heavens but in the cycle of life in worship and in everyday experiences. Even nature was part of God's reality, not just his dominion. Expectations of a Deliverer would usher in a golden age of messianic reign (Isa. 65:17–25) in which Jerusalem would be recreated and would not be inhabited by another power, such as the Assyrians. Isaiah's eschatological utterance was to give

---

13. Bruce M. Metzger and Michael D. Coogan, eds., *The Oxford Companion to the Bible* (New York: Oxford University Press 1993), 174.

14. For the development of the three-part Old Testament as reflected in Luke 24:44, see Julio C. Trebolle Barrera, "Origins of a Tripartite Old Testament Canon," in McDonald and Sanders, *Canon Debate,* 128–45.

15. James A. Sanders, *From Sacred Story to Sacred Text: Canon as Paradigm* (Philadelphia, Penn.: Fortress Press 1987), 30.

Israel hope no matter her condition and applied to the resurrection of all humankind.[16]

Christianity also effectively created a canon within the canon by selectively quoting the Old Testament verses that their leaders and theologians thought supported their version of how the last days would play out. Similar to Israel's authoritative view for how they read the Torah, Christians also found evidence for the perspective they wanted. James Barr stated, "Protestant orthodoxy in particular read into these evidences its own ideals and convictions of a religion strictly controlled by scripture and subservient to it, and never considered the possibility that the texts might, or even must, be read in another way."[17]

Barr's point here is well-taken. Christian expositors will often recast the *zitz im leben,* the real-life situation, from Israel's surroundings into a Christian fulfillment or expectation. Statements such as "Jesus is in every book of the Bible" and "Every promise made to David belongs to you" violate canonical hermeneutics in the worst possible way. Could it be that the promises to David were for him alone, and from them, we might learn what Yahweh can do to save his people in a general sense through lessons of faith? And, yes, the Old Testament pointed to the coming of the Divine Warrior, who was to be the suzerain of all nations (Isa. 18–20; 30:1–17; 31:1–3), in the house of either David (Isa. 9:7) or Joseph. And Jesus did become the new Moses and give new aspects of the Law from the mountain. But this dips into rhetorical criticism, where the interpreter identifies and understands a scriptural person's ministry by new data that is belatedly attributed to the revelation of the original writer.

The same situation happened with Isaiah 7:3, where Isaiah's son was seen as a coming ruler (Isa. 9:5b, which is a *hapax legomenon*) who would fight beside the people like an "Immanuel" (Isa. 7:14). Luke 1:31–35 effectively reinterprets this phrase from "the God who fights beside you in battle" to the sense of "God with us" in the form of God's Son. As a local application, the son of Isaiah was to be the Wonderful Counselor (Great Teacher) in ancient times (Isa. 9:6). He was to bring wisdom and justice to that generation (Isa. 9:7; 11:1–5). However, the names attributed to the

---

16. Sanford Ross Howard, לחיים *L'Chayim to Life: Finding the Light of Shalom—What the Rabbis Never Told You!* (Thorsby, Ala.: SAN Enterprises/Sabbath House, 1995), 176–77.

17. James Barr, *Holy Scripture: Canon, Authority, Criticism* (Oxford: Clarendon Press, 1983), 11.

coming Messiah are throne names to describe rule and authority, which appear in Isaiah 9:6. The expected parallel sense in Isaiah 9:7 opens with a spelling anomaly that puzzled the rabbis and introduced confusion about who was to rule and when. A modern person can turn to the Septuagint for a clear sense of the opening phrase of verse 7: "For the increase."[18] But the ancient Jewish sages had no such option until the Septuagint was fully developed sometime between the third and first century BC.[19] They had to struggle with the Hebrew text about whether the person who would bring an increase of God's government and peace had already come or was yet to appear, bearing ultimate rule and authority. Therefore, the prophecies that originally applied to the sons of Isaiah, the two kings, have within them a broader implication of what the Messiah would do when he would establish his throne in the future as the Davidic King and choose righteousness.[20] He would assume his authority and apply these throne names in a larger context and wider definition as the ruling Messiah. Thus the canonical process does maintain a development of God's kingdom in the Messiah's ministry until the ultimate result: the resurrection of humankind.

As accurate as Old Testament scribes attempted to be, there are some ancient texts that contain slightly different readings, such as those found in the Isaiah Scrolls of the Dead Sea Scrolls. These adjust the messianically significant passages of Isaiah 53 in the later Masoretic Text. The central point of these ancient texts remains clear—namely, that the Messiah would be a true wisdom teacher and usher in divine rule. In Isaiah's words, "of the increase of his government there shall be no end" (Isa. 9:7).

With various readings of the text, and additional prophets still yet to write, the Jewish canon continued to evolve. One scholar wrote,

> There seems to be little doubt that by ca. 200 BCE most of the Jewish people had recognized in some sense a collection of writings called the "Prophets" (*Nevi'im*), the bulk of which existed earlier than 400 BCE. We are probably correct in assuming that some parts of the prophetic literature, as well as the Law, were an exilic canon for the Jews in Babylon. This "prophetic" collection of writings included what was called the "Former Prophets" (Joshua, Judges, the Samuels, and the Kings), and four "Latter prophets" (Isaiah, Jeremiah, Ezekiel, and some of the books of the Twelve or the "Minor"

18. Andrew H. Bartelt, *The Book around Immanuel: Style and Structure in Isaiah 2–12*, vol. 4 of Biblical and Judaic Studies (Winona Lake, Ind.: Eisenbrauns, 1996), 122.

19. Melvin K. H. Peters, "Septuagint," in Freedman, *Anchor Bible Dictionary*, 5:1096–97.

20. Lancelot C. L. Brenton, *The Septuagint with Apocrypha: Greek and English* (Peabody, Mass.: Zondervan, 1980), 842.

> Prophets). Some of the latest of the Twelve prophets (Haggai, Zechariah, and Malachi) had not yet been written during the ministries of Ezra and Nehemiah. Pfeiffer claims that all of these books were adopted into Israel's canon not only because of growing public interest in them but also because of their recognized value "for enhancing the national pride and the hopes for a better future."[21]

Both the major and minor prophets, so termed by Christian canonization, characterized Israel's national literature and theology, and they also guided Israel's history and destiny. The canonical literature does not present history in the modern sense of the term. This very early literature framed a theologized reinterpretation of Israel's development and theology in her temple and synagogue. The Christian church often assumed that many New Testament concepts were totally foreign to Hebrew thought and practice because of the doctrine of supersessionism, wherein the church became the new covenant Israel. In truth, the old Israel had hopes of becoming the new Israel, with pilgrimages from many nations coming back to the land to prepare for the reign of the Messiah (see Isa. 2:2–4). In a similar fashion, the Qumran community viewed itself as the new Israel.[22] In the view of all these ancient groups, a filling of the spirit such as the prophets possessed would encompass the people of God's land (Joel 2:18, 28–32).

Church Fathers

In another vein, our modern perspective often dictates that we interpret the church fathers through the lens of textual integrity. This viewpoint creates the illusion that we may use them to verify certain textual readings from the four major textual groups of the Greek New Testament that grew out of the four translation centers in the Roman and Byzantine Empires: Rome, Antioch, Byzantium, and Alexandria. The practice was misapplied because the church fathers often took license from the original text reading and applied their own spiritual and theological model to show on which side of any number of doctrinal debates they stood. It is true that all but a few New Testament verses are cited by the desert fathers and other patristic sources. However, the allusions to the text are from memory or arose

21. Lee M. McDonald, *The Formation of the Christian Biblical Canon,* rev. and exp. ed. (Peabody, Mass.: Hendrickson Publishers, 1995), 32.

22. Florentino García Martínez, *The Dead Sea Scrolls Translated: The Qumran Texts in English,* 2nd ed., trans. Wilfred G. E. Watson (Leiden, Neth.: E. J. Brill, 1996), 3–19.

from oral traditions that do not correspond to known textual readings or to the modern use of the historical method. For example,

> first, the supposed "text of a Father" is based upon a gratuitous assumption: namely, that a Father in any single locale or at any particular time used one and only one manuscript. In fact, a Father may have switched manuscripts daily in some cases. This possibility alone precludes any suggestions that "the" [Greek New Testament] text used by a Father can indeed be reconstructed with confidence. Certainly, while a Father was in a single location, most manuscripts available to him in that region would reflect the local text of the area; but what if now and then another manuscript from a different region came his way? It becomes no surprise to find that some Fathers possess a text that is "mixed" in a significant degree. The fact is, we can only determine which *readings* a Father may have quoted at certain times in his works; the actual text of the manuscript(s) he may have used remains an open question.[23]

Melito of Sardis (died c. AD 190) came to the East to learn of the wisdom established by the desert fathers. In his letter to Onesimus, he expressed his desire to complete this task. In the letter's canonical list, Melito included most of the Apocryphal books, just as Athanasius did almost two centuries later, which were Judith, Tobit, Wisdom of Solomon, and a four-Gospel narrative. Since it was not typical of early Christians, it is amazing to think that Melito, the father of Western Logos Christology, upheld the Apocryphal literature in his writings. Two centuries later, in Athanasius's thirty-ninth festal letter, a key document from AD 367, he included Esther and four Apocryphal works—the Wisdom of Solomon, Sirach, Judith, and Tobit—that would find their way into the Old Testament Masoretic canon.[24]

The eastern fathers previously mentioned espoused a smaller Old Testament canon than the western fathers because the classifications of these

---

23. Maurice A. Robinson and William G. Pierpont, *The New Testament in the Original Greek according to the Byzantine/Majority Textform* (Atlanta: The Original Word Publishers, 1991), xxxiii, emphasis in original.

24. A cogent review of the theological, political, and ecclesiastical forces that influenced Athanasius's choice of books to fit into his canon is that of David Brakke, "Canon Formation and Social Conflict in Fourth-Century Egypt: Athanasius of Alexandria's Thirty-Ninth *Festal Letter*," *Harvard Theological Review* 87, no. 4 (October 1994): 395–419. For a general overview, consult Edmon L. Gallagher and John D. Meade, *The Biblical Canon Lists from Early Christianity: Texts and Analysis* (Oxford: Oxford University Press, 2017), 118–29; and Bruce M. Metzger, *The Canon of the New Testament: Its Origin, Development, and Significance* (New York: Oxford University Press, 1987), 130–35.

books were arranged in different canonical categories. For example, Origen's homily on the book of Numbers stated that Leviticus should be thrown out. He later utilized Psalm 25:1–2 with Jeremiah and 1 and 2 Maccabees in his homilies. Hilary followed Origen but added Tobit and Judith to his canonical listing. Cyprian with Ambrose included Jeremiah and Lamentations and reported them to be composed by the same author. Cyril, with his twenty-two-book Old Testament canon, accepted Baruch and the Epistle of Jeremiah.

By approximately AD 370, Gregory of Nazianzus divided Judges and Ruth so his canon could have twenty-two books and stated that Ezekiel and Song of Songs were to be for the mature reader who was no longer a novice or a catechumen in the faith. Catechumens were to learn the Psalms as beginning apprentices. Gregory's writings consisted of Hebrew texts and Aramaic Targums. Jerome (c. 342–420), in his great Latin Vulgate translation, declared the book of Psalms to be an incomplete corpus of literature and stated that the Hagiographa, the sacred writings, omitted Sirach but included Judith, Tobit, and the *Shepherd of Hermas.*

Later, Augustine (354–430) added Wisdom, Sirach, Esther, and Tobit to the list of books that he accepted as canonical. The Ethiopian Orthodox Church has a canonical arrangement of eighty-one to eighty-eight books, which includes extra books that are found in deuterocanonical lists depending on what is accepted by the local jurisdiction. We come upon the books of Josippon, *Enoch* from the Ethiopic text, *Jubilees,* Tobit, Judith, the additional psalm from the Septuagint, Baruch, Susanna, and others. The Proverbs are listed as two separate books: Messalë (Prov. 1–24) and Tägsas (Prov. 25–31).

In Eastern Orthodox tradition, the *Odes of Solomon* are recognized as canonical. This document was discovered in 1909 and points to the feminine nature of the Holy Spirit, who prepared the Son of God for his divine mission. Ode 36.1–3 states, "I rested on the Spirit of the Lord: and She raised me on high: and made me stand on my feet in the height of the Lord, before His perfection and His glory, while I was praising [Him] by the composition of His songs. She brought me forth before the face of the Lord: and although a son of man, I was named the illuminated one, the son of God."[25] In Roman Catholicism, by contrast, the *Prayer of Manasseh* is an

25. Stanley M. Burgess, *The Holy Spirit: Eastern Christian Traditions* (Peabody, Mass.: Hendrickson Publishers, 1989), 172–73.

appendix, but it is listed in the Eastern Orthodox Study Bible as an honored text. This document and others demonstrate the openness and the fluidity regarding the development of any orthodox canon.

It has long been observed that the early church fathers quoted all but a handful of verses contained in our New Testament. Until recent times, scholars of the Apocrypha did not explore the church fathers or the pseudepigrapha. With the advent of James Charlesworth's groundbreaking two-volume set of the pseudepigrapha,[26] scholars and laymen have access to this third category of ancient Near Eastern literature now paired with the Old and New Testaments. With the pseudepigrapha in hand, we can now better identify the literary trajectories that flowed from one group of canonical writings to another to form a literary train. Perhaps surprisingly, this train extends from Israel and its neighbors into the wisdom traditions of Solon in Greece, where Solon's proverbs were shared with Judah, and to the interaction of Psalms with the Canaanite collection of the same type, one example of which is Psalms 118 through 122.

The wisdom writings composed during the Axial Period, approximately the sixth century BC, were derived from one Mediterranean culture and were localized in smaller nation states, who promoted their own reactions to these international wisdom sayings. According to the *Letter of Aristeas,* by 280 BC the Septuagint translators in Egypt considered Israel's primary canon and Apocryphal writings to be the Holy Writings, or the Hagiographa. The Apocryphal books and versions of the Septuagint were often read thereafter in the Jewish diaspora because of the hidden wisdom they contained in interpreting Daniel and the other wisdom books that came into existence after the days of Ezra. The early church interpreted the wisdom of Daniel's prophecies within the time frame and structures set forth in the books of 2 Esdras, which the church understood to take place in their day. Modern scholarship now suggests there may be echoes from noncanonical writings in the words of Jesus. For example, Matthew 25:31 is an echo from *1 Enoch,* and Matthew 23:37 is from 2 Esdras 2.[27] Because this larger body

26. James A. Charlesworth, ed., *The Old Testament Pseudepigrapha*, 2 vols. (Garden City, N.Y.: Doubleday, 1983–85).

27. Lee Martin McDonald, "Recognizing Jewish Religious Texts as Scripture," and "Forming Jewish Scriptures as a Biblical Canon," in *Ancient Jewish and Christian Scriptures: New Developments in Canon Controversy,* ed. John J. Collins, Craig A. Evans, and Lee Martin McDonald (Louisville, Ky.: Westminster John Knox Press, 2020), 66 and 79 n. 24, respectively; for Esdras, see Bruce M. Metzger, "The Fourth Book of Ezra," in Charlesworth, *Old Testament Pseudepigrapha,* 1:527.

of original Hebrew literature was no longer in existence, it echoed principally through the Hellenistic synagogue outside ancient Palestine, where many of Jesus' statements in the Greek text follow within the Septuagint tradition. The church fathers had to rely on the writings of the Septuagint to draw upon the source material that was not included in the Masoretic Hebrew text, which became fixed in only the tenth century AD.

Traditional commentators often see the modern stable canonical process as originating from a four-stage model. They base this formula on (1) the Law, (2) the Prophets, (3) the Lord Jesus, and (4) his Apostles. The broader Christian approach reads the Old Testament through the lens of Jesus and the Apostles, and their canon is rooted in how the Christian faith began and how the corpus of our New Testament was framed. The church fathers add a fifth layer by establishing the traditions that early Christianity would develop and maintain.[28]

The Septuagint

The view that the canon remains open is still a minority position in western Christianity. When one holds to a closed canonical position of the text, one is locked into the historical and doctrinal positions that are held within the accepted canonical books, whatever their strengths and weaknesses may be. The character of the canon can vary in the relationships between the books that are canonized. But attempts to join to the canon theological works and other documents from the Apocrypha and pseudepigrapha are often met with a great deal of resistance. However, the discussions among scholars are changing, especially in regards to *1 Enoch*'s influence upon the New Testament, particularly in the book of Revelation. Until now, scholars assigned these references to apocryphal sources in an offhanded way that did not result in giving *Enoch* and other pseudepigraphal literature primary consideration for their theological importance. The extra Daniel literature contained in the Septuagint entitled Bel and the Dragon, as well as the additions to Esther, which the Masoretic Text compilers received from Jewish traditions as a minority report and, along with the Song of Solomon, were almost left out of the Jewish canon, have always been considered

28. Denis Farkasfalvy, "The Apostolic Gospels in the Early Church: The Concept of Canon and the Formation of the Four-Gospel Canon," in *Canon and Biblical Interpretation,* ed. Craig G. Bartholomew, Scott Hahn, Robin Parry, Christopher Seitz, and Al Wolters, vol. 7 of Scripture and Hermeneutics (Grand Rapids, Mich.: Zondervan, 2006), 113–14.

minority, secondary texts. The book of Esther and the erotic love poetry of the Song of Solomon were considered not to have primary standing in the canon because the name of God was not specifically mentioned.

Concerning the differing lengths of individual books, the Septuagint tradition generally follows the longer versions of these documents. The copies of the Song of Solomon text are very stable between the Masoretic tradition and the LXX. One notable exception in this case is Jeremiah.

> Tov argues that the Book of Jeremiah existed in two distinct Hebrew forms: a shorter edition from which the extant Greek was translated, and an expanded tradition that became the MT. He proposes that the shorter version of Jeremiah—reflected by 4QJer^{b,d} and the Greek version—is the older edition of Jeremiah. Fragments of both the shorter and longer Hebrew texts were found at Qumran. The oldest of the Jeremiah fragments, 4QJer^{a} (also called 4Q70)—as well as 2QJer (also called 2Q13) and 4QJer^{c} (also called 4Q72)—reflects the MT tradition and is thought to date from approximately 200 B.C.E., while 4QJer^{b,d} is dated somewhat later, to the first half of the second century B.C.E.[29]

In this case, the Dead Sea Scrolls contain both longer and shorter versions of the book of Jeremiah. Are they a compilation of the traditions, the Septuagint, and the Masoretic, or was there a distinct tradition of Jeremiah's record that was separate from the other two textual streams and brought together in the Qumran community?

Those who favor an open canon generally support the Septuagint readings and its additional documents, while the closed-canon position simply regards these writings as mere additions without primary canonical authority. The open-canon position sometimes assumes that the writings of a later date represent the theology and liturgical practices of earlier but now-lost writings that do not have a canonical classification. In a different but enlightening vein, the extra canonical documents go not only into time schemes for earth's redemptive history, as contained in *Jubilees,* but also into the seven to ten heavens from the ascension literature of Enoch's heavenly travels.

Moreover, there are additional stories about Jesus that add to the oral sayings in the literature of the Gospels, such as those about Jesus' childhood contained in the *Gospel of Thomas.* For example, the *Gospel of Thomas* 2:2 features a story about the clay bird the youthful Jesus made that came

29. Karen H. Jobes and Moisés Silva, *Invitation to the Septuagint* (Grand Rapids, Mich.: Baker Academic, 2000), 175–76.

to life at his command and flew away, showing his divinity from an early age. Most scholars have seen this as just a fanciful story reported at a later date in the Qur'an (sura 5:110) about the Lord Jesus, effectively underlining Jesus' genuine mortality in the face of viewpoints that held Jesus to be only a numinous person.

Additional stories exist about the potter's field that may have been part of the original composition of Jeremiah. In the New Testament, the reference appears in Matthew 27:9–10. Various attempts have been advanced throughout the centuries to explain how this reference fits into the death of Judas. Most scholars and commentators maintain that this insertion is out of context with the narrative in Matthew. However, several different reports lead to other possibilities.

> When we think of some of the things which *have* been said about it [the potter's field] by leading Christian scholars and commentators we cannot but feel shame. The devout and scholarly Alford, of all commentators, calls it a "slip of the pen" by Matthew! Bishop Wordsworth says it is a mistake allowed by the Holy Spirit to teach us not to trouble ourselves as to who the writers were, but to receive *all* prophecy as direct from God! Augustine suggests that Matthew was only quoting "from memory"! Eusebius and others say that the passage was originally in Jeremiah, but that the Jews cut it out, though they cannot prove this. Bishop Lightfoot and others suggest that Matthew puts Jeremiah as representing the whole body of the prophets, but *why* Matthew should do so is hard to see. Perhaps we are getting nearer the truth in the view of Origen and some others, that the passage which Matthew refers to was in *another* writing of Jeremiah which became lost. Or we may be still nearer the truth in the suggestion put forward in Smith's Bible Dictionary, that some annotator wrote "Jeremiah" in the margin and that it thereby crept into the text.[30]

No matter which textual explanation we adopt, the material attributed to Jeremiah was not yet fixed in any textual tradition.[31] The differences are apparent when one studies the larger Septuagint renderings.[32] It is

30. James Sidlow Baxter, *Studies in Problem Texts: Being a Short Series of Elucidatory and Applicatory Expositions of Certain Scripture Passages Which Have Occasioned Perplexity* (Grand Rapids, Mich.: Zondervan Publishing House, 1960), 140–41, emphasis in original.

31. More recent research has pointed to an undated *Apocryphon of Jeremiah* that Jerome saw. See William Adler, "The Pseudepigrapha in the Early Church," in McDonald and Sanders, *Canon Debate*, 226, also 213 n. 7.

32. Charles Lee Brenton, trans., *The Septuagint with Apocrypha: Greek and English* (Peabody, Mass.: Hendrickson Publishers, 1995), 971.

most likely that this reading in Jeremiah dropped out of use over time or was inserted into the so-called *Apocryphon of Jeremiah.* Let us remember the text says that "then was fulfilled that which was spoken by Jeremy the prophet" (Matt. 27:9). Evidently, the purchase of the potter's field followed the pattern of a purchase initiated by Jeremiah, although we have no specific citation for this fulfillment. The thirty pieces of silver, which was the "blood money," comes from Zechariah. Is there, then, a difference between the fulfillment of Jeremiah's prophecy and the reports which were circulated at the time of the death of Jesus?

Other texts such as the book of Wisdom are particularly helpful with our understanding of the wisdom traditions which had international acclaim during the Axial Period. The books of 1 and 2 Maccabees and the successful course of the Maccabean revolt have been viewed as possessing historically viable information. And the books of 1 and 2 Esdras established an early church eschatology that rested on Daniel chapters 2 and 7.

Conclusions

All this data supports the conclusion that the canon was both fixed and flexible in the literature of Judaism and early Christianity. The closing of the New Testament canon was probably an effort to stabilize the canon from the five canonical lists[33] that were accepted by various local communities and used primarily for local liturgical and worship practices. When the canon becomes too rigid and fixed, valuable additional theological and historical material is diminished or rejected wholesale. On the other hand, the problem with an open canonical concept is that there is greater tension with the primary canon because of the amount of potential source material that becomes available to add to scripture.

As examples, the current canon has the story of Jacob's ladder in Genesis 28:10–17, which has a description of exaltation but does not deal with the broader genre of Ascension literature that echoes this teaching. The Old Testament describes in Ezekiel and Isaiah the saints being exalted on the mountain of God (Ezek. 34:14; Isa. 2) and their odyssey being fulfilled at the top of the mountain, where complete restoration takes place in fulfillment of the Day of Atonement narrative. This theme is repeated in Micah 2. There is also tension and confusion created between the writers of Psalm 146:4 and Ecclesiastes 9:5, which seem to indicate that there is

33. Lists of accepted books by Clement of Alexandria, Origen, Athanasius, Irenaeus, and Valentinus.

no consciousness once the dead depart from this mortal life. If one holds a closed canonical position, this stance is quite tenable and ancient. However, with the Hellenization of Judaism through the Greek-speaking synagogue and the major prophets articulating the search for eternal life through exaltation and going up to the mountain, there is a clear affirmation of the consciousness of the departed dead (for example, Gen. 37:34–35). A tension develops between these two narrative approaches to the resurrection. Some resolve these issues by asserting that later revelation progressively clarifies the rest of the redemptive story. Others judge that Judaism went off the rails into pagan apostasy.

It is against this backdrop that the New Testament Apostles and early church fathers began the development of the church canon and New Testament streams of thought that diverged from Old Testament teachings. Where these narratives come together is in the motifs of judgment followed by resurrection and the new creation. The canonical positions of the Ethiopic Church, for example, have room in an open-canon context for all of this material. Even the Muratorian canon (late second century AD) listed books that were not accepted later by the church at large. This may be an indication that other books not contained in the current primary canon were accepted in the early church's liturgy and practice. When one reads the Gospel according to Phillip (second century AD), additional information about the Holy of Holies is entertained that connects with the Song of Solomon and eternal marriage. We also have the forty days of the appearances of the Risen Messiah, entitled *Evangelium Quadraginta Dierum,* that are joined with our Lord's other bodily manifestations after his Resurrection (Acts 1:3; 1 Cor. 15:5–8).[34] This is followed by the Ascension narrative in Acts 1:6 (see also Luke 24:30–51). As the church developed the doctrine of deification from the Ascension of Christ, the pseudepigraphal work that is called the *Evangelion of Mary* grew in acceptance, and her deification became prominent.[35]

The stabilization of the canonical process became paramount due to the scriptural and intellectual bulwark needed for the defense of Christ's redemption being the salvation of the world, a teaching which stood against

34. Hugh Nibley, *Mormonism and Early Christianity,* ed. Todd M. Compton and Stephen D. Ricks, vol. 4 of The Collected Works of Hugh Nibley (Salt Lake City: Deseret Book; Provo, Utah: Foundation for Ancient Research and Mormon Studies, 1987), 10–17.

35. Jaroslav Pelican, "Mary through the Centuries," in *Jesus through the Centuries—Mary through the Centuries* (New York: History Book Club, 2005), 42–45, 55–59, 97–104, 116–22, 128–36.

the Gnostic ideologies of an escape from the physical body and an evil world created by an imperfect creator-god. During the second and third centuries AD, Gnostic teachings about a pure spiritual resurrection challenged the church's view of Jesus' bodily Resurrection. The Gnostic position rested on a view borrowed from the Greek world that the body was evil. Moreover, the Gnostics held that only the true light and wisdom from the Demiurge, a creature subservient to the Unknowable Father, would enlighten men and women throughout the eons. Significant alternative texts and debates about the nature of celestial marriage in the resurrection would connect with the secret teachings about the Holy of Holies, the crowning of marriage, and temple liturgy, as seen in the writings of the early church fathers. These and other Alexandrian views about, for example, the premortality of all humans have been rejected by the church at large. But in the viewpoint of an open canonical connection, Gnostic literature and other ancient texts become a part of the theological spectrum of patristic Christianity and are essential to our full understanding of Christian theology and history.

Weighing the Authority of the New Testament on Restoration Scales

Andrew C. Skinner

In modern Christianity, when one speaks of authority, one usually refers to several interrelated issues associated with the New Testament text. The questions include to what extent we can view the New Testament doctrines, commandments, and covenants as authoritative—that is, as issuing from a divine source; to what extent statements in the biblical text accurately reflect God's mind and will; how statements in the Bible comport with history; which biblical authors possess authority; when the New Testament canon was being formed, how the authority or authenticity of a biblical book was determined; how the principle of authority relates to the belief in the idea of biblical inerrancy; and whether there are texts and writers outside the biblical canon who possess authority.

Locus of Authority

The Apostle Paul declared that "there is no authority [Greek, *exousia*] except by God" (Rom. 13:1).[1] Because authority in the New Testament was closely associated with "power" (though the two terms were sometimes differentiated),[2] the King James Version often renders *exousia* as power—"there is no power but of God." But the principle is the same: all authority and power are vested in and emanate from God, who delegates to his Beloved Son, and to other human beings through his Son, aspects and degrees of authority. This observation is demonstrated in the New Testament.

1. This translation comes from Robert K. Brown and Philip W. Comfort, trans., *The New Greek-English Interlinear New Testament,* 4th cor. ed. (Wheaton, Ill.: Tyndale House Publishers, 1993).

2. *The Interpreter's Dictionary of the Bible: An Illustrated Encyclopedia,* (Nashville: Abingdon Press, 1962), s.vv. "authority," "power of keys."

During his mortal ministry, Jesus said of his life that "no one takes it from me, but I lay it down from myself. I have authority [*exousia*] to lay it down and I have authority to receive it again. This command I received from my Father" (John 10:18).[3] Later, Jesus claimed that all authority in heaven and on earth was given to him by his Father (John 17:2; Matt. 28:18). After the Sermon on the Mount, Jesus was recognized by "the crowds" as teaching with authority, his own authority, and not as the scribes who appealed to the authority of other teacher-leaders in Judaism (Matt. 7:28–29). During that same sermon, Jesus presented his instructions as the omniscient God he truly was: "You have heard that it was said by them of old time, . . . but I say unto you . . ." (Matt. 5:21–22, 27–28, 31–34, 38–39, 43–44). All the sayings that Jesus attributed to the ancients came from the law of Moses. Such statements as these indicate that Jesus' teachings were intended to supersede the teachings of Moses, the great lawgiver.

That Jesus bestowed aspects of his own authority on others is well documented. To his Apostles, he gave "power [Greek, *dynamis*] and authority [Greek, *exousia*] over all the demons and to heal diseases" (Luke 9:1).[4] He also gave them the authority to forgive sins (John 20:33). To prophets and apostles, Jesus gave the authority to speak as though they themselves were the Lord: "Thus saith the Lord . . ." Stunningly, Jesus even permits Satan to have authority, but that is temporary, and it is only by his allowance that the adversary has any control (Rev. 2:10).

Thus the words and acts of Jesus of Nazareth carried foremost weight and authority for Christian disciples in terms of what they were to believe and how they were to conduct their lives. So it is today. Yet nothing about his life was written by him, so far as we know. He did not personally compose any of the books comprising the New Testament canon. That was largely left to his close followers—Apostles who were eyewitnesses of his life and teachings.

To be sure, there were other eyewitnesses to some of Jesus' activities. But as Ronald Heine notes in his study of classical Christian doctrine, these other witnesses "were not on a par with apostles as eyewitnesses, because the apostles were those closest followers who had been with him continually throughout his ministry."[5] They had witnessed his deeds

3. Brown and Comfort, *New Greek-English Interlinear New Testament.*

4. Brown and Comfort, *New Greek-English Interlinear New Testament.*

5. Ronald E. Heine, *Classical Christian Doctrine: Introducing the Essentials of the Ancient Faith* (Grand Rapids, Mich.: Baker Academic, 2013), 13–14. On the basis of Luke's

and heard his teachings firsthand from the beginning of his ministry. Latter-day scholars are in agreement but would emphasize that it is not just longevity of their firsthand association with Jesus that is critical. Rather, it is that the Apostles were chosen, ordained, and sent forth by Jesus to be special witnesses of his divinity and reality to all the world (Acts 1:8; D&C 107:23). At any rate, Heine, following many other scholars, also asserts that the Apostles "constituted the highest court of appeal when it came to authenticating what Jesus had done or said. When the words and deeds of Jesus began to be written down, it was natural for the Christians to treat these accounts as Scripture in the same way they treated the writings of Moses and the prophets."[6] After Jesus' Ascension, authority was vested in the ordained Apostles. The apostolic witness was of prime importance.

Heine goes on to provide a helpful paradigm for understanding how scriptural authority was determined and understood anciently. Heine turns to the Apostle Paul to illustrate. The latter recognized three sources of authority. First was the developing Old Testament—the law of Moses, the prophets, and the Psalms (Luke 24:44; see also John 1:45). "The main authority of the Hebrew Scriptures for Christians was the testimony that they were understood to bear to Christ."[7] Paul used various scriptural texts to support his message about Jesus. As he explained, "Whatever was written in former days was written for our instruction" (Rom. 15:4, NRSV). Second, Paul knew and drew upon "sayings of Jesus as a source of authority."[8] Sometimes he got those teachings from other Apostles (see 1 Cor. 15:3–8; Gal. 1:18–19).

Third, Paul considered the office of Apostle itself to carry authority. Heine cites the example of Paul's teachings on marriage in 1 Corinthians 7. "Paul carefully distinguishes the teaching of Jesus on the subject of marriage from what he himself says on a further matter about which he knows no teaching of Jesus. But it is quite clear that he expects his own words, as those of an apostle, to carry authority as well."[9]

---

testimony in Acts 1:21–23, there were others who traveled with Jesus for as long as the twelve Apostles had, some of whom may have been women (see Luke 8:1–3). But it was the authority held by the Apostles that was prized above all others.

6. Heine, *Classical Christian Doctrine,* 14.
7. Heine, *Classical Christian Doctrine,* 14.
8. Heine, *Classical Christian Doctrine,* 14.
9. Heine, *Classical Christian Doctrine,* 14–15.

Authority and Canon

Apostolic authority greatly influenced the formation of the New Testament canon. The word "canon" comes from a Greek term that means a standard or rule for measuring accuracy. The New Testament canon is that collection of writings judged by early Christian leaders of the first three centuries AD to accurately and authoritatively present the life and teachings of Jesus the Messiah. Eyewitness proximity to Jesus was the standard by which to measure which writings should be included in the authorized collection. This meant the Apostles. Thus "apostolic authorship appears to have been one of the chief means of determining canonicity."[10] As an example, the works of the Apostle Paul, the earliest Christian writings we know of to have circulated soon after their composition, "were readily accepted as canonical" by the Christian community because of his eyewitness testimony of Jesus' living reality.[11]

Statements from some early church fathers confirm the importance attached to the teachings and writings of the Apostles. Clement of Rome (died c. AD 99) stated, "The Apostles received the Gospel for us from the Lord Jesus Christ; Jesus the Christ was sent from God. The Christ therefore is from God and the Apostles from the Christ" (*1 Clem.* 42.1–2).[12] Irenaeus (c. AD 130–200), bishop of Lyon, France, spoke of the martyr Polycarp (c. AD 69–155) as "having always taught the things which he had learned from the apostles, and which the Church has handed down, and which alone are true."[13] Ignatius of Antioch (died AD 140), known as the "God-bearing," spoke with reverence regarding the two greatest Apostles of early Christianity while traveling as a prisoner to Rome: "I do not order you as did Peter and Paul; they were Apostles, I am a convict; they were free, I am even until now a slave" (*To the Romans* 4.3).[14]

There were exceptions to the primacy of direct apostolic witness of Jesus' life and teachings, the Gospels of Mark and Luke being examples.

---

10. Paul D. Wegner, *The Journey from Texts to Translations: The Origin and Development of the Bible,* corrected printing (Grand Rapids, Mich.: Baker Academic, 1999), 148.

11. Wegner, *Journey from Texts to Translation,* 148.

12. Kirsopp Lake, trans., *The Apostolic Fathers,* 2 vols. (Cambridge, Mass.: Harvard University Press, 1977), 1:79–81.

13. Irenaeus, *Against Heresies* 3.3.4, in *Ante-Nicene Fathers: Translations of the Writings of the Fathers Down to A.D. 325,* ed. Alexander Roberts and James Donaldson, 10 vols. (Grand Rapids, Mich.: Wm. B. Eerdmans, 1991), 1:416.

14. Lake, *Apostolic Fathers,* 1:231.

But apparently the "chain of authority could not reach any further away than immediate disciples of apostles. They had, at least, known the eyewitnesses and had heard their teachings."[15] Luke's Gospel seems to have been granted canonical status on the basis of the "author's relationship to Paul."[16]

Authority and Inerrancy of Scripture

Views on the authority of the Bible have been significantly influenced by the idea of biblical inerrancy. In its simplest formulation, biblical inerrancy is the belief that the Bible "is without error or fault in all its teaching."[17] This belief is rigidly upheld by various adherents of American evangelical Christianity, some of whom equate inerrancy with biblical infallibility, a step up in expressing the view that the Bible is without a single mistake.

Biblical inerrancy was officially formulated in the Chicago Statement on Biblical Inerrancy by an international conference of evangelical leaders in Chicago in October 1978 and signed by nearly three hundred evangelical scholars. It was obviously designed to defend the absolute authority of scripture against less literal, more liberal interpretations of the biblical text. The core of the statement avers that "Scripture in the original manuscripts does not affirm anything that is contrary to fact,"[18] with the stipulation that "inspiration, strictly speaking, applies only to the autographic text of Scripture."[19] Of course, there is no "autograph" of the biblical text or even an original composition of any biblical book. We possess only copies of copies. In a grudging acknowledgment of the lack of original copies, however, the statement goes on to declare, "We deny that any essential element of the Christian faith is affected by the absence of the autographs."[20] Furthermore, the autographic text of scripture "in the providence of God can be ascertained from available manuscripts with great accuracy."[21]

---

15. Heine, *Classical Christian Doctrine,* 21.

16. Wegner, *Journey from Text to Translation,* 149.

17. J. I. Packer, foreword to *Defending Inerrancy: Affirming the Accuracy of Scripture for a New Generation,* by Norman L. Geisler and William C. Roach (Grand Rapids, Mich.: Baker Books, 2011).

18. Wayne Gruden, *Systematic Theology: An Introduction to Biblical Doctrine* (Leicester, Eng.: Inter-Varsity Press, 1994), 91.

19. *Chicago Statement on Biblical Inerrancy,* article X.

20. *Chicago Statement on Biblical Inerrancy,* article X.

21. *Chicago Statement on Biblical Inerrancy,* article X.

The concept of biblical inerrancy certainly emphasizes the fact that "the authority of Scripture is a key issue for each generation of believers and in every age."[22] However, it is a controversial idea and has been called into question for a number of reasons by both Protestants and Roman Catholics. These reasons need not detain us here except to say that even some influential evangelical scholars disagree with the sweeping and unanswered critical questions flowing out of the Chicago Statement itself.[23] In our view, biblical inerrancy as articulated in the Chicago Statement and subsequent discussions does not harmonize well with Restoration scripture and modern prophets.

It ought to be acknowledged up front that The Church of Jesus Christ of Latter-day Saints regards the Bible with reverence. We place great authority in it. And we agree that, when it first came forth, "it contained the fulness of the gospel of the Lord, of whom the twelve apostles bear record; and they bear record according to the truth which is in the Lamb of God" (1 Ne. 13:24). Indeed, as Nephi indicated, the original apostolic witnesses were crucial to substantiating the authority of the Bible. But after scripture went forth by the hand of apostles and disciples of Christ, from the Jews unto the Gentiles, "many parts which are plain and most precious; and also many covenants of the Lord" were "taken away from the gospel of the Lamb" (1 Ne. 13:25–26).

Thus The Church of Jesus Christ of Latter-day Saints believes "the Bible to be the word of God as far as it is translated [and transmitted] correctly" (A of F 1:8) precisely because errors were made. Historical records confirm this point. An example comes from St. Jerome, the famous biblical translator who formulated a plan to produce a new, more trustworthy version of the Bible (later known as the Vulgate). Jerome sought to correct the problems existing in the Old Latin manuscripts of the biblical text then in circulation. In a letter to Pope Damasus in AD 383, Jerome described the challenge with existing Latin manuscripts of just the New Testament: "For if we are to pin our faith to the Latin texts, it is for our opponents to tell us *which*; for there are almost as many forms of texts as there are copies. If, on the other hand, we are to glean the truth from a comparison of many,

22. Peter Enns, "Inerrancy, However Defined, Does Not Describe What the Bible Does," in R. Albert Mohler and others, *Five Views on Biblical Inerrancy* (Grand Rapids, Mich.: Zondervan, 2013), 85.

23. For a thorough and accessible treatment of the scholarly positions on biblical inerrancy by evangelical leaders themselves, see Mohler and others, *Five Views on Biblical Inerrancy.*

why not go back to the original Greek and correct the mistakes introduced by inaccurate translators, and the blundering alterations of confident but ignorant critics, and further all that has been inserted or changed by copyists more asleep than awake?"[24]

Jerome recognized that at the very least a revision, if not a restoration, was needed in his day. Similarly, in these latter days, a doctrinal restoration was needed and has occurred. Latter-day Saints aver that for all its merits, ultimate authority does not rest in the King James Version, or in any other version of the Bible, or in any of the thousands of biblical manuscripts that exist in the original languages of Hebrew and Greek (from which, according to the Chicago Statement on Biblical Inerrancy, the autographic text of the Bible can be recaptured). Ultimate authority is vested in the Book of Mormon, Doctrine and Covenants, the Pearl of Great Price, the Joseph Smith Translation of the Bible, and the words of modern prophets.

In fact, a statement from the Church's First Presidency seems crafted to respond directly to the assertions put forward by proponents of biblical inerrancy: "Unfortunately, no original manuscripts of any portion of the Bible are available for comparison to determine the most accurate version. However, the Lord has revealed clearly the doctrines of the gospel in these latter days. The most reliable way to measure the accuracy of any biblical passage is not by comparing different texts, but by comparison with the Book of Mormon and modern-day revelations."[25] For Latter-day Saints, ultimate authority resides in "the most correct of any book on earth," the one book by which a person "would get nearer to God . . . than by any other book"[26]—the Book of Mormon—as well as in those reservoirs of scripture that present the very words of the Lord in modern times without having to be translated from an ancient language.

If we go back to the foundational principle that proclaims where ultimate authority is located, and that all, or most all, Christians agree on, we must have the authentic words of God preserved in the text. "For Christians the ultimate authority is God, revealed in Jesus Christ and His redeeming work."[27]

---

24. J. Stevenson, ed., *Creeds, Councils and Controversies: Documents Illustrating the History of the Church, A.D. 337–461*, rev. ed. (London: SPCK, 1989), 183, emphasis in original.

25. "First Presidency Statement on the King James Version of the Bible," *Ensign* 22, no. 8 (August 1992): 80.

26. *Teachings of the Presidents of the Church: Joseph Smith* (Salt Lake City: The Church of Jesus Christ of Latter-day Saints, 2007), 64.

27. *The Oxford Dictionary of the Christian Church*, 3rd rev. ed. (Oxford: Oxford University Press, 2005), s.v. "authority."

In this regard, the words of the Lord addressed to Sidney Rigdon, at a time when the Prophet Joseph Smith was engaged almost daily in making his inspired revision of the King James Version, are truly arresting: "And a commandment I give unto thee—thou shalt write for him [Joseph Smith]; and *the scriptures shall be given, even as they are in mine own bosom, to the salvation of mine own elect*; for they will hear my voice, and shall see me, and shall not be asleep, and shall abide the day of my coming; for they shall be purified, even as I am pure" (D&C 35:20–21, emphasis added).

For members of The Church of Jesus Christ of Latter-day Saints, authority rests in the direct word of the Lord and in ordained, authorized servants who speak in his name: "Whatsoever they shall speak when moved upon by the Holy Ghost shall be scripture, shall be the will of the Lord, shall be the mind of the Lord, shall be the word of the Lord, shall be the voice of the Lord, and the power of God unto salvation" (D&C 68:4). The living oracles supersede the written text if a discrepancy should arise.

Regarding authority and authorship in the Bible, it seems fair and defensible to say that the Latter-day Saint scholars who are involved in the present commentary project have begun their work with the assumption that the authorship of books in the New Testament, as well as the authority ascribed to them, is accurate and proper, unless there is evidence to the contrary. In other words, a burden of proof exists on the part of those who deny the traditional attribution of authorship or who deny the authority traditionally ascribed to a biblical text.

Ultimately, our love of the New Testament, its fundamental sanctity and authoritative soundness, and our continual reflection on its content cause us to join our voices with that of the Prophet Joseph Smith: "We take the sacred writings into our hands, and admit that they were given by direct inspiration for the good of man. We believe that God condescended to speak from the heavens and declare His will concerning the human family, to give them just and holy laws, to regulate their conduct, and guide them in a direct way, that in due time He might take them to Himself, and make them joint heirs with His Son."[28] And we are convinced that, to paraphrase the Prophet, whoever reads the New Testament "oftenest will like it best."[29]

---

28. *Teachings of the Presidents of the Church*, 66.

29. "Letter to the Church, circa March 1834," 142, Joseph Smith Papers, accessed February 11, 2022, https://www.josephsmithpapers.org/paper-summary/letter-to-the-church-circa-march-1834/1.

The Rise of Canonical and Apocryphal Literature

S. Kent Brown and David J. Larsen

All approaches toward understanding how the New Testament came to be must pass through the rather narrow narrative of what the term "canon" means and why it is important. Said another way, can we grasp what the scriptures are without understanding how they came to be the scriptures? The short answer is no. The long answer now presents itself.

Canon

The word "canon" enjoyed a long history before it became a part of the English language. Its first ancestor was the biblical Hebrew term קָנֶה (*qaneh*), which is related to similar terms in Akkadian and Ugaritic and bears the meaning "reed" or "measuring rod" as well as other related concepts.[1] From here, the term migrated into Greek—one of the few Hebrew words that was adopted by the Greeks—where it took the form κανών (*kanōn*). Significantly, in the Greek world, *kanōn* took on a metaphorical meaning of the standard, the ideal, the measure "by which the empirical world must be judged."[2] It is in this sense generally that the word *kanōn* came to be attached to the idea of scripture, or writings from God's authorized representatives that set the divine standards for personal conduct, personal and communal worship, and community interaction.[3]

---

1. Hedwig Lamberty-Zielinski, "qaneh," in *Theological Dictionary of the Old Testament,* ed. G. Johannes Botterweck, Helmer Ringgren, and Heinz-Josef Fabry, trans. David E. Green, 17 vols. (Grand Rapids: William B. Eerdmans, 1974–2021), 13:65–67, 69–70.

2. Wilhelm Schneemelcher, "General Introduction," trans. George Ogg, in *New Testament Apocrypha,* ed. Edgar Hennecke and Wilhelm Schneemelcher, 2 vols. (Philadelphia: Westminster Press, 1963), 1:21.

3. Hermann Wolfgang Beyer, "κανών," in *Theological Dictionary of the New Testament,* ed. Gerhard Kittel and Gerhard Freidrich, trans. Geoffery W. Bromiley, 10 vols. (Grand

In the New Testament, only two passages present themselves for review where the Greek term κανών appears, both from the Apostle Paul and written in the late AD 40s and mid-50s.[4] One passage is rather straightforward; the other is more complex. Let us begin with Galatians 6:15–16, which reads, "It does not matter[5] if a person is circumcised or not; what matters is for him to become an altogether new creature. Peace and mercy to all who follow this rule, who form the Israel of God" (Jerusalem Bible). Noting that the Greek κανών is translated "rule" in this passage, the meaning is plain. For Paul, the noun carries the sense of a "standard" that applies to one's attitude toward both those who are the same and those who are different from oneself, Jew or Gentile, circumcised or uncircumcised. Moreover, implicit is a "norm of action" that guides the believer to welcome into the faith those who are different, opening the believer to becoming a "new creature"[6] and to enjoying God's "peace and mercy" in this life. This person then becomes a member of the new "Israel of God" as it is now constituted in the wake of Jesus' ministry and Atonement.[7]

Paul's statement in 2 Corinthians 10:13–16 presents a different slant in a "linguistically difficult passage," as Beyer remarks.[8] It includes three occurrences of κανών—in verses 13, 15, and 16. Because no modern translation mirrors uniformly the occurrences of this term in the underlying Greek text of these passages, let us deal with them on a verse-by-verse basis. In the first passage, 10:13, Paul points out that the heart of the matter has to do with boasting—that is, taking credit for what another missionary has done, something that latecomers to Corinth have done at Paul's expense. After all, he was the first missionary to arrive in the city and to preach there (see Acts 18:1–7). In 10:13, we read of Paul that "we will not boast of things without [= *beyond*] our measure, but according to the measure of the rule which God hath distributed to us." Here the word "rule" translates κανών; the "rule" represents a "standard," but with a slightly different sense than

---

Rapids, Mich.: Wm. B. Eerdmans, 1964–76), 3:600–601; Schneemelcher, "General Introduction," 1:23–24 (hereafter cited as *TDNT*).

4. Frederick Fyvie Bruce, *Paul: Apostle of the Heart Set Free* (Grand Rapids, Mich.: William B. Eerdmans, 1977), 475.

5. Most of the fourth- and fifth-century manuscripts preserve the reading in the King James Version that opens Gal. 6:15: "For in Christ Jesus . . ." But the earliest papyrus manuscript that dates from about AD 200, the fragmentary $\mathfrak{P}^{46}$, and the fourth-century text Vaticanus (B) omit this phrase.

6. Schneemelcher, "General Introduction," 1:22.

7. Beyer, "κανών," 3:598.

8. Beyer, "κανών," 3:599.

that in Galatians 6:15–16. In this Corinthian passage, it refers to the call of Paul to his apostleship, effectively "the labor God has assigned to us" (2 Cor. 10:13),[9] an experience that set out the parameters of Paul's future ministry. The other occurrences of κανών flesh out this view.

Second Corinthians 10:15 offers to us the following: we have the "hope, when your faith is increased, that we shall be enlarged by you according to our rule abundantly." Again, κανών is translated as "rule." The sense is that as the members of the Corinthian congregation grow in their faith, Paul can then turn his attention to other places where the gospel has not yet been preached, "in the regions beyond you" (10:16), thus filling his apostolic commission more "abundantly."

The language of 2 Corinthians 10:16 is a little more difficult to elucidate. The King James Version reads, "not to boast in another man's line of things," where the term κανών is rendered "line of things." The sense has to do with not taking credit for another person's spiritual stewardship or spiritual responsibilities that he or she has been assigned and has fulfilled.[10] Thus the idea of a "standard" rests within this expression, a standard of generous missionary behavior toward the labors of other missionaries and preachers.[11]

Happily, after the days of Paul, early Christian sources document how standards came to play a significant role in the developing church (the word κανών itself came into prominence only in the fourth century). We will highlight three important developments. First, during the first century AD, church congregations that arose across the Mediterranean region and beyond exhibited a basic unity that took its character from a focus on Jesus and his Resurrection. But this fundamental unity was not to last. In one of the earliest New Testament documents, Paul's letter to the Galatians, written perhaps as early as AD 48,[12] Paul railed against certain believers who had introduced "another gospel" and who "would pervert the gospel of Christ" (Gal. 1:6–7). Though fellow Christians, these people were outsiders to the Galatian branches. In this way, as time went on, subtle and, in some cases, not-so-subtle differences exhibited themselves among congregations in what they taught about Christ, in the sacred books that they

9. Schneemelcher, "General Introduction," 1:22–23.

10. Frederick William Danker, ed., *A Greek-English Lexicon of the New Testament and Other Early Christian Literature,* 3rd ed. (Chicago: University of Chicago Press, 2000), s.v. ἀλλότριος.

11. Beyer, "κανών," 3:600.

12. Bruce, *Paul,* 475. Richard Lloyd Anderson, *Understanding Paul* (Salt Lake City: Deseret Book, 1983), 149 and 395, pushes the composition of Galatians as late as AD 58.

began to accept and read, and in their ecclesiastical practices. By the late first century and the beginning of the second, as apostolic authority waned, differences had become the norm according to preserved records. In some areas, what later came to be regarded as heretical was, in fact, the form that budding Christianity took.[13]

Next, during the second century, as Christians became more self-conscious of who they were in a Roman world that had turned hostile, church leaders perceived a need to establish boundaries that imposed norms on what to believe, how to worship, and how to govern the church. Admittedly, difficulties with Roman authorities were not the only challenges that church members faced. For example, we read in the surviving correspondence of Ignatius, the second-century bishop of Antioch in what is now southernmost Turkey, that competing forms of Christianity had by then emerged in cities and towns because of a crippling struggle over who held real authority in the church. What is more, it is impossible to determine whether Ignatius or his opponents possessed a purer form of Christian belief and standards. Let us look more closely.

Two of the major themes in Ignatius's seven letters have to do with a hoped-for unity behind the local bishops and a worrisome concern about an invading heresy. Clearly, something big was driving both his insistent appeals for believers to unite behind their bishops[14] and his warning of a cancerous heresy that, from his viewpoint, had invaded churches in Asia Minor and beyond. Philadelphia served as an example of other congregations in western Asia Minor where Ignatius knew of the existence of what he called "many specious wolves."[15] In William Schoedel's judgment, "A threat to Ignatius' authority by some Antiochene Christians evidently played a significant role in determining what Ignatius was to do and to say."[16]

---

13. Walter Bauer, *Orthodoxy and Heresy in Earliest Christianity,* ed. Robert A. Kraft and Gerhard Krodel (Philadelphia: Fortress Press, 1971), xxii.

14. Bauer, *Orthodoxy and Heresy,* 61, notes that for Ignatius, "the bishop . . . is like God or Christ in whose place he stands." William R. Schoedel, *Ignatius of Antioch: A Commentary on the Letters of Ignatius of Antioch,* ed. Helmut Koester, Hermeneia: A Critical and Historical Commentary on the Bible (Philadelphia: Fortress Press, 1985), 22, argues for a moderated view "that in Ignatius the bishop does not occupy the place of God or Christ and that we are still close to NT models." See also especially Hugh Nibley, *Apostles and Bishops in Early Christianity,* ed. John F. Hall and John W. Welch, vol. 15 of The Collected Works of Hugh Nibley (Salt Lake City: Deseret Book; Provo, Utah: Foundation for Ancient Research and Mormon Studies, 2005), 61–74.

15. *Letter to the Philadelphians* 2:2.

16. Schoedel, *Ignatius of Antioch,* 11.

Further, there was a "loss of control of the church in Antioch and the emergence of a group opposed to [Ignatius's] authority."[17] This group may have consisted of "Judaizers," who taught the observance of the Mosaic law, because Ignatius "seems to have been more or less prepared with arguments" against such groups in Magnesia and Philadelphia.[18] In addition, the grinding difficulties between Ignatius and his Christian opponents in Antioch seem to arise in part because of personal animosities.[19] Personalities simply got in the way of unity among the Christians. And none of these issues could be settled by Apostles; by then they were off the mortal stage.

Third, the final push for standardization came largely as a result of the church's convulsive confrontation with gnosticism, a loosely framed belief system that disparaged the God of the Old Testament as being too strict and generally emphasized that salvation came because of what a person knew rather than through the sacrificial death of Jesus Christ. This monumental struggle, which left the surviving church with deep wounds in its doctrines,[20] propelled church leaders toward standardizing a collection of scripture. Why? Because one of the important gnostic teachers, an anti-semitic man named Marcion, who hailed from the port city of Sinope on the south coast of the Black Sea, created a New Testament of sorts about AD 150 that consisted of an edited version of the Gospel of Luke and a collection of Paul's letters.[21] Other gnostic teachers simply produced their own sacred writings—Gospels, Epistles, and, later, Apocalypses—that they claimed went back to the early Apostles and prominent teachers. Although certain Christian writers from the late second and early third centuries, basing their work on the good sense of earlier unnamed leaders,[22] had begun to collect and assess documents that could stand side by side with "the law and the prophets" of the Old Testament, the fresh and growing gnostic productions of course sounded alarm bells throughout Christendom. Resting their judgment on what they trusted from the first generation

---

17. Schoedel, *Ignatius of Antioch,* 10.

18. Schoedel, *Ignatius of Antioch,* 11 and n. 62.

19. Schoedel, *Ignatius of Antioch,* 10–11 and n. 62.

20. Hugh Nibley, "The Passing of the Primitive Church (Forty Variations on an Unpopular Theme)," in *When the Lights Went Out: Three Studies on the Ancient Apostasy* (Salt Lake City: Deseret Book, 1970), 1–32.

21. Johannes Quasten, *Patrology,* 3 vols. (Utrecht, Neth.: Spectrum Publishers, 1950), 1:268–71; Schneemelcher, "General Introduction," 1:32–33.

22. Robert M. Grant, "The New Testament Canon," in *The Cambridge History of the Bible,* ed. Peter R. Ackroyd and Christopher F. Evans, 3 vols. (Cambridge: Cambridge University Press, 1970), 1:284–86.

of believers, including especially the Apostles, church leaders responded by drawing up lists of accepted writings.

One of the early efforts resulted in the intriguing list to be found in the fragmentary Muratori Canon that goes back to circa AD 200 and was initially composed in Rome.[23] The opening lines are missing, wherein a discussion of the Gospels of Matthew and Mark must have appeared. But the register of accepted books includes almost all those in our current New Testament except the Epistle to the Hebrews and the letters of Peter, James, and 3 John. Although later Christian authors raised questions about the suitability of the book of Revelation for worship, the Muratori Canon shows the inner good sense that the earliest Christians possessed in what they decided to read and discuss in their meetings; they were not deceived by compositions that grew far from the apostolic tree.

That said, during the second century and especially the third, the term κανών became linked to three expressions, which hardened into statements that included certain beliefs and excluded others. The so-called Rule of Truth "is binding truth as this is proclaimed by the Church and as it has taken shape in its preaching."[24] Its companion, the Rule of Faith, or the Latin *regula fidei,* has to do with "the norm that bounded the limits of the Christian search for truth." To put it another way, "it embraces not just a confession of faith, but also the observance of customs affirmed in the church."[25] The third expression, the Rule of the Church, or Ecclesiastical Rule, embraced these two and set out "the baptismal confession . . . [and] the whole sum of Christian doctrine . . . and the right execution of ecclesiastical actions."[26] Such rules or standards had come about because of "the coming to an end of the genuine authority" of the eyewitnesses of Jesus' ministry and Resurrection.[27]

From circa AD 400 onward, the meaning of the term κανών "was fixed more and more narrowly" as the church labored forward in its attempts to set "the norm" for its "ecclesiastical teaching."[28] In the western, Latin-speaking part of the church, the word "canon" mirrored this meaning. Specifically, the word was applied to "the resolutions of Church councils . . .

---

23. Schneemelcher, "General Introduction," 1:35–36, 42–45.

24. Beyer, "κανών," 3:600.

25. Vittorino Grossi, "Regula Fidei," in *Encyclopedia of the Early Church,* ed. Angelo Di Berardino, trans. Adrian Walford, 2 vols. (Cambridge: James Clarke, 1992), 2:732.

26. Beyer, "κανών," 3:600.

27. Schneemelcher, "General Introduction," 1:37; see also Nibley, *Apostles and Bishops in Early Christianity,* 7–23.

28. Schneemelcher, "General Introduction," 1:24.

after Nicea [in AD 325]." Beginning in the fifth century, decisions made in councils "were gathered in collections of canons"—that is, collections of rules that spelled out doctrine, church governance, and accepted modes of worship.[29] Most importantly, from the mid-fourth century, the term κανών was applied both to "the collection of the sacred writings" inherited from the synagogue, now known as the Old Testament or Old Covenant, and to the New Testament, "which had already taken essential shape from *c.* 200."[30] In different words, as Adolf Jülicher wrote, "In using the word 'canonical' the Christian of 200 had exactly the same feelings as if he had said: Divine, holy, infallible, an absolute standard."[31]

The Canonization of the New Testament

In the spring of AD 367, the thirty-ninth festal letter of Athanasius, bishop of Alexandria, set out for the first time the collection of books and letters that now make up our New Testament.[32] For almost two centuries before this moment, Christian writers and leaders had made efforts to create a list of works that would stand side by side with the Old Testament. In its Greek form, the list of works would be called the Septuagint. This process, made up of numerous local decisions in different areas of the Roman world, rested on books and letters from the apostolic period already adopted in many congregations for reading and teaching. After all, it was apparent that Paul intended at least some of his letters be read in church services, opening the possibility of collecting works from the era of the Apostles that would meet Christians' spiritual needs even though most had not been written for such a purpose (see 1 Thes. 5:27; Col. 4:16). These instructions from Paul were matched by directions in the book of Revelation that it be read and, under threat of a curse, its words not be changed (see Rev. 1:3; 22:18–19).[33]

---

29. Beyer, *TDNT* "κανών," 3:601.

30. Beyer, "κανών," 3:601.

31. Adolf Jülicher, *Einleitung in das Neue Testament,* Siebente Auflage; neubearbeitet in Verbindung mit Erich Fascher (Tübingen: J. C. B. Mohr, 1904), 555; Adolf Jülicher, *An Introduction to the New Testament,* trans. Janet Penrose Ward, 7th ed. (London: Smith, Elder, 1931), 563, quoted in Schneemelcher, "General Introduction," 1:23–24.

32. For Athanasius's list of works from the Old and New Testaments, see "Letters of Athanasius with Two Ancient Chronicles of His Life," in *Nicene and Post-Nicene Fathers of the Christian Church,* ed. Philip Schaff and Henry Wace, 2nd ser., 14 vols. (Grand Rapids, Mich.: William B. Eerdmans, 1978), 4:495–552.

33. Christopher F. Evans, "The New Testament in the Making," in *The Cambridge History of the Bible,* 1:232–36. The manner of reading, of course, would be to read aloud since that was the customary way that ancient people read, their ears making sense of what

Even though we understand that the New Testament frames "a collection of writings which in the first place were read and loved in the churches and only then were combined in a canon,"[34] the process of producing the New Testament labeled some works as acceptable and others not. One famous example involved a man named Serapion, the bishop of Antioch from AD 191 to 210. His writings exist only in fragmentary form and quotes by others. In an important passage, Eusebius quotes from a letter of Serapion to church members in Rhossus, which was located about thirty miles to the north of Antioch on the Gulf of Issus, the easternmost reach of the Mediterranean Sea. In this letter, Serapion reversed an earlier opinion he had about the *Gospel of Peter.* We read that initially he had instructed that "the Gospel put forward by them [of Rhossus] in the name of Peter, . . . let it be read." Later, however, after reading the text, he concluded that those "who studied this very Gospel [are] . . . Docetae," who did not accept that Jesus had a human nature. He decided that "the most part indeed was in accordance with the true teaching of the Saviour, but that some things were added."[35] It is from a large fragment of this Gospel, found at Akhmîm in Upper Egypt in the winter of 1886, that we can see items added to the New Testament accounts. The most notable centers on Jesus' Crucifixion—"And they brought two malefactors, and crucified the Lord betwixt them. But he kept silence, as one feeling no pain."[36] In this light, the *Gospel of Peter* understood that Jesus was beyond suffering in his mortal life, a point that completely reversed what was written in the earlier Gospel narratives (see, for example, Matt. 16:21; Mark 14:33–34; Luke 24:26). Therefore, this text was to be rejected on this basis alone.

Though a few exceptions are known, in a general way Jewish leaders and savants had already been making these kinds of decisions about documents that were candidates for their Bible, our Old Testament, discarding

---

was before them (there were no breaks between words or sentences and no punctuation). See 1 Ne. 1:13: "He [Lehi] read, saying [the words aloud]."

34. Schneemelcher, "General Introduction," 1:36.

35. Eusebius, *Ecclesiastical History* 6.12.3–6; the translation is from Hugh Jackson Lawlor and John Ernest Leonard Oulton, *Eusebius, Bishop of Caesarea: The Ecclesiastical History and the Martyrs of Palestine,* 2 vols. (London: SPCK, 1954), 1:187; see the notes in 2:196–97; see also Quasten, *Patrology,* 1:283–84. For further on Serapion, see Eusebius, *Ecclesiastical History* 5.19.1, in Lawlor and Oulton, *Eusebius, Bishop of Caesarea,* 1:165; and Jerome, *Lives of Illustrious Men* 41, in *Nicene and Post-Nicene Fathers of the Christian Church,* 3:371–72.

36. Montague Rhodes James, *The Apocryphal New Testament: Being the Apocryphal Gospels, Acts, Epistles, and Apocalypses* (Oxford: Clarendon Press, 1969), 91.

both the records now found among the fourteen books of the Old Testament Apocrypha and the so-called pseudepigrapha. For them, this process came to an end in the second century AD. Their criteria were simple: Did the doctrines and history expressed in a text stand within the parameters set out in the old, trusted accounts, and were the connections to known ancient personalities credible in the light of the same old accounts? But that is only part of the story. For them, the accepted records "represented the communication of revealed truth from God to man."[37]

Standing at a midpoint in the growth of Christian scripture, Clement of Alexandria (c. AD 150–215) could write about the conjoining of the Hebrew scriptures and the newly assembled Christian documents under the umbrella of the church: "The ecclesiastical rule [κανών] is the concord and harmony of the law and the prophets in the covenant delivered at the coming of the Lord."[38] The "covenant" here, of course, was the nascent New Testament, the still-growing body of Christian scripture that was taking its place next to the "the law and the prophets."[39] About the time of Clement's greatest activity as a teacher at the school of Alexandria (c. AD 190–202), the Muratori Canon took shape in Rome. As we have already seen, the only documents omitted from our current New Testament were Hebrews, James, 1 and 2 Peter, and 3 John. A little more than a century later, the historian Eusebius presented the books accepted in his congregation in Caesarea. His list admitted most New Testament books except those he called "disputed"—the Epistles of James and Jude, 2 Peter, and 3 John. Eusebius also hinted at a reluctance among some church members to embrace the Apocalypse of John by writing, "if it really seem right" to include it with the other sacred books.[40]

Naturally, a number of works were set aside. The reasons differed. In the case of the Muratori Canon, the *Shepherd of Hermas* and the *Apocalypse of Peter*—likely not the version of the *Apocalypse of Peter* found in

37. Roland Kenneth Harrison, *Introduction to the Old Testament* (Grand Rapids, Mich.: William B. Eerdmans, 1969), 260; for the more complete story, see 260–88.

38. Clement of Alexandria, *The Stromata, or Miscellanies* 6:15, in *The Ante-Nicene Fathers: Translations of the Writings of the Fathers down to A.D. 325*, ed. Alexander Roberts, James Donaldson, and A. Cleveland Coxe, 10 vols., American ed. (Grand Rapids, Mich.: William B. Eerdmans, 1956), 2:509; for the Greek text, see Geoffrey W. H. Lampe, ed., *A Patristic Greek Lexicon* (London: Oxford University Press, 1961), 701, s.v. "κανών."

39. The Book of Mormon calls this bifurcation "the records of the prophets and of the twelve apostles of the Lamb" (1 Ne. 13:39).

40. Eusebius, *Ecclesiastical History* 3.25.1–3, in Lawlor and Oulton, *Eusebius, Bishop of Caesarea,* 1:86–87.

1945 among the Nag Hammadi texts in Upper Egypt[41]—were judged to be acceptable for private instruction and worship but not to be read in the churches. The works of the heresiarchs Arsinous, Valentinus, Miltiades, and Basilides "of Asia Minor" were to be avoided at all costs.[42] Eusebius painted a different picture of forbidden delicacies and added to the earlier list. Even though he knew that certain books had been flirting with the status of scripture, he called "not genuine" five works that Christians had been reading for more than a hundred years—the *Acts of Paul,* the *Shepherd of Hermas,* the *Apocalypse of Peter,* the Epistle of Barnabas, and "the so-called Teachings of the Apostles." He was warm toward the *Gospel of the Hebrews* in which especially Jewish Christians "take a special pleasure." This document survives only in fragmentary form and recorded the visit of the resurrected Jesus to his brother James, a report found nowhere else (see 1 Cor. 15:7).[43] He dismissed the "Gospels of Peter and Thomas and Matthias" as well as the "Acts of Andrew and John and the other apostles" as "the forgeries of heretics."[44]

From such decisions were born the rejected books, the New Testament Apocrypha (see the following section). As we have learned, the process of selecting the New Testament scriptural canon did not come down to a simple decision by one or a handful of prominent Christian leaders. It rather grew out of the collected wisdom and experience of church members over a period of many decades. By the time of Eusebius, in the early fourth century, he could write about "those writings which the tradition of the Church has deemed true and genuine and acknowledged" in contrast to "the others outside their number."[45] To be sure, not all the loose ends would be tied up for another fifty years, until Athanasius wrote his celebratory letter for Easter in AD 367 wherein he lists the works that are now in our New Testament.

---

41. James Brashler and Roger A. Bullard, "The Apocalypse of Peter (VII,3)," in *The Nag Hammadi Library in English,* ed. James M. Robinson, rev. ed. (San Francisco: HarperCollins, 1990), 372–78; S. Kent Brown and C. Wilfred Griggs, "The Apocalypse of Peter: Introduction and Translation," *BYU Studies* 15, no. 2 (Winter 1975): 131–45.

42. Schneemelcher, "General Introduction," 1:42–45.

43. Jerome, *Lives of Illustrious Men* 2, in *Nicene and Post-Nicene Fathers of the Christian Church,* 3:362; see Philip Vielhauer, "Jewish-Christian Gospels," in Hennecke and Schneemelcher, *New Testament Apocrypha,* 1:160, 165.

44. Eusebius, *Ecclesiastical History* 3.25.4–7, in Lawlor and Oulton, *Eusebius, Bishop of Caesarea,* 1:87; see Lawlor and Oulton, *Eusebius, Bishop of Caesarea,* 2:94–97.

45. Eusebius, *Ecclesiastical History* 3.25.6, in Lawlor and Oulton, *Eusebius, Bishop of Caesarea,* 1:87.

Apocryphal Texts in the New Testament: Quotations and Allusions

Quotations of and allusions to the Old Testament that occur inside the New Testament are well-known. However, not many readers of the New Testament are familiar with how the apocryphal and pseudepigraphal writings influenced its authors. Some of the texts that appear to have affected them—the list is substantial—include the extracanonical books of *Enoch,* Baruch, Ezra or Esdras, Maccabees, Tobit, Sirach, *Jubilees,* the Psalms of Solomon, the *Testament or Assumption of Moses,* the *Life of Adam and Eve,* the *Ascension of Isaiah,* and others.

The collection of texts known as the Apocrypha consists of ancient religious texts incorporated into Catholic Bibles and others but are generally not considered to be canonical by Protestants. They are also known as deuterocanonical ("second canon") texts and are made up of books such as 1 and 2 Esdras, 1 and 2 Maccabees, Judith, Tobit, the Wisdom of Solomon, Baruch, the Song of the Three Children, the Story of Susanna, and Bel and the Dragon.

The books reckoned among the Apocrypha relate to Old Testament, or occasionally, intertestamental characters and events. Many texts are categorized as "New Testament Apocrypha" because they were written by early Christians about Jesus and the Apostles. Over time, disagreements arose between Christian groups regarding the canonical status of some of these. Examples include the *Protoevangelium of James,* the *Gospel of Thomas,* the *Gospel of the Ebionites,* the *Apocalypse of Paul,* the *Apocalypse of Peter,* the *Shepherd of Hermas,* and many more. Because most apocryphal texts were written after the New Testament documents, or at the same time in a few cases, most commentators do not believe that they influenced the New Testament. We shall discuss each Apocryphal text separately (see the following section).[46]

Several passages in the New Testament cite texts that were apparently thought to be authoritative then but now are not considered canonical. For example, in Colossians 4:16, Paul encourages the Saints to read his letter to the Laodiceans. This letter was never part of the New Testament and no

46. For more on New Testament apocryphal texts, see Thomas A. Wayment, *The Text of the New Testament Apocrypha (100–400 CE)* (New York: Bloomsbury, 2013); Bart D. Ehrman, *Lost Scriptures: Books That Did Not Make It into the New Testament* (Oxford: Oxford University Press, 2003); Bart D. Ehrman and Zlatko Pleše, *The Apocryphal Gospels: Texts and Translations* (Oxford: Oxford University Press, 2011).

longer exists. Jude 1:14–15 explicitly cites a prophecy of Enoch found in the text of *1 Enoch,*[47] which is widely available today. 2 Timothy 3:8 mentions Jannes and Jambres, Egyptian magicians who challenged Moses, but those names are only found in apocryphal texts and do not appear anywhere in the Old Testament. We can discover several similar examples of interactions between apocryphal texts and the New Testament records.

Let us examine a few specific examples of known apocryphal or pseudepigraphal texts that are quoted or alluded to in the New Testament. We begin with the important book known as *1 Enoch,* as it appears in Jude and also 1 and 2 Peter. Jude 1:14–15 reads as follows: "And Enoch also, the seventh from Adam, prophesied of these, saying, Behold, the Lord cometh with ten thousands of his saints. To execute judgment upon all, and to convince all that are ungodly among them of all their ungodly deeds which they have ungodly committed, and of all their hard speeches which ungodly sinners have spoken against him." This verse is a direct quote from *1 Enoch* 1:9. Jude apparently had access to this text and considered it a prophecy of enough legitimacy and authority that he felt comfortable quoting it verbatim in his letter. Furthermore, the discussion of the fallen angels in Jude 1:6 is generally understood by scholars to be drawing on the account of the "Watchers" in *1 Enoch* 6–19.[48] Jude appears to see the fulfillment of Enoch's prophecy in his own time, applying the prophecies about the "saints" and the "ungodly" to the church members of his day.

This same pericope from *1 Enoch* appears to have influenced the author of 1 and 2 Peter. Second Peter 2:4 evidently alludes to the story of the rebellious angels and their imprisonment in a similar manner to Jude.[49] First Peter is arguably even more influenced by *1 Enoch* in ways that are distinct from those of Jude and 2 Peter. George Nickelsburg outlined several parallel themes between 1 Peter and *1 Enoch* 108. The following chart represents some of his findings.[50]

---

47. Also known as the *Book of Enoch* or the *Ethiopic Book of Enoch.*

48. George W. E. Nickelsburg, *1 Enoch 1: A Commentary on the Book of 1 Enoch, Chapters 1–36; 81–108,* Hermeneia—A Critical and Historical Commentary on the Bible (Minneapolis, Minn.: Fortress Press, 2001), 86; Richard J. Bauckham, *Jude, 2 Peter,* vol. 50 of Word Biblical Commentary (Waco, Tex.: Word Books, 1983), 50–53; Thomas Wolthuis, "Jude and Jewish Traditions," *Calvin Theological Journal* 221 (1987): 21–41; J. Daryl Charles, *Literary Strategy in the Epistle of Jude* (Scranton, Penn.: University of Scranton Press, 1993), 108–16, 145–49. The "Watchers" is what *1 Enoch* calls the rebellious angels.

49. The influence may be indirect in the case of 2 Peter, as some argue that this Epistle draws on Jude for these themes. See, for example, Peter H. Davids, *The Letters of 2 Peter and Jude,* The Pillar New Testament Commentary (Grand Rapids, Mich.: William B. Eerdmans, 2006).

50. Nickelsburg, *1 Enoch 1: A Commentary on the Book of 1 Enoch,* 560.

Theme	1 Enoch 108	1 Peter
do evil	2, 6, 10	3:12
seed will perish	3	1:23
spirits punished/imprisoned	3–6	3:19–20
Noah and family saved	(106:16, 18)	3:20
prophets, books, angels	6–7	1:10–12
love God/Christ, heaven	8, 10	1:8
disdain silver, gold	8	1:7, 18
not desire food/desire milk	8	2:2
breath that passes/flesh as grass	9	1:24
spirits/faith tested, found pure/praiseworthy	9	1:7
bless, blessing	9–10	3:9
reproach, insult, abuse	7, 10	3:16; 4:4, 16
blessing by contrast	10	2:9
summoned from darkness to light	11	2:9
exaltation	12	5:4, 6
righteous judgment	13	1:17; 2:23

Scholars have long recognized the apocalyptic features of the Gospel of Matthew, and some argue that the book is heavily influenced by the texts of *1 Enoch* and possibly *2 Enoch.*[51] Recently, research compared the similar worldview shared by these texts, concluding that the main areas of Enochic influence can be found both in the first four chapters of Matthew and in the "Son of Man" sayings. For example, Amy Richter argues for significant influence of *1 Enoch* on the genealogy and infancy narrative found in the first two chapters of Matthew, albeit observing that Matthew does not quote from that text directly. Regarding the infancy narrative, the elements in Matthew that she asserts are dependent on *1 Enoch* are (1) Matthew's genealogy that features four women from the Old Testament record, (2) Joseph's unwillingness to accept Mary's explanation about her pregnancy, (3) the presence of revelatory dreams that shape and move the story forward, and (4) notables who, guided by astral signs, travel far to worship the child of promise.[52] Richter notes the similarities between the story of Jesus' conception and birth and that of Noah at the end of *1 Enoch.* Her findings can be summarized in the following chart.[53]

51. Also known as *2 (Slavonic) Enoch* or the *Slavonic Book of Enoch.*

52. Amy E. Richter, *Enoch and the Gospel of Matthew* (Eugene, Oreg.: Wipf and Stock, 2012), 3.

53. Richter, *Enoch,* 138–39.

	Lamech (Noah's father)	Joseph
Husband's Suspicion	Lamech suspects that the child is the product of a union between his wife and an angel.	Joseph suspects that the (unborn) child is the product of Mary and another man.
Informant	Methuselah goes to Enoch, who resides with the angels and has taken on angelomorphic qualities.	An angel of the Lord comes to Joseph.
Reality	Noah is truly the son of Lamech and his wife, a human child.	The child is the product of Mary and Deity.
Child's Identity and Purpose	His name will be Noah ("from whom you will find rest" or "he who gladdens the earth"). He will be righteous and blameless and will participate in the cleansing of the earth.	The child's name will be Jesus, "for he will save his people from their sins"; he is also called Emmanuel, "God is with us."
Husband's Response	The child is called Noah.	Joseph does all that the angel says, including naming the baby Jesus.

Additionally, Richter compares several elements in Matthew's account of Christ's ministry with the "Watchers" narrative. She points to the Watchers' "illicit pedagogy" versus Jesus' "righteous pedagogy,"[54] the Watchers' illicit sexual relationships versus Jesus' rejection of illicit sexual relationships,[55] the Watchers' violence versus Jesus' peace,[56] the Watchers or demons bringing disease versus Jesus healing and casting out demons,[57] and the Watchers teaching idolatry versus Jesus teaching true worship.[58]

Several scholars have noticed the parallels between the "Son of Man" sayings in Matthew and the Son of Man figure in the Enochic Book of Parables or Similitudes (*1 En.* 37–71).[59] According to George Nickelsburg

---

54. Richter, *Enoch,* 196–200.

55. Richter, *Enoch,* 201–2.

56. Richter, *Enoch,* 204–6.

57. Richter, *Enoch,* 206–10.

58. Richter, *Enoch,* 210–11.

59. See, for example, David R. Catchpole, "The Poor on Earth and the Son of Man in Heaven: A Reappraisal of Matthew xxv. 31–46," *Bulletin of the John Rylands Library* 61, no. 2 (1979): 378–83; Johannes Theisohn, *Der auserwählte Richter: Untersuchungen zum traditionsgeschichtlichen Ort der Menschensohngestalt der Bilderreden des Äthiopischen Henoch,* SUNT 12 (Göttingen: Vandenhoeck und Ruprecht, 1975), 149–201; Heinz

and James VanderKam, some consensus now exists that the author of Matthew knew the parables.[60] Notably, Leslie Walck explores this relationship in her monograph *The Son of Man in the Parables of Enoch and in Matthew.* She finds the highest concentration of similarities between the two texts in the parable of the tares (Matt. 13:36–43) and the description of the Final Judgment (Matt. 25:31–46), which are unique to Matthew in the synoptic Gospels. Both of these sections in Matthew treat the topic of the eschatological judgment. A principal feature of the Son of Man in both Matthew and this section of *1 Enoch* is that he is an eschatological judge.[61] In both, Walck notices, the Son of Man is seated on a throne of glory in the company of angels to judge the world. Thereupon, he divides the people of the earth into the righteous and wicked.

In this connection, the description of the Son of Man's throne as "the throne of his glory" appears only in the parables of Enoch and Matthew.[62] According to Walck, Matthew's theme of judgment bears deeper similarities to the concepts in *1 Enoch* than the other synoptics do. Furthermore, the judgment scenes in *1 Enoch* and Matthew are distinct from other similar scenarios in other texts.[63]

It could be argued that, although Matthew appears to know the apocalyptic traditions found in the Enochic literature well, he seems to be taking attributes described for Enoch and demonstrating that Christ is the ideal or true bearer of those attributes and that Christ is ultimately able to fulfill or complete what Enoch could not. Richter explains that Jesus repairs the damage that the Watchers did to the world and also sets out the important role of women in Matthew's narrative:

> The child Jesus is shown by Matthew to be the fulfiller to the legacy of Enoch, the promised one who will redeem and save his people, establish

---

Eduard Tödt, *The Son of Man in the Synoptic Tradition,* trans. Dorothea M. Barton, The New Testament Library (Philadelphia: Westminster Press, 1965), 94, 223; David Winston Suter, *Tradition and Composition in the Parables of Enoch,* SBL Dissertation Series 47 (Ann Arbor, Mich.: SBL/Edwards Brothers, 1979), 25–29.

60. George W. E. Nickelsburg and James C. VanderKam, *1 Enoch 2: A Commentary on the Book of 1 Enoch Chapters 37–82,* Hermeneia—a Critical and Historical Commentary on the Bible (Minneapolis, Minn.: Fortress Press, 2012), 72.

61. Leslie W. Walck, *The Son of Man in the Parables of Enoch and in Matthew* (New York: T&T Clark, 2011), 249.

62. Walck, *Son of Man,* 243.

63. Walck, *Son of Man,* 248–49, compares judgment scenes in *1 Enoch,* Matthew, Daniel 7, Revelation 20, the *Testament of Abraham* 12–13, the *Apocalypse of Elijah,* the *Apocalypse of Zephaniah,* the Greek *Apocalypse of Ezra,* and the *Sibylline Oracles* 2.

> righteousness on the earth, and ultimately redress the effects of the watchers' transgression. Moreover, by viewing Matthew's genealogy and infancy narratives through the lens of the Enochic watchers' template, one gains a view into how, according to Matthew's Gospel, women play a particular role in the story of Jesus. That is, alongside Joseph, Herod, the magi and some other notable male characters in the narrative, women's participation in Matthew's Gospel is prominent. . . . It is often in the examples of women and Jesus' interaction with women in the Gospel of Matthew that Jesus overcomes the watchers' transgression described in *1 Enoch*.[64]

It should be noted that, recently, Andrei Orlov has argued for the influence of the book of *2 Enoch* on Matthew's temptation narrative, asserting that the story of the ascension of Enoch may have been a template for the story of Jesus' temptation by Satan.[65] Many scholars now consider *2 Enoch* to be earlier than, or perhaps contemporary with, the writing of Matthew. Orlov explains that in *2 Enoch*, the patriarch is elevated to heaven to become the servant of God, and the angels there worship him. This sequence, Orlov points out, is also similar to what happens to Adam in some of the Adam texts, such as the primary Adam books—the angels bow down to Adam to worship him. In a few of those accounts, however, Satan and some of his followers refuse to worship Adam, rebel, and are cast out of heaven. Orlov observes that this theme can also be found in *2 Enoch*.

Orlov argues that Matthew picks up on these themes in his narrative where, like Enoch and Adam, Jesus is taken up to an elevated place and is there tempted to give Satan the honor that Satan refused to grant to Adam. Throughout the temptation narrative, we see Satan serving as a *psychopomp*, "transporting angel," for Jesus, taking him to the temple in Jerusalem and then to the highest mountain. This function is fulfilled by angels in many apocalyptic texts. In *2 Enoch*, two angels take Enoch to heaven. Perhaps importantly, the text also relates that Melchizedek was taken to the Garden of Eden by the angel Gabriel. In Matthew, instead of an angel being Jesus' psychopomp, Satan also serves as the *angelus interpres*, "interpreting angel," showing Jesus various scenes in vision and explaining them to him.[66]

---

64. Richter, *Enoch*, 3–4.

65. Andrei A. Orlov, "The Veneration Motif in the Temptation Narrative of the Gospel of Matthew: Lessons from the Enochic Tradition," in *Enoch and the Synoptic Gospels: Reminiscences, Allusions, Intertextuality*, ed. Loren T. Stuckenbruck and Gabriele Boccaccini (Atlanta: Society of Biblical Literature, 2016), 337–62.

66. Orlov, "Veneration Motif," 351–52.

Orlov observes that, much as the angels do with the visionary person of the Enochic and other apocalyptic texts, Satan takes Jesus on a "gradual upward progression . . . from the desert to a pinnacle in the temple and finally to a sacred mountain."[67] The highest point of the sacred mountain is often seen as the location of the throne of God (see *1 En.* 25:3). It is at this highest point (on the "exceeding high mountain") that, in the apocalyptic traditions, we would normally see, as mentioned previously, the visionary man humbling himself before God and worshiping him. We would also expect to see the motifs of veneration—such as anointing, clothing in glory, enthronement, and worship by the angels—applied to the exalted human himself. In Matthew, however, instead of these honors being bestowed on Jesus, we see the situation inverted and Satan asking Jesus to worship him. Satan assigns to himself the attributes and duties of Deity as he attempts to imitate God. Orlov explains that, in the apocalyptic texts, the goal of the visionary is usually to reach the highest heaven, prostrate himself before the throne of God, and become identified with the divine figure on the throne. What we may be seeing in Matthew, he argues, is Satan trying to persuade Jesus to bow down before him so that Jesus would be identified with Satan instead of God.[68]

Beyond the influence of the Enochic literature, we meet many additional quotations of and allusions to other apocryphal and pseudepigraphal texts. Besides the allusions to Enochic texts, Jude refers to a text known as the *Assumption of Moses.* Jude 1:9 reads, "Yet Michael the archangel, when contending with the devil he disputed about the body of Moses, durst not bring against him a railing accusation, but said, The Lord rebuke thee." Although portions of the *Assumption of Moses* are extant today, this section quoted by Jude is lost. The only reason we know that Jude is quoting this text is because the early Christian authors Clement of Alexandria[69] and Origen[70] affirmed that this was the case.

In the Epistle to the Hebrews, a verse seemingly draws from the apocryphal *Martyrdom and Ascension of Isaiah.*[71] Hebrews 11:37 describes the dreadful fate of some of God's prophets: "They were stoned, they were sawn asunder, were tempted, were slain with the sword: they wandered

67. Orlov, "Veneration Motif," 354.

68. Orlov, "Veneration Motif," 355.

69. Clement of Alexandria, *Comments on the Epistle of Jude* 9.

70. Origen, *On First Principles* 3.2.1.

71. This text is also known by the name of what is actually the second half of the work, the *Ascension of Isaiah.*

about in sheepskins and goatskins; being destitute, afflicted, tormented." The line about a prophet being sawn asunder echoes a similar description in the *Martyrdom and Ascension of Isaiah* 5:2, 11, 14: "And when Isaiah was being sawn in sunder, Belchira stood up, accusing him, and all the false prophets stood up, laughing and rejoicing because of Isaiah. . . . And they seized and sawed in sunder Isaiah, the son of Amoz, with a wooden saw. . . . And when Isaiah was being sawn in sunder, he neither cried aloud nor wept, but his lips spake with the Holy Spirit until he was sawn in twain." Hebrews does not produce a direct quote and the connection is somewhat speculative. The legend about Isaiah being sawn asunder was evidently a popular one at the beginning of the Christian era, and it appears in both the Jerusalem (*Sanhedrin* 10:2)[72] and Babylonian (*Yebamot* 49:2) Talmuds. Of the known references to this event, the *Martyrdom and Ascension of Isaiah* is the most likely to have informed the author of Hebrews.

First Corinthians 2:9 preserves a passage that the Apostle Paul considered to be a quotation of an older text: "But as it is written, Eye hath not seen, nor ear heard, neither have entered into the heart of man, the things which God hath prepared for them that love him." The way this passage is introduced ("as it is written") makes it look as if Paul is quoting a known authoritative text of scripture. However, there is no obvious source for this line. Something of a consensus exists that Paul may be citing a version of Isaiah 64:4 ("Men have not heard, nor perceived by the ear, neither hath the eye seen, O God, beside thee, what he hath prepared for him that waiteth for him"). The early Christian Fathers were not so sure and speculated widely on where the line came from, including within several apocryphal texts. Origen, Zacharias of Chrysopolis, and others believed that the words were derived from an apocryphal book, most likely the *Apocalypse of Elias*.[73] It seems more likely, however, that the passage is a loose rendering, or a different version, of Isaiah 64:4.

A similar case arises in Ephesians 5:14, which is also set up as an authoritative quotation: "Wherefore he saith, Awake thou that sleepest, and arise from the dead, and Christ shall give thee light." The "he" of the passage likely refers to God, here speaking through the scriptures. The closest Old

72. M. A. Knibb, "Isaiah, Martyrdom and Ascension of," in *The Old Testament Pseudepigrapha*, ed. James A. Charlesworth, 2 vols. (Garden City, N.Y.: Doubleday, 1983, 1985), 2:151.

73. Joseph Verheyden, "Origen on the Origin of 1 Cor 2,9," in *The Corinthian Correspondence*, ed. Reimund Bieringer (Leuven: Peeters, 1996), 504. See also Albrecht Oepke and Rudolf Meyer, "κρύπτω," *TDNT*, 3:988–89.

Testament verse is Isaiah 60:1, "Arise, shine; for thy light is come, and the glory of the Lord is risen upon thee." The ideas expressed in the two passages are similar, but the wording is quite different. Epiphanius said the source was the *Apocalypse of Elias,* and Euthalius believed it was a Jeremiah apocryphon.[74] It is difficult to establish the source, but it does appear to be ancient Christian poetry that Paul adopted in his text.

John 7:38 also comes into play: "He that believeth on me, as the scripture hath said, out of his belly shall flow rivers of living water." No passage in the Old Testament says this. However, the passage cannot be tied to any specific apocryphal text. It is possible that it stems from an alternate version of some canonical document, but it is not clear which text is a possible candidate.

Second Timothy 3:8 mentions a couple of characters whose names appear nowhere in the canonical scriptures: "Now as Jannes and Jambres withstood Moses, so do these also resist the truth." The names of these Egyptian magicians occur only in apocryphal tradition. The earliest known reference occurs in the Dead Sea Scrolls' *Damascus Document*: "For in times past Moses and Aaron stood in the power of the Prince of Lights and Belial raised up Yannes and his brother in his cunning when seeking to do evil to Israel the first time."[75]

These personalities are mentioned in various apocryphal texts, and Origen claims that 2 Timothy is quoting from the book of *Jannes and Jambre.*[76] It is reasonable to conclude that the author is making use of apocryphal traditions here.

New Testament Apocrypha

The aggregate of texts known in modern times as the "New Testament Apocrypha" was not gathered anciently into a recognizable collection. These texts are essentially derivative documents or imitation documents. That is, they model themselves largely on the New Testament books and include gospels, acts, epistles, and revelations. Often, they repeat events or important words that we find in the New Testament, but with a twist, evidently intending to replace or improve or cast doubt on the earlier New Testament version. Often, they attempt to fill in blank spots where we lack information, such as Jesus' childhood and his post-Resurrection ministry.

---

74. Oepke and Meyer, *TDNT,* 3:990.

75. Michael O. Wise, Martin G. Abegg Jr., and Edward M. Cook, *The Dead Sea Scrolls: A New Translation* (New York: HarperCollins, 1996), 56.

76. Oepke and Meyer, *TDNT,* 3:990.

Early Christians rejected these documents as authentic records of Jesus and the Apostles because, when set next to the texts that became accepted, these records appeared blemished or deficient. But this does not mean that they are without any value when reconstructing the world of the New Testament and what followed.

Many of these accounts survive by name only, mentioned scornfully in the written works of early church authors. The fact that only a limited number of these records have been discovered points to the energy with which authorities in the early church pursued and expunged them. Those texts that unexpectedly endured were found in out-of-the-way places, distant from the halls of power within the Roman Empire. They became linked with Christian interests following the Edict of Milan, agreed to by Constantine and Licinius, that introduced Roman tolerance for all religions in AD 313.

Upper Egypt, far from the immediate reach of the bishop of Alexandria and other church authorities, cradled some of these texts, which were discovered in a single ceramic jar in 1945 near the river town of Nag Hammadi. Of the fifty-two treatises preserved in thirteen books (some are duplicate copies), twenty exhibit clear ties to the New Testament. Of that number, only the *Gospel of Thomas* has risen in scholarly deliberations. Many scholars believe its roots go back to the time of the composition of the New Testament Gospels (c. AD 70–95) and therefore sheds light on the attempts to create a record of Jesus' mortal and post-mortal ministries.[77]

As a group, the New Testament apocryphal accounts preserve an astonishing diversity of doctrine and historical understanding. As we might expect, the Gospels dominate in numbers because of the interest in the Savior. These apocryphal texts fill in blank spots. For instance, we find accounts of Jesus' childhood—called infancy gospels—wherein, when angry with a playmate, Jesus turned the other child into an animal or bird, or crippled him, obliging the child's parents to plead with Mary and Joseph that they control their son or that the child be restored.[78] In another account, the five-year-old Jesus formed pools of water in a brook. When a playmate undid the pools so that the brook ran freely, Jesus was said to curse the boy

77. For a discussion and English translation of the *Gospel of Thomas*, see Helmut Koester, "The Gospel of Thomas (II,2)," trans. Thomas O. Lambdin, in Robinson, *Nag Hammadi Library*, 124–38.

78. The *Infancy Gospels* are collected in O. Cullmann, "Infancy Gospels," trans. A. J. B. Higgins, in Hennecke and Schneemelcher, *New Testament Apocrypha*, 1:363–417; and in James, *Apocryphal New Testament*, 38–90.

and to wither him as a diseased tree. The parents of the boy brought him to Joseph and rancorously accused him of lacking control over the child Jesus.[79] While such an account seems strange, one apparent motivation for rehearsing this kind of story is to show that Jesus was fully a part of this world, not some otherworldly personality, thus affirming the created order.

Other records claim to open windows onto Jesus' post-mortal ministering, usually emphasizing the secrets of salvation that he imparted to one or another of his disciples, with a complementary lack of stress on Jesus' atoning suffering and death. The disciple to whom the Risen Savior passed his special teaching therefore became the custodian of this doctrine. An example of such a text is the *First Apocalypse of James* from Codex V of the Nag Hammadi Library. Here the resurrected Savior interacted with his brother James—called in Christian literature "the brother of the Lord" or "the Just"—and revealed the secrets of eternity. In this document, Jesus' death and Resurrection were reduced to the expression "The Lord [Jesus] . . . fulfilled what was fitting," a clear shift of focus away from his Atonement (V.3.30.12–13).[80] Although important reasons exist for distrusting the historical accuracy of these "passion gospels," as M. R. James calls them,[81] a person cannot escape the overall impression that they reaffirm the strength and significance of Jesus' post-mortal ministry, as already disclosed in the Gospels and the book of Acts (see, for example, John 20:11–21:23; Acts 1:1–11).[82]

The apocryphal acts that are tied to the name of certain Apostles raise similar concerns about doctrine and historical reliability. The *Acts of John the Apostle* will illustrate. In one scene, John speaks of touching the Savior: "Sometimes when I would lay hold on [Jesus], I met with a material and solid body, and at other times, again, when I felt him, the substance was immaterial and as if it existed not at all" (*Acts of John* 93). This report clearly touches on the view that during Jesus' mortal ministry, his body was immaterial or otherworldly. In contrast, one tradition embedded in the *Acts of John* ties to the spot on the Mount of Olives where Jesus evidently taught his disciples about the fall of Jerusalem and the end of the world (see Matt. 24; Mark 13;

79. *Gospel of Thomas* 2.1–3.3, in James, *Apocryphal New Testament,* 49–50; and Cullmann, "Infancy Gospels," 1:392–93.

80. For an English translation of the *First Apocalypse of James,* see William R. Schoedel, "The (First) Apocalypse of James (V,3)," ed. Douglas M. Parrott, in Robinson, *Nag Hammadi Library,* 260–68.

81. James, *Apocryphal New Testament,* 90–165.

82. This was one of Nibley's conclusions in his *When the Lights Went Out,* 33–54.

Luke 21) as well as where he ascended into heaven (see Acts 1:9–12). The tradition says that, during the Crucifixion, John fled to "the cave"—obviously a well-known location—where the spiritual Christ appeared to him to offer sacred teaching, thus conferring a measure of holiness on the place (*Acts of John* 97).[83]

Other books of acts offer interesting tidbits. For example, the famous Hymn of the Pearl, embedded in the *Acts of Thomas the Apostle,* sketches the story of a heavenly son who descended into the world and was caught by its allures, in the process losing his memory of his celestial origins. He was then rescued by an awakening, saving word sent from above, which led him back to his heavenly parents and to his earlier glory (see *Acts of Thomas* 108–13).[84]

On balance, the apocryphal acts meet the standard received by Joseph Smith when he sought out the Lord to learn whether to translate the books forming the Old Testament Apocrypha that were bound in his Bible: "There are many things contained therein that are true, and it is mostly translated correctly; There are many things contained therein that are not true, which are interpolations by the hands of men" (D&C 91:1–2).

Of the few apocryphal Epistles, only the *Epistle to the Laodiceans* has caught the attention of scholars as a possibly authentic letter from Paul. Within its brief lines there is little of real interest.[85] We know such a letter existed because it is mentioned in Paul's Epistle to the Colossians in 4:16. But most students doubt that the sixth-century copy of this short letter preserves the one that Paul pointed to in his Colossian correspondence.[86]

---

83. For the *Acts of John,* see James, *Apocryphal New Testament,* 228–70; and K. Shäferdiek, "The Acts of John," trans. G. C. Stead, in Hennecke and Schneemelcher, *New Testament Apocrypha,* 2:188–259. On the traditions associated with the cave, see John Wilkinson, *Jerusalem as Jesus Knew It: Archaeology as Evidence* (London: Thames and Hudson, 1978), 119–22, 173–75.

84. Translations of the *Acts of Thomas* appear in James, *Apocryphal New Testament,* 364–438; The Hymn of the Pearl is on 411–15; and G. Bornkamm, "The Acts of Thomas," trans. R. McL. Wilson, in Hennecke and Schneemelcher, *New Testament Apocrypha,* 2:425–531; The Hymn of the Pearl is on 498–504. For LDS assessments, see Hugh Nibley, *The Message of the Joseph Smith Papyri: An Egyptian Endowment* (Salt Lake City: Deseret Book, 1975), 267–72; and John W. Welch and James V. Garrison, "The 'Hymn of the Pearl': An Ancient Counterpart to 'O My Father,'" *BYU Studies* 36, no. 1 (1996–97): 127–38.

85. James, *The Apocryphal New Testament,* 478, calls this short letter "wholly uninteresting."

86. For an assessment of the *Epistle to the Laodiceans,* see Charles P. Anderson, "Laodiceans, Epistle to the," in *The Anchor Bible Dictionary,* ed. David Noel Freedman, 6 vols. (New York: Doubleday, 1992), 4:231–33.

As the gifts of the Spirit receded into memory, a natural interest grew up among early Christians in the revelatory visions of past apostles and seers. Many visionary accounts were tied to the Old Testament, only a few to the New. Perhaps the most important of the apocryphal apocalypses is the *Apocalypse of Peter,* dated to the second century AD and known from a number of diverse sources, which underscores its broad Christian appeal.[87] Much of this text has to do with the next life, including the punishments that come upon the wicked. When a person reviews the account, it becomes clear that Christian art, which portrays the Judgment and the consequent punishments handed out therein, took inspiration from this kind of text, if not from the apocalypse itself. Heaven is described as "a very great region outside this world exceeding bright with light, and the air of that place illuminated with the beams of the sun, and the earth of itself flowering with blossoms that fade not" (*Apoc. of Peter* 15). In contrast, in a "very squalid . . . place of punishment" were to be seen "some . . . hanging by their tongues; and these were they that blasphemed the way of righteousness, and under them was laid fire flaming and tormenting them" (*Apoc. of Peter* 21–22).[88]

Aside from occasional unusual elements in the apocryphal New Testament documents, some students find little to interest them. The apocryphal accounts tend to find their inspiration from earlier New Testament books, imitating and adjusting them. While some of what we find in the apocryphal acts may go back to real historical events, caution arises because of untrustworthy aspects.[89] Again, the words of the Lord to Joseph Smith serve as a measure: "There are many things contained therein that are true, and it is mostly translated correctly; There are many things contained therein that are not true, which are interpolations by the hands of men" (D&C 91:1–2).

87. This text is not the same as the document of the same name found among the Nag Hammadi texts. See Brown and Griggs, "Apocalypse of Peter," 131–45.

88. For a translation of the *Apocalypse of Peter,* consult James, *Apocryphal New Testament,* 505–24. The quotations appear on 508–9. A discussion and translation of the Ethiopic version appear in Ch. Maurer, "Apocalypse of Peter," trans. H. Duensing, in Hennecke and Schneemelcher, *New Testament Apocrypha,* 2:663–83.

89. For a rather positive assessment of elements in the apocryphal books of acts, see S. Kent Brown, "Whither the Early Church?," in *Studies in Scripture: Volume Six, Acts to Revelation,* ed. Robert L. Millet (Salt Lake City: Deseret Book, 1987), 276–84; and S. Kent Brown, "Whither the Early Church?," *Ensign* 18 (October 1988): 6–10.

For Further Reading

Griggs, C. Wilfred, ed. *Apocryphal Writings and the Latter-day Saints.* Religious Studies Monograph Series no. 13. Provo, Utah: BYU Religious Studies Center, 1986.

James, Montague Rhodes. *The Apocryphal New Testament: Being the Apocryphal Gospels, Acts, Epistles, and Apocalypses.* Oxford: Clarendon Press, 1924.

Hennecke, Edgar, and Wilhelm Schneemelcher, eds. *New Testament Apocrypha.* 2 vols. Philadelphia: Westminster Press, 1963.

Nibley, Hugh. *When the Lights Went Out: Three Studies on the Ancient Apostasy.* Salt Lake City: Deseret Book, 1970.

Wayment, Thomas A. *The Text of the New Testament Apocrypha (100–400 CE).* New York: Bloomsbury, 2013.

Ehrman, Bart D. *Lost Scriptures: Books That Did Not Make It into the New Testament.* Oxford: Oxford University Press, 2003.

Ehrman, Bart D., and Zlatko Pleše. *The Apocryphal Gospels: Texts and Translations.* Oxford: Oxford University Press, 2011.

Versions

A Bible Fit for a King

How We Got the King James Version

Andrew C. Skinner

The English version of the Bible has been called "God's Bestseller."[1] According to Joseph Fielding Smith, President of The Church of Jesus Christ of Latter-day Saints, it "has had a greater influence on the world for good than any other book ever published."[2] It served as the foundation for the Restoration of the gospel of Jesus Christ in Joseph Smith's day, preparing the way for the dispensation of the fulness of times of which it prophesied (Eph. 1:10).

The publication of the King James Version in 1611 was the culmination of the process of translating the Bible into English, which began around the seventh century AD, when Christianity established itself in the British Isles with the arrival of missionaries in AD 597 sent by Pope Gregory I the Great (c. 540–604).[3] Generally speaking, the translation process started with interlinear English glosses of the Latin text of the Vulgate, the Bible the missionaries knew. Soon there were separate translations of specific passages in the biblical text, followed by translations of entire biblical books into the English of the period.

Best-known examples of early attempts to translate the Bible include English metrical renditions of parts of the Old and New Testaments done by a seventh-century monk named Caedmon (died c. 678). He turned certain biblical passages into Old English poems for people to memorize and sing. The venerable monk Bede (died c. 735), the "father of English history," is said to have translated portions of scripture into Old English. According to tradition, he was dictating an English version of John's Gospel as he lay

1. Note the title of Brian Moynahan, *God's Bestseller* (New York: St. Martin's Press, 2002).

2. Joseph Fielding Smith, *Doctrines of Salvation*, ed. Bruce R. McConkie, 3 vols. (Salt Lake City: Bookcraft, 1956), 3:184.

3. Bruce M. Metzger, *The Bible in Translation* (Grand Rapids, Mich.: Baker Academic, 2001), 55.

dying, though "no trace of this translation exists."[4] Other names involved in efforts to translate the Bible into English include Alcuin (735–804) and Alfred the Great (849–901).

John Wycliffe

Credit for producing the first whole Bible in English is usually given to Oxford don John Wycliffe (died 1384), though it is not clear how much of the translation Wycliffe did himself. The completed translation of both the Old and New Testaments was the work of various scholars, including Nicholas of Hereford and John Purvey. Different iterations appeared between 1382 and 1395.

However, there is little doubt that John Wycliffe initiated the project. He first began work on the New Testament and oversaw the production of the first draft of the whole because of its importance to him personally. By 1372, Wycliffe had become England's leading theologian and reformer. He believed the only true foundation for Christians was the Bible. The pope was not the voice of God on earth; the Bible was. Furthermore, "England belongs to no pope. The pope is but a man, subject to sin; but Christ is the Lord of lords, and this kingdom is held directly and solely of Christ alone."[5] A revival of biblical Christianity was desperately needed; a reformation of the church was required. The only way for that to happen was for the English people to possess the word of God in their own language. As Wycliffe said, "It helpeth Christian men to study the Gospel in that tongue in which they know best Christ's sentence."[6]

For Wycliffe, scriptural infallibility replaced papal infallibility; scripture alone was the sole basis for deciding doctrine and morals for every Christian. This conviction affected both Christianity and the history of the English Bible in monumental ways. It was the genesis for one of Protestantism's three

---

4. Philip W. Comfort, *Essential Guide to Bible Versions* (Wheaton, Ill.: Tyndale House, 2000), 38; Paul D. Wegner, *The Journey from Texts to Translations* (Grand Rapids, Mich.: Baker Academic, 2000), 276.

5. From Wycliffe's *Civil Dominion*, quoted in W. Kenneth Connolly, *The Indestructible Book* (Grand Rapids, Mich.: Baker Books, 1996), 73, https://lollardsociety.org/pdfs/Wyclif_de_Civili_Dominio_vol1.pdf.

6. Quoted in Wegner, *Journey from Texts to Translations*, 282; Henry Hargreaves, "The Wycliffite Versions," in *The Cambridge History of the Bible*, ed. G. W. H. Lampe, 3 vols. (Cambridge, Eng.: Cambridge University Press, 1963–70), 2:392; Henry Wheeler Robinson, *The Bible in its Ancient and English Versions* (Westport, Conn.: Greenwood Press, 1970), 138.

fundamental tenets: *sola scriptura,* "by scripture alone." However, efforts by like-minded scholars to translate the Bible into English in the fifteenth, sixteenth, and seventeenth centuries met with bitter opposition from Roman Catholic Church leaders. They inveighed against not just the notion of an English Bible but also the idea of common people having the word of God in their own hands. Henry Knighton, a Catholic writer of the time and a constant opponent of Wycliffe, summed up the church's view in telling fashion and provided an interesting window into the status of the laity in the minds of the church hierarchy.

> Christ gave his Gospel to the clergy and learned of the Church that they might give it to the laity and more infirm persons. . . . But this Master John Wyclif translated the Gospel from the Latin into the *Anglican* language not the *angelican.* And Wyclif, by thus translating the Bible made it the property of the masses and common to all and more open to the laity and even to women who were able to read. . . . And so the Gospel pearl is thrown before swine and trodden underfoot, . . . and this precious gem of the clergy has been turned into the sport of the laity, so that what used to be the highest gift of the clergy and the learned members of the Church has become common to the laity.[7]

Wycliffe remained undeterred in his pursuits and issued a clarion declaration for successors engaged in the work of translating the Bible into English.

> Christ and his Apostles taught the people in the language best known to them. It is certain that the truth of the Christian faith becomes more evident the more the faith itself is known. Therefore, the doctrine should not only be in Latin but in the common tongue, and as the faith of the Church is contained in the Scriptures, the more these are known in a true sense the better. The laity ought to understand the faith, and as the doctrines of our faith are in the Scriptures, believers should have the Scriptures in a language familiar to the people, and to this end indeed did the Holy Spirit endue them with the knowledge of all tongues. If it is heresy to read the Bible, then the Holy Ghost himself is condemned who gave in tongues to the Apostles of Christ to speak the Word of God in all languages that were ordained of God under heaven. If Christ was so merciful as to send the Holy Ghost to the heathen men to make them partakers of his blessed word, why should it be taken from us in this land that be Christian men?[8]

---

7. Quoted in David Fountain, *John Wycliffe: The Dawn of the Reformation* (Southampton, Eng.: Mayflower Christian Books, 1984), 45.

8. Quoted in Fountain, *Wycliffe: The Dawn of the Reformation,* 47.

William Tyndale

A little more than a century passed between the death of John Wycliffe (died 1384) and the coming of the man the world would recognize as the "Father of the English Bible"—William Tyndale (c. 1490–1536). Judging by any measure, Tyndale brought to English speakers the noblest of gifts—a new and improved version of the Bible in their own language—first the New Testament and then the Old. By the time Tyndale turned his considerable intellectual prowess to this endeavor, Martin Luther and Desiderius Erasmus were already working to reform of Roman Catholicism and would prepare new Bible translations of their own in German and Greek, respectively. Gutenberg had printed his now-famous forty-two-line Bible, inaugurated a new information age, and passed off the world's stage. Not least, individuals living in and out of England had become well acquainted with Wycliffe's first English Bible and had taken up the cause to make the scriptures the center of Christian theology.

Even the threat of church punishment—languishing in a dank prison cell or being consumed by agonizing fires at the stake—could not intimidate or dissuade these determined souls from studying the word of God directly in their own language. A set of laws called the Constitutions of Oxford of 1407–9 forbade the owning or making of English translations of the Bible, and yet "men and women were still being burned alive for the possession of such 'Lollard' material well over a hundred years later."[9] However, an increasingly greater challenge for English Bible readers was navigating the difficult and stilted translation left by Wycliffe and his collaborators.

Enter Master Tyndale. His resolve and sacrifice were exceeded only by his linguistic abilities. His work rendered the biblical text into beautiful contemporary English that was later taken by translators and made the direct expression of the King James Version published a little more than one hundred years (1611) after Tyndale's birth. "Through that King James Bible, which dominated the English-speaking world for 350 years, Tyndale has reached more people than Shakespeare."[10] It seems no exaggeration to say that the Restoration of the gospel of Jesus Christ is, in part, a product of William Tyndale and that God raised him up at the exact moment in history when he was needed.

---

9. David Daniell, "William Tyndale, the English Bible, and the English Language," in *The Bible as Book: The Reformation,* ed. Orlaith O'Sullivan (London: British Library; London: Oak Knoll Press, 2000), 39.

10. Daniell, "William Tyndale, the English Bible, and the English Language," 39.

Early Preparation

William Tyndale was born sometime between 1490 and 1495 to an affluent farming family in Gloucestershire, England. He went off to Oxford University at age twelve, and by 1515 (also the year of his ordination), he completed a master of arts degree. He became fluent in eight languages: English, German, French, Spanish, Italian, Greek, Hebrew, and Latin.[11] The sixteenth-century historian John Foxe described him as a thoroughgoing product of Oxford and one who was *addicted* to the scriptures! "[Tyndale was] brought up from a child in the University of Oxford, where he, by long continuance, increased as well in the knowledge of tongues, and other liberal arts, as especially in the knowledge of the Scriptures, whereunto his mind was singularly addicted; insomuch that he, lying then in Magdalen hall, read privily to certain students and fellows of Magdalen college some parcel of divinity; instructing them in the knowledge and truth of the Scriptures."[12]

After teaching at Oxford for a time, he moved to Cambridge, where he became "further ripened in the knowledge of God's Word."[13] There he also came in contact with new theological ideas promoted by scholars who supported church reform, including Miles Coverdale, John Frith, and Thomas Bilney. Luther's writings were, as we might say, served up as sumptuous fare for their theological feasts.[14] Moreover, not only was Cambridge at that time "a centre of aggressive Lutheranism," but it seems just before Tyndale was there, "the Lady Margaret's Professor of Divinity had been Erasmus himself, teaching Greek to, as he admitted, bored undergraduates."[15] During this time, Tyndale must have had access to the *Ovum Instrumentum* of 1516, the New Testament in the original Greek translated by Erasmus. In Gloucestershire, he began tutoring the children of a notable nobleman named Sir John Walsh. Fearlessly, Tyndale entered into spirited

11. Daniell, "William Tyndale, the English Bible, and the English Language," 41.

12. John Foxe, *Foxe's Book of Martyrs,* ed. W. Grinton Berry (New York: Eaton and Mains, 1907), 135.

13. Foxe, *Foxe's Book of Martyrs,* 136.

14. Ray L. Huntington and W. Jeffrey Marsh, "Revisiting William Tyndale, Father of the English Bible," *Religious Educator* 12, no. 2 (2011): 13–33; W. Kenneth Connolly, *The Indestructible Book: The Bible, Its Translators, and Their Sacrifices* (Grand Rapids, Mich.: Baker Books, 1996), 140–44.

15. David Daniell, "Introduction," in William Tyndale, trans., *The New Testament: A Facsimile of the 1526 Edition* (London: British Library; Peabody, Mass.: Hendrickson Publishers, 2008), [xi].

discussions on theology with various clergy and visitors to Little Sodbury Manor, which often took place around the Walshes' dinner table.

It is at this juncture we see Tyndale's views on the importance of an English Bible come into clearer focus. And we also see opponents attempt to thwart Tyndale. On one occasion, Tyndale had his now-famous encounter with the "learned man" who stated the church-supported view that people were better off without God's law found in scripture than without the pope's. "Master Tyndall hearing that, answered him, I defy the Pope and all his laws, and said, if God spare my life ere many years, I will cause a boy that driveth the plough, shall know more of scripture than thou dost."[16]

The die was cast. Tyndale possessed a conviction that he must provide for the plowboy's education by producing a reliable, readable edition of the Bible in English. For him, individuals in England must have access to the scriptures in order to withstand errors promulgated by church leaders. The laity deserved better than always having to be at the mercy of priests who tried to discredit teachings that Tyndale was convinced were true. He said, "I had perceived by experience how that it was impossible to establish the lay people in any truth, except that the scripture were plainly laid before their eyes in their mother tongue, that they might see the process, order and the meaning of the text."[17] Furthermore, Tyndale argued, "If [English] Christians possessed the Holy Scriptures in their own tongue, they could of themselves withstand these attacks. Without the Bible it is impossible to establish the people in truth. . . . Christians must read the New Testament [for themselves] in their own tongue."[18]

In 1524, with the help of Humphrey Monmouth, a wealthy cloth merchant, Tyndale left England—never to see it again—and moved to Hamburg, Germany. He believed he was on God's errand. He made his way to Wittenberg, where Luther had posted his Ninety-Five Theses, and got caught up in the discussion of Luther's doctrine of justification by faith alone. He met fellow Englishman William Roye, a linguist who assisted Tyndale in finishing his translation of the Greek New Testament into English in August 1525. They went to Cologne and found a printer, Peter Quentell. Why they chose to print in Cologne remains unclear. It was a very conservative center of

16. Daniell, "Introduction," [xii]; Foxe, *Book of Martyrs,* 139.

17. Quoted in Harold L. Phillips, *Translators and Translations* (Anderson, Ind.: Warner Press, 1958), 22, English modernized.

18. Quoted in M. Bayly, *The Story of Our English Bible and What It Cost* (London: James Nisbet, 1880), 90.

Catholicism. Unfortunately, Roye was an indiscrete braggart, especially after he had imbibed a few beers. Perhaps he was the one responsible for tipping off Johannes Cochlaeus about Tyndale's secret project. Cochlaeus was an enemy of reformation and alerted authorities, who shut down the printing operation. But Tyndale gathered up what had been done, fled to Worms in Germany, and finally got the complete New Testament printed by Peter Schoeffer.[19]

Once printed, several thousand copies of the new Bible were smuggled into England in barrels of flour and bolts of cloth. Humphrey Monmouth used his cloth operation to secretly distribute the copies. Tyndale's New Testament became an immediate bestseller. People were hungry for the word of God. Between 1525 and 1528, eighteen thousand copies were sold, which was no small feat. Sponsoring merchants priced each copy at half a crown, or two-and-one-half shillings. To provide perspective, it would have cost a brick mason five days' wages to purchase a Tyndale New Testament—the equivalent of at least $500 in today's economy![20] This may help modern readers appreciate what it cost our predecessors to possess the word of God, a treasure we may sometimes take for granted.

Tyndale's Bibles fomented national unrest. The bishop of London was enraged. King Henry VIII, though not yet a Protestant, was also angry. It should be remembered that this was eight years before Henry broke away from the Catholic Church over the issue of divorcing his first wife, Katherine. Johannes Cochlaeus, who had prevented the printing of Tyndale's New Testament in Cologne, expressed his intense opposition to and utter disdain for the whole notion of scripture being translated into the vernacular: "The New Testament translated into the vulgar tongue is in truth, the food of death, the fuel of sin, the veil of malice, the pretext of false liberty, the protection of disobedience, the corruption of discipline, the depravity of morals, the termination of Concord, the death of honesty, the well-spring of vices, the disease of virtues, the instigation of rebellion, the milk of pride, the nourishment of contempt, the death of peace, the destruction of charity, the enemy of unity, the murderer of truth."[21] Here was a man who knew how to hurl an insult!

19. John Stevens Kerr, *Ancient Texts Alive Today: The Story of the English Bible* (New York: ABS, 1999), 51–53.

20. Kerr, *Ancient Texts Alive Today,* 53.

21. Quoted in Kerr, *Ancient Texts Alive Today,* 54.

King Henry condemned Tyndale's New Testament and ordered copies to be burned publicly. He also began a policy of persecuting those found guilty of distributing or possessing copies. For his part, Bishop Tunstall authorized a certain merchant who was trading in Antwerp to act as a secret agent of the crown by using royal funds to buy up every copy he could of the new scripture and send them back to London for burning. What Tunstall didn't know is that the merchant was a sincere friend of Tyndale and thus happily began paying four times the amount it had cost to produce each Tyndale New Testament. "So, for every Bible Tunstall burned, the king paid for three more to be added to Tyndale's arsenal."[22]

A price was now put on Tyndale's head. Agents of the crown (bounty hunters really) traveled all over the Continent, sometimes in clever disguise, to track down their criminal. Some of them were bumbling and inept but still treacherous. They could be found bumping into each other but never quite managed to bump into Tyndale; he was spared. Tyndale next went to Marburg, Germany (1527–1531), and began working on the Old Testament—translating each word from the original Hebrew text. The Pentateuch (the first five books of Moses) appeared in 1530.[23]

In 1531, Tyndale moved to Antwerp. Controversies over his New Testament translation and subsequent revisions of it, as well as worries over being caught by authorities before his work was completed, distracted him from finishing the translation of the whole Old Testament. However, he was able to add Joshua through 2 Chronicles to the tally of completed books.[24] The rest of the Old Testament would be finished by John Rogers—friend, colleague, and confidante of Tyndale. But Tyndale never lived to see the whole of it printed.

By now, Tyndale was a fugitive, and he knew it. This kind of pressure and its attendant difficulties are known by many men and women. Unjust, unfair treatment in the face of attempting to follow God's promptings is often the worst kind of contradiction. It can make or break individuals. But Tyndale did not flinch; he did not become embittered or retreat from his own stated conviction that "scripture derives its authority from him who sent it."[25]

---

22. Connolly, *Indestructible Book,* 142.
23. Connolly, *Indestructible Book,* 142–44.
24. Kerr, *Ancient Texts Alive Today,* 56.
25. Connolly, *Indestructible Book,* 144.

It was in Antwerp that Tyndale was betrayed and caught by authorities. A secret agent of the English crown Henry Phillips offered to take Tyndale to dinner one night and lured him into taking a walk through town. As they entered an alley, upon a prearranged signal, two captors grabbed Tyndale and quietly whisked him off to a cold, damp dungeon in Vilvoorde fortress near Brussels. There he was imprisoned for almost a year and a half. Though friends and supporters petitioned authorities for his release (even King Henry was asked), Tyndale was given no reprieve. One of these petitioners Thomas Poyntz was himself arrested—guilty by association.[26]

Conditions in the Vilvoorde dungeon were miserable, as the only surviving letter from Tyndale during this period attests:

> I beg your Lordship and that by the Lord Jesus, that if I am to remain here through the winter, you will request the commissary to have the kindness to send me from the goods of mine which he has, a warmer cap: for I suffer greatly from cold in the head, and am afflicted by a perpetual catarrh [a cold] which is much increased in this cell. . . . But most of all I beg you clemency to be urgent with the commissary that he will kindly permit me to have the Hebrew Bible, Hebrew grammar, and Hebrew dictionary that I may pass the time in study. . . . I will be patient abiding the will of God, to the glory of the grace of my Lord Jesus Christ, whose spirit (pray) may ever direct your heart. Amen.[27]

It has been noted that this correspondence sounds very much like one of Paul's letters to Timothy[28] as the former awaited his fate and requested a visit from the latter, saying, "The cloke that I left at Troas with Carpus, when thou comest bring with thee, and the books, but especially the parchments" (2 Tim. 4:13). Tyndale's letter hints that he was probably still working on his unfinished translation of the Old Testament.

In August 1536, William Tyndale was found guilty of heresy by an ecclesiastical court and delivered over to secular officials, not church leaders, for public execution. Again, the principle invoked by the church, as with the case involving Wycliffe's exhumed body, was *Ecclesia non novit sanguinem*—"The Church does not shed blood."[29] Two months later, on October 6, 1536, Tyndale was taken from his cell, paraded into town, chained to a stake,

---

26. Kerr, *Ancient Texts Alive Today,* 60.

27. Kerr, *Ancient Texts Alive Today,* 60.

28. Stephen M. Miller and Robert V. Huber, *The Bible: A History, The Making and Impact of the Bible* (Intercourse, Penn.: Good Books, 2004), 171.

29. Moynahan, *God's Bestseller,* xi.

strangled openly by an executioner with a rope, and then burned. His last coherent words were "Lord, open the King of England's eyes."[30] One of the great minds and spiritual giants of an already impressive age was dead. He gave his life for a cause that he believed was God-inspired—a cause that would result in a Bible, in a restoration of scriptural accuracy, and in a changed language that would affect the whole world.

As it turned out, within a year of Tyndale's death, his dying wish was granted. Tyndale Bibles or versions that drew heavily upon his work were circulating in England—with King Henry's approval. Within two years, all parishes were encouraged to have a copy, and within five years, they were ordered to do so or face a fine levied by the government.

Tyndale's influence in other ways is hard to overstate. His translation changed the English language. He replaced certain terms with others that became widely accepted: "church" (Greek *ecclesia*) became "congregation," "priest" (Greek *presbyter*) became "elder," "do penance" (Greek *metanoia*) became "repent," "charity" (Greek *agape*) became "love."[31] More than that, literally dozens of words and phrases were coined by Tyndale to make his translation richer and more understandable. These include (but are not limited to) the following:

- alpha and omega
- apple of his eye
- beautiful
- brother's keeper
- busybody
- cast the first stone
- coat of many colors
- eat, drink, and be merry
- infidel
- Jehovah
- judge not
- no man can serve two masters
- Passover
- stiff-necked
- suffer fools gladly

30. Kerr, *Ancient Texts Alive Today,* 61; Foxe, *Book of Martyrs,* 152.
31. Kerr, *Ancient Texts Alive Today,* 55.

- two-edged sword
- undergird
- ungodly
- uproar

In fact, even the very word at the center of Christian theology, "atonement" (derived from the phrase "at-one-ment"), was appropriated by William Tyndale to describe the reconciliation that occurs between people and God through the redemptive suffering of Jesus Christ (Rom. 5:11). Though Tyndale has been credited with inventing the word "atonement," it was used in English texts as early as the fourteenth century. A form of the term appears in the oldest surviving Middle English romance, *King Horn* ("At one he was with the king").[32] And the 1395 edition of the Wycliffe Bible uses "onement" in Ezekiel 37:17 to describe the prophesied sticks of Judah and Ephraim that would "become one in thine hand" (King James Version) or "be in to onement in thin hond [*sic*]" (Wycliffe Bible).[33] "Atonement" appears in Sir Thomas More's manuscript history of Richard III in 1513.[34]

But William Tyndale was astute enough to see that "atonement" was the best equivalent of the Hebrew and Greek words used in the Old and New Testaments to refer to the act of bringing estranged beings into a state of union with God. Tyndale used the word only once in his 1526 edition of the New Testament, but he must be credited with giving "atonement" its powerful theological meaning, using it to translate the Greek *katallagan,* often rendered "reconciliation."

Only someone who understood the infinite and eternal power of Christ's sacrifice to put all humankind back into a right relationship with God the Father, after the wrenching estrangement brought about by sin, could have translated the Greek into the word "atonement." Only someone whose very soul was attuned to the nature of God and to the effects of sin, suffering, repentance, and reconciliation would have chosen "atonement." William Tyndale was such a man. Modern readers are the beneficiaries of his consecrated intellect and spiritual compass. Those of us who share the

---

32. Joseph Hall, ed., *King Horn: A Middle-English Romance* (Oxford, Eng.: Clarendon Press, 1901), 54.

33. Bible Study Tools, accessed October 30, 2023, https://www.biblestudytools.com/wyc/ezekiel/37.html.

34. Thomas More, *More's History of King Richard III,* ed. J. Rawson Lumby (Cambridge, Eng.: University Press; London: C. J. Clay, 1883), 13, https://books.google.gg/books?id=xQL154m8wxYC&printsec=frontcover.

English-language culture speak what we speak and are who we are because of William Tyndale.

All that William Tyndale endured was for the sake of bringing the word of God to an English-speaking population. Ultimately, he gave everything he possessed—even his own life—for God's work and word. He was a spiritual giant. His work profoundly, even monumentally, influenced future versions of the English Bible. They, in turn, all contributed to the crowning achievement in the chain of English Bibles—the King James Version. But none of these future versions equaled the significance of the work accomplished by William Tyndale. "Previous estimates of William Tyndale's contribution to the 1611 King James Version (or Authorized Version) of the Bible have run from a high of up to 90 percent . . . to a low of 18 percent." However, the most recent analysis by researchers at Brigham Young University concludes that for the New Testament, Tyndale's contribution is about 84 percent of the text, while in the Old Testament about 76 percent of his words have been retained.[35] Tyndale's influence continues to this day.

Persecution

William Tyndale's martyrdom caused his like-minded associates to steel their resolve and redouble their efforts to bring the best English Bible they could to the world. Tyndale's friend John Rogers was such a man. Rogers was responsible for completing the translation of the Old Testament into English, getting it to press, and ultimately becoming a martyr for the cause of truth.

John Rogers's brief friendship with Tyndale began in Antwerp. Rogers believed Tyndale's work and vision to be so important that he guarded with his life all the unpublished Old Testament translations and handwritten notes Tyndale had left with him for safekeeping. He initially published the completed Bible under the pseudonym of Thomas Matthew in 1537, just one year after Tyndale's death. At the insistence of Archbishop Thomas Cranmer, the "Matthews Bible" was granted the "Kings most gracious license" and officially recognized, as was Tyndale's work. Tyndale's heavenward plea at the time of his execution, to open the English king's eyes, was now answered in full!

Eventually, Rogers forsook the priesthood and the Roman Catholic Church, married a woman from Antwerp, and became pastor of a Protestant

35. Jon Nielsen and Royal Skousen, "How Much of the King James Bible Is William Tyndale's?," *Reformation* 3 (1998): 73.

congregation in Wittenberg, Germany (hometown of Martin Luther and, for a brief time, Tyndale himself). He then returned to England during the reign of King Edward VI (1547–1553), who was sympathetic to reform. In time, Rogers was recognized for his abilities at preaching and pastoring and was appointed lecturer in divinity at St. Paul's in London.[36]

When Queen Mary I (1553–1558), a staunch Catholic, ascended the English throne upon the death of Edward VI, there was a violent purge in England. The reform-friendly atmosphere evaporated, and many Reformation leaders fled to the continent. John Rogers, however, was defiant. In July 1553, he preached a sermon at St. Paul's on "the true doctrine taught in King Edward's days" and warned everyone to beware of returning to "pestilent Popery."[37] Ten days later, he was put under house arrest. In January 1554, he was sent to Newgate Prison in London for a year and then dispatched to the residence of a notorious persecutor of reformers to answer questions. Finally, in late January 1555, he was convicted by a papal commission of denying the Christian character of the Roman Catholic Church and rejecting the doctrine of transubstantiation by saying that the bread and wine of the Lord's Supper did not turn into the actual body and blood of Christ. For Rogers, such a denial was in perfect harmony with scriptural warrant. Transubstantiation was not a biblical doctrine. But biblical or not, Rogers was sentenced to death.[38]

Queen Mary I was the daughter of King Henry VIII and his first wife, Katherine of Aragon. She is described as being filled with resentment over the way Henry treated her mother.[39] Henry had tried to have their twenty-four-year marriage annulled because Katherine couldn't provide a surviving male heir to the English throne, and Henry didn't want Mary to become monarch. All of this set in motion events that resulted in the English Reformation. The quest for a new version of the Bible was an inextricable part of this reform. This was also a major factor contributing to the intensity of the Catholic restoration that Mary pursued and the bloodbath over which she presided. Between 1555 and 1558, Mary ordered 287 persons executed for religious convictions; most of these were by burning.[40] Mary was followed by Queen Elizabeth I and then King James.

---

36. Connolly, *Indestructible Book,* 149–50.
37. Connolly, *Indestructible Book,* 150.
38. Connolly, *Indestructible Book,* 150–51.
39. Kerr, *Ancient Texts Alive Today,* 86.
40. Kenneth O. Morgan, ed., *The Oxford Illustrated History of Britain* (Oxford: Oxford University, 2009), 259.

Bible Versions after Tyndale

When Queen Elizabeth I (1558–1603) ascended the throne of the English realm, Protestants everywhere breathed a sigh of relief. Many people had gone to prison or been put to death across Europe for supporting the spread of Bibles in the vernacular. But European religious reform in general, and the English Reformation in particular, could not now be stopped. In the British Isles, the Bible in English had become the heart and core of earthshaking change, as historian G. M. Trevelyan noted: "The English Reformation, which had begun as a Parliamentary attack on Church fees, and proceeded as a royal raid on Abbey lands, was at last to find its religious basis in the popular knowledge of the Scriptures which had been the dream of Wycliffe."[41]

By the time King James (r. 1603–1625) succeeded Queen Elizabeth to the throne of England, reactions to the language of Tyndale's Bible were not uniformly positive, as exemplified in the several versions of the English Bible that had appeared since Tyndale's New Testament was first published in 1526. The main ones were the Coverdale Bible of 1535 (named after its editor), the Great Bible of 1539 (named for its size), the Geneva Bible of 1560 (named for its place of printing), the Bishop's Bible of 1568 (authorized by the Church of England clergy), and the Catholic Douai-Rheims Bible of 1582 (so named for the place of translation—Douai Rheims College).[42]

Each of these Bibles favored a different doctrinal slant. The Geneva Bible contained a running commentary that was intensely antagonistic toward the pope as well as the Roman Catholic hierarchy, the Church of England, and the universities. However, the Geneva Bible was immensely popular with the people. It is the version Shakespeare likely used. It is the Bible that came to America on the Mayflower and certainly the version read by our Pilgrim forefathers. Yet, the Geneva Bible was understandably annoying to the bishops of the Church of England because it was too Protestant. Not least, it made King James unhappy because of notes in the margins that criticized kings.[43] The English clergy's response to the Geneva Bible was the Bishop's Bible, proposed by Matthew Parker, archbishop of Canterbury, and translated by a goodly number of church bishops.[44] Whereas the Geneva Bible was filled with anti-Catholic annotations, Parker ordered

41. Quoted in Kerr, *Ancient Texts Alive Today,* 63.
42. Miller and Huber, *Bible: A History,* 176–77.
43. Miller and Huber, *Bible: A History,* 178.
44. Connolly, *Indestructible Book,* 156.

that the Bishop's Bible "avoid notes of a doctrinal or controversial nature."[45] Still, the Puritans were not happy with it because it was not accurate, which was true for some portions.

The Puritans argued that the church and society needed to be "purified" of all remnants of Catholic influence. This meant getting rid of anything that resembled the Roman Catholic Church or distorted Christianity (from their point of view), which included such things as the office of bishop, clerical robes, emphasis on "high church" rituals, and the popular recent versions of the Bible currently in use. Therefore, before King James of Scotland even got to London to take up his new additional duties as king of England, he was presented with the Millenary Petition, so called because it was signed by one thousand Puritans who requested changes in the Church of England, including a new Bible.[46]

King James's Bible

James VI of Scotland had ruled over the Scottish realm for many years (since 1567) before he became king of England in 1603. He liked the episcopal structure of the Church of England, which was bishop centered. He especially liked the church's title for the king, "Defender of the Faith." He was not anxious to change things. Yet on one matter he agreed with the Puritans—the need for a new translation of the Bible.

In January 1604, during his first royal year in England, James called a conference at Hampton Court to evaluate the condition of the Church of England. The conference did not favor the Puritans' requests. But the king did agree to proceed with plans for a new Bible, with the provision that it omit controversial notes, like those in the Geneva Bible.[47]

Work began in July. The king claimed to have appointed fifty-four men to the translation team, although only fifty names can be found on various surviving lists. They were divided into six translation companies, two companies each working from three different cities in England (Oxford, Cambridge, and Westminster in London).[48] These teams included the finest biblical scholars of that era. Dr. Lancelot Andrewes, for example, was

---

45. Kerr, *Ancient Texts Alive Today,* 97–98.

46. Kerr, *Ancient Texts Alive Today,* 111.

47. Kerr, *Ancient Texts Alive Today,* 112–13.

48. S. L. Greenslade, "English Versions of the Bible, 1525–1611," in *The Cambridge History of the Bible,* vol. 3, *The West from the Reformation to the Present Day,* ed. S. L. Greenslade (Cambridge, Eng.: Cambridge University Press, 1963), 164–68.

a brilliant linguist, a master of fifteen languages, the dean of Westminster, and a famous preacher and devotional writer. William Bedwell of Cambridge University was the father of Arabic studies in England and the most distinguished Islamicist of his day. Dr. Miles Smith was a fine Semitist, energetic Puritan, and writer of the King James Version preface. Sir Henry Savile was eminent among Greek scholars.[49] Surely, these were men raised up for the very purpose to which they applied their considerable abilities.

These men sought not their own aggrandizement but the will of God. It was Miles Smith who said they didn't start out to make a new translation of the Bible because others were bad. Rather, they desired "to make a good one better, or out of many good ones, one principal good one . . . ; that hath been our endeavour, that our mark. To that purpose there were many [scholars] chosen, that were greater in other men's eyes than in their own, and that sought the truth rather than their own praise."[50]

It is no exaggeration to say these translators worked exceptionally long and hard to produce a new version of the word of God. In fact, some of them turned every waking moment to the task. One example is John Bois. Born in 1560, he could read Hebrew at age six and "write the Hebrew alphabet with elegance." As an undergraduate at Cambridge University, "he studied from 4:00 a.m. to 8:00 p.m." and turned down a career in medicine to pursue theology and humanities. He was assigned to the sixth company of translators working on the Apocrypha. He worked all week at St. John's College only to return to his country parish on weekends to prepare and deliver his Sunday sermons. Some objected to the appointment of this "country preacher" to a translation team filled with the ranks of such notable scholars from all over England. However, John Bois loved God and the common man. His work ethic was such that he did not waste a spare moment. And he believed in the importance of the work, though he did not believe himself to be important. Dr. Bois was ultimately chosen to do the final editing work on the entire biblical manuscript and prepare it for press.[51] The King James Version was printed in 1611.

One scholar who was not chosen for the original translation team became a vicious opponent of the new Bible, even though he had first argued for it. This was Hugh Broughton, a renowned professor who apparently became

---

49. Kerr, *Ancient Texts Alive Today,* 115.

50. Edgar J. Goodspeed, ed., *The Translators to the Reader: Preface to the King James Version 1611* (Chicago: University of Chicago Press, 1935), 33.

51. Kerr, *Ancient Texts Alive Today,* 121.

so incensed at being slighted by not receiving an invitation to participate that he would write in a letter, "Tell His Majesty, I had rather be rent in pieces with wild horses, than any such translation by my consent should be urged upon poor churches. . . . The new edition crosseth me. I require it to be burnt."[52] Though Broughton was admittedly a very bright man, he was also cantankerous and not missed owing to his eccentricity and bad temper. Neither did his absence on the translation team impoverish the work. However, the results of some work he did on a planned independent translation of the Bible did find its way into the hands of the King James translation team.[53]

The King James Version has also been called the "Authorized Version," though, oddly enough, no proof survives that the king formally approved the final product. The title page to the 1611 version read that it was "appointed to be read in churches,"[54] but there was no official law that said it had to be used, and it was a long time before the King James Version displaced the Geneva Bible as the Bible read by individuals.[55] Once established, however, the King James Version became entrenched. It was more than two hundred fifty years before a serious attempt was made to replace the King James Version with an updated translation. The English Revised Version appeared in 1885. From this revision sprang an American variation called the American Standard Version in 1901. This was followed by the Revised Standard Version in 1952 and the New Revised Standard Version in 1989.[56] In 1978 the New International Version appeared, with revisions in subsequent years.

Many of these versions undertook to correct mistakes found in the King James Version. Early editions of the King James Version were plagued with misprints, which were corrected in later printings. But one example of a misprint that never got corrected is found in Matthew 23:24: "strain at a gnat." It originally read "strain *out* a gnat." It has been corrected in other versions of the Bible.

52. Quoted in Miller and Huber, *Bible: A History,* 180; Hugh Broughton, *A Censure of the Late Translations for Our Churches* (R. Schilders, 1611), iii, https://books.google.com/books?id=eDX_FzFo3sEC&printsec=frontcover.

53. Kerr, *Ancient Texts Alive Today,* 115, 129.

54. *Holy Bible: 1611 King James Version,* 400th anniversary ed. (Grand Rapids, Mich.: Zondervan, 2011), ix.

55. "Publication of the King James Bible," *Christian History,* no. 28 (1990): 41; Kerr, *Ancient Texts Alive Today,* 129.

56. See the chart in Kerr, *Ancient Texts Alive Today,* 203–7.

Because of these so-called problems and the archaic nature of seventeenth-century English, some people say the King James Version is too outdated and will soon become obsolete (or *should* become obsolete). Even if readers eventually no longer use the King James Version, we have the King James translators to thank for many phrases still used today:[57]

- "the skin of my teeth" (Job 19:20)
- "Woe is me!" (Ps. 120:5)
- "a drop in a bucket" (Isa. 40:15)
- "my brother's keeper" (Gen. 4:9)
- "holier than thou" (Isa. 65:5)
- "at their wits' end" (Ps. 107:27)
- "hair stood on end" (Job 4:15)
- "apple of his eye" (Ps. 17:8)
- "lily of the valley" (Song 2:1)
- "line upon line" (Isa. 28:10)
- "set house in order" (Isa. 38:1)
- "Can a leopard change its spots?" (Jer. 13:23)
- "hollow of his hand" (Isa. 40:12)

Today, most people who can quote from the Bible quote the King James Version published in 1611. As one source notes, modern-day translators of new Bible revisions may "rightly feel humble, knowing they can never produce a work that will so mold a language and shape an entire culture" as did the King James Version.[58]

New translations of the Bible continue to be made for a variety of reasons: to keep apace with changes in the language, to facilitate ease of understanding, and to harmonize language with doctrinal understandings in the modern world. (It must be recognized that any translation is automatically an interpretation.) These new translations are valuable tools in helping students understand more deeply the meaning and intent of God's word. But perhaps it is not wrong to say as well that nothing has yet quite hit the high watermark left by the King James Version.

The King James Version was the culmination of a long process and many participants. We owe a great debt to all those who created the English Bible and made the King James Version possible. Their sacrifices were monumental, and their faith is inspiring.

---

57. "Publication of the King James Bible," 42.
58. "Publication of the King James Bible," 42.

Navigating the Textus Receptus

Understanding the Text upon which the King James Translation Rests

Eric Huntsman

The invention of moveable type by Johannes Gutenberg (c. AD 1400–1468) revolutionized how texts could be reproduced. Printing not only made duplicating texts cheaper and easier to produce in large numbers but also increased accuracy by reducing the errors from repeated copying. This limited the tendency for biblical textual traditions to produce numerous variant families, which were copies of the Greek New Testament text where minor differences developed and were perpetuated over time as the text was repeatedly copied. The first book printed by Gutenberg was an edition of Jerome's Latin translation of the Bible produced between 1450 and 1456. Whereas printed Latin editions multiplied throughout the remainder of the fifteenth century and the first edition of the Hebrew Old Testament was issued in 1488, the first Greek editions of the New Testament did not appear until 1514–15. The delay was due to the lack of standard Greek type for the many variants of Greek minuscule—or cursive, lowercase—handwriting and to the prestige of the Latin Vulgate.[1]

The first actual printing of a Greek text of the New Testament was part of a multilingual edition of the Bible produced in Alcalá, Spain, in 1514. Called the Complutensian Polyglot—from *Complutum,* the Latin name for Alcalá—this massive work contained the Hebrew text of the Old Testament, an Aramaic Targum, the Latin Vulgate, and the Greek Septuagint in the first three volumes and a Greek text of the New Testament drawn from unknown manuscripts of the Byzantine family in the fourth volume.[2]

1. Bruce M. Metzger and Bart D. Ehrman, *The Text of the New Testament: Its Transmission, Corruption, and Restoration,* 4th ed. (New York: Oxford University Press, 2005), 137–38.
2. Metzger and Ehrman, *Text of the New Testament,* 138–40, 222, 237–38.

While this was the first Greek edition printed, the first edition published and actually put on the market was one that Johann Froben, a printer in Basel, encouraged the Dutch humanist Desiderius Erasmus (1469–1536) to produce. Printing began in October 1515 and was completed in March 1516.[3] So hurriedly had Erasmus put his edition together, presumably so that Froben could market it before the Complutensian Polyglot was available, that he later remarked it was "precipitated rather than edited" (*praecipitatum verius quam editum*).[4]

Because Erasmus did not have a complete manuscript of the New Testament, he drew from half a dozen minuscules, most of them from the twelfth century and none earlier than the tenth century. Two manuscripts from the Dominican monastery at Basel provided most of his text, one codex containing most of the Gospels and another containing Acts and the Epistles. For Revelation, he relied upon a problematic manuscript that was completely lacking the final six verses, and much of the remaining text was frequently confused with the accompanying commentary. For this last section and for other portions where he could not separate the text itself from the commentary, Erasmus actually produced his own Greek text by translating it back into Greek from the Vulgate.[5] A similar example of creative text production may have occurred in Erasmus's third edition of 1522, in which he was pressured to insert the so-called "Johannine Comma," the Trinitarian reflection in 1 John 5:7–8 that was a standard part of the Latin Vulgate.[6] This passage is lacking in virtually every known Greek manuscript except for a Greek version of the passage thought to have been translated by a Franciscan friar named Froy in Oxford, which conveniently appeared before the 1522 edition.[7]

---

3. Desiderius Erasmus, *Novum Instrumentum omne, diligenter ad Erasmo Roterodamo recognitum & emendatum, non solum ad græcam veritatem . . .* (Basel, Switz.: Johann Froben, 1516), reprinted as a photographic facsimile, *Erasmus von Rotterdam. Novum Instrumentum. Basel 1516. Faksimile-Neudruck mit einer historischen, textkritischen und bibliographischen Einleitung von Heinz Holeczek* (Stuttgart, Ger.: Frommann-Holzboog, 1986).

4. Metzger and Ehrman, *Text of the New Testament,* 142–43.

5. Metzger and Ehrman, *Text of the New Testament*, 143, 145, 148; Philip W. Comfort, *Essential Guide to Bible Versions* (Wheaton, Ill.: Tyndale House, 2000), 102; Bruce M. Metzger, "The Text of the New Testament: Its Transmission, Corruption, and Restoration" (New York: Oxford University Press, 1964), 99.

6. See the summary of Carroll D. Osburn, "Johannine Comma," in *Anchor Bible Dictionary,* ed. David Noel Freedman, 6 vols. (New York: Doubleday, 1992), 3:882–83.

7. Metzger and Ehrman, *Text of the New Testament,* 146–47.

The manuscripts used by Erasmus all came from the Byzantine textual family, which underlies the majority of the New Testament manuscripts and whose character eliminates obscurities and features intelligibility.[8] According to tradition, the prototype for this text type was a recension, or edition, by Lucian of Antioch (c. AD 240–312) that was noted for its conflation of variant readings, harmonization, and smoothness of language.[9] Although this produced a more aesthetically and theologically pleasing version, Lucian's editing most likely produced a text further removed from the original autographs. Produced before the early fourth-century AD persecutions of Diocletian, when many copies of the Bible were destroyed, this recension became the basis for numerous copies made during and after the reign of Constantine.[10] Many historical factors combined to make Lucian's edition the standard text for Eastern Orthodoxy. The loss of much of the Middle East and North Africa to the Muslims, the effective loss of Greek literacy and the preference for Latin in western Europe, and the efforts of the eastern Roman government and church helped the Byzantine text family to survive antiquity and continue through the Middle Ages as the prevalent text family represented in most minuscule manuscripts.[11]

Despite being dependent upon poor manuscripts of the latest, and perhaps least reliable, textual family and notwithstanding its other weaknesses, Erasmus's 1516 Greek text was of supreme importance in the history of the Bible because it was the basis for both Luther's 1522 German translation and Tyndale's 1526 English translation.[12] Erasmus produced a fourth edition in 1527 that included the combination of a Greek text, the Vulgate, and Erasmus's own Latin translation in parallel columns. Robert Estienne (1503–1559), known as Stephanus, produced four versions of the Greek New Testament between 1546 and 1551.[13] He improved the Greek text by

---

8. "Lucianic Text," in *The Oxford Dictionary of the Christian Church,* ed. F. L. Cross and E. A. Livingstone, 3rd ed. (London: Oxford University Press, 1997), 1002.

9. Jerome, in *Patrologia Latina,* ed. Jacques-Paul Migne, 221 vols. (Paris: Imprimerie Catholique, 1841–55), vol. 29, col. 527.

10. Comfort, *Essential Guide to Bible Versions,* 90, 147–48.

11. Metzger and Ehrman, *Text of the New Testament,* 220.

12. William Tyndale, *The Newe Testament as It Was Written and Caused to Be Written by Them Which Herde Yt. to Whom Also Oure Saveour Christ Jesus Commaunded That They Shulde Preache It unto Al Creatures* (1526). See Comfort, *Essential Guide to Bible Versions,* 139.

13. Robert Estienne, *Novum Testamentum Græce. Lutetiæ: ex officiana Roberti Stephani Typographi, Typis Regiis* (Paris, 1546; 2nd ed., 1549; 3rd ed., 1550; 4th ed., Geneva, 1551).

consulting other manuscripts, began the practice of noting variant readings from different manuscripts, and was the first to divide the text into verses, although his practice of marking the verses while on bumpy horse-and-carriage rides (*inter equitandum*) sometimes produced awkward divisions. Stephanus's 1550 edition is significant because it was used in the English Geneva Bible of 1570. Between 1565 and 1611, Théodore de Bèze (1519–1605), or Beza, subsequently produced ten editions of the Greek text that were based on those of Stephanus,[14] and these were the texts largely "consulted" by the King James translators of 1611.[15]

In 1624 the Elzevir brothers of Leiden produced a popular edition of the Greek New Testament based on Beza's second edition of 1565.[16] Their own second edition of 1633 bore the following claim in its preface: "You have, therefore, the text now accepted by all, in which we present nothing altered or corrupted" (*Textum ergo habes nunc ab omnibus receptum: in quo nihil immutatum aut corruptum damus*). From this claim came *Textus Receptus,* the now common epithet given to the Greek text based on Erasmus's early efforts, which text lies behind the King James Version of the New Testament. Although Metzger notes that "its textual basis is essentially a handful of late and haphazardly collected minuscule manuscripts, and in a dozen passages its reading is supported by no known Greek witness,"[17] it nonetheless provided a sufficiently adequate basis for what was arguably the most influential English Bible, the King James Version—a translation that provided direction for the English Reformation and laid the groundwork for the Restoration.

---

14. Only four of these appeared as independent editions: Theodore Beza, *Novum Testamentum, cum versione Latina veteri, et nova Theodori Bezæ* (Geneva, 1565 [folio]; 2nd folio ed., 1582; 3rd folio ed., 1588–89; 4th folio ed., 1598).

15. Metzger and Ehrman, *Text of the New Testament,* 149–52.

16. Although Bonaventure and Abraham Elzevir received credit, the first edition was published by Abraham's brother Isaac; see Isaac Elzevir, *Novum Testamentum Græce* (Leiden, Neth., 1624); Bonaventure and Abraham Elzevir, *Novum Testamentum Græce,* 2nd ed. (Leiden, Neth., 1633).

17. Metzger and Ehrman, *Text of the New Testament,* 152.

Illuminating the Staying Power of the King James Version of the Bible among English-Speaking Latter-day Saints

Andrew C. Skinner

English-speaking members of The Church of Jesus Christ of Latter-day Saints reverence the King James Version of the Bible and demonstrate a preference for it over other English translations. This is a significant phenomenon when viewed against the number of English versions now available, and it reflects the official view of the Church toward the King James Version in particular and, perhaps surprisingly to some, a general preference among English speakers of various faiths in general.

The King James Version (KJV) was first published in 1611, the result of a process of trying to produce increasingly better English translations of the Bible depending on one's understanding of original biblical languages, one's theological orientation, and one's faith community. Two foundational works preceded the KJV. The first was John Wycliffe's New Testament, produced in AD 1380 (the entire Wycliffe Bible was finished in about 1382).[1] The second was William Tyndale's translation of the New Testament from the Greek, published in 1526.

The latter laid the foundation for the King James Version, also called the Authorized Version, which borrowed heavily from Tyndale's work. In fact, one authority on Tyndale stated that in "translating the Bible, Tyndale *fathered* what is probably the best known and certainly the most quoted work in the English language. A complete analysis of the Authorized Version, known down the generations as 'the AV' or 'the King James,' was made in 1998. It shows that Tyndale's words account for 84 per cent of the

1. There is debate about how much of the actual translating work was done by Wycliffe himself, especially the Old Testament, and exactly when the two Testaments appeared. The dates given are generally accepted.

New Testament, and for 75.8 per cent of the Old Testament books that he translated."[2]

A Proliferation of English Versions

The production of English versions did not cease in 1611. During the last century and a half, more translations of the Bible into English have appeared than most of us can keep track of. Revised versions of just the King James Bible itself include the following:[3]

- The Revised Version (the New Testament, 1881; entire Bible, 1885)
- The American Standard Version (1901)
- The Revised Standard Version (New Testament, 1946; entire Bible, 1952; Apocrypha, 1957)
- New American Standard Bible (1971)
- King James II Version (1971)
- The New King James Version (New Testament, 1979; entire Bible, 1982)
- New Revised Standard Version (1989)

Other English translations *not* categorized as revisions of the King James Version include the following:[4]

- *The Twentieth Century New Testament* (1901, revised 1904)
- Weymouth's New Testament (editions produced from 1903 through 1929)
- The Moffatt Version (New Testament, 1913; entire Bible, 1924)
- *An American Translation* (New Testament, 1923; entire Bible, 1927)
- The Confraternity Version (New Testament in 1941; entire Bible, 1970)

From 1950 onward, new English Translations of the Bible proliferated.[5] Included are the following:

- Phillips Bible (1958; revised, 1972)
- The Berkeley Version (New Testament, 1945; entire Bible, 1959)

---

2. Brian Moynahan, *William Tyndale: If God Spare My Life* (London: Abacus, 2003), 1, 402–3, emphasis added. Moynahan takes his figures from the work of BYU's very own Jon Nielsen and Royal Skousen, "How Much of the King James Bible Is William Tyndale's?," *Reformation* 3 (1998): 73.

3. List taken from Paul D. Wegner, *The Journey from Texts to Translations: The Origin and Development of the Bible* (Grand Rapids, Mich.: Baker Academic, 1999), 8.

4. Wegner, *Journey from Texts to Translations,* 8.

5. See Wegner, *Journey from Texts to Translations,* 357–97, where the author describes the essential characteristics of each of the translations listed herein.

- The New World Translation of the Holy Scriptures (New Testament, 1950; entire Bible, 1961; revised, 1981)
- *The New English Bible* (New Testament, 1961; entire Bible, 1970)
- *The Jerusalem Bible* (1966)
- *Good News Bible: Today's English Version* (New Testament, 1966; entire Bible, 1976)
- *The Living Bible* (New Testament, 1969; entire Bible, 1971)
- The New International Version (New Testament, 1973; entire Bible, 1978)
- The Revised English Bible (1989)
- *The Message* (New Testament, 1993; Old Testament Wisdom Books, 1997)
- The New Living Translation (1996)

This is a sampling of the English translations that have appeared since the publication of the King James Version in 1611. It is not a comprehensive list. The point here is to emphasize the large number of English Bible versions available to readers in modern times.

Reasons for New Versions

New versions or translations of the Bible since the King James Version appeared were and are undertaken for a variety of reasons. One is the archaic nature of seventeenth-century English and the desire to keep pace with changes in the English language. Even before 1800, the language of the KJV had already become antiquated. Only a few phrases from the 1611 edition are needed to illustrate the issue (other examples abound):

- "And Jacob sod pottage" (Gen. 25:29).
- "And mount Sinai was altogether on a smoke" (Ex. 19:18).
- "Thou shalt destroy them that speak leasing" (Ps. 5:6).
- "I trow not" (Luke 17:9).
- "And not as it was by one that sinned, so is the gift" (Rom. 5:16).

The meaning of some words used by the King James translation committee fell out of use to the point that the general populace no longer knew what they meant. And some words actually changed meaning over time, as the following examples indicate:

Term	Meaning in 1611	Modern Meaning
mean man	common man	cruel man
peculiar	belonging to one person	strange
cherish	to keep warm	to care about

Term	Meaning in 1611	Modern Meaning
prevent	to come before	to hinder
wealthy	happy	money or riches
knit	to let down	to weave

Another reason for needed changes is the increased understanding that has come to light with the discovery of additional early manuscripts. The sources available to the King James translation committee were significantly inferior to those available in our day. One scholar noted, "Of the five primary uncial manuscripts now received as authority for the purity of the text of the New Testament, only Codex Bezae was then available, and there is no evidence that it was used. Papyrus discoveries came three hundred years later. The King James scholars could have known fewer than twenty-five late manuscripts of the New Testament, and these were carelessly used. Today there are 5,358 known New Testament manuscripts and fragments. . . . The 1611 situation for the Old Testament was even poorer."[6]

Still another reason for revisions of the King James Version, as well as the creation of new translations over the years, involves concerns over style and content. The appearance of the newly published King James Version in 1611 immediately aroused detractors. Some of the most fervent were the pilgrims, some of whom brought the old Geneva Bible with them to the New World and rejected the KJV because it was seen as supporting the divine right of kings.[7] (And yet the King James Version was the first Bible printed in America in 1782.)

The 1611 King James Version included the Apocrypha, like previous English Bibles. This was strongly disapproved of by the Puritans. It became such a hot issue between those who were for its inclusion and those against it that in 1616, one Archbishop Abbot issued a decree stating that anyone who published an edition of the King James Version without the Apocrypha was to be thrown in prison for a year. The Apocrypha continued to be included in editions of the KJV fairly consistently until 1826, when it was omitted by the British Foreign Bible Society for financial reasons rather than real theological ones.[8]

---

6. Jack P. Lewis, *The English Bible from KJV to NIV: A History and Evaluation,* 2nd ed. (Grand Rapids, Mich.: Baker, 1991), 41–42.

7. C. Anderson, *The Annals of the English Bible* (New York: Robert Carter and Bros., 1849), 486, quoted in Wegner, *Journey from Texts to Translations,* 313.

8. Wegner, *Journey from Texts to Translations,* 312–13.

One of the most famous and intense, even vitriolic, opponents of the King James Version early on was Dr. Hugh Broughton, a distinguished scholar in the seventeenth century who was not invited to serve on the King James translation committee because of his disagreeable, even violent, temperament. He obviously saw a need for a new translation, or at least a revision of the existing Geneva Bible, because he had been working on such a revision for some thirty years before his death in 1612. Therefore, Broughton's outright rejection of the KJV does not seem to be based on lack of need (or desire) to improve the English text of the Bible but because the KJV was not well done in his view. Said he, "The late Bible . . . was sent to me to censure: which bred in me a sadness that will grieve me while I breathe, it is so ill done. Tell His Majesty that I had rather be rent in pieces with wild horses, than any such translation by my consent should be urged upon poor churches. . . . The new edition crosseth me. I require it to be burnt."[9]

In truth, early editions of the King James Version were plagued with misprints. Successive printings seemed to introduce new challenges. Sometimes the mistakes were so egregious that different editions of the King James Version acquired their own sobriquets. One of the most famous errors in an early edition of the KJV, printed in 1631, was the omission of the word "not" in the seventh commandment. Thus it read, "Thou shalt commit adultery." This edition came to be called the "Wicked Bible." In 1653 an edition called the "Unrighteous Bible" appeared, containing an error in 1 Corinthians 6:9, "the unrighteous shall inherit the earth," instead of "the righteous." In 1717 the "Vinegar Bible" was printed. It had many problems, but the misprint that gave this edition its nickname occurred in the chapter heading of Luke 20: "The Parable of the Vinegar" instead of "Vineyard." In the 1795 edition of the KJV, Mark 7:27 reads, "Let the children first be killed," instead of "be filled." Thus it is called the "Murderer's Bible."

Most misprints eventually got corrected. However, an example of an error that never got corrected in any of the King James editions until very recently is found in Matthew 23:24, "strain at a gnat." It did get corrected in other English translations and in modern-day revised editions of the King James Bible. (Readers are encouraged to see what their KJV says.) The New International Version (1973) reads, "Strain *out* a gnat," which reflects the original meaning. (In New Testament times, the strict Pharisee would carefully strain his drinking water through a cloth to make sure he did not swallow a gnat—the minutest of unclean animals.)

9. F. F. Bruce, *History of the Bible in English: From the Earliest Versions,* 3rd ed. (New York: Oxford University Press, 1978), 107.

From Rejection to Exalted Status

For eighty years after it was first published, "the King James Version endured bitter attacks. It was denounced as theologically unsound and ecclesiastically biased, as truckling to the king and unduly deferring to his belief in witchcraft, as untrue to the Hebrew text and relying too much on the Septuagint. The personal integrity of the translators was impugned. Among other things, they were accused of 'blasphemy,' 'most damnable corruptions,' 'intolerable deceit,' and 'vile imposture.' The critic who used these epithets was careful to say that they were not 'the dictates of passion, but the just resentment of a zealous mind.'"[10]

Eventually, the criticisms leveled against the King James Version faded away, and the King James Version ultimately gained standing so great that "its text acquired a sanctity properly ascribable only to the unmediated voice of God; to multitudes of English-speaking Christians it has seemed little less than blasphemy to tamper with the words of the King James Version," according to S. L. Greenslade, an editor of the *Cambridge History of the Bible.*[11]

Though the King James Version seemed the only divinely approved and proper version in the minds of people for a long time after this, with its archaic but sacred-sounding language, the Bible also seemed to be less and less familiar to average people in the view of some scholars and church leaders. In 1870, Samuel Wilberforce, bishop of Westminster, proposed that the King James Bible be revised. The principles and policies adopted by scholars and translators regarding what was to be allowed in the revision process were overly restrictive, and in the end, they produced a Bible in 1881 that was not very satisfying to anyone. Renowned preacher Charles Spurgeon said of the New Testament that the new version was "strong in Greek, weak in English."[12] But this effort at revision signaled both the very need for such improvements and the beginning of a slew of revised English versions.

Around this time, there also arose calls for new, modernized translations of the Bible that were not in the lineage of the King James Version. In 1891, for example, an idea was put forward by two laypeople in England: Mary

---

10. Luther A. Weigle, "English Versions since 1611," in *The Cambridge History of the Bible: The West from the Reformation to Present Day,* ed. S. L. Greenslade (Cambridge: Cambridge University Press, 1963), 361.

11. S. L. Greenslade, "English Versions of the Bible, 1525–1611," in Greenslade, *Cambridge History of the Bible,* 168.

12. Geddes MacGregor, *The Bible in the Making* (Washington, D.C.: University Press of America, 1982), 162.

Higgins, wife of a Congregational minister, and Ernest Malan, a telegraph engineer. They suggested a New Testament translation that would reflect "their own language."[13] This resulted in a translation called *The Twentieth Century New Testament: A Translation into Modern English Made from the Original Greek (Westcott & Hort's Text),* appearing in stages from 1898 to 1901.[14] In the preface to this translation the reason for its undertaking is explained:

> English-speaking people of today have not, until quite recently, had the opportunity of reading the Bible in the English of their own time. Though in the course of the last hundred years the Bible has been translated into the vernacular of most countries, the language of our Bible remains the English of three hundred years ago. This translation of the New Testament is an endeavor to do for the English nation what has been done already for the people of almost all other countries. . . . It had its origin in the recognition of the fact that the English of the Authorized Version (closely followed in that of the Revised Version), though widely valued for its antique charm, is in many passages difficult, or even quite unintelligible to the modern reader.[15]

Since the turn of the twentieth century, new English translations have proliferated, usually undertaken with the intent of making the biblical text more relevant to modern changing times. These attempts sought to harmonize language, and thus content, with changes in theological understandings. Translators also sought to make biblical concepts and language less rigid, less sexist, less racist, and so forth. (As a Latter-day Saint, one finds several changes to be helpful, but others not, like when translators skew the doctrinal intent of biblical passages as measured against the yardstick of restoration scripture.)

Yet the truly amazing thing in the history of the many English translations that have been published, each with its supportive constituency, is the staying power of the King James Version. With so many choices available to readers of the English Bible, the King James Version is the Bible that a majority of readers seem to stick with. A survey published in 2014 showed that 55 percent of the respondents who read the Bible in the United States reported using the King James Version, followed by 19 percent for the New International Version, with other versions used by fewer than 10 percent.[16]

---

13. Wegner, *Journey from Texts to Translations,* 341.

14. Wegner, *Journey from Texts to Translations,* 342.

15. *The Twentieth Century New Testament: A Translation into Modern English* (New York: Revell, 1904), iii.

16. Philip Goff, Arthur E. Farnsley II, and Peter J. Thuesen, "The Bible in American Life Today," in *The Bible in American Life,* ed. Philip Goff, Arthur E. Farnsley II, and

King James Usage among Latter-day Saints

Latter-day Saints as a whole are among those who love the King James Version and demonstrate a continuing preference for it over any other translation. One believes this is so for a number of reasons, some of which are as follows:

1. Though seventeenth-century King James English is regarded as archaic or outdated, twenty-first century English is still brimming with idioms and expressions from the King James Version. They are part of our culture, and we enjoy them. Here are some examples:

- "the skin of my teeth" (Job 19:20)
- "a drop in [the] bucket" (Isa. 40:15)
- "my brother's keeper" (Gen. 4:9)
- "holier than thou" (Isa. 65:5)
- "at their wits' end" (Ps. 107:27)
- "hair stood on end" (Job 4:15)
- "apple of his eye" (Ps. 17:8)
- "line upon line" (Isa. 28:10)
- "salt of the earth" (Matt. 5:13)
- "can a leopard change its spots" (Jer. 13:23)—and there are others.

2. The King James Version has received positive endorsements by Church leaders. President J. Reuben Clark said in his book *Why the King James Version,* published in 1956, that the King James Version was "the best version of any yet produced."[17] President M. Russell Ballard said, "It is not by chance or coincidence that we have the Bible today. . . . I believe even the scholars of King James had spiritual promptings in their translation work."[18]

3. Many luminaries outside the Church have viewed the King James Version as a high watermark in the history of the English language. H. L. Mencken called the King James Version "probably the most beautiful piece of writing in all the literature of the world."[19] Such views have influenced members of The Church of Jesus Christ of Latter-day Saints because we are

---

Peter J. Thuesen (New York: Oxford Academic, 2017), 5–32, https://doi.org/10.1093/acprof:oso/9780190468910.003.0001.

17. J. Reuben Clark, *Why the King James Version* (Salt Lake City: Deseret Book, 1956), 33.

18. M. Russell Ballard, "The Miracle of the Holy Bible," *Ensign* 37, no. 5 (April 2007): 80.

19. Quoted in D. Kelly Ogden, "King James Version," in *Encyclopedia of Mormonism,* ed. Daniel H. Ludlow, 4 vols. (New York: Macmillan, 1992), 1:109. See also H. L. Mencken, *Treatise on the Gods* (New York: Alfred A. Knopf, 1930), 243.

encouraged in scripture to be a wise, literature-loving people: "Yea, seek ye out of the best books words of wisdom" (D&C 88:118), and "study and learn, and become acquainted with all good books" (D&C 90:15).

4. Forty years ago, new enhanced editions of the triple combination and the King James Version of the Bible were published by the Church in 1979 and 1981, respectively. The four standard works of the Church became intricately tied to each other through footnotes and cross-references that mentioned all the standard works, and a new topical guide was published that provided very good references to scripture topics, which included passages from all the standard works.

5. Restoration scripture—the Book of Mormon, the Doctrine and Covenants, and the Pearl of Great Price—is written in King James English, or modified King James English, thus seamlessly tying each of the standard works to one another.

6. The King James Version is the foundation or basis for Joseph Smith's inspired revision of the Bible, called the Joseph Smith Translation (JST), which the Lord called "the scriptures . . . as they are in mine own bosom" (D&C 35:20). Additions in the JST to the various passages of the King James Version are presented in replicated seventeenth-century King James English.

7. One of the most significant reasons for the continued use of the King James Version among members of The Church of Jesus Christ of Latter-day Saints is a First Presidency letter dated May 22, 1992, that was addressed to all priesthood leaders serving in English-speaking units. It bears the signatures of Presidents Ezra Taft Benson, Gordon B. Hinckley, and Thomas S. Monson.

In part, the letter reads:

> Since the days of the Prophet Joseph Smith, The Church of Jesus Christ of Latter-day Saints has used the King James Version of the Bible for English-speaking members. . . .
>
> Many versions of the Bible are available today. Unfortunately, no original manuscripts of any portion of the Bible are available for comparison to determine the most accurate version. However, the Lord has revealed clearly the doctrines of the gospel in these latter-days. The most reliable way to measure the accuracy of any biblical passage is not by comparing different texts, but by comparison with the Book of Mormon and modern-day revelations.
>
> While other Bible versions may be easier to read than the King James Version, in doctrinal matters latter-day revelation supports the King James Version in preference to other English translations. All of the

> Presidents of the Church, beginning with the Prophet Joseph Smith, have supported the King James Version by encouraging its continued use in the Church. In light of all the above, it is the English language Bible used by The Church of Jesus Christ of Latter-day Saints.[20]

Concluding Reflections

The foregoing represent some reasons why, in my view, the King James Version resonates so deeply with members of The Church of Jesus Christ of Latter-day Saints and why it has such staying power in the face of so many other translations of the English Bible. The King James Version, along with the Joseph Smith Translation, helps teach the doctrines of the Restoration. The Restoration of the gospel of Jesus Christ in this last dispensation is tied to the King James Version. All English-language instructional and administrative materials produced by The Church of Jesus Christ of Latter-day Saints draw on the King James Version for biblical quotations.

Is the King James Version a perfect rendering of the Bible? Obviously not. Otherwise, the Lord would have seen no need to prompt his Prophet of the Restoration to undertake an inspired revision—the Joseph Smith Translation. In addition, since the time of Joseph Smith, the discovery of new biblical manuscripts, relevant historical documents, and our refined understanding of the Greek language have further expanded our understanding of the biblical text. This, combined with our increased knowledge of true doctrine from prophetic discourses, has motivated scholars to undertake a new English rendition of the Bible explicitly for Latter-day Saints based on the best available Greek versions plus insights from Restoration scripture. We also aim to provide an accompanying commentary written from the perspective of committed belief. This is a unique contribution. The translations and commentaries of the Brigham Young University New Testament Commentary series will be a helpful study aid.

---

20. "First Presidency Statement on the King James Version of the Bible," *Ensign* 22, no. 8 (August 1992): 80.

A King James Vocabulary Lesson

John W. Welch

In 2011, the Christian world celebrated the four-hundredth anniversary of the publication of the King James translation of the English Bible. The King James Version (KJV) has survived well and continues to stand as one of the more literal English translations. But as with all translations, any modern rendition of biblical language is accurate and fully dependable only "as far as it is translated correctly" (A of F 1:8).

Accordingly, LDS scholars continuously revisit ancient and modern texts as they seek to uncover nuances and clarify details that help to reveal or express the full meaning of every word in the scriptures. In this endeavor, this BYU New Testament Commentary series offers new renditions of New Testament books, with convenient parallel comparisons to the King James text. Readers of these commentary volumes will also find detailed discussions of many translational challenges and their possible solutions, especially arising in the main trouble spots that have been detected and discussed by others.[1] Of course, modern counterparts for most archaic or unfamiliar English words in the KJV can be found in footnotes of most Bible editions, including the LDS edition. But because some of these generally unfamiliar words appear multiple times in various spots in the Bible, we present here a convenient overview of these archaic words. In addition, a basic explanation for the thee/thou language is given. All this is offered in an effort to make modern readers more comfortable with King James idioms and manners of speech, since the KJV is still used by Latter-day Saints.

---

1. Some of the sources referenced for this article are Dewey M. Beegle, *God's Word into English* (Grand Rapids, Mich.: William B. Eerdmans, 1960); Ronald Bridges and Luther A. Weigle, *The Bible Word Book* (New York: Thomas Nelson and Sons, 1960); Alan S. Duthie, *How to Choose Your Bible Wisely,* 2nd ed. (Carlisle, U.K.: Paternoster, 1995); Melvin E. Elliott, *The Language of the King James Bible* (Garden City, N.Y.: Doubleday, 1967); Jacobus A. Naudé, review of Kenneth L. Barker, *The Balance of the NIV: What Makes a Good Translation, Review of Biblical Literature* (2002), https://www.sblcentral.org/home/book Details/1068; William Aldis Wright, *The Bible Word-Book* (London: Macmillan, 1884). I acknowledge the assistance of Kelsey Draper in researching several parts of this chapter.

Modern-day readers of the KJV may have difficulties understanding the intended meanings of various passages for a number of reasons and on many different levels. For one thing, since 1611 the English language has changed significantly (as all languages do over time).

In fact, some of the words in the KJV have dropped entirely out of modern English. In some cases, these words are simple, and the 1611 meaning may not seem to significantly alter the interpretation of the text today. But in other passages, even a slight misunderstanding of what one word might mean can change the doctrinal content of that passage significantly.

In addition, the translators in King James's court were Shakespearean contemporaries speaking or influenced by Elizabethan English, and readers of the KJV encounter some of the same obscure words and rhetoric. Words such as "propitiation" (Rom. 3:25; 1 John 2:2) or "staunched" (Luke 8:44) may press the vocabulary limits of many modern readers.

Another stumbling block to correct understanding is inaccurate translations, which pose problems that readers may miss entirely. These words may have a perfectly clear meaning in English today, but they do not quite convey the actual meaning of the words in the Greek originals of New Testament writings. For example, the virtues listed in 1 Timothy 3:2–4 and Titus 1:7–9 that should be exemplified by a bishop might better be translated as "attentive" (instead of "vigilant"), "prudent" (instead of "sober"), "righteous" (not "just"), "a friend to strangers or foreigners" (not "a lover of hospitality"), and "not autocratic or egotistical" (instead of "not self-willed"). Significant practical and ethical distinctions turn on how these Greek virtues are understood and applied.

Other times, readers think that they understand what a word means, but they may not grasp what the word actually referred to two thousand years ago. For example, the word "lamp" is perfectly understandable today, but if a child thinks of a modern electric lamp, he or she will have a hard time making any sense of the ten virgins putting oil into their "lamps."

In this short introductory chapter, we first look at problem words that fall into two categories: first, words that are now archaic and usually unfamiliar, especially to younger readers; and second, words that are easily misunderstood because their meanings have shifted.

Archaic Words

Some of the KJV's words are archaic and unfamiliar to modern readers. Fortunately, there are not many of these unknown words to deal with in the KJV. Here is a compilation and explanation of such words:

Anon. In its earliest usage, it means "straightway," "at once," "forthwith," or "instant." Servants said this in reply to a command: "Immediately!" (Matt. 13:20).

To *assay.* This word can mean "to try on" (clothing, gloves, etc.), "to try or examine" (as in a courtroom), "to attempt" (with the connotation of being tempted), or, as in Saul's case, "to try" or "to attempt" (Acts 9:26).

Divers in Elizabethan times meant "various" or "several," but as opposed to "diverse," it does not imply being different (Mark 8:3).

Draught. This refers to the disciples' act of "drawing in" a fishing net (Luke 5:4). However, it has a very different meaning in Matthew 15:17, where "draught" refers to an "outhouse" or "privy."

Fair shew. This expression refers to a "plausible" or "pleasing pretense" (Gal. 6:12).

Goodman of the house. The Latin word for "goodman" is *pater familias,* which means "man of the house" or "householder." However, the root of the Greek word for "goodman" is the same as the word "despot," likely implying a negative or tyrannical rule of the house (Matt. 24:43).

To *hale.* In Acts 8:3, "to hale" means to "drag," "pull," or "draw away from" with force or violence. Thus Saul was not merely summoning the men and women to jail; he was physically dragging them by force.

Halt. In the context of Matthew 18:8, "halt" is coupled with "maimed," and the two words' meanings are subtly differentiated. "Halt" means "lame" or "crippled," whereas "maimed" is used to describe mutilation or deformity.

To *list.* It means to "wish for" or "desire" something, much as the words "wish" and "want" today. One could "list" to taste a certain food or "list" to go to sleep when tired (Matt. 17:12).

Mote. In Matthew 7:3, the Savior is referring to a "minute particle," "speck," or "chip"—as small as flecks seen floating in a beam of light. It can also be used figuratively, referring to a "fault" or "blemish."

To set at *nought.* When Herod "set Christ at nought," it was not just an inconsequential brush-off (Luke 23:11). The Greek word means literally "from nothing." In this sense, "to set at nought" means to "value at nothing" or "despise." In its noun form, "nought" refers to "something that does not exist."

To *redound.* When Paul teaches "that the abundant grace might . . . redound to the glory of God," he means grace will "overflow" or "abound" (2 Cor. 4:15).

To *shew again.* When Christ told his disciples to "shew again," he meant "to report," "bring tidings" (from a person or a thing), or "make known openly" (Matt. 11:4).

Sore. Derived from the German word *sehr,* "very," "sore" is used in Matt. 17:6 as an adverb to intensify the Apostles' fear. Some synonyms are "very," "exceedingly," "extremely," and "severely."

To *straiten.* The Savior feels "straitened," which means "confined" or "pressed upon" on every side (Luke 12:50).

To *trow.* Like the German word *trauen,* it means "to trust." In the context of one of Jesus' parables, it is used to mean to "think," "believe," or "suppose" (Luke 17:9).

Ware. This is basically a shortened version of *aware,* with the same implicit meaning. It also denotes a conscious or cautious "awareness" (2 Tim. 4:15).

To *wist.* Christ corrects his mother, "Wist ye not," meaning "Didn't you know?" (Luke 2:49). The verb "to wist" is a cognate of the German word *wissen.* It means "to know" in the sense of knowledge or fact but does not refer to knowing people.

To *wot.* "To wot" implies a deeper understanding than "to wist"; it applies to something "perceived" or "discerned" (Acts 3:17).

Misunderstood Words

More problematic, however, are the words that people may think they understand, but they do not. These words can be particularly treacherous because readers can proceed reading with a misplaced sense of confidence. When readers come across these words, they need to do a double take, stop, and reprocess these words. They might look familiar, but for whatever reason, they are being used in an unfamiliar way. Here are a few examples:

To *adventure.* When Paul would not "adventure himself into the theatre" in Ephesus, it means he would not "give himself" or allow himself to go inside there (Acts 19:31).

To *approve.* As used in Philippians 1:10, this word means to "test" or "evaluate." It means more "to probe" rather than "approve."

Convenient. The things "not convenient" in Ephesians 5:4 are "unbecoming," "unseemly," and "improper."

Couch. This is a bed, not a sofa (Luke 5:19).

Emulation. By preaching to the Gentiles, Paul wishes to "provoke [some of the Jews] to emulation," which means that he wants to make them jealous (Rom. 11:14).

Hard. When one building was "hard to" another, it means that they shared an adjoining wall (Acts 18:7).

Instant. This word can have a lot of meanings. Jesus' accusers were "instant with loud voices," meaning "insistent" (Luke 23:23). When Paul exhorts people to "continue instant in prayer," the word means "persistent" (Rom. 12:12). When people besought Jesus "instantly," it means "urgently" or "hopefully" (Luke 7:4). When the tribes of Israel served God "instantly," it means "constantly" (Acts 26:7).

Lewdness. Lewdness today is defined as personal immorality or wickedness. In its earlier usage, however, "lewdness" meant "ignorant" or "unlearned" because of either ill-breeding or foolishness (Acts 18:14).

Mansions. In the Father's house (his temple, which models his heavenly realms) are many "resting places" or "dwelling places," but the Greek word *monai,* translated in John 14:2 as "mansions," may refer to relatively ordinary-sized abodes, resting places, or waystations.

Matter. The "matter" in James 3:5 is literally "fuel." A little fire can ignite a lot of fuel.

To *observe.* When Herod "observed" John the Baptist (Mark 6:20), the word means that Herod "respected" him. After all, he knew that he was "a just man and an holy."

To *occupy.* The servants were not just to occupy the property but to "negotiate" or "manage" it, as in a business occupation (Luke 19:13).

To *open.* In Acts 17:3, this means to "explain," as in "opening up one's understanding."

Particular. When Paul tells the Saints they are "members in particular" of "the body of Christ," he means "individually," not "especially" (1 Cor. 12:27).

Peculiar. Being a "peculiar people" (1 Pet. 2:9) does not mean being weird but being "distinctive," especially in the sense of being "peculiar to someone" or "belonging to someone." The word is borrowed directly from the Latin word *peculia,* which means "belongings" or "cattle." In other words, "belonging to" points to a personal possession.

Perfection. To bring "fruit to perfection" in Luke 8:14 means to bring "to maturity." The word "perfect" usually refers to completion or finishing, rather than being without error or defect.

Pitiful. Fortunately, when the Lord is "very pitiful," it does not mean pathetic but "compassionate," "tenderhearted," or having pity on us (James 5:11).

To *pray.* "We pray you" means "we beseech you," "we implore you" (2 Cor. 5:20).

To *prevent.* When Jesus entered the house, he did not "prevent" Peter, but he "spoke to him first" or "stood in front of him" (Matt. 17:25). The Latin translation of the Greek here uses the word *praevenit*, from which the English translators evidently got the idea of "prevent," but the Latin literally just means "to come (*venit*) in front of (*prae*)."

To *provoke.* Again, the problem stems from a transliteration of the Latin. When we are to "provoke" one another to good works (Heb. 10:24), this does not mean that we should annoy but "call forth" or "challenge" each other. The Latin *provocare* means "to call (*vocar*) forth (*pro*)."

Seal. Whenever this word is used in scripture, it does not mean "to close," as in "licking and sealing an envelope," but rather it means to "stamp with an official seal or impression."

Several. As used in the parable of the talents, each person was given an amount according to his "several ability," which should not be understood to mean each one's many abilities. This word means according to their "individual or personal abilities" (Matt. 25:15). Legally, when two people are obligated under a contractual liability that is denominated as a "joint and several" obligation, this means that the parties can be held liable either together—"jointly," each contributing their own share—or "severally, individually"—meaning each for the whole amount. The word "several" in Matthew 25:15 is used in this personal sense.

Spent. When Paul says that he "will very gladly spend and be *spent* for you," he is saying that he will "spend money freely and be *completely used up*" in the service of his brothers and sisters (2 Cor. 12:15).

Thought. The words "take no thought for your life" in the Sermon on the Mount actually mean "don't be worried for the sake of your soul" (Matt. 6:25).

Virtue. When "virtue" went out of Jesus (Luke 8:46), he did not become what we would call less virtuous. In this case, virtue means "power" (the Greek word here is *dynamis*), and the Latin word translated as "strength" in this verse is *virtutem*, from which the English word directly derives.

Worship. Being promised to "have worship in the presence of them that sit at meat with thee" (Luke 14:10) means to have the "respect" or "esteem" of the people who eat together with one another, as companions or close associates.

Using Thee/Thou Language

In his May 1993 general conference address, Elder Dallin H. Oaks encouraged Latter-day Saints to address God by using "special words that have been sanctified by use in inspired communications, words that have been recommended to us and modeled for us by those we sustain as prophets and inspired teachers."[2] In particular, he mentioned the use of the pronouns "thee," "thou," "thy," and "thine" to show respect to God,[3] even though those words may seem "archaic . . . unfamiliar and difficult."[4] Indeed, using these reverent forms of speech when addressing God in prayer or encountering them in the scriptures can be confusing or awkward. But with a little effort, this small hurdle can be removed for people who wish to use these pronouns more comfortably.

The use of "thee" and "thou" has shifted somewhat over the centuries;[5] however, the following six guidelines may be helpful in teaching people, especially readers for whom English is not their primary language. These few basic patterns may also prove useful in raising the comfort level of readers as they engage with the King James language, which is filled with such expressions.

Reminders to use thee/thou language are not intended to create rigid constraints on the free flow of words, especially those of prayer uttered in love and humility before the Lord, for the essence of prayer is not found in the parts of speech but in the sincerity of a person's heart. The following patterns, however, may increase familiarity with these forms and raise comfort levels, thus building confidence and openness in speaking this way before the Lord. Learning to use thee/thou language may also help English speakers as they strive to learn foreign languages, most of which also have two forms of "you" that are regularly used in particular circumstances, depending on local cultures.

---

2. Dallin H. Oaks, "The Language of Prayer," *Ensign* 23, no. 5 (May 1993): 15–16.

3. On the rules of English grammar in the 1830s pertaining to the use of *thee* and *thou* in respectful discourse, see Noah Webster, *An Improved Grammar of the English Language* (New Haven, Conn.: Hezekiah Howe, 1831), 25; Samuel Kirkham, *English Grammar* (Rochester, N.Y.: W. Alling, 1835), 142–47.

4. Oaks, "Language of Prayer," 16.

5. The use of *you* began to replace *thou* and *ye* as nominatives in the fourteenth century, eventually becoming common in sixteenth-century speech. Yet "for a long while the old and the new forms often alternated with each other," and by the eighteenth century, *you* became the standard in English prose. George O. Curme, *A Grammar of the English Language* (Essex, Conn.: Verbatim, 1977), 2:15–16; see also 2:527–29; and J. N. Hook and E. G. Matthews, *Modern American Grammar and Usage* (New York: Ronald Press, 1956), 170. During Elizabethan times, when the King James Version of the Bible was being produced, "there is strong evidence that, while the older 'eth' ending continued to be *written*, it was *pronounced* as if it were '-s.'" Alister E. McGrath, *In the Beginning: The Story of the King James Bible and How It Changed a Nation, a Language, and a Culture* (New York: Doubleday, 2001), 272. Considering this, we cannot insist that the distinctions between these forms must be rigidly or dogmatically enforced.

Guideline 1: **Thee** *is like* **me. Thy** *is like* **my. Thine** *is like* **mine.**

In other words, in places where it would sound right to use the first-person pronouns "me," "my," or "mine," it is appropriate to use the rhyming second-person forms. For example, a person would say, "Walk with *me.*" So, in speaking of God, one would say, "Walk with *thee*" (not "walk with *thou*"). Similar pairs illustrate this point further: People thank *me* / People thank *thee.* My mother knows *me* / My mother knows *thee.* This is *my* church / This is *thy* church. The glory be *mine* / The glory be *thine.*

Indeed, when praying, we can formulate a thought negatively in the first person and then resolve it positively in the second person with respect to God: That they will glorify not *me,* but *thee.* Not *my* will, but *thy* will be done. The thanks be not *mine,* but *thine.*

Obviously, thinking "not me, but thee" and "not my, but thy" can shift our attention away from ourselves and to our Father in Heaven. Speaking this way in prayer also reinforces the close relationship that God desires to foster between us and him, the *me* and *thee.*

Guideline 2: Use **thine** *instead of* **thy** *when the next word starts with a vowel—that is,* **A, E I, O,** *or* **U.**

These cases are exceptions to the first guideline. Accordingly, *thy* son / *thine* only son. *Thy* word / *thine* own word. This rule is similar to what happens in using *a* or *an.* English usage requires the use of *an* when the next word begins with a vowel sound: *a* son / *an* only son. *A* day / *an* extraordinary day.

When the main word begins with an *h,* the usage can go either way. The King James Version treats the initial *h* as a vowel, but modern usage is mixed: *thy* foot / *thine* hand (alternatively, *thy* hand). *Thy* mind / *thine* heart (alternatively, *thy* heart).

Guideline 3: Use **thou** *as the subject of a sentence or of a dependent clause when you would normally use* **you** *in the singular.* **Ye** *is the plural form of* **you.**

In grammatical terms, "thou" is the nominative form of this pronoun. This rule is a little more difficult to apply than the first rule because, as the following example shows, the same word "you" can be used either as a subject (in the nominative case) or as an object (in the accusative case): *You* [the subject] love us, and we love *you* [the object]. The first "you" in this example is doing the loving; the second "you" refers to the one who is loved.

This then becomes as follows: *Thou* [the subject] lovest us (see guideline 3), and we love *thee* [the object] (as stated in guideline 1). It also helps to note the similarity in spelling between "you" and "thou," even though the letters *-ou* are pronounced differently. Nevertheless, these two words are closely related (through the German word for the familiar form of "you": *du*).

This third rule is further illustrated by other examples: *I* am here / *Thou* art here. *I* see / *Thou* seest. *You* know our needs / *Thou* knowest our needs. *You* have given us / *Thou* hast given us.

Guideline 4: Use **ye** *as the plural equivalent of* **thou.**

The word "ye" is not likely to be used in prayers, but it appears frequently in scripture. For example,[6] when Jesus instructs individuals how to pray alone in their closets, he says, "When thou prayest." When he instructs people regarding group prayers, he says, "After this manner therefore pray ye" (3 Ne. 13:6, 9).

Guideline 5: When **thou** *is the subject, the indicative verb ends in* **-st** *or* **-t.**

For example: You *have* / Thou *hast.* You *had* / Thou *hadst.* You *would* / Thou *wouldst* (or *wouldest*). You *should* / Thou *shouldst* (or *shouldest*). You *know* / Thou *knowest.* You *love* / Thou *lovest.* "Yea, Lord; thou knowest that I love thee" (John 21:16).

A simple *-t* is added to the end of some English verbs where the *-s* has dropped out: You *will* / Thou *wilt* (not *willst*). You *are* / Thou *art* (not *arst*).

Other verbs remain the same as in normal speech.[7] Even a verb in the imperative mood with "thou" as the subject does not change: "Father, glorify [not glorifieth] thou me with thine own self" (John 17:5).

One of the best ways to learn to appreciate the rhythm and distinctive sound of thee/thou language is to read the scriptures out loud. Especially rich is the entire chapter of John 17, where Jesus prays to the Father. The King James translation renders Jesus' words as follows: "I have finished the work which *thou gavest* me" (v. 4). "They have believed that *thou didst send* me" (v. 8). "I pray not that *thou shouldest take* them out of the world" (v 15).

---

6. "In Biblical language *ye* is now uniformly employed as nominative [plural] and *you* as dative and accusative [plural]. . . . In the original text of [the King James] version this usage was not so uniform, as there were in it a number of *you's* where we now find *ye.*" Curme, *Grammar,* 2:15.

7. For a chart of the full inflection of English verbs, see Curme, *Grammar,* 1:327–33.

"Sanctify them through *thy* truth" (v. 17). "That the world may know that *thou hast sent* me, and *hast loved* them, as *thou hast loved* me" (v. 23).

Guideline 6: When the word **who** *stands in place of* **thou** *or refers to God, the verb that follows may likewise end in* **-st** *or* **-t.**

For example, our Father, [thou] who *art* in heaven. But this usage is flexible—in the sacrament hymn we sing, "O God the Eternal Father, who *dwells* (not *dwellst*) amid the sky."[8]

These six guidelines are the main rules a person needs to know to use thee/thou language. Strictness is not crucial; many variations exist within the King James Version of the Bible. And if ever in doubt, we can usually avoid awkward or uncertain constructions by rephrasing while still retaining the respectful tone. For example, to avoid a sentence like "We ask thee *that thou mightest lend* us thy mercy," we might say simply, "We ask thee *to lend* us thy mercy" or just "Please lend us mercy." The Lord, who looks upon the heart, will understand and answer the humble prayer that is offered with real intent.

Conclusion

Word studies are important building blocks in our ability to read and understand the scriptures. Without too much difficulty, readers can notice the few archaic words in the KJV and learn their meaning. More effort is required to detect words that appear to be clear and readily understood but may say something quite different or even unexpected.

A few short studies of Greek New Testament words have been published in the *Ensign*, and this explanation of the use of thee/thou language has been published in the *Religious Educator.*[9] Nevertheless, more work on word usages would yet sharpen our understanding of truths contained in the New Testament. The publication of this multivolume commentary on the New Testament, covering every word and phrase in the writings of the early Apostles and disciples who followed the Lord and Savior

---

8. "O God, the Eternal Father," *Hymns of The Church of Jesus Christ of Latter-day Saints* (Salt Lake City: The Church of Jesus Christ of Latter-day Saints, 1985), no. 175.

9. John W. Welch, "New Testament Word Studies," *Ensign* 23, no. 4 (April 1993): 28–30; John W. Welch, "Word Studies from the New Testament," *Ensign* 25, no. 1 (January 1995): 28–30; John W. Welch, "Teaching the Usage of *Thee* and *Thou,*" *Religious Educator* 4, no. 1 (2003): 49–53.

Jesus Christ in the meridian of time, hopefully brings to light the meaning of many obscure words and phrases in the New Testament, helping to illuminate and clarify the wording of the King James Version for faithful modern readers.

Archaic Words

Word	Definition	Reference
anon	immediately	Matt. 13:20
to assay	to attempt, try	Acts 9:26
divers	various, several	Mark 8:3
draught	the act of drawing a net	Luke 5:4
draught	an outhouse, privy	Matt. 15:17
fair shew	a plausible pretense	Gal. 6:12
goodman	man of the house, despot	Matt. 24:43
to hale	to drag, draw, pull	Acts 8:3
halt	crippled, deformed	Matt. 18:8
to list	to wish, will, desire	Matt. 17:12
mote	a speck, chip	Matt. 7:3
to set at nought	to value at nothing, despise	Luke 23:11
to redound	to abound, overflow	2 Cor. 4:15
to shew again	to report	Matt. 11:4
sore	very, exceedingly, extremely, severely	Matt. 17:6
to straiten	to make tense, confine	Luke 12:50
to trow	to think, believe, suppose	Luke 17:9
ware	aware, conscious, cautious	2 Tim. 4:15
to wist	to know	Luke 2:49
to wot	to perceive, discern, know	Acts 3:17

Familiar Words with Unexpected Meanings

Word	Definition	Reference
to adventure	to arrive, happen	Acts 19:31
amazed	afraid, confounded, bewildered	Mark 6:51
to approve	to test	Philip. 1:10
convenient	becoming, seemly, proper	Eph. 5:4
couch	bed	Luke 5:19
dog	person who is wicked in some way	Rev. 22:15

Word	Definition	Reference
emulation	envy, jealousy	Rom. 11:14
hard	close, near	Acts 18:7
instant	insistent	Luke 23:23
instant	persistent	Rom. 12:12
instantly	urgently, hopefully	Luke 7:4
instantly	constantly	Acts 26:7
lewdness	ignorant, unlearned	Acts 18:14
mansions	dwelling or resting places	John 14:2
matter	fuel	James 3:5
to observe	to respect, treat with reverence	Mark 6:20
to occupy	to negotiate, manage	Luke 19:13
to open	to expound, interpret, explain	Acts 17:3
in particular	individually	1 Cor. 12:27
passion	suffering	Acts 1:3
peculiar	distinctive, belonging to	1 Pet. 2:9
perfection	maturity	Luke 8:14
pitiful	compassionate, tenderhearted	James 5:11
to pray	to beseech, implore	2 Cor. 5:20
to prevent	to question	Matt. 17:25
to provoke	to call forth, challenge, incite	Heb. 10:24
to seal	to stamp with official seal or impression	John 3:33
several	individual	Matt. 25:15
spent	consumed	2 Cor. 12:15
strait	narrow, strict	Matt. 7:13
to tax	to register or enroll in a list	Luke 2:1–5
thought	worry, anxiety, melancholy	Matt. 6:25
virtue	power or energy in a miraculous sense	Luke 8:46
worship	honor or respect	Luke 14:10

Making Sense of All Those New Testament Translations

Why and How They Differ

Andrew C. Skinner

In addition to the many translations of the Bible into different languages, some 371 by the opening of the twenty-first century,[1] there are many versions of the Bible in English. The majority of these appeared in the twentieth century. It seems self-evident as to why the Bible has been translated into so many languages and dialects. In the words of John Wycliffe, creator of the first complete Bible in English, "It helpeth Christian [people] to study the Gospel in that tongue in which they know best Christ's sentence."[2] Reasons for the proliferation of English versions are more complicated. To understand them, we need to go back to the King James Version (KJV).

In the seventeenth and eighteenth centuries, the KJV acquired the stature of the standard English Bible. First, the KJV was known as the Authorized Version because it was authorized by the king, who, in his view and the view of his subjects, held his position by divine right. A Bible authorized by one invested with divine authority, as it were, seemed to be endowed with special authority. Second, the KJV "captured the best of all the preceding English translations and far exceeded all of them."[3] The Authorized Version

1. Bruce M. Metzger, *The Bible in Translation: Ancient and English Versions* (Grand Rapids, Mich.: Baker Academic, 2001), 9.

2. Quoted in Paul D. Wegner, *The Journey from Texts to Translations* (Grand Rapids, Mich.: Baker Academic, 2000), 282; Henry Hargreaves, "The Wycliffite Versions," in *The Cambridge History of the Bible,* vol. 2, *The West from the Fathers to the Reformation,* ed. G. W. H. Lampe (Cambridge, Eng.: Cambridge University Press, 1969), 392; Henry Wheeler Robinson, *The Bible in Its Ancient and English Versions* (Westport, Conn.: Greenwood Press, 1970), 138.

3. Philip W. Comfort, *The Complete Guide to Bible Versions* (Wheaton, Ill.: Tyndale House, 1996), 48. See also Adam Nicolson, *God's Secretaries: The Making of the King James Bible* (New York: HarperCollins, 2003).

"gathered to itself the virtues of the long and brilliant royal line of English Bible translations; it united high scholarship with Christian devotion and piety. It came into being at a time when the English language was vigorous and young, and its scholars had a remarkable mastery of the instrument which Providence had prepared for them. Their version has justifiably been called 'the noblest monument of English prose.'"[4]

Indeed, the influence of the KJV was monumental, not only on the spirituality of English-speaking peoples but also on the English language, English literature, and English culture. "No other translation has touched the lives of so many English-speaking people for centuries and centuries, even until the present day,"[5] including Latter-day Saints.

The King James translators did exceptional work given their charge and the resources available to them. The fifty-plus scholars called upon to make the new translation were trained in Hebrew and Greek and were people of deep spirituality. "They have a ghost presence in our lives, invisible but constantly heard, enriching with the 'civility, learning and eloquence' of their translation."[6] They formed subcommittees, each tasked with translating a portion of the Bible. The work of each subcommittee then passed through several reviews by other members of the greater team of translators.

In addition, all the scholars were instructed to follow the Bishop's Bible as their template but to consult the Tyndale, Matthews, Coverdale, Great, and Geneva Bibles when they thought those versions reflected better or more accurate renderings of the original languages. Possessing this mandate, the King James translators recognized that they needed the work of previous translators to complete their task. Their dependence on the work of those who went before was emphasized in the original KJV preface: "Truly (good Christian Reader) we never thought from the beginning that we should need to make a new translation, nor yet to make a bad one a good one, . . . but to make a good one better, or out of many good ones one principal good one."[7]

---

4. John Livingston Lowes, *Essays in Appreciation* (Boston: Houghton Mifflin, 1936), 3, quoted in J. H. Skilton, "English Versions of the Bible," in *New Bible Dictionary,* ed. J. D. Douglas (Grand Rapids, Mich.: William B. Eerdmans, 1962), 373–74.

5. Comfort, *Complete Guide to Bible Versions,* 49.

6. Nicolson, *God's Secretaries,* xi.

7. Erroll F. Rhodes and Liana Lupas, eds., *The Translators to the Reader: The Original Preface of the King James Version of 1611 Revisited* (New York: American Bible Society, 1997), 54; see also p. 18.

But over time, biblical scholars found that the KJV possessed some deficiencies. For the Old Testament, the translators relied upon the Masoretic Text of the Hebrew Bible. It was adequate, but the translators' thorough understanding of the Hebrew language was deemed lacking. For the New Testament, "the Greek text [used was] an inferior" one, known as the *Textus Receptus* (Latin for "received text"), which was based on the work of the great northern Renaissance humanist scholar Erasmus of Rotterdam (1466–1536). He compiled "the first Greek text to be produced on a printing press" using "five or six very late manuscripts dating from the tenth to the thirteenth centuries" that "were far inferior to earlier manuscripts." This Greek text was printed around 1516. Both Martin Luther and William Tyndale used a version of this Greek text in making their translations. Luther's version was completed in the 1520s, and Tyndale's translation appeared in 1525.[8]

Erasmus's Greek text went through a few more revisions, most notably undertaken by Robert Stephanus and Theodore Beza. The latter's work was published in 1624 and again in 1633 by the Elzevir brothers. The preface to the second edition announced that it contained "the text which is now received by all, in which we give nothing changed or corrupted."[9] Thus it received the name *Textus Receptus* and thereafter was used by translators of the King James New Testament.

Not long after the KJV was published (1611), older, superior manuscripts began to be discovered. "Around 1630, Codex Alexandrinus, a fifth-century manuscript of the Greek Bible, was brought to England" and gave scholars a text that was considered closer to the original New Testament witness.[10]

Two hundred years later, the German scholar Constantin von Tischendorf (1815–1874) made his famous discovery of the Codex Sinaiticus in the library of St. Catherine's Monastery at the foot of the traditional Mount Sinai. This manuscript is dated to the fourth century and is one of the two oldest vellum (treated animal hide) manuscripts of the New Testament. The Sinaiticus and the Codex Vaticanus are considered by most modern scholars to be the best available texts of the Greek New Testament. The Codex Vaticanus, named after the Vatican Library, where it has been held since at least the fifteenth century (c. 1475 or 1481), is usually regarded as

---

8. Philip W. Comfort, *Essential Guide to Bible Versions* (Wheaton, Ill.: Tyndale House, 2000), 147–48. This is a greatly expanded version of Comfort's *Complete Guide to Bible Versions*.

9. Quoted in Comfort, *Essential Guide to Bible Versions,* 148–49.

10. Comfort, *Essential Guide to Bible Versions,* 149.

the oldest extant manuscript of the complete Greek Bible (Old and New Testaments), dating to the fourth century as well.[11]

Nineteenth-century scholars began to produce versions of the New Testament based on these earlier manuscripts. Samuel Tregelles, for example, published a Greek text in which he sought "to exhibit the text of the New Testament in the very words in which it has been transmitted on the evidence of ancient authority."[12] Disfavor toward the *Textus Receptus,* and hence toward the King James New Testament, was solidified by the work of two British scholars, Brooke Westcott and Fenton Hort, who produced an edition entitled *The New Testament in the Original Greek* (1881).[13] They argued that Codex Vaticanus and Codex Sinaiticus, along with other early manuscripts, represented the version of the New Testament that most closely replicated the original writings of the ancient authors. Westcott and Hort stated that Codex Vaticanus "preserved not only a very ancient text, but a very pure line of very ancient text."[14]

In the twentieth century, second- and third-century New Testament manuscripts written on papyrus were discovered. Several of these present a text very similar to Codex Vaticanus; others are more similar to Codex Sinaiticus. Among the most important early papyrus manuscripts is 𝔓[75], dated to around AD 175–200. It bears a close resemblance to Codex Vaticanus.[15] These manuscripts are invaluable to New Testament text critics—that is, those who strive to produce the most accurate Greek text of the New Testament.

Also at the beginning of the twentieth century, Eberhard Nestle used the best manuscripts and editions of the Greek New Testament that were produced in the nineteenth century and compiled a version of the Greek text that won wide acceptance. This project was carried on for several years by

---

11. Paul D. Wegner, *The Journey from Texts to Translations* (Grand Rapids, Mich.: Baker Academic, 2004), 195–96; Brent Nongbri, "The Date of the Codex Sinaiticus," *Journal of Theological Studies* 73, no. 2 (October 2022): 516–34, https://doi.org/10.1093/jts/flac083.

12. Quoted in Comfort, *Essential Guide to Bible Versions,* 149–50; Samuel Prideaux Tregelles, *An Account of the Printed Text of the Greek New Testament* (London: Samuel Baxter, 1854), 160, 173–74.

13. Brooke Foss Westcott and Fenton John Anthony Hort, *The New Testament in the Original Greek* (Cambridge, Eng.: Macmillan, 1881).

14. B. F. Westcott and F. J. A. Hort, *Introduction to the New Testament in the Original Greek* (New York: Harper and Brothers, 1882; Peabody, Mass.: Hendrickson Publishers, 1988), 250–51.

15. Bruce M. Metzger, *The Test of the New Testament: Its Transmission, Corruption, and Restoration,* 3rd ed. (New York: Oxford University Press, 1992), 41.

his son and then by Kurt Aland. The latest edition (28th) of Nestle-Aland's *Novum Testamentum Graece* appeared in 2012.[16] The same Greek text of Nestle-Aland was used to produce a volume published by the United Bible Societies entitled simply *The Greek New Testament.*[17] Most modern scholars and translators today use one of these two critical editions.[18]

Because most modern English versions of the New Testament use one or the other of the two Greek editions mentioned above, they are shorter than the KJV and the New King James Version (NKJV) by as much as a thousand words in some instances. As one scholar notes, "The New Testament of the King James Version has fifty more verses than do most modern versions. This is because the King James Version is based on an edition of the Greek New Testament known as the *Textus Receptus,* which has about fifty more verses than do other modern critical editions of the Greek New Testament, such as the text of Westcott and Hort, or the Nestle-Aland text."[19]

The fact that the current Nestle-Aland edition of the New Testament is a far better representation of the original text than the *Textus Receptus* or the KJV raises the issue of theological differences. Does this mean, practically speaking, that readers of modern English versions of the New Testament that are closely based on the Nestle-Aland Greek text are reading a different gospel or receiving different theology than readers of the KJV? Perhaps in some instances. (This becomes an important argument in support of modern revelation.) Maybe a better way of stating the issue is to say that readers of the KJV are reading a version of the New Testament text that was not read in the first three centuries of the Christian church. "Most of the significant theological differences between the TR [and the KJV] and modern critical editions of the Greek text pertain to issues of Christology, especially as reflected in titles or descriptions of Christ."[20] Here again the richness and importance of restoration theology is highlighted against the backdrop of the KJV.

---

16. ed. Barbara Aland and others, *Novum Testamentum Graece,* 28th rev. ed. (Stuttgart, Ger.: Deutsche Bibelgesellschaft, 2012).

17. ed. Barbara Aland and others, *The Greek New Testament,* 4th rev. ed. (Stuttgart, Ger.: Deutsche Bibelgesellschaff/United Bible Societies, 1998).

18. A "critical edition" of a text is not a copy of any one manuscript, but rather a text produced by consulting the best manuscripts to arrive at what text critics regard as the best reading of a passage.

19. Comfort, *Essential Guide to Bible Versions,* 151.

20. Comfort, *Essential Guide to Bible Versions,* 156.

Another matter that is highlighted when comparing various versions of the New Testament in English is the philosophy of translation. Some translators employed a literal word-for-word translation methodology, while others preferred a thought-for-thought approach. For example, the Revised Standard Version (RSV) and the New American Standard Bible (NASB) "are more literal than most versions." The New Revised Standard Version (NRSV) is still a fairly literal translation but with revisions leaning toward a freer thought-for-thought approach when deemed appropriate. The New International Version (NIV) was produced by a translation committee seeking a thought-for-thought creation. Some modern versions are based on a "dynamic equivalence" methodology, seeking to produce a translation in the idiom of the modern speech of certain population segments.[21]

Philip Comfort has categorized some well-known English versions of the Bible to help us get a sense of the methodologies employed.[22]

Strictly literal: *New American Standard Bible*

Literal: *King James Version, American Standard Version, New King James Version, Revised Standard Version, New American Bible*

Literal with freedom to be idiomatic: *New Revised Standard Version*

Thought-for-thought: *New International Version, New Jerusalem Bible, Revised English Bible*

Functional equivalent (modern speech): *Today's English Version, New Living Translation, Comtemporary English Version*

Paraphrastic: *The Living Bible, The Message*

As Comfort notes, "A word-for-word rendering can be executed more easily than a thought-for-thought one; for in doing the latter, the translator must enter into the same thought as the author—and who can always know with certainty what the author's original, intended meaning was? Therefore, a dynamic-equivalent or thought-for-thought translation should be done by a group of scholars (to guard against personal subjectivism)."[23] In my view, it is critical to emphasize that a translation is axiomatically or self-evidently an interpretation!

---

21. Comfort, *Complete Guide to Bible Versions,* 90–95, referencing Eugene A. Nida and Charles R. Taber, *The Theory and Practice of Translation* (Leiden, Neth.: E. J. Brill, 1969), 202.

22. Comfort, *Essential Guide to Bible Versions,* 235.

23. Comfort, *Complete Guide to Bible Versions,* 93.

John Beekman and John Callow proffer a profound summary of the foundational principle which lies at the heart of all translation efforts: "Translating faithfully involves knowing what Scripture means. This is fundamental to all idiomatic translation, and it is at this point that exegesis comes in. . . . In other words, its immediate purpose is to ascertain, as accurately as possible, using all the means available, just what the original writer, 'moved by the Holy Spirit,' meant as he dictated or penned his words, phrases, and sentences. Exegesis thus lies at the heart of all translation work, for if the translator does not know what the original means, then it is impossible for him to translate faithfully."[24]

By the last decades of the twentieth century, the English-speaking world seemed to have enough new Bible translations that the time had come for committee revisions of existing versions, as was seen in 1605–1611 when the KJV was produced. An excellent example is the New Revised Standard Version of 1990. The chair of the committee, the late and great dean of New Testament text critics, Bruce M. Metzger, spoke of three reasons revisions are made, which also apply to the rationale behind the Brigham Young University New Testament Commentary series: requisition of still older biblical manuscripts, further (closer) investigation of linguistic features of the text, and changes in the usage (meaning) of the English language.[25] To these we may add a fourth reason: the flood of light, truth, and knowledge of God's intended meaning for his children that has proceeded forth from the Restoration of the gospel, beginning with Joseph Smith. To this end, the BYU New Testament Commentary series was inaugurated.

---

24. John Beekman and John Callow, *Translating the Word of God* (Grand Rapids, Mich.: Zondervan, 1974), 34–35.

25. Bruce M. Metzger, "To the Reader," in *The Holy Bible: New Revised Standard Version* (New York: Oxford University Press, 1989), xi–xvi.

Plumbing the Depths of the New Testament

Published Works by Our Commentary Authors

Selected works by each author are listed in reverse chronological order.

Lincoln H. Blumell

Blumell, Lincoln H., ed. *New Testament: History, Culture, and Society: A Background to the Texts of the New Testament.* Provo, Utah: Religious Studies Center, Brigham Young University; Salt Lake City: Deseret Book, 2019.

———. "An Amulet Containing Acts 9:1." *Bulletin of the American Society of Papyrologists* 54 (2017): 31–43.

———. "Luke 22:43–44: An Anti-Docetic Interpolation or an Apologetic Omission?" *TC: A Journal of Biblical Textual Criticism* 19 (2014): 1–35.

———. "The Message and the Medium: Some Observations on Epistolary Communication in Late Antiquity." *Journal of Greco-Roman Christianity and Judaism* 10 (2014): 24–67.

Blumell, Lincoln H., and Thomas A. Wayment. "Coptic New Testament Fragments in the Brigham Young University Collection." *Journal of the Canadian Society for Coptic Studies* 6 (2014): 59–88.

Blumell, Lincoln H. "P.Vindob. G 42417(= P116): Codex Fragment of the Epistle to the Hebrews 2:9–11 & 3:3–6 Reconsidered." *Zeitschrift für Papyrologie und Epigraphik* 171 (2009): 65–69.

S. Kent Brown

Brown, S. Kent. *The Epistle to the Ephesians.* Brigham Young University New Testament Commentary. Provo, Utah: BYU Studies, 2023.

———. "Jesus' First Visit to the Temple." In *The Temple: Symbols, Sermons, and Settings; Proceedings of the Fourth Interpreter Foundation Matthew B. Brown Memorial Conference, 10 November 2018,* vol. 5, *Temple on Mount Zion,* ed. Stephen D. Ricks and Jeffrey M. Bradshaw, 235–66. Orem, Utah: Interpreter Foundation; Salt Lake City: Eborn Books, 2024.

———. *The Testimony of Luke.* Brigham Young University New Testament Commentary. Provo, Utah: BYU Studies, 2015.

———. "Peter's Keys." In *The Ministry of Peter, the Chief Apostle,* ed. Frank F. Judd Jr., Eric D. Huntsman, and Shon D. Hopkin, 91–102. 43rd Annual Brigham Young University Sidney B. Sperry Symposium. Provo, Utah: Religious Studies Center, Brigham Young University; Salt Lake City: Deseret Book, 2014.

Brown, S. Kent, Richard Neitzel Holzapfel, and Dawn C. Pheysey. *Beholding Salvation: The Life of Christ in Word and Image.* Salt Lake City: Deseret Book, 2006.

Brown, S. Kent. *Mary and Elisabeth: Noble Daughters of God.* American Fork, Utah: Covenant Communications, 2002.

Richard D. Draper

Draper, Richard D., and Michael D. Rhodes. *Epistle to the Hebrews.* Brigham Young University New Testament Commentary. Provo, Utah: BYU Studies, 2021.

Draper, Richard D. "'By His Own Blood He Entered in Once into the Holy Place': Jesus in Hebrews 9." In *Thou Art the Christ, the Son of the Living God: The Person and Work of Jesus in the New Testament,* ed. Eric D. Huntsman, Lincoln H. Blumell, and Tyler J. Griffin, 244–59. 47th Annual Brigham Young University Sidney B. Sperry Symposium. Provo, Utah: Religious Studies Center, Brigham Young University; Salt Lake City: Deseret Book, 2018.

Draper, Richard D., and Michael D. Rhodes. *Paul's First Epistle to the Corinthians.* Brigham Young University New Testament Commentary. Provo, Utah: BYU Studies, 2015.

———. *The Revelation of John the Apostle.* Brigham Young University New Testament Commentary. Provo, Utah: BYU Studies, 2016.

Draper, Richard D. *The Savior's Prophecies.* American Fork, Utah: Covenant Communications, 2001.

———. *Opening the Seven Seals: The Visions of John the Revelator.* Salt Lake City: Deseret Book, 1991.

John Gee

Gee, John. "The Cares of This World: Roman Economics and the New Testament." In *New Testament History, Culture, and Society: A Background to the Texts of the New Testament,* ed. Lincoln H. Blumell, 210–29. Provo, Utah: Religious Studies Center, Brigham Young University; Salt Lake City: Deseret Book, 2019.

———. "Not Just Sour Grapes: Jesus's Interpretation of Isaiah's Song of the Vineyard." *Interpreter: A Journal of Latter-day Saint Faith and Scholarship* 28 (2018): 21–36.

———. "Jesus's Courtroom in John." In *"To Seek the Law of the Lord": Essays in Honor of John W. Welch,* ed. Paul Y. Hoskisson and Daniel C. Peterson, 135–50. Orem, Utah: Interpreter Foundation, 2017.

Gee, John, and Thomas A. Wayment. "Did Paul Address His Wife in Philippi?" *Studies in the Bible and Antiquity* 4 (2012): 71–93.

Gee, John. "James, First and Second Peter, and Jude: Epistles of Persecution." In *The Life and Teachings of the New Testament Apostles: From the Day of Pentecost to the*

Apocalypse, ed. Richard Neitzel Hotzapfel and Thomas A. Wayment, 171–90. Salt Lake City: Deseret Book, 2010.

———. "The Great and Last Sacrifice." In *"Behold the Lamb of God": An Easter Celebration,* ed. Richard Neitzel Holzapfel, Frank F. Judd Jr., and Thomas A. Wayment, 139–54. Provo, Utah: Religious Studies Center, Brigham Young University, 2008.

———. "The Corruption of Scripture in Early Christianity." In *Early Christians in Disarray: Contemporary LDS Perspectives on the Christian Apostasy,* ed. Noel B. Reynolds, 163–204. Provo, Utah: Foundation for Ancient Research and Mormon Studies, 2005.

John F. Hall

Hall, John F., and John W. Welch, eds. *Masada and the World of the New Testament.* Provo, Utah: BYU Studies, 1997.

Hall, John F. *New Testament Witnesses of Christ: Peter, John, James, and Paul.* American Fork, Utah: Covenant Communications, 2002.

Hall, John F., and John W. Welch. *Charting the New Testament.* Provo, Utah: Foundation for Ancient Research and Mormon Studies, 2002.

———, eds. *Apostles and Bishops in Early Christianity.* Vol. 15 of The Collected Works of Hugh Nibley. Salt Lake City: Deseret Book; Provo, Utah: Foundation for Ancient Research and Mormon Studies, 2005.

Eric D. Huntsman

Huntsman, Eric D. "The Gospel of John." In *New Testament History, Culture, and Society: A Background to the Texts of the New Testament,* ed. Lincoln H. Blumell, 304–21. Provo, Utah: Religious Studies Center; Salt Lake City: Deseret Book, 2019.

———. *Becoming the Beloved Disciple: Coming unto Christ with the Gospel of John.* Springville, Utah: Cedar Fort, 2018.

———. "Luke's Jesus: The Compassionate and Saving Son of God." In *Thou Art the Christ, the Son of the Living God: The Person and Work of Jesus in the New Testament,* ed. Eric D. Huntsman, Lincoln H. Blumell, and Tyler J. Griffin, 112–35. 47th Annual Brigham Young University Sidney B. Sperry Symposium. Provo, Utah: Religious Studies Center, Brigham Young University; Salt Lake City: Deseret Book, 2018.

———. "The Unveiling of Christ and of Angels: Apocalyptic Mediation in The Book of Revelation." In *Latter-day Saint Readings of Revelation 21–22,* ed. Julie M. Smith, 85–98. Provo, Utah: Neal A. Maxwell Institute for Religious Scholarship, 2016.

———. "Jesus on Jesus: John 5 and 7." In *Perspectives on Mormon Theology,* vol. 1, *Scriptural Theology,* ed. James E. Faulconer and Joseph M. Spencer, 69–80. Salt Lake City: Greg Kofford Books, 2015.

———. "The Petrine *Kērygma* and the Gospel according to Mark." In *The Ministry of Peter, the Chief Apostle,* ed. Frank F. Judd Jr., Eric D. Huntsman, and Shon D. Hopkin, 169–90. 43rd Annual Brigham Young University Sidney B. Sperry

Symposium. Provo, Utah: Religious Studies Center; Salt Lake City: Deseret Book, 2014.

———. "The Accounts of Peter's Denial: Understanding the Texts and Motifs." In *The Ministry of Peter, the Chief Apostle,* ed. Frank F. Judd Jr., Eric D. Huntsman, and Shon D. Hopkin, 127–49. 43rd Annual Brigham Young University Sidney B. Sperry Symposium. Provo, Utah: Religious Studies Center, Brigham Young University; Salt Lake City: Deseret Book, 2014.

Joshua M. Matson

Matson, Joshua. "Between the Testaments: The History of Judea between the Testaments of the Bible." In *New Testament History, Culture, and Society: A Background to the Texts of the New Testament,* ed. Lincoln Blumell, 3–18. Provo, Utah: Religious Studies Center, Brigham Young University; Salt Lake City: Deseret Book, 2019.

———. "The Fourth Gospel and Expectations of the Jewish Messiah." In *Thou Art the Christ, the Son of the Living God: The Person and Work of Jesus in the New Testament,* ed. Eric D. Huntsman, Lincoln H. Blumell, and Tyler J. Griffin, 175–91. 47th Annual Brigham Young University Sidney B. Sperry Symposium. Provo, Utah: Religious Studies Center, Brigham Young University; Salt Lake City: Deseret Book, 2018.

Cecilia M. Peek

Peek, Cecilia M., Lincoln H. Blumell, Jason R. Combs, Mark D. Ellison, and Frank F. Judd Jr., eds. *The Household of God: Families and Belonging in the Social World of the New Testament.* Provo, Utah: Religious Studies Center, Brigham Young University, 2022.

Peek, Cecilia M. "Receiving Christ: Atonement, Grace, and Eternal Salvation." In *Ancient Christians: An Introduction for Latter-day Saints,* ed. Jason Combs, Mark D. Ellison, Catherine Gines Taylor, and Kristian Heal, 329–67. Provo, Utah: Neal A. Maxwell Institute, 2022.

———. "The Greeks and Alexander the Great." In *A Bible Reader's History of the Ancient World,* ed. Kent P. Jackson, 286–97. Provo, Utah: Jerusalem Center for Near Eastern Studies, Brigham Young University, 2016.

Peek, Cecilia M., and Eric D. Huntsman. "Imperial Cult and The Beasts of Revelation." In *The Life and Teachings of the New Testament Apostles,* ed. Richard N. Holzapfel and Thomas A. Wayment, 221–49. Salt Lake City: Deseret Book, 2010.

Peek, Cecilia M. "The Death of John the Baptist." In *The Life and Teachings of Jesus Christ,* vol. 2, *From the Transfiguration through the Triumphal Entry,* ed. Richard N. Holzapfel and Thomas A. Wayment, 208–35. Salt Lake City: Deseret Book, 2006.

———. "Early Galilean Ministry and Miracles." In *The Life and Teachings of Jesus Christ,* vol. 1, *From Bethlehem through the Sermon on the Mount,* ed. Richard

Neitzel Holzapfel and Thomas A. Wayment, 269–305. Salt Lake City: Deseret Book, 2005.

———. "The Burial." In *The Life and Teachings of Jesus Christ,* vol. 3, *From the Last Supper through the Resurrection: The Savior's Final Hours,* ed. Richard N. Holzapfel and Thomas A. Wayment, 338–77. Salt Lake City: Deseret Book, 2003.

Tom R. Roberts

Roberts, Tom R. *Divorce and Remarriage: A Middle Eastern Biblical Approach.* Eugene, Ore.: Wipf and Stock Publishers, 2018.

———. "Exportation of Middle Eastern Culture to North America." *Ancient American* 18, no. 104 (2014): 8–11.

———. *From Sacral Kingship to Sacred Marriage: A Theological Analysis of Literary Borrowing.* New York: Vantage Press, 2003.

———. *Systematic Theology: Addendum; The Law, Sabbath, and Redemption.* Meridian, Idaho: Church of God Publishing House, 2003.

Brent J. Schmidt

Schmidt, Brent J. *Relational Faith: The Transformation and Restoration of* Pistis *as Knowledge, Trust, Confidence, and Covenantal Faithfulness.* Provo, Utah: BYU Studies, 2022.

———. *Relational Grace: The Reciprocal and Binding Covenant of* Charis. Provo, Utah: BYU Studies, 2015.

———. *Utopia and Community in the Ancient World: The Ancient Utopian Societies of Pythagoras, the Essenes, Pachomius, and Late Pagan Athens.* Lewiston, N.Y.: Edwin Mellen Press, 2010.

Andrew C. Skinner

Skinner, Andrew C. "The Life of Jesus of Nazareth: An Overview." In *New Testament History, Culture, and Society: A Background to the Texts of the New Testament,* ed. Lincoln H. Blumell, 245–77. Provo, Utah: Religious Studies Center, Brigham Young University; Salt Lake City: Deseret Book, 2019.

———. "In Praise of the Resurrection of Jesus Christ: The Culmination of His Saving Work." In *Thou Art the Christ, the Son of the Living God: The Person and Work of Jesus in the New Testament,* ed. Eric D. Huntsman, Lincoln H. Blumell, and Tyler J. Griffin, 26–48. 47th Annual Brigham Young University Sidney B. Sperry Symposium. Provo, Utah: Religious Studies Center; Salt Lake City: Deseret Book, 2018.

———. *The Savior's Final Week: Gethsemane, Golgotha, The Garden Tomb.* Salt Lake City: Deseret Book, 2014.

Skinner, Andrew C., and D. Kelly Ogden. *Verse by Verse: The Four Gospels.* Salt Lake City: Deseret Book, 2006.

———. *Verse by Verse: Acts through Revelation.* Salt Lake City: Deseret Book, 2006.

Julie M. Smith

Smith, Julie M. "The Resurrection." In *New Testament History, Culture, and Society: A Background to the Texts of the New Testament,* ed. Lincoln H. Blumell, 377–90. Provo, Utah: Religious Studies Center; Salt Lake City: Deseret Book, 2019.

———. *The Gospel according to Mark.* Brigham Young University New Testament Commentary. Provo, Utah: BYU Studies, 2018.

———, ed. *Latter-day Saint Readings of Revelation 21–22.* Provo, Utah: Neal A. Maxwell Institute for Religious Scholarship, 2016.

———. "Mark and Luke: Women's Roles." In *As Iron Sharpens Iron: Listening to the Various Voices of Scripture,* ed. Julie M. Smith, 95–104. Salt Lake City: Greg Kofford Books, 2016.

———. *Search, Ponder, and Pray: A Guide to the Gospels.* Salt Lake City: Greg Kofford Books, 2014.

John S. Thompson

Thompson, John S. "How Luke's Gospel Portrays Jesus as the Exodus or Way of the Temple." In *Proceedings of the Sixth Interpreter Foundation Matthew B. Brown Memorial Conference, 4–5 November 2022,* vol. 7, *Temple on Mount Zion,* ed. Stephen D. Ricks and Jeffrey M. Bradshaw. Orem, Utah: Interpreter Foundation; Salt Lake City: Eborn Books, forthcoming.

———. "Arrayed in Dazzling White: The Goddess Ta'it and Clothing in Ancient Egyptian Rituals of the Old Kingdom." In *Sacred Space, Sacred Thread: Perspectives across Time and Traditions,* ed. John W. Welch and Jacob Rennaker, 134–45. Eugene, Ore.: Wipf and Stock, 2019.

———. "How John's Gospel Portrays Jesus as the Way of the Temple." In *The Temple: Ancient and Restored,* vol. 3, *Temple on Mount Zion,* ed. Matthew B. Brown, Jeffrey M. Bradshaw, Stephen D. Ricks, and John S. Thompson, 307–33. Orem, Utah: Interpreter Foundation; Salt Lake City: Eborn Books, 2016.

John W. Welch

Welch, John W., and Jeannie Welch. *The Parables of Jesus: Revealing the Plan of Salvation.* American Fork, Utah: Covenant Communications, 2019.

Welch, John W. "The Symbolism of Two Sons in the Parable of the Prodigal Son." In *Seek Ye Words of Wisdom: Studies of the Book of Mormon, Bible, and Temple in Honor of Stephen D. Ricks,* ed. Donald W. Parry, Gaye Strathearn, and Shon D. Hopkin, 265–90. Orem, Utah: Interpreter Foundation; Provo, Utah: Religious Education, 2020.

———. "Roman Law Relating to the New Testament." In *New Testament: History, Culture, and Society: A Background to the Texts of the New Testament,* ed. Lincoln H. Blumell, 160–77. Provo, Utah: Religious Studies Center, Brigham Young University; Salt Lake City: Deseret Book, 2019.

———. "Symbolism in the Parable of the Willing and Unwilling Two Sons in Matthew 21." In *Let Us Reason Together: Essays in Honor of the Life's Work of Robert L. Millet,* 97–116. Religious Studies Center, Brigham Young University; Salt Lake City: Deseret Book, 2016.

———. *The Sermon on the Mount in the Light of the Temple.* London: Ashgate, 2009.

———. "Miracles, *Maleficium,* and *Maiestas* in the Trial of Jesus." In *Jesus and Archaeology,* ed. James H. Charlesworth, 349–83. Grand Rapids, Mich.: William B. Eerdmans, 2006.

———. "Modern Revelation: A Guide to Research about the Apostasy." In *Early Christians in Disarray: Contemporary LDS Perspectives on the Christian Apostasy,* ed. Noel B. Reynolds, 101–32. Provo, Utah: Foundation for Ancient Research and Mormon Studies, 2005.

About the Contributors

Lincoln H. Blumell

Lincoln H. Blumell is a Full Professor in the Department of Ancient Scripture at Brigham Young University. He holds graduate degrees from the University of Calgary, University of Oxford, and University of Toronto. He specializes in Early Christianity and Greek and Coptic papyrology and epigraphy.

S. Kent Brown

S. Kent Brown is an emeritus professor of Ancient Scripture at Brigham Young University (BYU) and a former director of the BYU Jerusalem Center for Near Eastern Studies. In the world of documentary films, he was the executive producer for *Journey of Faith, Journey of Faith: The New World,* and *Messiah: Behold the Lamb of God.* He and his wife, Gayle, have five children, twenty-five grandchildren, and six great-grandchildren.

Tad R. Callister

Born in 1945 in Glendale, California, Elder Tad R. Callister was an attorney, pursuing a career that grew out of his education at BYU, UCLA, and New York University. After serving as a missionary, bishop, stake president, regional representative, and mission president for The Church of Jesus Christ of Latter-day Saints, he was called to be a member of the Second Quorum of the Seventy in 2008 and was later appointed to the Presidency of the Seventy. He was released from that calling in April 2014 and was sustained as the twenty-first Sunday School General President, helping the Church to launch the "Come, Follow Me" curriculum. He authored three books: *The Blueprint of Christ's Church, The Infinite Atonement,* and *The Inevitable Apostasy and the Promised Restoration.* He and his wife, Kathryn, are the parents of six children.

Richard D. Draper

Richard D. Draper is an emeritus professor of Ancient Scripture at BYU and a former graduate coordinator and associate dean of Religious Education. For the BYU New Testament Commentary series, he and Michael Rhodes authored the volumes on First and Second Corinthians, First and Second Thessalonians, Hebrews, and Revelation. He and his wife, Barbara, are the parents of six children and the grandparents of sixteen grandchildren.

John Gee

John Gee is the William (Bill) Gay Research Professor in the Department of Asian and Near Eastern Languages at BYU. He has published on New Testament philology, economics, social institutions, textual criticism, historical authenticity, and the use of the Old Testament in the New Testament. He is working on the commentary for the Epistle of James in the BYU New Testament Commentary series.

John F. Hall III

The late John F. Hall (1951–2023) earned his BA from BYU, his MA from Princeton University, and his PhD from the University of Pennsylvania, specializing in ancient Roman studies from the time of the Etruscans to the reign of Augustus. At his retirement, he was a professor of Classics and Ancient History at BYU, where he was the Eliza R. Snow University Fellow. At his death, he was survived by three sons, six grandchildren, and his wife, Dena.

Eric D. Huntsman

Eric D. Huntsman received his BA in classical Greek and Latin from BYU and his MA and PhD in ancient history from the University of Pennsylvania. He joined the BYU faculty in 1994 in the Department of Classics and Ancient History. He transferred to Religious Education in 2003 and became a full professor of Ancient Scripture in 2015, serving from 2012 to 2021 as the coordinator of the Ancient Near Eastern Studies program in the Kennedy Center and currently serving as the associate director for academics at the BYU Jerusalem Center for Near Eastern Studies (since 2022). He and his wife, Elaine, are the parents of two children, Rachel and Samuel.

Kelsey Draper Lambert

Kelsey Lambert (BYU '05) received a master's degree in English from Indiana University and worked as a writer in high tech for sixteen years. She currently manages technical writers at Salesforce, focusing on engineering and security documentation. She works from her home office in Midway, Utah.

David J. Larsen

David J. Larsen received a BA in Near East studies from BYU, an MA in biblical theology from Marquette University, and a PhD in biblical studies from the University of St. Andrews in Scotland. His research interests include Jewish and Christian apocalyptic and mysticism, the Psalms, royal/messianic themes in the Bible and in the Dead Sea Scrolls, and "ascent to heaven" traditions. He currently lives in Charles Town, West Virginia, with his wife, Marluce, and the youngest two of their five children.

Joshua M. Matson

Joshua M. Matson is a scholar of the Bible and the Dead Sea Scrolls and an assistant professor in Ancient Scripture and the Jerusalem Center at BYU. He received a PhD in religion from Florida State University and has published articles on the Old and New Testaments, with a particular emphasis on the Minor Prophets, the Second Temple period, and the Jewish context of the New Testament. Dr. Matson grew up in Chubbuck, Idaho, and is married to Erin Barnes. They are the parents of four children.

Cecilia M. Peek

Cecilia M. Peek is an associate professor of Classical Studies in BYU's Department of Comparative Arts and Letters. Her research interests shine light on Hellenistic history, with particular emphasis on Ptolemaic Egypt (especially Cleopatra VII), Roman imperial history, classical historiography, and early Christian history. She received a BA in classics with a minor in German from BYU and an MA and PhD in ancient history and Mediterranean archaeology from the University of California at Berkeley. Professor Peek and her husband, Ken, are the parents of four children.

Tom R. Roberts

Tom R. Roberts holds a BA in theology from Triune Biblical University, a master of theology from Covenant Bible College and Seminary, and a master of divinity and a PhD in theology from Hellenic Orthodox University in Athens, Greece. He is currently pursuing doctoral studies at EUCLID University. Dr. Roberts has published two books, *From Sacral Kingship to Sacred Marriage: A Theological Analysis of Literary Borrowing* and *Divorce and Remarriage: A Middle Eastern View.* Dr. Roberts's articles have appeared in *Ancient American, Convergent Streams,* and other professional publications; he has presented at Kent State University's Communal Studies Group conference and at the Society for Mormon Philosophy and Theology. He has also reviewed books and articles for the Interpreter Foundation.

Brent J. Schmidt

Brent J. Schmidt teaches at BYU–Idaho in the religion and humanities departments. He earned degrees in history and classics from the University of Utah and a PhD in classics from the University of Colorado–Boulder, specializing in philology and late antiquity. He enjoys traveling, skiing, gardening, and studying ancient and modern languages.

Avram R. Shannon

Avram R. Shannon received a BA in ancient Near Eastern studies from BYU, a master's degree in Jewish studies from the University of Oxford, and a PhD from Ohio State University in Near Eastern languages and cultures, with a graduate interdisciplinary specialization in religions of the ancient Mediterranean. As a longtime student of Rabbinic Judaism, ancient Mediterranean religions, Jewish studies, and ancient biblical interpretation, he focuses his research on idolatry and image worship, Jewish/non-Jewish interactions, tribal and affinity groups, and kingship and priesthood in the ancient world. He and his wife, Thora, are the parents of nine children.

Andrew C. Skinner

Andrew C. Skinner is an emeritus professor of Ancient Scripture at BYU, where he served in various administrative posts, including dean of Religious Education, founding executive director of the Neal A. Maxwell Institute for Religious Scholarship, and associate director of the Jerusalem

Center for Near Eastern Studies. He is the author or coauthor of twenty-one books and over two hundred articles. He also edited seven volumes and has written much on the New Testament. He is currently working on volumes for the Book of Acts and the Epistle to Philemon for the BYU New Testament Commentary series.

John S. Thompson

John S. Thompson obtained his BA and MA in ancient Near Eastern studies (Hebrew Bible) from BYU and the University of California Berkeley, respectively, and completed a PhD in Egyptology at the University of Pennsylvania. He was an employee of the Seminaries and Institutes of Religion for twenty-eight years, most recently as a coordinator and institute director in the Cambridge, Massachusetts area. Now a full-time researcher and writer for Scripture Central, he and his wife, Stacey, live in Orem, Utah, where they welcome their nine children and four grandchildren.

John W. Welch

Dr. Welch's name is synonymous with discoveries such as identifying chiasmus in the Book of Mormon, seeing the Sermon on the Mount in the light of the temple, and understanding the Good Samaritan as an allegory of the Plan of Salvation. With degrees in history, Latin, Greek, and the law, he is well positioned to contribute textual and contextual insights into the Gospel of Matthew, which he is currently working on for the BYU New Testament Commentary series. He and his wife, Jeannie—both of whom are retired BYU faculty members—have recently returned home after teaching religion classes for two academic years as full-time missionaries at BYU–Hawaii.

Scripture Index

This index is ordered by book under Old Testament, New Testament, Book of Mormon, Other Ancient Sources, Pearl of Great Price, and Doctrine and Covenants.

John

Acts

Romans

Pearl of Great Price

Joseph Smith—History

Articles of Faith

Doctrine and Covenants